Microsoft Reporting Services in Acti

Microsoft Reporting Services in Action

TEO LACHEV

MANNING
Greenwich
(74° w. long.)

For online information and ordering of this and other Manning books, please go to www.manning.com. The publisher offers discounts on this book when ordered in quantity. For more information, please contact:

Special Sales Department
Manning Publications Co.
209 Bruce Park Avenue
Greenwich, CT 06830
Fax: (203) 661-9018
email: orders@manning.com

Manning Publications Co.
209 Bruce Park Avenue
Greenwich, CT 06830

Copyeditor: Linda Recktenwald
Typesetter: Denis Dalinnik
Cover designer: Leslie Haimes

ISBN 1-932394-22-2

Printed in the United States of America
1 2 3 4 5 6 7 8 9 10 – VHG – 08 07 06 05 04

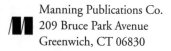

To my beautiful wife, Elena,
and our lovely children, Maya and Martin,
for your sacrifices in making this book a reality

To my parents
for supporting my decisions to take the road less traveled
and for always being very proud of me

brief contents

contents

foreword

Let me let you in on a little secret: creating software at Microsoft is pretty similar to creating software at any other company. I think many people's perception is that Microsoft designs products by having an army of market researchers carefully examining competitive products and surveying consumers to determine exactly what features to put in the next release.

The reality is that most of the ideas that go into Microsoft products are the result of small teams of people brainstorming in front of whiteboards or chatting in hallways. I'm not saying we don't know what competitors are doing or what customers are asking for, but the process of translating real-world scenarios to requirements and designs is much more organic than you might think. This flexible approach allows teams to take a fresh look at existing problems as well as adapt to industry trends and customer demands.

Case in point: when we started building Reporting Services, we didn't set out to copy what other companies had already done. Instead, we asked questions like "What does it mean to build an enterprise reporting product?" "How do we enable people to create powerful data visualizations without writing code?" and, most important of all, "How can we build a platform that people can leverage in their own applications?" The answer to this final question ended up driving a major part of the product's design.

Building a platform is not something to be taken lightly. It requires that you spend extra time factoring and documenting the interfaces between software components. It means that your components should not use any "back doors" that are not available to other developers using the platform. It also can change the order in which you build the product—you have to focus on the nonvisual parts of the product *before* you work on the user-facing ones. For example, the Reporting Services report processing engine was up and running about a year before the graphical report design tool was ready. During this time, report definition files had to be hand-coded in order to test any new report processing features.

The decision to build a platform also means that you will have to spend time on infrastructure and interfaces at the expense of end-user features. We knew that this trade-off would mean the first version of Reporting Services might look less feature-rich than other more "mature" reporting products. We felt like this was the right long-term strategy, as a strong platform would enable others to fill the gaps instead of having to wait for us to add every feature. When asked about this approach, I sometimes pose the question, "Is it better to build a car with a powerful engine and fewer lights on the dashboard or one with lots of lights that can't go anywhere?"

One decision we made for our new platform was to bet on another new platform: .NET. As we had no legacy code to support, we decided early on to make Reporting Services a 100 percent .NET application. While this may seem like a no-brainer today, when we started building Reporting Services the CLR and the .NET Framework had not yet been released. Although building an enterprise-quality server product on such a new technology stack was a little risky at the time, the decision has paid major dividends in developer productivity and product quality.

Ultimately, the barometer of whether we have succeeded is what our customers and partners are able to build on the platform. Since we released the first version of the product earlier this year, I have seen applications built by customers leveraging the Reporting Services platform in ways I never imagined. But a platform isn't useful if *all* developers don't have the know-how to take advantage of it. Because the product is so new, detailed information and good examples have been sparse and hard to find.

That's where resources like Teo's excellent book come in. This book starts by providing a solid foundation for using the built-in tools included with Reporting Services but quickly takes you to the next level by focusing on the programmability and extensibility aspects of the product. The focus on these parts of Reporting Services will help you leverage and extend the product feature set in your own applications. Teo's approach is to provide real-world examples and useful scenarios that walk you through the details and give you new ideas to explore. Teo has the ability to take complex topics and break them into smaller sections that can be easily understood. I enjoyed being one of the book's technical reviewers as I was able see how various parts of the product came to life on the page. I encourage you to use the ideas in this book and take Reporting Services to the next level.

BRIAN WELCKER
Group Program Manager
Microsoft SQL Server Reporting Services

preface

In archeology, the Rosetta stone was the key that solved the mysteries of Egyptian hieroglyphics. I believe that with the release of Microsoft SQL Server 2000 Reporting Services, code-named Rosetta, Microsoft gives organizations the key they need to unlock the secrets of enterprise data and unleash the power hidden within.

Looking retrospectively, Microsoft's reporting strategy has been confusing, at least for me. Microsoft Access debuted in the early 90s with a powerful report designer that made desktop reporting child's play.

Enterprise developers, however, have not been that lucky. The lack of comprehensive native reporting capabilities continues even today in the .NET framework. True, some progress has been made with the advent of print-related controls, such as PrintDocument, PrintPreviewControl, and so on, but still, dealing with the GDI+ (Graphics Device Interface) API is usually the last thing a developer wants to tackle when creating the next line-of-business application. For reasons such as these, report-enabling Microsoft-centric solutions has been traditionally regarded as a tedious chore.

To address this problem, many of us defected to third-party tools. Others chose to fill the void with homegrown, customized solutions. While these solutions address particular needs, they can also be costly, time-consuming, and difficult to implement.

I remember with nostalgia a project that I worked on about five years ago. It called for developing a reporting solution for a major Fortune 100 company. I implemented the solution as a server-based framework, following a design pattern similar to the one discussed in chapter 13. I used Microsoft Access as a reporting tool to generate reports and save them as snapshot files. Once the report was ready, the Report Server would e-mail it back to the user or send the user a link to the snapshot file.

Implementing this solution was a lot of fun, but it took a significant development effort. I wouldn't have had to do all of this if I had had Reporting Services back then. Instead of implementing a homegrown solution, I could have used RS to report-enable the applications.

For this reason, I was very excited when I heard about Reporting Services in late 2003. Finally, there was an easy way to report-enable different types of applications. Subsequently, I was involved in a project where I was able to confirm to myself that, indeed, RS was the reporting platform I had been dreaming about for years.

To share my enthusiasm I decided to write a book about Reporting Services. While I contemplated what the book's scope would be, it dawned on me that I could bring the most value by following my heart and approaching Reporting Services from a developer's point of view. I put myself in a position that many developers could relate to. Here I am, a developer, consultant, and architect, who is tasked with adding reporting features to a given application. How would I go about this?

To answer this question, my book takes a solution-oriented approach, and more than half of it is devoted to integrating different types of applications with RS. As you read this book, you will discover a common pattern. It starts by discussing the requirements and design goals of a given reporting scenario. Then it discusses the implementation choices, and finally it explains how the solution is implemented.

I firmly believe that a technical book should go beyond rehashing the product documentation. I tried my best to follow this path and take up where the RS documentation (which, by the way, is excellent) leaves off. For this reason, my book should be used in conjunction with it. When you read the book, you will notice that sometimes, when I believe I can't explain things any better, I refer you to the product documentation.

Microsoft Reporting Services in Action is written for report authors, administrators, and developers who need a detailed and practical guide to the functionality provided by RS. In the first half, report authors will master the skills they need to create versatile reports. Administrators will learn the ropes of managing and securing the report environment.

The second half of the book is primarily aimed at intermediate-to-advanced .NET developers who are planning to leverage RS to add reporting capabilities to their Windows Forms or web-based applications. However, because of the service-oriented architecture of Reporting Services, the book will also benefit developers who target other platforms but want to integrate their applications with RS.

Microsoft SQL Server 2000 Reporting Services is a great piece of technology. With RS, report authors can create reports as easily as you would do it in Microsoft Access. Make no mistake, though. RS is a sophisticated server-based platform, and its feature set goes well beyond that of a desktop reporting tool. To use RS effectively, you need to have a solid grasp of how it works and how it can be integrated with different types of client applications. I hope this book makes this endeavor easier.

acknowledgments

Writing this book has been a lot of fun and a lot of work. Although you see only my name on the front cover, this book has been a team effort involving many people.

First and foremost, I would like to acknowledge my family for their kind support in making this book a reality. My wife, Elena, contributed directly to the book by helping me recover what was lost in the process of translation. To my family I owe my greatest thanks.

Thanks to the Reporting Services team at Redmond for giving us this great product and working hard to make it even more successful. You can judge by yourself Microsoft's commitment to customer satisfaction by looking at the number of messages answered by Microsoft engineers on the RS discussion list (microsoft.public.sqlserver.reportingsvcs).

Brian Welcker, Microsoft Group Product Manager for SQL Server Business Intelligence, has been phenomenal in helping me with my project on several fronts, including reviewing the book and providing valuable technical feedback, as well as writing the foreword.

Thanks go to several Microsoft engineers—Brian Hartman, Bryan Keller, Daniel Reib, and Tudor Trufinescu—for reviewing parts of this book. Not only did these folks not mind my constant pestering, but they were even more eager to help make this book as technically accurate as possible.

I am grateful to the Manning team for publishing *Microsoft Reporting Services in Action* and demanding my best to ensure that this book meets the highest standards. Thanks to Dr. Marjan Bace for giving a chance to an aspiring author. Thanks to my development editors, Ann Navarro and Lianna Wlasiuk, for not losing faith that my incoherent writings could turn into something readable. As project editor, Mary Piergies has been outstanding in orchestrating the production process. My copy editors, Liz Welch and Linda Recktenwald, did a great job in polishing my manuscript. Kudos to my tech editor, Todd Meister, for verifying that the book is technically correct, and to Susan Forsyth for proofreading the manuscript. Thanks also to Dr. Dave Roberson for organizing the technical review process and to my technical reviewers, Alexzander Nepomnjashiy and Mark Monster, for reviewing the manuscript. Thanks to the book's publicist, Helen Times, for getting the word out. I am grateful to the rest of the Manning production team for their many contributions to this book.

I must also acknowledge my coworkers from Extreme Logic, now part of the Hewlett-Packard Enterprise Services group, for the productive and competitive environment that I found so exciting and invigorating. I consider myself very fortunate for having been part of this community for the past four years.

There are a few other people who contributed indirectly to the book. Thanks to Steven Gould for his Open Source OpenForecast package that I used in chapter 6 for the report-forecasting example. Thanks to Dino Esposito for his CodeDom sample. Kudos to Peter Bromberg for the ASP.NET menu control and to Christian Weyer for the dynamic Web services invocation sample.

My thanks also to the many unnamed developers for their altruistic support on the .NET discussion lists. I admire your willingness to help. Your contributions kept me sane during many dire moments in my career! Thanks also to Google for archiving the newsgroup content and making it easily accessible.

I would especially like to acknowledge my parents, Zlatka and Stefan Lachev, for supporting me in my choice of studying computer engineering, despite the fact that a career in medicine or in the army looked much more promising at the time.

Finally, thank *you* for purchasing this book! I sincerely hope that you will find it as enjoyable to read as it has been for me to write!

Thanks and happy reporting!

roadmap

Following the report lifecycle's logical path, this book explains how you can *author*, *manage*, and *deliver* RS-based reports.

Chapter 1 provides a panoramic overview of Reporting Services. The chapter is intended to give you a firm grounding in what RS really is. We look at how RS addresses the reporting problem area, its feature set, and its architecture. To round out the chapter we jump right in and create our first report. The chapter concludes with discussing RS strengths and weaknesses.

Part 1, "Authoring reports," teaches you the skills that you will need as a report author to create RS-based reports. It encompasses chapters 2–6.

Chapter 2 focuses on discussing various options for authoring reports. We start by explaining the report-authoring process. We continue by looking at how we can author reports with Visual Studio .NET by using the Report Wizard and the Report Designer and by importing from Microsoft Access. We also discuss how developers can leverage the open nature of the report definition schema by creating reports programmatically. We conclude the chapter by mentioning two third-party tools that you can use to author reports ad hoc or import them from Crystal Reports.

Chapter 3 gets to the gist of the report-authoring process by teaching you how to work with report data. It discusses the RS data architecture and shows you how to work with data sources, datasets, and report queries. It emphasizes the role of parameters and walks you through the steps for creating parameterized reports.

Chapter 4 teaches you the practical skills needed for authoring different types of reports with the Report Designer. We create various report samples to complement our discussion, including tabular, freeform, chart, crosstab, subreports, and multicolumn reports.

Chapter 5 shows you how to use expressions and functions to extend your reports programmatically. It starts by emphasizing the role of expressions and how they can be used to manipulate the report item properties. It continues by giving you an in-depth understanding of the RS object model and its collections. Next, we look at the RS internal functions and how they can be leveraged to add interactive features to our reports, such as reports with navigational features and document maps, as well as localized reports.

Chapter 6 explains how you can supercharge the capabilities of your reports by using embedded Visual Basic .NET code and external code in the form of .NET assemblies. It presents an end-to-end example that demonstrates how you can leverage custom .NET code to add forecasting features to your reports.

Part 2, "Managing reports," explains how report administrators can manage and secure the report repository. It includes chapters 7–8.

Chapter 7 discuses different ways of managing the report catalog. It starts by explaining how report administrators can use the Report Manager to perform various management activities. Then, it presents other management options, including using the RS Web service, WMI provider, RS script host, and other utilities.

Chapter 8 teaches you how you can secure the report catalog. It explores the RS role-based security model and how it can be leveraged to enforce restricted access to the Report Server. Then, it explains how code access security works and how you can adjust it to grant permissions selectively to custom code.

Part 3, "Delivering reports," discusses how developers can integrate RS with different application scenarios. This part includes chapters 9–14.

Chapter 9 provides an overview of the two application integration options available with RS, URL and Web service, and how they compare with each other.

Chapter 10 teaches you the skills you need to report-enable WinForm-based applications. It starts by discussing how RS can be leveraged with different application designs. The chapter walks you through an end-to-end sample, the Report Wizard, that demonstrates various practical techniques that you can use to integrate this type of application with RS.

Chapter 11 covers integrating RS with web-based applications. It demonstrates various techniques for generating reports on the client side and server side of the application. Here, we create an enhanced version of the Report Viewer sample control that facilitates server-side web reporting.

In Chapter 12, you learn how RS can be used in conjunction with OLAP for implementing synergetic reporting solutions. It walks you through the steps for creating a sample Analysis Services cube and implementing a WinForm front end with Office Web Components for generating dynamic and standard reports.

Chapter 13 shows how you can address some common enterprise reporting needs. Specifically, this chapter shows you how you can implement a façade layer that supports multiple reporting providers. In addition, it showcases a possible approach to implement an application-based security layer by leveraging the Windows 2003 Authorization Manager.

Chapter 14 demonstrates how you can distribute reports via subscriptions. It starts by explaining how the RS subscribed-delivery process works. Then, it looks at how you can distribute reports via e-mail and file-share delivery extensions.

Part 4, "Advanced reporting," teaches you advanced techniques so you can make the most out of Reporting Services. It consists of chapters 15 and 16.

Chapter 15 discusses the implementation details of three custom extensions that you can use to extend the features of RS. It starts by implementing a custom dataset extension to report off ADO.NET datasets. Then, we discuss a custom delivery extension that can be used to distribute reports to an arbitrary Web service. Next, we author a custom security extension. Finally, we show how to plug in custom HTTP modules to implement preprocessing tasks before the request reaches the Report Server.

Chapter 16 shows you how to conduct a capacity-planning study to evaluate RS in terms of performance and scalability. You learn how to establish performance goals, how to create test scripts with the Application Center Test, and how to stress test your Report Server installation. You can apply the skills you harvest in this chapter for stress testing not only the Report Server but any web-based application as well.

source code

The book's source code can be downloaded from Manning's web site at http://www.manning.com/lachev. The next sections discuss the software requirements for executing the code and the steps to set it up.

Instead of partitioning the source code on a per-chapter basis, we decided to consolidate most of it in two applications: a WinForm-based AWReporterWin application and a web-based AWReporterWeb application. This approach has several advantages, including the following:

- Simplifies the setup—For example, you need only one virtual folder to host the AWReporterWeb web application.
- Allows the reader to launch the samples conveniently from a single application menu.
- Simulates real-world applications—For example, you can encapsulate the code logic in a set of common classes.

The trade-off is that you may not have all the software dependencies required to compile the sample applications and you may run into compilation errors, as explained in the next section.

SOFTWARE REQUIREMENTS

Table 1 outlines the software requirements needed to run all code samples.

Table 1. Software requirements

Software	Reason	Used in Chapters
Reporting Services 1.0 (Developer or Enterprise edition)	The Standard edition doesn't include custom security extensions and data-driven subscriptions.	All
Microsoft Windows 2003 Server	For the Authorization Manager component. If you want to skip this sample, you can use Windows XP or Windows 2000.	13
Microsoft Visual Studio 2003 with .NET Framework 1.1	Required by Reporting Services.	All

continued on next page

Table 1. Software requirements *(continued)*

Software	Reason	Used in Chapters
Microsoft SQL Server 2000	Required by Reporting Services. You will need to install the AdventureWorks2000 database from the RS Setup program.	All
Microsoft Office 2003	For Office Web Components and Access reporting. You will also need to install the Office 2003 Primary Interop Assemblies (PIAs).	12, 13
DynWSLib	The Dynamic XML Web Services Invocation sample for invoking web services dynamically. Can be downloaded for free from gotdotnet.com.	15
Microsoft WebService Behavior	For invoking Web services on the client side of a web application. Can be downloaded for free from MSDN.	11
Application Center Test	ACT is included with Visual Studio .NET 2003.	16
Analog Web Analyzer	For analyzing IIS logs. Can be downloaded for free from http://www.analog.cx/.	16
Report Magic	For reporting off analog files. Can be downloaded for free from http://www.report-magic.org/.	16

Some samples have more involved setup requirements. For example, chapter 12 requires the Office Web Components Primary Interop Assemblies (PIAs) to be installed, while chapter 13 requires the Authorization Manager (available only on Windows 2003 and Windows 2000 as a separate download) to be installed. To prevent compilation errors because of missing external dependencies, we excluded the source code for these two chapters, the AWReporterWin and AWReporterWeb projects, respectively. Please follow the setup instructions found in the readme files in the sample folders to run these samples successfully.

In case you still experience compilation errors as a result of missing external dependencies, we suggest that you resolve the issue by excluding the samples. For example, let's say you don't have Office 2003 and you can't compile AWReporterWin. To fix this, right-click on the corresponding folder that contains the sample code in the Visual Studio .NET 2003 Solution Explorer and choose the Exclude from Project menu item. Then, compile the project and fix the compilation errors (if any) by commenting out any references to the excluded code.

SETTING UP THE SOURCE CODE

Once you download the source code archive, you can extract the zip file to any folder of your hard drive. Once this is done, the folders listed in table 2 will be created.

Table 2. Source code folders

Folder	Purpose	Used in Chapters
AWReporterWeb	An ASP.NET web-based application that demonstrates various web-based reporting techniques. You will need to set up an IIS virtual folder pointing to this folder.	9, 10, 11, 12, 13, 15
AWReporterWin	A WinForm-based application that demonstrates how you can add reporting features to WinForm applications.	2, 7, 9, 10, 11, 12,13
AWReportViewer	The enhanced version of the ReportViewer sample control for server-side web reporting.	11
AWRsLibrary	For report forecasting.	6
Database	A database projects that includes SQL scripts to create stored procedures and views in the AdventureWorks2000 database.	As dictated by the code sample setup instructions
Extensions	Includes the custom data, delivery, and security extensions.	15
OpenForecast	The converted to J# OpenForecast package.	6
Performance Testing	Includes the test scripts for performance testing RS.	16
Reports	Includes the sample reports that we author in this book.	All

Most of the code samples include readme files with specific step-by-step instructions that you follow to set up the code sample.

Running the sample reports in Visual Studio .NET

Perhaps most of you will be eager to run the sample reports immediately. To execute the reports successfully under the Visual Studio .NET Report Designer, follow these steps:

Step 1 Copy the AWC.RS.Library.dll and OpenForecast.dll to the Report Designer binary folder, C:\Program Files\Microsoft SQL Server\80\Tools\Report Designer.

Step 2 Open the AWReporter.rptproj (found under the Reports folder) in Visual Studio .NET 2003.

Step 3 Change the data source credentials of the AW2000 Shared DS data source by double-clicking the AW2000 Shared DS.rds file and switching to the Credentials tab. Enter the user name and password of a database login that has at least Read permissions to the tables in the AdventureWorks2000 database.

At this point, you should be able to run most of the reports.

Some reports require a more involved setup process. For example, there are reports that require that additional assemblies, such as AWC.RS.Extensions.dll and AWC.RS.Library.dll, be configured properly. The readme files that accompany the sample code include specific step-by-step instructions about how to configure these assemblies.

Deploying the reports to the Report Server

To run most of the code samples successfully, you need to deploy the sample reports to the Report Server. Assuming that you have Administrator rights to the report catalog, the easiest way to do this is to follow these steps:

Step 1 Copy the AWC.RS.Library.dll and OpenForecast.dll to the Report Server binary folder, C:\Program Files\Microsoft SQL Server\MSSQL\Reporting Services\ReportServer\bin. This step is needed because some reports reference these assemblies, and the deployment process will fail if these assemblies are not found in the Report Server binary folder.

Step 2 If you haven't done this already, copy the AWC.RS.Library.dll and OpenForecast.dll to the Report Designer binary folder C:\Program Files\Microsoft SQL Server\80\Tools\Report Designer.

Step 3 Open the AWReporter.rptproj project (found under the Reports folder) in Visual Studio .NET 2003.

Step 4 Right-click the AWReporter project in the Visual Studio .NET Solution Explorer and choose Properties to open the project's properties.

Step 5 Verify that the TargetFolder setting is set to AWReporter and the TargetServerURL setting is set to http://<servername>/ReportServer, where <servername> is the computer name where the Report Server is installed. If RS is installed locally, the TargetServerURL setting should be http://localhost/ReportServer.

Step 6 Click the Configuration Manager button and verify that both the Build and Deploy check boxes are selected for Debug configuration. Click OK to dismiss the Property Pages dialog.

Step 7 Right-click the AWReporter project again and choose Deploy. This will build the reports and then deploy them to the report catalog.

Step 8 To verify the setup, open the Report Manager web portal. If RS is installed locally, the default Report Manager URL will be http://localhost/reports. Under the Home folder, verify that the AWReporter folder exists. Click its link and run the Sales By Territory report. If everything is okay, the report will render in the browser.

Configuring the AWReporterWeb application

To configure the web-based samples, you need to set up the AWReporterWeb virtual folder by following these steps:

Step 1 Right-click the AWReporterWeb folder in Windows Explorer and choose Properties.

Step 2 Select the Web Sharing tab.

Step 3 Click the Share This Folder radio button.

Step 4 In the Edit Alias dialog, enter **AWReporterWeb** as an alias.

Step 5 Make sure that the Read Access Permission check box is selected and the Scripts radio button is selected. Click OK to close the Edit Alias dialog.

Step 6 Open the Internet Information Manager (IIS) console. Right-click the AWReporterWeb folder, choose Properties, and then select the Directory Security tab. Click the Edit button in the Authentication and Access Control panel. Uncheck the Enable Anonymous Access check box. Make sure that the Integrated Windows Authentication check box is selected.

author online

Your purchase of *Microsoft Reporting Services in Action* includes free access to a private web forum run by Manning Publications, where you can make comments about the book, ask technical questions, and receive help from the author and from other users. To access the forum and subscribe to it, point your web browser to www.manning.com/lachev. This page provides information on how to get on the forum once you are registered, what kind of help is available, and the rules of conduct on the forum.

Manning's commitment to our readers is to provide a venue where a meaningful dialog among individual readers and between readers and the author can take place. It is not a commitment to any specific amount of participation on the part of the author, whose contribution to the AO remains voluntary (and unpaid). We suggest you try asking the author some challenging questions, lest his interest stray! The Author Online forum and the archives of previous discussions will be accessible from the publisher's web site as long as the book is in print.

ABOUT THE AUTHOR

Teo Lachev has more than 11 years of experience designing and developing Microsoft-centered solutions. He currently works as a technology consultant for the Enterprise Application Services practice of Hewlett-Packard. Teo is a Microsoft Certified Solution Developer and Microsoft Certified Trainer. He lives in Atlanta, Georgia.

You can contact Teo through the Author Online forum, by sending him e-mail at teo@prologika.com, or by visiting his web site at http://www.prologika.com.

about the title and cover

By combining introductions, overviews, and how-to examples, Manning's *In Action* books are designed to help learning *and* remembering. According to research in cognitive science, the things people remember are things they discover during self-motivated exploration. Although no one at Manning is a cognitive scientist, we are convinced that for learning to become permanent it must pass through stages of exploration, play, and, interestingly, re-telling of what is being learned. People understand and remember new things, which is to say they master them, only after actively exploring them. Humans learn *in action*. An essential part of an *In Action* guide is that it is example-driven. It encourages the reader to try things out, to play with new code, and explore new ideas.

There is another, more mundane, reason for the title of this book: our readers are busy. They use books to do a job or solve a problem. They need books that allow them to jump in and jump out easily and learn just what they want, just when they want it. They need books that aid them *in action*. The books in this series are designed for such readers.

ABOUT THE COVER ILLUSTRATION

The figure on the cover of *Microsoft Reporting Services in Action* is a "Giancataro," who, judging by his attire, might be a tradesman or basket weaver. We know the illustration is taken from an Italian source estimated to be about 200 years old. Our efforts to get a translation of "Giancataro" have failed. The first reader who correctly solves the puzzle of what the word means will receive a free Manning book of his or her choice. Please post your translations to the Author Online forum at www.manning.com/lachev.

We at Manning celebrate the inventiveness, the initiative, and the fun of the computer business with book covers based on the rich diversity of regional life of two centuries ago brought back to life by pictures assembled from various collections. This was a time when the dress codes of two regions separated by a few dozen miles identified people uniquely as belonging to one or the other. Dress codes have changed since then and it is now often hard to tell the inhabitant of one continent from another. Perhaps, trying to view it optimistically, we have traded a cultural and visual diversity for a more varied and interesting personal, intellectual—and technical life.

Introducing Microsoft Reporting Services

So much information, so little time ... the character "Poison Ivy" would likely say if the Batman saga was taking place in today's enterprise.

We all know that the dot.com boom is history and so are the lavish IT budgets. In the doldrums of the economic recovery, organizations tend to spend their money on streamlining internal processes to gain a competitive advantage. According to Microsoft, today's information workers spend as much as 80 percent of their time gathering information, with only 20 percent left to analyze it and make a decision. In many organizations, such requests consume significant IT and development resources. Too often, Excel spreadsheets are the prevalent reporting tools today and manual data entry or "pencil-pushing" is among the top reasons for inaccurate data and wrong decisions. Aware of these issues, Microsoft initiated the Microsoft SQL Server 2000 Reporting Services project at the beginning of the new millennium, with a bold vision to "enable employees at all levels of an organization to realize the promise of Business Intelligence to promote better decision making."

This chapter provides a panoramic view of Reporting Services (RS). Throughout the rest of this book I will use the terms *Reporting Services* and *RS* interchangeably. You will see

- Why RS is such a compelling choice for enterprise reporting
- The main parts of the RS architecture
- The report-generation process and report lifecycle
- The steps for creating your first RS report

1.1 WHAT IS RS?

Regardless of the alphabet soup of terms and acronyms that are popping up like daisies almost every day and that have probably become a part of your IT vocabulary—terms such as BI (business intelligence), OLAP (online analytical processing), data mining, DSSs (decision support systems), EISs (executive information systems), digital dashboards, enterprise portals, and enterprise data buses—the purpose of enterprise reporting is to simply "get out" what was "put in." Therefore, for many applications, reporting represents the last, and often most important, stage of the IT pipeline.

To clarify the last point, let's consider a typical scenario that RS can address effectively. Let's say that an organization has built a web portal for submitting orders online. As the business grows, the same organization may need to implement a reporting infrastructure to analyze sales data and understand its business, for example, to find out the top-selling products, customer demographics, and so forth. To accomplish this goal, the organization could leverage RS.

We use the term *report* to refer to the web-based or saved-to-file counterpart of a standard paper-oriented report. For example, an organization may want to give its customers an option to generate various reports online—an Order History report, for instance. Web reporting has traditionally been difficult to implement. Even more difficult has been exporting reports to different file formats. RS solve both problems elegantly, for two reasons. First, out-of-the-box RS is web-enabled. Second, most popular export formats are natively supported.

1.1.1 Why do we need RS?

Ironically, despite the important role that reporting plays in today's enterprise, creating and distributing reports have been traditionally painstaking and laborious chores. To understand why we need RS, let's analyze the reporting problem space.

Table 1.1 lists some of the most pressing issues surrounding the reporting arena and how RS addresses them.

Table 1.1 How Microsoft RS deals with the reporting problem space

Reporting Need	How RS addresses it?
Report authoring can be labor intensive.	By using the powerful Report Designer, you can author reports as easily as you can with Microsoft Access.
Centralized report management is needed.	RS enables you to save your reports in a single report repository.

continued on next page

Table 1.1 How Microsoft RS deals with the reporting problem space *(continued)*

Reporting Need	How RS addresses it?
Reports need to be distributed to various destinations.	RS supports both on-demand and subscription-based reporting. Reports can be requested on-demand by Win-Form and web-based applications. Alternatively, reports can be distributed to a list of subscribers.
Reports often need to be exported in different electronic formats.	RS supports many popular export formats out of the box.
Proprietary nature of reporting tools doesn't allow you to extend them.	RS has a flexible architecture that allows you to extend RS capabilities by writing custom code.
Reports need to be secured.	RS offers a comprehensive security model that administrators can leverage to enforce secured access to reports by assigning users to roles. When the default Windows-based authentication is not a good fit, it can be replaced with custom security implementations.
Enterprise reporting solutions can be costly.	To minimize cost, RS is bundled and licensed with SQL Server. If you have a licensed copy of SQL Server 2000, you may run RS on the same server for no additional license fee.

Depending on your particular situation you may find other compelling reasons to target RS as your reporting platform of choice. We revisit the RS features throughout this chapter.

Supported report types

Your reporting requirements may call for authoring various types of reports that differ in complexity. For example, your users may request that a large report include a document map for easy navigation. RS lets you design a variety of report types, as listed in table 1.2.

Table 1.2 RS supports various report types

Report Type	Purpose	Example
Tabular	Displays data in a table format with a fixed number or rows and columns.	Excel-type reports
Freeform	Data regions are positioned arbitrarily on the page by the report author.	Invoice-invoice details report
Chart	Presents data graphically.	Employee performance chart
Crosstab (matrix)	Data is rotated to present row data as columns.	A report that shows products on rows and time on columns
Drilldown	Includes expandable sections.	A company performance crosstab report where product can be expanded by category and brand

continued on next page

Table 1.2 **RS supports various report types *(continued)***

Report Type	Purpose	Example
Drillthrough	Generated from clicking on a hyperlink.	Customer Order History with hyperlinks on the order identifier to show the order details report
Interactive	Includes interactive features, such as document maps, hyperlinks, visible-on-demand sections, and so forth.	Adobe Acrobat–type reports with document maps on the left side

Although most popular reporting tools support many of the report types shown in table 1.2, RS makes the report-authoring process as easy as working with Microsoft Access reporting functionality. For example, report authors can drag and drop items to define the report's appearance.

Now that we understand what RS is, let's see how it fits in the Microsoft BI vision.

1.1.2 How is RS implemented?

Microsoft released version 1.0 of RS at the beginning of 2004 as an add-on to Microsoft SQL Server 2000. At a very high level, RS can be defined as a server-based platform for authoring, managing, and distributing reports. We discuss the RS architecture in more detail in a moment. For now, note that RS is integrated with and requires several other Microsoft products, including:

- Windows 2000 or above as a server operating system
- Microsoft SQL Server 2000 (with Service Pack 3a) and above
- Internet Information Server (IIS) 5.0 or above
- .NET Framework 1.1
- Visual Studio .NET 2003 for report authoring and testing

For more information about installing RS, please refer to appendix A.

RS editions

To address different user needs, RS is available in several editions, as you can see by looking at table 1.3.

Table 1.3 RS supports editions to meet various reporting needs

Edition	Choose when...
Standard	You need to install RS on a single computer. The Standard edition doesn't support clustered deployment to load-balance multiple RS instances.
Enterprise	You need all RS features, including load balancing.
Developer	You have to integrate RS with client applications or extend its capabilities by writing .NET code. The Developer edition supports the same feature set as the Enterprise edition, but it is for use as a test and development system, not as a production server.
Evaluation	You need to evaluate RS. The Evaluation edition expires after 120 days.

For more information about how the RS editions differ, refer to the product documentation or the "Reporting Services Features Comparison" section in the RS official website at http://microsoft.com/sql/reporting/productinfo/features.asp.

For information about RS licensing requirements, visit the "How to License Reporting Services" page at http://www.microsoft.com/sql/reporting/howtobuy/howtolicensers.asp.

1.1.3 RS and the Microsoft BI platform

RS is positioned as an integral part of Microsoft's business intelligence (BI) platform. This platform is a multiproduct offering whose goal is to address the most common data management and analysis challenges that many organizations face every day, such as analyzing vast volumes of data, trend discovery, data management, and of course, comprehensive reporting.

During the RS official launch presentation on January 27, 2004, Paul Flessner, Microsoft senior vice president of Enterprise Services, outlined the place of RS in the Microsoft BI platform offering, as shown in figure 1.1.

Table 1.4 outlines the purpose of the major building blocks within the Microsoft BI platform.

Most of you have probably used more than one of these products in the past to solve your data management and analysis needs. Indeed, most of them have been around for a while. What was missing was a product for authoring, managing, and

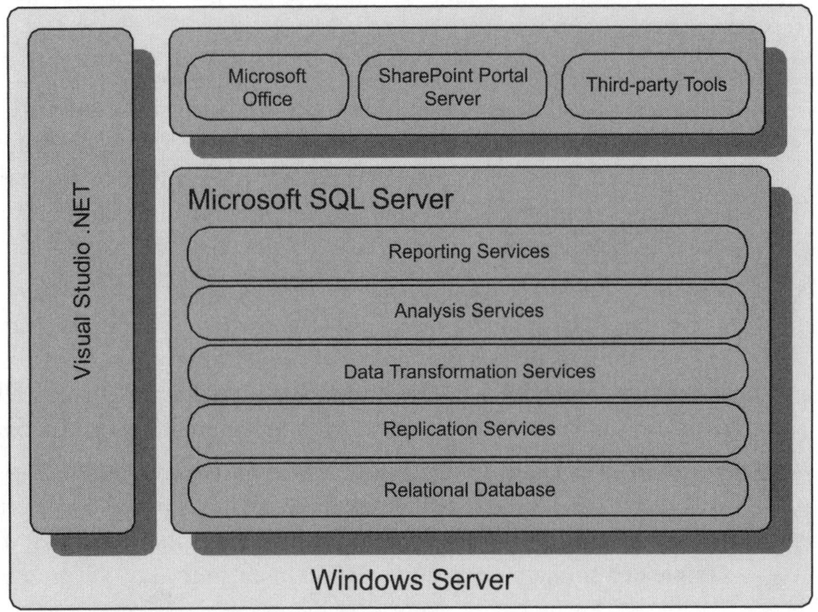

Figure 1.1 The Microsoft BI platform consists of several products layered on top of the SQL Server database engine and addresses various data management and reporting needs.

Table 1.4 The key Microsoft BI platform components

Component	Purpose
Microsoft SQL Server	A relational database to store data
Analysis Services	An analytical processing (OLAP) engine
Data Transformation Services	Tools for extracting, transforming and loading data
Reporting Services	Server-based reporting platform for report authoring, management and delivery
Replication Services	Replicates data to heterogeneous data sources
Microsoft Office	Desktop applications for data analysis and reporting
SharePoint Portal Server	Business Intelligence collaboration
Visual Studio.NET	A development tool to create .NET-based applications, including analytical and reporting solutions.

generating reports that could be easily integrated with all types of applications. RS fills the bill nicely.

Having introduced you to RS, let's take a panoramic view of its features to understand why it can be such a compelling choice for enterprise reporting.

1.2 RS AT A GLANCE

Even in its first release, RS offers a broad array of features that can address various reporting needs:

- *Information workers can leverage RS to author both standard ("canned") reports and reports with interactive features.* Here, we use the term "standard" to refer to reports that display static data. An interesting aspect of RS is that your reports can include a variety of features that provide interactivity to users. For example, the end user can show or hide items in a report and click links that launch other reports or web pages.
- *Third-party vendors can target RS to package reports as a part of their applications.* For example, if customers have RS installed, the vendor setup program can upload the report files to the Report Server. You'll see this done in chapter 2. Note that the next version of RS is expected to include stand-alone controls for generating reports directly from report files and will not require RS to be installed.
- *Organizations can use RS to report-enable their business-to-business (B2B) or business-to-consumer (B2C) applications.* For example, an organization can selectively expose some of its data in the form of reports to its business partners. You'll see an example of a similar integration scenario in chapter 11.

Let's now get a glimpse of the RS landscape and observe some of RS's most prominent landmarks. Don't worry if you find you are not getting the Big Picture yet. In section 1.3, we take a closer look at the main pieces of the RS architecture.

1.2.1 Authoring features

As a report author, with RS you have several choices for creating reports. We discuss each of these options in detail in chapter 2. For now, we'd like to introduce you to the Report Designer; this will likely be the option that you will use most of the time for report authoring.

Introducing the Report Designer

Using the Report Designer graphical environment, you can create reports of different types, such as crosstab drilldown reports, like the one shown in figure 1.2.

RS doesn't restrict your report-authoring options to static paper-oriented reports. Instead, you can make your reports more versatile and easy to use by adding interactive features, such as expandable sections, hyperlinks, and document maps. Given its tight integration with the Visual Studio. NET integrated development environment (IDE), the Report Designer provides you with access to all report design features as well as team development features, such as source code management.

About the Report Definition Language

At this point, you may be wondering what an RS-based report file looks like and how it is stored. RS saves the report as an Extensible Markup Language (XML) file that is described in a Report Definition Language schema.

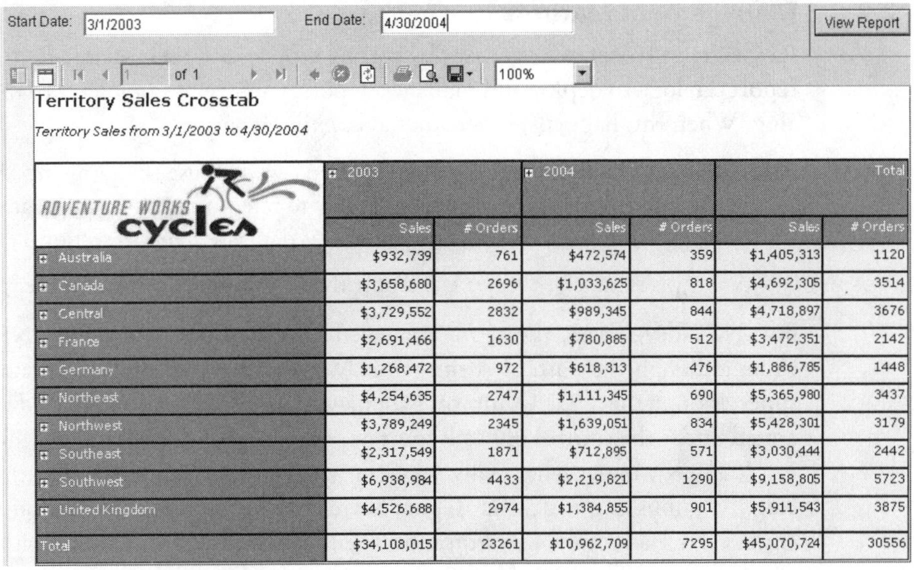

Start Date: 3/1/2003 End Date: 4/30/2004 View Report

of 1 100%

Territory Sales Crosstab

Territory Sales from 3/1/2003 to 4/30/2004

ADVENTURE WORKS cycles	2003		2004		Total	
	Sales	# Orders	Sales	# Orders	Sales	# Orders
Australia	$932,739	761	$472,574	359	$1,405,313	1120
Canada	$3,658,680	2696	$1,033,625	818	$4,692,305	3514
Central	$3,729,552	2832	$989,345	844	$4,718,897	3676
France	$2,691,466	1630	$780,885	512	$3,472,351	2142
Germany	$1,268,472	972	$618,313	476	$1,886,785	1448
Northeast	$4,254,635	2747	$1,111,345	690	$5,365,980	3437
Northwest	$3,789,249	2345	$1,639,051	834	$5,428,301	3179
Southeast	$2,317,549	1871	$712,895	571	$3,030,444	2442
Southwest	$6,938,984	4433	$2,219,821	1290	$9,158,805	5723
United Kingdom	$4,526,688	2974	$1,384,855	901	$5,911,543	3875
Total	$34,108,015	23261	$10,962,709	7295	$45,070,724	30556

Figure 1.2 With RS you can create various types of reports, including drilldown crosstab reports like this one.

DEFINITION A *report definition* contains report data retrieval and layout information. The report definition is described in an XML schema, called the Report Definition Language (RDL).

Saving reports as XML-based report definition files offers two main advantages:

- *It makes the report format open and extensible.* Using the XML-based RDL format is beneficial for achieving interoperability among applications and vendors. Microsoft is working with other industry leaders to promote RDL as an XML-based standard for report definitions. Visit the RS official website (check the Resources section for the link) for a list of Microsoft RS partners.
- *It makes the report portable.* For example, you can easily save the report to a file and upload it to another Report Server. In chapter 2 you'll see how a third-party reporting tool leverages this feature for ad-hoc reporting.

If you use the Report Designer to create your report, its definition will be automatically generated for you. However, just as you don't have to use Visual Studio .NET to write .NET applications, you can write the report definition using an editor of your choice, such as Notepad, or generate it programmatically (as you will see in chapter 2). Of course, the Report Designer makes authoring reports a whole lot easier. Third-party tools will most likely emerge at some point to provide alternative RDL editors.

1.2.2 Management features

RS facilitates report management by storing reports and their related items in a central report catalog. To deploy and manage a report, you need to upload it to the report catalog. When this happens, it becomes a *managed* report.

DEFINITIONS Throughout the rest of this book we will use the terms *report catalog* and *report repository* interchangeably to refer to the RS Configuration Database. For more information about this database, refer to section 1.3.2.

A *managed report* is a report that is uploaded to the report catalog.

For .NET developers, the term "managed" has nothing to do with .NET managed code, although the pattern is the same. While .NET managed code runs under the supervision of the .NET Common Language Runtime (CLR), a managed report is generated under the control of the Report Server.

You may wonder what really happens when a report is uploaded to the report catalog. At publishing time, the Report Server parses the report definition (RDL), generates a .NET assembly, and stores the assembly in the Report Configuration Database for the report. The RDL file is never used again. When the report is processed, the assembly is loaded and executed by the Report Server.

A report can include other items, such as images and data source–related information. These report-related items are also stored in the report catalog. Finally, the report catalog captures additional information, called *metadata*, associated with reports. For example, just as you can organize physical files in folders, RS allows you to organize reports in folders.

DEFINITION The report *metadata* describes additional configuration information associated with a report, such as security permissions, the parent folder, and so forth.

RS offers centralized report management that administrators will appreciate. To simplify the administration of the report catalog, RS comes with a tool called the Report Manager. The Report Manager is implemented as a web-based application, and as such it is easily accessible. This tool empowers you to manage just about any aspect of the report repository, including

- Report information and metadata, such as the folder structure and report properties
- Data sources from which the report will draw data
- Report parameters (for parameterized reports)
- Security

1.2.3 Delivery features

Reports hosted under RS can be delivered using on-demand ("pulled") delivery or subscribed ("pushed") delivery. The more common scenario is on-demand delivery, where the user requests the report explicitly. As a report author, you don't have to do anything special to web-enable your report because RS does this for you once it is uploaded to the report catalog.

The "pushed" delivery option alone can justify implementing RS. This option gives end users the ability to subscribe to reports, so reports will be sent to them when a certain event is triggered—when a timing event triggers, for instance, for report subscriptions based on a schedule. As another example, a financial institution could allow its customers to opt in and subscribe to certain reports of interest, such as a monthly bank statement. Then, at the end of the month, the bank statement report could be generated and sent to users via e-mail.

We'll discuss the report-delivery process in more detail in section 1.5.

1.2.4 Extensibility features

An important characteristic of every enterprise-oriented product, such as RS, is that it has to be easily extendable. Simply put, extensibility relates to the system's ability to accommodate new features that are built out of old ones. One of the things I like most about RS is the extensibility features it includes by virtue of its open and flexible architecture. Developers can easily extend RS by writing .NET code in their preferred .NET language. Specifically, you can extend RS in the following areas:

- *Custom .NET code*—.NET developers can enhance reports programmatically by writing .NET custom code. Chapter 6 demonstrates how you can add forecasting features to your reports by using prepackaged code in the form of .NET assemblies.

- *Data processing extensions*—Out of the box, RS can connect to any data source that has an ODBC or OLE DB provider. In addition, you can write your own custom data extensions to report off other data structures, as chapter 15 illustrates.
- *Delivery extensions*—Out of the box, subscribed reports can be delivered via e-mail or file share delivery extensions. Developers can write their own delivery extensions to deliver the report to other destinations, such as to web services, as you'll learn in chapter 15.
- *Security extensions*—By default, RS uses the Windows-based security model to enforce restricted access to the report catalog. If Windows-based security is not an option, you can replace it with custom security models. You'll see an example of how this could be done in chapter 15, where we'll implement custom authentication and authorization for Internet-oriented reporting.
- *Rendering extensions*—Generating reports in other export formats than the ones supported natively can be accomplished by writing custom rendering extensions. See section 1.4.2 for more information about the supported export formats.

1.2.5 Scalability features

A *scalable* application responds well under increased loads. RS can scale up and out to address the high-volume reporting requirements of large organizations. It is designed from the ground up to process reports efficiently. For example, it supports several report caching options, such as report execution caching, snapshots, and report sessions, as we discuss in chapter 7.

Reporting Services Enterprise Edition supports clustered deployment, which you can use to load-balance several RS servers on multiple machines. This allows enterprise organizations with high-scalability requirements to scale out RS and provides fault tolerance. RS performance is the subject of chapter 16.

1.2.6 Security features

RS is designed to provide a secured environment from the ground up. It offers a comprehensive security model for accessing reports that leverages Windows authentication. This model maps the user Windows account or group to a *role*, and the role describes what permissions the user has to access items in the report catalog. Report administrators can add Windows users to predefined roles or create new ones.

Once again, when the default Windows-based security model is not a good fit, you can replace it by plugging in your own custom authentication and authorization implementations in the form of custom security extensions.

To promote trustworthy computing, RS leverages the .NET code-based security to "sandbox" custom code based on configurable security policies. We discuss the RS security model in chapter 8.

1.2.7 Deployment features

Because it is server-based, RS has zero deployment requirements for integrating with client applications. For this reason, any type of client applications can target RS, not only .NET-based applications. Because you can access RS through the two most popular web protocols, HTTP-GET and Simple Object Access Protocol (SOAP), any web-capable application can be integrated with RS, regardless of the targeted platform and development language.

DEFINITIONS The Hypertext Transfer Protocol (HTTP), on which the Internet is based, comes in two flavors: HTTP-GET and HTTP-POST. While HTTP-GET passes request parameters as a part of the URL, HTTP-POST passes them as name/value pairs inside the actual message.

Simple Object Access Protocol (SOAP) is a lightweight XML-based protocol, layered on top of HTTP, for exchanging structured and type information on the Web. In recent years, SOAP has become the industry-standard protocol for communicating with web services.

Integrating your applications with RS requires a good grasp of its architecture. The next section outlines the major RS building blocks.

1.3 RS ARCHITECTURE

An important feature of the RS architecture is that it is *service*-oriented as opposed to *object*-oriented. Don Box, a Microsoft prominent architect working on the next-generation web services, outlines the following four characteristics of a service-oriented architecture:

- *Boundaries are explicit.* Cross-application communication uses explicit messaging rather than implicit method call invocation.
- *Services are autonomous.* The lifetime of a service-oriented application is not controlled by its clients.
- *Services share schema and contract, not class.* Service-oriented applications advertise their functionality to the outside world using XML-based schemas.
- *Service compatibility is determined based on policies.* By using policies, service-oriented applications indicate which conditions must be true in order for the service to function properly.

You may have used object-oriented reporting tools in the past in which the report consumer instantiates an object instance of the report provider. A characteristic of this model is that both the report consumer and the report provider instances share the same process space. For example, to render a Microsoft Access report, you need to instantiate an object of type `Access.Application`. Then, you use OLE automation to instruct Access to open the report database and render the report.

You will probably agree that as useful and widespread as the object-oriented model is, it is subject to some well-known shortcomings. For example, both the consumer and provider are usually installed on the same machine. As a consequence, the reports hosted by the report provider are not easily accessible by geographically dispersed clients. For instance, only COM-capable clients can interface with Microsoft Access.

A second shortcoming involves application interdependencies. Object-oriented applications are typically deployed as a unit. All Microsoft Access clients, for example, need to have the Access type library installed locally in order to establish a reference to it.

To address these shortcomings, RS departs radically from the object-oriented paradigm. In terms of reporting, the RS service-oriented architecture offers two distinct advantages: (1) Administrators can centralize the report storage and management in one place, and (2) it promotes application interoperability—report consumers can request reports over standard web protocols, such as HTTP-GET and SOAP.

The RS service-oriented architecture can be better explained in the context of a three-tier application deployment view, as shown in figure 1.3.

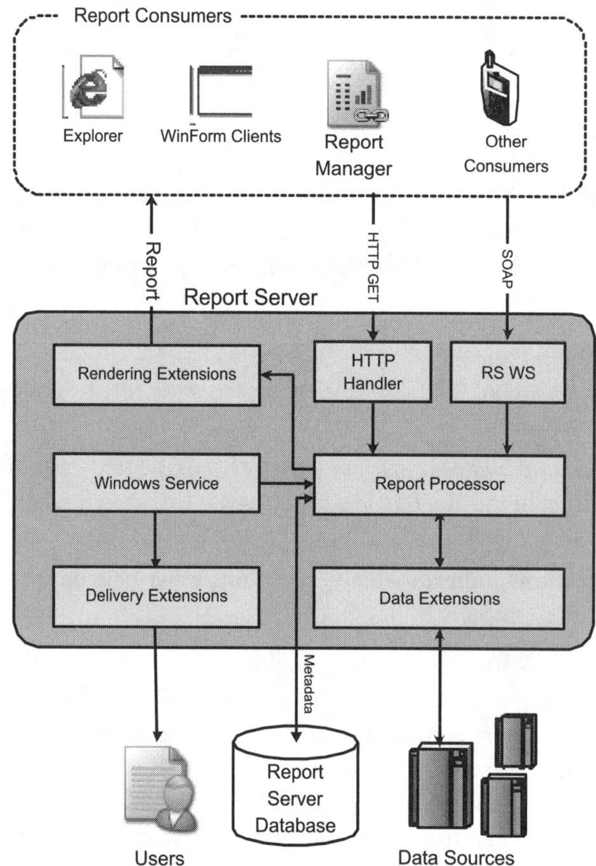

Figure 1.3
Report consumers submit report requests to the Report Server, which queries data sources to retrieve the report data and generate the report.

The RS architecture includes the following main components:

- The Report Server, whose main task is to generate reports
- The Report Server Configuration Database (the report catalog), which serves as a centralized report repository
- The Report Manager, a web-based tool for managing the report catalog and requesting reports.

Let's explain the role of each component in more detail, starting with the Report Server.

1.3.1 The Report Server

At the heart of the RS architecture is the Report Server engine. The Report Server performs the following main tasks:

- Handles the report requests sent by the report consumers. I will use the term "*report consumer*" to describe any client application that requests reports from the Report Server. Once again, this could be *any* application regardless of the language in which it was written or the platform it runs on.
- Performs all chores needed to process the report, including executing and rendering the report, as we discuss in detail shortly.
- Provides additional services, such as snapshots and report caching, authorization and security policy enforcement, session management, scheduling, and subscribed delivery.

DEFINITION We will use the term "report request" to refer to the set of input arguments that the report consumer has to pass to the Report Server to generate a report successfully. At minimum, the report request must specify the path to the report and the report name. Other arguments can be passed as report parameters, including rendering format, whether the report should include the standard toolbar, and so forth.

Looking at figure 1.3, you can see that the Report Server encompasses several components, including the Report Processor, Windows Service, and extensions. From an implementation standpoint, perhaps the best way to describe the Report Server is to say that it is implemented as a set of .NET assemblies located in the C:\Program Files\Microsoft SQL Server\MSSQL\RS\ReportServer\bin folder.

NOTE An interesting fact about the Report Server is that it is 100% written in C# code. As far as I can tell, this qualifies it as the first true .NET server. No, unfortunately the source code is not provided. Moreover, the Report Server assemblies are obfuscated to prevent reverse engineering, reuse, and abuse.

As you know, the Report Server's main role is to generate reports. To accomplish this, the server retrieves the report definition from the report catalog, combines it with data from the data source, and generates the report.

Figure 1.3 and the product documentation indicate that the Report Processor component is responsible for report processing. The implementation details of the processor are not disclosed at the time of this writing, but most likely the majority of its functionality is encapsulated in the Microsoft.ReportingServices.Processing.dll assembly. For the remainder of this book we use the terms *Report Processor* and *Report Server* interchangeably.

Section 1.4 explains the purpose of each of the Report Server components and shows how they relate to report processing.

From an integration standpoint, perhaps the most important observation that you need to draw from figure 1.3 is that the Report Server has two web-based communication façades that expose its functionality to external clients: HTTP Handler, which accepts URL-based report requests submitted via HTTP-GET, and the Web service (shown in figure 1.3 as RS WS), which handles SOAP requests. You will see how these façades impact the report-delivery process in section 1.5.

1.3.2 The Report Server database

When you install RS, the setup program creates the Report Server database. This database is implemented as two physical SQL Server 2000 databases: The Reporting Services Configuration Database, ReportServer, hosts the report catalog and metadata. In this section, we'll take a closer look at each.

The Reporting Services Configuration Database

The Reporting Services Configuration Database, ReportServer, hosts the report catalog and metadata. As we mentioned earlier, in order for a report to be available to the end users, its report definition file must be uploaded (published) to the catalog.

If you open this database in the SQL Server Enterprise Manager, you will be able to deduce the purpose of most of its tables. For example, the Report Server Configuration Database keeps the catalog items in the Catalog table, the data source information in the Data-Source table, and so forth. Note that querying the report catalog directly is discouraged by Microsoft. Instead, the recommended way to access the report catalog is through the Report Server APIs. Microsoft also discourages you from making data changes directly to the catalog. The reason behind this is that Microsoft may change the catalog schema in the future but will maintain backward compatibility through the Report Server API.

As you may recall, RS can be deployed in a load-balanced cluster environment. In this deployment model, the Report Server database is shared among all nodes of the cluster.

The Reporting Services Temporary Database

The RS setup program also creates a second database, ReportServerTempDB, which is used by RS for caching purposes. For example, once the report is executed, the Report Server saves a copy of the report in the ReportServerTempDB database.

DEFINITION *Report caching* describes the Report Server feature of keeping the report intermediate format in the Report Server database for a certain duration.

We'll return to the topic of report caching in chapter 7.

The Adventure Works 2000 sample database

Finally, if you install the RS samples, the setup program installs a sample database called AdventureWorks2000. This database is also used by other Microsoft products, such as Commerce Server and Notification Services.

The AdventureWorks2000 database includes a much more "realistic" sales ordering database model than the SQL Server sample databases, Northwind or Pubs. You will quickly realize this by surveying the data held in the more than 60 tables. We'll work with this sample database in section 1.7, where you'll have a chance to create a report using RS.

1.3.3 The Report Manager

Implemented as an ASP.NET web application, the Report Manager performs two main tasks: report management and requests for reports. You can think of the Report Manager as an application façade that communicates with the Report Server via the Report Server APIs. From the Report Server perspective, the Report Manager is no different than any other client application.

Report management

Users familiar with SharePoint Portal Server will find the Report Manager similar to this product both in terms of user interface and purpose. As you can with SharePoint, you can use the Report Manager to create folders, upload resources, manage subscriptions, and set up security.

For example, figure 1.4 shows that I used the Report Manager to navigate to a folder AWReporter and to retrieve a list of the catalog items under this folder. You can click on a report link to run a report or access and change the report properties.

In case you're wondering where the items shown in figure 1.4 come from, we will create them in the next few chapters when we discuss the report-authoring process.

Keep in mind that in RS you work with virtual folders. Neither the folders nor the report definition files actually exist in a file system. Instead, they exist in the Report Server Database as metadata, but they appear as folders and items when you access the Report Server through the Report Manager.

Requesting reports

Sometimes, building a reporting application might be overkill. Or small companies might not have the IT resources to do so quickly or simply cannot afford the effort. In such cases, the Report Manager can be used as a reporting tool. Users can navigate to the Report Manager portal and request reports on the spot, as figure 1.5 shows.

Even better, users can use the handy toolbar, which the Report Server generates automatically, to perform various report-related tasks, including specifying parameter values for reports that take parameters (more on this in chapter 3), paging, zooming, and exporting the report to different formats.

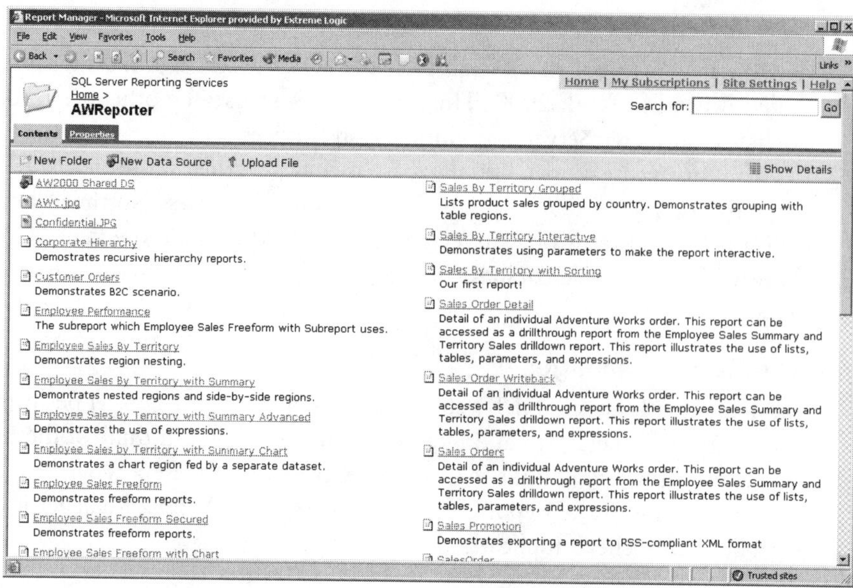

Figure 1.4 Users can use the Report Manager portal to generate or manage reports.

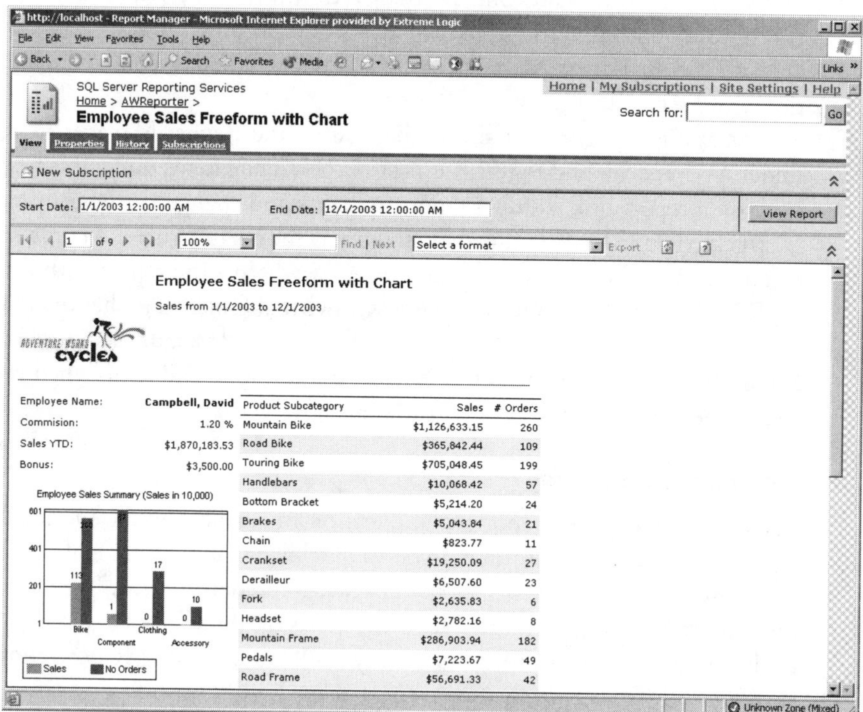

Product Subcategory	Sales	# Orders
Mountain Bike	$1,126,633.15	260
Road Bike	$365,842.44	109
Touring Bike	$705,048.45	199
Handlebars	$10,068.42	57
Bottom Bracket	$5,214.20	24
Brakes	$5,043.84	21
Chain	$823.77	11
Crankset	$19,250.09	27
Derailleur	$6,507.60	23
Fork	$2,635.83	6
Headset	$2,782.16	8
Mountain Frame	$286,903.94	182
Pedals	$7,223.67	49
Road Frame	$56,691.33	42

Figure 1.5 Small organizations that don't need to create report-enabled applications can use the Report Manager to request reports. This figures shows the Employee Sales Freeform with Chart report generated in HTML.

Now that we've had a 100-foot view tour of the major building blocks of RS, let's peek under its hood to see how it processes, renders, and delivers reports.

1.4 UNDERSTANDING REPORT PROCESSING

Report processing encompasses all activities performed by the Report Server to generate a report. To understand how the Report Server processes a report, let's see what happens when the report is requested on demand.

Figure 1.6 depicts what happens when a report hosted under the Report Server is requested by a report consumer. First, the consumer submits (1) a report request to the Report Server.

Once the report request is intercepted by the Report Server, it is forwarded (2) to the Report Processor. The Report Processor parses the request and retrieves (3) the report definition and metadata from the Report Server Database. The Report Processor checks whether the user is authorized to access this report. If so, the Report Processor processes the report, which involves two stages: execution and rendering.

Let's get more insight into each of these stages, starting with the execution stage.

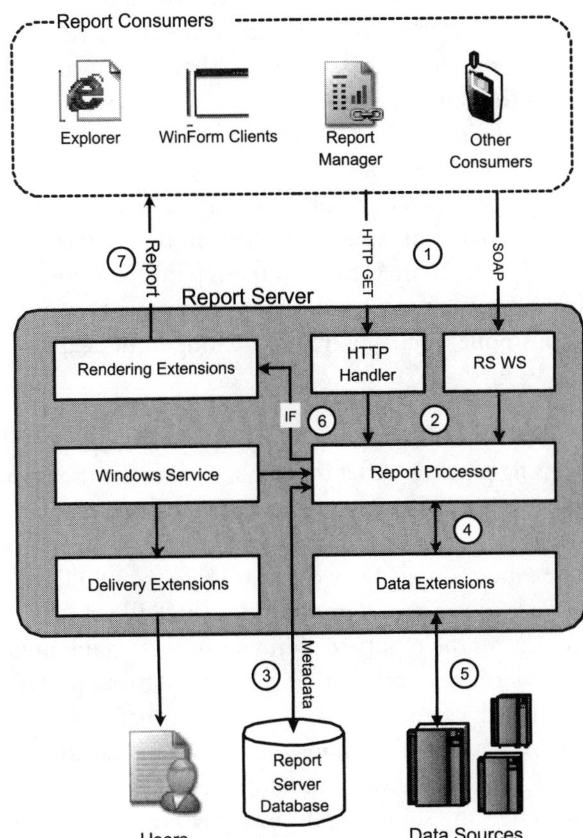

Figure 1.6
You can integrate your applications with RS by using the two web communication façades: HTTP Handler and the RS Web service.

1.4.1 Execution stage

The report execution phase starts when the Report Server begins processing the report and finishes when the report is ready for rendering. For the sake of simplicity, let's assume that the report is requested for the first time.

Generating the raw report

As we explained earlier, when the report is published, the Report Server parses its report definition (RDL), generates a .NET assembly, and saves the assembly in the catalog for the report. During the execution phase, the Report Server loads and executes the assembly. Referring back to figure 1.6, you can see that the Report Server uses a data extension (4) to query (5) the data source to retrieve the report data, combines the resulting dataset and report layout information, and produces (6) the report in a raw form, called *intermediate format* (IF).

Having the report generated in an intermediate format before it is finally rendered is beneficial in terms of performance. It allows the Report Server to reuse the same IF regardless of the requested export format. Developers who are familiar with the intermediate language (IL) code execution model in .NET can think of IF in a similar way. IL abstracts the platform on which the code executes, while IF abstracts the rendering format. For example, one report consumer can request the report in an HTML format, while another can request the same report as PDF. In either case, the Report Server already has the raw report; the only thing left is to transform it into its final presentation format. During the rendering stage, the Report Server loads the report IF and renders (7) the report in the requested format using a rendering extension.

Once the report IF is generated, it is saved (cached) in the Report Server Temporary Database. Note that if the report is cached, the report execution phase may be bypassed completely for subsequent requests because the Report Server decides to use the cached IF. We will postpone discussing report caching until chapter 7.

1.4.2 Rendering stage

As shown in figure 1.6, the report-rendering stage represents the second (and last) stage in the report-processing pipeline. After the Report Server has the report IF, it renders the report in its final presentation format as per the export format requested by the user. You will be pleasantly surprised to see the plethora of natively supported formats that a report can be exported to. My favorites are HTML and PDF. For example, as figure 1.7 shows, I have loaded a report exported to a PDF file in Adobe Acrobat.

The Report Server delegates the report-rendering process to rendering extensions. RS comes with various rendering extensions that correspond to supported export formats. If the report consumer does not specify the export format explicitly, the report will be rendered in HTML 3.2 or 4.0, depending on the browser capabilities. Table 1.5 lists each out-of-the box RS supported rendering formats.

As we've said before, when the supported formats are not enough, you can write your own rendering extensions.

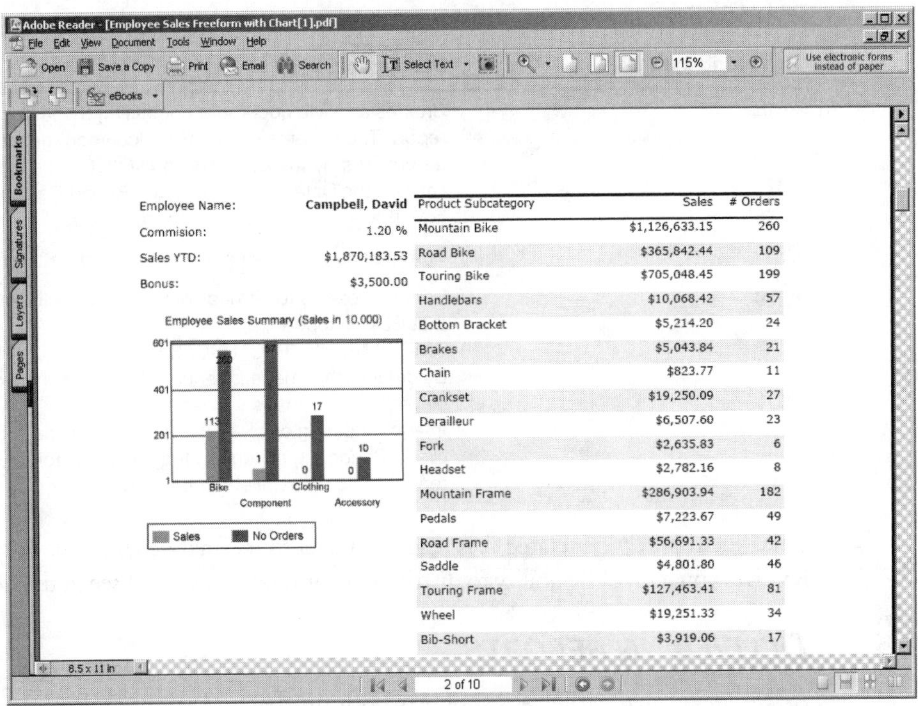

Figure 1.7 With RS you can export your reports to many formats, including Adobe Acrobat PDF. Here, I have exported this report to Adobe PDF and loaded it in Adobe Reader.

Table 1.5 Report rendering options

Rendering Extension	Description
HTML	HTML 4.0 (Internet Explorer 5.0 and above), Netscape (6.2 and above), HTML 3.2 otherwise.
HTML with Office Web Components	HTML 4.0 with Office Web Components (OWC). Charts are rendered using the OWC chart control and matrixes are rendered using the PivotTable OWC.
MHTML	MIME encapsulation of the Aggregate HTML Documents standard, which embeds resources such as images, documents, or other binary files as MIME structures within the report. This is a good option to minimize the number of round trips between the browser and server to fetch resources. MHTML is most useful for sending reports through e-mail, as we see in chapter 14.
PDF	Adobe Acrobat files.
Excel	Creates a visual representation of the report in an Excel workbook and translates Excel formulas whenever possible. Users can open the report in Excel to change it.

continued on next page

Table 1.5 Report rendering options *(continued)*

Rendering Extension	Description
XML	Creates an XML document containing the information in the report. The schema of the XML document generated is determined by the contents and layout of the report. Users can use the Data Output tab in the Report Designer to control how the elements will be rendered.
CSV	Comma-separated value file, with no formatting.
Image	Renders reports to bitmaps or metafiles, including any format that GDI+ supports: BMP, EMF, GIF, JPEG, PNG, RIFF, and WMF. By default, the image is rendered in TIFF, which can be displayed with an image viewer. Image rendering ensures the report looks the same on every client. Rendering occurs on the server; all fonts used in the report must be installed on the server.

Once the report is generated it is ready to travel to its final destination: the report user. RS gives you a lot of flexibility to distribute your reports, as you'll see in the next section.

1.5 DELIVERING REPORTS

As we mentioned earlier, RS supports both on-demand (pull) and subscribed (push) report delivery. To view a report on demand, the user explicitly requests the report from the Report Server. Alternatively, the user can choose to subscribe to a report. With this option, the report is pushed to the subscribers when the report data is refreshed or on a specified schedule.

Let's take a closer look at each delivery option.

1.5.1 On-demand delivery

One of the most important decisions you have to make when integrating RS reports in your application is how the application will access the Report Server to request reports. While in some cases the system design may dictate the integration option, occasionally the choice won't be so straightforward and you may have to carefully evaluate the application requirements to determine the best approach. We revisit the on-demand delivery options in more detail in chapter 9. For now, note that reports can be requested on-demand in two ways: URL access and the Web service.

URL-based report access

The report consumer requests a report by URL by submitting an HTTP-GET request to the Report Server. The advantages of URL access are its simplicity and better performance. In the simplest case, the consumer can embed the report URL into a hyperlink.

For example, a web-based application can have a drop-down Reports menu where each link targets a RS report. With the URL access option, the report arguments are passed as query parameters in the report URL. For example, assuming that you have installed the sample reports included with book source code, the following URL will run the Territory Sales Crosstab sample report with the start date 3/1/2003 and an end date of 4/30/2003.

```
http://localhost/ReportServer?/AWReporter/Territory Sales Crosstab&Start-
Date=3/1/2003&EndDate=4/30/2004
```

Web service

With RS, reports can also be requested by submitting SOAP-based requests to the Report Server Web service. The main advantage of this service is that its feature set goes well beyond just report rendering. It also encompasses an extensive set of methods to manage all aspects of the Report Server, such as uploading reports, retrieving a list of resources from the report catalog, and securing RS.

You can think of the Report Server Web service as a façade to the Report Server that allows RS to be integrated with a broad array of platforms. For example, if you are building an enterprise application integration (EAI) solution, a BizTalk schedule might invoke the Web service `Render()` method, get the XML representation of the report, retrieve some data from it, and pass it on to another application. Or, if your reporting application is B2B oriented and your partner has a Web service, you can send the report results to it in XML.

In some cases, a report consumer will use a combination of both access options to integrate with RS. For example, a report consumer can use the RS Web service to find out what parameters a report takes. Then, the application presentation layer can present the parameters to the user so that the user can enter the parameter values. When the user submits the report request, the application can use URL access to send the request to the Report Server.

1.5.2 Subscribed delivery

In the "push" report delivery scenario, the reports are generated and delivered automatically by the Report Server to a delivery target. Reports can also be delivered at a scheduled time. For example, a financial institution can set up a portfolio balance report to be generated and delivered through e-mail to its customers at the end of each month.

The Report Server Windows service (ReportingServicesService.exe) works in tandem with the SQL Server Agent service to generate and deliver subscribed reports.

> **NOTE** SQL Server Agent is a component of Microsoft SQL Server, and it is responsible for running scheduled SQL Server tasks.

For example, if the report is to be generated according to a set schedule, the SQL Server Agent will create a job and move the subscription to the Subscriptions table when the time is up. The RS Windows service periodically polls the Report Configuration Database to find out whether there are any new subscription jobs. If this is the case, the Windows service picks up the job, generates the report, and delivers it to the end users through a delivery extension.

Out of the box, RS comes with two delivery extensions: the e-mail delivery extension and the file share delivery extension. The e-mail delivery extension delivers the report via e-mail. The report can be delivered to either subscribed users (opt-in subscription) or to a data-driven list of recipients. The file share extension delivers reports to a network share. When these two options are not enough, you can write custom delivery extensions.

Note that the Report Server Windows service doesn't communicate with the Report Server through the HTTP Handler or Web service façades. Instead, because it is installed on the same machine as the Report Server, the Windows service directly loads and calls the Report Server assemblies. This is beneficial for two reasons. The first relates to availability. Even if the IIS server is down, the Windows service will still execute scheduled tasks and deliver reports to subscribers. The other reason is better performance—the web façades are completely bypassed.

Another task that the Report Services Windows service is responsible for is performing background database integrity checks, as well as other administrative tasks.

Before we see RS in action, it may be beneficial to get a good high-level understanding of the report lifecycle. This is important because the remaining chapters of this book follow an identical flow.

1.6 What is the report lifecycle?

By now, you probably realize that the Report Server is a sophisticated reporting platform with a feature set that goes well beyond a desktop reporting tool. To minimize the learning curve, this book follows a logical path based on the *report lifecycle*. The report lifecycle is the process that you typically follow to work with reports, and it involves three stages: authoring, management, and delivery. Figure 1.8 depicts the report lifecycle stages.

In the report-authoring stage, you create the RDL file through the use of report-authoring tools. For example, you can use the Visual Studio .NET Report Designer to lay out the report. Recall that both report data retrieval and layout information are described in the RDL file. We'll discuss many more details of the report authoring stage in chapters 2–6.

In the report-management stage, you manage the report catalog. As you recall, the report catalog is stored in the Reporting Services Configuration Database. The report catalog keeps the report and all related items. Typical management tasks include organizing reports in folders, uploading reports, and granting users access to run reports. We'll take a closer look at report management in chapters 7 and 8.

The report-delivery stage is concerned with distributing the reports to their final destinations, including end users, printers, or archive folders. A managed report can be delivered either on-demand or pushed to the subscribed users. Report delivery is discussed in detail in chapters 9–14.

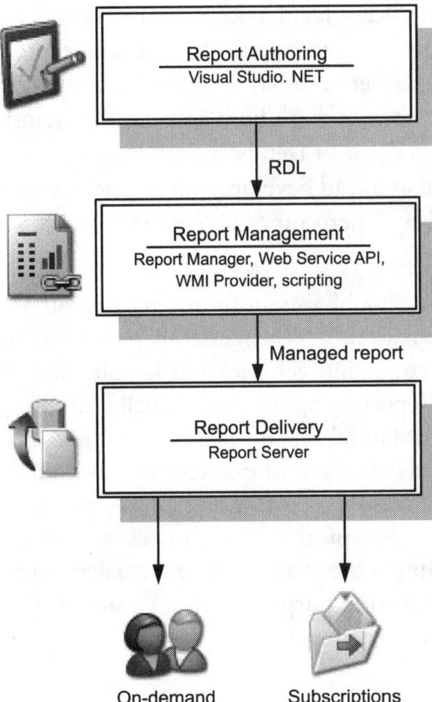

Figure 1.8 Report lifecycle phases include report authoring, management, and delivery. In the report-authoring stage, you lay out the report. In the report-management stage, you deploy and manage the report. Finally, RS gives you many ways to distribute your reports to their final destination.

Enough theory! Let's put in practice what we learned so far and get our hands on RS.

1.7 RS IN ACTION

This section has two main objectives. First, we introduce an imaginary company, Adventure Works Cycles (AWC), which we reference throughout the rest of this book. We will discuss various hypothetical reporting challenges that AWC faces and implement solutions to address them.

Second, we get our feet wet and create our first report using the Visual Studio .NET Report Wizard and the AdventureWorks2000 sample database. Granted, this is going to be a simple tabular-style report, but as simple as it is, it showcases all the phases of the report lifecycle. We also use this report in the next three chapters as a practical example to expand our knowledge about RS.

1.7.1 About the Adventure Works Reporter

Let's start with a hypothetical problem statement. You are a developer with AWC, which manufactures and sells goods to individuals and retailers. The company has enjoyed tremendous success the last few years. Sales are going up exponentially and the customer base is growing fast. Today, AWC has customers both in the United States and overseas. It has already implemented a web-based ordering online transaction processing (OLTP) system to capture sales orders online.

However, success does not come cheap. Data inaccuracy and slow decision making are among the top complaints by the sales managers. Often, data is captured and consolidated in the form of Excel spreadsheets. What is needed is a reporting system to present the company with data in a format that's both easy to understand and analyze and to allow AWC's management to discover trends and see how the company is performing. You have been designated as a lead developer for the new Adventure Works (AW) Reporter system. Fascinated by Microsoft SQL Server 2000 RS, you decide to base your reporting system on it.

NOTE In the real world, you should abstain from reporting off an OLTP database for performance reasons. As the name suggests, OLTP systems must scale to meet large transaction volumes and handle hundreds and even thousands of users. Reporting applications usually submit queries to retrieve and analyze substantial sets of data, which impose data locks on many records in the database. This can severely tax your OLTP system performance. For this reason, reporting and OLTP are usually two mutually exclusive options. A typical solution involves consolidating OLTP data and then uploading it to a data warehouse database that is optimized and designated for reporting purposes only. We discuss OLAP and data warehousing in detail in chapter 12.

1.7.2 Your first report

One crucial piece of information that the AW management would probably like to know is what the yearly products sales per territory are. With such a report in hand, managers can determine how well AW is doing in each sales region. To meet this requirement, let's create the Sales by Territory report. Figure 1.9 shows the final version of the report that we'll create in this section.

Sales By Territory

Territory	Product Category	Sales
Australia	Accessory	$8,359.74
	Bike	$773,111.46
	Clothing	$18,665.74
	Component	$96,911.11
Canada	Accessory	$32,835.84
	Bike	$2,315,632.98
	Clothing	$86,657.62
	Component	$457,317.56

Figure 1.9 Our first report is Sales by Territory.

This is just one of the many sample reports we'll design throughout the course of this book. We'll use the Sales by Territory report in subsequent chapters to demonstrate other RS features.

Table 1.6 shows the list of tasks that we need to accomplish to create the report organized by the report lifecycle phases.

Table 1.6 The task map for creating our first report

Phase	Task	Description
Authoring	Create BI project.	Create a new BI project in Visual Studio .NET.
	Create the report data source.	Use the Report Designer Data tab to configure a database connection to the AdventureWorks2000 database.
	Set the report dataset.	Define a dataset query to retrieve the report data.
	Lay out the report.	Use the Report Wizard and Report Designer to author the report.
	Test the report.	Use the Report Designer Preview tab to preview and test the report.
Management	Deploy the report.	Use Visual Studio .NET to deploy the report to the Report Server catalog.
Delivery	Ensure on-demand report delivery.	Use the Report Manager to navigate and render the report.

As you'll recall, the first phase of the report lifecycle is authoring the report.

Authoring the report

Let's develop our first report using the Report Designer. To do so, we need to create a new Visual Studio .NET Business Intelligence (BI) project.

Task: Create a Business Intelligence Project

To create a project, complete the following steps (see figure 1.10):

Step 1 Open Visual Studio .NET and choose File → New → Project.

Step 2 From Project Types, select Business Intelligence Projects.

Step 3 From Templates, select Report Project.

Step 4 In the Location field, enter **AWReporter**, specify a location, and click OK.

Step 5 Once the project is created, right-click on the AWReporter project node in the Solution Explorer window and select Properties. The Property Pages dialog box appears, as shown in figure 1.11.

Step 6 Verify that the TargetFolder setting is set to AWReporter. This specifies the folder name in the report catalog where all reports defined in the project will be deployed.

Step 7 In the TargetServerURL field, enter the Report Server URL. If RS is installed locally on your machine and you have accepted the defaults during setup, the

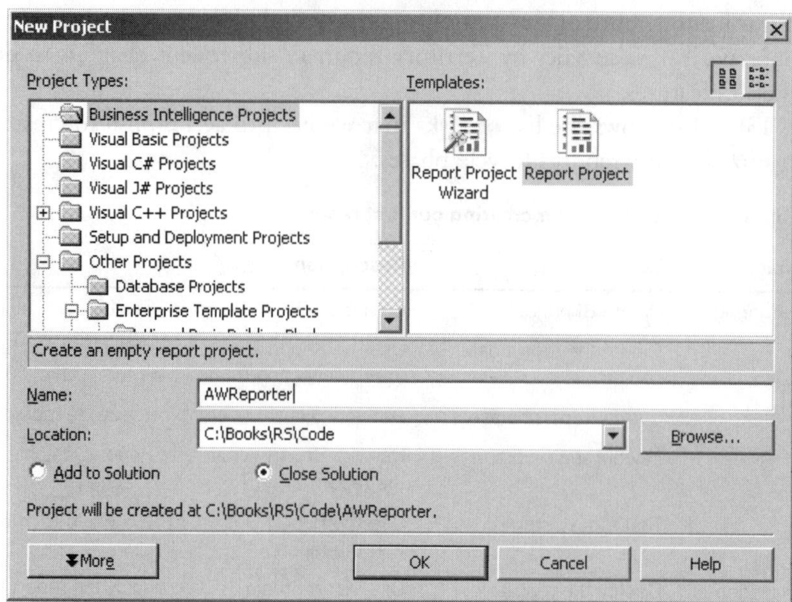

Figure 1.10 Use Visual Studio .NET to create a new BI project.

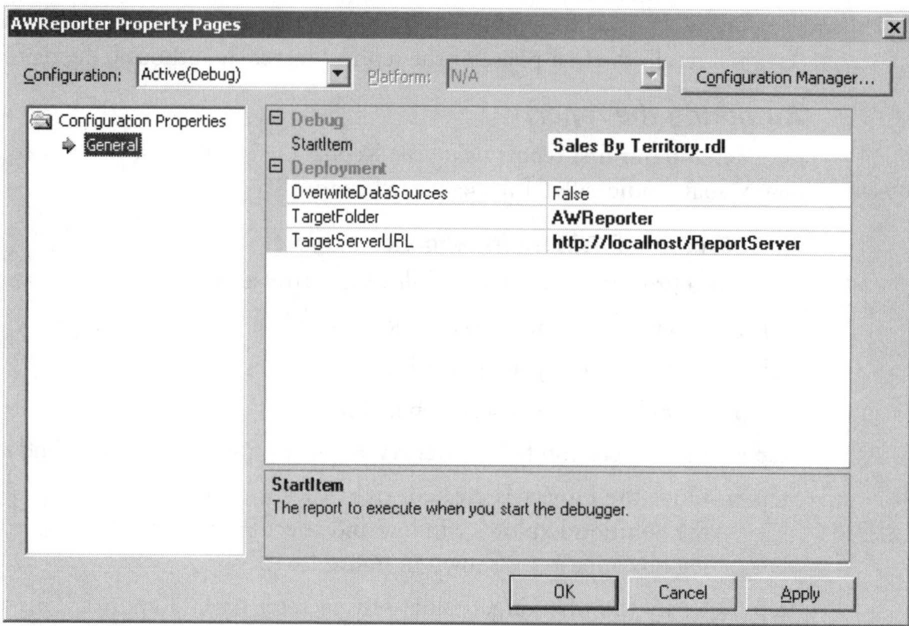

Figure 1.11 Use the report property page to set up the project properties.

URL of the Report Server should be http://localhost/ReportServer. Click OK to close the Property Pages dialog box.

Task: Create the Report Data Source

Next, we create a shared data source pointing to the AdventureWorks2000 sample database. Don't worry if the concept of a shared data source is not immediately clear. When we get to chapter 3 it will all begin to make sense.

Step 1 Right-click on the Shared Data Sources node in the Solution Explorer and choose Add New Data Source. The familiar Data Links Properties appears, as shown in figure 1.12.

Switch to the Provider tab and verify that the Microsoft OLE DB Provider for SQL Server is selected (we will be connecting to a SQL Server database). Back to the Connection tab, specify:

- The name of the SQL Server that you use to install RS. In my case, the database is installed locally, which is why the data source name is "."
- A valid username and password combination for an SQL Server account that has permissions to query the tables in the Adventure-Works2000 database. Select the Allow Saving Password check box.
- Select the AdventureWorks2000 database from the "Select the database on the server" drop-down list. Test the connection by clicking the Test Connection button. If all is well, click OK.

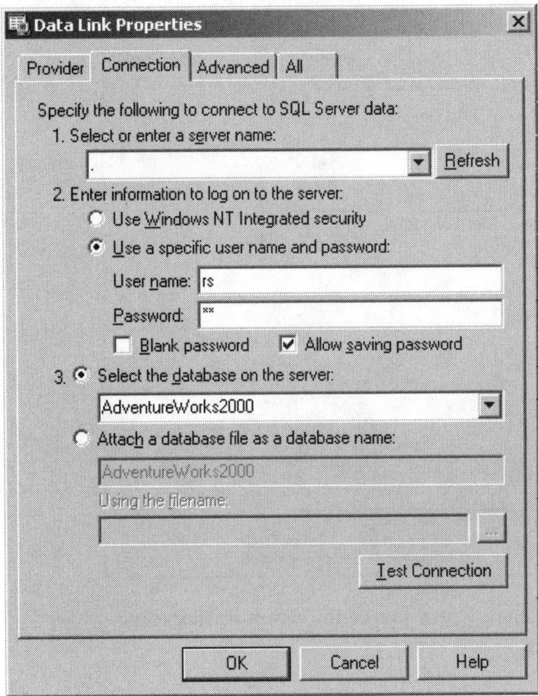

Figure 1.12
Use the Data Link Properties dialog box to establish to set up a data source pointing to the AdventureWorks2000 database.

Step 2 By default, RS names the data source with the same name as the database. Since we are going to use this data source for most of the sample reports in this book, let's make the name more descriptive.

Double-click on the AdventureWorks2000.rds file. The Shared Data Source dialog box appears, as shown in figure 1.13.

Change the Name property of the data source to AW2000 Shared DS and click OK. Optionally, in the Solution Explorer rename the data source file to AW2000 Shared DS.rds.

Now it's time to author the report. We'll use the handy Report Wizard to save some time.

Task: Set the Report Dataset

Step 1 Right-click on the Reports node in the Solution Explorer and choose Add New Report.

Step 2 On the Report Wizard welcome screen, click Next.

Step 3 On the Select the Data Source screen, make sure that the Shared Data Source radio option is selected and that AW2000 Shared DS appears in the Shared Data Source drop-down list. Click Next.

Step 4 In the Design the Query screen, click the Edit button. The familiar query designer window appears.

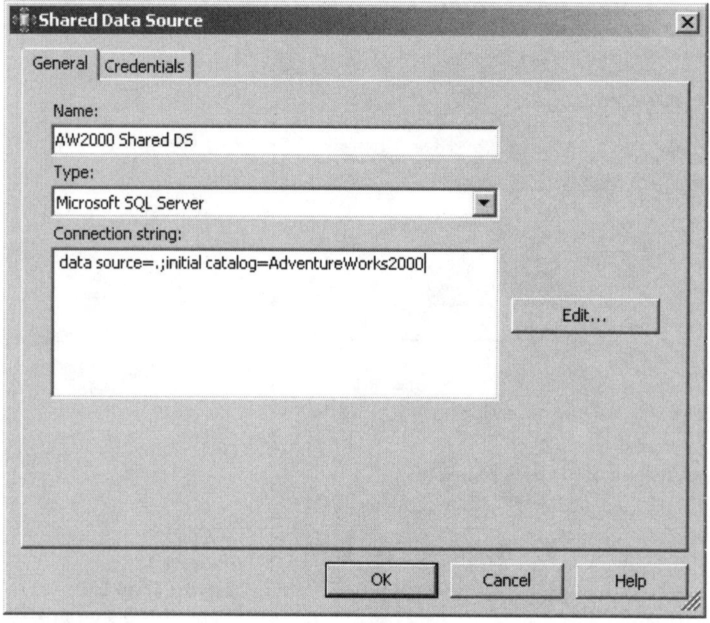

Figure 1.13 Setting up the shared data source to AdventureWorks2000 database.

Step 5 Enter the following SQL statement in the query pane:

```
SELECT        ST.Name AS Territory, PC.ProductCategoryID,
              PC.Name AS ProductCategory,
              SUM(SOD.UnitPrice * SOD.OrderQty) AS Sales
FROM          SalesOrderDetail SOD
INNER JOIN    Product P ON SOD.ProductID = P.ProductID
INNER JOIN    SalesOrderHeader SOH ON
              SOD.SalesOrderID = SOH.SalesOrderID
INNER JOIN    SalesTerritory ST ON
              SOH.TerritoryID = ST.TerritoryID
INNER JOIN    ProductSubCategory PSC ON
              P.ProductSubCategoryID = PSC.ProductSubCategoryID
INNER JOIN    ProductCategory PC ON PSC.ProductCategoryID =
              PC.ProductCategoryID
WHERE         DATEPART(YY, SOH.OrderDate) = DATEPART(yy, GETDATE())
GROUP BY      ST.Name, PC.Name, PC.ProductCategoryID
ORDER BY      ST.Name, PC.Name
```

This query retrieves the product sales orders grouped by territory and product category. The AW database groups products in subcategories, which are then rolled up to product categories. For the purposes of this report, we summarize the sales data by product categories since this represents the most consolidated level in the product hierarchy, which is exactly what upper management is interested in seeing. The sales amount is retrieved from the SalesOrderDetail table. In addition, the query filters the orders created for the current year. In chapter 3, we'll make the report parameter driven by allowing the user to pass an arbitrary date. At this point, click Next.

Task: Lay Out the Report

To lay out the report, perform the following steps:

Step 1 On the Select the Report Type screen, leave the report type set to Tabular. Click Next.

Step 2 On the Design the Table screen, select all fields except ProductCategoryID and click Details so the fields appear in the report details section, as shown in figure 1.14. Click Next.

Step 3 On the Choose the Table Style screen, click Corporate, the click Next.

Step 4 Finally, on the Completing the Report Wizard screen, enter **Sales by Territory** as the name of the report. Click Finish, and we're done!

Visual Studio displays the Report Designer with the Layout tab selected, as shown in figure 1.15.

The integration with Visual Studio.NET Report Designer allows you to easily preview and test your reports without leaving the Visual Studio .NET IDE.

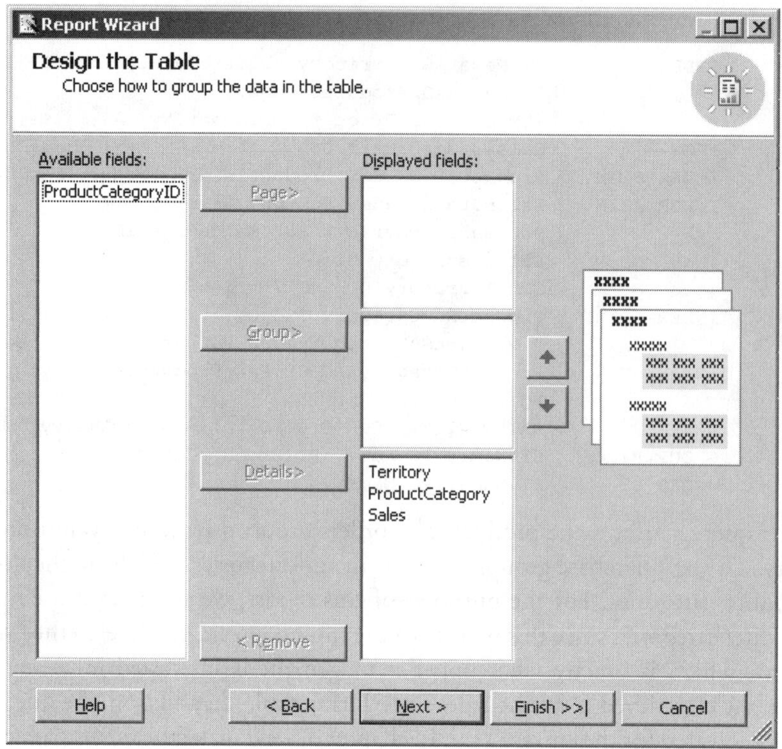

Figure 1.14 In the Design the Table step, you choose which fields will appear on the report and how data will be grouped.

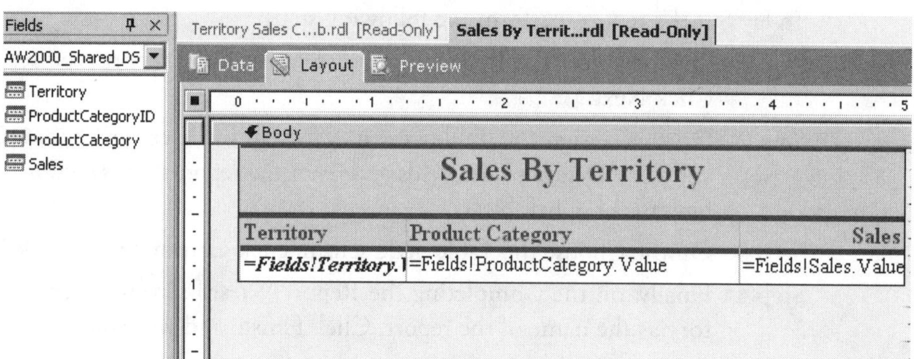

Figure 1.15 Use the Report Designer Layout tab to lay out your report.

Task: Test the Report

Let's make some cosmetic changes to enhance our report.

Step 1 Click on the Report Designer Preview tab to see the HTML representation of the report. Notice the report toolbar at the top, which allows you to zoom, print, and save the report in different formats. The Sales field needs some formatting work.

Step 2 Click the Layout tab again to go back to design mode.

Step 3 Right-click on the Sales text box and choose Properties. Specify the format settings, as shown in figure 1.16.

Click OK to close the Textbox Properties dialog box.

Step 4 Increase the width of the Territory and Product Category columns; stretch them out as far as there is space within the report width.

Step 5 Right-click again on the Territory text box and go to the field properties.

Step 6 Click the Advanced button and, in the Font tab, change the font weight to bold and style to Italic. Click OK.

Step 7 Back to the Textbox Properties dialog box, hide the repeating territory names by selecting the Hide Duplicates check box, as shown in figure 1.17.

Preview the report again. Now it should look like the report shown in figure 1.9. Still not very pleasing to the eye, but not bad for a few minutes of work!

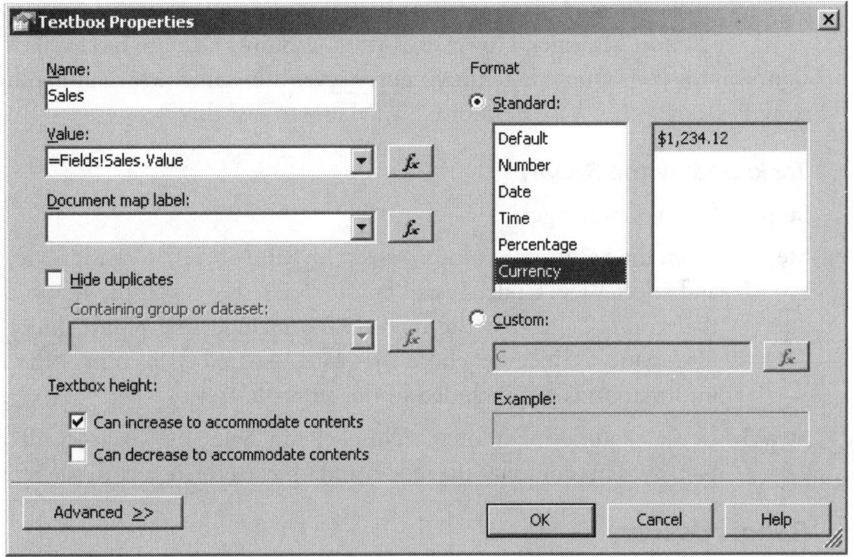

Figure 1.16 Use the Textbox properties page to set up format settings.

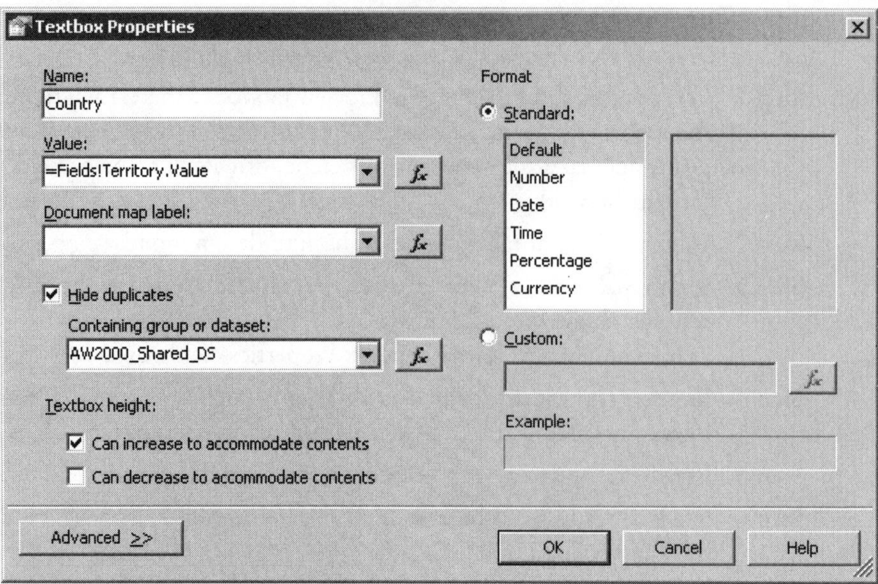

Figure 1.17 Select the Hide Duplicates check box to hide the territory name duplicates.

Report management

Once you are satisfied with the report, you will probably need to deploy it to make it available to all users. This is a report management task that you can accomplish by using the Report Manager. However, if your Windows account has local administrator rights on the computer where the Report Server is installed, you can deploy the report straight from within Visual Studio .NET. Let's do just that.

Task: Deploy the Report

Step 1 Save your changes.

Step 2 From the Solution Explorer, select the Sales by Territory.rdl node, right-click, and select View Code. Visual Studio .NET shows you the report definition of the report. Note that the report RDL includes the report query and layout information. Since we chose to create a shared data source, the data source information is not included in the report RDL.

Step 3 In the Solution Explorer, right-click on Sales by Territory.rdl and choose Deploy. This compiles the report and uploads the report to the report catalog.

Report delivery

Once the report has been promoted to a managed report, it can be delivered to your end users. Let's see how users can request the report on-demand by using the Report Manager as a quick-and-easy report-delivery tool.

Task: On-Demand Report Delivery

Step 1 Open the browser and navigate to the Report Manager URL, which by default is http://<reportservername>/reports. Notice that below the Report Manager Home folder there is a new folder, AWReporter, and that its name matches the TargetFolder setting you specified in the report project settings.

Step 2 Click on the AWReporter folder link to see its content. You should find the AW2000 Shared DS data source and Sales by Territory report links.

Step 3 Click on the Sales by Territory report link to request the report with the Report Manager.

As you can see, authoring, managing, and delivering reports with RS is straightforward. At this point, you may decide to compare RS at a high level with other reporting tools you've used in the past. The next section discusses how RS stacks up against the competition.

1.8 EVALUATING RS

By the time you read this book, comparison charts will probably be available from Microsoft and other sources to show how RS compares with other popular reporting tools. For example, the Resource section at the end of this chapter lists a link to a detailed feature comparison document between RS and Crystal Reports.

Based on my experience with integrating applications with third-party reporting packages, I think that as a first iteration, RS is surprisingly feature-rich. My favorite top ten features, where I believe RS excels, are as follows:

1. Natively exposed as a Web service—The RS reports are widely accessible, and you don't have to do anything special to publish your reports as web services because they are hosted under the Report Server, which provides a web service façade.
2. Support of plethora of export formats—You may be delighted to learn that the ability to export reports to PDF and Excel is provided out the box. In addition, reports can be delivered in many other popular formats, including web formats (HTML), popular image formats (such as TIFF and JPEG), and data formats (Excel, XML, CSV).
3. On-demand and subscribed report delivery—Another huge plus is the subscribed report delivery option, which allows developers to implement opt-in report features in their applications.
4. Documented report definition format—Developers can create reports to be published to the Report Server using Microsoft or third-party design tools that support the RS XML RDL.
5. .NET Framework integration—In the extensibility area, you'll appreciate the fact that you are not locked from a programmability standpoint. As we mentioned earlier, when built-in features are not enough, you can reach out and

borrow from the power of the .NET Framework by integrating your reports with .NET code. In addition, the Report Services programming model is 100 percent .NET-based.

6 Extensible architecture—The RS architecture is fully extensible and allows developers to plug in their own security, data, delivery, and rendering extensions.

7 Zero deployment—Thanks to its service-oriented architecture, RS has no client footprint and offers true zero deployment for all application types.

8 Scalability—RS can scale better, since it is designed from the ground up to scale in web farm environments.

9 Visual Studio .NET integration—Report authors will enjoy the familiar IDE environment when designing and testing reports.

10 Cost—From a cost perspective, it is hard to beat the bundled with the SQL Server RS pricing model, especially if you compare it with the five-digit price tag of third-party reporting tools.

Of course, nothing is perfect, and Report Services has its own shortcomings, some of which I would like to mention here. As a .NET developer, I would like to see a future version of RS bring a tighter integration with Visual Studio .NET. Ideally, working with BI projects should not be much different than working with .NET code projects, for example, Windows Forms. In the future, I would expect RS to evolve and add the following features:

- Allow developers to add code-behind files to their reports.
- Instead of Visual Basic .NET only, support all .NET-compatible languages for writing expressions and report-specific code.
- Use the Visual Studio .NET code editor instead of the Notepad-like Custom Code Editor.
- Support events; currently, developers cannot write event handlers to respond to runtime conditions. Microsoft Access, for example, has been enjoying a report object model with events since its first release. Since the RS generation process is not event-driven, the only option for implementing runtime code customization with Report Services is to use expressions.
- Include more flexible object model, for example, creating report elements dynamically, and referencing and changing report items from custom code.
- Convert reports from reporting tools other than Microsoft Access.

I hope that the above shortcomings will be addressed in future releases of RS to make this tool an even more compelling choice for enterprise reporting.

1.9 SUMMARY

This chapter took you on a whirlwind tour of the RS platform. We've discussed its role in the Microsoft BI initiative, as well as its features and high-level architecture. You have even had a chance to use RS and create a simple report based on the AdventureWorks2000 sample database. Now that you have a good high-level understanding of its features, you can begin using RS to report-enable your own applications.

By now, you should understand the major components of RS and their role in the report lifecycle. In addition, you should see the advantages that the service-oriented and web-enabled RS architecture has to offer.

Perhaps most important, you should be familiar with the three stages of the report lifecycle: report authoring, management, and delivery. The remaining chapters explore each of these stages in this order. In the next chapter, we discuss different ways to create RS reports.

1.10 RESOURCES

Microsoft RS website
(www.microsoft.com/sql/reporting/)—First stop for the latest on RS.

Microsoft Business Intelligence Platform website
(www.microsoft.com/sql/evaluation/BI/default.asp) —The Microsoft BI portal home page.

A feature comparison between RS vs. Crystal Reports
(http://certia.ramblainf.com/pdf/RSvsBO_En_v1.pdf)—Ceria's Business Intelligence Team has developed a detailed feature comparison document that outlines how Microsoft RS stacks against Crystal Enterprise.

A Guide to Developing and Running Connected Systems with Indigo
(http://msdn.microsoft.com/msdnmag/issues/04/01/Indigo/)—In section 1.3 I emphasized the role of the RS service-oriented programming model. Read Don Box's article for more information about SOA.

PART 1

Authoring reports

The report lifecycle starts with the report-authoring phase. Part 1 teaches you the skills that you will need to master as a report author to create Reporting Services–based reports.

We will start by discussing the options RS offers for creating reports. Since most report authors will probably rely on the integrated with VS.NET Report Designer, we will explore its report-authoring features in detail.

We will find out how to set up the report data source and work with datasets. We will also lay out best practices for data management.

The best way to acquire report-authoring skills is by example. For this reason, we will author various reports, including tabular, freeform, crosstab, chart, and multicolumn reports and reports with navigational features.

Often, you may need to enhance your report features programmatically. We will show how you can do just this by using expressions and functions.

One of the most prominent features of Reporting Services that many developers, including myself, appreciate is its extensible nature. One way you can extend the capabilities of your reports is to integrate them with custom .NET code that you or somebody else has written. You will learn how to leverage custom code to supercharge the capabilities of your reports.

C H A P T E R 2

Report authoring basics

In chapter 1 we discussed the report lifecycle and identified the first stage as the report-authoring process. Recall that in this stage, you set up the report data and lay out the report itself. The report data and layout information are described in a report definition file.

You may wonder what options are available to you as report authors with RS. As you will see shortly, RS offers not one but several ways to create reports. In this chapter we discuss

- The report-authoring process
- Authoring reports using Visual Studio .NET (VS.NET)
- Generating the report definition language (RDL) report manually
- Third-party tools for report authoring

Although you will probably rely most of the time on the Report Designer to author reports, it is important to understand when and how to use the other options. In this chapter, we provide a panoramic view of report-authoring techniques. In chapter 4 we discuss how you can use the Report Designer to lay out different types of reports.

2.1 THE REPORT-AUTHORING PROCESS: STEP BY STEP

Before we discuss specific report-authoring options, it may make sense to step back and reflect on the authoring process to learn how you can create reports that meet user requirements. Although there is no magic formula for creating successful reports, I recommend that you follow a guided process for authoring reports similar to the software development methodology in general.

Figure 2.1 shows the typical steps you should follow when authoring your reports.

Experienced developers will probably recognize these steps immediately. Just as with software projects, you should resist the temptation to jump into "construction" (report authoring) before you have a good understanding of what your users want. Once the report is ready, it has to be meticulously tested before it is deployed to the report catalog.

Below the name of each step, we've listed the typical ways to accomplish the step. For example, you can author the report with VS.NET, generate the report definition programmatically, or use third-party tools.

Let's explain each step in more detail.

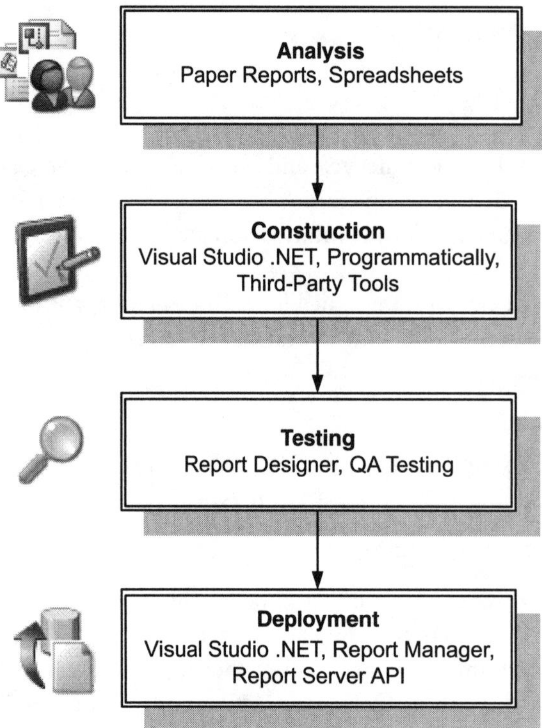

Figure 2.1 The report-authoring process typically consists of analysis, construction, testing, and deployment steps.

2.1.1 Analysis

The objective of the Analysis step is to collect the user requirements and prototype the report. In this stage, you typically examine existing report artifacts and other data sources, such as paper reports, spreadsheets, and standard forms, to understand what data is needed and how it is related. In addition, you conduct Joint Application Development (JAD) sessions with your users to clarify the reporting requirements, create throwaway report prototypes, and in general, do whatever possible to reach a consensus with your users about what the report should look like.

For example, in chapter 1 we created the Sales by Territory report requested by the Adventure Works management. Here, we've assumed that the Analysis step has been completed and we know exactly what our users want. If that were not the case, however, we would've started with prototyping the report. First, we could've determined what reporting sources the AWC managers currently use to obtain the same data. Perhaps they use Excel spreadsheets that we can use to see what the report looks like. Once we've determined the report layout, we need to find where the report data originates. In this case, we need to find out where the sales data resides—in mainframe, Oracle, or SQL Server databases?

Sometimes, you will find that you don't have all the data you need to satisfy the user requirements. For example, you might discover that some of the information is buried deep within the mainframe abyss and getting it out to daylight will require another project or two altogether.

NOTE I was involved once in a project with a major corporation to build an ASP.NET-based prototype whose main objective was to showcase .NET best development practices. During the requirements-gathering phase, I worked with one of the in-house business analysts. The application had to simulate an online food delivery service and allow customers to browse food categories, select an item, and so forth—in other words, a typical shopping cart e-store application. One of the client requirements stipulated that we had to follow the client process methodology, and its first stage was creating use cases. The business analyst and I divided the use cases among us. You can imagine my surprise when I was reading the "Cook food" and "Deliver food" use cases that she had come up with. The "Cook food" use case included such tasks as "get ingredients," "heat utensils," "mix ingredients," and "taste food," whereas "Deliver food" called for the driver checking the gas tank, filling the tank, and similar tasks. Obviously the analyst was more familiar with the food-cooking process than software development.

A good approach at the end of this phase is to come up with a paper prototype of the report that defines the report look and feel. Next, during the report design phase, you can use this prototype to flesh out the actual report.

Discussing the Analysis step in any greater detail is outside the scope of this book. However, to emphasize the importance of requirements gathering and analysis, we use a common pattern for the reporting solutions that we'll build in subsequent chapters. Notice that each reporting solution starts with defining the user requirements and high-level design goals that must be addressed before moving on to the actual implementation.

2.1.2 Construction

If you make it successfully out of the analysis, you graduate to the report-construction phase. The main deliverable of the Construction step is the RS-based report. Here, you will use one of the report-authoring options described in this chapter to create the report. As we've mentioned, there are several techniques you can use to do this, ranging from taking advantage of the integration with VS.NET Report Designer to generating the report definition programmatically.

If you create your reports interactively by using the reporting tools we discuss in this chapter, you will find that report construction is typically a two-stage process and consists of (1) setting up report data, and (2) arranging report items on the report canvas.

With RS, to set up the report data you first specify a data source and define one or more queries, as we discuss in detail in chapter 3. Next, you can use data regions (such as tables, matrixes, lists, and charts) to display the data on the report and add other report items to the layout. Chapter 4 shows you how to do just that.

2.1.3 Testing

Similar to how you test software projects, you should perform unit testing with your reports, as well as QA testing. With VS.NET you can easily preview the report to ensure that its layout meets the requirements and executes successfully. Once you are satisfied with the layout, inside the VS.NET IDE you can fully simulate the production report server environment and determine whether the report will render under given configurations. You'll see how the Report Designer facilitates the report unit testing process in section 2.2.2.

Once you have finished unit testing, the report goes to QA for final preproduction testing. If possible, you should designate a separate staging test Report Server for performance and logistics reasons.

2.1.4 Deployment

As we mentioned in chapter 1, to make your report available to end users you have to deploy it to the report catalog. RS gives you several options for uploading your reports:

- Uploading the report definition file manually using the Report Manager. We've already seen how in chapter 1.
- Uploading the report from within the VS.NET IDE. We explain this technique in section 2.2.2.
- Uploading the report definition programmatically by calling the Report Server Web service (see chapter 7 for more on this approach).

The focus of this chapter is to discuss the available options for authoring RS reports. Let's begin by finding out how we can do that with VS.NET.

2.2 AUTHORING REPORTS IN VS.NET

Visual Studio .NET provides several options for authoring RS reports:

- The Report Wizard
- The Report Designer
- Importing reports from Microsoft Access

Let's take a closer look at each of these tools, starting with the Report Wizard.

2.2.1 Authoring reports with the Report Wizard

You are already familiar with the Report Wizard because we used it in chapter 1 to create our first report. To start the Report Wizard within VS.NET, right-click on the project node, then choose Add New Item. Alternatively, as a shortcut you can right-click on the Reports node and select Add New Report.

As figure 2.2 shows, the Report Wizard supports two report types:

- Tabular, where the report data is laid out in a tabular format. Optionally, you can define one or more report groups. Grouping allows you to logically organize the data into different sections, as well as provide subtotals or other summary information in the group footer.
- Matrix (crosstab), where the report data can be grouped both in rows and columns. With matrix reports, you can define dynamic (expanding) columns to give the user an option to "drill down" for analyzing data further. We discuss this type of report in more detail in chapter 4.

One thing that is not that obvious is how the Report Wizard uses report styles to format the report in one of several predefined styles, including Bold, Casual, Corporate, Compact, and Plain. If for some reason you want to modify the existing styles or create new ones, you can do so by changing the StyleTemplates.xml file located by default in C:\Program Files\Microsoft SQL Server\80\Tools\Report Designer\Business Intelligence Wizards\Reports\Styles. This file enumerates the report styles as Extensible Markup Language (XML) elements, which you can change using your favorite text editor.

NOTE The styles that the Report Wizard lets you choose from are used only once, during the process of generating the report definition (RDL) file, to define the report appearance. Currently, RS does not support style templates ("skins") that define a common look and feel across reports, similar to the way web developers would use Cascading Style Sheets (CSS) or themes to control the page appearance. This feature has been slated for a future RS version.

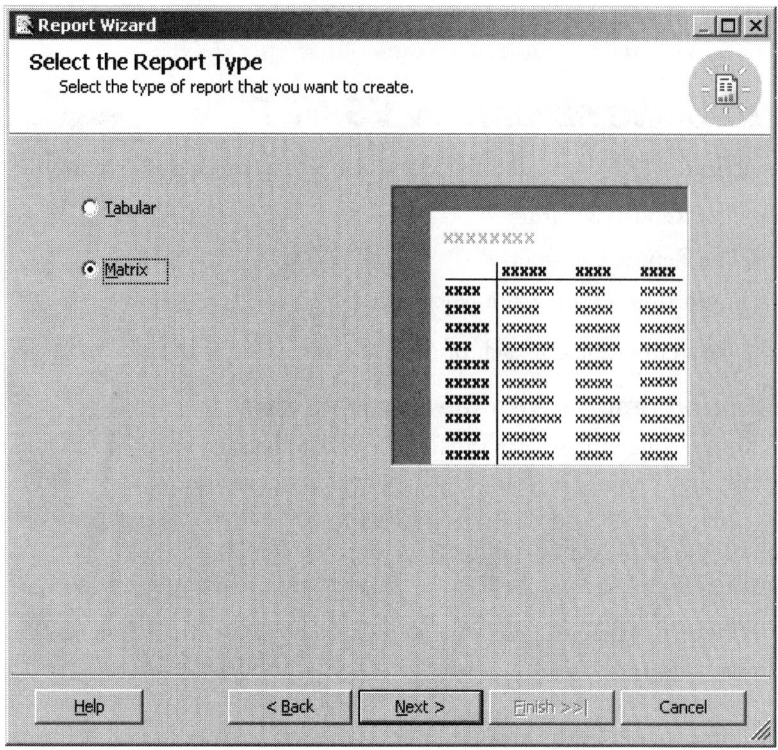

Figure 2.2 The report types supported by the Report Wizard

Most of you will probably agree that the Report Wizard is a good starting point when you need to generate a report quickly. It saves you time by automating some of the mundane report-authoring tasks, such as laying out the dataset fields. But, as with any wizard, it has its own limitations. For example, the Report Wizard design options are limited to Tabular and Matrix reports only. In addition, the Report Wizard doesn't support multiple regions, region nesting, or multiple datasets. To get the full design feature set supported by RS, you need to switch to the Report Designer.

2.2.2 Authoring reports with the Report Designer

Most of us will rely exclusively on the powerful Report Designer to create and design reports. For this reason, I would like to take some time and give you an overview of the essentials. Chapter 3 shows you how to use the Report Designer to set up the report data source and query. In chapters 4 and 5 you'll learn how the Report Designer makes authoring different types of reports a breeze.

NOTE Although most .NET developers will probably enjoy designing and running reports inside the familiar VS.NET environment, for other report authors, the full environment could be overkill if they purchase and install VS.NET solely for the purposes of creating reports. There are plans for a future version of RS that might include a stand-alone Designer, which would operate outside VS.NET. Third-party tools would also probably emerge, as mentioned in section 2.4.

If you haven't done this already, start VS.NET 2003 and open the AWReporter project (AWReporter.rptproj) that we created in chapter 1. (If you skipped this step, you can find the AWReporter project included with the book source code.) Then, double-click on the Sales by Territory report in the Solution Explorer pane to open the report in layout mode inside the VS.NET Report Designer, as shown in figure 2.3.

The Report Designer itself has a tabbed user interface with Data, Layout, and Preview tabs. Their display order corresponds to the sequence of steps you typically follow to author the report:

- *Data tab*—First, you use the Data tab to set up the report data. We discuss this further in chapter 3.
- *Layout tab*—Second, you design the report layout. Chapters 4 and 5 examine designing reports.
- *Preview tab*—Finally, you test report changes using the Preview tab.

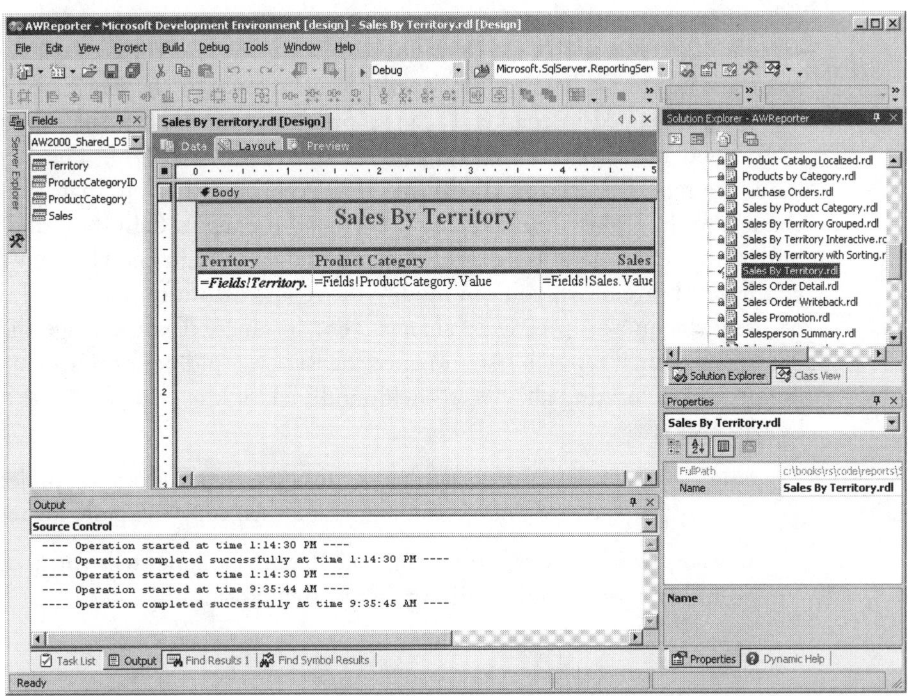

Figure 2.3 The VS.NET Report Designer tabbed window allows you to switch easily from one mode to another.

Working with BI projects

You may wonder how business intelligence (BI) projects differ from other types of projects supported by VS.NET. When you open a BI project, the VS IDE changes to accommodate the new project type, as follows:

- Two new menu items (Report and Format) are added to the main menu.
- When the report is in layout mode (the Layout tab is selected), several new toolbars appear to facilitate report formatting, such as Layout, Report Borders, Report Formatting, and Standard.
- A new Fields toolbox is lets you display the report dataset fields. Don't worry if its purpose is not immediately clear—we discuss working with data in chapter 3.
- The Report Items section is added to the toolbox (not shown in figure 2.3). You'll learn how to work with report items in Chapter 4.

As with any other VS.NET solution, you can add more than one project as a part of a single solution. One scenario where this could be useful is when you need to step through custom code executed by a given report, as you'll see in chapter 6.

You manage the BI project items using the VS.NET Solution Explorer. Each project has two folders: Shared Data Sources and Reports. As its name suggests, the Shared Data Sources folder holds the definitions of the data sources, in other words, the connections, which are shared among all projects. The shared data sources are saved in XML files with the extension .rds. Don't worry if the concept of shared data sources is not immediately clear. It will all make sense in chapter 3.

As we explained in chapter 1, the report definition file describes the report in an XML-based format called Report Definition Language (RDL). The Reports folder holds the report definition (*.rdl) files. It is important to note that when you make changes to the report, you are actually changing the report definition file. To view the underlying report definition, right-click on the report item and choose View Code. If you have a brave heart, you can modify the report definition file directly. This could be useful to quickly propagate changes. For instance, if you change the name of a dataset column, it is much faster to open the RDL file and perform search-and-replace, as opposed to locating all affected fields and making the changes in the layout mode by trial and error.

NOTE I've found that the fastest way to copy a report from one project to another is to create a new blank report and then copy and paste the report RDL.

If you make errors in the report schema, the Report Designer tells you about the problem promptly, with an informative message, such as this one:

```
Microsoft Development Environment is unable to load this document.
Deserialization failed: This is an unexpected token. The expected
token is 'NAME'. Line 7, position 9.
```

Besides the report definition files, you can add other external resources to the BI project, such as image files and Extensible Stylesheet Language Transformations (XSLT) transformation files. We will talk more about images and exporting reports to XML in chapters 4 and 5, respectively. Although I call them "external," note that when you upload the report to the report catalog, its associated resources get uploaded to the Catalog table in the Report Server Configuration Database.

Strangely, VS.NET doesn't allow you to create new folders below the Reports folder, although the Report Manager doesn't prevent you from creating nested folders within a project folder. Actually, I don't consider this to be a disadvantage because I would usually try to keep the folder structure as flat as possible. I recommend that you either stick with one folder per project or organize the folder structure logically and physically per applications. For example, an HR and Payroll application can have separate report folders to hold application-specific reports. We discuss folder management in chapter 7.

Previewing reports

As I mentioned earlier, you can unit-test a report on your development machine by previewing the report. The Report Designer actually provides two ways to preview a report: the Preview tab and Preview window. Both modes render the report locally. By "locally," we mean outside the Report Server. In fact, you don't even need the Report Server to preview a report. Being able to work in an offline, "disconnected" mode is useful for several reasons. The report administrator might enforce secured access to the Report Server. All new reports may have to go through a verification and approval process before they are deployed to the production Report Server. For this reason, you could install only VS.NET and the Report Designer on your development machine. The Report Designer allows you to execute the whole report-authoring process on your computer. Once you are ready, you can ask the report administrator to publish the report.

You might be curious to know how it is possible to preview the report outside the Report Server because we mentioned in chapter 1 that a report is processed by the Report Server. You see, when you install the Report Designer, it installs the whole binary stack of the Report Server into the Report Designer installation folder. The Report Designer simply delegates the report rendering to the Report Server binaries, without asking the Report Server explicitly to do so, as shown in figure 2.4.

As figure 2.4 shows, when a report consumer requests a managed report it asks the Report Server to generate and return the report. However, when the report is previewed with the Report Designer, no request is made to the Report Server. Instead, the Report Designer calls the Report Server binaries that are copied during the RS setup process in the Report Designer folder. For this reason, you can think of the Report Designer as a scaled-down Report Server. Of course, its capabilities are limited to report processing and rendering only.

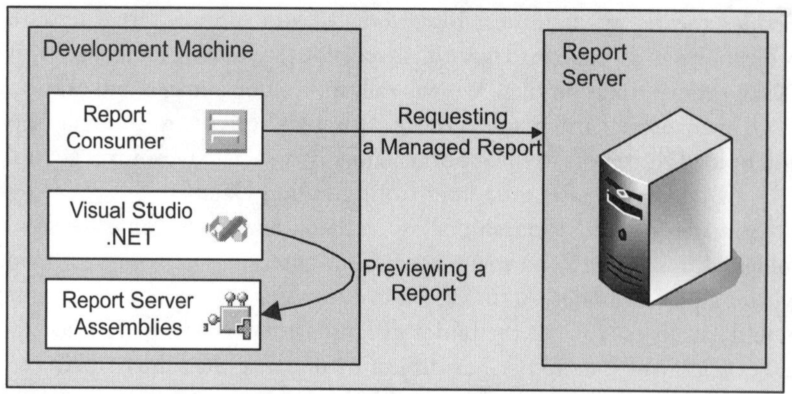

Figure 2.4 When the report is previewed, the Report Designer calls directly the Report Server binaries.

Previewing reports using the Preview Tab

During the report design process, you will find yourself switching often to the Preview tab to quickly see what the report looks like in its rendered form. The Preview tab is a mini Report Server by itself, as shown in figure 2.5.

Just as it does when you render a report through the Report Server, the Preview tab adds the standard report toolbar on the top of the report. The standard toolbar automatically generates parameter placeholders for parameterized reports. In addition, it provides zooming, paging, and printing of the report. Preview mode also allows you to export the report as a file to any of supported rendering formats.

It is important to note that previewing a report using the Preview tab bypasses the custom code security policy rules defined in the Report Designer configuration file (rspreviewpolicy.config). As a result, all custom code is granted the FullTrust permission set. If this security jargon doesn't make sense now, wait until chapter 8, where we discuss code access security in detail.

Data | Layout | Preview

StartDate 4/1/2003 12:00:00 AM EndDate 3/31/2004 12:00:00 AM View Report

Forecasted Months: 3

1 of 1 100%

Sales by Product Category

Sales from 4/1/2003 to 3/31/2004

ADVENTURE WORKS cycles	2003					
	Apr	May	Jun	Jul	Aug	
Accessory	$9,914	$12,482	$10,790	$52,101	$108,505	$10
Bike	$2,327,267	$3,383,223	$2,410,859	$3,405,714	$4,870,610	$4,82
Clothing	$58,157	$83,589	$69,421	$102,357	$172,110	$16
Component	$361,482	$550,141	$459,898	$780,521	$1,148,594	$1,19
Service	$0	$0	$0	$0	$0	

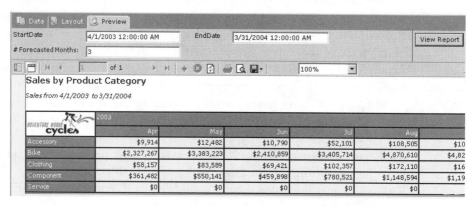

Figure 2.5 The Report Designer Preview tab allows you test the report in the VS.NET IDE.

Previewing reports using the Preview window

To preview a report in the Preview window, do one of the following:

- Right-click on the report, then choose Run.

or

- Set the StartItem property in the project settings to the name of the report you want to preview, then press F5.

Why do we need another option for previewing the report? The Preview window offers two additional features that the Preview tab doesn't have:

- It facilitates debugging external code by loading the report in a stand-alone report host process.
- It gives the report author an option to simulate the targeted Report Server environment.

As you will see in chapters 6 and 15, debugging custom code can be tricky. To facilitate the debugging process, the Preview window loads the report and the custom assembly inside a separate process, called ReportHost. This makes debugging a lot easier because developers can add the custom assembly to the BI solution, set the StartItem project setting to the report that uses the custom code, and press F5 to debug the project. When the report calls the custom code, the breakpoints will be hit.

The second reason why the Preview window could be useful is that it can be used to simulate the Report Server environment as close as possible. The Report Designer settings are stored in a few configuration files, which mirror the Report Server configuration files. For example, the Report Designer code access security policy is stored in the rspreviewpolicy.config file, while the Report Server reads its policy from the rssrvpolicy.config file.

Unlike the Preview tab, when the report is rendered (run) in the Preview window, the Report Designer applies the settings from these configuration files. If the Report Designer and the Report Server settings are identical, the report will be subject to the same security checks as it would if run on the Report Server. We examine RS code security in chapter 8.

For example, although previewing the Sales by Product Category report (which we'll create in chapter 6) under the Preview tab succeeds, it fails when run in the Preview window, as shown in figure 2.6.

In case you are curious, the reason for the failure is that this report references custom assemblies that require elevated code security rights than those defined by the default permission set. We discuss code access security chapter 8.

What happens when you press F5 to run the report depends on the Configuration Manager properties, defined for the active project configuration. Figure 2.7 shows these properties for the AWReporter project.

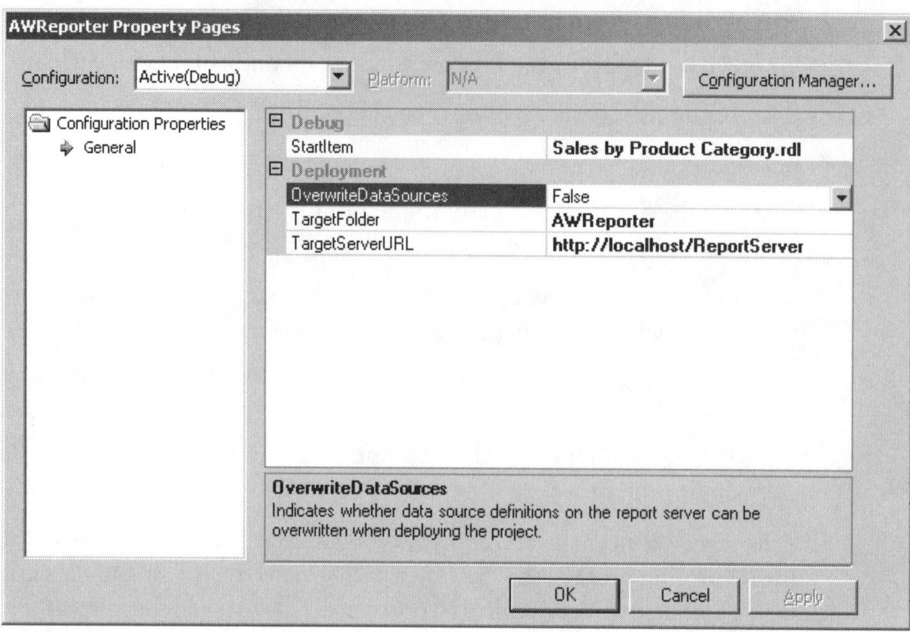

Figure 2.6 You can use the Report Designer Preview window to find out if the report will render successfully in production.

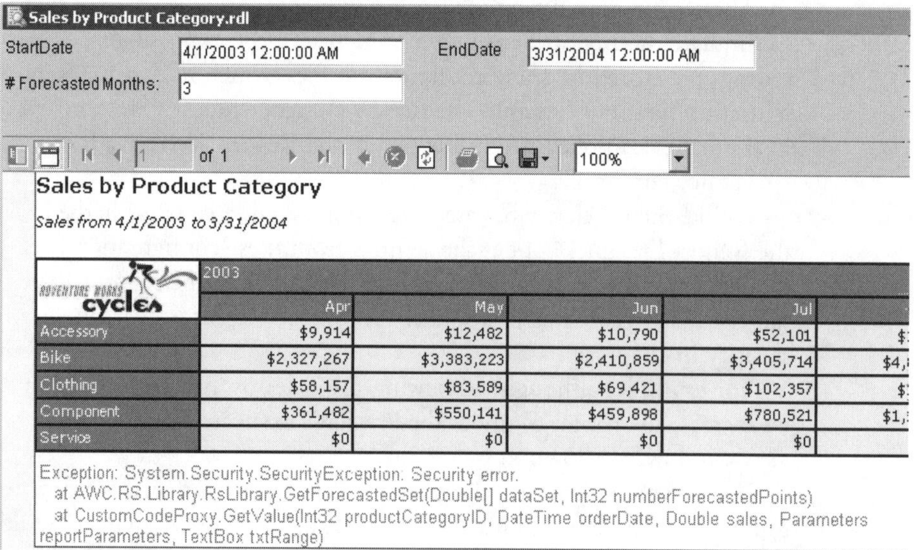

Figure 2.7 Configuration Manager properties determine what happens when you run a BI project. If the Build option is selected, VS.NET will build the project. If the Deploy option is selected, VS.NET will deploy the report items to the report catalog.

In our case, both the Build and the Deploy check boxes are selected. As a result, when we press F5, VS.NET will build and deploy all reports within our BI project.

TIP If both the Build and the Deploy options are on, VS.NET will build and redeploy all reports inside your BI project before the report is loaded in the Preview window. This could take a substantial amount of time. Once the reports are uploaded to the report catalog, you typically don't want to rebuild and redeploy them each time you press F5. To skip these two steps and get to the Preview window faster, clear the Build and Deploy check boxes.

Once you've tested the report successfully, you can promote it to a managed report by deploying it to the Report Server.

Building reports

As a part of the testing process, you need to check if the report can be generated successfully by *building* the report. Using the Report Designer, you can do this in two ways:

- *Explicitly*—To build the whole project, use the Build menu or right-click on the project node in the Solution Explorer and choose Build. To build specific reports, you can select multiple reports by holding the Ctrl key and then build them by right-clicking on the report and selecting Build.
- *Implicitly*—Switching to any of the preview modes or deploying the report causes the Report Designer to build the report automatically.

Building a report doesn't result in a binary, as you would expect when working with .NET development projects. Instead, the build process simply verifies that the report is structured properly and that all field references and expressions are resolvable. If the Report Designer determines that a validation rule is broken, it reports an exception in the Task List. For example, if you misspell a field name, the Report Designer will complain with the following exception:

```
The value expression for the textbox '<textbox name>' refers
to the field '<field name>'.  Report item expressions can only
refer to fields within the current data set scope or, if inside
an aggregate, the specified data set scope.
```

Only a report that compiles successfully can be uploaded to the report catalog. Upon deploying the report, the Report Server enforces this rule by performing the same checks that the Report Designer does when you build the report. For example, you may try to upload a report with syntax errors directly to the report catalog using the Report Manager. However, the attempt will fail with the same error as the one that the Report Designer would report in the Task List if you build the report.

Deploying reports

Finally, once the report is tested successfully it is ready to be promoted to a managed report.

If you have rights to update the report catalog, you can publish the report straight from VS.NET. As a prerequisite for this to happen, you have to set the TargetFolder and TargetServerURL settings in the project properties, as shown in figure 2.8.

The TargetFolder setting specifies the name of the catalog folder that the report will be uploaded to. If the folder doesn't exist, it will be created. The TargetServerURL setting defines the Report Server URL.

BI projects in VS.NET support separate configurations to address different deployment scenarios. For example, during the QA testing lifecycle, you would typically use a staging Report Server. Once the report is tested, you would deploy to production. To address these deployment needs, the project settings include several predefined configurations, among them DebugLocal, Release, and Production. You can use these configurations any way you want. For example, assuming that you have set up separate staging and production environments, you can set these configurations as shown in table 2.1.

You can also define additional configurations if needed by clicking on the Configuration Manager button.

To deploy a single report from the VS.NET, right-click on its file in the Solution Explorer and choose Deploy. The Deploy command first builds the report. Then, it invokes the Report Server Web service to deploy the report to the Report Server. Similar to building reports, you can deploy multiple reports by selecting them and choosing Deploy from the context menu.

Finally, just as with any other development project, I strongly suggest that you put your BI projects under source control, e.g. by using Microsoft Visual SourceSafe. To accomplish this, right-click on the project node and choose Add Solution to Source Control.

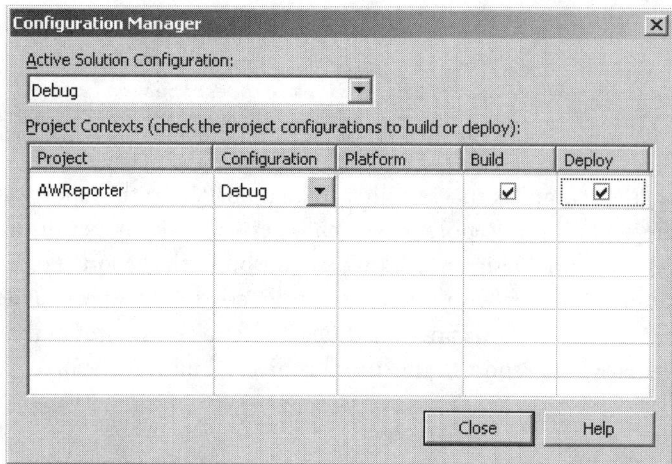

Figure 2.8 Using the project properties you can specify different configurations to address various deployment needs.

Table 2.1 Use different configurations to address different deployment needs.

Configuration	Environment	Purpose
DebugLocal	Local machine	For unit testing with a local instance of Report Server. For example, TargetURL set to http://localhost/ReportServer.
Release	Staging	For QA testing.
Production	Production	The production Report Server.

You will get more insight into the Report Designer because we'll be using it throughout the next few chapters to author various sample reports.

2.2.3 Importing reports from Microsoft Access

There is a good chance that you may be using Microsoft Access for your reporting needs. Although Access is a great reporting tool and it is getting more enterprise-oriented with each new release, you may find that moving to Reporting Services could be beneficial for several reasons:

- RS is designed from the ground up for scalability and performance under high loads. As we explained in Chapter 1, the Reporting Services architecture is service-oriented and facilitates integrating RS with all types of client applications. If you want to integrate Access reports with other applications, you have to rely on legacy technologies, such as OLE Automation, or create your own homegrown solutions, which can take significant up-front development effort.
- Some RS features simply do not have Access equivalents, such as report scheduling and delivery, report management, and so forth. For example, with RS you can export reports to many different formats, while Access restricts you to viewing reports with the Access viewer and exporting is limited to HTML.
- The RS architecture is extensible, while the Access one is proprietary.

There may be other reasons for upgrading from Access to RS depending on your situation.

Reporting Services supports importing reports from Microsoft Access 2002 and above only. Microsoft claims that importing from Access preserves 80% of the Access report features. For a full list of the supported features, please consult the "Importing Reports from Access" topic in the RS documentation. The most noticeable unsupported feature, which will probably cause quite a bit of pain and suffering during the migration process, is Access custom modules and events. Since the report generation process in RS is not event-driven, any custom events that you have defined in your Access report will be lost. As a remedy, you need to find ways to replace your custom code with expressions.

Importing Northwind reports

If you decide to move to RS, you can speed the report-migration process by importing your Access reports. For the time being, Microsoft Access it the only importing option natively provided by RS. However, by the time you read this book, third-party vendors will most likely have released converters from other formats. We mention such a tool in section 2.4.

To demonstrate how this report authoring option works, let's import reports from the Northwind database that comes with the Microsoft Access samples.

NOTE The Importing from Access feature is only available if Access 2002 or later is installed.

Step 1 Create a new BI project and name it Northwind.

Step 2 Right-click on the project (or Reports) node in the Solution Explorer, choose Import Reports from the context menu, and then select Microsoft Access.

Step 3 Specify the location of the Northwind database and click OK.

You will see the imported reports added one by one to the Northwind BI project. Because VS.NET doesn't allow you to pick individual reports, all reports will be imported.

Let's open the Alphabetical List of Products report in the Report Designer by double-clicking on its file. The Report Designer opens the report in a layout mode, as shown in figure 2.9.

As you can see, VS.NET has preserved the report layout. Now, try to preview the report. The Preview window complains about compilation errors. A look at Task List reveals that the culprit is the expression defined in the FirstLetterOfName field, which references the ProductName text box as a report item. Change the expression to

```
=Left(Fields!ProductName.Value,1)
```

Now the report runs fine, as shown in figure 2.10.

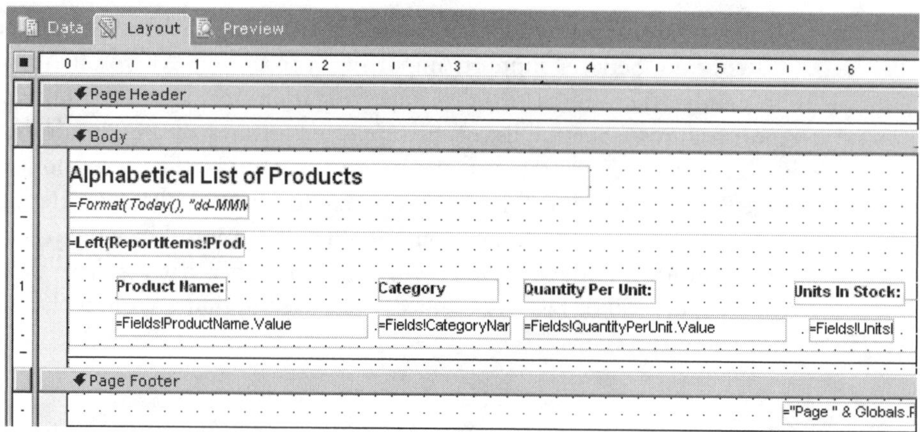

Figure 2.9 The Alphabetical List of Products report after importing it from Microsoft Access

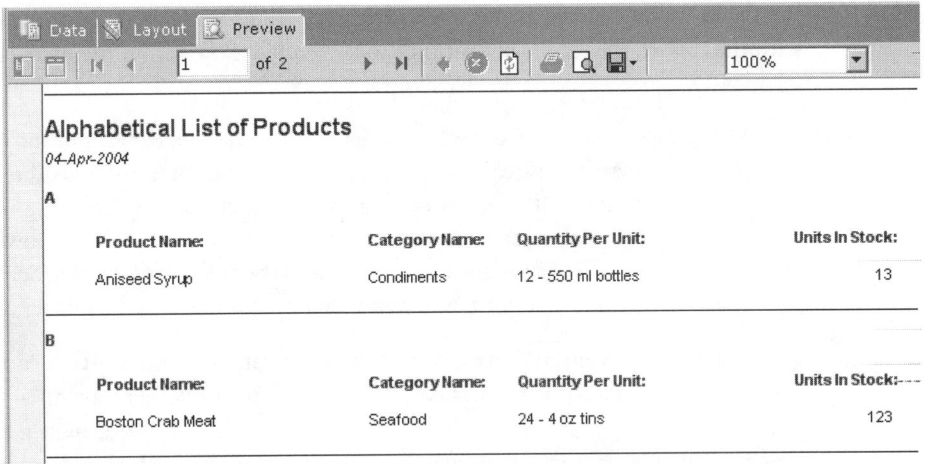

Figure 2.10 The Alphabetical List of Products in Preview mode

Strictly speaking, this report could be rendered more efficiently using a table region instead of using a rectangle item and a list region, but it's still not bad for a few minutes of work.

If you are experienced in Access, you can use the import feature not only to facilitate the upgrade process but also to minimize the learning curve and come up to speed quickly with RS. For instance, RS automatically converts Access expressions to their RS VB.NET equivalents, e.g., [Page] to Globals.PageNumber. It is not perfect, but it will save you quite a bit of effort to just lay out the report in the Report Designer.

With RS you are not limited to creating reports interactively. Instead, thanks to the open XML nature of the report definition schema, you can produce reports programmatically.

2.3 CREATING REPORTS PROGRAMMATICALLY

Recall that the report definition of an RS-based report is described in a specification, called Report Definition Language (RDL). See the Resources section for a link to the RDL schema on the Microsoft website. RDL is composed of XML elements that conform to an XML grammar, which Microsoft created specifically for RS. Microsoft has worked with other industry leaders to promote this grammar as an XML-based standard for report definitions. If this effort is successful, RDL may become the de facto report interchange format of the future.

Widespread RDL adoption will increase the level of interoperability among report vendors and consumers, just like XML today facilitates interoperability between different platforms. This will open a new world of possibilities. Customers will be able to choose the best-of-breed products, without having to worry about vendor lock-in. Vendors can add reporting capabilities to their applications, without having to distribute report engines for report rendering. As long as the reports conform to RDL, any RDL-compliant tool can be used as a report generator. For example, a report vendor can create an ad hoc reporting tool, which generates RDL files. Once the user is ready with the report, the report definition can be rendered by any reporting tool that understands RDL.

NOTE Currently RS doesn't support stand-alone reporting from the report definition file. Instead, to generate the report you need to upload the report definition to the report catalog. If you are third-party vendor, this means that your customers must have RS installed to run your reports. However, the next version of RS, which is expected to be bundled with the SQL Server 2005, will include WinForm and web-based controls for stand-alone reporting.

Creating reports programmatically by generating the report definition can also be useful if you need to author reports on the fly. I had to implement a similar approach in one of my recent real-life projects. Imagine that you need to design a multisection report, where each section shows the sales performance of a particular Adventure Works office. A client front-end application could let the user select arbitrary sections to be included in the report. How would you implement this?

One implementation approach could be to filter the report sections at the data source. Then, you can use a data-bound list region to repeat the sections returned by the report query. But what if the database-driven approach is not an option? Ideally, in this case you would want to generate the report sections programmatically, similar to the way you can create dynamic controls in WinForm or web-based .NET applications. Unfortunately, dynamically generating report items is currently not supported by RS.

As a workaround, you can programmatically generate the report definition. Once you get the list of the selected sections by the user, you can load the report RDL in an XML Document Object Model (DOM) and create as many report list items as the number of the selected sections. Next, you can call the Report Server Web service API to upload RDL to the report catalog, for example, to the user's My Reports folder, and render the report.

2.3.1 The AW Ad Hoc Reporter sample

Because the RDL schema is XML-based, every developer who is familiar with manipulating XML documents with the XML DOM can generate RS report definitions programatically. Before you do that, take some time to review the RDL schema specification, which is described in the RS documentation.

The RDL schema is open and allows developers and vendors to extend it by adding custom elements and namespaces. For example, you might need to develop a custom rendering extension to render a report in a format not supported by RS—for example, fixed text format—and you need to pass the name of the output file to it. Microsoft has already thought about this and provided a Custom element defined in the schema, which can be used as a placeholder to pass additional information. You can add your custom extension parameters to the Custom element. This element is ignored by RS, which allows you to add whatever you need to it.

A common reporting need for many organizations is empowering the information workers by giving them options to generate reports ad hoc. To show you how this could be done with RS, I've developed the world's poorest ad hoc report generator, the AW Ad Hoc Reporter. The design goals of the AW Ad Hoc Reporter are to

- Allow the user to report off an arbitrary database table
- Allow the user to define a tabular report ad hoc by dragging and dropping columns
- Generate the report definition programmatically

You can find the AW Ad Hoc Reporter under the chapter 2 menu in the AWReporterWin sample application included in the book source code. Figure 2.11 shows the AW Ad Hoc Reporter in action.

Here, I used the Ad Hoc Reporter to author a simple report that has four fields. Once the Get RDL button is clicked, the Ad Hoc Reporter generates the report definition.

Using the Ad Hoc Reporter

The user specifies the connection string and the full path to the output RDL file. Once you change the settings, the application "remembers" by storing them in the .NET isolated storage.

After the connection string is specified, you can list the tables in the requested catalog by clicking the Get Schema button. At this point, a call to the database is made to retrieve the table schema from the requested database.

The list of table names is loaded in the Tables drop-down list. Each time you change the table in the drop-down list, its column schema is fetched from the database and shown in the Columns list.

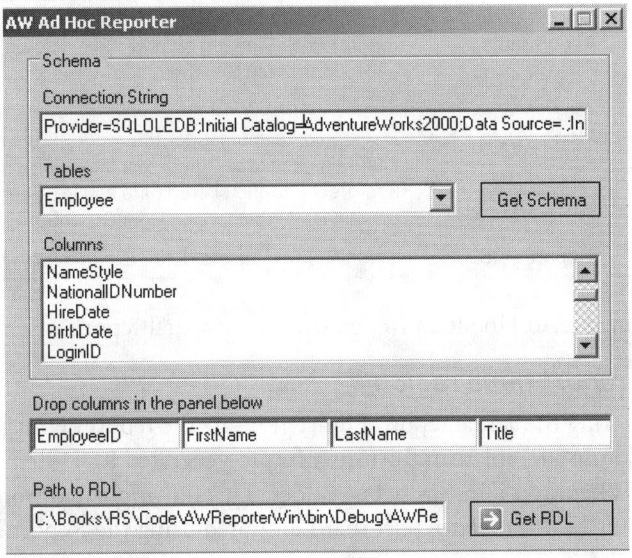

Figure 2.11 The AW Ad Hoc Reporter allows you to create simple ad hoc reports by generating the report definition file.

To specify which columns will be shown on the report, you drag them from the Columns list and drop them on the panel below. Once a column is dropped, the application creates a text box to display the column name and adds it to the panel. You can drop as many columns as there is space available in the panel (about four columns). Removing columns from the panel is currently not supported.

Once the report layout is defined, you can generate the report definition by clicking the Get RDL button. Before doing so, make sure that the predefined RDL schema (Schema.xml) is located in the application build folder, which by default is bin\debug.

Uploading the report definition file

After the report definition file is generated, you can upload the report to the report catalog and make it available to your end users. You can do this manually by using the Report Manager. Alternatively, you can use the Report Server Web service API to upload it programmatically. You'll see an example of the latter approach in chapter 7.

Now that you've seen how you can use the Ad Hoc Reporter to author report definitions programatically, let's peek under its hood to find out how it is implemented.

2.3.2 Implementation details

Table 2.2 lists some of the RDL schema elements that we are dealing with for the purposes of this example. It by no means provides full coverage of RDL schema. See the Resources section at the end of this chapter for a link to the RDL section in the RS online documentation.

Table 2.2 The RDL schema elements used in the Ad Hoc Reporter sample

Element Name	XPath	Description
ReportItems	/Report/Body/ReportItems	Contains the report items that define the contents of a report region. The region may have its own ReportItems collection, which lists the report items that belong to this region.
DataSources	/Report/DataSources	Lists the data sources for the report. If the report uses a shared data source, the datasource element will contain a reference to the shared data source. Otherwise, it will contain DataProvider and ConnectionString elements.
DataSets	/Report/DataSets	Contains the datasets defined in this report.

Let's now see how the Ad Hoc Reporter generates the actual report.

Creating the report table region

To simplify authoring the actual report, I don't generate the report definition file from scratch. Instead, I use a template in the form of a pre-generated RDL file, Schema.xml, located in the AWReporterWin/bin/debug folder. This file originated from the report definition of a very basic tabular report that I authored using the Report Designer, as shown in listing 2.1.

Listing 2.1 The predefined tabular report schema

```
<Table Name="table1">                    <-- Defines a table with the name "tablel"
  <Height>0.25in</Height>
  <Details>
    <TableRows>
      <TableRow>
        <Height>0.25in</Height>
        <TableCells>                     <-- Defines the table cells
          <TableCell>
            <ReportItems>
              <Textbox Name="textbox1">
                <Style />
                <Value />
              </Textbox>
            </ReportItems>
          </TableCell>
        </TableCells>
      </TableRow>
    </TableRows>
  </Details>
  <DataSetName>AWReporter</DataSetName>  <-- Defines the table dataset
  <Top>0.375in</Top>
  <Width>1.66667in</Width>
  <Style />
  <TableColumns>
    <TableColumn>
      <Width>1.66667in</Width>           <-- Defines the table columns
    </TableColumn>
  </TableColumns>
</Table>
```

As you can see, the predefined schema has a table region with one column and one cell only. For the first column that the user drags and drops, I have to update only the name of the cell. For any subsequent column, I generate a new column and cell in the table region.

Generating RDL

Let's now put on our developers' hats and write some .NET code to generate the report definition. The bulk of the report-generation logic is encapsulated in the `CreateRDL` function, as shown in listing 2.2.

Listing 2.2 Creating the report definition programmatically by loading the report schema in the XML DOM

```
private void CreateRDL()
{
   XmlDocument xmlDoc = new XmlDocument();
```

```
    xmlDoc.Load (System.IO.Path.Combine(Application.StartupPath,
                 "Schema.xml"));

XmlNamespaceManager xmlnsManager =
    new XmlNamespaceManager(xmlDoc.NameTable);
xmlnsManager.AddNamespace("rs","http://schemas.microsoft.com" _
    & "/sqlserver/reporting/2003/10/reportdefinition");
xmlnsManager.AddNamespace("rd","http://schemas.microsoft.com" _
    & "/sqlserver/reporting/reportdesigner");

    GenerateColumns(xmlDoc, xmlnsManager);
    GenerateCells (xmlDoc, xmlnsManager);
    UpdateDataSource(xmlDoc, xmlnsManager);
    xmlDoc.Save(txtRDLPath.Text);
}
```

Adds the namespaces used in the RDL schema

Generates the table region columns

Generates the table region cells

Defines the report data source

The application loads the schema using the XML DOM. Because the schema defines XML namespaces, we use the XmlNamespaceManager to add the namespaces to the XML document. Then, we generate the table region columns and cells. For each cell, we set the field name to be the same as the column name. After that, we embed the data source information into the report definition, which includes the connection string and dataset schema. Finally, we save the RDL file to a location specified by the user in the Path to RDL text box. Once the report definition is generated, we can test the report by loading the file in a BI project and previewing the report.

There will be cases when the AW Ad Hoc Reporter will not be enough (OK, I am also modest, am I not?). Currently, Microsoft doesn't provide an ad hoc reporting tool. To fill the void, you can use third-party offerings, as you see in the next section.

2.4 CREATING REPORTS WITH THIRD-PARTY TOOLS

Microsoft is partnering with a number of independent software vendors (ISVs) to create add-ons to RS to extend its capabilities. I would like to finish this chapter by mentioning two third-party reporting tools, Cizer's Quick Query for Microsoft Reporting Services and Hitachi's RDL Generator. You may find these products interesting because they address two popular needs: ad hoc reporting and converting Crystal Reports.

For a full list of the Microsoft partners for RS visit http://www.microsoft.com/sql/reporting/partners/default.asp.

2.4.1 Cizer's Quick Query

As of time of this writing, Microsoft doesn't offer a tool for ad hoc reporting that integrates with RS. To respond to this need, Cizer has developed the Quick Query as a web-based tool that allows users to craft simple ad hoc reports in a fast and easy way. No knowledge of report authoring with the Report Designer is required. Many organizations don't have dedicated IT resources or expertise to create reports using the

VS.NET Report Designer. This is where Quick Query can be useful because it allows information workers to generate easily their own reports.

Cizer's Quick Query embraces the Microsoft RDL schema as a report storage medium and integrates seamlessly with RS. The report administrator can define which data sources users can report off, such as tables, stored procedures, or SQL statements. Once the report data sources are set up, users can navigate to the Quick Query portal. Figure 2.12 shows the Quick Query web portal.

Users can select a data source from the Select Data Source drop-down list. Then, they can pick which fields from the data source they want to see on the report. Quick Query supports data grouping, filtering, and parameterized queries.

Once the fields are selected, users can define the report layout and request to see the report. At this point, behind the scenes Quick Query uploads the report definition to RS using the Report Server Web service API.

Then, Quick Query requests the report from Report Server by URL and displays it to the user. Users also have an option to save the ad hoc report definition as an RDL file. In this case, the tool calls down to Report Server Web services by invoking the `GetReportDefinition()` method. This downloads the report definition file to the user machine.

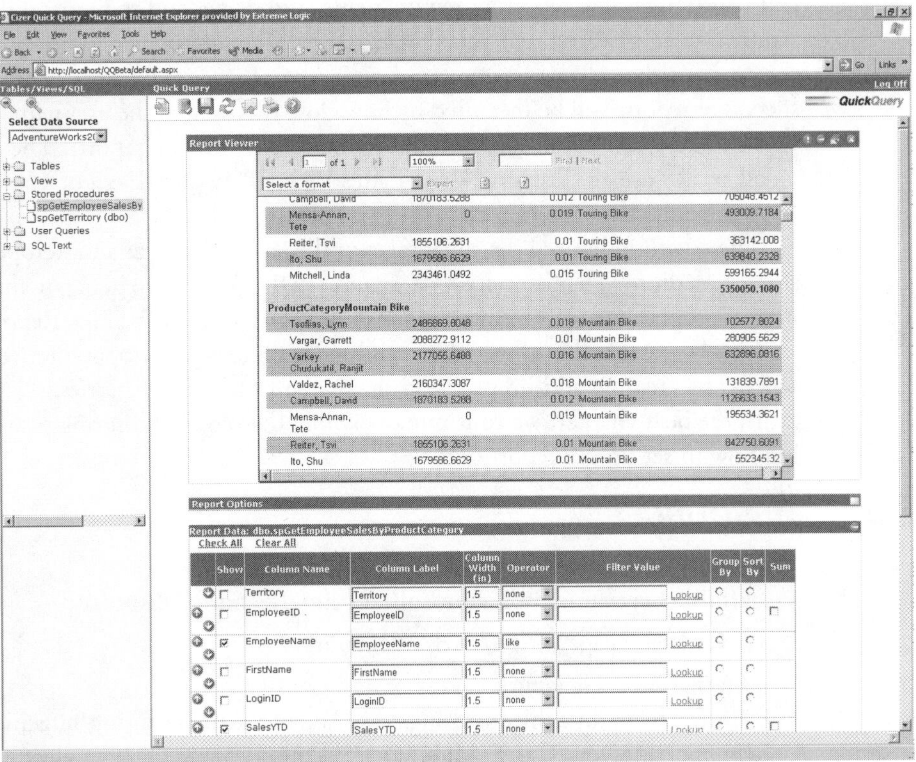

Figure 2.12 Cizer's Quick Query has a web-based front end that allows end users to create ad hoc reports.

Cizer also offers another product, called Report Builder, that is a report designing tool, similar to the VS.NET Report Designer. It is also web-based and requires no client installation.

Check out the Resources section for the URL to Cizer's home page.

2.4.2 Hitachi's RDL Generator

Another tool that you may find interesting is the Hitachi's RDL Generator. It is a conversion tool that processes existing Crystal Reports (.rpt) formats and converts them to RDL.

RDL Generator sponsors a simple WinForm interface that allows the user to specify the location of the Crystal report file. Then, it parses the report, generates the RS report definition and outputs it in the Preview pane. Once you have the report definition, you can save it as a file and upload it to the report catalog.

See the Resources section for the URL to this tool.

2.5 SUMMARY

In this chapter we explored the report-authoring process. This process encompasses several stages: analyzing reporting requirements, authoring, and testing and deploying the report. We emphasized that you should resist the temptation of jumping into creating the report without having a good understanding of what your users want. After all, the success of reports will be measured by how close they match the user requirements.

In this chapter we also discussed different ways to create reports. The options provided by RS are the Report Wizard, the VS.NET Report Designer, and importing reports from Microsoft Access.

Then, we emphasized the advantages of the RDL schema as an interoperable report storage medium. Thanks to its XML syntax, RDL allows us to generate the report definition programmatically, as we demonstrated with the AW Ad Hoc Reporter sample.

Finally, we saw that third-party vendors can leverage the open nature of the RDL schema by creating add-on products that extend the RS capabilities.

In the next chapter, we continue to explore the report-authoring process by learning how to set up the report data.

2.6 RESOURCES

Report Definition Language Specification
(http://www.microsoft.com/sql/reporting/techinfo/rdlspec.asp)

Cizer's home page (http://www.cizer.com)

Hitachi's RDL Generator
(http://www.hitachiconsulting.com/Apps/hitachiconsulting/hitachiconsulting/supportingDocs/CaseStudies/SO-MS%20RDL%20Generator-electronic.pdf)

Report Services Partners
http://www.microsoft.com/sql/reporting/partners/default.asp

CHAPTER 3

Working with data

By now, you know that the report-authoring process involves working with the report data. Specifically, you set up the data in the construction phase of the process.

In this chapter, we provide more in-depth coverage about the Report Designer. You will learn how to use the Report Designer Data tab to set up the report data. We cover the following topics:

- Setting up the data source
- Defining report datasets
- Creating dataset queries with the Graphical and Generic query designers
- Creating parameter-driven reports

3.1 WORKING WITH DATA SOURCES

In the simplest scenario, you won't need to integrate your report with a database at all. Before ruling out this possibility, consider an e-mail campaign scenario where you need to send reports to subscribers. For example, Adventure Works Cycles may want to notify its customer base about a new product. In this case, the report will not be data-driven at all, because it needs only static text and images. If this is the case, you can proceed to laying out the report itself, as discussed in chapter 4.

Most reporting requirements, however, call for data-driven reports. With the proliferation of database standards and providers, reporting off heterogeneous databases has traditionally been difficult even with the most popular reporting tools. For example, Microsoft Access is limited to supporting only ODBC-compliant databases. One of the most prominent strengths of RS is that it can draw data from any data source that has an ODBC or OLE DB driver. Don't despair if your data source doesn't support ODBC or OLE DB. Developers can extend RS to report off pretty much any data source that exposes data in a tabular format, as you will see in chapter 15.

While I am not excluding the possibility of reporting off less popular data sources, such as flat files or Excel spreadsheets, usually your reports will draw data from designated Online Transaction Processing (OLTP) or Online Analytical Processing (OLAP) databases.

The first step to creating a data-driven report is to set up a connection to the database where the report data resides.

NOTE The RS documentation uses the term *data source* to refer to the definition of a database connection, which, I think, is confusing because the name "data source" is usually associated with the database itself. Perhaps the reason behind this is to differentiate between the connection specification (connection string, credentials, etc.) and the actual physical connection. For sake of simplicity, I will use the terms *data source* and *connection* interchangeably.

3.1.1 Connecting to the database

Before we show you how to define a database connection, note that with RS your reports are not limited to drawing data from a single data store. Instead, data can originate from multiple heterogeneous databases. For example, let's say you need to create an Employee Sales Summary report that shows salespeople's performance alongside human resources (HR)-related data. You may have the sales data captured in a SQL Server database, whereas the HR data is stored in an Oracle database. One way to consolidate data from these two data sources is to link the Oracle database to the SQL Server. In this case, you will need to connect to the SQL Server database only.

NOTE Microsoft SQL Server 2000 allows you to attach (link) to OLE DB-compliant data sources called *linked servers*. Once the linked server is set up, you can create stored procedures or statements that span both servers.

When using linked servers is not possible, you can define two database connections that your report will use to draw data from each database, as shown in figure 3.1.

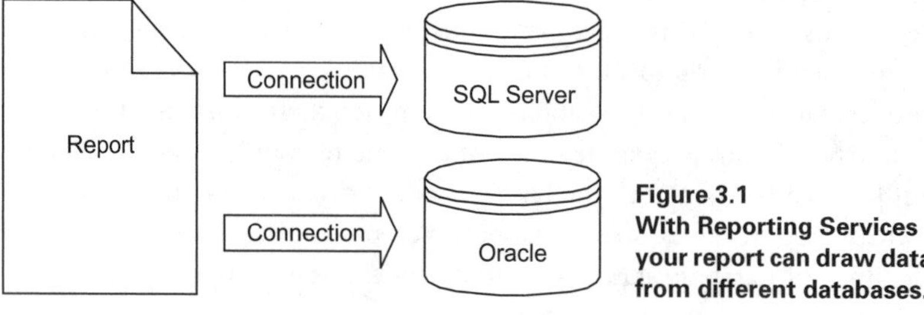

Figure 3.1 With Reporting Services your report can draw data from different databases.

Whether you need to fetch data from one database or several, you will have to make some decisions when setting up the database connection. First, you must decide if the connection will be set up as report-specific or shared.

Report-specific data source

A report-specific connection gets embedded into the report definition (RDL) file. Use a report-specific connection when

- You need to encapsulate the database information inside the report definition file.
- You want to simplify the report distribution and setup.

A report-specific connection makes it possible to distribute both the report layout and connection information in one file. For example, a third-party vendor might choose to store database connection information in the RDL file to simplify the process of distributing the report to its customers. In this case, the connection should be defined as report-specific.

You create a report-specific connection as a part of setting up the report dataset (more on this in section 3.2). The process of creating a report-specific connection is similar to setting up a shared connection, as we discuss in the next section. The only difference is that you need to deselect the "Use shared data source reference" check box in the Data Source dialog box, as shown in figure 3.2.

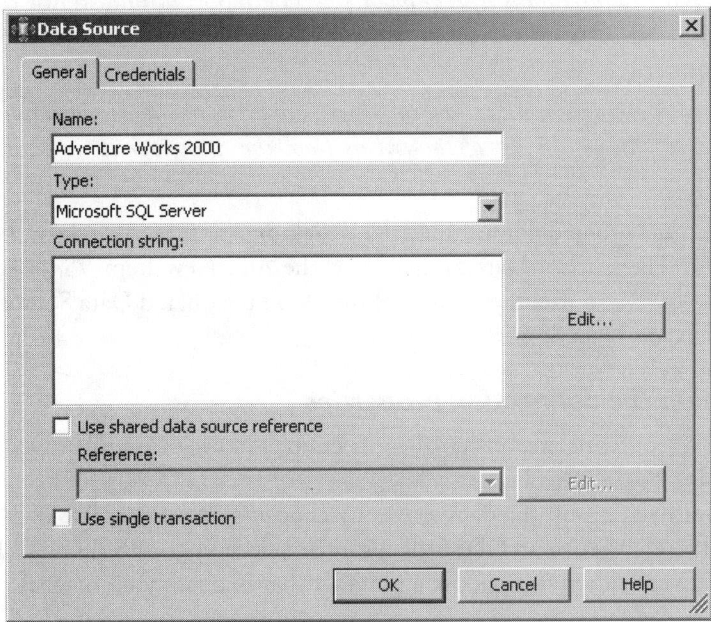

Figure 3.2 To create a report-specific connection, be sure that the "Use shared data source reference" option is not selected.

You can open this dialog box by selecting the dataset in the Dataset drop-down list (on the Data tab) and clicking the "..." button to open the Dataset Properties dialog box. Clicking the "..." button located to the right of the Data source drop-down (see figure 3.10) displays the Data Source dialog box.

Once you finish configuring the data source, its definition will be embedded in the report, as you can see by inspecting the `DataSources` element in the report definition file. As you'll recall from the Employee Sales Summary example at the beginning of this chapter, one report can draw its data from more than one data source (report-specific or shared).

Shared data source

As its name suggests, a shared data source can be used by all reports within the same Visual Studio .NET (VS.NET) business intelligence (BI) project. A shared data source offers the following advantages over a report-specific connection:

- *Ensures that all physical connections that use the same shared data source specification utilize identical connection strings.* This is a prerequisite for connection pooling (more on this in section 3.1.2).
- *Centralizes connection management.* For example, the report administrator can use the Report Manager to change the connection authentication settings and all reports in the project that share the connection will pick up the new settings.
- *A shared connection is a securable item.* The report administrator can enforce a role-based security policy to control which users can change the connection information.
- *When working with data-driven report subscriptions, a shared connection can be used to retrieve the list of subscribers from the subscriber store.* More on this in chapter 14.

To create a new shared connection, right-click on the project node and choose Add New Item. Then, select Data Source from the Add New Item VS.NET dialog box. Alternatively, as a shortcut, you can right-click on the Shared Data Sources folder and select Add New Data Source.

Setting up the connection properties

To set up a report-specific or shared connection, you use the familiar Data Link Properties dialog box, shown in figure 3.3.

You start setting up the data source by choosing an appropriate data provider. If you need to connect to an ODBC data source, select Microsoft OLE DB Provider for ODBC Drivers; otherwise, choose a provider that matches your database.

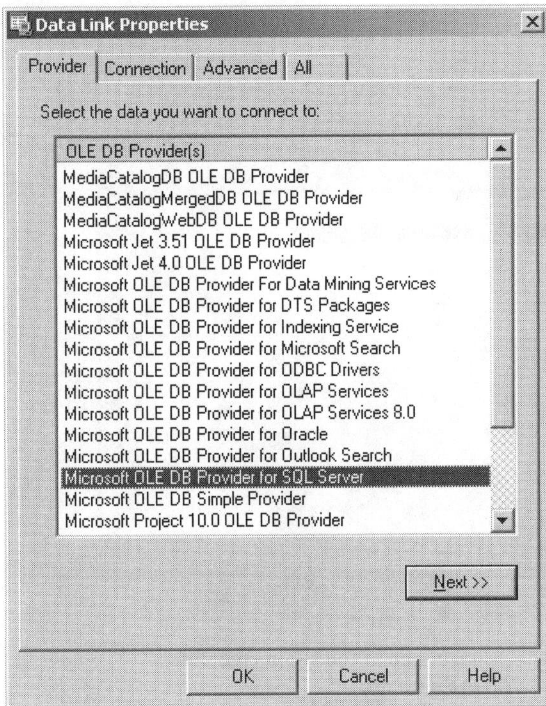

Figure 3.3
Use the Data Link Properties dialog box to choose a data provider.

NOTE Unfortunately, with version 1.0 of Reporting Services, connection strings cannot be based on expressions. As a result, you may need to change the connection string manually when moving from a development to a production environment. To minimize the migration impact, consider defining data sources as shared. Using connection strings expressions—for example, to get the connection string from a report parameter—has been slated for the next version of RS.

Regardless of the provider choice you make in this dialog box, the Report Server will use one of four *data extensions* to talk to the provider, as shown in figure 3.4. To see this dialog box, once the data source is created, double-click on its file in the Solution Explorer.

Experienced .NET developers will instantly understand why the number of extensions is limited to four, as we explain next.

Working with data extensions

The number of the supported data extensions for the report data source corresponds to the number of the .NET data providers included in the .NET Framework.

NOTE In .NET, a data provider is used for connecting the application to a database, executing commands, and retrieving results.

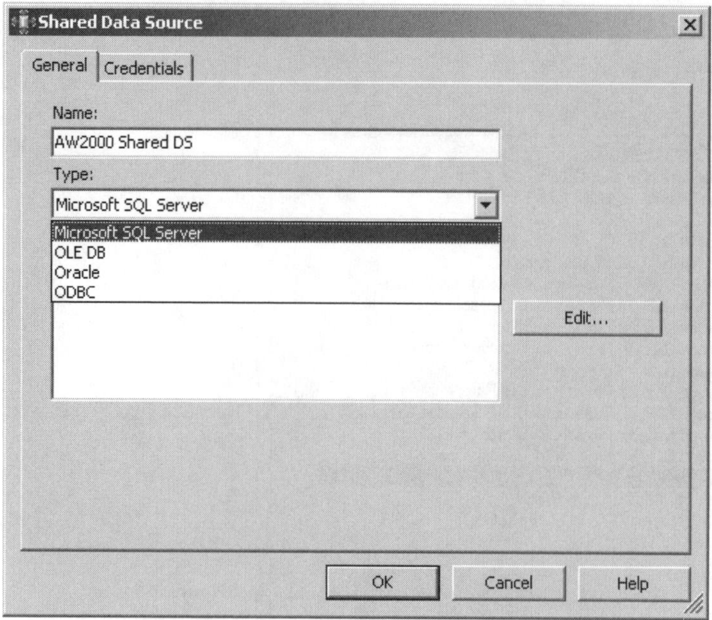

Figure 3.4 The Report Server will use one of the supported data extensions to communicate with the data provider.

Table 3.1 lists the available .NET data providers.

Behind the scenes, the Report Server maps your provider choice to one of the supported RS data extensions, as shown in figure 3.5.

The Report Server data extensions are just wrappers on top of the .NET data providers. You can think about them as the Report Server Data layer. The data extensions are implemented in the Microsoft.ReportingServices.DataExtensions assembly.

NOTE I mention the Microsoft.ReportingServices.DataExtensions assembly for completeness only. You don't need to reference it explicitly in your BI project.

The extensions supported by the Report Server are enumerated in the Reporting Services configuration files. For example, only the extensions listed under the `<Data>` element in the RSReportDesigner.config configuration file will appear in the Report Designer

Table 3.1 The available .NET data providers

.NET Provider	Description
System.Data.SqlClient	Data provider for SQL Server
System.Data.OleDb	Data provider for OLE DB-compatible data sources
System.Data.OracleClient	Data provider for Oracle
System.Data.Odbc	Data provider for ODBC

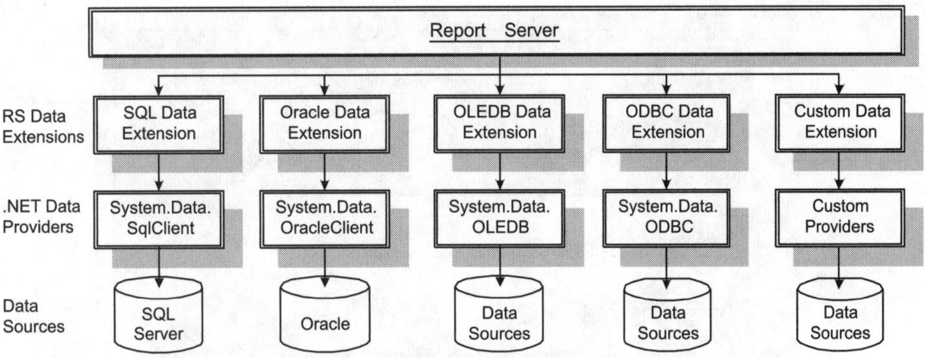

Figure 3.5 RS supports four data extensions, which correspond to the available .NET data providers.

Data Source dialog box. Similarly, the Report Server will allow only the extensions listed under the `<Data>` element in the RSReportServer.config file to execute.

It is important to note that the Report Server data access options are not restricted to these four data extensions. Developers can extend the Report Server by creating custom data extensions, as you'll see in chapter 15.

Once the data provider is selected, you will have to decide how the user will be authenticated against the data source.

3.1.2 Choosing an authentication mechanism

The second decision that you have to make when setting up the report data source is what authentication mechanism RS will use to establish the connection. RS provides four credential options that the Report Server can use to log into the database.

Use the Credentials tab in the Shared Data Source dialog box to specify the authentication settings, as shown in figure 3.6.

During design time, the Report Designer will use the credentials settings to authenticate against the data source. Note that for security reasons the credential settings are not saved in the data source definition. Instead, VS.NET caches these settings in memory. If you need to save the credentials it in the data source definition, you can manually change the report RDL file (for a report-specific data source) or to the RDS data source file (for a shared data source).

> **NOTE** You will notice that VS.NET doesn't reflect changes to the credentials settings and may still establish database connections using the old credentials. This is probably a bug, which we hope will be fixed in Report Services Service Pack 1. To avoid this anomaly, close and reopen VS.NET after the change.

The Report Designer Data Source dialog box (shown in figure 3.6) is somewhat inadequate and doesn't show all the authentication options that RS supports. For this reason, let's discuss the full-blown Report Manager Data Source tab, as shown in figure 3.7.

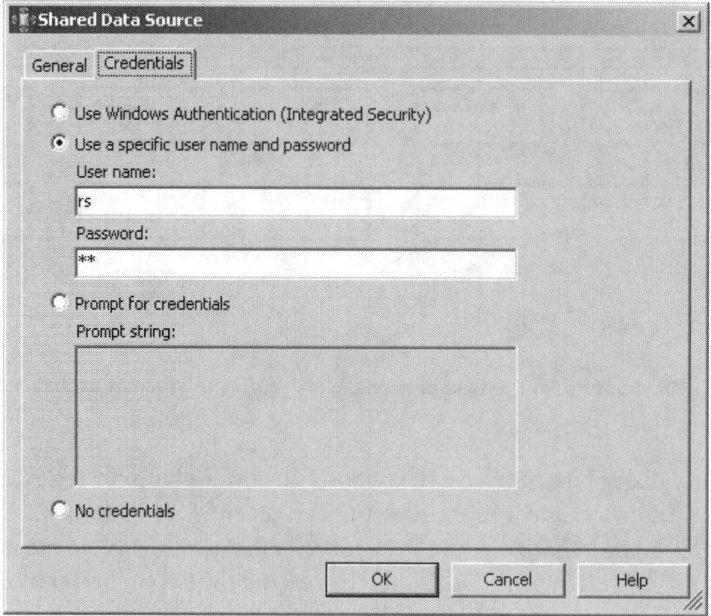

Figure 3.6 Use the Credentials tab to set the connection authentication settings.

As shown in figure 3.7, you can choose one of the following data source authentication options:

- The credentials supplied by the user running the report
- Credentials stored securely in the report server
- Windows NT Integrated Security
- Credentials are not required

NOTE To access the screen shown in figure 3.7, use the Report Manager web application. Assuming that you have deployed the shared data source to the AWReporter folder, you can see the share data source properties by requesting the Report Manager URL in your browser (e.g., http://localhost/reports), navigating to the AWReporter folder, and clicking on AW2000 Shared DS link.

These authentication choices might seem bewildering at first, so let's spend some time exploring each one.

The credentials supplied by the user running the report

This first option prompts the user for the login credentials. It will cause the Report Server to generate two fields, Log In Name and Password, in the standard report toolbar. If the "Use as Windows credentials…" check box is not selected, the Report Server

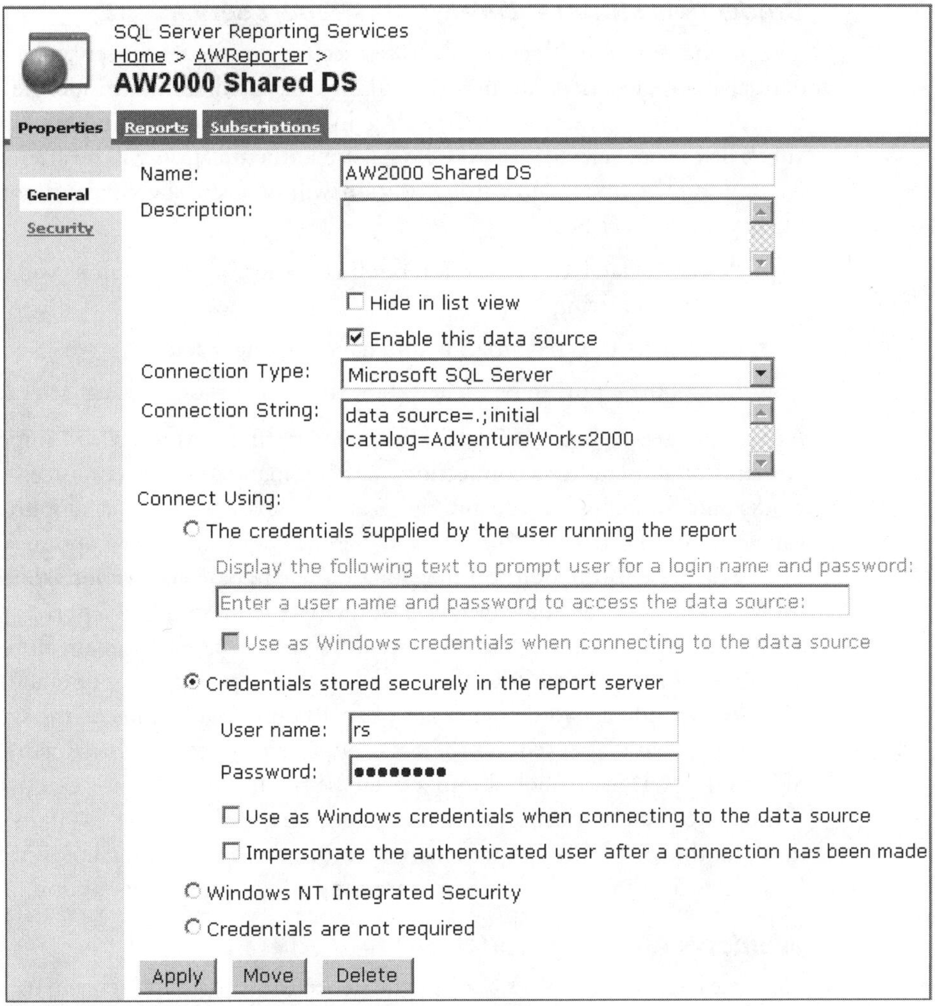

Figure 3.7 **Use Report Manager to set up the connection authentication settings that the Report Server will use to connect to the data source.**

will attempt to authenticate the user through standard database authentication. Otherwise, Windows Authentication will be used.

The "Credentials supplied by the user running the report" option is useful for testing purposes because you can run the report under different login credentials—for example, to troubleshoot end-user authentication issues. However, in a production environment, I recommend you avoid this option. In this case, asking the users to supply the database login credentials may present a security risk. In addition, this option cannot be used with subscribed "pushed" reports because they are generated in an unattended mode.

Credentials stored securely in the report server

The second option is "Credentials stored securely in the report server." The login credentials you enter here are persisted in an encrypted format inside the DataSource table in the ReportServer database. Again, if the "Use as Windows credentials…" check box is not selected, standard database authentication will be attempted; otherwise, Windows Integrated Authentication will be used. This second option is most likely your best bet because it

- Promotes database connection pooling because all connections will use the same connection string.
- Centralizes the credentials maintenance in one place.
- Allows the report to be cached—for more details on caching, refer to chapter 7.

As you can see in figure 3.7, there is an interesting option called "Impersonate the authenticated user after a connection has been made to the data source." This option works only for logins with admin rights and database servers that support user impersonation. In the case of SQL Server, behind the scenes this option executes the SETUSER system function to impersonate the database connection, so it runs under the identity of the Windows account of the user requesting the report.

For example, imagine that you log into Windows as AWDomain\Bob. The report administrator has chosen the "Credentials stored securely…" option and has entered User Name and Password credentials of an account that belongs to the sysadmin SQL Server role. Now, you request the Sales by Territory report. The Report Server calls SETUSER AWDomain\bob. From a database point of view, this is exactly the same as if Integrated Authentication were used. Because the SQL Server 2000 documentation says that the SETUSER option may not be supported in future releases of SQL Server, I advise against using the "Impersonate the authenticated user" option.

Windows NT Integrated Security

Next, we have the Windows NT Integrated Security option. When you use this option, the Report Server will attempt to establish the connection under the context of the Windows account of the user requesting the report. If you are a .NET developer, this is the exactly the same as if you'd specified the "Integrated Security=SSPI" setting in the connection string. The important thing to remember here is that the Report Server impersonates the call to the database to run under the context of the report user.

For example, in the previous scenario where Bob is requesting a report, the call to the database goes under the AWDomain\Bob account. Of course, in order for this to work, the database administrator has to create a database login for this Windows account and grant the right privileges. Using the Windows identity for database authentication is convenient because it allows the database administrator to simplify the database security model by using existing Windows accounts.

However, for performance reasons, I don't recommend you use this option for large reporting applications. Because the connection string for each user will be different

(Windows account names and passwords are different), the connections will not be pooled. Actually, to be more accurate, you will end up with as many connection pools as the number of users requesting the report. Not good!

Credentials are not required

You can configure a data source connection to use no credentials. This could be useful in the following circumstances:

- *The data source doesn't support authentication.* For example, in chapter 15 we create a custom dataset extension to report off ADO.NET datasets. Because in this case we won't have a database to connect to, we can use the "Credentials are not required" option.
- *The credentials are specified in the connection string.* As we mentioned at the beginning of this section, you can store the credentials in the connection string by manually changing the data source definition.
- *The report is a subreport that use the credentials of the parent report to connect to its data source.* In this case the subreport will inherit the data source credentials from the parent and there is no reason to set up specific credentials.

When you select the "Credentials are not required" option, the Report Server uses a special account to make the connection. For more information about how to set up this account, refer to the "Configuring an Account for Unattended Report Processing" section in the product documentation.

Monitoring database connection pooling

If you have experience in writing Microsoft-centric, data-driven applications, you have probably heard about *database connection pooling*. Database connections are expensive resources. Many database providers, such as the .NET SqlClient provider, perform connection pooling behind the scenes to minimize the number of open database connections. When a connection is closed, it is returned to the pool. When the application needs to connect to the database again, the provider checks the pool for available connections. If it finds one, it uses that connection; otherwise, it creates a new one.

So, connection pooling makes your application (in our case, the Report Server) more scalable. The catch is that two connections can share the same pool only if their connection strings are exactly the same, including the login credentials. The "Credentials stored securely in the report server" option enforces this rule and enables connection pooling. Therefore, this is my preferred option for better performance results.

To see how each authentication option affects the number of open database connections, open the Performance console from the Administrative Tools program group, as shown in figure 3.8.

Let's first experiment with the "Credentials stored securely in the report server" option. Before we start, you may want to change the Report Server session timeout from its default value of 600 to the minimum allowed value of 60 (the SessionTimeout

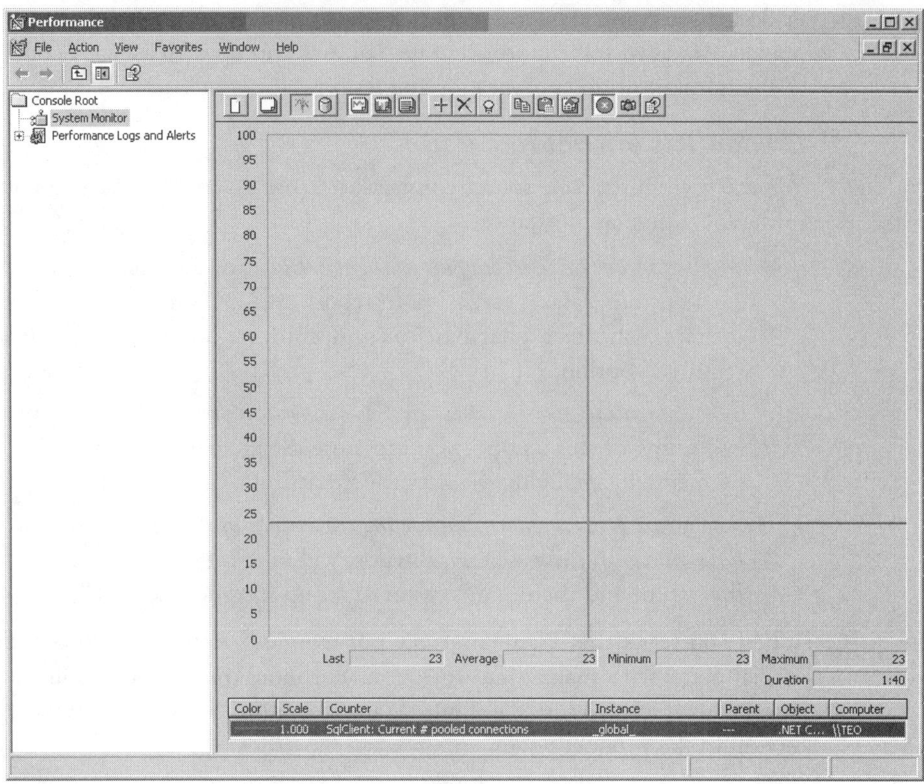

Figure 3.8 Use the "SqlClient: Current # pooled connections" counter found under the .NET CLR DATA category to monitor database connection pooling.

column in the ConfigurationInfo table in the ReportServer SQL Server database). This causes the report session to expire sooner, which in turn forces the Report Server to query the database when processing the report.

NOTE When you experiment with different authentication options, you might be surprised to find that no connection to the database is created with the new credentials. In the case of SQL Server, you may not see the connection when using the Process Info screen in Enterprise Manager or executing the sp_who system procedure. The reason for this is most likely the report session caching that the Report Server does behind the scenes. The default session timeout specified in the SessionTimeout field in the ConfigurationInfo table (ReportServer database) is 600 seconds. This means that if the Report Server decides to reuse the report intermediate format when the report is requested again, it won't query the data source within that period. Instead, it will use the report IF serialized in the Report Server Temporary Database.

We discuss report caching in detail in chapter 7. For the time being, when you experiment with different authentication connection options, you may want to decrease the SessionTimeout value so that the report session expires sooner. My experiments show that you cannot completely disable the ReportServer session caching. The minimum value you can set the SessionTimeout field to is 60 seconds. If you decide to change SessionTimeout, don't forget to restart IIS. Alternatively, you can manually delete the record in the table SessionData (ReportServerTempDb database) or set its Expiration column to a date in the past.

To monitor database connection pooling, follow these steps:

Step 1 Assuming that RS is installed locally on your computer, open the Report Manager by navigating to http://localhost/reports in the browser. Navigate to the AWReporter folder and click on the AW2000 Shared DS data source.

Step 2 Select the "Credentials stored securely…" option and specify the credentials of a database login that has rights to query the Adventure Works database.

Step 3 Open the Performance Console and add the "SqlClient:Current # pooled connections" counter found under the .NET CLR Data performance category for the _global_ domain.

Step 4 Open another instance of the browser and request the Sales by Territory report (the encoded report URL should be: http://localhost/Reports/Pages/Report. aspx?ItemPath=%2fAWReporter%2fSales+By+Territory). Assuming that there is no other connection with the same credentials, you should see the pooled connection counter going up. Wait for one minute or remove the session record from the SessionData table in the ReportServerTempDB.

Step 5 Repeat the process by opening up another instance of the browser and requesting the report again. The pooled connection counter should remain unchanged. This means that the .NET SqlClient provider uses connection pooling behind the scenes and reuses the already existing connection.

Let's now change the authentication options of the data source to Windows NT Integrated Security. For the new test, you will need two Windows user accounts, which are members of the Administrator group. You can use regular user accounts, but you have to specifically give them rights to the database, while members of the Administrator group automatically get admin privileges. Fire up the browser again and request the Sales by Territory report.

Observe the pooled connection performance counter. Now, right-click on the Internet Explorer shortcut and choose Run as. Specify the user name and password for the second user account. Run the report again, and you will see the counter going up instead of remaining unchanged. This proves that the Report Server doesn't pool connections.

Let's wrap up our overview of authentication options with some recommendations.

Authentication best practices

To summarize, I recommend that you follow these guidelines for data source authentication:

- Use shared data sources. For example, almost all reports from the AWReporter project use the AW2000 Shared DS.rds shared data source.
- Use the "Credentials stored securely in the report server" option with standard or Windows-based authentication.
- Don't use an account with admin database privileges! Instead, create a new database login and assign it to a role that has only read permissions to the database you need to report off.

If you use SQL Server, you can assign the login to the db_datareader role, as shown in figure 3.9.

In my case, I created a new SQL Server login, named it "rs", and assigned it to the db_datareader role. Also, I granted the new login rights to the AdventureWorks2000 database.

As we explained in chapter 2, before the report is run by end users it has to be uploaded to the report catalog. As a part of the deployment process, you need to ensure that all data sources that the report uses have also been deployed to the report catalog.

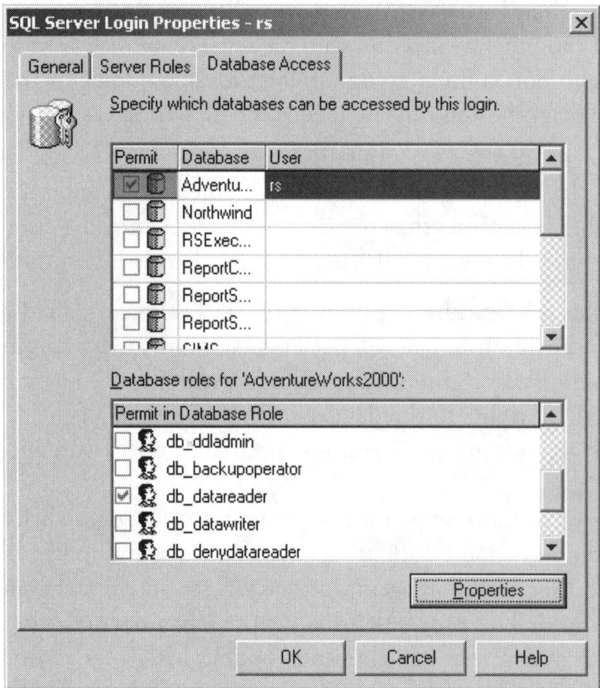

Figure 3.9
With SQL Server you can set up a database login with restricted read-only rights by assigning it to the db-datareader role.

3.1.3 Deploying data sources

You don't need to take any extra steps to upload a report-specific data source. As you'll recall, its definition is a part of the report RDL file and travels with it.

Because a shared data source is saved in a separate file, it must be uploaded to the report catalog so it is available to all reports that use it. Assuming that you have "Manage data sources" rights, you can deploy a shared data source straight from the VS.NET by right-clicking on its file and choosing the Deploy command. Alternatively, the report administrator can upload the file manually using the Report Manager.

What happens when you redeploy the shared data source from the VS.NET IDE depends on the OverwriteDataSources project setting (click on the project node in the VS.NET Solution Explorer and choose Properties). If this setting is false (the default), once the new data source has been created, any subsequent changes made to that data source inside the VS.NET project will not be propagated (will not overwrite) the data source settings in the Report Server database.

Setting OverwriteDataSources to false can be both useful and dangerous. It can be useful because during the design phase you can change the data source to point to a local or staging database. You don't have to know the login credentials for the production reporting database. You can use your own set of credentials or use Windows authentication. It is also dangerous because your development data source may have more rights to that database than the account that will be used in production environment. As a result, when you deploy your report to the production Report Server, it may fail to execute when attempting to retrieve data.

If OverwriteDataSources is false, then you will see the following warning when you try to deploy the project within VS.NET:

```
Cannot deploy data source <data source name> to the server
because it already exists and OverwriteDataSources is not specified.
```

Once you have the data source connection all set, it is time to craft the dataset(s) that the report will use.

3.2 WORKING WITH REPORT DATASETS

Just as .NET datasets are used as data carriers in .NET applications, RS datasets are used to expose data to your report. However, the term *dataset* as used by RS has nothing to do with ADO.NET datasets. Instead, it refers to the specification that describes how the data from the database is retrieved and what that data schema looks like. In this fashion, an RS dataset can be loosely related to a hybrid between a .NET dataset and the data adapter used to fill it in with data. Specifically, in RS dataset spells out

- The SQL query or statement that will be used to retrieve the report data
- The data source (connection) that the query will use
- List of database fields (columns) to be used by the report
- Other information that you specify when you set your dataset, such as the options on the Data Options, Parameters, and Filters tabs

You use the Report Designer to set up one or more datasets. As with all report-related elements, the dataset definition is stored in the report definition file.

3.2.1 Understanding the dataset definition

The dataset specification becomes a part of the report definition file and can be found under the `<DataSets>` element. For example, listing 3.1 shows the abbreviated dataset definition for the Sales by Territory report that we created in chapter 1. To open the report definition, right-click on the Sales by Territory.rdl item in the VS.NET Solution Explorer and choose the View Code command.

Listing 3.1 The DataSet element contains the report dataset definition.

```
  <DataSets>
    <DataSet Name="AW2000_Shared_DS">
      <Fields>   <-- Defines the dataset fields
        <Field Name="Territory">
          <DataField>Territory</DataField>
          <rd:TypeName>System.String</rd:TypeName>
        </Field>
        <Field Name="ProductCategoryID">
          <DataField>ProductCategoryID</DataField>
          <rd:TypeName>System.Byte</rd:TypeName>
        </Field>
<!--more dataset fields...-->
      <Query>
        <DataSourceName>AW2000 Shared DS</DataSourceName>   <-- Defines the dataset data source
        <CommandText>   <-- Defines the dataset query
SELECT     ST.Name AS Territory, PC.ProductCategoryID, PC.Name AS
<!--the rest of the SQL statement here-->
</CommandText>
      </Query>
    </DataSet>
  </DataSets>
</DataSet>
```

Unfortunately, you can't define a dataset as shared inside a VS.NET BI project. Therefore, the dataset definition is always report-specific. It would be nice if you could reuse the dataset definition among reports, similar to the way you can create typed datasets in .NET development projects but this is not possible with version 1.0 of Reporting Services.

NOTE Microsoft hints that shared queries, which definitions could be shared among reports, will be supported in a future release of Reporting Services.

Let's now see how we can set up a report dataset.

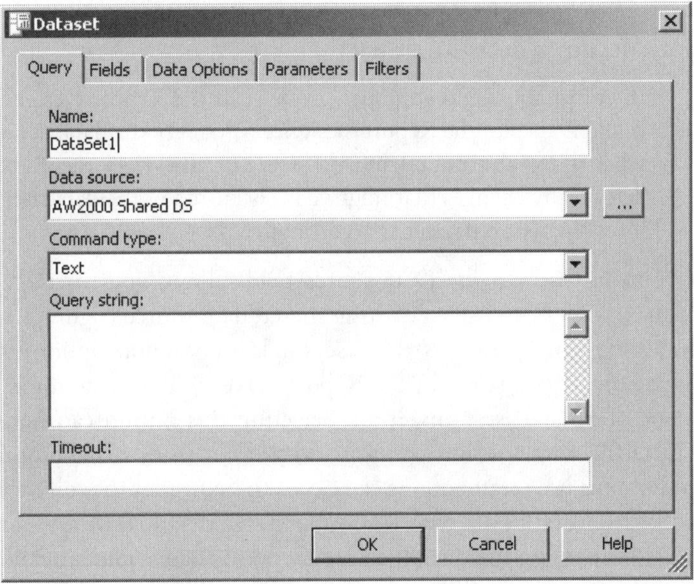

Figure 3.10 Use the Query tab in the Dataset dialog box to specify the dataset name, data source, and query string.

3.2.2 Creating a report dataset

To create a report dataset, you will use the Report Designer Data tab. To create a new dataset, you select New Dataset from the Dataset drop-down control. This brings up the Dataset dialog box, shown in figure 3.10.

Let's now discuss briefly each tab, starting with the Query tab.

The Query tab

The Query tab contains the following fields:

- *Name*—Consider changing the dataset name to something more meaningful, especially if you need more than one dataset for your report.
- *Data source*—Clicking the ellipsis button brings you to the Data Source dialog box (figure 3.11) that you can use to set up a report-specific or shared data source.
- *Command type*—The command type can be Text if the query string you enter is a SQL statement, a stored procedure, or TableDirect, in case you want to specify just the table name and get all data from that table (currently TableDirect is not supported by the .NET SqlClient provider, so this option cannot be used with SQL Server).
- *Query string*—You can type the query text (or stored procedure name) here or copy and paste it from somewhere else. Alternatively, if you prefer to author your query in a civilized manner, you can leave the Query string text box blank and later use the Graphical Query Designer.

- *Timeout*—You can define a timeout value for the query execution. If you leave it empty, the query doesn't time out.

NOTE Interestingly, when you open a report in the Report Designer and switch to the Data tab, the Report Designer will query the database to retrieve the schema for the underlying datasets. In this way, the Report Designer detects any changes that might have occurred in the database and synchronizes the report dataset(s) accordingly.

The ellipsis button (next to the Data source field) allows you to create a new data source, or connection, or to use an existing shared data source (figure 3.11).

The interesting setting here is the Use single transaction option, which is not checked by default. If you select it, the Report Server will execute the report queries within a scope of a database transaction. Selecting this option can be useful if you report off an OLTP database and you want to prevent reading uncommitted "dirty" data. To understand how transactions can be useful, consider the following example.

Let's say you have a report with a summary and detail sections—for example, a summary section showing the overall company performance and a detail section that breaks down sales by territory. To create this report you've decided to use two queries: one for the summary section and another for the report details. By default the Report Server will execute these two report queries in parallel. Let's also assume that you are reporting off an OLTP database and data is volatile. What will happen if the data

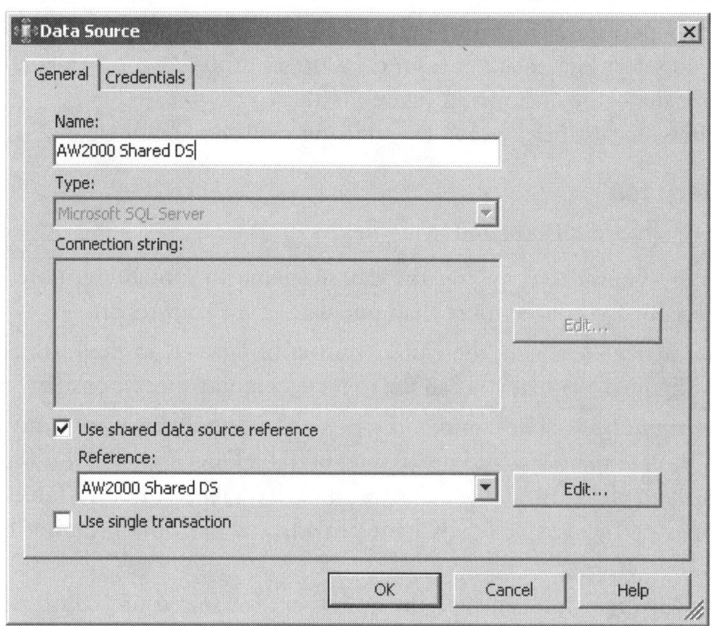

Figure 3.11 You associate the dataset with a data source from the Dataset dialog box.

changes while the report is executing? The numbers in both sections may not match at all, right? To ensure data consistency, you may want to enclose both queries in a single transaction.

There is a good reason for having the Use single transaction option disabled by default. Transactions enforce data integrity by means of database locks, and the higher the transaction isolation level, the more locks are imposed. Database locks and performance are mutually exclusive things, so leave that option deselected unless you have a good reason to enable it.

The Fields tab

The Fields tab in the Dataset dialog box show the dataset fields once the query is executed. Sometimes you may notice that the field list doesn't get refreshed after the underlying query is changed. If this happens, you have to manually synchronize the dataset fields. To synchronize the dataset and database schema, you click the Refresh Fields button. Alternatively, you can use the Fields toolbox to change the fields manually.

For example, let's say you add a new field to your SQL statement and the field doesn't appear in the Report Designer. To fix this, right-click on any field in the Fields toolbox and select Add New Field to open the dialog box shown in figure 3.12.

You can also create calculated dataset fields. A calculated field is a field based on an expression. Because expressions can reference methods in external .NET assemblies, the sky is the limit on what the content of a calculated field can be. (We cover

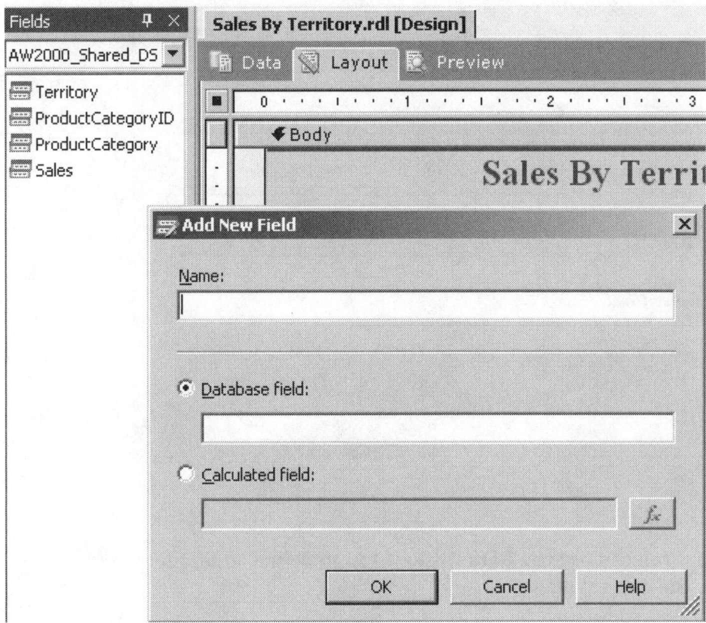

Figure 3.12 Adding a new dataset field using the Fields toolbox

expressions in chapter 5.) Of course, if the expression involves only database columns, you will be better off using expressions supported by the targeted data source for performance reasons.

If for some reason you want to change the dataset field name to something other than the database column name, you can do this by changing the value of the Field Name property.

The Data Options tab

The Data Options allows you to set additional data options for the query, such as case sensitivity, as shown in figure 3.13.

For example, when you set the Case sensitivity option to True, the clause `where FirstName = 'john'` will not bring up records where the first name start with capital J.

By default, RS will attempt to derive the values of data options from the data provider when the report runs. For more information about the query data options, see the product documentation.

The Parameters tab

The Parameters tab allows you to define parameters for your query. We discuss working with dataset parameters in section 3.4.

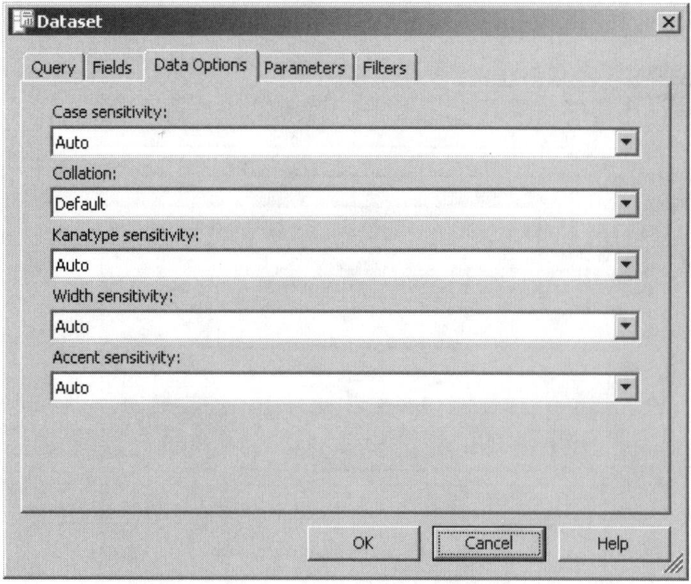

Figure 3.13 You can use the Data Options tab to define additional options for the dataset query.

The Filters tab

Use the Filters tab in the Dataset dialog box to limit the data fetched by the query. A dataset filter works like a SQL WHERE clause but an important distinction exists. While you can use a WHERE clause in your SQL statement to filter data at a data-source level, a dataset filter limits the data *after* it has been retrieved from the data source.

For example, if you want to filter a Products Sales by Quarter report to show sales product sales only in 2004, you can do so in one of two ways:

- Use a SQL WHERE clause to filter the results at the data source.
- Get the product sales for all years and then eliminate the unwanted records during the report generation using a dataset filter.

As you can imagine, filtering at the data source is much more efficient, so report filters should be used with caution. One possible scenario where filtering can be useful is when you need to enforce security. Let's say that the Sales by Territory report takes a parameter that allows privileged users to request the report for a given territory. However, you want to prevent regional managers who will run the report from requesting a territory they don't supervise. To implement this, create a lookup dataset for parameter available values. Then, set a filter based on an expression, which restricts the parameter choices based on the user's Windows identity. We implement such an example in chapter 8.

Another scenario where filters can be useful is when you need to work with data sources that don't support filtering. If you wonder which data sources don't support filtering, check out chapter 15 where we write a custom dataset data extension. The extension allows you to "bind" a report to a .NET dataset. ADO.NET datasets doesn't currently support a SQL-like WHERE clause, so you cannot easily filter data at the dataset level. However, you can use a report filter to limit the dataset rows.

Sometimes, one dataset may not be enough to meet the data requirements of your report. Fortunately, with RS you can define more than one dataset per a report.

3.2.3 Using multiple datasets

To add another dataset to your report, return to the Data tab, expand the Dataset drop-down list, and select New Dataset. This opens the Dataset dialog box shown earlier in figure 3.10.

Having multiple datasets can be useful for two main reasons:

- For parameterized reports you can make the report parameters data-driven from a separate dataset. For example, a typical reporting requirement is to restrict the parameter choice to a predefined set of values. To accomplish this with RS, you can use one dataset for the report data and a second one for the parameter lookup values. We'll see an example of this in section 3.4.4.
- Different sections of the report can be driven by different datasets, as you'll see in chapter 4. As we mentioned earlier, multiple datasets don't have to fetch their data from the same data source.

There are a few important points about multiple datasets that we would like to mention. You cannot join datasets as you could join database tables by using relations, even if they have the same fields. As a result, you cannot mix fields from different datasets in a single report region. We look at report regions in chapter 4, but for time being note that RS supports various report items called regions for different report types, including charts, tables, pivots, and other regions. To display data in a region, you need to associate (bind) it with exactly one dataset.

While the Report Designer allows you to drag fields from one dataset to a region bound to another, you can use only aggregate functions, such as `First()`, `Sum()`, and `Avg()`, when referencing its fields. If you try to reference the field directly (outside an aggregate function), then you will see the following exception during the report compilation process:

```
Report item expressions can only refer to fields within the
current data set scope or, if inside an aggregate, the
specified data set scope.
```

Chapter 5 details the expression scope rules.

For best performance results, I suggest you minimize the number of the report datasets in your reports. In the best case, you will need only one dataset as an underlying source for the report data. You should carefully evaluate if you need additional datasets for the available values of report parameters.

One scenario where you may require an additional dataset is when you have to restrict the parameter choices in the report toolbar for reports requested by URL. With other integration scenarios, the client application may be responsible for collecting and validating parameters. If this is the case, you won't need another dataset to define the parameter lookup values.

3.3 AUTHORING DATASET QUERIES

To fill in a dataset with data, you need to set up a dataset query. One dataset can be associated with exactly one query. When the report is processed, the Report Server will execute the dataset query statement against the data source and load the dataset.

To help you with setting up the database queries, the Report Designer comes with not one but two query designers: Graphical and Generic. The main characteristic of the first one is convenience, while the second excels in flexibility.

3.3.1 Using the Graphical Query Designer

Figure 3.14 shows the Sales by Territory dataset open in the Report Services Graphical Query Designer.

You may be familiar with the Graphical Query Designer because it is the same one that SQL Server Enterprise Manager, VS.NET, and a plethora of other development tools use. It makes authoring complex SQL statements a breeze. Even users unfamiliar with the intricacies of SQL can create sophisticated queries in a matter of minutes.

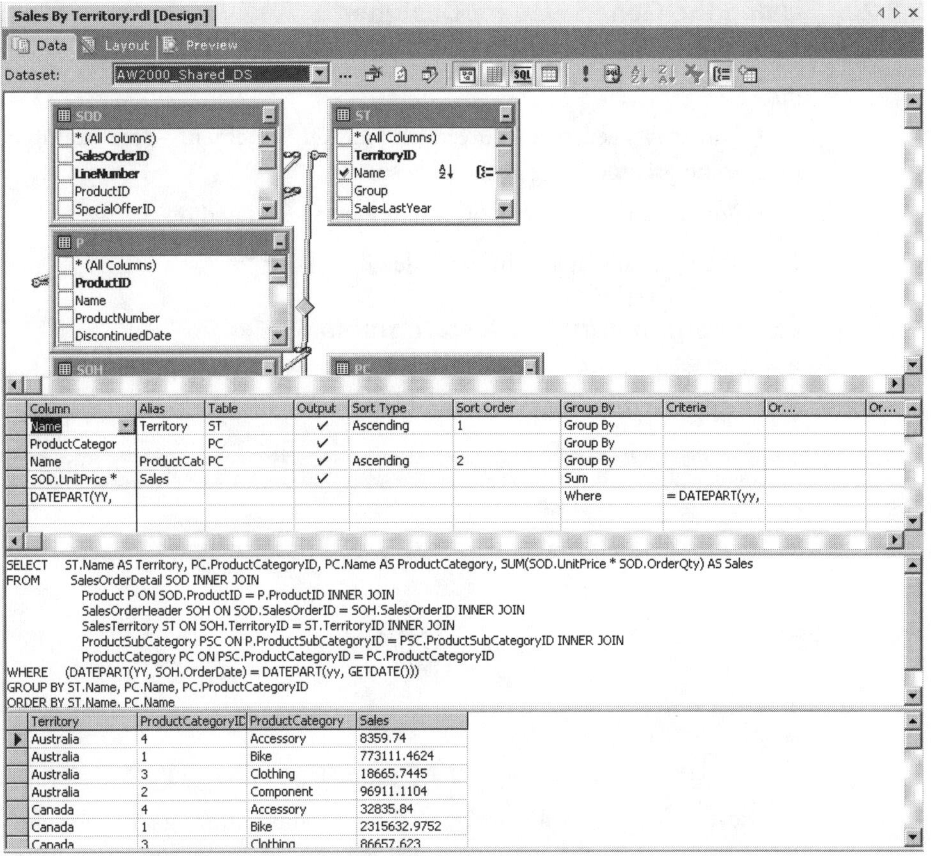

Figure 3.14 Use the Graphical Query Designer to author, test, and run queries.

The Graphical Query Designer also has SQL syntax checking to make sure that query text you specify makes sense and conforms to the SQL grammar supported by the targeted database. Once you craft your query and execute it, the dataset fields will be shown in the Fields toolbar on the left, as well as on the Fields tab of the dataset properties.

Authoring a dataset query with the Graphical Query Designer is a matter of completing the following steps:

Step 1 Right-click on the Diagram pane empty area and choose Add Table. Add as many tables from the data source as needed.

Step 2 Select table columns as needed. The Graphical Query Designer shows the resulting SQL statement in the SQL pane.

Step 3 Modify the statement as per your requirements using the SQL pane or the Grid pane.

Step 4 Run the query by clicking the Run button (the one with the exclamation point) to see the results in the Results pane.

3.3.2 Using the Generic Query Designer

Sometimes you will reach the limits of the Graphical Query Designer, as in the following two cases:

- You may need to execute multiple SQL statements—for example, to perform some preprocessing at the data source.
- You need to work with SQL statements generated on the fly.

Let's discuss each scenario in more detail.

Executing multiple SQL statements

Say you need to run an update query to the SalesOrderDetail table before the sales order data is retrieved, as shown in listing 3.2.

Listing 3.2 Using batches of statements to update and retrieve data

```
DECLARE @SalesOrderID int
SET     @SalesOrderID = 1

UPDATE  SalesOrderDetail
SET     UnitPrice = 100
WHERE   (SalesOrderID = @SalesOrderID )

SELECT  *
FROM     SalesOrderDetail
```

NOTE In the real world, you should avoid retrieving all table columns using the "*" wildcard in your queries. Instead, for performance reasons you should limit the number of columns to the ones you need.

Granted, this could be accomplished by encapsulating both statements inside a stored procedure, but sometimes you may not have this choice.

You may try using the Graphical Query Designer to execute this batch, but you wouldn't get too far. The Graphical Query Designer complains with the following error:

```
This designer does not graphically support the DECLARE CURSOR SQL construct.
```

My example doesn't use a SQL cursor at all, but in any case, the Graphical Query Designer refuses to cooperate. As a workaround, we can switch to the Generic Query Designer (figure 3.15) by clicking on its button (the one before the exclamation point button).

If the data source credentials have update rights to the database, the SQL block will execute fine and the dataset fields will be populated based on the columns defined in the select statement (in this case, all columns from the SalesOrderDetail table).

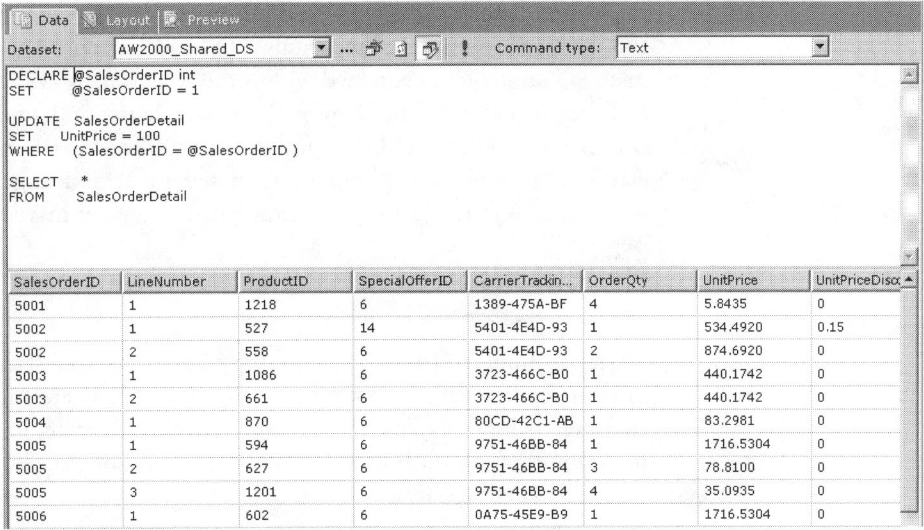

Figure 3.15 **Executing multiple SQL statements in the Generic Query Designer**

NOTE The previous query requires UPDATE rights to the AdventureWorks2000 database. If the data source account is restricted, the report will fail to execute even if the report doesn't use any of the dataset fields. The reason for this is that when a report is requested, the Report Server executes all report queries to populate the report datasets. For this reason, I recommend that you delete this dataset as soon as you are done experimenting so that it doesn't interfere with report processing.

Using expression-based queries

The second scenario where you must use the Generic Query Designer is when you need to work with expression-based queries. Unlike the Graphical Query Designer, the Generic Query Designer doesn't attempt to parse the query text to ensure it is syntactically correct. Instead, it allows you to type whatever you want, and once the query is constructed, it passes the query directly to the data source. For users familiar with Microsoft Access, the Access equivalent is a pass-through query.

We haven't covered expressions yet (see chapter 5), but consider the case where you want to restrict the results returned from the SalesOrderDetail table only if the OrderID is specified. To achieve this use a Visual Basic .NET (VB.NET) expression, similar to this one:

```
= "select * from SalesOrderDetail " & _
Iif(Parameters!OrderID.Value Is Nothing, "", _
" where SalesOrderID =" & Parameters!OrderID.Value)
```

NOTE Expression-based queries are susceptible to *SQL injection attacks*. SQL injection happens when some (malicious) SQL code is appended to the legitimate SQL statement contained within the report query. For example, the SQL statement we've just discussed is vulnerable to a SQL injection attack. A hacker could pass another SQL statement to the OrderID report parameter—for example, a data modification statement to change, append, or delete data. As a result, the expression-based statement may look like this:

```
= "select * from SalesOrderDetail where
SalesOrderID = 1;UPDATE SalesOrderDetail
(SET // perform data changes here
```

There are number of strategies for using expression-based statements safely in your reports. One is to filter out the report parameters for valid SQL characters—for example, the semicolon delimiter character in our case. For more information on how to prevent SQL injection attacks, refer to the security-related resources listed in chapter 7.

When the Generic Query Designer determines that expressions are used, it doesn't give you a choice to execute the query by clicking on the exclamation point. As a result, you won't be able to get the dataset fields. Instead, you need to add the fields manually, using either the Fields toolbox or the Fields tab in the dataset properties. Once you have done this, you can drag the fields to the report layout and execute the report. Finally, if the query is based on an expression, as in the above case, don't forget to prefix the text with "=".

I would like to fast-forward a bit and mention that the ability to use an expression to generate the SQL statement on the fly opens a whole new world of opportunities. Your report can call a piece of code defined as an expression or in an external assembly to get the query statement custom-tailored based on certain conditions. The example that follows is simple but illustrates the expression's flexibility. Say you have a function that returns a SQL statement, like the one shown here:

```
Function GetSQL (ByVal orderID as Integer) as String
   Return "select * from SalesOrderDetail where " _
   & "SalesOrderID = " _ & orderID
End Function
```

The `GetSQL` function can be defined as an embedded function in the report or located in an external assembly—for example, in the application data layer. We discuss extending RS with custom code in detail in chapter 6.

Once the `GetSQL` function is ready, using the Generic Query Designer you can set your query text to

```
= Code.GetSQL(Parameters!OrderID.Value)
```

In this case, we are calling the `GetSQL` function and passing the value of the `OrderID` report parameter. Once we manually define the fields that the query returns, we can base our report on the results of this generated on-the-fly query. Talking about flexibility!

Another popular scenario where expression-based queries can be useful is when the report takes a multivalue parameter. Chapter 10 shows how this can be done.

Now that you know how to create basic dataset queries, let's see how we can make them more flexible by using parameters.

3.4 PARAMETER-DRIVEN REPORTS

Your dataset queries won't be very useful if they don't allow users to pass parameters. Report and query parameters give users the option to alter the report execution and subset of data shown in the report. For example, you can add a parameter to the Sales by Territory report to enable users to specify the sales year rather than defaulting to the current year. We'll see exactly how to do this in section 3.4.2.

3.4.1 The role of parameters

Recall from chapter 1 that the Report Server enjoys a service-oriented architecture that is entirely server based. We also said that with RS reports can be requested by URL and SOAP.

The Report Server doesn't offer an object model that can be instantiated and manipulated locally by the report consumer, as you would have probably done in the past with other reporting tools—for example, using OLE Automation to control Microsoft Access. Instead, the only way to control the report-generation process from outside is by using parameters, as shown in figure 3.16.

If you are accustomed to object-oriented programming, this may seem strange at first. But consider the benefits. The service-oriented architecture of the Report Server eliminates tight coupling between the consumer and server. If the Report Server had an object model that could be instantiated locally by the report consumer, then most likely its client base would have been restricted to .NET-based applications only. Instead, thanks to its service-oriented architecture, RS can be integrated with any type of consumer. Developers familiar with designing stateless web services will find the Report Server programming model similar.

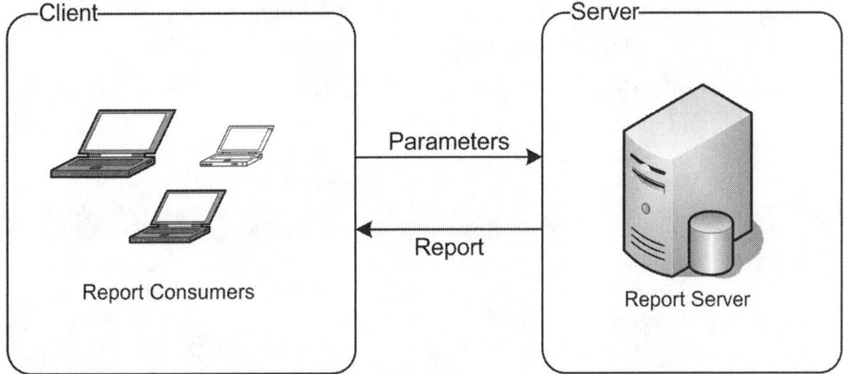

Figure 3.16 From the report consumer perspective, the Report Server can be viewed as a black box that accepts report requests and optionally parameters and returns reports.

The RS report-processing model is stateless because once the report is generated, the Report Server discards any state associated with the report request. As far as the report-generation process is concerned, you can think of the Report Server as a black box that accepts a report request (optionally parameterized) and returns the generated report. Do you want to sort the report data in a different way? Do you want to filter out the data that the data source returns? Do you want to show or hide certain report items based on runtime conditions?

By using parameters, coupled with custom expressions inside the report, you can achieve just about anything you can otherwise accomplish with an object model. For example, hardcoding criteria in your queries is convenient for the developer but not very useful for the end users. Often, you will need to make the report interactive by allowing the users to pass report parameters. To accomplish this, a parameter value can be passed to the dataset query or stored procedure to filter out the report data.

3.4.2 Building parameter-driven queries

Let's see how we can make our Sales by Territory report interactive by allowing the user to specify the sales year instead of always defaulting to the current year. We can easily change the report dataset query to use a query parameter. Since we are using SQL Server as a database, we need to use named parameters.

NOTE The named parameter syntax is specific to the data extension. In the SQL .NET provider you use named parameters (`@varname`). With the Oracle data extension you use named parameters but with a different prefix (`:varname`). The OLE DB provider doesn't support named parameters, but you can use the question mark (`?`) for parameter placeholders.

Let's make the query parameter-driven by following these steps:

Step 1 Start by saving the Sales by Territory report to Sales by Territory Interactive report. The easiest way to accomplish this is to right-click on the Sales by Territory report in the Solution Explorer and choose Copy.

Step 2 Right-click on the project node (AWReporter) and choose Paste. Rename the new report to Sales by Territory Interactive.

Step 3 Open the AW2000_Shared_DS dataset inside the Graphical Query Designer and replace the `DATEPART(yy, GETDATE())` criteria with `@Year`, as shown in listing 3.3:

Listing 3.3 Using a query parameter to filter the query data

```
SELECT ST.Name AS Territory, PC.ProductCategoryID, PC.Name AS
       ProductCategory,SUM(SOD.UnitPrice*SOD.OrderQty) AS Sales
FROM   SalesOrderDetail SOD INNER JOIN
       Product P ON SOD.ProductID = P.ProductID INNER JOIN
       SalesOrderHeader SOH ON SOD.SalesOrderID=SOH.SalesOrderID
INNER JOIN SalesTerritory ST ON SOH.TerritoryID = ST.TerritoryID
INNER JOIN ProductSubCategory PSC ON P.ProductSubCategoryID =
```

```
        PSC.ProductSubCategoryID
INNER JOIN ProductCategory PC ON PSC.ProductCategoryID =
        PC.ProductCategoryID
WHERE DATEPART(YY, SOH.OrderDate) = @Year
GROUP BY ST.Name, PC.Name, PC.ProductCategoryID
ORDER BY ST.Name, PC.Name
```

In the listing, we are specifying a named report parameter called Year. Now run the query. When the Graphical Query Designer parses the query, it discovers the parameter and displays the Define Query Parameters dialog box, as shown in figure 3.17.

Step 4 Enter *2003* and click OK. The query retrieves the sales orders placed in 2003.

Once the Graphical Query Designer parses the parameter, it will add the parameter to the parameter list defined for this query, which can be seen on the Parameters tab of

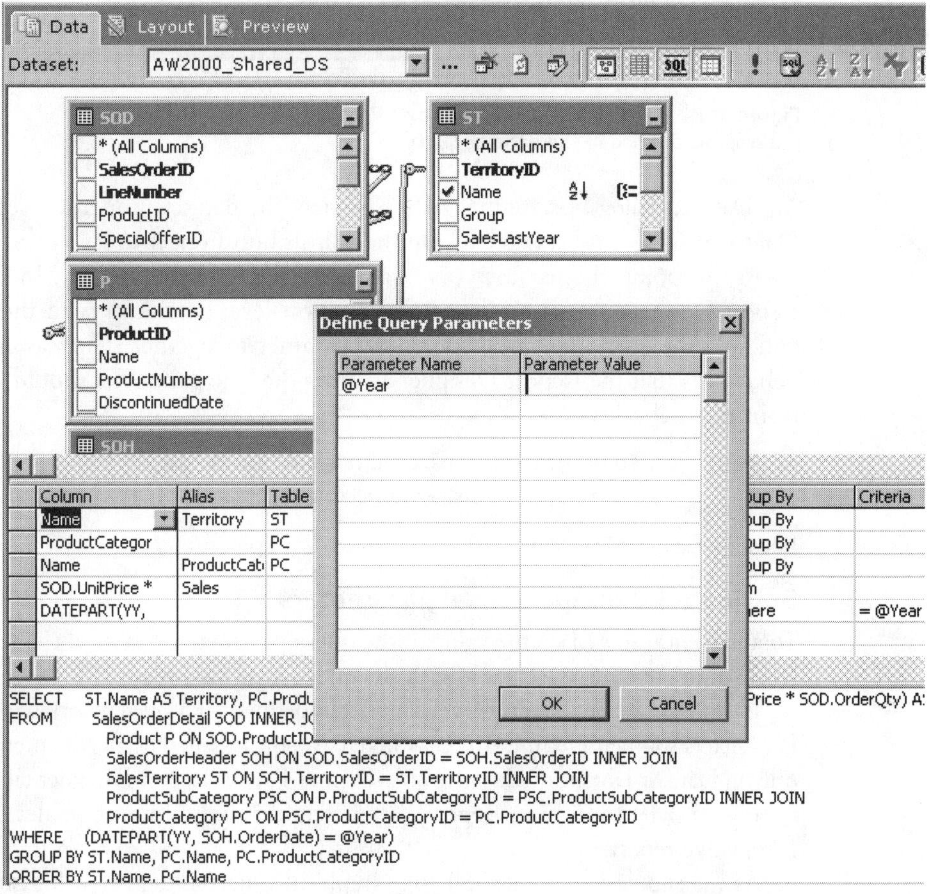

Figure 3.17 To set up a parameter-driven query, specify parameter placeholders.

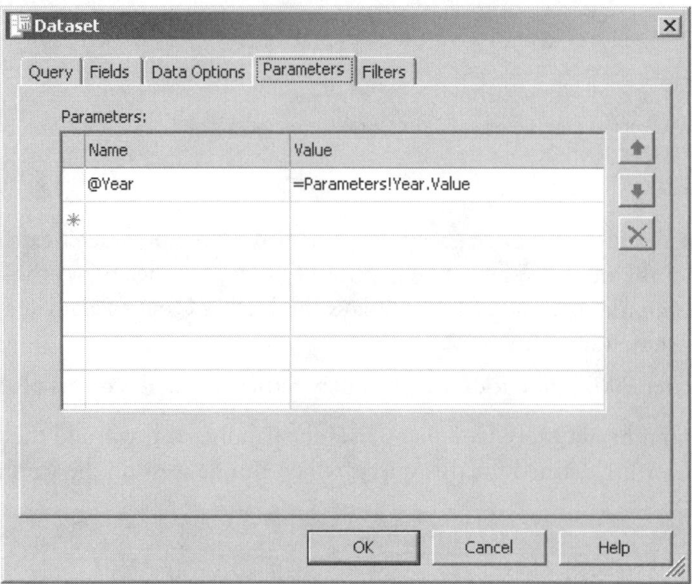

Figure 3.18 Use the Dataset dialog box's Parameters tab to see all parameters defined in the dataset query.

the Dataset dialog box (figure 3.18). To view the dataset properties, select it in the Dataset drop-down list and click on the ellipsis button next to it.

At this point, the parameter is associated with the dataset query. In addition, the Report Designer automatically creates a report-level parameter with the same name and links the query-level and report-level parameters together. The reason behind this behavior is that the Report Designer assumes that the parameter should be accessible from external callers.

NOTE To pass the parameter value from outside the report—for example, from client applications—you need to create a report-level parameter.

Let's now see how we can work with report-level parameters.

3.4.3 Setting up the report-level parameters

To allow end users to set the value of the query parameter, you need to create a report-level parameter and associate it with the query-level parameter.

If you want to see all report-level parameters defined for a given report, select the Report Parameters submenu item from the VS.NET Report menu. The Report menu is available only in Data or Layout mode (when the Data or Layout Report Designer tabs are active).

Figure 3.19 shows the Report Parameters dialog box for the Sales by Territory Interactive report.

As we said earlier, by default the Graphical Query Designer will assume that the report parameter will be publicly accessible and pairs each query-level parameter with

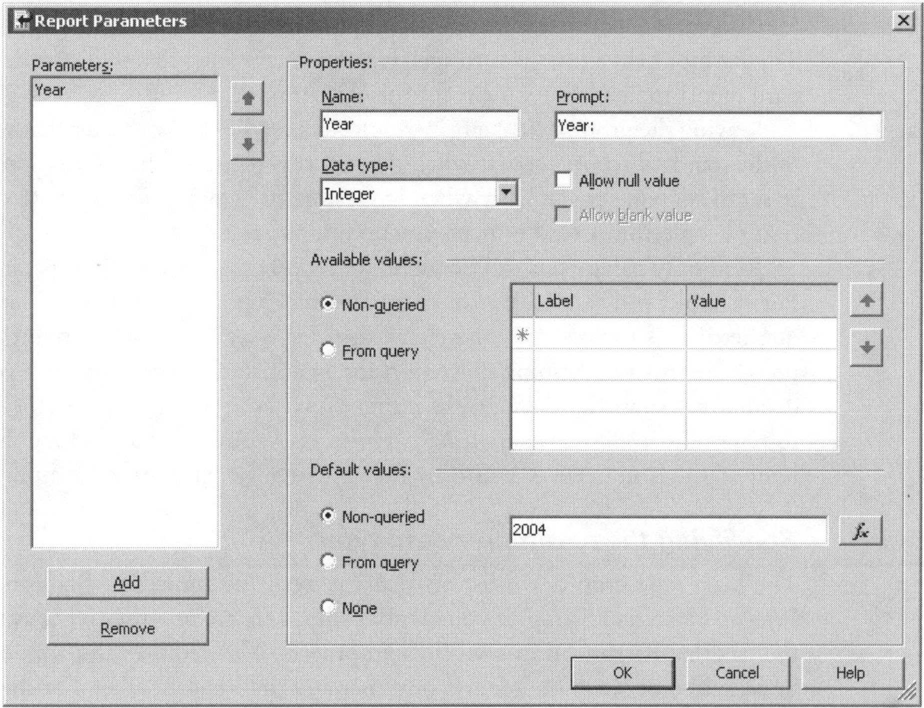

Figure 3.19 Use the Report Parameters dialog box to set up the report parameters.

a report-level parameter. However, you can manually add or remove report-level parameters if needed.

One scenario that calls for adding parameters manually is when you need more parameters than the report query(s) takes. For example, you may need a parameter to pass some value that is used in an expression.

Why would you want to remove a report-level parameter? This can be useful if you don't want the users to pass values to it. For example, the query parameter may be derived internally using an expression and it may not make sense to expose it to the end user. Parameters don't have a Visibility property you can set to hide them. Instead, you achieve the same effect by removing them from the Report Parameters dialog box.

NOTE When you remove a query parameter, the Report Designer doesn't assume that you want to remove the report parameter as well. It leaves the report parameter in the report, which may result in an orphaned publicly accessible parameter. To "fix" this, open the Report Parameters dialog box and remove the parameter.

Using the Prompt field

The Prompt field allows you to specify a parameter label that will appear on the standard report toolbar. Enter **Year:** for the Year prompt.

Leaving the prompt field empty results in a read-only parameter that will not show in the standard report toolbar when the report is requested by URL. Moreover, trying to set the parameter explicitly when requesting the report either by URL or SOAP will result in an error. A read-only parameter must have a default value associated with it.

Read-only parameters can be useful for reports that require fixed parameter values. For example, you may have a "Sales by Quarter" report that shows the data for a given quarter that is passed as a parameter value. Let's say that at some point you want to prevent users from running this report for an arbitrary quarter. Instead, you decide to default the parameter value to the current quarter. One way to hide the parameter is to remove it from the report-level parameters. Another option to hide the parameter temporarily is to make it read-only by removing the parameter prompt.

Specifying the parameter data type

The Data type drop-down list restricts the available choices to Boolean, DateTime, Integer, Float, and String. If you wonder why there are no other types available, recall the fact that RS runs in its own isolated process. This requires all parameter values to be serialized between the report consumer and the Report Server. For this reason, the choice of the parameter data types is restricted only to .NET primitive types that can be passed by value.

Note that the Report Server automatically casts the parameter values to the data type you specify. For this reason, you can use the methods of the .NET data type structure to retrieve or set the parameter value. For example, if you set the parameter type to DateTime, you can use the `DateTime.Year` property to get to the year because the values of date type in .NET are represented by the DateTime structure.

We will see more expression examples in chapter 5.

Passing default values

The Allow null value option in the Report Parameters dialog box indicates if NULL can be passed as a report value. If a default parameter value is not specified, clearing the check box in effect makes the parameter required. The Allow blank value option is available only for the String data type and means that an empty string can be passed as a report value.

Let's go back to the Sales by Territory Interactive report and change the data type of the Year parameter to Integer. Finally, to make the parameter required, make sure that the Allow null value check box is cleared. Now, let's preview the report (figure 3.20).

The report toolbar changes to accommodate the Year parameter. Note that if you leave the year field empty, the report is not generated because the year is a required parameter.

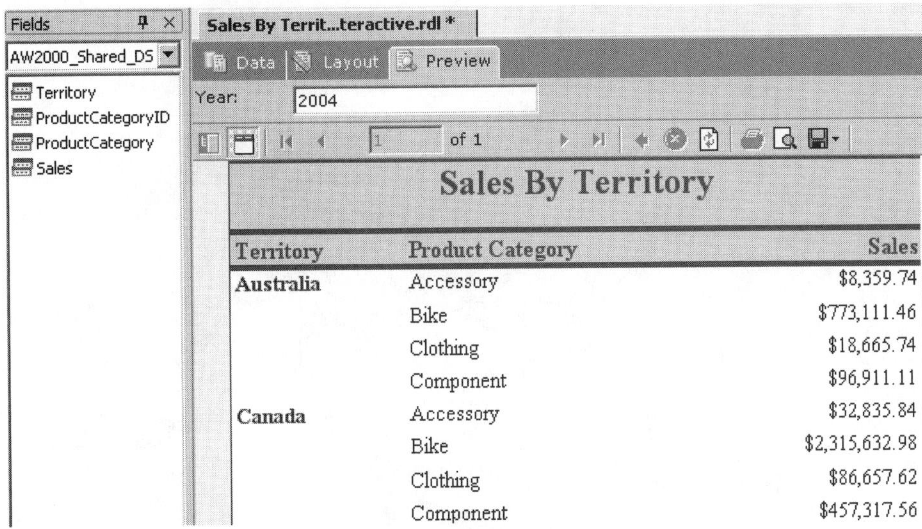

Figure 3.20 The parameterized version of the report takes the year as a parameter.

Defining nonqueried lookup parameter values

So far, so good. But what if we want to restrict the user to select a year from a predefined list of years? For example, it doesn't make sense to allow the user to type 2005 if there are no sales orders placed in that year. To accomplish this, we can define parameter available (lookup) values.

In the Report Parameter dialog box, make sure that the Non-queried radio button is selected in the Available values radio group. Then, type the allowed years in the grid, as shown in figure 3.21. Let's also default the Year parameter to 2004 by entering this value as a Non-queried default value.

Preview the report again using the Preview tab and note that the report is generated for the default year of 2004 and the Select Year field is now a drop-down list from which the user can pick one of the available values.

With RS you are not restricted to static available values. You can make the list data-driven by basing it on a query or expression. If it is based on a query, you can specify which dataset column will be used for the default value. If the query results in more than one row, the first one is used.

Next, let's see how to implement a data-driven lookup list based on a dataset retrieved from a stored procedure call.

3.4.4 Working with stored procedures

To demonstrate query-driven lookups, let's pretend that users have requested the ability to filter out the product sales by territory by choosing the sales territory from a lookup list. To make the list data-driven, we will create a second dataset that will be

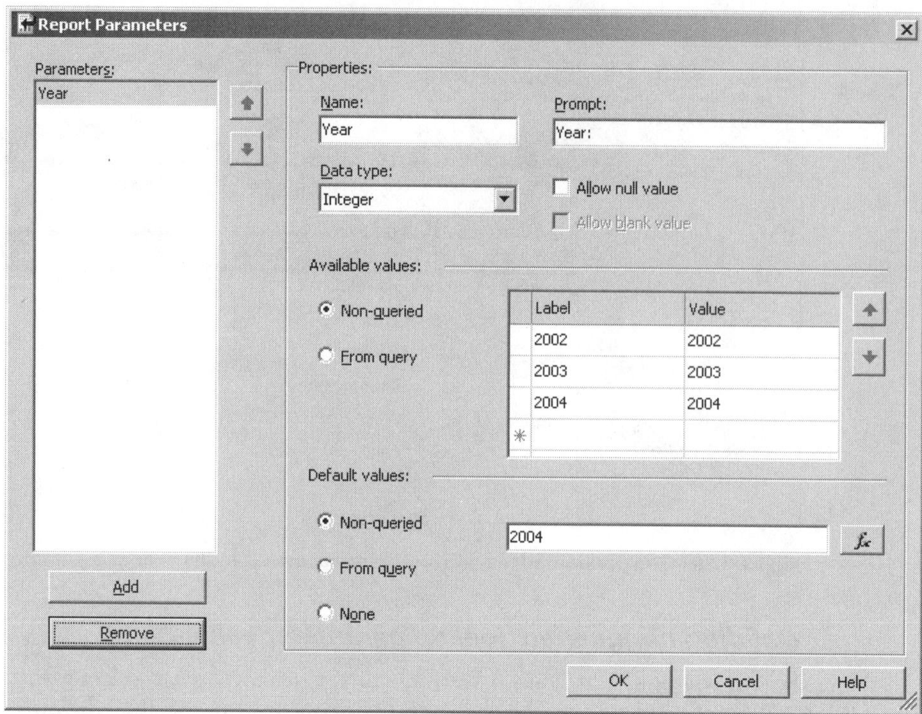

Figure 3.21 Use the Non-queried option to specify a fixed list of report parameter available values.

generated by a stored procedure. In addition, we will synchronize the Year and Territory parameters, so that only territories that have sales in that year will be shown.

Because the Adventure Works 2000 database doesn't come with any stored procedures, I wrote a simple stored procedure called `spGetTerritory` that takes an `@Year` input argument. You can find the `spGetTerritory` source code in the sp.sql script found in the Database.dbp project.

Stored procedures advantages

As you've seen, the Graphical Query Designer makes generating free SQL statement easy. However, the easy way is not always the right way. I highly recommend that in real life you use stored procedures instead of free SQL statements. Stored procedures offer the following advantages:

- *Faster performance*—The database servers parse and compile the stored procedure statements.
- *Reuse*—The SQL statements are located in one place and can be easily reused by another report.

- *Encapsulation*—As long as you keep the input and output the same, you can change the stored procedure inner implementation as much as you like.
- *Security*—Stored procedures can be secured at a database level. In addition, using stored procedures could help preventing SQL Injection attacks.

In SQL addition, a stored procedure can be used as a substitute of an expression-based query. Instead of using expression-based queries—for example, to generate SQL WHERE clauses conditionally—you can do this inside stored procedures.

For these reasons, we use stored procedures in this book wherever it makes sense to do so.

Using a stored procedure as a dataset query

You can fill your report datasets with data from stored procedures. Let's see how using the Graphical Query Designer.

Once you install the `spGetTerritory` stored procedure, make sure to grant EXECUTE permissions to the database login that the AW2000 Shared DS shared data source uses.

The `spGetTerritory` procedure retrieves the list of the sales territories that have orders placed in a given year, as shown here:

```
CREATE PROCEDURE spGetTerritory (@Year int)
AS
SET NOCOUNT ON

SELECT DISTINCT ST.TerritoryID, ST.Name AS Territory
FROM   SalesTerritory ST INNER JOIN
       SalesOrderHeader SOH ON ST.TerritoryID = SOH.TerritoryID
WHERE  DATEPART(YY, SOH.OrderDate) = @Year
ORDER BY ST.Name
```

To use this stored procedure as a source for the lookup dataset, follow these steps:

Step 1 Create a new dataset dsTerritory and set the command type to StoredProcedure, as shown in figure 3.22.

Step 2 Enter **spGetTerritory** in the "Query text" textbox or leave the query string blank at this point and click OK to select it later. The Graphical Query Designer shows the Stored Procedure drop-down list, which lists all stored procedures that the AW2000 Shared DS database login has permissions to execute. Select spGetTerritory, as shown in figure 3.23, and run the query.

The designer displays the familiar Define Query Parameters dialog box.

Step 3 Enter **2004** and click OK to see the stored procedure call results.

Step 4 Now, open the dataset properties. Switch to the Parameters tab and observe that there is a `@Year` parameter and its value is set to Parameters!Year.Value. Because we already have a Year report parameter, which we needed for the first dataset, the designer has correctly linked the dsTerritory Year parameter to the Year report parameter.

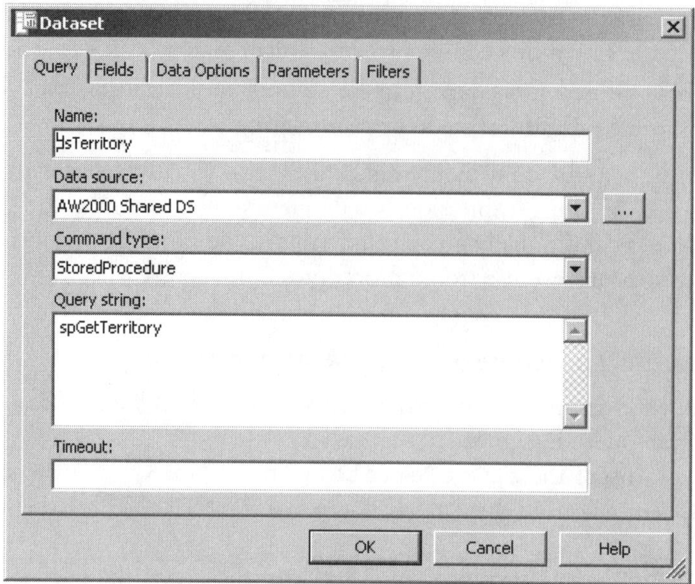

Figure 3.22 To use a stored procedure as a query statement, enter its name in the Query string text area.

Defining query-based lookup parameter values

Now, it is time to set up the available values for the Territory parameter. Open the Report Parameters menu from the Reports main menu and set up the Territory parameter settings, as shown in figure 3.24.

Go back to the Data tab, select the report dataset in the Datasets drop-down list, and in the Query pane of the Graphical Query Designer change the SQL WHERE clause of the dataset query to filter data by the Territory parameter, as follows:

```
WHERE (DATEPART(YY, SOH.OrderDate) = @Year) AND
  (ST.TerritoryID = @Territory)
```

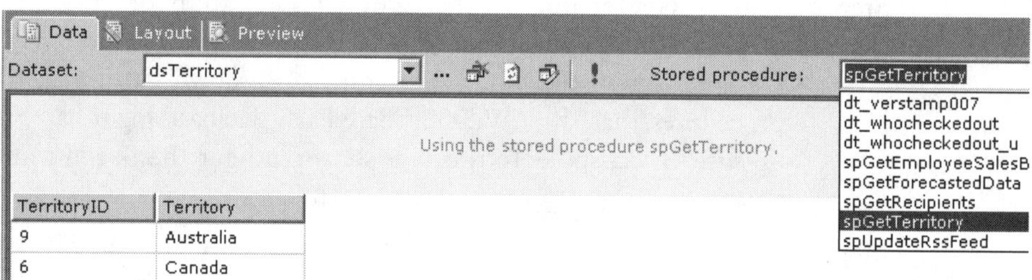

Figure 3.23 When a stored procedure is used as a query text, the Graphical Query Designer shows the list of stored procedures.

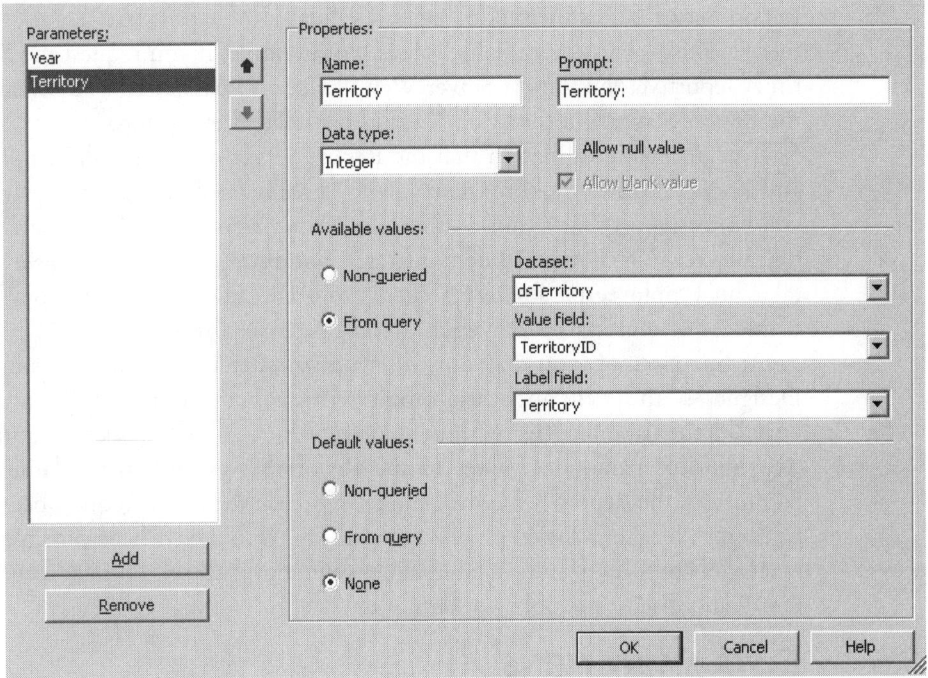

Figure 3.24 Use the From query settings to define data-driven lookup parameter datasets.

Now preview the report, as shown in figure 3.25. Note that changing the year results in refreshing the Product Category drop-down list so only product categories associated with that year are shown.

You may think that the parameter settings (available, default, and null values) that you set using the Report Parameters dialog box are useful only if the report includes the standard report toolbar. Actually, this is not the case. Before the report is processed, the

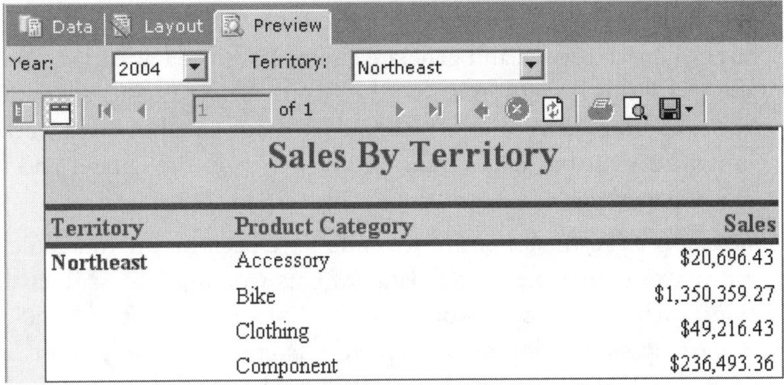

Figure 3.25 The Sales by Territory report with Year and Product Categories parameters

Report Server parses the report request, validates the report parameters, and matches them against the list of available values. For example, if you request the Sales by Territory report via the Report Server Web service and pass 2010 as the year parameter, the Report Server will throw an "invalid parameter" exception.

The automatic validation that the Report Server performs can be both a blessing and a curse. It could backfire when you don't really need it. This may be the case when you have a report that requires multiselect parameters, as the Purchase Orders report that we create in chapter 10 demonstrates. For example, you could have a report that takes an Employee parameter. A client front end may allow users to select a single employee or multiple employees from an Employee list.

At first attempt, you may opt to set up parameter available values in the Report Designer, so the client application could retrieve them from the Report Server to prepopulate the parameter list with the lookup values. All will work well until you try to pass multiple parameter values to the Report Server. When validating the report parameters, the Report Server will choke and reject the report request because it won't find a match against the employee column. This would have been possible if there had been a way to turn off the available values validation. We see a similar scenario in chapter 10 and discuss possible workarounds.

3.5 Data limitations

Reporting Services goes a long way to satisfy various data needs, but it has its own limitations. This section discusses a few you may encounter when you set up your report data.

3.5.1 Data source limitations

The following are not supported:

- *Dataset "binding".* First, binding to external datasets—or any other structures for that matter—is not supported. By external, I mean a dataset that is not produced as a result of a report query, but rather is passed by another application. For example, a .NET application may want to retrieve a dataset from its business layer or a web service and generate a report off its data. As I've pointed out, the reason for this limitation is that the Report Server doesn't share the client process space so passing objects by reference is not possible. As a workaround, you can write a custom data extension that serializes the dataset and passes it as a report parameter, as you will see in chapter 15.
- *Reporting off XML documents.* It would have been nice if you could use an XML schema to define the report dataset. This would allow XML-enabled applications, such as Microsoft Word or Excel 2003, to integrate with RS and generate reports by submitting saved-to-XML documents to the Report Server. In the case of SQL Server, it could have made it also possible to use FOR XML statements. Again, you have to put on your developer's hat and create a custom data extension if the requirements call for reporting off XML.

- *Multiple-resultset stored procedures.* Only the first resultset is exposed. Output stored procedure parameters are not supported either.

3.5.2 Parameter limitations

- Custom parameter validation is not supported with RS version 1.0.
- Available values validation cannot be turned off.

There are also other parameter limitations specific to the report toolbar that we discuss in chapter 9.

3.6 SUMMARY

In this chapter, you learned how to set up report data, which is a prerequisite for creating data-driven reports. We emphasized the fact that with RS you can report off virtually any data store that exposes its data in a tabular format.

We began by showing you how to set up the report data source. Then, we explored how to create one or more datasets to feed the report with data.

You saw how to use the Graphical and Generic query designers to author queries, and we examined the role that parameters play in custom-tailoring report queries. Along the way, we showed you how to create parameter-driven reports. Finally, we looked at some limitations of the RS data architecture.

You will use the knowledge you have harvested in this chapter to create many interactive parameter-driven reports throughout the rest of this book. In addition, you have probably started seeing the advantages of the RS service-oriented architecture in terms of deployment, such as zero client deployment requirements and interoperability with wide range of clients.

Now that you have a good grasp of working with report data, it is time to see how you can use the Report Designer to lay out reports. The next chapter will demonstrate how to design various kinds of professional-looking reports with the Report Designer.

3.7 RESOURCES

Accessing Data with ADO.NET (http://msdn.microsoft.com/library/default.asp?url=/library/en-us/cpguide/html/cpconConnectionPoolingForSQLServerNETDataProvider.asp)—A chapter from the VS.NET documentation that discusses database connection pooling.

Designing Data Tier Components and Passing Data Through Tiers (http://msdn.microsoft.com/architecture/application/default.aspx?pull=/library/en-us/dnbda/html/BOAGag.asp)

A good best practices read from the MSDN .NET Architecture Center, which might be interesting for .NET developers. Learn how to best expose your data to Microsoft .NET applications and how to implement an effective strategy for passing data between the tiers in a distributed application.

CHAPTER 4

Designing reports

Once you've set up the report data, you can proceed with laying out the report itself. To accomplish this task with the Report Designer, use the Layout tab. As we saw in chapter 1, Reporting Services supports various report types. In this chapter, we see how the Report Designer can help us design many versatile and professional-looking reports. In the following sections, we

- Discuss the main parts of the report layout
- Explain how to use data regions and report items
- Create many sample reports to put what we've learned into practice

Because the report design process is very interactive, the best way to present this chapter is by example. After each report type explanation we will create a sample report. At the end, we will have worked through creating tabular, freeform, chart, and matrix reports, as well as subreports and multicolumn reports.

Unlike chapter 1, in which we used the Report Wizard to quickly create the Sales by Territory report, we will create the sample reports in this chapter using the Report Designer.

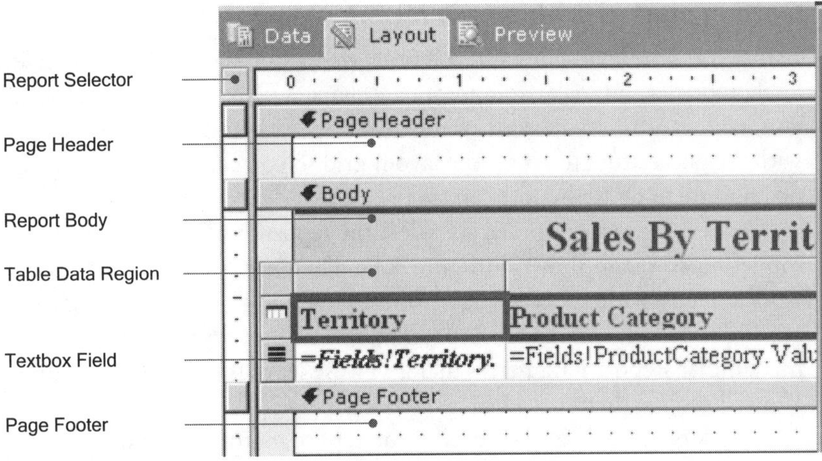

Figure 4.1 A report includes header, body, and footer sections.

4.1 ANATOMY OF A REPORT

To be an effective report author, you need to have a good grasp of a report's anatomy. RS reports consist of *sections* (also called *bands*) that can contain *report elements*. Report elements include *data regions* and *report items*. Take, for example, the Sales by Territory report shown in figure 4.1.

We have enabled the Page Header and Page Footer options from the Visual Studio .NET Reports menu, so the Page Header and Page Footer bands are visible.

The report sections are the page header, report body, and page footer. To lay out a report, you drag and drop report elements from the Report Items toolbar (shown in figure 4.2) to the report body section.

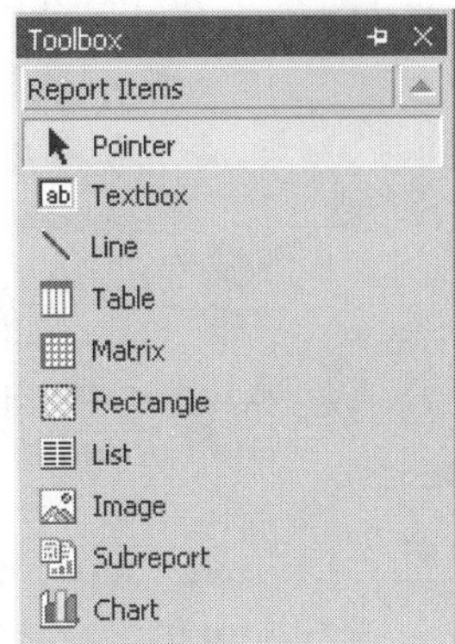

Figure 4.2 You can drag data regions and items from the Report Items toolbar to the report body.

NOTE In my opinion, the Report Items toolbar should have been named Report Elements because it contains not only report items but data regions as well. To avoid confusion, I will use the term "report elements" to refer to both report items and data regions.

For example, instead of using the Report Wizard, we could have authored the Sales by Territory tabular report from scratch by dragging the table region from the Report Items toolbar and dropping it in the body section. Then, we could have dragged and dropped the report dataset fields inside the table region. If we had done this, the table region would have created textbox report items behind the scenes to display the dataset data.

4.1.1 Getting started with a new report

Before you start laying out a new report, we would suggest that you review the report-level properties and make the appropriate changes right from the beginning. For example, you may want to review and change the page size and margins settings. Experiment with the grid setting to set up the layout grid so you can "snap" the report items as you position them on the report canvas.

To view the report properties, select the report by clicking the Report Selector (the top leftmost square shown in figure 4.1). Then, right-click and choose Properties, or work directly with the VS.NET Properties window. You will recognize some of the report properties, such as the ReportParameters property, which, when selected, opens the familiar Report Parameters dialog. Please leave the rest of the properties for now. We will discuss them on an as-needed basis.

Let's look at each of the parts of the report anatomy in more detail.

4.1.2 Understanding report sections

An RS-based report consists of three main sections:

- *Page Header*—The page header content is displayed at the top of each page.
- *Report Body*—A report always has a body section, which is where most of the report content will be located.
- *Page Footer*—The page footer content is displayed at the end of each page.

A report can optionally have Page Header and Page Footer bands, displayed at the top and bottom of each page, respectively. By default, the page header and footer content appear on every report page, including the first and the last. You can suppress the header and/or footer on the first and/or last page of the report by changing the PrintOnFirstPage and PrintOnLastPage setting from the properties.

Headers and footers can contain only static text and images. RS reports don't have designated report header and footer elements. Instead, you can use the Report Body band to place items that need to appear once at the beginning or end of the report.

Let's now discuss the various building blocks included with the Report Designer and how they can be used to lay out different types of reports. By no means will we try to enumerate each property of every report element. For this, you'll need to turn to the RS documentation, which provides excellent step-by-step instructions. Instead, after providing a high-level overview of the report structure and elements, we will walk you through the process of creating various reports by example.

4.1.3 Understanding report items

With RS you can use the following report items to display data and graphical elements, as shown in table 4.1.

Table 4.1 Use report items to display data and graphical elements.

Report Item	Description
Textbox	The textbox is the report item that you will use most often to display text information. Textbox elements can contain static text or data from the underlying data source. You can use expressions for the textbox content.
Image	You use the image item to display binary images for visual effects (backgrounds, logos, etc.) or to display data stored as images from the report data source.
Subreport	The subreport item defines a placeholder that points to another report.
Line	The line item is a graphical element that you can use to enhance the presentation of your report, e.g., to separate a report group from its details.
Rectangle	Rectangles can be used in two ways: as a graphical element and as a container for other report items. Users familiar with .NET development can make an analogy to the panel element. Similarly to the panel, you can place report items within a rectangle and you can move them with the rectangle.

Some of the report items shown in table 4.1 deserve more attention.

Working with images

The Report Server supports the following image formats: JPG, BMP, GIF, and PNG. To display the actual image in the image report item, you set the Source property. The image source can be defined as

- *Embedded*—In this case, the image data is serialized (MIME-encoded) and embedded in the report definition file. When the report is uploaded to the report catalog, the image is saved in the Report Server database. If you embed the same image in different reports, each report gets its own copy of the image. Similarly to working with report-specific data sources, you use the embedded image option when you want to distribute all report-related items in one file.
- *External*—The image refers to an image file that is located in the same project. With this option, only the name of the image is stored in the report definition file. The actual image is shared across all reports that use it. This simplifies image maintenance because if the image is updated, the change will propagate through all reports that reference the image. You typically use external images for implementing report banners and logos. For example, all the reports inside the AWReporter project use an external image (AWC.jpg) to display the company logo.
- *Database*—The image is bound to an image column from the report dataset. For example, the Product Catalog report included in the RS samples uses this option to show the product image for each product.

The external image option deserves additional attention. We usually try to shy away from storing images in the database for performance and maintenance reasons. A better approach would be to store just the image URL that points to the image file located on a network share or another web server.

For example, let's say you have an employee table that stores the employees' pictures among other employee-related data. You have two implementation options:

- You can define that column as an image type and store the employee pictures in binary format.
- Better, you can store just the image URL path, e.g., //imageserver/images/empid.gif.

The release version of RS restricts the external image option to images defined in the local project only. In fact, it doesn't allow you to specify image URLs that point to anywhere else but to image files located in the same Business Intelligence project. However, the RS Service Pack 1 (SP1), which will probably be out by the time you read this book, will support referencing image files by URL. The preliminary feedback we got from the RS team is that external images will work the same way as the images stored in the catalog. A configurable low-privileged user account will be used to retrieve the image from the given URL. This will allow you to use true "external" images in your reports.

Working with subreports

The subreport item defines a placeholder that points to another report. Usually, you opt for subreports when you need to reuse an existing report. Subreports are a popular reporting technique used to display separate groups of data with many reporting tools, such as Microsoft Access.

With RS, you should consider using nested data regions instead of subreports for performance reasons. If you use a subreport within your report, the Report Server has to process both reports separately. This is less efficient than using a single report with two regions. However, sometimes you won't have a choice. For example, nested data regions have a restriction that they must use the same dataset. If you want to use different datasets that need to display correlated data, then the only choice is to create a subreport. We will look at subreports in more detail in section 4.6.

Working with rectangles

An important (but not so obvious) use for the rectangle item is to group things together so that they move as a unit. In this respect, the rectangle item represents a WinForm panel control that can be used to enclose other controls.

Sometimes, items will get pushed out of alignment with other items on the page. You can group them together with an invisible rectangle and they will get moved together. You will see an example of when this could be useful in section 4.3.1.

4.1.4 Understanding data regions

Besides report items, the Report Items toolbar includes more sophisticated report elements referred to as *data regions.*

While you can use stand-alone textbox and image report items to display data, they are most useful when they display repeating rows of data from a report dataset. In chapter 3 you saw how RS uses datasets to represent the results of queries returned by data providers. To bind report items to datasets, you use data regions. In this respect, .NET developers may relate RS data regions to ASP.NET data-bound controls, such as the data repeater control.

Table 4.2 lists the data regions that RS supports and how they can be used to create different types of reports.

Table 4.2 Reporting Services comes with a number of data regions for different types of reports.

Region	Report Type	Description
Table	Tabular	The table data region generates as many rows as the number of records in the underlying dataset. You can optionally group or sort data by fields or expressions. For example, for the Sales by Territory report, the Report Wizard automatically generated a table data region to render the report data in tabular format.
List	Freeform	When using the list region, you are not restricted to static columns as with the table region. Instead, you can arrange report items any way you want. Microsoft Access users will find that the list region allows them to place items arbitrarily, similarly to how they lay out a report in Access.
Matrix	Matrix (crosstab)	The matrix region can include dynamic columns. Dynamic columns can be configured as hidden. The user can expand a hidden dynamic column to see more data, i.e., drill down into the data.
Chart	Chart	As its name suggests, the chart region displays the report data in chart format. Various kinds of chart types are supported, such as bar, pie, graph, and many more.

To fill in a data region with data you bind the data region to a dataset by setting its DataSetName property.

> **NOTE** The Report Designer automatically associates a dataset with a data region when you drag and drop a dataset field to the data region.

Data regions are designed to generate repeating sections of data. For example, to display the sales numbers of the Adventure Works sales territories in the Sales by Territory report, we use a table region. During the report processing stage, the Report Server executes the dataset query, populates the dataset, and passes it to all data regions bound to it so they can render themselves.

All data regions except the chart region can act as containers for other report items. Considering again the Sales by Territory report, you can see that the table data region is a container for the textbox report items that generate the data in the table columns.

At this point, you may ask, "Why do we need data regions at all, when we can place report items directly onto the report?" The short answer is flexibility. The next section should make this clear.

Data region advantages

The advantages of using data regions are as follows:

- They can be used as "supercharged" subreports, as we explain next.
- They can be placed side by side and draw data from separate datasets.

Reports can vary greatly in their layout and complexity. A very simple report might need to display the data in a tabular format only. A more complicated report, however, may include different sections, each of which might be rendered in a different way. Those of you familiar with Microsoft Access know that complex reports need to be broken into subreports. We will discuss subreports in more detail in section 4.6.

With RS, you will find that in most cases you don't need subreports. Instead, you can use individual data regions. This is possible because the data regions can be nested inside other data regions, as we will see shortly in this chapter. In addition, you can place a data region anywhere you want inside the report body.

You can also position data regions side by side, and each of them can have its own datasets and be independent from the others. For example, you can place a chart and table region side by side. The chart region can display the company sales per territory in chart format, while the table region can provide a breakdown per product and territory.

Another example where side-by-side data regions could be useful is in a multisection report. For example, imagine that you need to author a sophisticated report that includes a few sections. Based on some business rules, the report may not show certain sections. One way to achieve this requirement would be to break down the report data in sections and implement each section as a separate data region. Then, you could programmatically hide the sections during the report runtime using expressions.

Binding data regions to report datasets

In order for the data regions to display data they must be associated with a dataset. You don't have to manually bind a data region to a dataset. Once you drag and drop a dataset field to the data region, the Report Designer links that region to the dataset, as you can see by inspecting the DataSetName property of the region. You can also manually associate a region to a dataset. This could be useful, for example, if you change the dataset name.

You can customize the message that is displayed inside a data region if the underlying dataset has no rows by using the NoRows property, which every data region has. The default setting is an empty string. For example, if the report query results in no rows, you can let the user know by setting the NoRows property to No Data to Display.

Setting up paging

As explained in chapter 1, a report can be requested in any RS-supported rendering format. Some formats, such as image and PDF, support page sizes and will repaginate the report based on the page size you specify. Others, such as HTML, will not honor the page size settings and render all data in one page (please see the "Working with Multiple Pages" topic in the RS documentation for more information). In such cases, you can use page breaks to improve the report performance.

It may seems strange at first that RS doesn't specifically include a page break element to allow you to arbitrarily force a page break at specific point of the report. Instead, each data region has several page break–related properties that you can use to force a page break before and/or after the region. You can also enforce page breaks before and after region groups. You will see how to use region groups to group related data together in section 4.2.1.

Version 1.0 of Reporting Services doesn't support predefined page layouts and sizes. Instead, you have to explicitly define the page size in units on the Report Properties dialog.

TIP Sometimes, you may need to have control over the number of rows per page for tabular reports. You can accomplish this by using details groupings (discussed in 4.2.1) based on expressions. For example to display 25 rows per page, follow these steps:

- Add a group to the table and group on the following expression: `=Ceiling(RowNumber(Nothing)/25)`
- Turn off the group header and footer.
- Turn on PageBreakAtEnd on the group.

If you need web-style paging, you could try using report hyperlinks, the approach we describe in chapter 5.

Now that you've learned about the report layout at a high level, let's see how to put this knowledge in practice by creating different types of reports, starting with tabular reports.

4.2 DESIGNING TABULAR REPORTS

You create tabular reports by using the table data region. You can optionally define report groups by grouping the table region data by fields or expressions.

Tabular reports with groups

The first report that we created in chapter 1, the Sales by Territory report, is an example of a tabular report. Let's enhance it by grouping data.

If you preview this report, you will notice that we didn't quite meet the original requirements. The sales management requested that we group the sales data by territory. However, we've just hidden the duplicated territory names. Let's fix this by using table region groups. The final version of the report is shown in Figure 4.3.

Sales By Territory

Territory	Product Category	Sales
Australia		
	Accessory	$8,359.74
	Bike	$773,111.46
	Clothing	$18,665.74
	Component	$96,911.11
Australia Totals:		*$897,048.06*
Canada		
	Accessory	$32,835.84
	Bike	$2,315,632.98
	Clothing	$86,657.62
	Component	$457,317.56
Canada Totals:		*$2,892,444.00*
Central		
	Accessory	$9,618.56
	Bike	$1,670,230.04
	Clothing	$29,913.86

Figure 4.3 Sales by Territory report grouped by territory

Creating a table region group

To group the report data by territory, complete the following steps:

Step 1 Open the Sales by Territory Interactive report.

Step 2 Click the table so that the row and column handles appear next to and above the table region.

Step 3 Right-click the handle of any row and select Insert Group. The Grouping and Sorting Properties dialog appears, as shown in figure 4.4.

Step 4 Change the group name to grpTerritory.

> **NOTE** I highly recommend that you come up with a good naming convention for report item names and use it consistently. It doesn't matter what it is; what does matter is that you have one. You will realize its benefits when you start referencing the report items in expressions. I try to use three-letter prefixes, e.g., *txt* for textboxes, *grp* for groups.

Step 5 From the Group On field, select the Fields!Territory.Value field from the drop-down list.

Step 6 Select the Include Group Footer checkbox to generate group footers after each group to include the sales totals per territory, and then click OK.

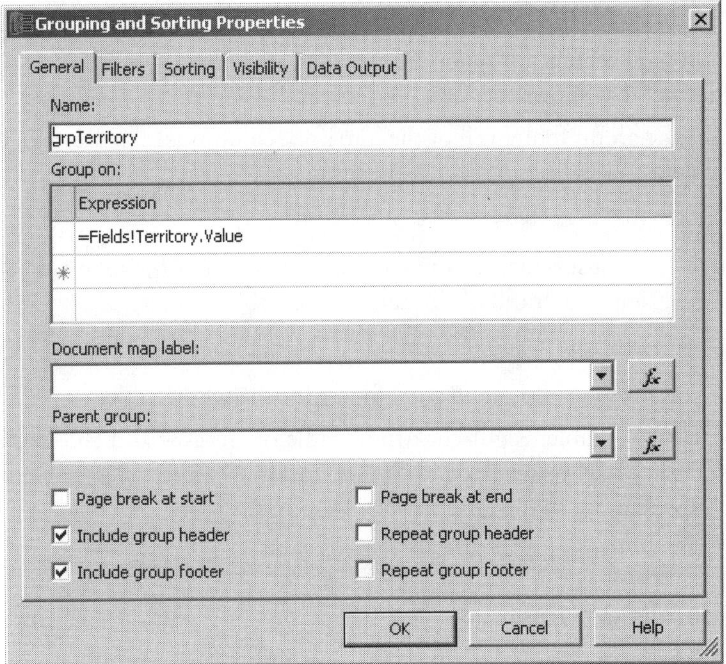

Figure 4.4 Creating a new group

Step 7 Next, move the Fields!Territory.Value to the group header by dragging the field (select the field and click on the selection border) from the group detail section to the group header. At this point, your report layout should look like the one shown in figure 4.5.

Moving the textbox to the group header let us display the territory name only once, at the beginning of each new group.

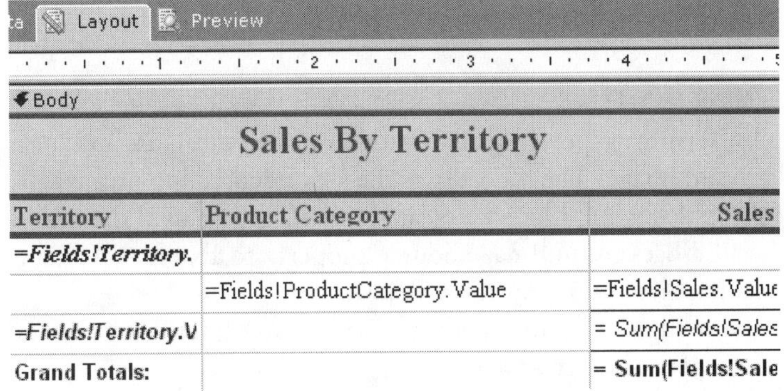

Figure 4.5 Adding the territory group headers and footers

Creating group subtotals

A common requirement for report groups is to include group subtotals. Let's create a group subtotal that shows the sales per territory.

Step 1 In the group footer cell of the Territory column (see figure 4.5), type the following Visual Basic .NET expression:

```
= Fields!Territory.Value & " Totals:"
```

Step 2 To create a subtotal for the territory group, enter the following expression in the group footer cell of the Sales column:

```
= Sum(Fields!Sales.Value)
```

Now, let's create a grand total footer for the whole table.

Step 3 Select the table. Right-click the handle of any row and choose Table Footer. In the Territory cell type **Grand Totals:**. In the Sales cell type the same expression as in the group footer:

```
= Sum(Fields!Sales.Value)
```

Using details grouping

The table region grouping capabilities are not limited to creating group headers and footers only. Instead, the table details data can also be grouped. For example, imagine that the table dataset contains the daily sales data, but you need to consolidate it by quarters. One option would be to perform the consolidation at the database by changing your dataset query. This will also be the best option in terms of performance.

When this is not possible, you can group the details by using the Details Grouping button on the Groups tab of the table region properties. In our case, to consolidate the data in quarters, we will need to add two expressions to the Group On grid: one to group the data by years and one by quarters. If the dataset field that contains the sales date is named Date, then the expressions will be `Fields!Date.Value.Year` and `DatePart("q", Fields!Date.Value)`, respectively.

Using image items

The Sales by Territory report also demonstrates how you can use an external image file as a background image. The report uses the Confidential.jpg image as a background image of the table region. Once we created the image, we used the table region properties to set the BackgroundImage Source property to External, Value to Confidential.jpg, and BackgroundRepeat to NoRepeat.

Finally, you might want to experiment with borders, fonts, colors, and formatting to make the report more eye-catching.

4.2.1 Parameterized tabular reports

Because we can almost feel your resentment toward the Sales by Territory report growing, we'll create a new report from scratch to learn more about working with table regions. Let's say that the AWC management has requested a report that tracks the employee performance for a given period of time. To allow users to see the sales data filtered for a given time period and salesperson, the report needs to be designed as parameterized. The employee sales data needs to be grouped by employee and then by product subcategory and sorted by the employee sales total in descending order.

In its final version, the report will look like the one in figure 4.6.

Because you are already familiar with the table region, I'll highlight a few things worth mentioning rather than provide step-by-step implementation instructions.

Setting up the report parameter lookup values

Let's start by setting up the report data. For this report, we have defined two datasets.

First, we have set up a dataset (dsEmployeeSales) to retrieve the available parameters for the Employee parameter. This dataset gets its results from the spGetEmployeeSalesByProductSubcategory stored procedure, which you can find in the Database project included with the book source code.

We decided to use a stored procedure to encapsulate the data query. If we had chosen a free SQL statement, we would have had to use an expression to inject the `where` clause in the case where the user has requested to see all employees' sales data. The stored procedure takes a start date, end date, and EmployeeID as parameters. The report defaults the start date parameter to 1/1/2003 and the end date to 12/1/2003.

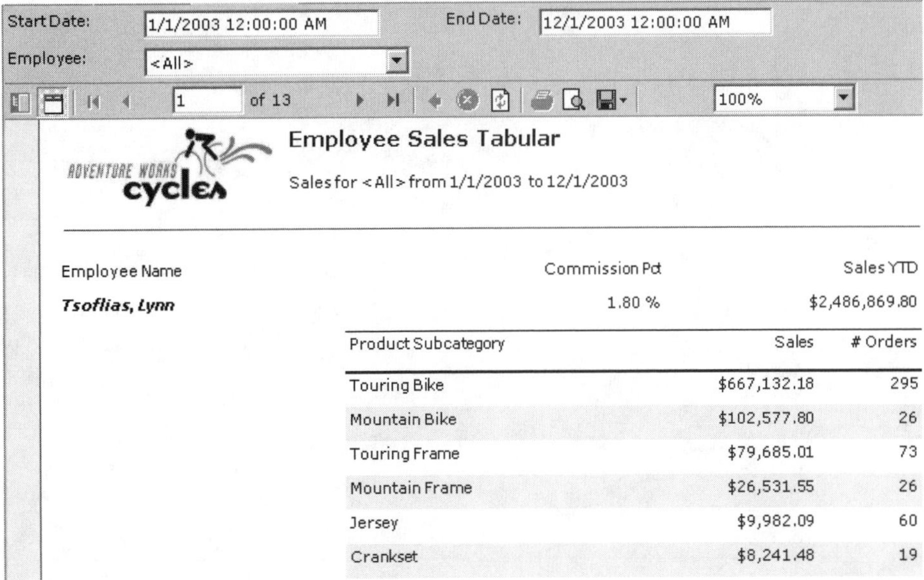

Figure 4.6 The Employee Sales Tabular report with a query-based Employee parameter

Next, we created the dsSalesPerson dataset to retrieve a list of all employees from the Employee table who are also salespeople. This dataset defines the available values for the Employee parameter. It also gives the user the option to see all employees by using the `UNION SQL` operator and adding an additional record with a label of `<All>` and a value of `-1`.

Once you have the lookup dataset defined, use the Report Parameters dialog to configure the report parameters, as shown in figure 4.7.

To set up the available values for the Employee parameter, select the From Query option and choose the dsSalesPerson dataset from the Dataset dropdown. We will use the EmployeeID column from the dataset as an input parameter to the stored procedure.

Setting up the report header

After we set up the report data, we designed the report as a tabular report.

First, we created the report header. As we mentioned in section 4.1.2, RS doesn't provide designated report header and footer sections. Instead, you can achieve the same effect by placing elements at the top of the body section. For the purposes of the Employee Sales Tabular report, in the body section of the header, we added a rectangle report item with two textboxes: one for the name of the report and another

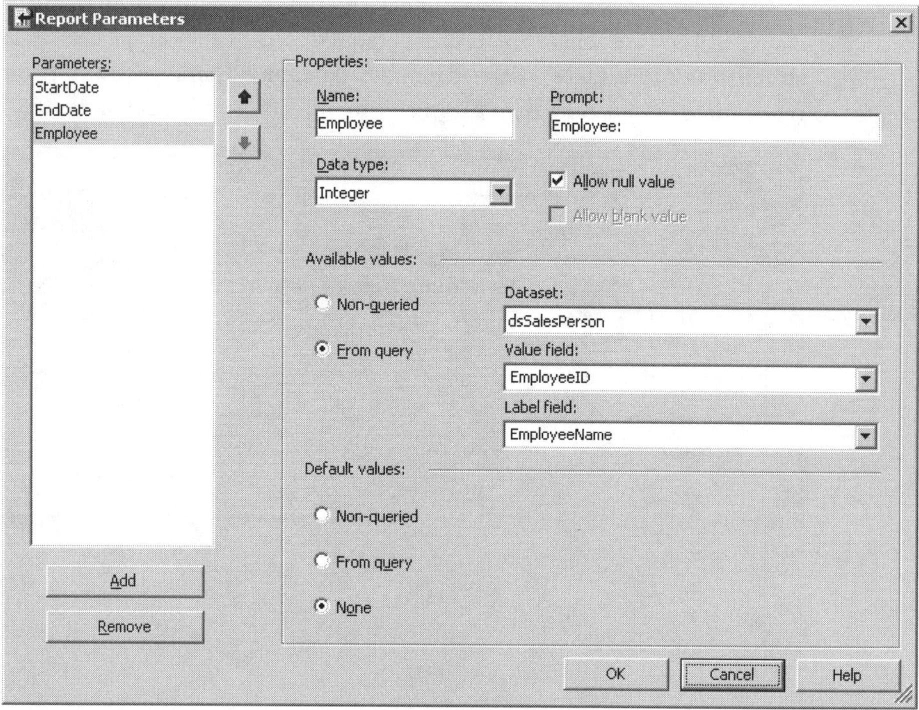

Figure 4.7 Setting up the Employee parameter available values

to display the parameter information. The second textbox is based on the following VB.NET expression:

```
="Sales for " & Parameters!Employee.Label & " from " _
& Parameters!StartDate.Value & " to " & Parameters!EndDate.Value
```

We will postpone discussing expressions until the next chapter. For now, this is a simple VB.NET expression, which concatenates the label (the visible text) of the Employee parameter with the requested date range.

In addition, we used a rectangle for the report header. Inside, we dragged and dropped the AWC.jpg image file, which you can find included in the project. Because this image can be potentially used by all corporate reports, for easier maintenance we decided to reference the image as an external image. The easiest way to do that is to add the image file to the project. Then, you drag and drop the image to your report. Another option is to drag and drop the image item from the report toolbox, which starts the Image Wizard. Please note that as a part of the report deployment process, you have to deploy all external images that the report uses.

Laying out the tabular report

Now it's time for the fun part. For the tabular portion of the report we used a table region called tblEmployeeSales. First, we dragged and dropped a table region from the toolbox, as shown in figure 4.8. By default, the table region has a table header, details, footer rows, and three columns.

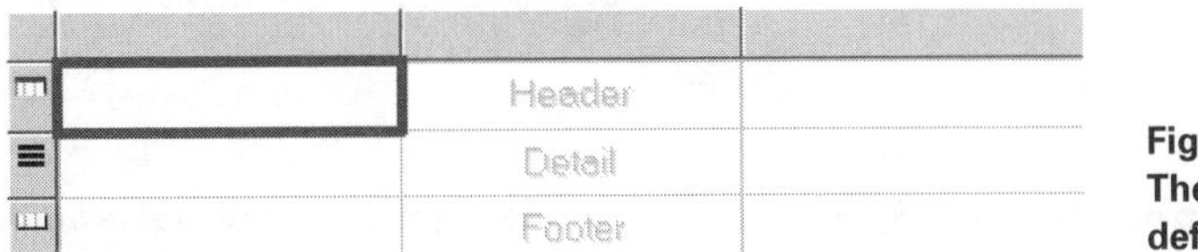

Figure 4.8 The table region with default settings

Once we dragged and dropped the table region below the header rectangle, we populated it with the dataset fields, as shown in figure 4.9.

The easiest way to accomplish this is by dragging and dropping the fields from the Fields window to the appropriate cells. Once you drag the first field and drop it onto the table region, the Report Designer associates the data region and the dataset, as you can see by looking at the DataSetName region property.

You can manually associate a region with a dataset by expanding the DataSetName dropdown and specifying a dataset explicitly. Manually associating a region with a dataset is necessary when you rename the region dataset and when you want to replace

Employee Name	Commission Pct		Sales YTD
	=Fields!ProductSubCategory.Val	=Fields!Sales.Value	=Fields!NoOrders.Value

Figure 4.9 To populate a table region, drag and drop these dataset fields.

the dataset with another one. The Report Designer automatically generates a textbox report item once the field is dropped into a cell.

Next, we need to create the appropriate table regions groups to group data by employee and product subcategory.

Grouping the table region data

We defined two groups: grpEmployee and grpProductSubcategory. You can view the group definitions by clicking anywhere within the table region, selecting the group selector located on the left row handle, and choosing Edit Group from the context menu.

Alternatively, to get to the Group dialog, you can follow these steps:

Step 1 Once the table is selected, click on the table selector square (the top left-most square). At this point, the table selection border changes, as shown in figure 4.10.

This puts the table region in Edit mode, so you can resize it or drag it to a new location.

Step 2 Now, you can right-click anywhere on the border and choose Properties to view the table region properties.

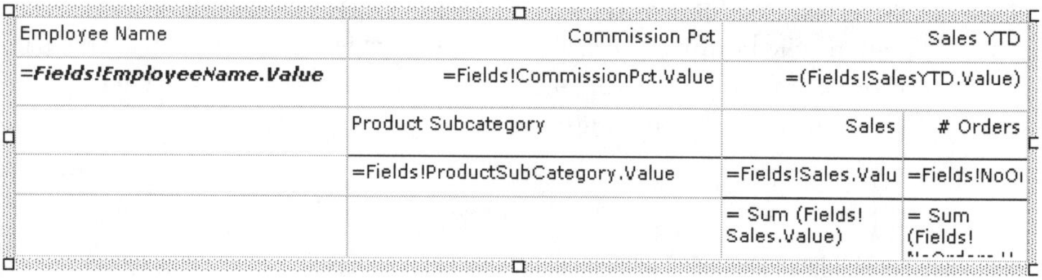

Employee Name	Commission Pct	Sales YTD	
=Fields!EmployeeName.Value	=Fields!CommissionPct.Value	=(Fields!SalesYTD.Value)	
	Product Subcategory	Sales	# Orders
	=Fields!ProductSubCategory.Value	=Fields!Sales.Valu	=Fields!NoO
		= Sum (Fields! Sales.Value)	= Sum (Fields!

Figure 4.10 To put the table region in Edit mode, click twice so that the table border selection changes as shown.

The Groups tab shows the defined groups, which in our case look like the ones shown in figure 4.11.

If you click the Edit button, you will see that the `Group on` expression for the first group is set to `Fields!EmployeeName.Value`. This groups the report data by employee. The second group is set to `Fields!ProductSubcategory.Value`. It groups the product data by category and creates the product subcategory header and footer.

NOTE In general, if you want to achieve better performance, I recommend that you delegate as much data manipulation and massaging as possible to the database. This is what the database is designed for. For example, the Employee Sales Tabular report does all the grouping and sorting in the spGetEmployeeSalesByProductSubcategory stored procedure. It sorts the data by Employee Name in ascending order and then by sales amount in descending order. I use report grouping only to define labels for the columns and totals in the footers.

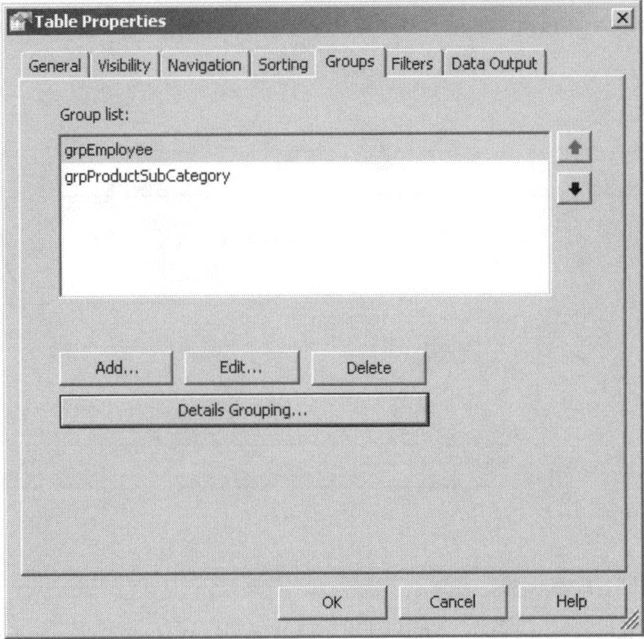

Figure 4.11 Defining table region groups

4.2.2 Tabular reports with interactive features

Another interactive feature, besides parameters, that you can add to your tabular reports is *visible-on-demand* groups. For example, if the table region has two groups nested one within the other, the parent group can act as a toggle to show/hide the nested group. The table region automatically generates an image that the user can click to expand/collapse the nested group. This visible-on-demand technique can give your tabular reports a "briefing" look.

The Employee Sales Tabular Interactive report shown in figure 4.12 demonstrates the visible-on-demand interactive feature.

The new version of the report hides the product subcategory group by default. The user can click the plus indicator to expand the Product Subcategory section and see its details. Users experienced with designing web content will probably agree that designing collapsible sections using JavaScript code and DHTML is not that straightforward. The process usually involves wrapping the section in a DIV element and calling client-side JavaScript code to show/hide the section.

Using the Report Designer, creating a visible-on-demand section is a matter of setting the nested group visibility to be toggled by the parent group, as shown in figure 4.13.

The choice of which textbox item you select in the Report Item drop-down is important because the expandable plus image will be placed immediately before this item. In this case, in the Report Item drop-down, we selected lblProductSubCategory, which is the name of the textbox with a value of Product Subcategory.

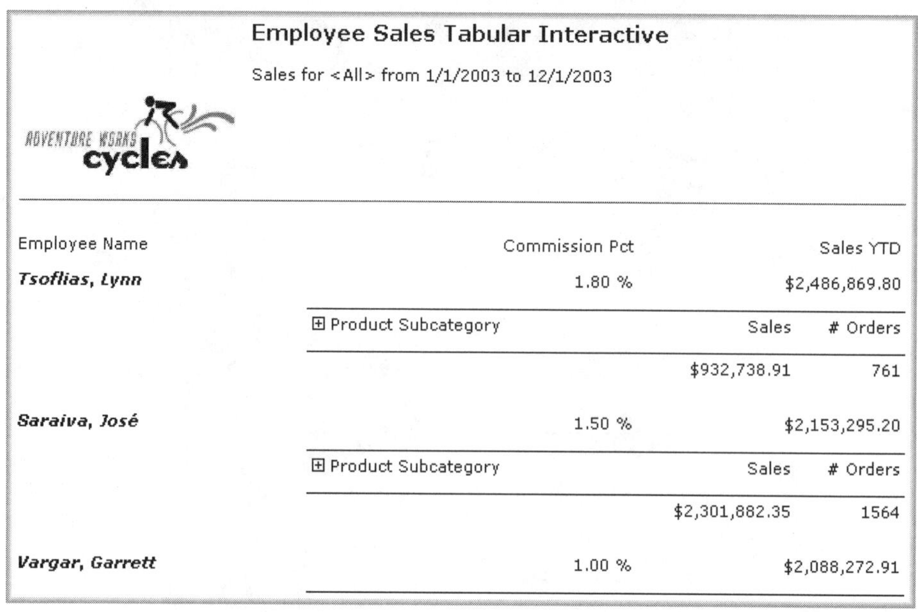

Figure 4.12 This tabular report has visible-on-demand groups that can be expanded by clicking the plus sign next to them.

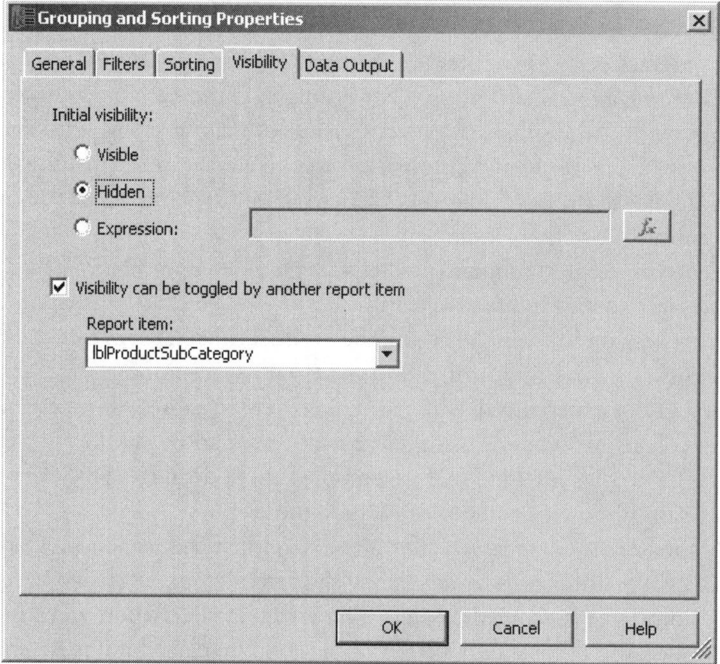

Figure 4.13 Creating visible-on-demand groups

4.2.3 Table region limitations

To summarize, the table region works great for simple tabular reports. However, when report complexity increases, you might find the tabular layout restrictive. For example, with the table region, your layout options are restricted to static columns. If the group header and table details have the same number of columns, everything is great. Otherwise, you will find yourself creating new columns and merging existing ones.

For example, the Employee Sales Tabular report sample needs three columns for the Employee group, while it needs four for the Product subcategory group. To solve this, we defined four columns at the table level. Then, for the Employee group, we merged the last two columns by selecting both of them and choosing Merge Cells from the context menu. As you can see, as the complexity of report layout increases, the table region might soon get in the way.

4.3 *DESIGNING FREEFORM REPORTS*

When the table region is not enough, you can use the list region to create freeform reports. As their name suggests, freeform reports allow you to arrange items arbitrarily inside the list region.

4.3.1 Freeform reports with nested regions

Figure 4.14 shows the new version of the Employee Sales report (Employee Sales Freeform), which now uses list and table regions, with the table region nested inside the list region.

At first glance, the report looks the same. However, the employee information section is now located to the left of the product sales section and its text boxes are arranged in a freeform way, one below the other.

ADVENTURE WORKS cycles

Employee Sales Freeform

Sales for <All> from 1/1/2003 to 12/1/2003

		Product Subcategory	Sales	# Orders
Employee Name:	**Tsoflias, Lynn**			
Commision:	1.80 %	Touring Bike	$667,132.18	295
Sales YTD:	$2,486,869.80	Mountain Bike	$102,577.80	26
Bonus:	$5,650.00	Touring Frame	$79,685.01	73
		Mountain Frame	$26,531.55	26
		Jersey	$9,982.09	60
		Crankset	$8,241.48	19
		Vest	$5,819.78	21
		Bike Racks	$5,112.00	13
		Derailleur	$4,643.46	26

Figure 4.14 Use freeform reports when you need to lay out items arbitrarily on the report canvas.

Working with list regions

Here's how we authored the report:

First, we dragged and dropped a list region from the report toolbar and named it lstEmployeeSales. Then, we grouped the list by Employee Name, similar to how the table region was grouped before. To accomplish this, we selected the list region, right-clicked, and chose Properties. Then, we clicked the Edit Details Group button, as shown in figure 4.15.

This brought us to the familiar Grouping Properties dialog where we defined a new group based on the following grouping expression:

```
=Fields!EmployeeName.Value
```

The screenshot in figure 4.15 was taken with Reporting Services Beta 2. Unfortunately, there is a bug in the RTM that the PageBreakAtEnd element does not appear in the List Group dialog for list regions. The functionality is still there, but you have to edit the RDL by hand and add `<PageBreakAtEnd>True</PageBreakAtEnd>` inside the Grouping element. For the Employee Sales Freeform report this should look like this:

```
<Grouping Name="grpEmployee">
  <GroupExpressions>
    <GroupExpression>=Fields!EmployeeName.Value</GroupExpression>
   </GroupExpressions>
   <PageBreakAtEnd>true</PageBreakAtEnd>
</Grouping>
```

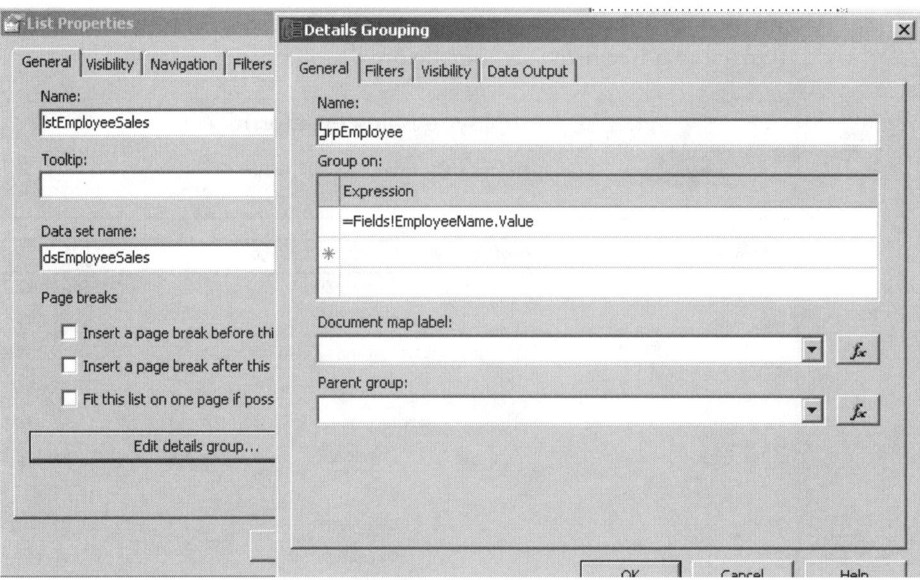

Figure 4.15 Defining list item groups

This PageBreakAtEnd bug will be fixed in RS Service Pack 1 slated for a release in June 2004.

On the same dialog, we also selected the Page Break At End option to generate a page break after the employee group is generated. Then, we moved the tblEmployee-Sales region inside the list region and removed all groups from it. As a result, the table region is now nested inside the list region, so both regions are synchronized.

Laying out the report

Given that we are no longer confined to static columns, we could choose to lay out the employee fields anywhere we want. We can also add as many fields as we want without being restricted to static columns. For instance, we added the Bonus field from the report dataset. Had the Adventure Works database stored pictures of the employees, we could have added an image report item to display the employee photos as well.

Finally, we enclosed all employee fields in a rectangle to prevent some of the fields from being pushed down by the table region. Because the list region now groups the data by employee, the table region needs to show only the product sales in a tabular form. We defined a table header and footer to show the table region labels and totals, respectively.

NOTE As we noted before, the rectangle report item can serve as a container for other items. When enclosing other items, it prevents the table region from pushing down other items. For example, if we hadn't used a rectangle to enclose the employee fields, the last field would have been pushed down when the report was generated.

4.3.2 Grouping freeform data

While table and matrix regions provide multiple levels of grouping within a single data region, lists can have only one group. This limitation might not be that obvious from the Grouping Properties dialog because it allows you to define multiple `Group on` expressions. It is important to note, though, that this will not result in true nested groups because you won't be able to aggregate the results at a group level. Instead, to create two nested groups using lists, you must place a list within another list.

Let's consider an example. What if, for the Employee Sales report, we wanted to group by territory first and then by salesperson, so we could see the total sales amount per territory. Figure 4.16 shows what the revised Employee Sales by Territory report should look like.

There is a new group now, which breaks down the employee sales data by territory. Although the screenshot doesn't show it, before the end of each territory group there is a textbox that totals the sales by that territory.

At your first attempt, you might think that to create the new group you could define a new `Group on` expression using the Grouping Properties dialog. If you did this, however, you would find out that you couldn't create subtotals on the territory level. Instead, what you need to do is to add a new list (lstTerritory) and nest the

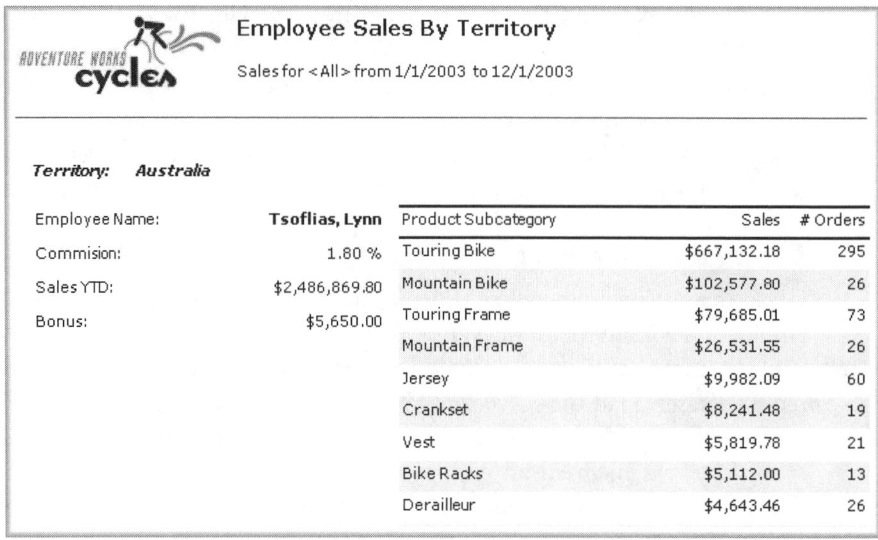

Figure 4.16 To achieve additional levels of grouping with freeform reports, you can nest data regions within other data regions.

lstEmployee list within it. The prior list will group the data per territory, while the latter per employee. Figure 4.17 shows lstEmployee nested inside lstTerritory.

TIP As you add items to the report, you might find it difficult to select items. For example, it is almost impossible to select an enclosing rectangle by trying to click on its boundaries. You can tab among fields until you select the item you need, but a better way is to use the VS.NET Properties window and select the item from the drop-down. This will select the item in the Report Designer as well.

Another even faster way to select the item container is to hit the Esc key object when the child is selected.

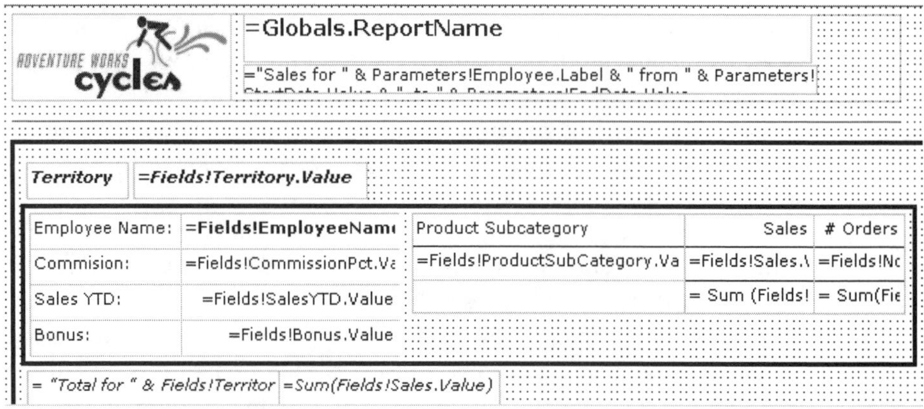

Figure 4.17 Nesting lists for additional levels of grouping

4.3.3 Freeform reports with side-by-side data regions

As we said at the beginning of this chapter, data regions can coexist peacefully next to one another and each of them can be bound to its own dataset. This could be useful when you need to have sections in your report that draw data from separate datasets.

One practical application of using side-by-side regions is creating summary reports. The Employee Sales by Territory with Summary report does exactly this. Figure 4.18 shows the new report.

The report has a summary section at the top to summarize territory sales data. To design the report, we created a new dataset (dsTerritorySummary). Then, we added a new table region (tblSummary) before the lstTerritory region and populated it with the fields from the dataset, as shown in figure 4.19.

With RS, one report can have many regions of different types placed side by side. However, as we mentioned in chapter 3, you should try to limit the number of the report datasets for performance reasons.

Giving only text-oriented reports to users may not be enough. For example, marketing people love charts so that they can spot business trends more easily. The next section teaches you how to design chart reports.

ADVENTURE WORKS cycles

Employee Sales By Territory with Summary

Sales for <All> from 1/1/2003 to 12/1/2003

Territory	Sales YTD	# Customers
Australia	$2,486,869.80	40
Canada	$6,169,098.67	114
Central	$3,985,928.65	76
France	$2,177,055.65	40
Germany	$2,160,347.31	40
Northeast	$4,825,355.27	77
Northwest	$4,358,526.04	76
Southeast	$4,201,294.95	80
Southwest	$6,643,143.71	118
United Kingdom	$2,568,244.05	40
Grand Total	**$39,575,864.11**	**701**

Territory: Australia

Employee Name:	**Tsoflias, Lynn**
Commision:	1.80 %
Sales YTD:	$2,486,869.80
Bonus:	$5,650.00

Product Subcategory	Sales	# Orders
Touring Bike	$667,132.18	295
Mountain Bike	$102,577.80	26
Touring Frame	$79,685.01	73
Mountain Frame	$26,531.55	26

Figure 4.18 To work with more than one dataset, use side-by-side data regions.

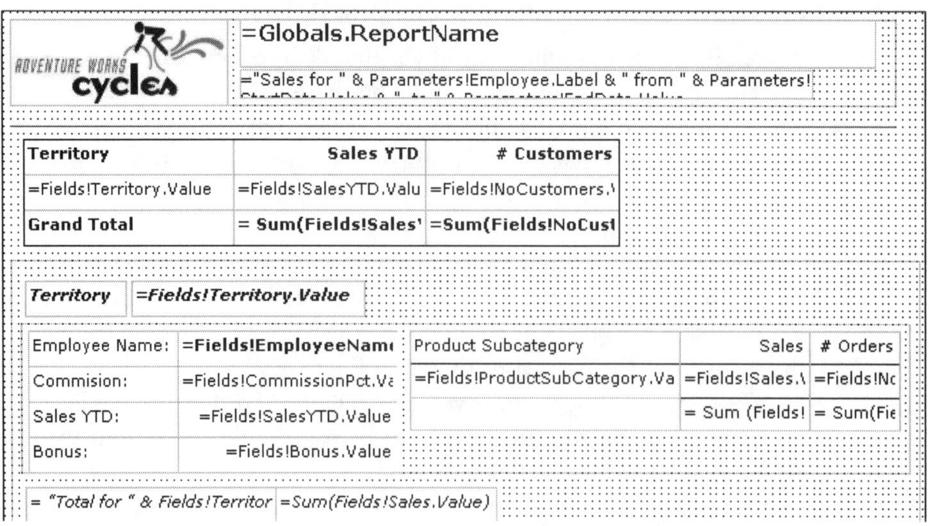

Figure 4.19 Your reports can have data regions of different types placed side by side.

4.4 DESIGNING CHART REPORTS

Chart reports display data in an easy-to-understand graphical format. With RS, you can add different types of charts to your reports, including column, bar, area, line, pie, doughnut, scatter, bubble, and stock chart types.

4.4.1 The chart data region

The chart data region is a sophisticated control, and explaining it in detail could easily fill in a whole chapter. Most of you who have experience in authoring chart reports using other reporting tools, such as Microsoft Graph for charting with Access-based reports, will probably find the RS chart region similar. In this section we will give you only the essential knowledge for working with the RS chart region. If you need more information, please refer to the product documentation.

NOTE If you have experience using the Dundas Software chart control, you'll find yourself in familiar waters, since RS uses this control for charting.

To set up a chart report, you drag and drop the chart data region. Figure 4.20 shows the default appearance of the chart region.

Once the chart region is placed on the report canvas, you can change the chart type by right-clicking it and using the context menu or by selecting the General tab from the Chart Properties dialog, as shown in figure 4.21.

Once you have selected the chart type, you need to set up the chart data by defining the chart values, categories, and series.

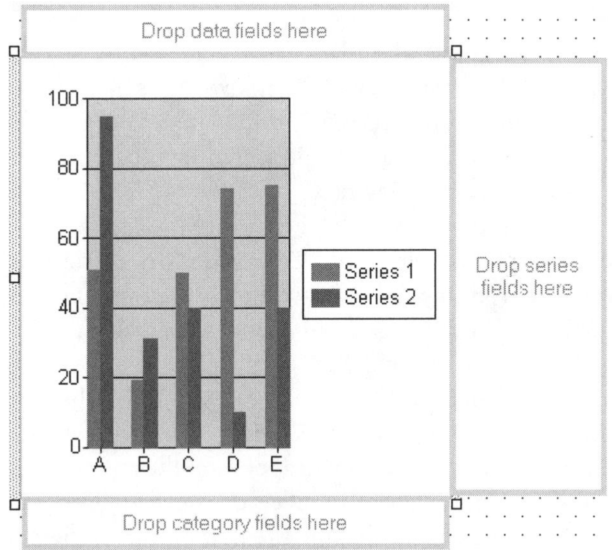

Figure 4.20
The chart region has data, series, and category fields.

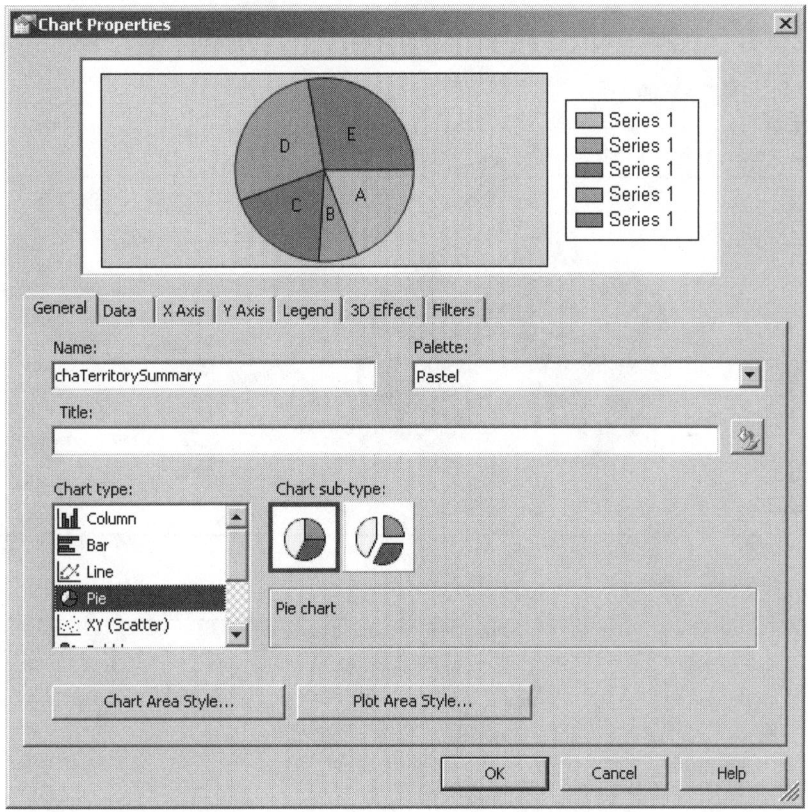

Figure 4.21 Changing the chart type to a pie chart.

4.4.2 Working with charts

To demonstrate a practical example of a chart report, let's assume that the AWC sales management has requested that we change the Employee Sales by Territory with Summary report. Instead of having the report display the territory sales in a tabular fashion, the management has requested the data to be presented in a chart format, so they can easily see which countries are performing best.

Figure 4.22 shows the Employee Sales by Territory with Summary Chart report.

This report uses an exploded pie chart. Once we changed the chart type, we dragged the Territory field from the dsTerritorySummary dataset and dropped it into the data fields section. Then, we dragged and dropped the Sales YTD field into the data fields section, as shown in figure 4.23.

As a result, the chart was configured to display Sales YTD as values and group the sales data by Territory. In addition, using the Category Groups properties, we sorted the data by Sales YTD so that the countries will appear on the top of the chart legend.

Also, we enabled the chart point labels (numbers on the slices) by going to the Data tab on the Chart Properties dialog and clicking the Edit button of the Values section. We defined the data labels as shown in figure 4.24.

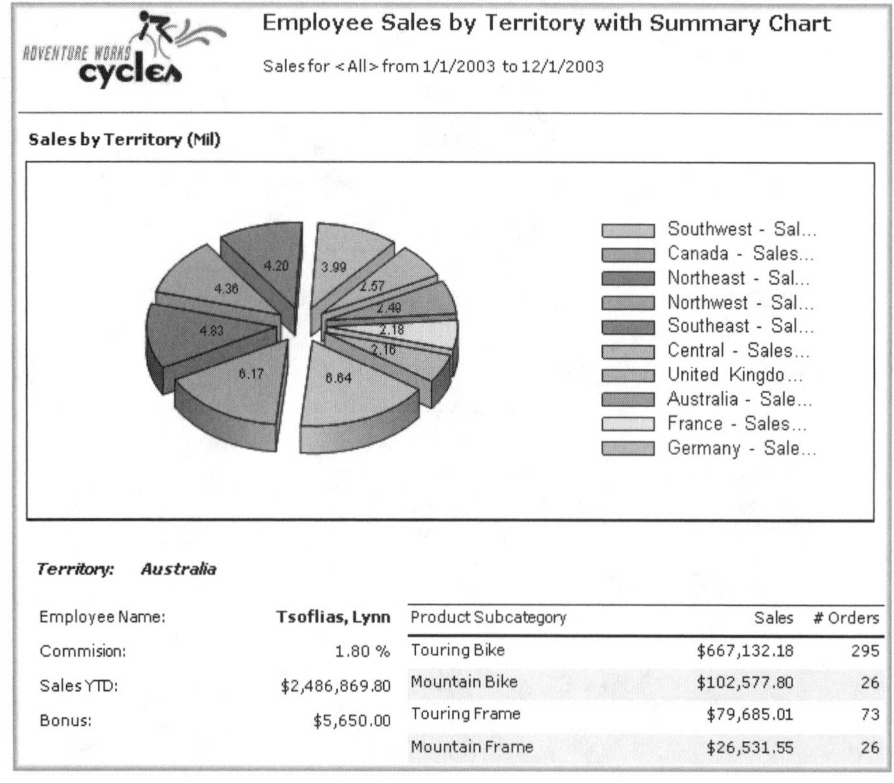

Figure 4.22 You can use chart report to display the report data in an-easy-to-understand graphical format.

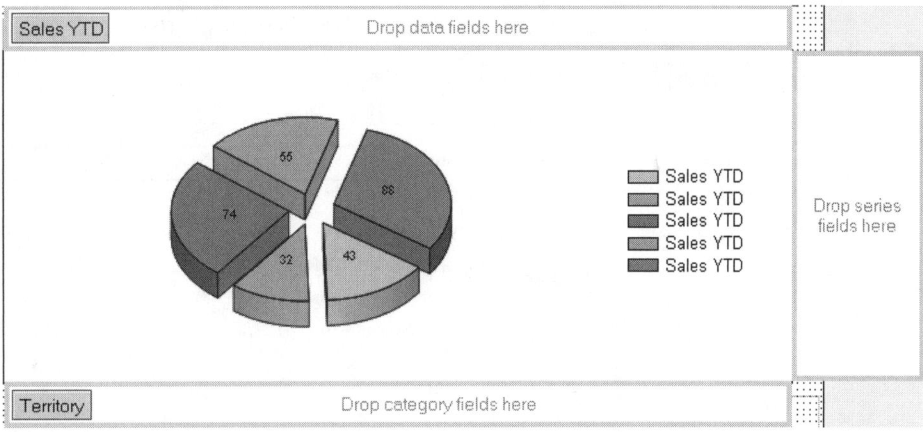

Figure 4.23 Setting up the chart data

Because of the limited space on the chart, we used an expression to show the sales value in millions. In addition, we enabled the chart legend and set the chart display type to 3D by making changes to the Legend and 3D Effect tabs, respectively.

4.4.3 Nesting chart regions

Let's look at another example. This time, we need to include a chart in each employee section showing the employee performance at a glance. The performance metrics (chart data fields) will consist of the sales amount and number of orders and will be grouped by product subcategory. Figure 4.25 shows the new Employee Sales Freeform with Chart report.

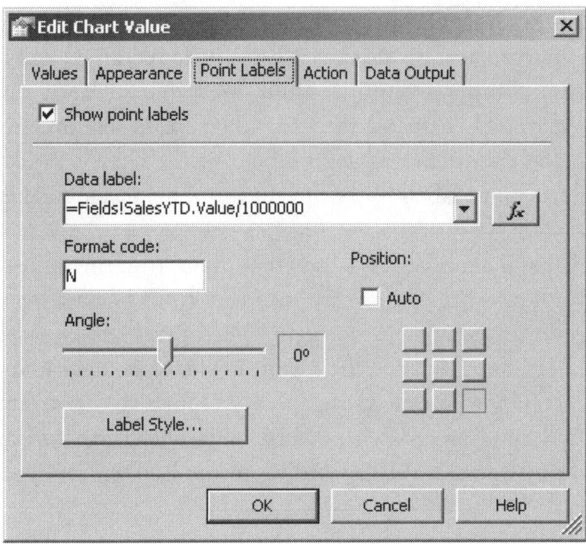

Figure 4.24 Setting up the chart point labels

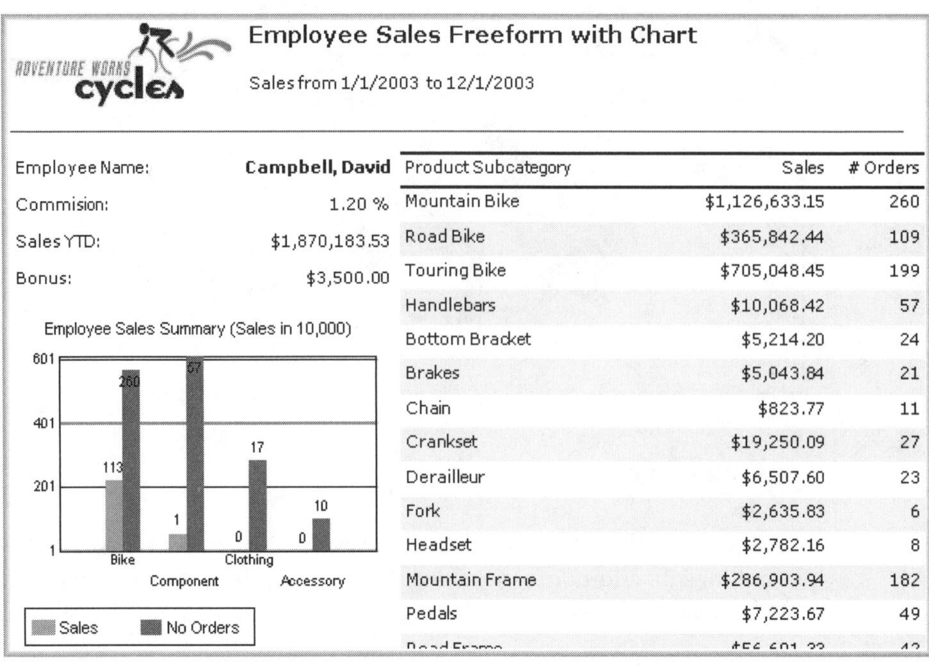

Figure 4.25 You can nest the chart region inside another region.

For the purposes of this report, we changed the data source to use a free SQL statement that includes an additional `group by` clause to group the data by product category. In addition, we simplified the report by removing the employee filter. This reduces the report datasets to one because we removed the dsEmployee dataset, which was used to define the available values for the Employee parameter.

Next, we added a chart region inside the recEmployee rectangle and changed the chart type to Column, Simple Column. Then, we selected both the Sales and NoOrders fields and dropped them on the chart data fields section. After that, we dragged and dropped the ProductSubCategory field to the chart category fields section. We also enabled the point labels for both values and made a few other minor formatting changes.

Because both the list and chart regions draw their data from the same dataset, they are in sync with each other. If the chart region needs to fetch its data from a different dataset, you have to take an extra step to synchronize both regions, for example, by passing the EmployeeID value from the list region to the chart dataset query.

Sometimes, it is necessary to rotate results in your reports so that columns are presented horizontally and rows are presented vertically. This is known as creating a *crosstab (pivot) report*, or a *matrix report* according to the RS terminology.

4.5 DESIGNING CROSSTAB REPORTS

To create crosstab reports with RS, you use the matrix data region. Those of you who are familiar with Microsoft Access will find the matrix region similar to Access crosstab queries. Many of you who have created crosstab reports in the past will probably agree that rotating the data to create this type of report is not easy. The matrix region takes the burden away from developers by allowing even inexperienced users to create crosstab reports in minutes.

4.5.1 Matrix region advantages

This control brings this type of report to a whole new level by

- Supporting virtual columns to rotate data automatically
- Including interactive features by supporting expanding rows and columns to allow the user to drill down into the data

Rotating data with the matrix region

Retrieving data from the database in a crosstab format is not an easy endeavor. In the case of SQL Server, you have to be well versed in SQL to craft complicated statements using CASE expressions. This is what a possible SQL Server query might look like if you want to transpose the sales data from the Adventure Works 2000 database in quarters as columns:

```
SELECT  SUM(CASE DATEPART(QQ, OrderDate)
        WHEN 1 THEN UnitPrice*OrderQty ELSE 0 END) AS Q1,
        SUM(CASE DATEPART(QQ, OrderDate)
        WHEN 2 THEN UnitPrice*OrderQty ELSE 0 END) AS Q2,
        SUM(CASE DATEPART(QQ, OrderDate)
        WHEN 3 THEN UnitPrice*OrderQty ELSE 0 END) AS Q3,
        SUM(CASE DATEPART(QQ, OrderDate)
        WHEN 4 THEN UnitPrice*OrderQty ELSE 0 END) AS Q4
FROM    SalesOrderDetail  AS SOD INNER JOIN
SalesOrderHeader AS SOH ON SOH.SalesOrderID = SOD.SalesOrderID
WHERE    DATEPART(YY,OrderDate) = 2003
GROUP BY DATEPART(yy, OrderDate)
```

And this is what the result looks like:

```
Q1           Q2            Q3            Q4
------------ ------------- ------------- -------------
7776157.6018 9737223.6868  16937272.0506 15226227.5317
```

Now, imagine that you need to display the data in a crosstab report not by quarter but by month, within a user-defined date range, and you will start appreciating the work that the matrix region does behind the scenes for you! The matrix region makes crafting sophisticated queries to rotate data unnecessary. Instead, once you've defined the virtual columns, the matrix region transposes and aggregates data automatically.

Interactive crosstab reports

Making crosstab reports interactive allows users to drill down through data. For instance, top managers are usually interested in the high-level view of the company performance, e.g., sales by country. The mid-level management is concerned with a more detailed view of information, specific to their domain, e.g., sales by stores.

Crosstab reports with expandable groups allow each tier of users to see the level of detail they need. In this respect, developers who have used Microsoft Office Web Components in the past will find the matrix region similar (although less powerful) to the Pivot Table component. We will talk about building reports using Microsoft Office Web Components in more detail in chapter 12.

The best way to explain how the matrix region works is to see an example, as the next section demonstrates.

4.5.2 Working with the matrix region

Going back to our fictitious scenario, the Adventure Works sales management has requested that you create a Territory Sales report, which will be used by the company's top- and mid-level sales managers. The top management would like to see the territory sales consolidated by country on a yearly basis, while the mid-level management would need a breakdown by salesperson per month. Instead of creating two reports, you prudently decide to leverage the power of the matrix region and author only one dynamic report. Figure 4.26 shows the Territory Sales Crosstab report.

The users can expand both rows (territories) and columns (time) to drill down into employees' sales data and months respectively. For example, the snapshot shows that the user has expanded Canada to see the sales data broken down by all salespersons who handle the Canada region. In addition, the user has decided to see the monthly sales data for 2004, while the sales data for 2003 is displayed consolidated.

Let's discuss the essential points of this report design process.

Territory Sales Crosstab

Territory Sales from 3/1/2003 to 4/30/2004

ADVENTURE WORKS cycles	2003		2004		Total	
	Sales	# Orders	Sales	# Orders	Sales	# Orders
Australia	$932,739	761	$472,574	359	$1,405,313	1120
Canada	$3,658,680	2696	$1,033,625	818	$4,692,305	3514
Central	$3,729,552	2832	$989,345	844	$4,718,897	3676
France	$2,691,466	1630	$780,885	512	$3,472,351	2142
Germany	$1,268,472	972	$618,313	476	$1,886,785	1448
Northeast	$4,254,635	2747	$1,111,345	690	$5,365,980	3437
Northwest	$3,789,249	2345	$1,639,051	834	$5,428,301	3179
Southeast	$2,317,549	1871	$712,895	571	$3,030,444	2442
Southwest	$6,938,984	4433	$2,219,821	1290	$9,158,805	5723
United Kingdom	$4,526,688	2974	$1,384,855	901	$5,911,543	3875
Total	$34,108,015	23261	$10,962,709	7295	$45,070,724	30556

Figure 4.26 Using the matrix region, creating crosstab reports is easy.

Setting up the report data

First, we set up the dsTerritorySales report dataset with the following SQL statement:

```
SELECT     ST.TerritoryID, ST.Name AS Territory, SP.SalesPersonID,
           E.LastName + N', ' + E.FirstName AS EmployeeName,
           SOH.OrderDate AS Date,SUM(SOD.UnitPrice*SOD.OrderQty)AS
           Sales, COUNT(SOH.SalesOrderID) AS NoOrders
FROM       SalesOrderDetail SOD
INNER JOIN SalesOrderHeader SOH
           ON SOD.SalesOrderID = SOH.SalesOrderID
INNER JOIN SalesPerson SP
           ON SOH.SalesPersonID = SP.SalesPersonID
INNER JOIN Employee E ON SP.SalesPersonID = E.EmployeeID
INNER JOIN SalesTerritory ST
           ON SP.TerritoryID = ST.TerritoryID
WHERE      (SOH.OrderDate BETWEEN @StartDate AND @EndDate)
GROUP BY   ST.TerritoryID,ST.Name,SOH.OrderDate,
           SP.SalesPersonID, E.LastName + N', ' + E.FirstName
ORDER BY   ST.Name, SOH.OrderDate
```

Since the matrix rows of this report summarize the information in territories and salespersons, the query statement provides these groups. Drilldown per year is achieved with expressions based on the OrderDate field inside the report. The query also takes start and end dates as parameters.

Adding the matrix region

Next, we switch to the layout mode and drag and drop the matrix region into the report, as shown in figure 4.27.

The upper-left cell of the matrix region is the corner cell. You can use it to display a title for the matrix region. In our case, we used that cell as a container for the AWC logo image.

The matrix data region makes defining the rows and columns in the crosstab easy. To group the data into rows and columns you must define the row and column dynamic groups.

Defining dynamic groups

Dynamic row and column groups can nest within other dynamic row and column groups. You add dynamic groups by dragging and dropping dataset fields to the Rows and Columns areas. Report Designer displays a helpful bar hint when you drag the field over the row or column headers to show you valid places where you can drop the field to nest the new group inside an existing group.

For example, to drill down by territory and salesperson, we dragged and dropped the Territory and EmployeeName fields from the dsTerritorySales dataset into the

	Columns
Rows	Data

Figure 4.27
You define dynamic and static matrix groups by dragging and dropping dataset fields into the respective areas.

Rows section. As a result, the matrix region created two dynamic row groups, which we renamed rowTerritory and rowEmployee respectively, as shown in figure 4.28.

The Columns section is little bit trickier. Here, we need to define dynamic columns for years and months. To achieve this, we created two column groups, colYear and colMonth, and set them to be based on the `Fields!Date.Value.Year` and `Format(Fields!Date.Value, "MMM")` expressions respectively. Because the Date field from the report dataset is of type DateTime, you could use the methods and properties of the .NET DateTime structure to retrieve the year and month portions. We also formatted the month value to show the abbreviated version of the month, for example, *Jan* for January.

Defining static groups

To display the actual data (intersected cells for dynamic row and column groups), you define static rows or column groups. You are not restricted to one static group. When you add more than one static group under a given dynamic column, the dynamic header splits to accommodate the new group. To demonstrate this, we dragged and dropped both the Sales and NoOrders dataset fields to the matrix region data section, so the users could see the sales dollar amount alongside the number of orders placed per territory segment.

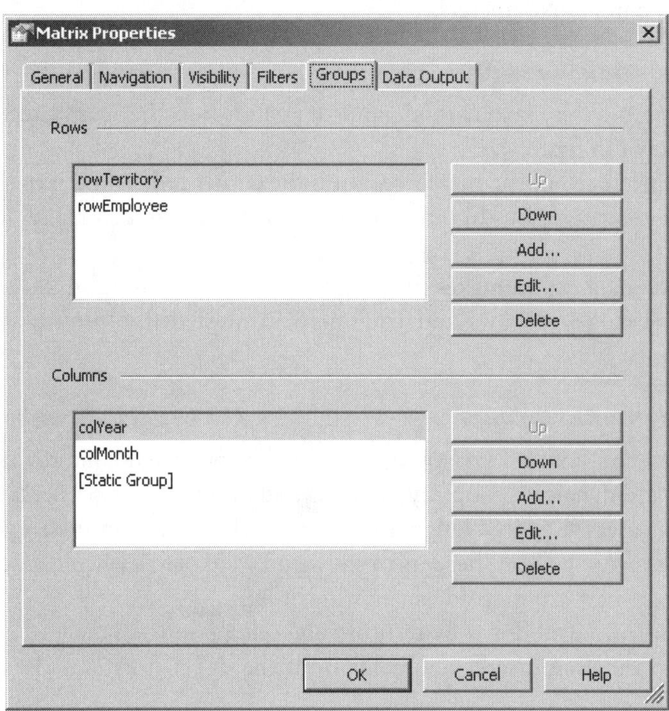

Figure 4.28 You can achieve data drilldown with the matrix region by creating nested column and row dynamic groups.

To get the expand/collapse magic working, we had to change the visibility for the rowEmployee and colMonth groups. Figure 4.29 shows the visibility settings for the rowEmployee group.

These settings make the rowEmployee group invisible initially. Only when the user expands the higher-level Territory group does the Employee group become visible. In a similar way, we set the visibility of colMonth to be toggled by the txtYear field.

One limitation with the interactive features of the matrix region with version 1.0 of Reporting Services is that it doesn't allow the user to expand all groups at once.

Creating subtotals

With many crosstab reports you may want to sum numeric data horizontally and vertically. The matrix region also allows you to define subtotals to sum the data on row and column groups. The only aggregate operation supported is summing. You create subtotals by right-clicking the header of a row or column dynamic group and selecting Subtotal from the context menu. For the Territory Sales report, we defined subtotals on the Territory and Year levels. We also made numerous formatting changes, such as setting border styles, background colors, and formatting settings to make the report looks better, as shown in figure 4.30.

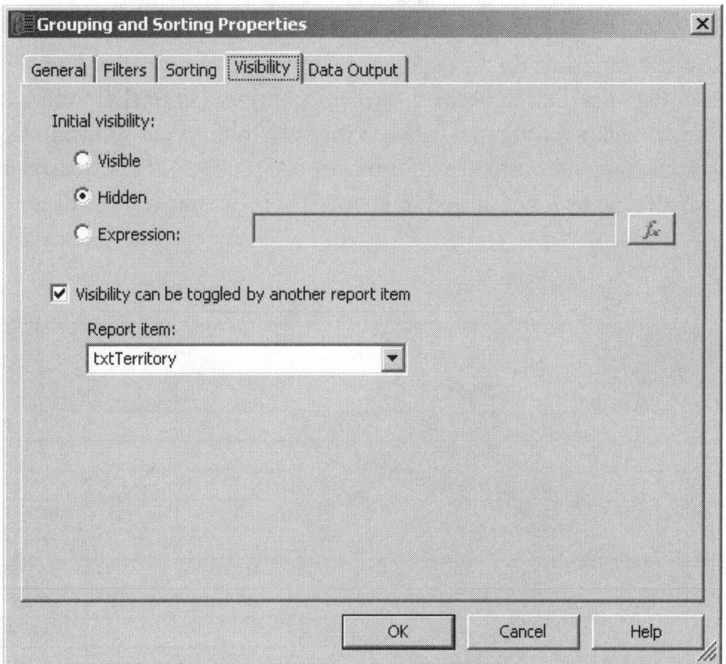

Figure 4.29 You can toggle the group visibility by changing the Visibility settings.

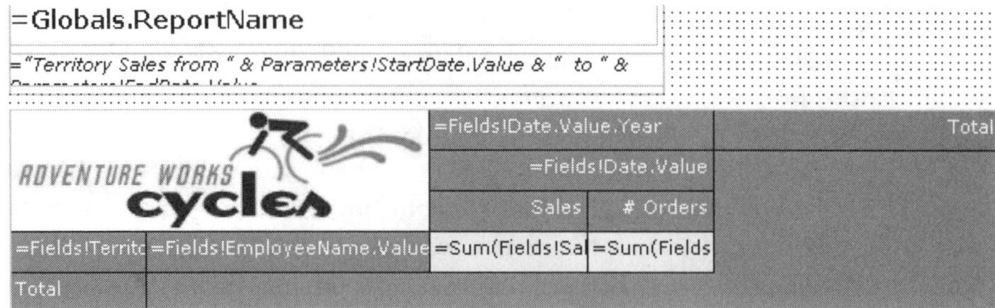

Figure 4.30 To create a row or column subtotal, right-click the header and choose Subtotal.

Currently, the matrix region doesn't support headers and footers per grouping. It is designed for a traditional crosstab layout, which has only subtotals. There are plans that Reporting Services might hybridize the table and matrix regions (most likely by adding table-like features to the matrix) in the next version.

4.5.3 Adjusting the report layout

The matrix region doesn't confine you to a fixed row and column layout. For example, you can get an inverted mirrored layout by changing the Direction property from LTR (left to right) to RTL (right to left). Also, you can move a given number of columns before the row header by using the GroupsBeforeRowHeaders property. For example, if you request sales data that falls in between two years and set GroupsBeforeRowHeaders to 1, the row header will be positioned between the year columns, as shown in figure 4.31.

One interesting performance optimization detail about the matrix region inner workings is that, as we mentioned in chapter 1, it doesn't render all the data at once

Territory Sales Crosstab

Territory Sales from 3/1/2003 to 4/30/2004

2003		ADVENTURE WORKS cycles	2004		Total	
Sales	# Orders		Sales	# Orders	Sales	# Orders
$932,739	761	Australia	$472,574	359	$1,405,313	1120
$3,658,680	2696	Canada	$1,033,625	818	$4,692,305	3514
$3,729,552	2832	Central	$989,345	844	$4,718,897	3676
$2,691,466	1630	France	$780,885	512	$3,472,351	2142
$1,268,472	972	Germany	$618,313	476	$1,886,785	1448
$4,254,635	2747	Northeast	$1,111,345	690	$5,365,980	3437
$3,789,249	2345	Northwest	$1,639,051	834	$5,428,301	3179
$2,317,549	1871	Southeast	$712,895	571	$3,030,444	2442
$6,938,984	4433	Southwest	$2,219,821	1290	$9,158,805	5723
$4,526,688	2974	United Kingdom	$1,384,855	901	$5,911,543	3875
$34,108,015	23261	Total	$10,962,709	7295	$45,070,724	30556

Figure 4.31 Using the GroupsBeforeRowHeaders property

when the report is rendered in HTML. Instead, you will notice that each time you expand a section, a round trip (HTTP-GET request) occurs to the Report Server to fetch the data for the expanded section. To be more specific, a matrix report retrieves all data from the data source when the query is executed, produces the report in intermediate format, and serializes it into data chunks in the ReportServerTempDb database. This process is known as *report session caching*, and we will discuss this topic in detail in chapter 7.

When a report row or column is expanded, the matrix region posts back to the server to retrieve the report for that section. This improves the report performance because sections are rendered on an as-needed basis. The session management occurs only when the Report Server renders the report in HTML.

You will see more of the matrix region in chapter 6 when we discuss how to use expressions in crosstab reports to see forecasted data.

4.6 DESIGNING SUBREPORTS

A subreport is a report item that points to another report. As you have seen, RS gives you plenty of design choices, and in many cases you won't need to use subreports at all. There are two main situations, however, that will necessitate using subreports:

- *Reusing existing reports*—You can use the subreport region as a placeholder to host an existing report. For example, you may already have a company sales summary report, like one of the summary reports we created before. For easier maintenance, you might want to reuse the report. Each time you change the report, the change will be propagated to all reports of which this report is part. Also, in some cases you simply have no other choice.
- *Nesting report sections that use different datasets*—This will be the case when you need to nest a data region inside another region and each region uses a different dataset, as in the following example:

Imagine that the AWC management has requested that we change the Employee Sales Freeform with Chart report to show an Employee Performance Summary chart that outlines the employee sales for the past 12 months. In other words, the Employee Performance Summary chart needs to ignore the start date parameter and show the sales summary for the previous 12 months relative to the end date parameter.

For example, if the user has requested to see the Employee Sales report from 10/1/2003 to 12/1/2003, the Employee Performance Summary needs to show the monthly breakdown of employee sales starting with 1/1/2003, as shown in figure 4.32.

The report requirements call for creating a new dataset for the Employee Performance Summary chart. Our first impulse might be to base a chart region on the new dataset and nest it inside the list region. However, the chart region needs to follow the employee breakdown of the list region. In other words, the chart needs to be synchronized with the employee grouping of the list region.

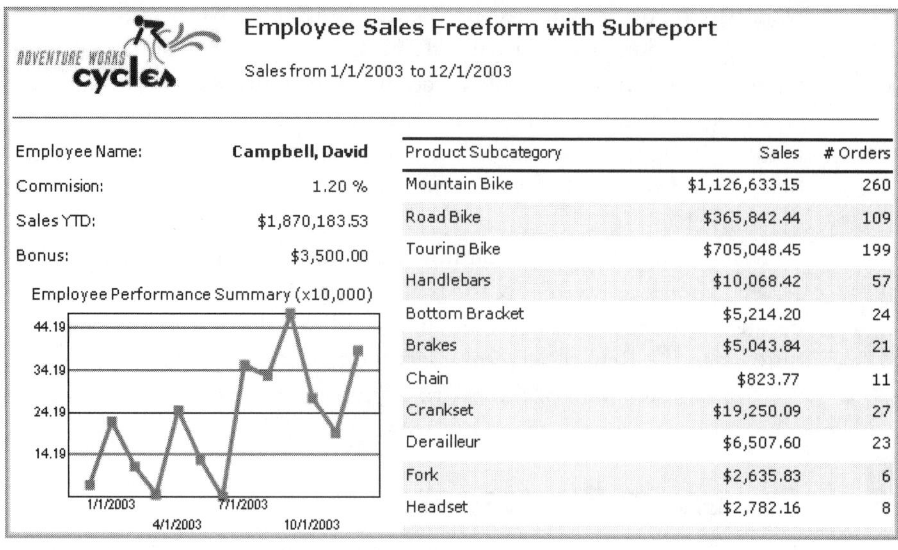

Figure 4.32 Use subreports when you need to nest report sections that draw data from separate datasets.

This presents a problem, though, because synchronized nested regions, which use the same groupings, must use the same dataset. The solution is to create a new subreport for the chart and synchronize the subreport with the main report. Let's create the Employee Performance subreport.

4.6.1 Laying out the report

There is really nothing different about creating a subreport than creating an ordinary report. As you know by now, we'll start by setting up the report data.

Setting up the report data

To create the report dataset, we used a free SQL statement as our dataset source, as shown below:

```
SELECT     E.EmployeeID, E.LastName + N', ' +
           E.FirstName AS EmployeeName,
           SUM(SOD.UnitPrice * SOD.OrderQty) AS Sales,
           COUNT(SOH.SalesOrderID) AS NoOrders,
           DATEPART(yy, SOH.OrderDate) AS Year,
           DATEPART(m, SOH.OrderDate) AS Month
FROM       SalesPerson SP
INNER JOIN SalesOrderHeader SOH
           ON SP.SalesPersonID = SOH.SalesPersonID
INNER JOIN Employee E ON SP.SalesPersonID = E.EmployeeID
INNER JOIN SalesOrderDetail SOD
           ON SOH.SalesOrderID = SOD.SalesOrderID
WHERE      (SOH.OrderDate BETWEEN DATEADD(mm, - 12, @Date)
           AND @Date)
```

```
AND         (E.EmployeeID = @EmployeeID)
GROUP BY    E.EmployeeID, E.LastName + N', ' + E.FirstName,
DATEPART    (m, SOH.OrderDate), DATEPART(yy, SOH.OrderDate)
ORDER BY    DATEPART(yy, SOH.OrderDate), DATEPART(m, SOH.OrderDate)
```

This statement groups the sales data per employee for the past year relative to the @Date parameter. It defines two parameters: EmployeeID and @Date. In addition, the statement breaks down the order date by month and year. This is needed to summarize the sales data per month. To achieve this, we created a new calculated dataset field called Date, which is based on the following expression:

```
= new DateTime (Fields!Year.Value, Fields!Month.Value,1)
```

This expression simply converts the month and year back to a date that starts at 12:00 A.M. We could have converted the date in the statement itself using SQL expressions, but we wanted to demonstrate calculated dataset fields.

Configuring the subreport

Next, let's use a chart region to present the data in graphical format. Figure 4.33 shows the subreport in a layout mode. You have already seen how to configure a chart, but this time the chart type is Line.

Once the subreport is created, we are ready to place it inside a subreport region. The easiest way to do that is to drag the report from the Solution Explorer and drop it inside the main report. Because we want to nest the subreport inside the lstEmployeeSales region, make sure you drop the subreport into the recEmployee rectangle.

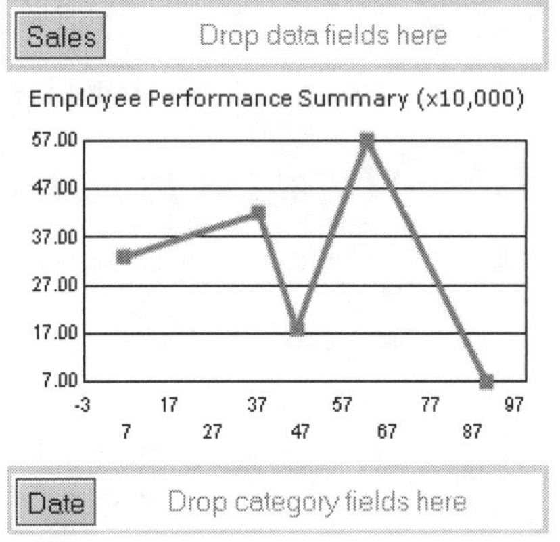

Figure 4.33 Creating a subreport is no different than creating an ordinary report.

4.6.2 Synchronizing the subreport with the master report

Finally, we need to synchronize both reports by passing the required parameters to the subreport. You can set the subreport parameters by using the VS.NET Properties window. Alternatively, you can right-click on the subreport, choose Properties, and select the Parameters tab from the Subreport Properties dialog, as shown in figure 4.34.

In our case, for the @Date parameter of the subreport we pass the @EndDate parameter of the main report. We link the @EmployeeID subreport parameter to the EmployeeID field of the main report dataset. As a result, each time the main report starts a new Employee group it passes the Employee ID to the subreport to display the summary data for that employee only.

Be careful to set all required subreport parameters. If you miss some or set them up incorrectly, the subreport will not be shown. Instead, the subreport region will report an exception, "Error: the subreport could not be shown."

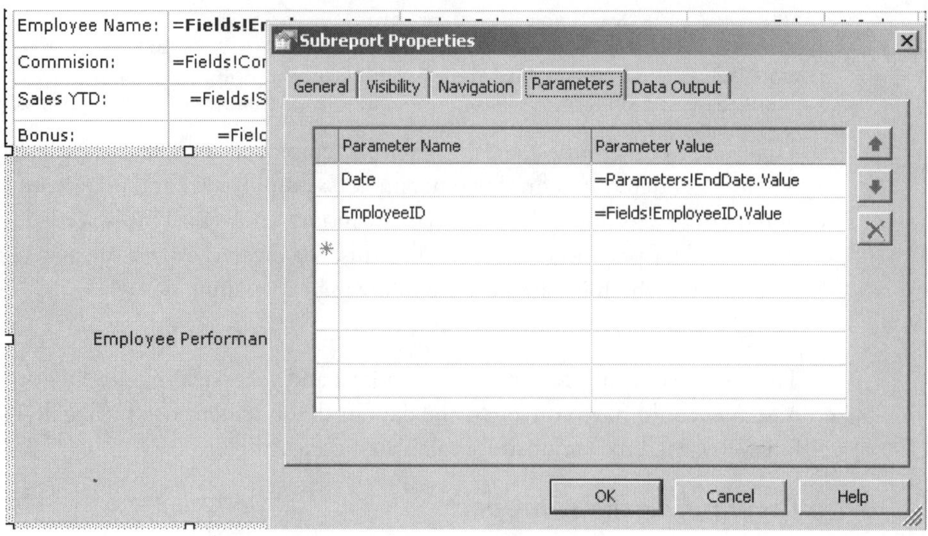

Figure 4.34 Integrating the main report with a subreport

4.7 DESIGNING MULTICOLUMN REPORTS

The Report Designer allows you to easily create multicolumn (shaking) reports. Just like a newspaper, a multicolumn report can conserve space by displaying the report data in more than one column.

The Products by Subcategory report demonstrates how you can author such reports, as shown in figure 4.35.

Let's find out how we can split the report data in multiple columns.

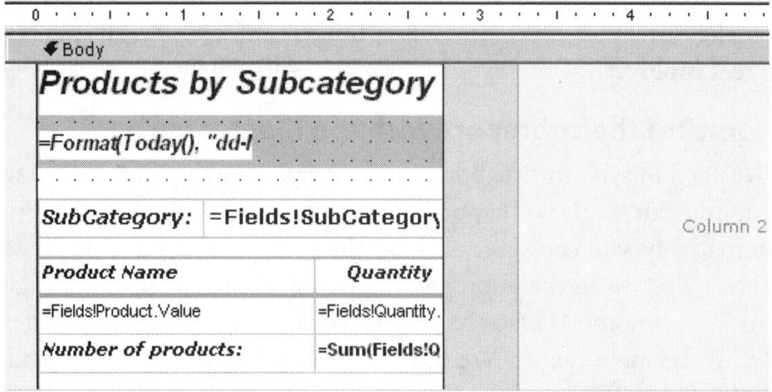

Figure 4.35 Creating multicolumn reports with Reporting Services is easy.

Products by Subcategory

05-Apr-2004

SubCategory: Bike Racks

Product Name	*Quantity*
Hitch rack - 4 bike	0
Number of products:	**0**

SubCategory: Bike Stand

Product Name	*Quantity*
All-purpose bike stand	144
Number of products:	**144**

SubCategory: Bottles & Cages

Product Name	*Quantity*

SubCategory: Helmet

Product Name	*Quantity*
Sport-100 helmet, Black	324
Sport-100 helmet, Blue	216
Sport-100 helmet, Red	288
Number of products:	**828**

SubCategory: Hydration Pack

Product Name	*Quantity*
Hydration pack -70oz	108
Number of products:	**108**

SubCategory: Lights

Product Name	*Quantity*
Headlights - dual-beam	180
Headlights - weatherproof	216

SubCategory: Tires & Tubes

Product Name	*Quantity*
Patch kit with 8 patches	180
Number of products:	**180**

SubCategory: Mountain Bike

Product Name	*Quantity*
Mountain-100 Black, 38	99
Mountain-100 Black, 42	78
Mountain-100 Black, 44	49
Mountain-100 Black, 48	88
Mountain-100 Silver, 38	49
Mountain-100 Silver, 42	88
Mountain-100 Silver, 44	83
Mountain-100 Silver, 48	62
Mountain-200 Black, 38	100

Figure 4.36 The Products by Subcategory report in a design mode

4.7.1 Setting up multiple columns

The report shows the product inventory data arranged in three columns to conserve paper space. The trick to creating this report is to make sure that the report data width doesn't exceed the column width, as shown in figure 4.36.

To create the report, we used a list region for the subcategory section and a nested table region for the product details. We set the body width of the report to 2.75 in. To achieve the multicolumn layout, we went to the Report Properties dialog (select

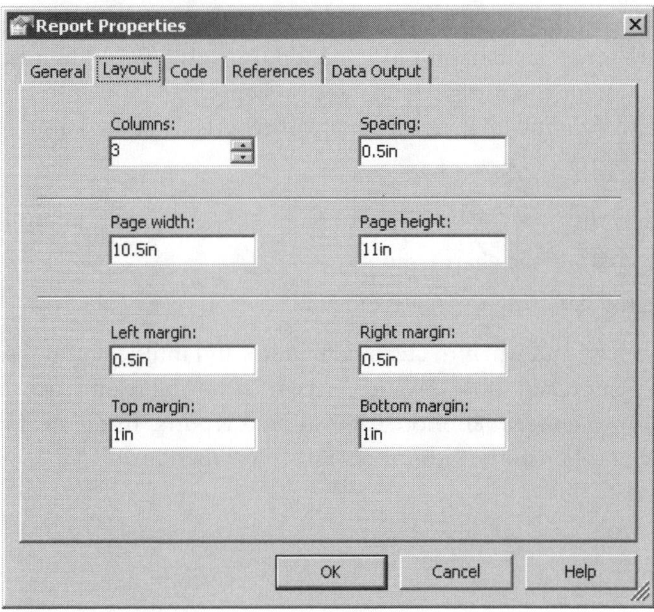

Figure 4.37 Setting up the number of columns

the report by clicking the Report Selector, right-click, and choose Properties) and set the number of columns to 3, as shown in figure 4.37.

Currently, RS supports defining multiple columns only at the report level. You cannot, for example, define a multicolumn layout per region, for example, a table region.

4.7.2 Testing multicolumn reports

When setting up the column widths, you have to ensure that you have enough page space to accommodate the number of columns, per the formula below:

```
Page width-(left margin + right margin) >= number of columns *
column width + (number of columns - 1) * column spacing
```

The Report Designer makes the trial-and-error fitting game unnecessary by showing you the outline of the columns in layout mode. This allows you to easily see whether the report width exceeds the page width.

A final note: to see the report rendered correctly in multiple columns, make sure that you preview the report using the Print Preview button. If you just preview the report, you won't see the data flowing in columns because the preview mode doesn't take in consideration the page settings.

4.8 SUMMARY

One of main strengths of RS is that it gives us the right tools to easily design many different types of reports. The Report Designer enables even novice users to create professional-looking reports in a matter of minutes. We've seen that the report data regions give us a lot of flexibility for laying out our reports. We've discussed the effects of data region nesting and using regions side by side.

We've also shown how to create a variety of reports using regions:

- Tabular reports use the table region.
- Freeform reports use the list region.
- Chart reports use the chart region.
- Crosstab reports using the matrix region.

We've seen also how and when to create subreports and multicolumn reports.

Now, it is time to add more advanced report authoring techniques to our arsenal that will help us to create even more sophisticated reports. In the next chapter we'll learn how to enhance reports with expressions and functions.

4.9 RESOURCES

The Dundas Software web site (http://www.dundas.com/)

Creating crosstab reports using SQL statements with Microsoft SQL Server http://msdn.microsoft.com/library/default.asp?url=/library/en-us/acdata/ac_8_qd_14_04j7.asp

CHAPTER 5

Using expressions and functions

Sometimes, reporting requirements may call for advanced techniques that go beyond the scope of the Report Designer. For example, you may need to implement conditional formatting to change the color of report items based on the some conditions.

Most modern reporting tools support programming primitives of some sort that developers can use to write expressions and programmatically manipulate report elements. In this chapter, we will explore how we can use expressions and functions with Reporting Services to enhance the report capabilities.

Our discussion will cover the following topics:

- Writing expressions
- Working with the Report Object Model global collections
- Using functions
- Using expressions to author reports with interactive features
- Examining RS export formats and how formatting can impact the interactive features of a report
- Creating localized reports

To round out this chapter, we will show how we can use expressions to add interactive features to our reports, including reports with navigational features and reports with document maps.

5.1 UNDERSTANDING EXPRESSIONS

An RS *expression* is custom code written in Visual Basic .NET that uses a combination of keywords, operators, functions, and constant values to calculate the value of a report item or its properties during runtime. You are already familiar with one of most basic type of inline expressions: the field expression. We used field expressions on many occasions to display the value of a dataset field by referencing the Fields collection, for example, `=Fields!Sales.Value`.

You have probably used expressions with other reporting tools to achieve some degree of runtime customization, such as implementing calculated fields. For example, say you want to combine the employee first and last names into one string to set the value of a textbox report item called txtEmployeeName. With RS, you can achieve this by using the following inline expression for the Value property of the textbox:

```
= Fields!FirstName.Value & " " & Fields!LastName.Value
```

RS does not limit your use of expressions to setting values of textbox report items. Instead, by using expressions you can manipulate programmatically just about any property of a report item and region.

NOTE In my opinion, Reporting Services is a bit too expression-oriented. For example, using expressions is the only way to programmatically change the values and properties of report items, because you cannot reference them outside expressions. Trying to change the value of a textbox item inside custom code is not possible because its value is read-only.

I personally hope future releases will deemphasize the use of expressions. As a developer accustomed to writing event-driven code, I feel challenged by the prospect of scattering expressions all over the report. Haven't we passed the spaghetti-code era yet? Besides, it will present a maintenance issue for more complicated reports. Similar to the ASP.NET code-behind paradigm, my dream reporting programming model would support structured event handling.

Memorizing the expression syntax can be tedious. To address this, the Report Designer offers you a helping hand by giving you an Expression Editor.

5.1.1 Using the Expression Editor

The Report Designer allows you to write report expressions by typing the expression text manually or using the Expression Editor. You will probably find the first method handy when you want to quickly change the expression text or enter simple expressions. For example, you can click inside a text box and directly type a field expression to bind the textbox to a dataset field, e.g., `=Fields!Sales.Value`.

Alternatively, you can use the Expression Editor. To open the editor, use one of the following options from within the Report Designer:

- Using the item's VS.NET Properties window, choose the Expression item from the available options for any property that can be manipulated by an expression, for example, the TextBox.Value property.
- From the item's Properties dialog (right-click the item and choose Properties), click the *fx* button located to the right of any property that supports expressions.
- As a shortcut when entering an expression for the textbox Value property, you can right-click the textbox and choose Expression from the context menu.

Figure 5.1 shows the Expression Editor, which we brought up by right-clicking one of the textboxes inside the Employee Sales Freeform report and choosing Expression from the context menu.

As shown in figure 5.1, in this case the Expression Editor shows the fields of the dsEmployeeSales dataset. As far as manipulating the expression itself, the Expression Editor gives you options to replace the selected text, insert the expression at the cursor location, or append the expression at the end by choosing the proper button located in the center of the dialog.

The Expression Editor doesn't validate the expression in any way. Sorry, no IntelliSense either! Have you started missing the VS.NET editor yet?

For your convenience, the three most used *collections* from the Report Server object model (Globals, Parameters, and Fields) are shown on the left side of the dialog, so you don't have to memorize the names of their members. We will revisit these collections in section 5.2.

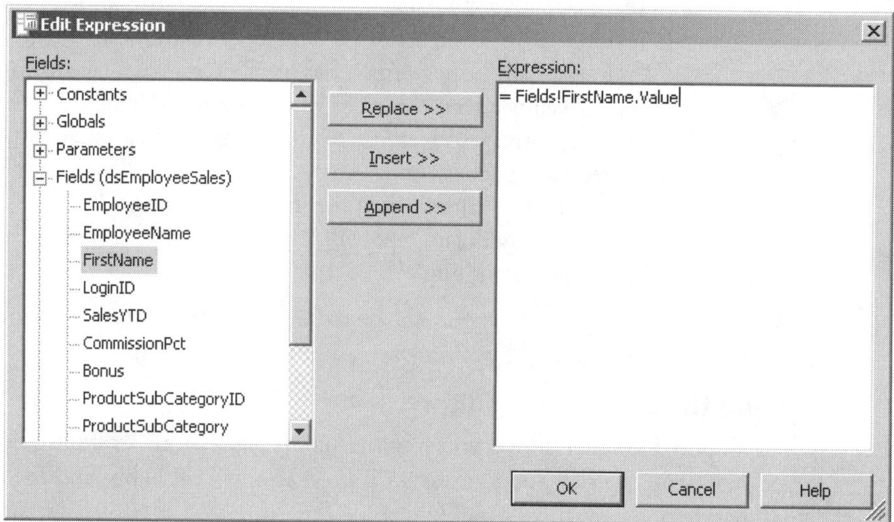

Figure 5.1 Use the Expression Editor to create expressions.

5.1.2 Expression syntax

As we explained in chapter 3, the Report Designer verifies the expression syntax during the report-building process. Just as with any programming environment, you need to learn to play by the compiler's rules. There are a few syntax-related rules about expressions worth mentioning before we see some examples.

First, because you author expressions in VB.NET, the expression syntax is not case-sensitive. For this reason, fields!Sales.value and Fields!Sales.Value are interchangeable. Be aware, though, that for some reason RS requires that the field names match exactly the dataset field names despite the fact the Visual Basic is not case-sensitive. If they don't, a compilation exception is thrown. For example, if the dataset field is SalesYTD but you use Fields!salesYTD in your expression, the Report Designer errors out with the following exception:

```
The value expression for the textbox 'txtTerritorySalesYTDTotal' refers to
the field 'salesYTD'.  Report item expressions can only refer to fields
within the current data set scope or, if inside an aggregate, the specified
data set scope.
```

Second, to tell RS that you want to use an expression, you must prefix the expression text with an equal sign (=). I've personally forgotten about this rule countless times! The Report Designer reacts in different ways to remind you about this rule. For example, if you type the expression in the Properties window, an invalid property exception dialog is shown. Or, it won't complain at all for textbox values. In this case, the Report Designer will assume that you are entering static text, which will be shown as-is when the report is rendered.

Besides these two rules, your expression syntax needs to comply with the syntax of VB.NET. For VB.NET language reference, please check the VS.NET product documentation.

5.1.3 Determining expression execution order

The Report Server has a rule processor that involves some sophisticated decision making to determine the order in which the expressions are executed. For the lack of a better term, we will refer to it as an expression sequence processor. When the processor parses expressions, it also discovers any interdependencies that may exist and ranks the expressions accordingly. For example, say you have three textbox items, A, B, and C, inside a list region. A gets its value from a dataset field. B references A, and C references B. The expression sequence processor will discover that these expressions are interdependent and sort their execution order accordingly. In our example, the value of A will be set first, followed by the values of B and then C.

If the expressions are not interdependent, our experiments show that they are executed sequentially according to their location in the report. For example, expressions that set properties of the Body band are executed before the expressions in items located in the body section. Is this important? Well, knowing the order in which the expression will be executed allows you to write "pseudo" events to do some preprocessing to compensate for the lack of "real" events in Reporting Services.

Say you want to initialize some class-level variables in custom code before you call a custom function inside an expression. Also assume that the expression is used to set the value of a textbox item in a table region. Because currently Reporting Services doesn't support events, you may think that you are of out of luck. However, you can use an expression in the Body band, for example, an expression to set the BorderStyle property, which will fire before the table region is rendered.

Because there is only one Body band inside the report, this expression will fire once, which is exactly what you want in order to perform the initialization tasks. Inside the expression you can call a method in the custom code, which will set the required state. As you will see in chapter 8, this is exactly the approach we take to author the Show Security Policy report, so we can initialize the Report Server web service proxy before we call its methods.

5.1.4 Understanding expression scope

One of the things that you need to consider when referencing report items in expressions is the concept of *expression scope*. Simply put, the expression scope defines the boundaries in which the expression can operate. Each dataset, region, and grouping defines a scope. The scope rules can get complicated, but the simple rule of thumb is that an expression cannot reference other items outside its current or containing (outer) scope.

The following example should make this clear. Consider the report layout shown in figure 5.2.

You may find this layout similar to that of the Employee Sales by Territory with Summary Advanced report we created in the chapter 4. Here, we have a table region A placed side-by-side with a list region and another table region B nested inside the list. This layout defines several scopes, including

- A scope of the report body section
- A scope of table region A
- A scope of the list region
- A scope of table region B

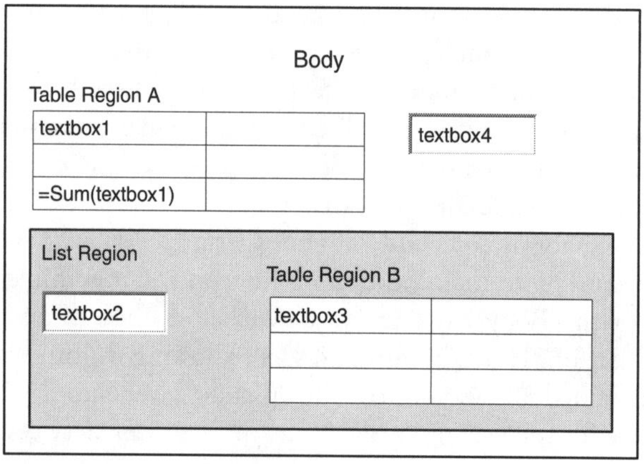

Figure 5.2
Each dataset, region, and grouping defines an expression scope.

There may be other scopes, such as those for groups defined inside a region. Based on the current or containing scope rule we mentioned before, there are some valid and invalid reference combinations, as shown in table 5.1.

Table 5.1 Expression reference examples

Valid References	Invalid References
An expression for the value of textbox3 that references textbox2.	An expression for the value of textbox2 that references textbox3. (Table region B is nested in the list region and it is not in the list's current or containing scope.)
An expression for the value of textbox3 that references textbox4. (The table region is inside the body region.) However, an expression for the value of textbox4 cannot reference textbox3.	An expression for the value of textbox3 that references textbox1 and vice versa; an expression for the value of textbox1 that references textbox3; neither can it reference textbox2.

How about referencing the `SUM()` aggregate in table region A from either the list region or table region B? At first, you might think that this is not possible because table A is not in the containing scope of both regions. But as with every rule there are exceptions, and the truth is that this combination is allowed. The exception here seems to be a result of the fact that an expression can reference an aggregate value regardless of its scope.

At first, the scope rules may seem mind-boggling, but with some experience it gets easier. Besides, the Report Designer is kind enough to remind us each time we fail to comply to this rule with one of the following two exceptions:

```
The value expression for the textbox '<textboxname>' refers to the report
item '<reportitemname>'.  Report item expressions can only refer to other
report items within the same grouping scope or a containing grouping scope.
```

Or, if the referenced textbox gets its value from a dataset field:

```
The value expression for the textbox '<textboxname>' refers to the field
'<reportitemname>'.  Report item expressions can only refer to fields within
the current data set scope or, if inside an aggregate, the specified data
set scope.
```

5.1.5 Dealing with expression errors

Similar to programming in other languages, report expression code goes through compilation and execution phases. When you build the report or just request to preview it, the Report Designer parses the report expressions to ensure that the code you entered actually makes sense. If there are syntax and reference errors, the Report Designer informs you about them by showing an error message in the Preview tab, as shown in figure 5.3.

The compilation errors are shown in the Task List. The error messages seem to be very descriptive and informative. For example, if we misspell the name of the Sales dataset field as Sale (Fields!Sale.Value), the exception text pinpoints the exact problem:

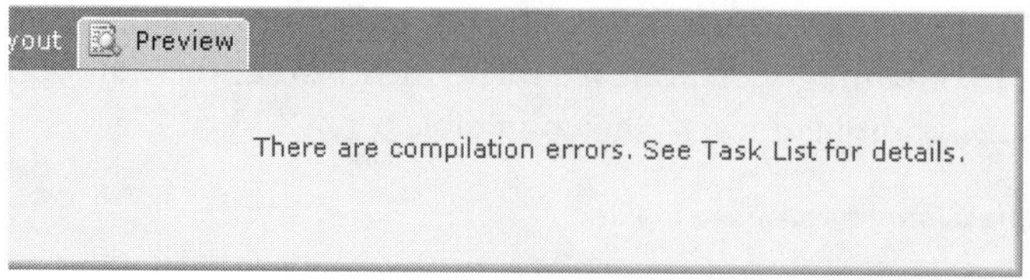

Figure 5.3 If an expression cannot be compiled, an error message is shown in the Preview tab.

```
The value expression for the textbox 'txtSales' refers to the field 'Sale'.
Report item expressions can only refer to fields within the current data set
scope or, if inside an aggregate, the specified data set scope.
```

When the exception references a report item, you can double-click on the exception text to navigate to the item and inspect it.

Some error conditions are discovered only during runtime. For example, you may have an expression for a calculated field that results in a division-by-zero exception. The way in which runtime errors are reported depends on how the expression is used. If the expression is used to get the value of a textbox, #Error is shown in the textbox. Otherwise, the exception is ignored. For example, if you have an expression to conditionally change the color of a line item from black to red, and the expression errors out, it will be ignored and the line will be shown in black.

The most common source of runtime errors, which will probably bite you at the beginning, is omitting the Value property when you reference dataset fields, for example, Fields!Sales as opposed to Fields!Sales.Value. Because Fields!Sales references an object of type field, you will get a runtime error with #Error as the textbox value without any other complaints from the Report Designer.

Circular references are not allowed even if the expression scope is valid. For example, if textbox A references textbox B and textbox B references textbox A, you won't get a compilation error, but when the report is rendered, the value of B will be set to #Error.

To make programming with expressions easier, RS exposes report items as collections referred to as the Report Services Object Model.

5.2 EXPLORING THE REPORT OBJECT MODEL

To use expressions in your reports, you have to have a good grasp of the Report Object Model. Reporting Services offers a simplified object model, exposed in the form of global object collections that you can reference in your expressions.

The Report Object Model can be referenced only internally, that is, from code running inside the report. You cannot instantiate a report object externally, as you might have been accustomed to doing with other reporting tools and applications. For example, Microsoft Access exposes its object model as an externally creatable object of type Access.Application that external callers can instantiate using OLE Automation.

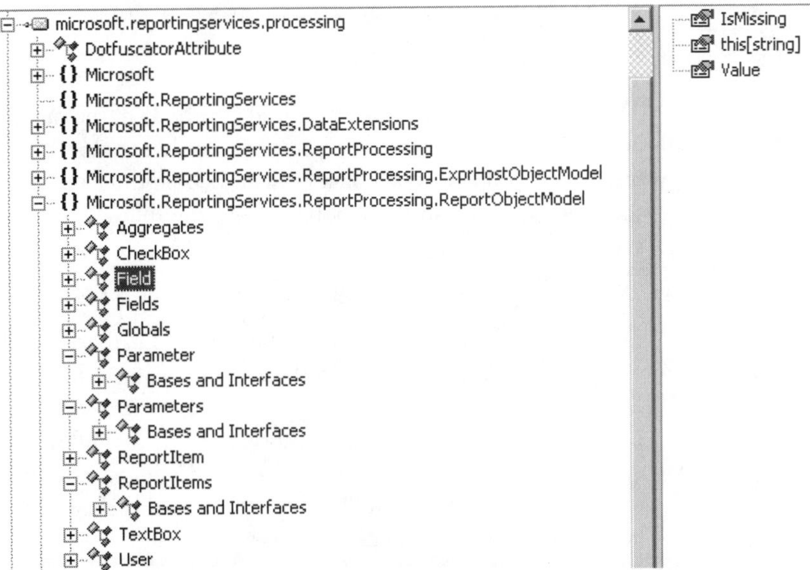

Figure 5.4 The Report Object Model is implemented in the Microsoft. ReportingServices.Processing assembly. It contains five object collections that you can access programmatically in expressions or custom code.

At first, the inability to create and manipulate the Report Object Model from outside might seem restrictive. In my opinion, though, I see it as a compromise, given the other advantages that the Reporting Services architecture has to offer. You may understand this better if you consider the fact that the RS architecture is entirely server-based. The RS process lifetime is not controlled by the client application. Instead, Reporting Services runs in its own process and, thanks to its service-oriented architecture, any consumer capable of submitting HTTP GET and SOAP requests can access it. Because RS runs in its own process, it is not possible to instantiate an RS object locally.

The object model is implemented in the Microsoft.ReportingServices.Processing assembly, under the `Microsoft.ReportingServices.ReportProcessing.ReportObjectModel` namespace, as shown in figure 5.4.

You can find the Microsoft.ReportingServices.Processing assembly in the Report Server binary folder (C:\Program Files\Microsoft SQL Server\MSSQL\Reporting Services\ReportServer\bin) or in the Report Designer folder (C:\Program Files\Microsoft SQL Server\80\Tools\Report Designer). To browse the object model using the VS.NET Object Browser, create a new C# or VB.NET project, reference this assembly, and press Ctrl-Alt-J.

NOTE How do I know where the Report Object Model is implemented? When I was experimenting with the object model, I wrote a simple but useful function called `ShowItem`, which you can find in the AWC.RS.Library assembly, as shown in the following:

```
public static string ShowItem( object item){
return "Success";
}
```

The idea was to put a breakpoint inside the body of the function, so I could break when I called it from expressions inside the report. For example, to inspect the properties of a dataset field, I could drag and drop a field from the report dataset on the report and use the following expression for the textbox value:

```
=AWC.RS.Library.RsLibrary.ShowItem(Fields!<field name>)
```

Once I break inside the `ShowItem` function, I can explore the item argument in the Watch window. In the case of passing a dataset field, the type of the argument was `Microsoft.ReportingServices.ReportProcessing.ReportObjectModel.Field`. Following this hint, I open the Microsoft.ReportingServices.Processing assembly, which reveals the object model shown in figure 5.4. Later in this chapter, I will show you how to debug code in an external assembly.

As we said in chapter 3, the only two ways to control the report output are externally by using parameters and internally by using expressions.

As we mentioned already, currently the RS Report Object Model doesn't support events. Personally, I hope a future release will change this and introduce an eventing mechanism, similar to the one found in Microsoft Access. For example, a BeforeReportStart event could make it possible for developers to write a custom event handler to check some business rules and, if certain conditions are not met, stop the report processing and throw an exception. Or, such an event could make it possible to perform some report preprocessing before the report is rendered.

The Report Object Model exposes five collections that are accessible to you as a developer, as listed in table 5.2.

Table 5.2 RS exposes valuable runtime information in the form of five read-only collections.

Collection	Purpose
ReportItems	Exposes the textbox items in the report
Fields	Wraps the fields of a report dataset
Globals	Encapsulates some global report properties, such as the number of pages
Parameters	Represents the report parameters
User	Includes user-related properties

You can access the items in these collections using all variations of the standard Visual Basic collection syntax: `Collection!ItemName`, `Collection("ItemName")`, and `Collection.Item("ItemName")`. Because the `Collection!ItemName` syntax is the shortest of the three, we will use it the most. The items inside the Globals and User collections are also exposed as properties and can be accessed by `Collection.ItemName`.

Let's now discuss each of these collections and how they can be used.

5.2.1 Using the ReportItems collection

The ReportItems collection contains all textbox report items of the type `Microsoft.ReportingServices.ReportProcessing.ReportObjectModel.ReportItem`. It allows the report author to reference the values of other textbox items subject to the scope rules we discussed previously. Please note that we said textbox items, because the collection contains nothing else.

NOTE Strictly speaking, the ReportItem class serves as a base type, which the objects inside the ReportItems collection derive from. For example, if you pass a textbox item to the `ShowItem` function, mentioned previously, you will see that its type is `Microsoft.ReportingServices.ReportProcessing.ReportObjectModel.TextBox` and it inherits from ReportItem. In addition, if you examine the `Microsoft.ReportingServices.ReportProcessing.ReportObjectModel` namespace in the Object Browser or .NET Reflector, you will find out that there is a `CheckBox` type defined, which is not currently used. I expect the Report Object Model to evolve in the future and ReportItems collections to include additional report items besides textboxes.

You would expect the ReportItems collection to include all report items placed on the report (not just textboxes), but this is not the case. Why? Because with version 1.0 of Reporting Services the report item properties can be changed only by expressions and the textbox values are read-only, there is really no good reason to do so. I hope the next version will enhance the object model to expose not only all report items but also their properties (in read-write mode) similar to the WinForm and ASP.NET object models.

Even better, a future RS object model could support creating report items dynamically in code. This would make it possible to generate report sections conditionally. For instance, a Body_OnLoad event handler could check some business rules and generate different report regions based on the result, such as a chart or tabular region. For now, the best you can do is to hide a region pragmatically by using an expression.

Implementing conditional formatting

A common requirement is to add conditional formatting features to reports, where the visual appearance of report items (font, color, size, and so on) changes based on some runtime conditions. Consider an example to demonstrate how the ReportItems collection could be used to customize the appearance of textbox report items.

Let's change the Employee Sales by Territory with Summary report to check whether the salesperson has exceeded a certain goal, e.g., $2,500,000. If she has exceeded her goal, the report will show an indicator and highlight the person's name

Territory: Central			
Employee Name:	**Caro, Fernando**	Product Subcategory	Sales
Commission:	1.50 %	Road Bike	$2,083,024.71
Sales YTD:	$1,958,815.81	Mountain Bike	$1,114,406.63
Bonus:	$2,500.00	Road Frame	$352,405.13
Exceeded Goal!		Touring Bike	$302,816.90
		Mountain Frame	$255,327.66
		Touring Frame	$44,790.62

Figure 5.5 Using expressions to implement conditional formatting

in bold. I saved the revised version of the report as Employee Sales by Territory with Summary Advanced.

Figure 5.5 shows what the report looks like when a salesperson has exceeded the goal. Please note that the conditional formatting is based on the Sales total amount (not shown on figure 5.5) and not on the Sales YTD amount.

To implement the new report features, we added a new textbox called txtExceeded-Goal inside the recEmployee rectangle and set its value to Exceeded Goal! and its foreground color to red. Then, in the Advanced Textbox Properties dialog (right-click txtExceededGoal, choose Properties, and in the TextBox Properties dialog click the Advanced button), we set its initial visibility to be based on the expression shown in figure 5.6.

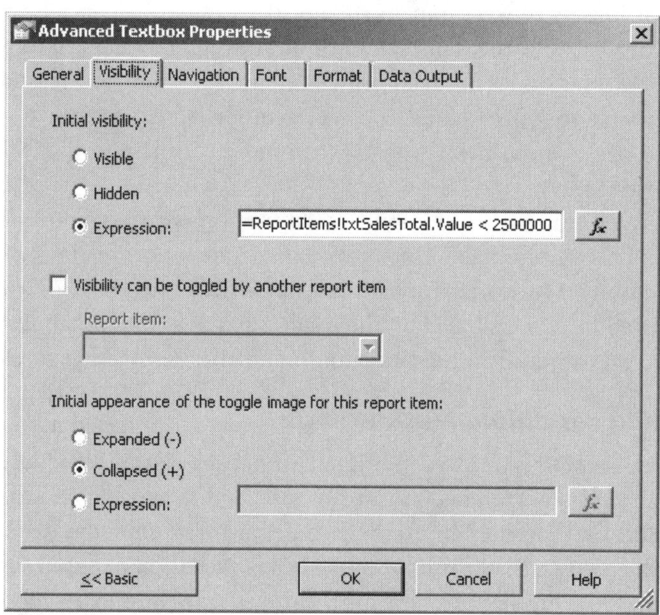

Figure 5.6 Using an expression to format conditionally the visibility of the txtExceededGoal textbox

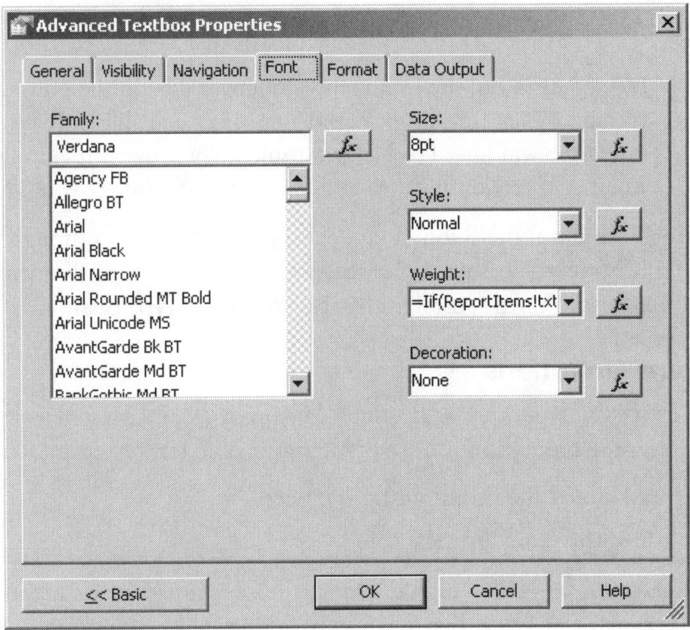

Figure 5.7 Using an expression to set the font weight of the txtEmployeeName textbox

To retrieve the employee sales total, we used the txtSalesTotal textbox, which happens to be the one that holds the sales total amount in the tblEmployeeSales table. In terms of performance, this is also the fastest way to get to the aggregate figure, because we don't have to recalculate it. We used the 2,500,000 threshold to toggle the visibility of txtExceededGoal. Strangely, the Boolean logic for the initial visibility is reversed. If the expression evaluates to false, the item is visible; otherwise it is hidden.

Similarly, to change the font of the txtEmployeeName field to bold, we implemented this expression:

```
=Iif(ReportItems!txtSalesTotal.Value < 2500000, "Normal", "Bold")
```

Figure 5.7 shows this expression in the Weight field of the Advanced Textbox Properties dialog:

The VB.NET `Iif` operator will be probably the one you will most often use in your expressions. In this case, if the sales total is less than the targeted amount, the font weight is normal; otherwise it is bold.

When the three-part `Iif` syntax gets in the way, you may find the `Switch` function useful. For example, if we wanted to check for more than one condition and change the color of txtSalesTotal accordingly, we could have used the `Switch` function, as shown here:

```
=Switch(ReportItems!txtSalesTotal.Value < 2500000, "Red",
ReportItems!txtSalesTotal.Value >= 250000 AND
```

```
ReportItems!txtSalesTotal.Value < 500000, "Yellow",
ReportItems!txtSalesTotal.Value >= 500000, "Green")
```

NOTE For some reason, the font color is not available on the Font tab under the Advanced TextBox Properties dialog. It is available only on the VS.NET Properties window. To change the font color programmatically, expand the Color property drop-down and select its first item, <Expression…>.

An interesting note about the ReportItem.Value property is that although it references the value in a textbox item, it preserves the underlying data type. For this reason, we were able to reference the sales total amount without any type casting.

ReportItems limitations

These two expressions get the work done. However, as any seasoned developer will point out, our implementation is not very maintainable for two primary reasons:

- We've hard-coded the threshold figure twice.
- We've coded the same business rule twice.

The first issue could be easily corrected by defining a constant in custom embedded code for this report. The second issue could be addressed by moving the business logic inside a VB.NET function defined in embedded code or an external assembly, as we will discuss in chapter 6. The custom function could then return a Boolean value that we can evaluate in both expressions.

What if we want to get rid of expressions altogether? For instance, can we replace both expressions in our case with a call to a single function or use an internal event to centralize all formatting and data manipulation logic in a single place? We've already said that RS doesn't support events, so the event option is out. What about the first option? Can we write a function and pass the whole ReportItems collection? Unfortunately, the answer is no.

First, the ReportItems collection exposes only the textbox items inside the report, so we don't have access to data regions and other report items. You might say that in our case this is not an issue, because we want to manipulate only textboxes anyway. However, it so happens that the Value property is the only property available to us. Second, to make the things even more difficult, the Value property is read-only. In other words, if we decide to get innovative and pass the txtExceededGoal and txtEmployeeName items as objects to a custom function, we won't get too far because we cannot change the textbox value inside the function. As you are starting to see, the current Reporting Services programming model leaves some space for future improvements.

So, to recap, the ReportItems collection contains all textbox report items inside the report, and each ReportItem object has one read-only, publicly accessible property, Value. This means that the only way to change the textbox value programmatically is to attach an expression to the Value property inside the Report Designer. By the way, to reference the value of the current textbox item, you can use Me.Value or just Value.

5.2.2 Using the Fields collection

The Fields collection exposes the fields (columns) from a given row of the report dataset as objects of the type `Microsoft.ReportingServices.ReportProcessing.ReportObjectModel.Field`. .NET developers can draw an analogy between the RS Field object and DataColumn of the ADO.NET DataTable class. Unlike the DataColumn class, however, each Field object inside the Fields collection has only two public read-only properties, Value and IsMissing.

The Value property can return one of the following:

- Nothing (null in C#), in case there is missing data or the data is NULL. To check for Nothing you can use the VB.NET function `IsNothing()` or `<fieldname.Value> Is Nothing`.
- The field value, whose type is cast to one of the standard .NET data types, such as Int32, DateTime, and so on. The type translation that Reporting Services performs behind the scenes is great because it allows you reference the field value directly in strongly typed .NET functions. For example, you might recall that for the Year column in the Territory Sales Crosstab report we used the expression Fields!Date.Value.Year. This was possible because the value of the Date field was exposed as a .NET DateTime structure.

Dealing with null and missing values

Unfortunately, the automatic conversion that RS does to translate NULL values and missing data to Nothing may be more trouble than it is worth because sometimes you do need to differentiate between both conditions. For example, in a matrix report you may need to react in a different way when there is no data for a given row and column combination and when the aggregate value is NULL.

One workaround is to replace the NULL values at the data source or in the report query statement with whatever value makes sense, e.g., 'NULL'. Then, you can write a simple VB.NET function like the one below to check for both conditions:

```
Function GetValue(value As Object) As Object
        If value is Nothing Then
            Return "N/A"  ' missing data
        Else
            Return value  ' has value or 'NULL'
        End If
   End Function
```

Another way to differentiate between missing data and NULL values is to base the textbox on an expression that uses the `CountRows()` function. We will see an example of how this could be implemented in chapter 6.

Checking for missing fields

To make dealing with missing values more confusing, the Field object exposes a property called IsMissing. It is important to note that it doesn't check for missing values. Instead, it returns true if the field is not found in the report dataset. If you trying to understand the practical use of this, consider the case when the report dataset is returned by a call to a stored procedure.

For example, consider the Employee Sales by Territory report that we developed in the previous chapter to show employee performance. Users belonging to various security roles, such as administrators and clerks, can request this report. In the second case, you might not want to reveal the employee-sensitive information, such commissions and bonuses.

You can hide these fields using expressions. Alternatively, you can pass a parameter to the spGetEmployeeSalesByProductSubcategory stored procedure to exclude these fields entirely. If you use the latter approach, you can use the IsMissing property to exclude these fields from expressions that use them. If you don't check whether they are available, they will show #Error.

Finally, the Field object also implements an indexer. Currently, its implementation returns NULL. The next version of Reporting Services may include additional properties that data providers, such as the SQL Server .NET provider, could return.

Using the Fields collection in expressions

Here's an example showcasing the Fields collection. We'll change the Employee Sales by Territory with Summary Advanced report and replace the # Orders column with the Percentage of Employee's Total column. The new column will show the sales amount for each product subcategory as a percentage of the sales total, as shown in figure 5.8.

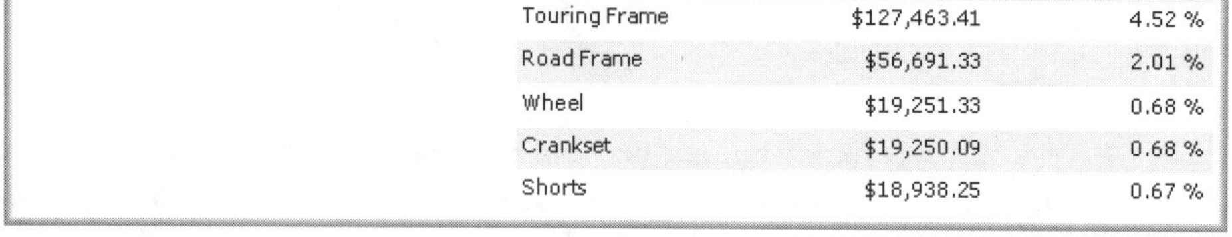

Territory: Northwest

Employee Name:	**Campbell, David**
Commission:	1.20 %
Sales YTD:	$1,870,183.53
Bonus:	$3,500.00
Exceeded Goal!	

Product Subcategory	Sales	Percentage of Employee's Total
Mountain Bike	$1,126,633.15	39.94 %
Touring Bike	$705,048.45	25.00 %
Road Bike	$365,842.44	12.97 %
Mountain Frame	$286,903.94	10.17 %
Touring Frame	$127,463.41	4.52 %
Road Frame	$56,691.33	2.01 %
Wheel	$19,251.33	0.68 %
Crankset	$19,250.09	0.68 %
Shorts	$18,938.25	0.67 %

Figure 5.8 Using the Fields collection to implement the calculated field Percentage of Employee's Total

To implement the new requirements, we have to change the expression of the corresponding textbox item to

```
=Fields!Sales.Value/ReportItems!txtSalesTotal.Value
```

To express the data as a percentage, we changed the textbox format accordingly.

Another way of implementing Percentage of Employee's Total is to rewrite the above expression to use the txtSales report item, as follows:

```
= ReportItems!txtSales.Value/ReportItems!txtSalesTotal.Value
```

So, should we use the ReportItems or Fields collection? In terms of performance, there is really not that much difference, because both are exposed internally as collections. However, if we need to use an aggregate or calculated result that is already available in a textbox, we would reference it using the ReportItems collection. For example, the above expression will produce the same result, if it is changed to

```
=Fields!Sales.Value/Sum(Fields!Sales.Value)
```

This expression, however, will calculate the sales total for each row in the tblEmployeeSales table, which is less efficient than getting the value from the txtSalesTotal textbox.

5.2.3 Using the Parameters collection

The Parameters collection exposes the report parameters as objects of the type `Microsoft.ReportingServices.ReportProcessing.ReportObjectModel.Parameter`. Each Parameter object has two publicly accessible read-only properties: Label and Value.

Using parameter labels and values

As we saw in chapter 3, you can define a list of available values for a report parameter, and the list could be explicitly set or dataset-driven. Similarly to a drop-down control, if you decide to set available values, you can use a pair of values for each report parameter: a label for the visible portion and a value for the actual parameter value.

For example, in the Sales by Territory Interactive report, we used the TerritoryID column from the dsTerritory dataset as the parameter value and the Territory column as the parameter value. In this case, the Label and Value parameters map to the parameter Label and Value properties, respectively. If you don't use available values, the Label property returns Nothing, while the Value property returns the parameter value.

We have already seen examples that use the Parameters collection. For example, the Territory Sales Crosstab report has a subtitle (txtRange), which shows the requested date range using the passed parameter values.

Implementing dynamic sorting

Now look at another example that will demonstrate how we can leverage report parameters to implement dynamic sorting. We'll enhance the Sales by Territory report to sort the report data by category and sales. We saved the new version of the report as Sales by Territory with Sorting.

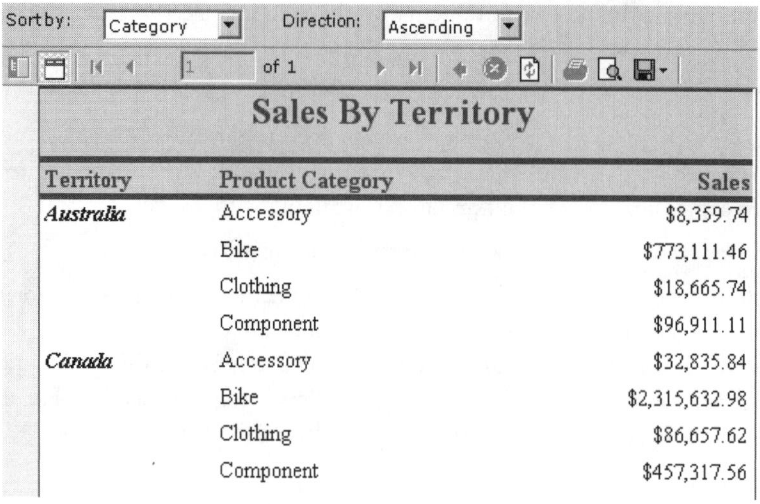

Sort by: Category Direction: Ascending

1 of 1

Sales By Territory

Territory	Product Category	Sales
Australia	Accessory	$8,359.74
	Bike	$773,111.46
	Clothing	$18,665.74
	Component	$96,911.11
Canada	Accessory	$32,835.84
	Bike	$2,315,632.98
	Clothing	$86,657.62
	Component	$457,317.56

Figure 5.9 Using the Parameters collection to implement dynamic sorting allows the user to specify which column to sort on and in which direction.

Figure 5.9 shows what our new sample report looks like.

The table region in version 1.0 of Reporting Services doesn't support dynamic sorting, e.g., by clicking on the table header. However, we can get around this limitation by setting up report parameters that the user can pass to specify which column to sort on and in which direction. For this reason, we defined two report parameters: SortBy and Direction.

Then, we set the Sorting tab in the table region properties, as shown in figure 5.10.

We sorted the table region data by Territory first. Then, we used two expressions to dynamically sort by either category or sales, based on the user selection. For example, if the user has selected to sort by sales in descending order, the third expression result will evaluate to Sales and the direction to Descending. If the condition is not met, the expression will return zero, which makes the table region ignore the expression.

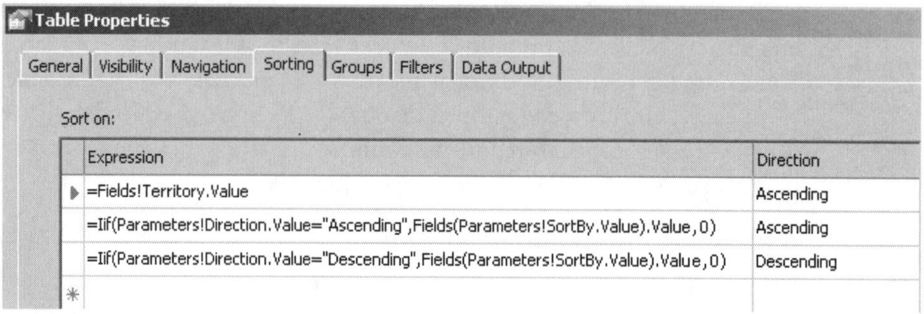

Table Properties

General | Visibility | Navigation | Sorting | Groups | Filters | Data Output

Sort on:

Expression	Direction
=Fields!Territory.Value	Ascending
=Iif(Parameters!Direction.Value="Ascending",Fields(Parameters!SortBy.Value).Value,0)	Ascending
=Iif(Parameters!Direction.Value="Descending",Fields(Parameters!SortBy.Value).Value,0)	Descending

Figure 5.10 Use the sorting properties to implement expression-based dynamic sorting.

5.2.4 Using the Globals collection

The Report Server exposes some useful global report properties in the Globals collection, as shown in table 5.3.

Table 5.3 The Globals collection includes some common report properties.

Property	.NET Data Type	Purpose
ExecutionTime	DateTime	The date and time when the Report Server started processing the report
PageNumber	Int32	The current page number
ReportFolder	String	The full path to the report, e.g., /AWReporter
ReportName	String	The report name, e.g., Territory Sales
ReportServerUrl	String	The Report Server URL, e.g., http://servername/Reports
TotalPages	Int32	The number of pages

The ExecutionTime property can come in handy when you experiment with report caching. We will discuss how caching affects the report execution process in chapter 7. When the Report Server determines that it can use the cached report copy, the report is not processed at all. Instead, the cached copy of the report is returned to the user. Hence, the ExecutionTime property will not change within the expiration period.

We have already used the ReportName property in some of the reports we created so far to display the report name as a report title.

The PageNumber and TotalPages properties can be used only inside the report page header and footer. For example, the Products by Category multicolumn report displays the current page in the page footer using the following expression:

```
="Page " & Globals.PageNumber
```

5.2.5 Using the User collection

Finally, the User collection contains information about the user who is currently requesting the report. Specifically, the User collection exposes the following two properties:

- *UserID*—When Windows authentication is used, UserID returns the Windows domain account of the user who runs the report. For example, if Terri has logged in as Terri to the adventure-works domain, the User.UserID will return adventure-works\Terri. If custom authentication is used, then UserID will return whatever the extension sets as a user principal. We will see an example of how we can use this property to enforce a secured access to report data in the next chapter.
- *Language*—The language ID of the user running the report, for example, en-US, if the language is set to English (United States). The Language property allows us to localize our reports, as we will see in section 5.5.

Often, to increase expression power, you will need to call some piece of prepackaged code, exposed as a function, as we will discuss next.

5.3 WORKING WITH FUNCTIONS

Reporting Services allows you to reference external and internal (native) functions. You can use external functions located in .NET standard or custom assemblies.

In addition, RS comes with some native functions that encapsulate commonly used programming logic, such as functions that produce aggregate values, count dataset rows, and so forth. We will discuss the RS native functions in section 5.3.2.

5.3.1 Referencing external functions

How you reference external functions depends on where the function is located. RS has two commonly used .NET assemblies pre-referenced for you: Microsoft.VisualBasic and mscorlib. Microsoft.VisualBasic contains the types that form the Visual Basic runtime. Mscorlib is a special .NET assembly that defines the .NET data types, such as System.String and System.Int32, as well as many frequently used functions and types defined under namespaces starting with System, such as `System.Collections` and `System.Diagnostics`.

The following namespaces from the above two assemblies have been already imported by RS, so you can use their types and methods without having to specify namespaces:

- *`Microsoft.VisualBasic`*—This namespace allows you to access many of the common VB runtime functions. For example, in the Territory Sales report, we used the VB.NET `Format` function located in the Microsoft.VisualBasic assembly to create a dynamic group, so we can group the report data by month. The expression we used for this purpose was `=Format(Fields!Date.Value, "MMM")`. Or, you can use the `MsgBox` function to help you while debugging your embedded code. As you will see in chapter 6, the Report Designer Code Editor has left a lot to be desired and doesn't provide debugging capabilities. Please remember, though, to remove the `MsgBox` calls before you deploy your report to the Report Server. If you don't, you will get #Error in all textboxes that reference functions with `MsgBox` in your embedded code.
- *`System.Convert`*—Allows you to perform runtime conversion between types, for example, from string to double using `System.Convert.ToDouble()`.
- *`System.Math`*—Provides constants and static methods for trigonometric, logarithmic, and other common mathematical functions.

To reference the rest of the System namespaces, you need to specify the fully qualified class name including the namespace. For example, if you need to use a collection of the type ArrayList in an expression, you have to use its fully qualified name, `System.Collections.ArrayList`.

To use functions located in other .NET assemblies, you need to reference the assembly first. We will discuss working with custom code in detail in chapter 6.

RS comes with a number of native functions that you can use in your expressions. Most of these functions are *aggregate* functions.

5.3.2 Using aggregate functions

Aggregate functions perform a calculation on set of values from data in datasets, data regions, and groupings and return a single value. Aggregate functions are often used with data region groups to produce data aggregates in the group footer.

We have already seen many examples where we used the most common aggregate function, `Sum()`, to get an aggregated total of the data, such as the Sales Total per employee or product category in the Employee Sales by Territory report.

Another aggregate function that we used to implement conditional formatting was the `RowNumber()` function. The `RowNumber()` function produces a running count of the rows within a specified scope. For example, in the Employee Sales by Territory report, we used `RowNumber` to alternate the background color for the rows in the tblEmployeeSales table region between white and beige. To achieve this effect, we used the following expression for the BackgroundColor property of the tblEmployeeSales table row to determine whether the row number is odd or even and to format it accordingly:

```
=Iif(RowNumber("tblEmployeeSales") Mod 2, "White", "Beige")
```

Understanding the aggregate scope

If you look at the syntax of the RS aggregate functions, you will notice that all of them take the argument Scope. This scope can be set to the name of a group, data region, or dataset. We have already talked about the expression scope, but we would like to discuss this concept once again in the context of aggregate functions.

To understand how scopes affect aggregates, please recall that a report can have multiple datasets and data regions. The data regions can coexist side-by-side or be nested one within the other. But how does an aggregate function determine which dataset or region provides the data for the aggregate calculation? For example, if you look at the Employee Sales by Territory Advanced report, we have several expressions that use the `Sum()` function to calculate the total sales amount. First, we used it in the expression that defines the txtTerritorySalesYTDTotal textbox value inside the tblSummary table region to show the sales total for all sales territories. Second, we used it inside lstTerritory to get the sales total per territory. Finally, we used the same expression inside tblEmployeeSales to get the sales total per salesperson. How does `Sum()` resolve to the right scope?

Obviously, the `Sum()` function has some intelligence built into it to determine the right scope of operation. It so happens that if a scope is not explicitly specified, it defaults to the innermost containing data region or grouping in which the aggregate is defined. So, in our example, the scope of the `Sum()` function defaulted to tblSummary, lstTerritory, and tblEmployeeSales, in that order.

Setting the aggregate scope explicitly

Let's see one more example. We'll change the Employee Sales by Territory with Summary Advanced report and add another column to tblEmployeeSales that will show the percentage of the salesperson's total relative to the territory total. To achieve this, we can copy and paste the third table column (Percentage of Employee's Total) and use the following expression for the new column:

```
=Fields!Sales.Value/Sum(Fields!Sales.Value, "grpTerritory")
```

Now, we explicitly set the aggregate scope to the grpTerritory group scope of the lstTerritory list region, which groups the data by territory. In this way, we can get to the territory sales total. Figure 5.11 shows the new version of the Employee Sales by Territory with Summary Advanced report.

Of course, in this particular case, we could have used the value in the txtTerritoryTotal textbox, which conveniently displays the territory total, but we wanted to show you how the scope affects the aggregate calculation.

Understanding aggregate scope rules

There are some rules that govern the valid use of scopes. Failure to follow them results in the following exception, which you will probably run into quite often at the beginning:

```
The value expression for the textbox 'txtTerritoryGrandTotal' uses an
aggregate expression without a scope.  A scope is required for all aggre-
gates used outside of a data region unless the report contains exactly one
data set.
```

As the exception text says, one of the rules is that you can specify only an aggregate scope of a containing group, region, or dataset. To demonstrate this, we'll change the Employee Sales by Territory with Summary Advanced report to show the grand total for all territories for the given time period. At first attempt, you might think that you can accomplish this by adding a new textbox outside the lstTerritory list region and setting its value to Sum(Fields!Sales.Value).

Territory: ***Canada***

Employee Name:	Saraiva, José
Commission:	1.50 %
Sales YTD:	$2,153,295.20
Bonus:	$5,000.00

Product Subcategory	Sales	Percentage of Employee's Total	Percentage of Territory's Total
Road Bike	$687,096.62	29.85 %	29.85 %
Mountain Bike	$641,178.50	27.85 %	27.85 %
Touring Bike	$487,603.52	21.18 %	21.18 %
Mountain Frame	$148,812.58	6.46 %	6.46 %
Road Frame	$108,689.19	4.72 %	4.72 %
Touring Frame	$87,352.57	3.79 %	3.79 %
Jersey	$22,922.69	1.00 %	1.00 %
Shorts	$12,952.62	0.56 %	0.56 %

Figure 5.11 With aggregate functions, you can set the aggregate scope explicitly.

However, when you run the report, you will get the "wrong scope" exception that we just discussed. The problem is that because there is no containing scope, the `Sum()` function has no idea how to calculate the expression.

You may try to solve this issue by changing the expression to `Sum(Fields!Sales.Value, "lstTerritory")` so you "tell" the function to use the lstTerritory list region. This won't work either, because you can request only a containing scope. In our case, because the textbox is outside any region, there is no containing scope.

The right expression in this scenario is `Sum(Fields!Sales.Value, "dsEmployeeSales")`, so the `Sum()` function calculates the total for the whole dataset, as shown in figure 5.12.

Please note that if the report uses only one dataset, you don't have to explicitly specify the dataset name, because the aggregate will default to it if it has no containing scope.

The Report Designer helps you somewhat to adopt the scope mentality. When you drag and drop a dataset field from another dataset to a region, it automatically generates an aggregate expression for the textbox value. If the field is numeric, the following expression is generated:

```
=Sum("<field name>", "<dataset name>")
```

As you can see, the Report Designer explicitly sets the scope to the dataset name that the field belongs to. If the field is the numeric `Sum()`, the Report Designer defaults to `Sum()`; otherwise it uses the `First()` aggregate function to retrieve the field value from the first data row.

Implementing running totals

There are a few other aggregate functions available with RS that allow you to perform various aggregate calculations, such as counting (`Count()`, `CountDistinct()`, `CountRows()`) and getting the minimum, average, and maximum values, as well as

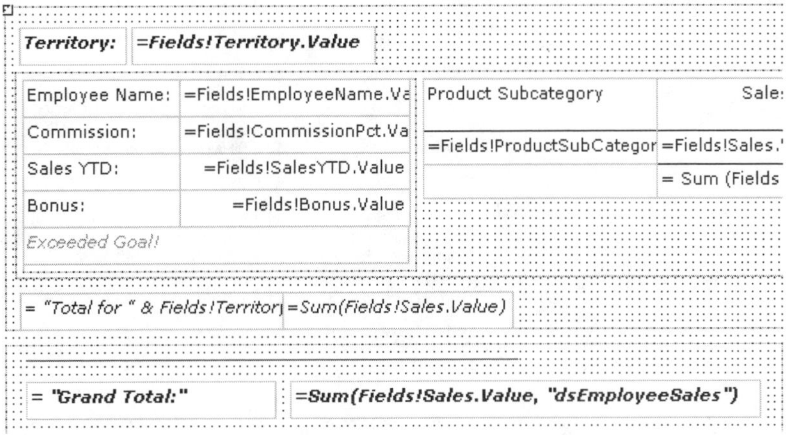

Figure 5.12 Creating a grand total by using aggregate functions

variance and deviation values. Please consult the documentation for a full list of all aggregate functions supported by RS. Those of you familiar with SQL will find the RS aggregate functions similar to the ones supported by most databases. The SQL specification defines five aggregate functions that databases must support (`MAX`, `MIN`, `AVG`, `SUM`, and `COUNT`).

An interesting function that we would like to mention is `RunningValue()`. This function allows you to implement running total aggregate calculations, as the Monthly Sales by Product Category report shown in figure 5.13 demonstrates.

The Running Totals column carries over the total from the previous months so the user can see the accumulated-by-month amount. Running totals reports are not easily done using straight SQL. With the helpful `RunningValue()` function, though, authoring this report with RS is a matter of minutes. The only thing that we have to do is set the Running Total column expression to

```
=RunningValue(Fields!Sales.Value, Sum, "dsSales")
```

Of course, if you need aggregate operations other than summing, we can replace the `Sum` function in `RunningValue` with any other aggregate function with the exception of `RunningValue`, `RowNumber`, or `Aggregate`.

The `Aggregate()` function returns a custom aggregate if the database provider supports user-defined aggregates. Currently, SQL Server 2000 does not support custom aggregates. However, the next release, code-named Yukon, will allow developers

ADVENTURE WORKS cycles

Monthly Sales by Product Category

Sales for Bike Racks from 5/1/2003 to 5/31/2004

SubCategory	Year	Month	Sales	Running Totals
Bike Racks	2003	Jul	$16,992.00	$16,992.00
	2003	Aug	$29,136.00	$46,128.00
	2003	Sep	$32,544.00	$78,672.00
	2003	Oct	$15,864.00	$94,536.00
	2003	Nov	$24,048.00	$118,584.00
	2003	Dec	$21,768.00	$140,352.00
	2004	Jan	$10,512.00	$150,864.00
	2004	Feb	$13,104.00	$163,968.00
	2004	Mar	$13,560.00	$177,528.00
	2004	Apr	$15,480.00	$193,008.00
	2004	May	$26,352.00	$219,360.00
Total:			**$219,360.00**	

Figure 5.13 Use the `RunningTotal()` function to implement running totals.

to create user-defined aggregate functions. Similar to user-defined functions (UDF), custom aggregates return a single value and they can be written in any of the supported .NET languages.

5.3.3 Using other internal functions

RS provides three other helpful functions that you can use in your expressions: `InScope`, `Level`, and `Previous`.

The `InScope()` function indicates whether the current report item is within the specified scope. This is especially useful with matrix regions, as we will see in section 5.4.1 when we discuss reports with navigational features.

Implementing recursive hierarchies

The `Level()` function returns the level offset as an integer value for recursive hierarchy reports. Recursive hierarchy reports are based on self-referential data, which has a parent-child relationship already defined. A typical example is an organizational hierarchy, where each employee record in the database has a ManagerID column pointing to the employee supervisor record. RS allows us to quickly generate reports that take advantage of such recursive data relationships.

For example, let's create a report that displays the AWC organizational structure. Figure 5.14 shows the Corporate Hierarchy report.

The report shows the employee name, his title, and the name and title of his direct supervisor. In addition, the report gives the user two options to filter the report data. First, the user can choose to see whom a given employee reports to, and second, it allows the user to see the employee's subordinates.

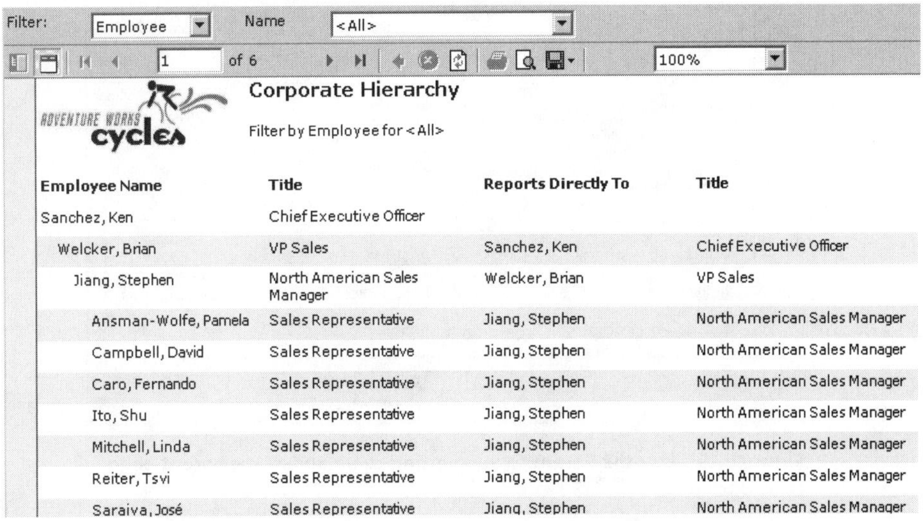

Filter: Employee Name <All>

1 of 6 100%

ADVENTURE WORKS cycles

Corporate Hierarchy

Filter by Employee for <All>

Employee Name	Title	Reports Directly To	Title
Sanchez, Ken	Chief Executive Officer		
Welcker, Brian	VP Sales	Sanchez, Ken	Chief Executive Officer
Jiang, Stephen	North American Sales Manager	Welcker, Brian	VP Sales
Ansman-Wolfe, Pamela	Sales Representative	Jiang, Stephen	North American Sales Manager
Campbell, David	Sales Representative	Jiang, Stephen	North American Sales Manager
Caro, Fernando	Sales Representative	Jiang, Stephen	North American Sales Manager
Ito, Shu	Sales Representative	Jiang, Stephen	North American Sales Manager
Mitchell, Linda	Sales Representative	Jiang, Stephen	North American Sales Manager
Reiter, Tsvi	Sales Representative	Jiang, Stephen	North American Sales Manager
Saraiva, José	Sales Representative	Jiang, Stephen	North American Sales Manager

Figure 5.14 Use the `Level()` function to create recursive hierarchy reports.

The trick to creating a recursive hierarchy report with RS is to configure the Parent Group setting on the region Grouping and Sorting Properties dialog, as shown in figure 5.15.

In our case, we set the Parent Group to the employee's manager. Once this is done, RS walks recursively through the employee data, starting with the top manager and going all the way down. To offset the table region rows in accordance with the employee hierarchical level, we used the following expression for the left padding setting of the Employee Name textbox (txtName):

```
=Convert.ToString(2 + (Level()*10)) & "pt", 2pt, 2pt, 2pt
```

The `Level` function returns an integer value indicating the hierarchical level of a row. Thus, for the top manager, Level returns 0; its subordinates have a level of 1, and so on. We simply use the return value from the `Level` function to offset the text accordingly. To give the user an option to switch between employees and managers, we added the Filter parameter with two available values, Employee and Manager, respectively. Then, we based the report dataset query on an expression that appends the appropriate `WHERE` clause accordingly.

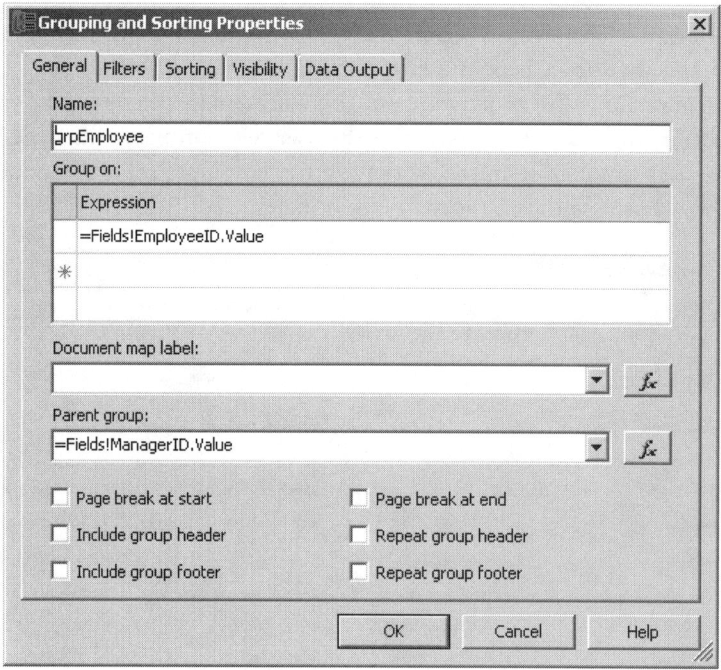

Figure 5.15 Use the Parent Group setting to establish the parent-child relationship.

Monthly Sales by Product Category

Sales for Bike Racks from 5/1/2003 to 5/31/2004

SubCategory	Year	Month	Sales	% Change	Running Totals
Bike Racks	2003	Jul	$16,992.00	N/A	$16,992.00
	2003	Aug	$29,136.00	71 %	$46,128.00
	2003	Sep	$32,544.00	12 %	$78,672.00
	2003	Oct	$15,864.00	-51 %	$94,536.00
	2003	Nov	$24,048.00	52 %	$118,584.00
	2003	Dec	$21,768.00	-9 %	$140,352.00
	2004	Jan	$10,512.00	-52 %	$150,864.00
	2004	Feb	$13,104.00	25 %	$163,968.00
	2004	Mar	$13,560.00	3 %	$177,528.00

Figure 5.16 Using the `Previous` function to implement the percentage increase

Implementing data differentials

The `Previous()` function is useful to return the previous aggregate value from the current or another scope. For example, we can enhance the Monthly Sales by Product Category and add a % Change column to show the change in percentage from one month to the next. Figure 5.16 shows the new version of the report.

Looking at the report, the user can see that, for example, the sales were up 71 percent from July to August. We used to the following expression for the value of the txtPerChange textbox:

```
=Iif(Previous(Fields!Sales.Value)>0, _
(Fields!Sales.Value - Previous(Fields!Sales.Value)) _
/Previous(Fields!Sales.Value), "N/A")
```

First, this expression checks to see whether we have data from the previous month. If not, N/A is displayed. Otherwise, we use the `Previous` function to get the sales amount for the previous month and calculate the difference.

Now that we know how to use expressions and functions, we can make our reports more interactive by taking advantage of the navigational features that RS provides.

5.4 DESIGNING REPORTS WITH NAVIGATIONAL FEATURES

With Reporting Services you can add navigational features to your reports in the form of hyperlinks and document maps. By using these features, you can give the report user the option to jump quickly to a specific area of a large report or navigate to an external URL-addressable resource.

5.4.1 Reports with hyperlinks

All data regions (including the chart region) support hyperlinks. Hyperlinks in reports can be used to allow the user to navigate to

- Another report
- A bookmark inside a report, similarly to the way you can use bookmarks in Microsoft Word documents
- A URL address—The currently supported options are mailto, http, https, news, and ftp. The URL address can be defined as static text or produced by an expression. For example, in a report that shows a list of vendors, the vendor name hyperlink could navigate the user to the vendor's web site.

NOTE Unfortunately, to prevent executing client-side malicious code, Reporting Services currently doesn't support calling JavaScript functions from hyperlinks. Microsoft hints that a future version may allow the administrator to configure RS to allow additional protocols.

One common use of hyperlinks is to navigate the user to a URL address.

Using hyperlinks to send e-mail

The Territory Sales Drillthrough report (shown in figure 5.17) demonstrates how you can incorporate navigation capabilities in your reports with hyperlinks.

Now the report displays the salesperson's name as a hyperlink, so the user can conveniently click it to send the salesperson an e-mail message. You can define hyperlinks for textbox and image report items from the Navigation tab of the item's Advanced Properties dialog, as shown in figure 5.18.

In this case, we defined the following expression for the Jump to URL hyperlink action property:

```
="mailto:" & Fields!EmailAddress.Value
```

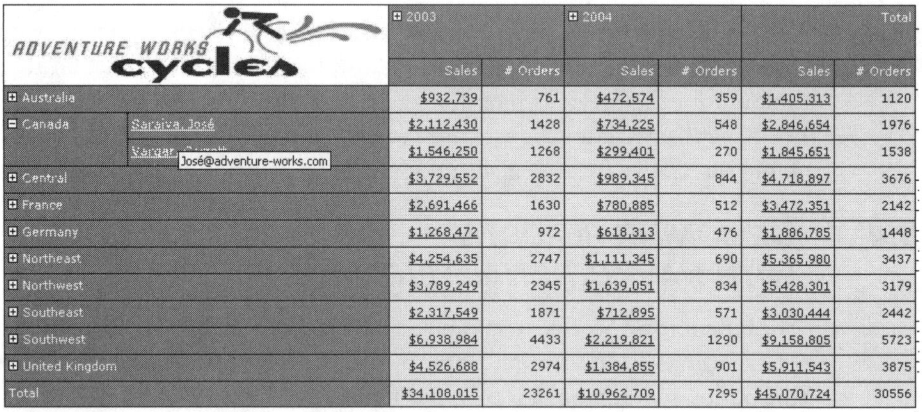

ADVENTURE WORKS cycles		2003		2004		Total	
		Sales	# Orders	Sales	# Orders	Sales	# Orders
Australia		$932,739	761	$472,574	359	$1,405,313	1120
Canada	Saraiva, José	$2,112,430	1428	$734,225	548	$2,846,654	1976
	Vargar, … José@adventure-works.com	$1,546,250	1268	$299,401	270	$1,845,651	1538
Central		$3,729,552	2832	$989,345	844	$4,718,897	3676
France		$2,691,466	1630	$780,885	512	$3,472,351	2142
Germany		$1,268,472	972	$618,313	476	$1,886,785	1448
Northeast		$4,254,635	2747	$1,111,345	690	$5,365,980	3437
Northwest		$3,789,249	2345	$1,639,051	834	$5,428,301	3179
Southeast		$2,317,549	1871	$712,895	571	$3,030,444	2442
Southwest		$6,938,984	4433	$2,219,821	1290	$9,158,805	5723
United Kingdom		$4,526,688	2974	$1,384,855	901	$5,911,543	3875
Total		$34,108,015	23261	$10,962,709	7295	$45,070,724	30556

Figure 5.17 Use hyperlinks to navigate the user to a URL address.

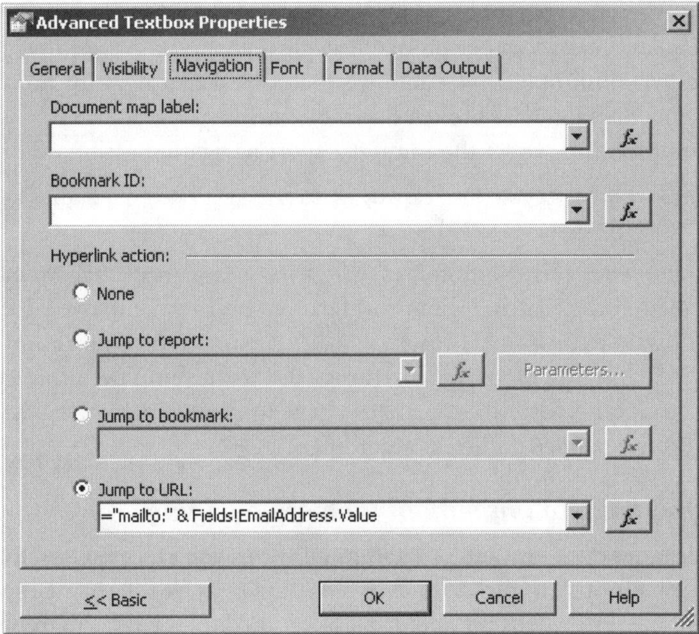

Figure 5.18 To add navigational features to your reports, use the Navigation tab of the report item's Advanced Properties dialog.

Once you set the hyperlink action, RS automatically changes the mouse cursor to a hand when the user hovers on top of an item with a hyperlink. In addition, we implemented conditional formatting to underline the person's name only if the EmailAddress field is not null.

Finally, we implemented a tooltip to show the person's e-mail address by setting the Tooltip property (VS.NET Properties window) of txtEmployee to the following expression:

```
= Fields!EmailAddress.Value
```

Hyperlinks are frequently used to create drillthrough reports.

Creating drillthrough reports

The same sample report, Territory Sales Drillthrough, also demonstrates how you can add drillthrough features to your reports by setting the hyperlink action to open another report that could show more detailed data for the currently selected item. With RS, you are not restricted to hard-coding the name of the drillthrough report. Again, you can use expressions to evaluate a condition and return the report name.

For example, the Territory Sales Drillthrough report evaluates the row grouping scope of the matrix region using the `InScope()` function. If the user has expanded the Employee row group (to drill down and see the salesperson's data), the sales amount hyperlink navigates the user to the Employee Sales Freeform report so the user can see the sales breakdown per product category. If the Employee row group is collapsed, the hyperlink opens the Employee Sales by Territory with Summary Chart report to show the sales data broken down by territory.

To accomplish this we set the Jump to report navigation action of txtSales to

```
=Iif(InScope("rowEmployee"), "Employee Sales Freeform", "Employee Sales By
Territory with Summary Chart")
```

To understand what this expression evaluates to, please recall that we have two row groups defined in the matrix region: rowTerritory and rowEmployee. InScope("rowTerritory") always returns true, because the sales territory represents the outermost row grouping. InScope("rowEmployee") returns false if the Employee row group is collapsed and true otherwise. InScope allows you to determine which row or column group has been expanded and react accordingly.

Using hyperlinks to implement web-style paging

With a little bit of creativity and programming effort, you can use links in your reports to implement various custom actions. For example, say you have a large report that takes a very long time to execute and displays hundreds of records. To improve the user experience, you may want to implement custom paging similar to the familiar web-based application-paging concept.

The report could retrieve the report data in chunks, for example, a hundred records at a time. At the end of the report, you can add a textbox with the text "Next page…." You can make the textbox clickable by defining a link that will point to the same report. You can use an expression for the link URL to "remember" the current selection criteria and send it back to the report when a new page is requested.

5.4.2 Reports with document maps

Reports can grow large, which could make it difficult navigating through them and finding the right information easily. For example, suppose that Adventure Works Cycles would like to expose its product catalog report online. There are several reasons of why this could be beneficial:

- Customers and salespersons would be able to access the company product catalog over the Internet.
- The catalog would always contain the up-to-date product information.
- Exposing the product catalog as a report would save substantial time in comparison with authoring it and maintaining it using web pages, not to mention that the users would be able to export the product catalog to one of the many supported formats.

What is a document map?

One potential implementation area of concern is that the product catalog may include hundreds of products and the user may not be able to find the information of interest quickly. RS solves this issue elegantly by allowing report authors to implement *document maps* with links to report areas. Similarly to Table of Contents in books, report document maps present an outline of the report data. In the previous example, the product catalog map could organize the product data in categories, subcategories, and products for faster navigation. By the way, this is exactly what the Product Catalog report, which is included in the Reporting Services samples, does.

Let's see an example to showcase the advantages of using document maps. We'll assume that the AWC management would like to see the company sales quarterly performance for a given period broken out by sales territory and store. Because a sales territory could potentially include many stores, the management has requested that we implement some sort of navigational features so users can find a particular store easily. There are at least two possible implementation approaches:

- Pass the store name as a parameter. However, this implementation would require regenerating the report for each store needed.
- Create a document map to organize the sales data in territories and stores.

Figure 5.19 shows the Territory Sales by Store with Map report, which includes a data map for easier navigation.

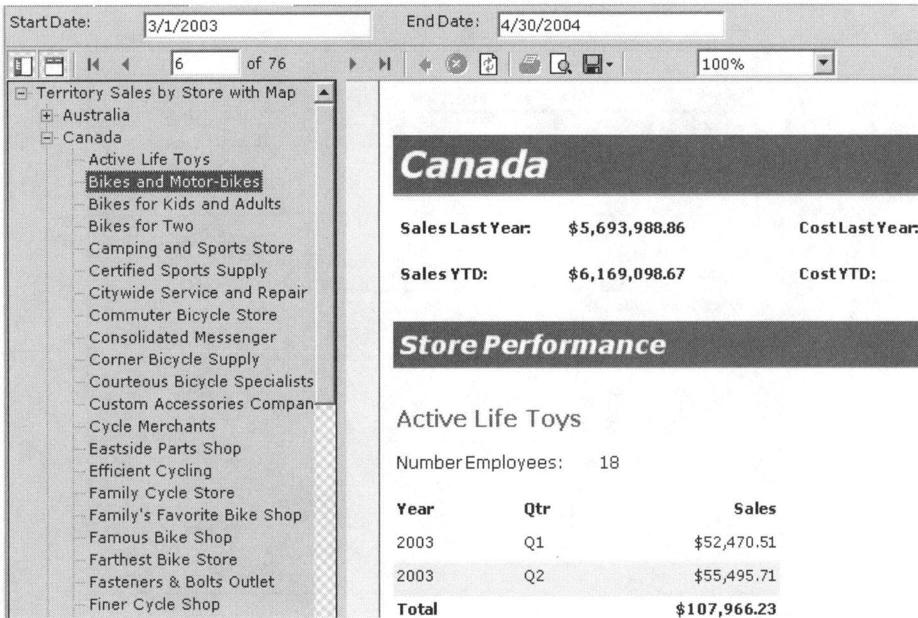

Figure 5.19 Adding a document map to the Territory Sales by Store report makes it easy for users to view and navigate to a store in any given territory.

As you can see, the report displays a hierarchical document map on the left side listing territories and stores alphabetically. The user doesn't have to page through the report to find a particular store. Instead, he can expand the document map and locate the store quickly.

Implementing document maps

Authoring the actual report is nothing we haven't seen so far. We used three regions, one table and two list regions, to group the data by country, store, and quarter. The table region (tblStoreSales) is nested inside the store list (lstStore), which in turn is nested inside the territory list (lstTerritory).

Now comes the fun part. You may think that implementing a document map might require creating new datasets and expressions. Actually, it really can't be simpler. The only thing that we had to do was to associate the Label property of the lstTerritory and lstStore groups to the corresponding document map label, as shown in figure 5.20.

To achieve the two-level hierarchy of territory and store, for the Territory list we set the document map label to Fields!Territory.Value, while for the Store list we set it to the Fields!Store.Value. That's all there is to it! RS does the heavy lifting to parse the data recursively and generate the document map when the report is processed.

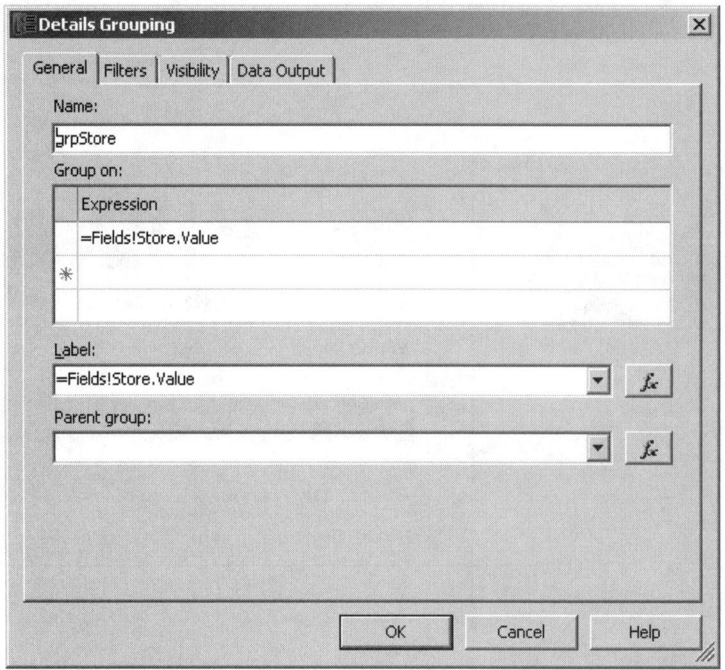

Figure 5.20 Implement a document map in your reports by associating the Label property of the group to a document map label.

As you've seen in this section as well as in chapter 4, RS allows you to add a variety of interactive features to your reports, such as a report toolbar, toggled visibility, navigational features, and document maps. One thing that may not be clear is how different export formats impact these features. We'll round out this discussion by looking at some considerations that you need to keep in mind with regard to report rendering.

5.5 REPORT RENDERING CONSIDERATIONS

The area of functionality that is most impacted by exporting is the report interactive features. Table 5.4 shows the set of supported interactive features for each export format.

Table 5.4 Interactive features that are supported for each export format

Feature	HTML	MHTML	HTML OWC	Excel	Image	PDF	CSV	XML
Report toolbar	✓		✓					
Toggled visibility	✓		✓					
Navigational features	✓	✓	✓[1]	✓				
Document maps	✓		✓			✓		

(✓[1]) Hyperlinks to static URLs in rows and column groups only

With version 1.0 of Reporting Services, export formats are not securable items. In other words, if the user has rights to render the report, she can export it in any registered format. If you need to limit the export options, the simple solution will be to do this in your client application. The disadvantage is that an adept user can bypass the client application and export the report directly from the Report Server. If this is an issue, you can implement a façade layer between the client application and the Report Server to validate the report requests. This approach is similar to the scenario that we will discuss in chapters 11 and 13.

Alternatively, you can also remove the rendering extension elements in the RSReportServer.config configuration file (found under the `<Render>` section) to eliminate the possibility that the export format can be used altogether.

5.5.1 Exporting reports to HTML

The Report Server uses the HTML rendering extension to render the report to HTML by default if a rendering format is not specified. HTML 4.0 is used for up-level browsers, such as Internet Explorer 4.0 or above or Netscape 7.0 or above; otherwise, HTML 3.2 is used.

The report formatting settings, such as fonts, colors, and borders, are encapsulated in an inline stylesheet included in the page. Charts are always saved as image files.

If not already cached by the browser, images are fetched via additional requests to the Report Server. In essence, the browser asks the Report Server to send the image by submitting a URL request to the server, such as the following:

```
http://localhost/ReportServer?/AWReporter/Employee Sales Freeform with
Chart&rs:Format=HTML4.0&rs:ImageID=0b326371-9aec-4705-87bf-1af02b3d5e78
```

One interesting option that exporting to HTML supports is auto-refreshing reports. For example, you can author a company stock performance report that automatically refreshes itself on a set schedule to get the latest stock value. You can set up the report to automatically refresh itself at a certain interval by using the AutoRefresh report property. You can find this property both on the General tab of the Report Properties dialog (select the report by clicking the Report Selector, right-clicking the report, and choosing Properties) and on the report's Properties window. Behind the scenes, this property emits a meta browser tag, e.g., `<META HTTP-EQUIV="Refresh" CONTENT="5">` if you set the AutoRefresh property to 5 seconds.

In terms of preserving the report fidelity, HTML is your best choice because it supports all interactive features, such as hyperlinks, document maps, and expandable crosstab reports.

There's one performance consideration when exporting reports to HTML. To render an HTML report, the browser loads the report in memory. For large reports, this could result in an "out of memory" exception. To prevent this and display HTML reports faster, you can define page breaks wherever it makes sense. For example, you can place a page break at the beginning or end of region groupings.

To enhance the report performance, the Report Server automatically generates a soft page break after the first page when repaginating HTML reports. Therefore, the first page of report loads quickly even with large reports.

5.5.2 Exporting reports to MHTML

The MHTML (MIME Encapsulation of Aggregate HTML Documents) format, listed as Web Archive in the standard report toolbar, encapsulates the report and its images in a single file. This eliminates the round-tripping to the Report Server to fetch the report images.

Because MHTML is based on MIME, rendering reports in MHTML format will be probably the best export option when you need to push the report to the users via e-mail subscribed delivery, as we will discuss in more detail in chapter 14. MHTML is more compact than PDF and TIFF formats. Please note, though, that all interactive features except hyperlinks (drillthrough reports) will be disabled when you export to MHTML.

5.5.3 Exporting reports to HTML with Office Web Components

This option is the same as HTML with an additional twist: chart and matrix regions are exported as chart and pivot Office Web Components, respectively. Of course, this requires that the Microsoft Office Web Components package be installed locally. The package is available as a stand-alone component of Microsoft Office.

If the Office Web Components package is not installed, the user will be prompted to download and install it from the Microsoft Office web site, where several localized versions are available, as you can see by examining the `OWCConfiguration` section in the RSReportServer.config configuration file. If the user doesn't have a valid Office license, OWC will be installed in read-only mode and all interactive features will be disabled.

Why would you export a report to HTML OWC? This export format is especially useful for chart and crosstab reports because it allows the end users to see data from different angles by adding/removing columns at will. Figure 5.21 shows the Territory Sales Crosstab report exported in HTML OWC.

Without any effort on our part the pivot report now has many more interactive features. Not only can the users drill down through data, but they can also remove, replace, and change groups. For example, how about if we want to see data grouped by time in rows and by territory in columns. To accomplish this we need to just drag the groups to their new places and remove the groups we don't want.

OWC is a marvelous piece of technology that we will talk more about in Chapter 12 when we will see how to integrate Reporting Services with OLAP applications. For now, we would like to mention one limitation that the HTML OWC format is a subject to. Typically, to tap into the full power of Office Web Components you will use them in a client/server model, where they are connected to the backend database, such as SQL Server or Analysis Services. However, reports that are exported to HTML OWC use OWC in a disconnected mode, where all the report data is downloaded as XML and fed into the component using a special data provider called

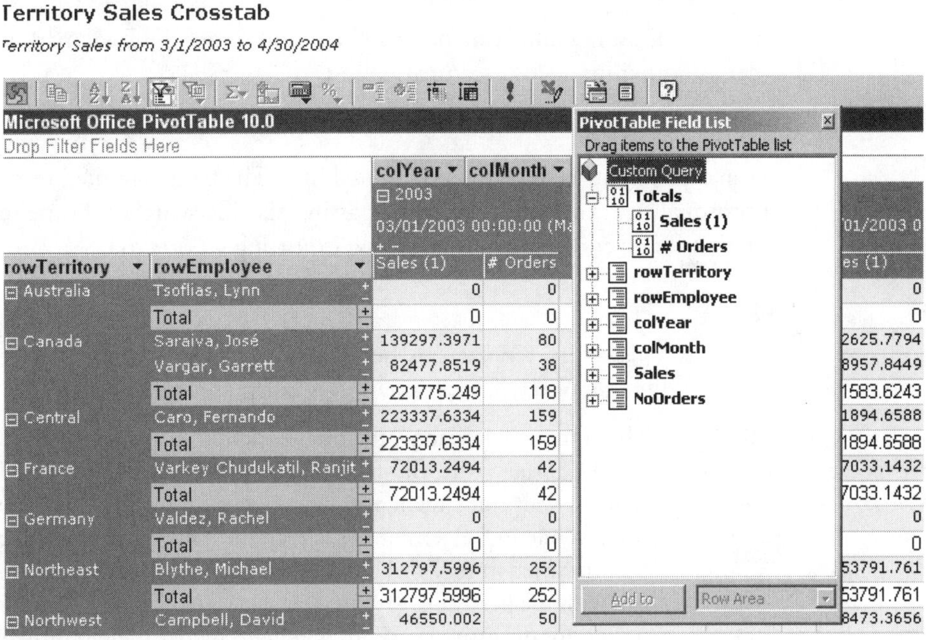

Figure 5.21 Exporting reports to HTML OWC format

MSPersist. As a result, the data shown on the report is always limited to the data returned by the report query.

5.5.4 Exporting reports to other formats

Here's a quick recap about the rest of the export formats.

Excel

This format could be useful when you want to manipulate the report data offline in Microsoft Excel XP or later versions. Exporting to Excel doesn't require the use of Office Web Components for matrix and charts regions. Please consult with the documentation about other considerations when exporting reports to Excel.

Image

Exporting a report as an image allows the report to be rendered in BMP, EMF, GIF, JPEG, PNG, TIFF, and WMF image formats. The default option is TIF. Different formats can be requested by passing device settings parameters. We will discuss how to use device settings in chapter 9.

Exporting a report as an image could be useful if you want to show the report easily on a web page or print it consistently regardless of the printer capabilities. On the downside, all interactive report features will be lost. Another disadvantage of exporting to image files is that it substantially increases the report size.

PDF

If the report has a document map, it can be found under the Bookmark tab in Adobe Reader. All other interactive features are lost.

CSV

You can export reports to comma-delimited files. The field delimiter, record delimiter, and text qualifier can be fine-tuned by passing specific switches. Please see the documentation for all considerations regarding exporting reports to CSV.

XML

As you have just seen, reports can be exported to XML. Only the report data is exported and the report layout information is not preserved.

NOTE Microsoft will probably provide a rendering extension for exporting reports to RTF format with the next release of Reporting Services. If you don't want to wait until then, you have two options. First, you can use third-party rendering extensions, such as the SoftArtisians's OfficeWriter, to export the report to Word format (for more information refer to chapter 16). Or, with the persisting to XML feature available with Office 2003, another option for exporting to Word will be to render the report in XML format, compliant with the Word schema.

5.6 DESIGNING LOCALIZED REPORTS

So far, we have been blissfully ignorant about designing our reports in such a way that they could support localized user interfaces and regional settings in multiple cultures. For example, when calculating the sales total we didn't take in consideration the fact that the AdventureWorks2000 database captures the currency code along with the sales data.

NOTE The AdventureWorks2000 database demonstrates a few localization aspects that you commonly have to deal with. First, as we said, it stores the currency code in the SalesOrderHeader table. Second, it maintains a currency conversation table that captures the currency exchange rate on a daily basis. Also, it stores the product description in several languages in the ProductDescription table. If you have never localized applications before, you might want to review the AdventureWorks2000 database schema to understand the complexity surrounding this issue.

In addition, on a few occasions, we have been formatting currency amounts as dollars explicitly, such as $##0.00. For the purpose of demonstrating the report design process with Reporting Services this is fine, but in real life you need to be aware of how globalization requirements affect reporting, and you should author your reports accordingly.

At minimum, if the reports will be requested by international users, I would recommend that you use culture-neutral format strings to format dates and numbers, such as "d" for short dates as opposed to mm-dd-yyyy, or N for numbers as opposed to #,##0. Please check the .NET documentation for a full list of date and numeric culture-neutral format strings.

5.6.1 Report localization basics

Reporting Services helps you in two ways to localize your reports:

- It exposes the user language code, e.g., en-US, under the User.Language property, so you can pass it to the database or react to it programmatically.
- If culture-neutral formatting is used, the Report Server formats the text inside textboxes in accordance with the user language settings that the browser passes to the Report Server. In addition, RS sets the Calendar, NumericalLanguage, and NumericalVariant accordingly.

Beyond that you are on your own. For example, you must take care of translating the report text into different languages, perform currency conversions, and so on. To demonstrate some localization techniques we modified the Product Catalog sample report that comes with the RS samples and saved it as Product Catalog Localized inside the AWReporter project.

Figure 5.22 depicts the algorithm that the Report Server follows to localize the content inside a textbox report item that is formatted with the currency culture-neutral format specifiers, such as "c".

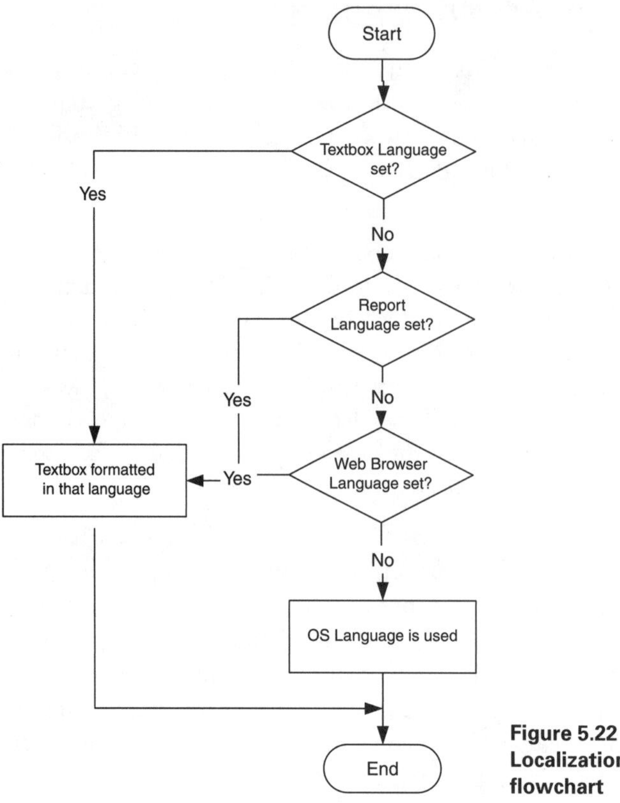

Figure 5.22 Localization flowchart

Each textbox has a Language property that you can explicitly set to a specific locale. If you do so, the textbox content will be formatted according to the specified language. Take, for example, the Product Catalog Localized report. You may want to show the product list price always formatted as dollars, regardless of the fact that international users can request the report with various language settings. To do this, you change the Language property of the ListPrice textbox item to English (United States). Of course, another way to accomplish this would be to use user-defined format specifiers instead of culture-neutral, such as $#.#00.00. However, I would advise against this practice because of the rework involved if you change your mind later and decide to localize the textbox item.

If the textbox language is not set, the report language will be used. To change the locale at a report level, you change the report Language property.

If the report language is not set, the Report Server will honor the browser language settings. For example, in the case of Internet Explorer, the user can specify multiple languages that will be treated by the browser and prioritize them when viewing web content. In Internet Explorer end users can specify preferred languages by using the Language Preference dialog, as shown in figure 5.23.

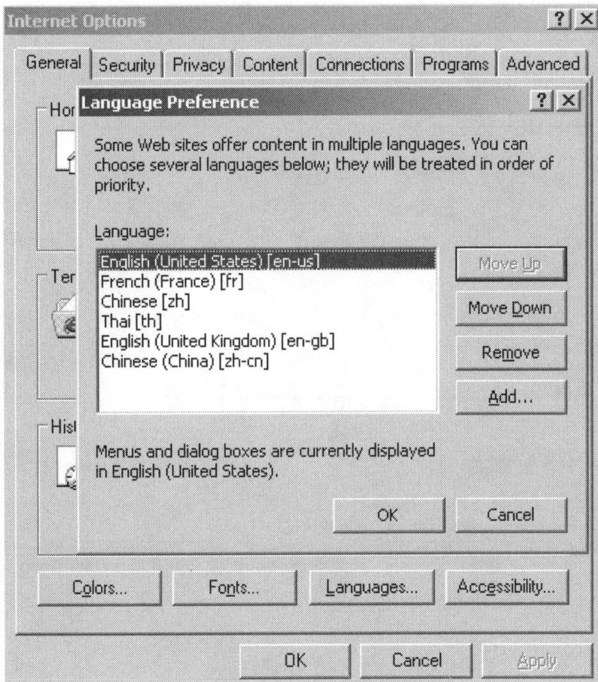

Figure 5.23
End users can use the Internet Explorer Language Preference dialog to specify their preferred languages.

If the browser language settings are not set, the Report Server will use the operating system language settings. Windows users can change these settings by accessing the Regional and Language Options Control Panel applet.

5.6.2 Localization techniques

So far, we have talked only about how localization affects formatting. What if you need to localize the report content in different languages or perform currency conversion? As the AdventureWorks2000 database demonstrates, you can adopt a data-driven approach.

Data-driven localization

The Product Catalog Localized report demonstrates this technique by displaying the translated product description according the user locale settings. For example, let's open the IE Language Preference dialog (see figure 5.23) and move the French (France) [fr] locale to the top of the browser languages. When we request the report, it localizes the product description, as shown in figure 5.24.

Here, we are taking advantage of the fact that AdventureWorks2000 database stores localized product descriptions in the ProductDescription and ProductDescription-XLocale tables.

To retrieve the correct translated product description, we pass the two-letter language code to the @Language query parameter. The two-letter language code is returned by the `GetTwoLetterISOLanguageName` embedded function, as follows:

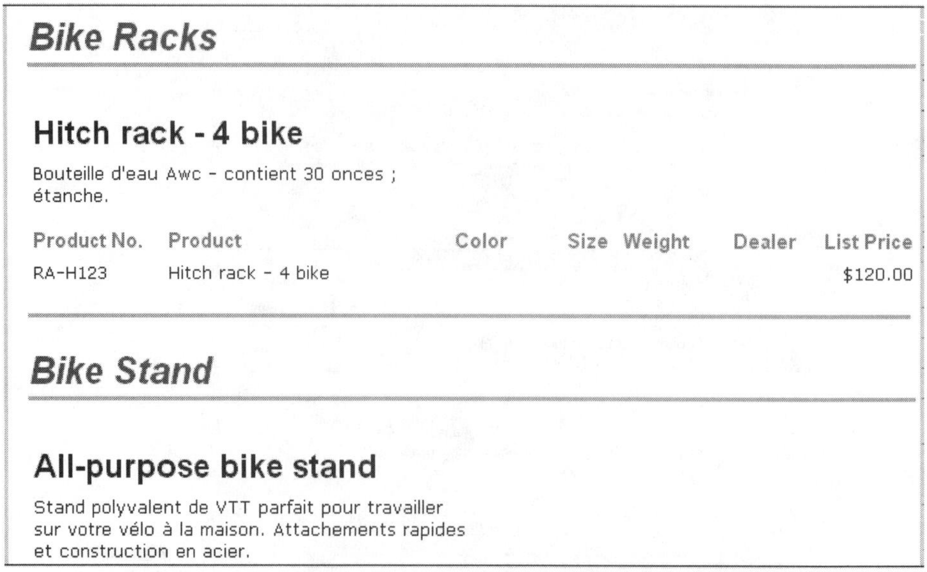

Bike Racks

Hitch rack - 4 bike

Bouteille d'eau Awc - contient 30 onces ; étanche.

Product No.	Product	Color	Size	Weight	Dealer	List Price
RA-H123	Hitch rack - 4 bike					$120.00

Bike Stand

All-purpose bike stand

Stand polyvalent de VTT parfait pour travailler sur votre vélo à la maison. Attachements rapides et construction en acier.

Figure 5.24 Localizing the product description

```
Function GetTwoLetterISOLanguageName(LocaleID as String) as String
    Dim ci As New System.Globalization.CultureInfo(LocaleID,False)
    return ci.TwoLetterISOLanguageName
End Function
```

In the @Language query parameter, we pass User.Language to the LocaleID argument. User.Language returns the four-letter language code, e.g., fr-FR, so we need this function to get the two-letter code.

Please notice that we have set the List Price locale explicitly to English (United States). If we hadn't done so, the list price would appear formatted in Euros, which is definitely not what we need. If we had wanted to convert the price to another currency, we could have used the currency exchange rates stored in the CurrencyRate table.

We also provided another simple function inside the report embedded code, `GetLanguageNativeName`, to display the language native name on the first page of the report. For example, for French users it returns français (France), so you can easily see which locale the user has selected. You can also see how choosing a different locale impacts the format of dates by looking at the current date displayed on the first page of the report.

Defaulting the user culture

Okay, but what if you want your report to support only a subset of locales? For example, the AdventureWorks2000 database supports only seven languages, and Japanese happens not to be among the ones supported. What would happen if a user with Japanese language settings requests our report? Well, as far as the currency conversion is concerned, we can handle this at the database level. If the language is not supported, we could default to English and convert the sales amount to dollars.

However, we would need to also take care of changing the language settings of the report itself to English. If we left the textbox items to use culture-neutral format specifiers, then RS would happily format the textbox values according to the Japanese regional settings. We would end up with the sales amount calculated in dollars at the data source but shown in yens on the report. What a mess!

How can we solve this issue? One option is to base the format settings of all localized textboxes on expressions. Similar to the database approach, the expressions could call a custom function, which could check for supported locales and default to English. However, this approach could easily become messy and difficult to maintain.

A better option, in our opinion, would be to check the locale before the report is rendered and revert the user culture to the default language in case the locale is not supported. If we could do this, we would solve both the database and formatting issues. Unfortunately, this approach cannot be implemented with version 1.0 of Reporting Services. First, with the lack of events, we cannot perform some preprocessing before the report is generated. Using a custom HTTP module to intercept the report request and change the thread culture will not work either. The reason for this limitation is that currently the Report Server uses the "accept-language" HTTP header to determine the user-preferred language. Unfortunately, the request headers collection is read-only at the time the request arrives at the Report Server.

5.7 SUMMARY

You can greatly enhance your report features by using expressions coupled with functions. You can write expressions manually or use the Expression Editor. The Reporting Services object model exposes five collections that you can reference in expressions:

- The Fields collection allows you to reference the report's dataset fields.
- The ReportItems collection exposes all textbox items.
- The Parameters collection allows you to reference the parameter values passed to the report.
- The Globals and User collections contain some useful global and user-specific values.

To expand your expression capabilities, you can use native functions that come from RS or external functions from the prereferenced standard .NET assemblies.

You can use expressions to add interactive features to your reports, such as links and document maps. You need to be aware of how different export formats impact the report's interactive features. The richest format that offers the most interactive features is HTML.

Finally, if international users will see your reports, you can localize your report by using various techniques, including formatting and expressions based on the user language.

With RS, you can accomplish much more with expressions than creating calculated fields and calling a limited number of functions. In chapter 6 we will see how to unleash the expression capabilities by integrating them with custom code.

5.8 RESOURCES

Globalizing and Localizing Applications (http://msdn.microsoft.com/library/default.asp?url=/library/en-us/vbcon/html/vboriInternationalization.asp)
A chapter from the Visual Studio .NET documentation that will introduce you to the internationalization features built into .NET.

CHAPTER 6

Using custom code

Reporting Services doesn't limit your programming options to using inline expressions and functions. In this chapter, we will show you how to supercharge the expression capabilities of your reports by integrating them with custom code. Writing custom code allows us to use advanced programming techniques to meet the most demanding reporting needs.

In this chapter, you will

- See what custom code options RS offers
- Learn how to write embedded code
- Find out how to integrate reports with external .NET assemblies
- Use XSL transformations to produce XML reports

We will put our custom code knowledge into practice by creating an advanced report that will show forecasted sales data.

With the widespread adoption of the XML as an interoperable data exchange format, we will also see how we can export reports to XML and custom-tailor the report output by using XSL transformations.

6.1 UNDERSTANDING CUSTOM CODE

As we mentioned in chapter 1, one of the most prominent features of Reporting Services is its extensible architecture. One way you can extend the RS capabilities is by integrating your reports with custom code that you or somebody else wrote. In general, you have two options for doing so:

- Write embedded (report-specific) code using Visual Basic .NET.
- Use custom code located in an external .NET assembly.

We'll now discuss each custom code option in more detail.

6.1.1 Using embedded code

As its name suggests, *embedded* code gets saved inside the Report Definition Language (RDL) file. Before we jump to a code example, we would like to mention some limitations that embedded code is a subject to:

- You can call embedded code only from within the report that contains the code. Because embedded code is saved in the RDL file, it is always scoped at the report level. For this reason, code embedded in one report cannot be referenced from another report. To create global and reusable functions that could be shared among reports, you have to move them to an external .NET assembly.
- You are restricted to using Visual Basic .NET only as a programming language for writing embedded code.
- As we pointed out in chapter 5, inside custom code you cannot directly reference the report object global collections, such as Fields, ReportItems, and so on. Instead, you have to pass them to your embedded methods as arguments.

To call embedded code in your report, you reference its methods using the globally defined *Code* member. For example, if you have authored an embedded code function called `GetValue`, you can call it from your expressions by using the following syntax:

```
=Code.GetValue()
```

DEFINITION *Shared* (called static in C#) methods can be invoked directly through the class name without first creating an instance of the class. To designate a method as shared, you use the VB.NET Shared modifier. The embedded code option doesn't support shared methods. On the other hand, *instance* methods are accessed through instances of the class and don't require a special modifier.

With the exception of shared methods, your embedded code can include any VB.NET-compliant code. In fact, if you think of the embedded code as a private class inside your project, you won't be far from the truth. You can declare class-level members and constants, private or public methods, and so on.

Maintaining state

One not-so-obvious aspect of working with embedded code is that you can maintain state in it. For example, you can use class-level members to preserve the values of the variables between calls to embedded code methods from the moment the report processing starts until the report is fully processed. We will demonstrate this technique in the forecasting example that we will explore in section 6.2.

Please note that state can be maintained within the duration of single report request only. As we explained in chapter 2, the RS report-processing model is stateless. For this reason, the report state gets discarded at the end of the report processing. Reporting Services is a web-based application, and just like any other web application, once the request is handled, its runtime state gets released. For this reason, subsequent requests to the same report cannot share state stored in class-level variables.

Let's now look at a practical example where embedded code can be useful.

Writing embedded code

You can write embedded code to create reusable utility functions that can be called from several expressions in your report. Let's examine an example of how we can do just that.

Suppose that the Adventure Works users have requested that we change the Territory Sales Crosstab report to display N/A when data is missing, as shown in figure 6.1.

Territory Sales Crosstab

Territory Sales from 3/1/2003 to 4/30/2004

ADVENTURE WORKS cycles	2003			
	Mar		Apr	
	Sales	# Orders	Sales	# Orders
Australia	N/A	N/A	N/A	N/A
Canada	$221,775	118	$66,553	74
Central	$223,338	159	$483,000	279
France	$72,013	42	$68,080	84
Germany	N/A	N/A	N/A	N/A
Northeast	$312,798	252	$380,409	169
Northwest	$83,069	80	$258,606	139
Southeast	$151,121	70	$207,179	179
Southwest	$422,127	277	$211,994	181
United Kingdom	$390,492	216	$520,473	296
Total	$1,876,733	1214	$2,196,294	1401

Figure 6.1 You can use embedded code to implement useful utility functions scoped at the report level.

Further, let's assume that we need to differentiate between missing data and NULL values. When the underlying value is NULL, we will translate it to zero. To meet this requirement, we could write a simple embedded function called `GetValue`.

Using the Code Editor

To write custom embedded code, you use the Report Designer Code Editor, which you can invoke from the Report Properties dialog. You can open this dialog in either of two ways:

- Select the report by right-clicking the Report Selector and choosing Properties.
- Right-click anywhere on the report outside the body area, and choose Properties.

Then, from the Report Properties dialog, choose the Code tab, as shown in figure 6.2.

Granted, function GetValue can easily be replaced with an Iif-based expression. However, encapsulating the logic in an embedded function has two advantages. First, it centralizes the logic of the expression in one place instead of using Iif functions for every field in the report. Second, it makes the report more maintainable because if you decide to make a logical change to your function, you do not have to track down and change every Iif function in the report.

As you can see, the Code Editor is nothing to brag about. It is implemented as a simple text area control, and its feature set doesn't go beyond copying and pasting text. For this reason, I highly recommend that you use a standard VB Windows Forms or Console application to write your VB.NET code in a civilized manner and then copy and paste it inside the Code Editor.

The Report Designer saves embedded code under the `<Code>` element in the RDL file. When doing so, the Report Designer URL-encodes the text. Be aware of this if you decide to change the `<Code>` element directly for some reason.

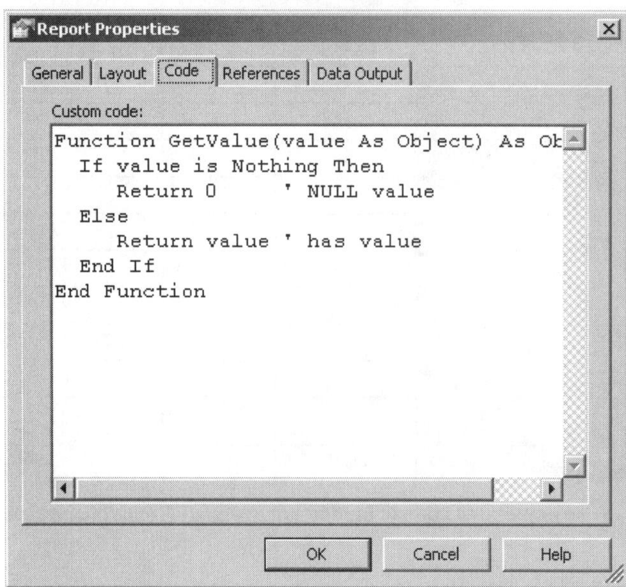

Figure 6.2
Use the Code Editor for writing embedded code. The `GetValue` function, shown in the Code Editor, determines whether a value is missing or NULL.

Handling missing data

Once the `GetValue` function is ready, to differentiate between NULL and missing data in our report, we could base the txtSales and txtNoOrders values on the following expressions:

```
=Iif(CountRows()=0, "N/A", Code.GetValue(Sum(Fields!Sales.Value)))
```

and

```
=Iif(CountRows()=0, "N/A", Code.GetValue(Sum(Fields!NoOrders.Value)))
```

respectively.

The `CountRows` function returns the count of rows within a specified scope. If no scope is specified, it defaults to the innermost scope, which in our case resolves to the static group that defines the values in the data cells. Both expressions first check for missing data (no rows) by using `CountRows` and display N/A if no missing data is found. Otherwise, they call the `GetValue` embedded function to translate the NULL values.

We recommend that you use embedded code for writing simple report-specific utility-like functions. When your programming logic gets more involved, you should consider moving your code to external assemblies, as we discuss next.

6.1.2 Using external assemblies

The second way of extending RS programmatically is by using prepackaged logic located in external .NET assemblies that can be written in any .NET-supported language. The ability to integrate reports with custom code in external assemblies increases your programming options dramatically. For example, by using custom code, you can do the following:

- Leverage the rich feature set of the .NET Framework. For example, let's say you need a collection to store crosstab data of a matrix region in order to perform some calculations. You can "borrow" any of the collection classes that come with .NET, such as Array, ArrayList, Hashtable, and so on.
- Integrate your reports with custom .NET assemblies, written by you or third-party vendors. For example, to add forecasting features to the Sales by Product Category report in section 6.2, we leveraged the Open Source OpenForecast package.
- Write code a whole lot easier by leveraging the powerful Visual Studio .NET IDE instead of the primitive Code Editor.

I hope that at some point in future, RS will get better integrated with the Visual Studio .NET IDE and support other .NET languages besides VB.NET. Ideally, RS should allow developers to add custom classes to their business intelligence projects and write code using the Visual Studio .NET editor. If this gets implemented, enhancing RS programmatically will be no different than writing code in traditional .NET development projects.

Based on preliminary feedback that I got from Microsoft, this seems to be the long-term direction that RS will follow.

Referencing external assemblies

To use types located in an external assembly, you have to first let the Report Designer know about it by using the References tab in the Report Properties dialog, as shown in figure 6.3.

Assuming that our report needs to use the custom AWC.RS.Library assembly (included with this book's source code), we must first reference it using the References tab. While this tab allows you to browse and reference an assembly from an arbitrary folder, note that when the report is executed, the .NET Common Language Runtime (CLR) will try to locate the assembly according to CLR probing rules. In a nutshell, these rules give you two options for deploying the custom assembly:

- Deploy the assembly as a private assembly.
- Deploy the assembly as a shared assembly in the .NET Global Assembly Cache (GAC). As a prerequisite, you have to strong-name your assembly. For more information about how to do this, please refer to the .NET documentation.

If you choose the first option, you will need to deploy the assembly to the Report Designer folder so that the assembly is available during the report-testing process. Assuming that you have accepted the default installation settings, to deploy the assembly to the Report Designer folder, copy the assembly to C:\Program Files\Microsoft SQL Server\80\Tools\Report Designer. Once you have done this, you can build and render the report in preview mode inside VS.NET.

Before the report goes live, you need to deploy the assembly to the Report Server binary folder. Specifically, you need to copy to the assembly to the Report Server binary

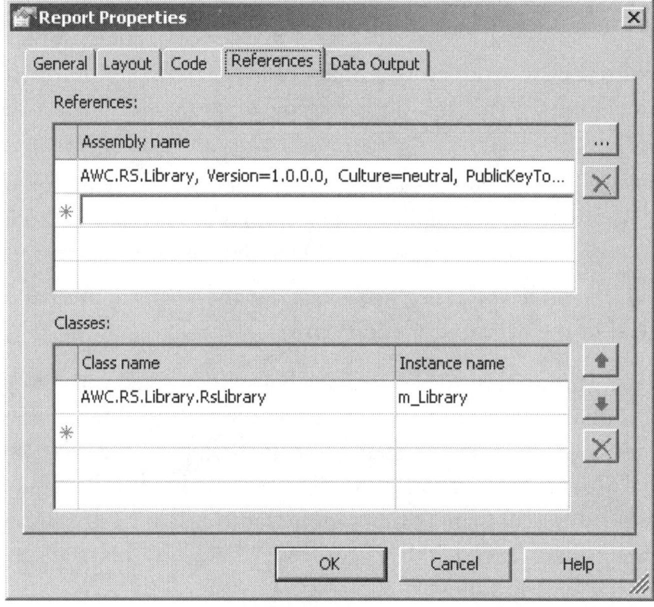

Figure 6.3 Use the Report Properties dialog to reference an external assembly.

folder, which by default is C:\Program Files\Microsoft SQL Server\MSSQL\ Reporting Services\ReportServer\bin.

Please note that deploying the custom assembly to the right location is only half of the deployment story. Depending on what your code does, you may need also to adjust the code access security policy so the assembly code can execute successfully. We will discuss the code access security model in chapter 8. If you need more information about deploying custom assemblies, please refer to the "Using Custom Assemblies with Reports" section in the RS documentation.

Calling shared methods

When using custom code in external assemblies, you can call both instance and shared methods. If you need to call only shared methods (also called static in C#) inside the assembly, you are ready to go because shared methods are available globally within the report.

You can call shared methods by using the fully qualified type name using the following syntax:

```
<Namespace>.<Type>.<Method>(argument1, argument2, …, argumentN)
```

For example, if we need to call the `GetForecastedSet` shared method located in the RsLibrary class (AWC.RS.Library assembly) from an expression or embedded code, we would use the following syntax:

```
=AWC.RS.Library.RsLibrary.GetForecastedSet(forecastedSet, forecastedMonths)
```

where `AWC.RS.Library` is the namespace, `RsLibrary` is the type, `GetForecastedSet` is the method, and `forecastedSet` and `forecastedMonths` are the arguments.

If the custom assembly is your own, how can you decide whether to define your methods as shared or instance? My short answer is to use shared methods if you don't need instance methods. Shared methods are convenient to call. However, instance methods allow you to maintain state within the duration of the report request. For example, you can preserve the class-level variable values between multiple method invocations of the same type. The state considerations for using code in external .NET assemblies are the same as the ones we discussed in the section 6.1.1 for embedded code.

One thing to watch for is using shared class-level fields to maintain state because their values are shared across all instances of the same report. So, depending on how many users are accessing a single report at any one time, the value of a shared field may be changing. In addition, the values of shared fields are not private to a report user, so sensitive user-only data should never be accessed through a shared field or property. Finally, static class-level fields are subject to multithreading locking issues. To avoid these issues, create your classes as stateless classes that don't have class-level shared fields or use instance class-level fields and methods. For more information about shared vs. instance methods, see the Visual Studio .NET documentation.

Sometimes, you simply won't have a choice and your applications requirements will dictate the type of method invocation. For example, if the method needs to be also invoked remotely via .NET Remoting, it has to be an instance method.

Calling instance methods

To invoke an instance method, you have some extra work left to do. First, you have to enumerate all instance classes (types) that you need to instantiate in the Classes grid (see figure 6.3). For each class, you have to assign an instance name. Behind the scenes, RS will create a variable with that name to hold a reference to the instance of the type.

NOTE When you specify the class name in the Classes grid, make sure that you enter the fully qualified type name (namespace included). In our example (shown previously in figure 6.3), the namespace is `AWC.RS.Library` while the class name is RsLibrary. When you are in doubt as to what the fully qualified class name is, use the VS.NET Object Browser or another utility, such as Lutz Roeder's excellent .NET Reflector (see section 6.5 for information on this utility), to browse to the class name and find out its namespace.

For example, assuming that we need to call an instance method in the AWC.RS.Library assembly, we have to declare an instance variable m_Library, as shown in figure 6.3. In our case, this variable will hold a reference to the RsLibrary class.

If you declare more than one variable pointing to the same type, each will reference a separate instance of that type. Behind the scenes, when the report is processed, RS will instantiate as many instances of the referenced type as the number of instance variables.

Once you have finished with the reference settings, you are ready to call the instance methods via the instance type name that you specified. Just as with embedded code, you use the `Code` keyword to call an instance method. The difference between a shared and an instance method is that instead of using the class name, you use the variable name to call the method.

For example, if the `RsLibrary` type had an instance method named `DummyMethod()`, we could invoke it from an expression or embedded code like this:

```
Code.m_Library.DummyMethod().
```

Having seen what options we have as developers for programmatically expanding our report features, let's see how we can apply them in practice. In the next section, we will find out how we can use embedded and external code to add advanced features to our reports.

6.2 CUSTOM CODE IN ACTION: IMPLEMENTING REPORT FORECASTING

In this section, we will show you how to incorporate forecasting capabilities in our reports. These are the design goals of the sample report that we are going to create:

- Allow the user to generate a crosstab report of sales data for an arbitrary period.
- Allow the user to specify the number of forecasted columns.
- Use data extrapolation to forecast the sales data.

Here is our fictitious scenario. Imagine that the AWC management has requested to see forecasted monthly sales data grouped by product category. To make these things more interesting, let's allow the report users to specify a data range to filter the sales data, as well as the number of forecasted months. To accomplish the above requirements, we will author a crosstab report, Sales by Product Category, as shown in figure 6.4.

The user can enter a start date and an end date to filter the sales data. In addition, the user can specify how many months of forecasted data will be shown on the report. The report shows the data in a crosstab fashion, with product categories on rows and time periods on columns. The data portion of the report shows first the actual sales within the requested period, followed by the forecasted sales in bold font.

For example, if the user enters 4/30/2003 as a start date and 3/31/2004 as an end date and requests to see three forecasted months, the report will show the forecasted data for April, May, and June 2004 (to conserve space, figure 6.4 shows only one month of forecasted data).

As you would probably agree, implementing forecasting features on your own is not an easy undertaking. But what if there is already prepackaged code that does this for us? If this code can run on .NET, our report can access it as custom code. Enter OpenForecast.

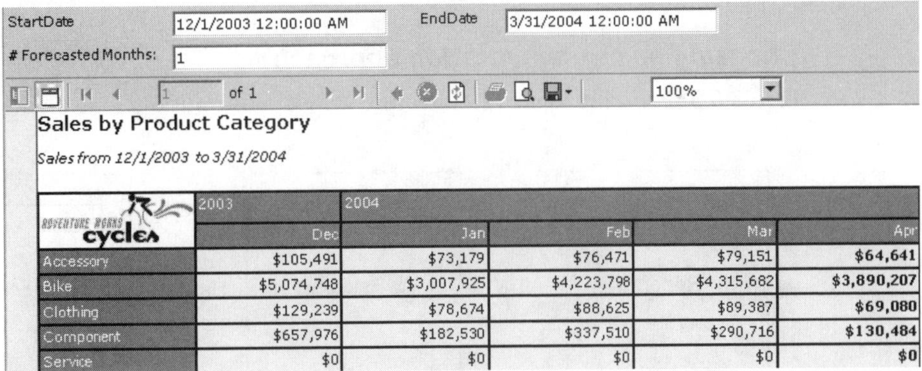
StartDate 12/1/2003 12:00:00 AM EndDate 3/31/2004 12:00:00 AM

Forecasted Months: 1

1 of 1 100%

Sales by Product Category

Sales from 12/1/2003 to 3/31/2004

	2003	2004			
ADVENTURE WORKS cycles	Dec	Jan	Feb	Mar	Apr
Accessory	$105,491	$73,179	$76,471	$79,151	**$64,641**
Bike	$5,074,748	$3,007,925	$4,223,798	$4,315,682	**$3,890,207**
Clothing	$129,239	$78,674	$88,625	$89,387	**$69,080**
Component	$657,976	$182,530	$337,510	$290,716	**$130,484**
Service	$0	$0	$0	$0	**$0**

Figure 6.4 The Sales by Product Category report uses embedded and external custom code for forecasting.

6.2.1 Forecasting with OpenForecast

Forecasting is a science in itself. Generally speaking, forecasting is concerned with the process used to predict the unknown. Instead of looking at a crystal ball, forecasting practitioners use mathematical models to analyze data, discover trends, and make educated conclusions. In our example, the Sales by Product Category report will predict the future sales data by using the data extrapolating method.

There are number of well-known mathematical models for extrapolating a set of data, such as polynomial regression and simple exponential smoothing. Implementing one of those models, though, is not a simple task. Instead, for the purposes of our sales forecasting example, we will use the excellent Open Source OpenForecast package, written by Steven Gould.

OpenForecast is a general-purpose package that includes Java-based forecasting models that can be applied to any data series. The package require no knowledge of forecasting, which is great for those of us who have decided to focus on solving pure business problems and kissed mathematics goodbye a long time ago.

OpenForecast supports several mathematical forecasting models, including single-variable linear regression, multi-variable linear regression, and so on. The current OpenForecast version as of the time of this writing is 0.3, but version 0.4 is under development and probably will be released by the time you read this book. Please see section 6.5 for a link to the OpenForecast web site.

Let's now see how we can implement our forecasting example and integrate with OpenForecast by writing some embedded and external code.

6.2.2 Implementing report forecasting features

Creating a crosstab report with forecasting capabilities requires several implementation steps. Let's start with a high-level view of our envisioned approach and then drill down into the implementation details.

Choosing an implementation approach

Figure 6.5 shows the logical architecture view of our solution.

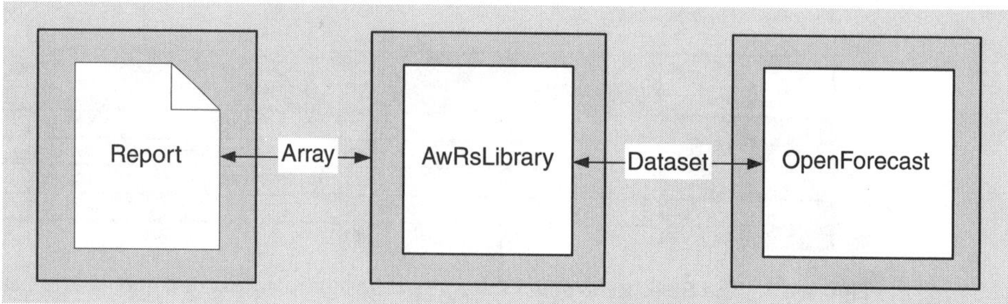

Figure 6.5 The Sales by Product Category report uses embedded code to call the AwRsLibrary assembly, which in turns calls the `J# OpenForecast` package.

Our report will use embedded code to call a shared method in a custom assembly (AwRsLibrary) and get the forecasted data. AwRsLibrary will load the existing sales data into an OpenForecast dataset and obtain a forecasting model from OpenForecast. Then, it will call down to OpenForecast to get the forecasted values for the requested number of months. AwRsLibrary will return the forecasted data to the report, which in turn will display it.

We have at least two implementation options for passing the crosstab sales data to AwRsLibrary:

- Fetch the sales data again from the database. To accomplish this, the report could pass the selected product category and month values on a row-by-row basis. Then, AwRsLibrary could make a database call to retrieve the matching sales data.
- Load the existing sales data in a structure of some kind using embedded code inside the report and pass the structure to AwRsLibrary.

The advantages of the latter approach are as follows:

- *The custom code logic is self-contained.* We don't have to query the database again.
- *It uses the default custom code security policy.* We don't have to elevate the default code access security policy for the AwRsLibrary assembly. If we choose the first option, we won't be able to get away with the default code access security setup, because RS will grant our custom assemblies only Execution rights, which are not sufficient to make a database call. Actually, in the case of OpenForecast, we had to grant both assemblies FullTrust rights because any J# code requires FullTrust to execute successfully. However, we wouldn't have had to do this if we had chosen C# as a programming language.
- *No data synchronization is required.* We don't have to worry about synchronizing the data containers, the matrix region and the AwRsLibrary dataset.

For the above reasons, we will choose the second approach. To get it implemented, we will use an expression to populate the matrix region data values. The expression will call our embedded code to load an array structure on a row-by-row basis. Once a given row is loaded, we will pass the array to AwRsLibrary to get the forecasted data.

Now, let's discuss the implementation details, starting with converting OpenForecast to .NET.

Migrating OpenForecast to .NET

OpenForecast is written in Java, so one of the first hurdles that we had to overcome was to integrate it with .NET. We had two options to do so:

- *Use a third-party Java-to-.NET gateway to integrate both platforms.* Given the complexities of this approach we quickly dismissed it.

- *Port OpenForecast to one of the supported .NET languages.* Microsoft provides two options for this. First, we can use the Microsoft Java Language Conversion Assistant (see section 6.5 for more information) to convert Java-language code to C#. Second, we could convert OpenForecast to J#. The latter option would have preserved the Java syntax although that code will execute under the control of the .NET Common Language Runtime instead of the Java Virtual Machine.

We decided to port OpenForecast to J#. The added benefit to this approach is that the Open Source developers could maintain only one Java-based version of OpenForecast. Porting OpenForecast to J# turned out to be easier than we thought. We created a new J# library project, named it OpenForecast, and loaded all *.java source files inside it. We included the .NET version of OpenForecast in the source code that comes with this book.

Figure 6.6 shows the converted to J# version of OpenForecast open in Visual Studio.NET.

We had take care of only a few compilation errors inside the MultipleLinearRegression, because several Java hashtable methods are not supported in J#, such as `keySet()`, `entries()`, and hashtable cloning. We also included a WinForm application (TestHarness) that you can use to test the converted OpenForecast. We included the OpenForecast DLL so you could still run the report even if you don't have J# installed.

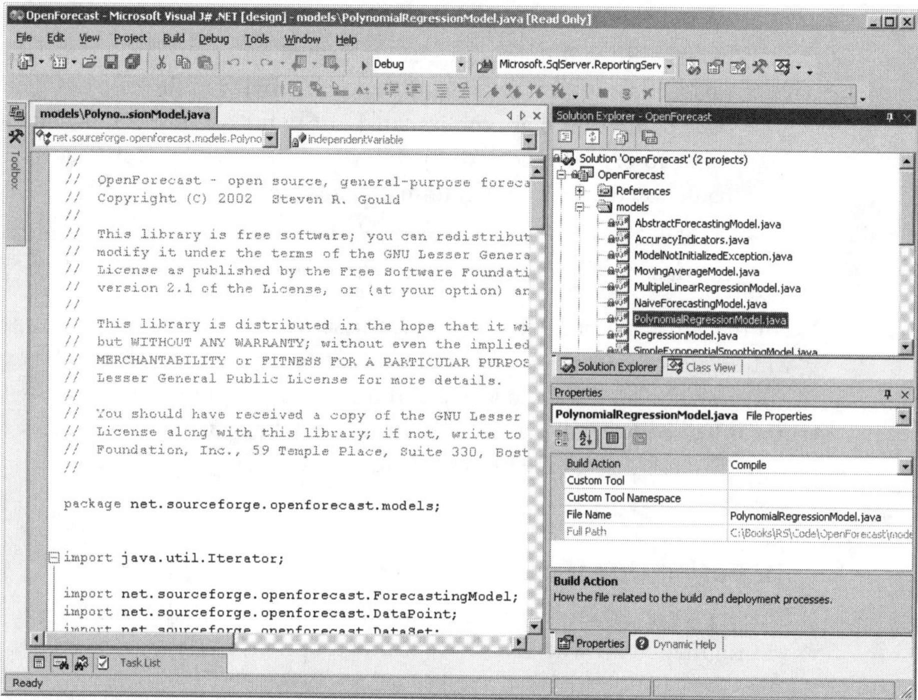

Figure 6.6 To convert Java-based OpenForecast to .NET, we migrated its code to J#.

Implementing the AwRsLibrary assembly

The next step was to create the custom .NET assembly, AwRsLibrary, that will bridge the report-embedded code and OpenForecast. We implemented AwRsLibrary as a C# class library project. Inside it we created the class RsLibrary that exposes a static (shared) method, `GetForecastedSet`. The abbreviated code of this method is shown in listing 6.1.

Listing 6.1 The report-embedded code calls the AwRsLibrary `GetForecastedSet` method, which in turns calls OpenForecast.

```
public static void GetForecastedSet(double[] dataSet,
  int numberForecastedPoints ) {
  DataSet observedData = new DataSet();          <-- Define an OpenForecast dataset and load it with the matrix row array
  Observation dp;
  for (int i=0;i<dataSet.Length-numberForecastedPoints;i++) {
    dp = new Observation( dataSet[i]);
    dp.setIndependentValue( "x", i);
    observedData.add( dp );
  }

  ForecastingModel forecaster = new MultipleLinearRegressionModel();   <-- Obtain a forecasting model from OpenForecast
  forecaster.init(observedData);
  DataSet requiredObservations = new DataSet();   <-- Specify placeholders for the forecasted data
 for ( int i=dataSet.Length-numberForecastedPoints;
  i < dataSet.Length; i++ ) {
    dp = new Observation( 0.0 );
    dp.setIndependentValue( "x", i );
    requiredObservations.add( dp );
  }

  forecaster.forecast( requiredObservations );   <-- Perform forecasting

  int index =  dataSet.Length - numberForecastedPoints;
  Iterator it = requiredObservations.iterator();
  while ( it.hasNext() ) {   <-- Populate the input array
    dataSet[index] = ((DataPoint)it.next()).getDependentValue();
    index++;
  }
}
```

The `GetForecastedSet` method receives the existing sales data for a given product category in the form of a dataSet array, as well as the number of the requested months for forecasted data. Next, integrating with OpenForecast is a matter of five steps.

Step 1 We create a new OpenForecast dataset and load it with the existing data from the matrix row array.

Step 2 We obtain a given forecasting model. OpenForecast allows developers to get the optimal forecasting mathematical model based on the given data series by calling the `getBestForecast` method. This method will examine the dataset and will try a few forecasting models to select the most optimal. If the returned model is not a good fit, you can request a forecasting model explicitly by instantiating any of the classes found under the model's project folder.

NOTE When testing the report, I noticed that with my sales data `getBestForecast()` returns the PolynomialRegressionModel model, which returns negative values when the sales data varies considerably. For this reason, I explicitly request the MultipleLinearRegressionModel model. I recommend that you try `getBestForecast()` first for your forecasting applications, and only if the returned model doesn't meet your needs should you request a model explicitly.

Step 3 We prepare another dataset to hold the forecasted data and initialize it with as many elements as the number of forecasted months.

Step 4 We call the forecast method to extrapolate the data and return the forecasted results.

Step 5 We load the forecasted data back to the dataSet array so we can pass it back to the report's embedded code.

Once we have finished with both the AwRsLibrary and OpenForecast .NET assemblies, we need to deploy them.

Deploying custom assemblies

As we explained in section 6.1, we need to deploy custom assemblies to both the Report Designer and Report Server binary folders. The custom assembly deployment process consists of the following steps:

Step 1 Copy the assemblies to the Report Designer and Report Server binary folders.

Step 2 Adjust the code-based security if the custom code needs an elevated set of code access security permissions.

To make both assemblies, AwRsLibrary and OpenForecast, available during design time, we have to copy AWC.RS.Library.dll and OpenForecast.dll to the Report Designer folder, which by default is C:\Program Files\Microsoft SQL Server\80\Tools\Report Designer.

Similarly, to successfully render the deployed report under the Report Server, we have to deploy both assemblies to the Report Server binary folder, which by default is C:\Program Files\Microsoft SQL Server\MSSQL\Reporting Services\ReportServer\bin. In fact, the Report Server will not let you deploy a report from within the VS.NET IDE if all referenced custom assemblies are not already deployed.

The default RS code access security policy grants Execution rights to all custom assemblies by default. However, J# assemblies require FullTrust code access rights. Because the .NET Common Language Runtime walks up the call stack to verify that all callers have the required permission set, we need to elevate the code access security policy for both assemblies to full trust. This will require changes to the Report Designer and Report Server security configuration files.

We will provide more details about how code access security works and how it can be configured in chapter 8. If you don't want to wait until then, you can find a copy of our rssrvpolicy.config configuration file enclosed with the AwRsLibrary project. Toward the end of the file, you will see two CodeGroup XML elements that point to the AwRsLibrary and OpenForecast files. You will need to copy these elements to the Report Server security configuration file (rssrvpolicy.config).

In addition, as we discussed in chapter 2, if you want to preview (run) the report in the Preview window from the Report Designer, you will need to propagate the changes to the Report Designer security configuration file (rspreviewpolicy.config) as well.

Once the custom assemlies are deployed, we will need to write some VB.NET embedded code in our report to call the AwRsLibrary assembly, as we will discuss next.

Writing report embedded code

To integrate the report with AwRsLibrary we added an embedded function called `GetValue` to the Sales by Product Category report as shown in listing 6.2.

Listing 6.2 The embedded `GetValue` function calls the AwRsLibrary assembly.

```
Dim forecastedSet() As Double  ' array with sales data
Dim productCategoryID As Integer = -1
Dim bNewSeries As Boolean = False
Public Dim m_ExString = String.Empty

Function GetValue(productCategoryID As Integer, _
  orderDate As DateTime, _
sales As Double, reportParameters as Parameters, _
txtRange as TextBox) As Double

  Dim startDate as DateTime = reportParameters!StartDate.Value
  Dim endDate as DateTime = reportParameters!EndDate.Value
Dim forecastedMonths as Integer = _
  reportParameters!ForecastedMonths.Value

  If (forecastedSet Is Nothing) Then
    ReDim forecastedSet(DateDiff(DateInterval.Month, _
       startDate, endDate) + forecastedMonths)
  End If

  If Me.productCategoryID <> productCategoryID Then
    Me.productCategoryID = productCategoryID
    bNewSeries = True
    Array.Clear(forecastedSet, 0, forecastedSet.Length - 1)
  End If

  Dim i = DateDiff(DateInterval.Month, startDate , orderDate)
```

Redim the array only once to hold existing sales data plus forecasted sales

The array holds sales data per product category

```
    'Is this a forecasted value?
     If orderDate <= endDate Then
              ' No, just load the value in the array
              forecastedSet(i) = sales
     Else
        If bNewSeries Then
           Try
             AWC.RS.Library.RsLibrary.GetForecastedSet(_      <-- Call AwRsLibrary
               forecastedSet, _                                    to get the
               forecastedMonths)                                   forecasted set
             bNewSeries = False
           Catch ex As Exception
             m_ExString  = "Exception: " & ex.Message
             System.Diagnostics.Trace.WriteLine(ex.ToString())
             throw ex
           End Try
       End If
     End If ' is it forecasted value
     Return forecastedSet(i)
End Function
```

Because the matrix region data cells use an expression that references the `GetValue` function, this function gets called by each data cell. Table 6.1 lists the input arguments that the `GetValue` function takes.

Table 6.1 Each data cell inside the matrix region will call the `GetValue` embedded function and pass the following input arguments.

Argument	Purpose
productCategoryID	The productCategoryID value from the rowProductCategory row grouping corresponding to the cell
orderDate	The orderDate value from the colMonth column grouping corresponding to the cell
sales	The aggregated sales total for this cell
reportParameters	To calculate the array dimensions, `GetValue` needs the values of the report parameters. Instead of passing the parameters individually using Parameters!ParameterName.Value, we pass a reference to the report Parameters collection.
txtRange	A variable that holds the error message in case an exception occurs when getting the forecasted data

To understand how `GetValue` works, note that each data cell inside the matrix region is fed from the forecastedSet array. If the cell doesn't need forecasting (its corresponding date is within the requested date range), we just load the cell value in the array and pass it back to display it in the matrix region. To get this working, we need to initialize the array to have a rank equal to the number of requested months plus the number of forecasted months. Once the matrix region moves to a new row and calls our function, we are ready to forecast the data by calling the `AwRsLibrary.GetForecastedSet` method.

Implementing the Sales by Product Category crosstab report

The most difficult part of authoring the report itself was setting up its data to ensure that we always have the correct number of columns in the matrix region to show the forecasted columns. By default, the matrix region won't show columns that don't have data. This will interfere with calculating the right offset to feed the cells from the array.

Therefore, we have to ensure that the database returns records for all months within the requested data range. To implement this, we need to preprocess the sales data at the database. This is exactly what the spGetForecastedData stored procedure does. Inside the stored procedure, we prepopulate a custom table with all monthly periods within the requested date range, as shown in listing 6.3.

Listing 6.3 The spGetForecastedData stored procedure ensures that the returned rowset has the correct number of columns.

```
CREATE  PROCEDURE spGetForecastedData (
  @StartDate smalldatetime,
  @EndDate smalldatetime
)
AS

DECLARE @tempDate smalldatetime

DECLARE @dateSet TABLE        <-- Define a custom table to hold all months
  (                               within the requested date range
  ProductCategoryID   tinyint,
  OrderDate    smalldatetime
  )

SET   @tempDate = @EndDate

WHILE (@StartDate <= @tempDate)      <-- Insert the
BEGIN                                    month records
  INSERT INTO @dateSet
  SELECT ProductCategoryID,  @tempDate
  FROM ProductCategory

  SET @tempDate = DATEADD(mm, -1, @tempDate)
END

SELECT     DS.ProductCategoryID, PC.Name as ProductCategory,
           OrderDate AS Date, NULL AS Sales
FROM       @dateSet DS INNER JOIN ProductCategory PC ON
           DS.ProductCategoryID=PC.ProductCategoryID
UNION ALL     <-- Return the actual sales data
                  plus the dummy records
```

```
SELECT     PC.ProductCategoryID, PC.Name AS ProductCategory,
           SOH.OrderDate AS Date,
           SUM(SOD.UnitPrice * SOD.OrderQty) AS Sales
FROM       ProductSubCategory PSC INNER JOIN
           ProductCategory PC ON PSC.ProductCategoryID =
           PC.ProductCategoryID
INNER JOIN
           Product P ON PSC.ProductSubCategoryID =
           P.ProductSubCategoryID
INNER JOIN SalesOrderHeader SOH INNER JOIN
           SalesOrderDetail SOD ON SOH.SalesOrderID =
           SOD.SalesOrderID
ON         P.ProductID = SOD.ProductID
WHERE      (SOH.OrderDate BETWEEN @StartDate AND @EndDate)
GROUP BY SOH.OrderDate, PC.Name, PC.ProductCategoryID
ORDER BY PC.Name, OrderDate
```

Finally, we union all records from the @dateSet table (its Sales column values are set to NULL) with the actual SQL statement that fetches the sales data.

Once the dataset is set, authoring the rest of the report is easy. We use a matrix region for the crosstab portion of the report. To understand how the matrix region magic works and how it invokes the embedded `GetValue` function, you may want to replace the expression of the txtSales textbox with the following expression:

```
= Fields!ProductCategoryID.Value & "," & Fields!Date.Value _
  & "," &  Format(Fields!Sales.Value, "C")
```

Figure 6.7 shows what the Sales by Product Category crosstab report looks like when this expression is applied.

As you can see, we can easily get to the corresponding row and column group values that the matrix region uses to calculate the aggregate values in the region data cells. Now we have a way to identify each data cell. The matrix region is set up as shown in table 6.2.

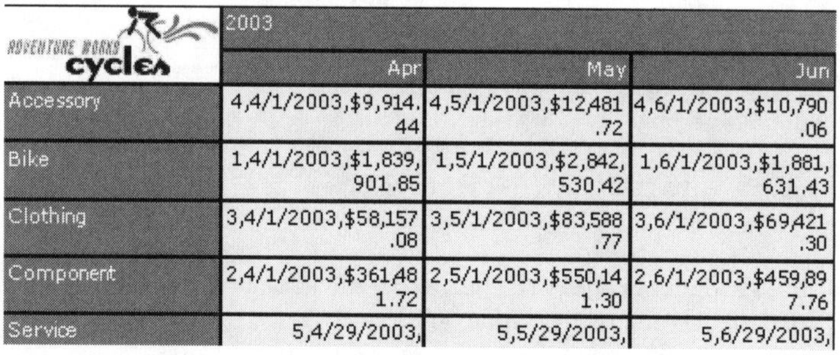

ADVENTURE WORKS cycles	2003		
	Apr	May	Jun
Accessory	4,4/1/2003,$9,914.44	4,5/1/2003,$12,481.72	4,6/1/2003,$10,790.06
Bike	1,4/1/2003,$1,839,901.85	1,5/1/2003,$2,842,530.42	1,6/1/2003,$1,881,631.43
Clothing	3,4/1/2003,$58,157.08	3,5/1/2003,$83,588.77	3,6/1/2003,$69,421.30
Component	2,4/1/2003,$361,481.72	2,5/1/2003,$550,141.30	2,6/1/2003,$459,897.76
Service	5,4/29/2003,	5,5/29/2003,	5,6/29/2003,

Figure 6.7 How the matrix region aggregates data

Table 6.2 The trick to getting the matrix region populated with forecasted values is to base its data cells on an expression.

Matrix Area	Name	Expression
Rows	rowProductGroup	=Fields!ProductCategory.Value
Columns	colYear	=Fields!Date.Value.Year
	colMonth	=Fields!Date.Value.Month
Data	txtSales	=Code.GetValue(Fields!ProductCategoryID.Value, Fields!Date.Value, Sum(Fields!Sales.Value), Parameters, ReportItems!txtRange)

To implement conditional formatting for the forecasted columns (show them in bold), we used the following expression for the font property of the txtSales textbox:

```
=Iif(Code.IsForecasted(Fields!Date.Value, Parameters!EndDate.Value),
"Bold", "Normal")
```

This expression calls the `IsForecasted` function located in the report-embedded code. The function simply compares the sales monthly date with the requested end date and, if the sales date is before the end date, returns false.

The only thing left for us to do is to reference the AwRsLibrary assembly using the Report Properties dialog's References tab, as shown previously in figure 6.3. Please note that for the purposes of this report, we don't need to set up an Instance Name (no need to enter anything in the Classes grid), because we don't call any instance methods.

Debugging custom code

You may find debugging custom code challenging. For this reason, I would like to share with you a few techniques that I have found useful for custom code debugging.

There aren't many options for debugging embedded code. The only one I have found so far is to use the `MsgBox` function to output messages and variable values when the report is rendered inside the Report Designer. Make sure to remove the calls to `MsgBox` before deploying the report to the Report Server. If you don't, all `MsgBox` calls will result in an exception. For some reason, trace messages using System.Diagnostics.Trace (OutputDebugString API) inside embedded code get "swallowed" and don't appear either in the VS.NET Output window or by using an external tracing tool.

When working with external assemblies, you have at least two debugging options:

- Output trace messages.
- Use the VS.NET debugger to step through the custom code.

Tracing

For example, in the `AwRsLibrary.GetForecastedSet` method, we are outputting trace messages using System.Dianogistics.Trace.WriteLine to display the observed and forecasted values. To see these messages when running the report inside VS.NET or Report Server, you can use Mark Russinovich's excellent DebugView tool, shown in figure 6.8.

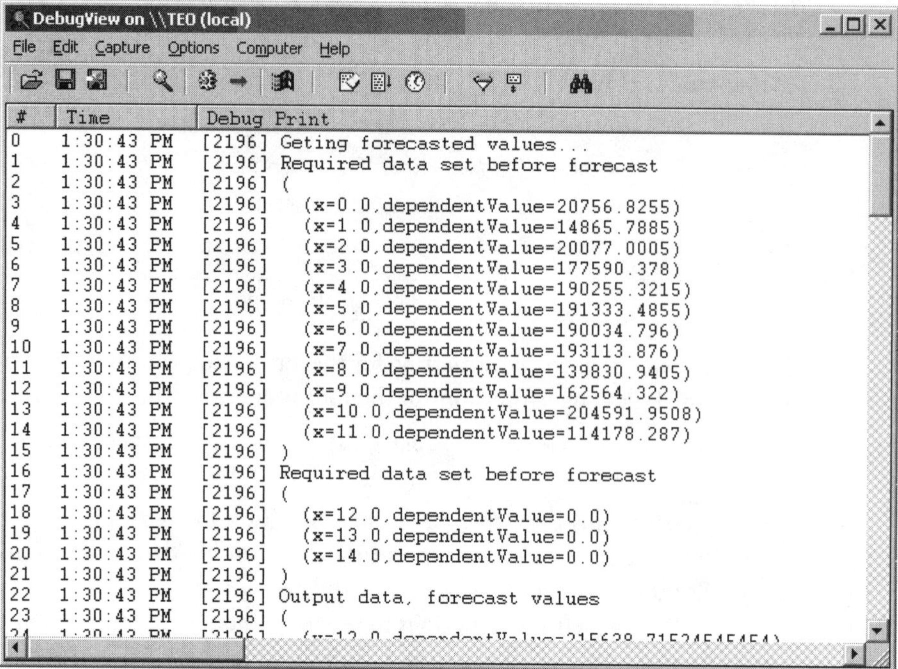

Figure 6.8 Outputting trace messages from external assemblies in DebugView

For more information about DebugView, see section 6.5.

Debugging custom code

You can also step through the custom assembly code using the VS.NET debugger by attaching to the Report Designer process, as follows:

Step 1 Open the custom assembly that you want to debug in a new instance of VS.NET. Set breakpoints in your code as usual.

Step 2 In your custom assembly project properties, expand the Configuration Properties node and select Debugging. Set Debug Mode to Wait to Attach to an External Process.

Step 3 Open your business intelligence project in another instance of VS.NET.

Step 4 Back at the custom assembly project, click on the Debug menu and then choose Processes. Locate the devevn process that hosts that the Business Intelligence project and attach to it. In the Attach To Process dialog, make sure that the Common Language Runtime check box is selected, and click Attach. At this point, your Processes dialog should look like the one shown in figure 6.9.

In this case, we want to debug the code in the AwRsLibrary assembly when it is invoked by the Sales by Product Category report. For this reason, in the AwRsLibrary project we attach to the AWReporter devenv process.

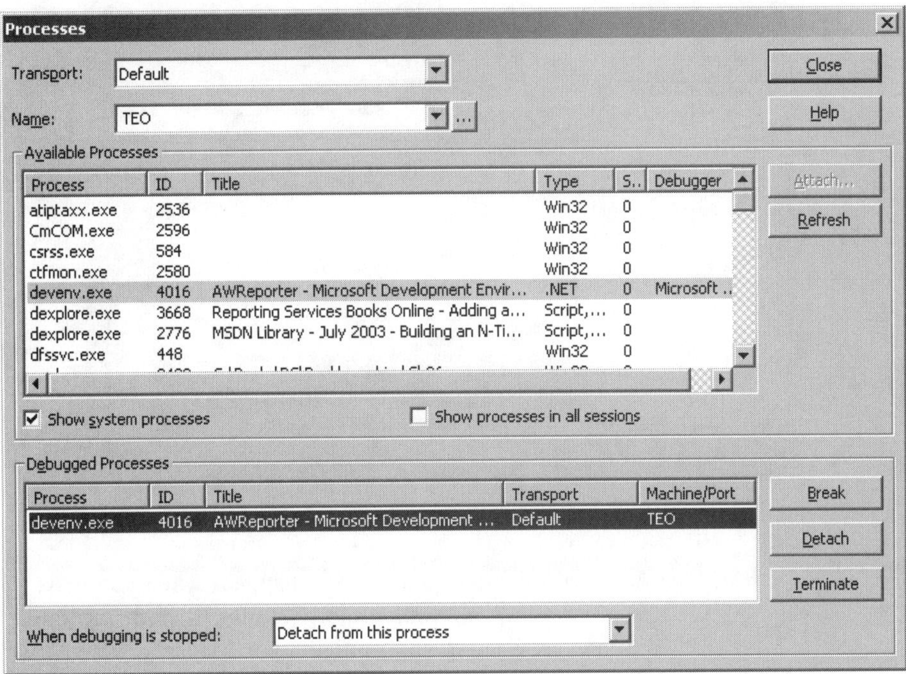

Figure 6.9 To debug custom assemblies, attach to the Visual Studio instance that hosts your BI project.

Step 5 In the Business Intelligence project, preview the report that calls the custom assembly. Or, if you have already been previewing the report, press the Refresh Report button on the Preview Tab toolbar. At this point, your breakpoints should be hit by the VS.NET debugger.

As you will soon find out, if you need to make code changes and recompile the custom assembly, trying to redeploy it to the Report Designer folder results in the following exception:

```
Cannot copy <assembly name>: It is being used by another person or program.
```

The problem is that VS.NET IDE holds a reference to the custom assembly. You will need to shut down VS.NET and then redeploy the new assembly. To avoid this situation and make the debugging process even easier, you could debug the custom assembly code by using the Report Host (Preview Window). To do this, follow these steps:

Step 1 Add the custom assembly to the VS.NET solution that includes your BI project.

Step 2 Change the BI project start item to the report that calls the custom code, as shown in figure 6.10.

Step 3 Press F5 to run the report in the Preview window. When the report calls the custom code, your breakpoints will be hit.

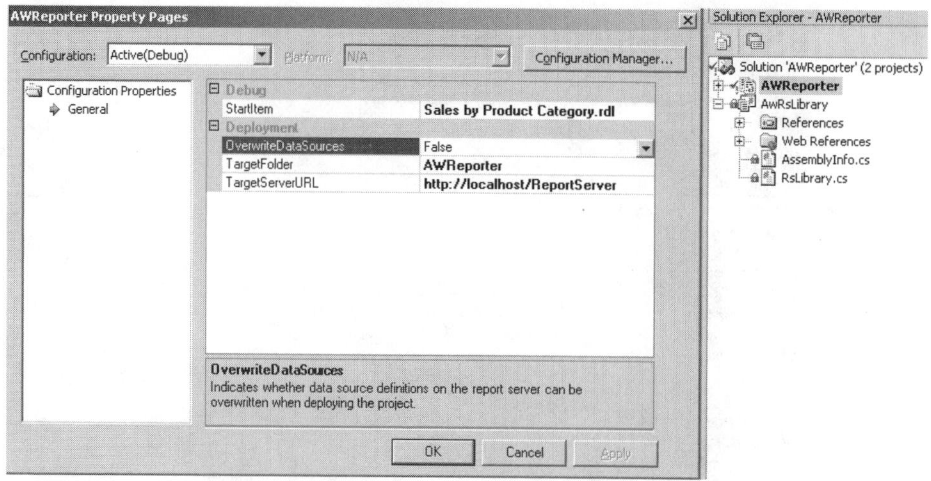

Figure 6.10 Use the Report Host debug option to avoid locking assemblies.

NOTE As explained in chapter 2, what happens when you press F5 to debug a report depends on your project settings. If both the Build and Deploy options are selected in Configuration Manager, VS.NET will build and deploy all reports in your Business Intelligence project before the report is displayed in the Preview window. To avoid this problem and launch your report faster, clear these options or switch to DebugLocal configuration. This configuration doesn't include the Deploy option by default.

When using the Preview window approach, VS.NET doesn't lock the custom assemblies. This allows you to change the build location of your assembly to the Report Designer folder so that it always includes the most recent copy when you rebuild the assembly. As we explained in chapter 2, running your projects in the Preview window is a result of the code access security policy settings specified in the Report Designer configuration file (rspreviewpolicy.config).

Let's now look at another way of using custom code in reports in the form of XSL transformations.

6.3 USING XML-BASED REPORTS

So far in this chapter, we've seen how we can use custom code to extend report capabilities programmatically. For all its flexibility, custom code has its limitations. For example, besides hiding report items, you cannot control the report output programmatically. However, if you export your reports to XML, you can use custom code in the form of XSL transformations to precisely control the XML presentation of the report, as we will discuss next.

Strictly speaking, from an implementation standpoint, exporting a report to XML is no different than exporting it to any other rendering format, because the actual work is performed by the XML rendering extension (Microsoft.ReportingServices.XmlRendering.dll), which happens to be one of the supported RS extensions. However, I decided to devote a special place for it because, in my opinion, this is an extremely useful and important option.

Given the fact that the IT industry has embraced XML as the de facto standard for data exchange between heterogeneous platforms, exporting a report to XML opens a whole new world of opportunity. For example, in the B2B (business-to-business) scenario, an organization could expose an inventory report to its vendors. A vendor could request the report in XML to find out the current inventory product levels. The XML document could then be sent to a BizTalk server, which could extract the product information and send it to the manufacturing department. We will implement a similar solution in chapter 11.

6.3.1 Understanding XML exporting

The content of the following report elements could be exported to XML: textbox, rectangle, subreport, table region, list region, and matrix region. As a report author, you have full control over the XML presentation of these elements. To customize the XML-rendered output of the report, you use the Data Output tab of the report element's property pages. Which settings can be customized depends on the type of the element. In general, you can specify the following:

- Whether the report element and its content (for regions, groups, and rectangles) will be exported
- The XML element name
- Whether the report element will be rendered as an XML attribute or element

For example, at a report level, you can specify the root node name and XML schema. At the region level, you can specify whether the region and its items will be rendered at all. At the textbox level, you can tell the Report Server whether the textbox content will be rendered as an XML attribute or element.

When the Data Output settings are not enough, you can further fine-tune the XML output by using custom XSL transformations. For example, while skipping report elements is easy, adding additional XML nodes is not. In cases such as this, you can write an XSL transformation that will be applied by the Report Server after the report is rendered to XML.

Let's now look at a practical example that demonstrates how exporting to XML could be useful.

6.3.2 Exposing the report content as an RSS feed

While I was trying to figure out what a good XML report could be, my favorite RSS reader (IntraVNews) popped up a new window to let me know about the current news headlines. For those of you who are not familiar with this great information medium, RSS (which stands for all of the following: RDF Site Summary, Rich Site Summary, or Really Simple Syndication) is an XML-based format that allows information workers to describe and syndicate web content. Many organizations and individuals use RSS for *blogging*.

DEFINITION A *blog*, short for *web log*, is a personal journal that is frequently updated and intended for general public consumption.

This inspired me to see if we could expose a report as an RSS feed. To give our example a touch of reality, let's say that Adventure Works Cycles would like to take advantage of the increasing popularity of blogging with RSS feeds. In particular, the company management has requested these requirements:

- Future promotional campaigns must be exposed as an RSS feed. The AWC customers could subscribe to the feed using their favorite RSS newsreader and be notified about future product promotions.
- Each promotional item must include a hyperlink that will show more details about the campaign, such as discounted products and their sale prices.

Implementation options

How can we implement the above requirements? One approach could be to add the promotional information as static or dynamic web content to the company's web portal. For example, the products page could include a section that lists the current promotions. As far as exporting the promotional data as XML for the purposes of the RSS feed, we could create a Web Service that would query the Adventure Works database, retrieve the promotion details in XML, and write them into an RSS blog file.

Another implementation option could be to author an RS report that would supply both the HTML and XML content. The RSS Web Service could then request the report as XML and append the promotional information to the RSS blog file. The RSS item hyperlink could bring the customer to the HTML version of same report. Of course, the latter option assumes that you are willing to allow web users to access your Report Server directly by URL. This is not as bad as it sounds. If Windows authentication is an issue, you can replace it with a custom security extension to authenticate and authorize your web users, as we will discuss in Chapter 15.

Which approach will work better for you depends on your particular needs and limitations. In our case, we will go for the latter to demonstrate the exporting-to-XML feature. To recap, our design goals for the new report sample will be as follows:

- Export the report to RSS-compliant XML format.
- Append the report XML to an RSS feed (we will postpone the actual implementation to chapter 9).

Implementing the report

Let's start by creating a new report called Sales Promotion. The report gets the promotional data from the SpecialOffer and SpecialOfferProduct tables. In addition, it takes one parameter, Campaign ID, which the user can use to request a specific campaign.

For example, figure 6.11 shows the second page of the Sales Promotion report when the user requests a campaign with an ID of 2.

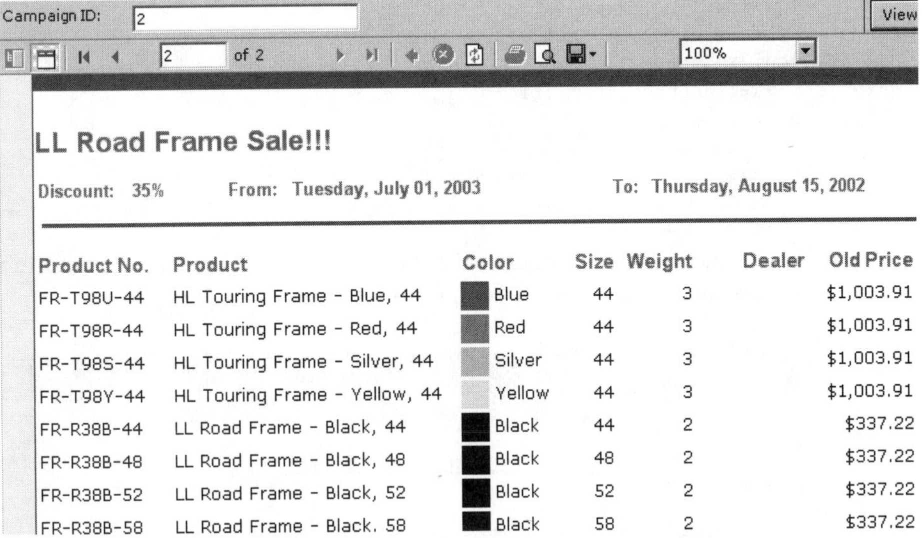

Campaign ID: 2

2 of 2 100% View

LL Road Frame Sale!!!

Discount: 35% From: Tuesday, July 01, 2003 To: Thursday, August 15, 2002

Product No.	Product	Color	Size	Weight	Dealer	Old Price
FR-T98U-44	HL Touring Frame - Blue, 44	Blue	44	3		$1,003.91
FR-T98R-44	HL Touring Frame - Red, 44	Red	44	3		$1,003.91
FR-T98S-44	HL Touring Frame - Silver, 44	Silver	44	3		$1,003.91
FR-T98Y-44	HL Touring Frame - Yellow, 44	Yellow	44	3		$1,003.91
FR-R38B-44	LL Road Frame - Black, 44	Black	44	2		$337.22
FR-R38B-48	LL Road Frame - Black, 48	Black	48	2		$337.22
FR-R38B-52	LL Road Frame - Black, 52	Black	52	2		$337.22
FR-R38B-58	LL Road Frame - Black, 58	Black	58	2		$337.22

Figure 6.11 The Sales Promotion report serves as both the RSS feed source and the HTML campaign details page.

As you can see, this report is very similar to the RS Product Catalog report sample, so we won't spend much time discussing its implementation details. Instead, we will focus on explaining how to export the report's content to XML.

Understanding the RSS schema

What the report's XML output needs to be depends on which version of the RSS specification you have to support. For example, listing 6.4 shows what the sales promotion RSS feed should look like if it conforms to RSS version 2.0.

Listing 6.4 The Sales Promotion RSS feed to which the AWC subscribers will subscribe to be notified about sales promotions

```
<rss version="2.0">
<channel>    <— General feed-related header
  <title>AWC Promotions</title>
  <link>http://www.adventure-works.com/</link>
  <description>Great discounted deals!</description>
  <language>en-us</language>
  <ttl>1440</ttl>
  <item xmlns:n1="http://www.awc.com/sales" xmlns:xs="http://www.w3.org/
2001/XMLSchema">    <— Feed item
    <title>LL Road Frame Sale!!!</title>
    <link>http://localhost/reportserver?/AWReporter/Sales
            Promotion&SpecialOfferID=2&rs:Command=Render&rs:Format=XML
    </link>
    <description>Great LL Road Frame Sale!!!</description>
    <pubDate>Saturday, January 10, 2004</pubDate>
```

```
  </item>
  <item xmlns:n1="http://www.awc.com/sales" xmlns:xs="http://www.w3.org/
2001/XMLSchema">
    <!-Another item information here-
  </item>
</channel>
</rss>
```

Given the above feed, figure 6.12 shows how it gets rendered in the IntraVNews RSS Reader, which is integrated with Outlook:

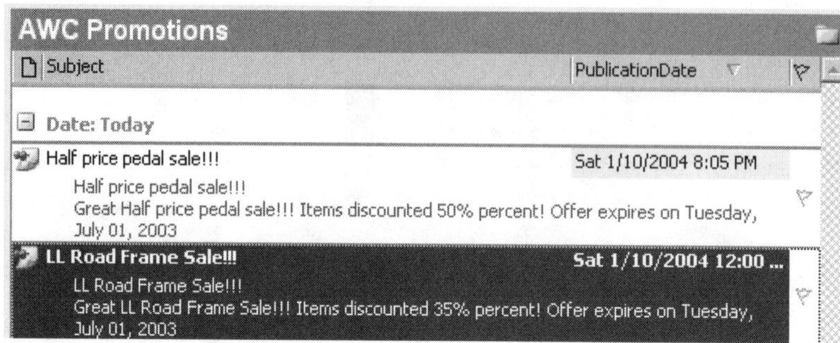

Figure 6.12 The AWC Promotions feed rendered in IntraVNews

Let's now examine what needs to be done to massage the report output in order to make it compliant with the RSS schema.

Defining the report XML output

The first step required to export the report to an RSS-compliant format is to fine-tune its XML output. We've made a few changes using the Data Output tab for various elements, so the report renders to the abbreviated XML schema shown in listing 6.5.

Listing 6.5 The Sales Promotion report rendered in XML

```
<SalesPromotion xmlns="http://www.awc.com/sales" xmlns:xsi="http://
www.w3.org/2001/XMLSchema-instance" xsi:schemaLocation="..." Name="Sales
Promotion" Date="2004-01-10T00:00:00.0000000-05:00">
  <Promotions>
    <Promotion Description="LL Road Frame Sale!!!">    <-- The Promotion element will represent an item in the RSS feed
      <ProductInfo>
        <Products>
          <Product ProductNumber="FR-T98U-44"
             Product="HL Touring Frame - Blue, 44" Color="Blue"
             Size="44" Weight="2.92" ListPrice="1003.9100"/>
          <Product ProductNumber="FR-T98R-44" Product="HL Touring Frame -
Red, 44" Color="Red"
             Size="44" Weight="2.92" ListPrice="1003.9100"/>
        </Products>
```

```
      </ProductInfo>
    </Promotion>
  </Promotions>
</SalesPromotion>
```

The most important change that you have to make is to explicitly set the XML Schema setting at the report level, as shown in figure 6.13.

If the Data Schema setting is not specified, the Report Server will autogenerate the XML document global namespace to include the date when the report is processed. This will interfere with referencing the document elements from an XSL transformation, so make sure you explicitly set the schema namespace.

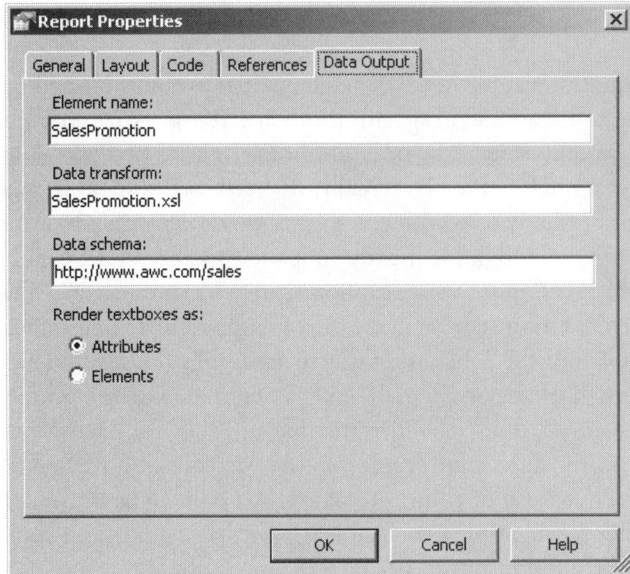

Figure 6.13
Use the Data Output report settings to define the report XML root element name and namespace.

Writing the XSL tranformation

Once you have finished making adjustments to the XML schema, the next step will be to write an XSL transformation to transform the XML output to an RSS-compliant format. To fit the Sales Promotion output to the RSS schema, we wrote the simple XSL transformation shown in listing 6.6.

Listing 6.6 Use XSL transformations to fine-tune the report's XML output.

```
<?xml version="1.0" encoding="UTF-8"?>
<xsl:stylesheet version="1.0"
xmlns:n1="http://www.awc.com/sales"
xmlns:xs="http://www.w3.org/2001/XMLSchema">
  <xsl:template match="/">
   <xsl:for-each select="n1:SalesPromotion/n1:Promotions/
```

```
      n1:Promotion">     <-- Loop through all Promotion elements
     <item>    <-- Generate an RSS item
      <title><xsl:value-of select="./@Description"/></title>
      <link>http://www.adventure-workds.com/promotions</link>
      <description>Great <xsl:value-of select="./@Description"/>
        Items discounted
        <xsl:value-of select="./@DiscountPct"/> percent! Offer
           expires on
         <xsl:value-of select="./@StartDate"/>
       </description>
      <pubDate><xsl:value-of select="./@StartDate"/></pubDate>
     </item>
    </xsl:for-each>
  </xsl:template>
</xsl:stylesheet>
```

The XSL transformation simply loops through all sales promotions and outputs them in XML according to the RSS item specification. Strictly speaking, in our case there is always going to be only one XML sales promotion node, because we use a report parameter to select a single campaign. Finally, we need to add the XSL transformation file to our project. Similarly to working with images, we have to add the XSLT file to the same report project and subsequently upload it to the report catalog when the report is deployed. The Report Server cannot reference external XSLT files.

The last implementation step is to take care of appending the current sales promotion item to the RSS blog file. The easiest way to accomplish this would be to manually update the RSS feed XML file on the web server when there is a new promotional campaign. RSS newsreaders could reference this file directly, for example, by going to http://www.adventure-works.com/promotions.rss. Of course, if the requirements call for it, the process could also be fully automated. We will see how this could be done in chapter 9, where we will implement a table trigger that invokes a custom web service when a new sales promotion record is added to the database.

To subscribe to the RSS feed, AWC customers would configure their favorite RSS readers to point to the blog file. Once they do so, they will be notified each time the blog file is updated.

6.4 SUMMARY

In this chapter we learned how to integrate our reports with custom code that we or someone else wrote.

For simple report-specific programming logic, you can use embedded VB.NET code. When the code complexity increases or you prefer to use programming languages other than VB.NET, you can move your code to external assemblies.

For interoperability with different platforms and languages, you can export your reports to XML. You can control precisely the report output by using the Data Output tab coupled with custom XSL transformations.

By now, you should have enough knowledge to be able to author reports with Reporting Services. We'll now move on to the second phase of the report lifecycle: report management.

6.5 Resources

The OpenForecast web site (http://openforecast.sourceforge.net/)

Microsoft Java Language Conversion Assistant
(http://msdn.microsoft.com/vstudio/downloads/tools/jlca/default.aspx)
Converts Java-language code to C#

Mark Russinovich's DebugView tool
(http://www.sysinternals.com/ntw2k/freeware/debugview.shtml)

What is RSS?
(http://www.xml.com/pub/a/2002/12/18/dive-into-xml.html)
A good introduction to RSS

Lutz Roeder's .NET Reflector
(http://www.aisto.com/roeder/dotnet/)
Similar to the VS.NET Object Browser, Reflector is a class browser for .NET components.

PART 2

Managing reports

Once your report is ready, you will probably need to make it available to the end users. A common requirement posed to enterprise-wide reporting frameworks, such as Reporting Services, is to facilitate report access and management by keeping all report configuration in a single place. To respond to this need, RS captures reports and their related items in a centralized report catalog.

In part 2 we will put on our report manager's hats to find out what techniques are available for carrying out the second phase of the report lifecycle—report management. Most of our time will be spent discussing how we can leverage the Report Manager web application to perform various management tasks, such as uploading reports, organizing reports in folders, configuring and working with server-side settings, configuring report caching, and so forth.

As a versatile reporting platform, RS provide ways to address various management needs. We will explore other management options supported by RS, such as the RS Web service, WMI provider, RS Scripting Host, and specialized utilities.

An important task that every report manager needs to master is how to secure the report catalog. We will look at how the RS role-based security mechanism works and how it can be configured to enforce restricted access to the report catalog. Finally, you will learn how to configure RS code access security to grant the minimum set of permissions that reports with custom code need to execute successfully.

C H A P T E R 7

Managing the Reporting Services environment

Reporting Services provides all the tools you need to support the full lifecycle of a report. In a typical enterprise environment, there are usually three different groups of people who get involved with each of the three phases of a report's lifecycle:

- Report authors focus on authoring reports using the Report Designer.
- Administrators are concerned with managing the report repository.
- Developers report-enable their applications to allow users to request reports on-demand or via subscriptions.

In this chapter, we will wear administrators' hats and discuss how we can manage the report environment. As we will find out, Reporting Services provides not one but several maintenance options for performing various administration tasks. We'll discuss each option as follows:

- The Report Manager
- The RS Web service
- The Reporting Services WMI Provider

- The Scripting Host
- Other administration utilities

Let's start our tour by looking at how report administrators can leverage the Report Manager web portal to manage the report catalog.

7.1 MANAGING RS WITH THE REPORT MANAGER

The report administrator's responsibilities typically include performing various day-to-day tasks to maintain the report catalog. For example, the administrator may want to grant rights to certain users or Windows groups to run a given report.

To reduce the management effort, Reporting Services includes a user-friendly web-based tool called the Report Manager.

The Report Manager serves the following main tasks:

- *Report delivery*—End users can use the Report Manager to request reports on demand.
- *Report management*—Report administrators can use the Report Manager to manage all aspects of the report catalog.

Before we explore the Report Manager portal, it will be beneficial to start with a 1,000-foot view of its architecture.

7.1.1 How the Report Manager works

From an implementation perspective, the Report Manager is simply a web-based front end to the Report Server, as shown in figure 7.1.

From an application standpoint, the Report Manager is implemented as an ASP.NET application, consisting of maintenance pages, styles, images, and other web resources.

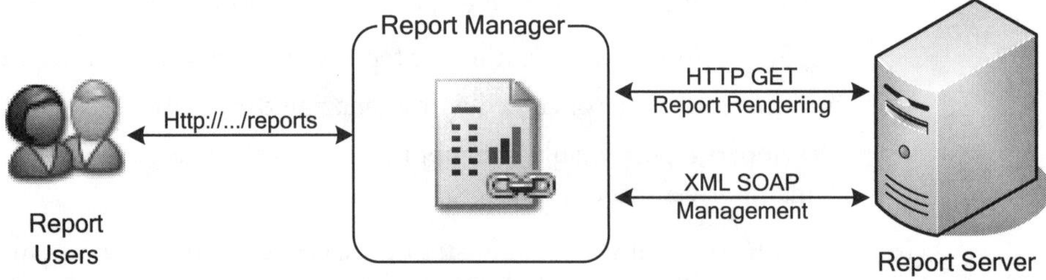

Figure 7.1 The Report Manager is implemented as an ASP.NET application that accesses the Report Server via HTTP-GET and XML SOAP. HTTP-GET requests are used to render reports; XML SOAP requests are used for all other report management tasks.

Installing the Report Manager

The Report Manager's default installation settings are listed in table 7.1.

Table 7.1 The Report Manager's default installation settings

Setting	Value
Vroot	Reports
Physical Folder	C:\Program Files\Microsoft SQL Server\MSSQL\Reporting Services\ReportManager
URL	http://<reportserver>/reports

The Reporting Services Setup program doesn't allow you install the Report Manager separately from the Report Server, which forces you to have both components installed on the same box. This is because deploying the Report Manager on a separate computer requires that you use Kerberos as an authentication protocol so that the user credentials are properly delegated between the Report Manager and the Report Server.

NOTE The Kerberos protocol originated at MIT more than a decade ago. The Windows implementation of Kerberos allows an application to flow an authenticated identity across multiple physical tiers of the application. For more information about how to configure Kerberos, refer to section 7.7.

If enabling Kerberos is not a problem, moving the Report Manager to a separate machine is not difficult. Thanks to the xcopy ASP.NET deployment, this is as easy as creating a new IIS virtual root and copying all Report Manager files to it. Once you have done this, you should verify that the ReportServerUrl setting in the RSWebApplication configuration file points to the correct Report Server URL.

Configuring the Report Manager

The ASP.NET and Report Manager–specific configuration settings are defined in the web.config and RSWebApplication.config configuration files, respectively. Some of the configuration settings worth mentioning are listed in table 7.2.

Table 7.2 The Report Manager configuration settings

Setting	File	Description
DefaultTraceSwitch	Web.config	Defines the level of tracing information output
ReportServerUrl	RSWebApplication.config	Specifies the URL address of the Report Server
MaxActiveReqForOneUser	RSWebApplication.config	Limits the number of open HTTP requests by user. Useful for preventing denial of service attacks.

The Report Manager uses ASP.NET sessions to maintain folder view preferences, such as showing/hiding folder details. For this reason, the Report Manager ASP.NET session state cannot be turned off.

The Report Manager is configured to use Windows-based authentication to authenticate users. In addition, it is configured by default to impersonate the user, as you can see by examining the `<identity>` element in the web.config configuration file. As a result, all requests to the Report Web Server for both report rendering and management go out under the identity of the Windows user.

The Report Manager web application

To access the Report Manager portal, enter its URL address in a browser, which by default is http://<servername>/reports, where <servername> is the name of the computer where the Report Manager is installed.

Figure 7.2 shows the Contents tab of Report Manager Home page. Your Contents tab may differ from mine, depending on what custom folders you have created below the Home folder and if the My Reports feature has been enabled (see section 7.1.2).

Users familiar with Microsoft SharePoint will find the Report Manager look and feel similar. The UI interface is very intuitive, so I won't spend much time discussing each individual page. Instead, I will focus on a few topics that warrant more explanation. If you need more information about working with the Report Manager, please consult the Reporting Services documentation.

Using the Report Manager for report delivery

The Report Manager can be used as a quick-and-easy report delivery tool. Organizations that cannot afford or don't need customized reporting applications will appreciate this option.

To render a report using the Report Manager, navigate through the folder structure and click the Report link. Behind the scenes, report rendering is accomplished through client-side URL (HTTP-GET) requests to the Report Server. To accomplish all tasks

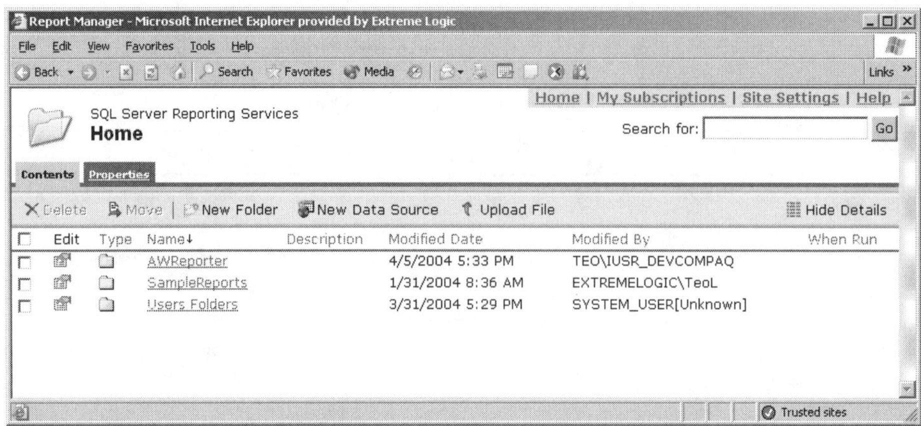

Figure 7.2 The Report Manager Portal is used for rendering reports and managing the report catalog.

other than report rendering, the Report Manager calls the RS Web service on the server side using XML SOAP requests.

7.1.2 Managing Report Server settings

The Site Settings menu of the Report Manager allows the report administrator to manage some important Report Server settings and tasks, including role-based security, shared schedules, execution logging, and report history.

The Site Settings page is shown in figure 7.3.

The changes that you make on the Site Settings page are saved in the ConfigurationInfo table in the Report Server Configuration database. Some of the settings are self-explanatory. For example, the Report Execution timeout setting limits the report execution time to the specified number of seconds.

We'll explain how to manage the My Reports, schedule, and job features here, but we will postpone discussing role-based security to chapter 8. If you feel you need more information about the system settings, please check the "Report Server System Properties" section in the product documentation.

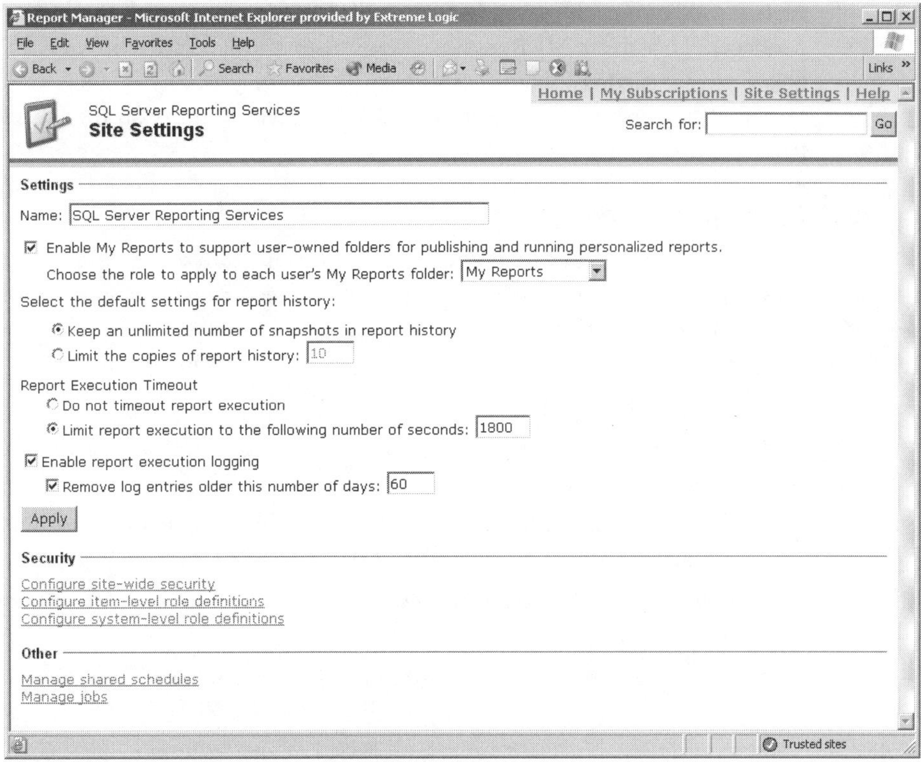

Figure 7.3 Use the Site Settings page to manage server-side settings, enable the MyReports feature, and manage shared schedules, jobs, and so on.

Enabling My Reports

An interesting Reporting Services feature is My Reports. My Reports provides a personal, private workspace per user. In a typical enterprise environment, the administrator may restrict public access to report folders but grant users restricted rights to upload, manage, and view their own reports in the "sandboxed" My Reports area.

To enable the My Reports feature (it is disabled by default), select the Enable My Reports To Support User-Owned Folders For Publishing And Running Personalized Reports check box.

The administrator can specify which security role will be mapped to My Reports to further restrict the allowable tasks that users can perform. The choices are the Browser, Content Manager, My Reports, and Publisher roles. We will postpone discussing these roles to chapter 8. For the time being, note that the default role (My Reports) grants the users rights to create and manage reports, folders, and resources in their private workspace.

When My Reports is enabled, two things happen. First, the Report Manager creates a catalog folder called Users Folders. This folder will contain a personal folder for each Windows user. Next, a My Reports link is added to the Home page of the Report Manager. To activate My Reports, a report user must click this link, which in turn creates a private catalog folder for this user.

After the personal folder is created, clicking My Reports on the Home page navigates the user to her personal folder.

Managing schedules

Using the Report Manager, the report administrator can schedule certain report activities to run in an unattended mode once or on a recurring basis. For example, you may need to distribute a report on a regular basis to subscribed users. To accomplish this, you can create a shared schedule to trigger the subscription event.

The following activities can be scheduled:

- *Delivering reports through subscriptions ("pushed" reports)*—We will look at subscribed report delivery in chapter 14.
- *Generating report snapshots*—We will explain what report snapshots are in section 7.1.4.
- *Adding report snapshots to the report history*—We will discuss report snapshot history in section 7.1.4.
- *Expiring a cached report copy*—Caching is also explained in section 7.1.4.

Similarly to working with data sources, you can create two types of schedules:

- *Report-specific schedules*—A report-specific schedule is associated with a single report. You can create a report-specific schedule from the report's Execution property page.

- *Shared schedules*—As its name suggests, a shared report schedule can be shared by reports and subscriptions that need to occur at the same time. Once the shared schedule is created, you can select its name from a drop-down list during the process of scheduling the activity, as we will show in section 7.1.4.

You should use shared schedules whenever you can because of the following advantages they offer:

- *Centralized maintenance*—Let's say the employees of the Sales department have subscribed to some monthly summary reports to be e-mailed to them on the first day of each month. To simplify the report maintenance, you decide to use a shared schedule to initiate the subscribed delivery. If the users later change their mind and request the reports to be delivered on the last day of the month, you need only update the shared schedule.
- *Security*—Similar to a shared data source, a shared schedule is a securable item and can be managed by users who have rights to execute the Manage Shared Schedules task.

You create or manage shared schedules using the Manage Shared Schedules link under the Other section of the Site Settings page. This will bring you to the Schedule page, as shown in figure 7.4. The SQL Server Agent service must be running to make changes to a schedule.

For example, the screenshot in figure 7.4 shows that we have created a schedule that runs on a quarterly basis. To see all reports that depend on the shared schedule, click the Reports link.

The RS Windows service (not to be confused with the RS Web service) (ReportingServicesService.exe) works with the SQL Server Agent to coordinate the running of scheduled tasks. Here is a simplified picture of what happens behind the scenes. When a schedule is created, the Report Server creates a SQL Server Agent job and schedules it to run when the event is due. When the time is up, the SQL Server Agent creates a record in the Event table in the Report Server database.

The RS Windows service periodically polls this table for new events. The polling interval can be controlled by the PollingInterval setting in the RSReportServer.config configuration file. The default value is 10 seconds. In case there is a new event, the Windows service queries the report catalog to get a list of the scheduled tasks that are up. Then, it calls down to the Report Server (directly, not via the web façades) to execute the tasks. Finally, if the schedule is reoccurring, the Windows service creates a new SQL Server Agent job and schedules it to run according to the specified schedule interval.

As a developer, you can programmatically log an event in the Report Server database by invoking the FireEvent SOAP API. This could be useful if you want to disregard the schedule and initiate the execution of a certain task explicitly. For example, as a report administrator, you may have set up the product catalog report to be e-mailed automatically to Internet customers on a monthly basis. However, you may also need to send the report immediately when a new product is entered into the sales database.

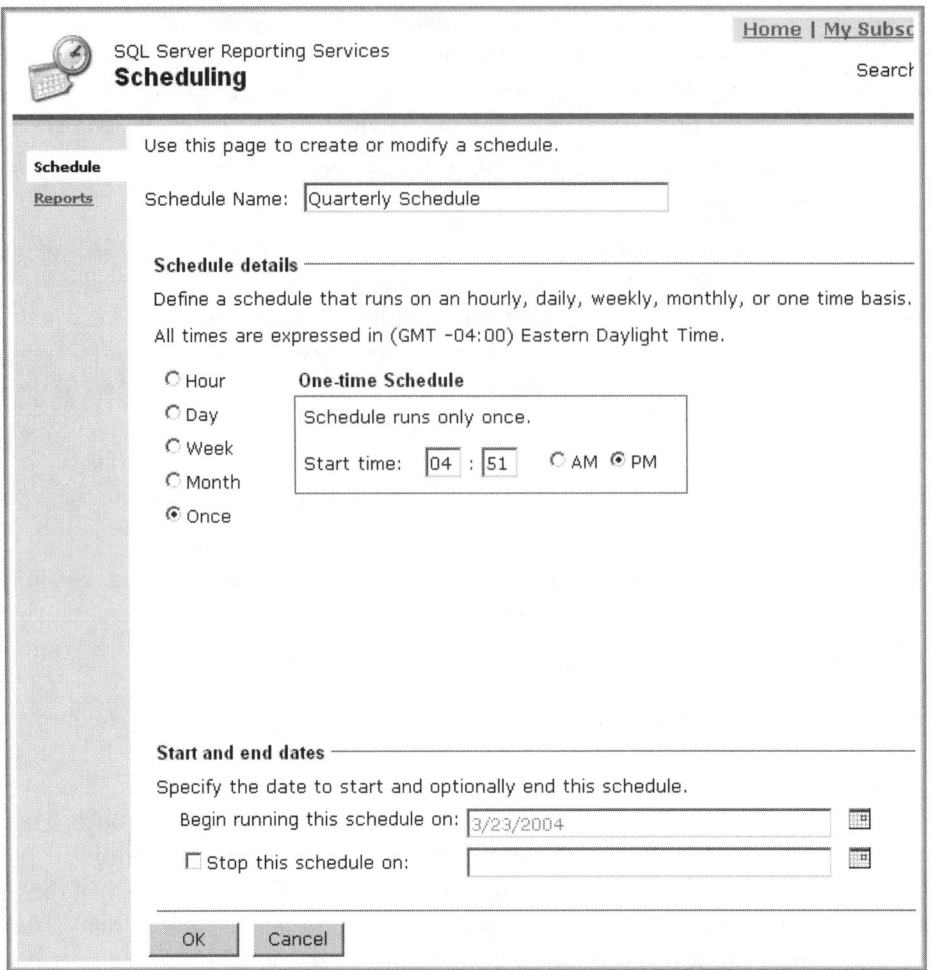

Figure 7.4 Use the Schedule page to specify the shared schedule settings.

To meet this objective, you can use a table trigger attached to the Product table to invoke FireEvent when a new record is added to this table. We will see an example of how this scenario could be implemented in chapter 14.

Managing jobs

Sometimes, you may need to examine the current task activity of the Report Server. For example, users may complain that reports are taking a long time to execute and you need to find out how many report requests are pending.

To see the list of all running jobs, click the Manage Jobs link in the Other section of the Site Settings page. For example, figure 7.5 shows that we are currently executing the Sales By Territory Interactive report.

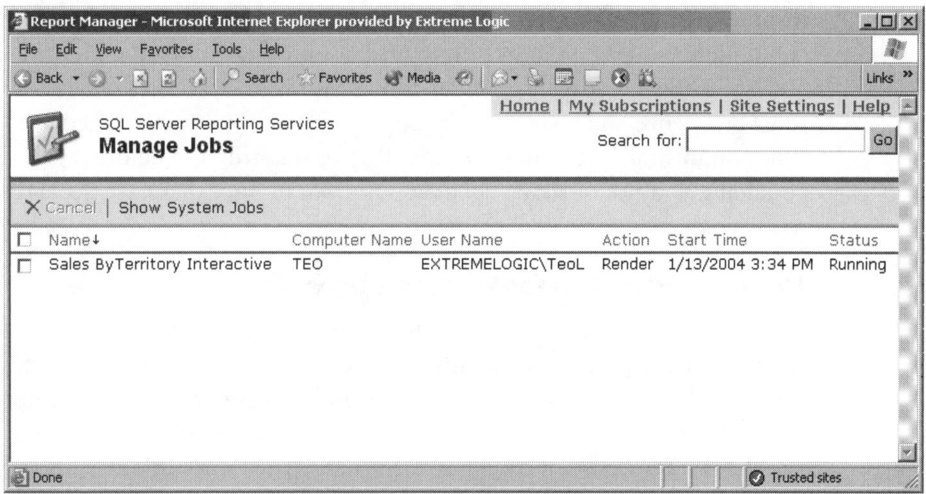

Figure 7.5 Use the Manage Jobs page to see a list of all running user and system jobs.

There are two types of running jobs that the Report Server supports: user jobs and system jobs. A user job is any job that is explicitly initiated by a user, such as all actions that the user can initiate through the Report Manager. These include requesting a report, viewing the report history, subscribing to a report, and so on. A system job is a job running in unattended mode and initiated by the Report Server. System jobs include scheduled snapshots and data-driven subscriptions.

The list of running jobs is retrieved from the RunningJobs table in the Report Server database. When the Report Server initiates a new user or system job, it creates a record in this table. The RS Windows service periodically scans this table at an interval specified under the RunningRequestsDbCycle setting in the RSReportServer.config configuration file.

The administrator can attempt to cancel a running job by selecting the job and clicking the Cancel button. This in turns invokes the CancelJob web method of the RS Web service, which attempts to terminate the background thread servicing the report request. Canceling a job doesn't guarantee that the job will be immediately terminated. Sometimes, hung jobs may require you to manually restart the Report Server. Because the Report Server's lifetime is controlled by IIS, to restart it you will need to restart IIS.

Let's now see how we can use the Report Manager to manage the report catalog.

7.1.3 Managing content

In a typical enterprise environment, the report administrator will spend most of her time managing *content*. Content management tasks include creating folders, uploading resources in these folders, and managing resources. For example, just as you would avoid saving all your files in the root folder of your hard drive, you would stay away from uploading all reports to the Home folder. Instead, from the Home page you could use the New Folder button to create subfolders below the Home folder.

While how you organize folder content on your PC hard drive is a matter of personal preference, the RS folder namespace is publicly accessible. Therefore, as a responsible administrator you need to carefully plan its structure before reports go "live." If you don't, you risk breaking client applications or links that have dependencies on the report folders.

Understanding the folder namespace

Similarly to an OS file system, the Report Manager organizes reports in folders. The RS folder namespace is a hierarchy that contains predefined (Home and My Reports) folders and user-defined folders that the administrator creates. For example, figure 7.2 shows that we have created two folders, AWReporter and SampleReports.

The main purpose of having a folder namespace is to uniquely identify a resource in the report catalog. For example, just as you could have many files named readme.doc on your PC hard drive, you could have many reports named the same in the report catalog. However, you cannot have two reports with the same name uploaded to the same folder.

Although you may find the folder concept similar to the Windows folder structure, please note that the folders that you create in the Report Manager are virtual and they do not map to physical folders. Instead, the folders and their contents are uploaded to the Report Server Configuration database and stored in the report catalog (Catalog table). This table defines a self-referential integrity relationship where each record references its parent. The top folder is predefined and is called Home. When you click a folder link, the Report Manager simply calls down to the RS SOAP API to query the Report Server Configuration database and find out which child records are linked to this folder.

Using the Report Manager, the report administrator can perform the folder tasks listed in table 7.3.

Table 7.3 Use the Report Manager to perform a variety of management tasks.

Task	Example
Upload content to a folder	Once a new report is created, the administrator has to upload it to the report catalog to make the report globally available.
Move content between folders	Sometimes, the administrator may need to reorganize report content just as you may need to use Windows Explorer to move files from one folder to another.
Create subfolders	Establishing a good hierarchical structure is an important task that every administrator must carefully evaluate. For example, one of the decisions that you must make as early as possible before setting up the report catalog is how the folder namespace should be organized, i.e., per department, application, and so on.

continued on next page

Table 7.3 Use the Report Manager to perform a variety of management tasks. *(continued)*

Task	Example
Move folders and all of their content to another folder	The Report Manager allows you to move the entire content of a folder to another folder. For example, a company may go through a reorganization in which some departments are consolidated into one department. Using the Report Manager, you could update the report catalog to reflect the new organizational structure.
Delete folders and all of their content	With the Report Manager you delete resources when they are no longer needed.
Hide folders and resources	To reduce folder clutter, users can exclude resources from the folder view by hiding them.
Modify folder names	Similarly to using Windows Explorer, the report administrator can rename folders.

To perform these folder tasks, the administrator would access the folder or resource properties and initiate the appropriate action from there. For example, figure 7.6 shows the Properties page of the AWReporter folder that contains our sample reports.

Use the folder's Properties page to perform various management tasks. For example, to delete the folder, click the Delete button.

For some reason, copying folders and resources is not supported. As a workaround, you could upload the files manually.

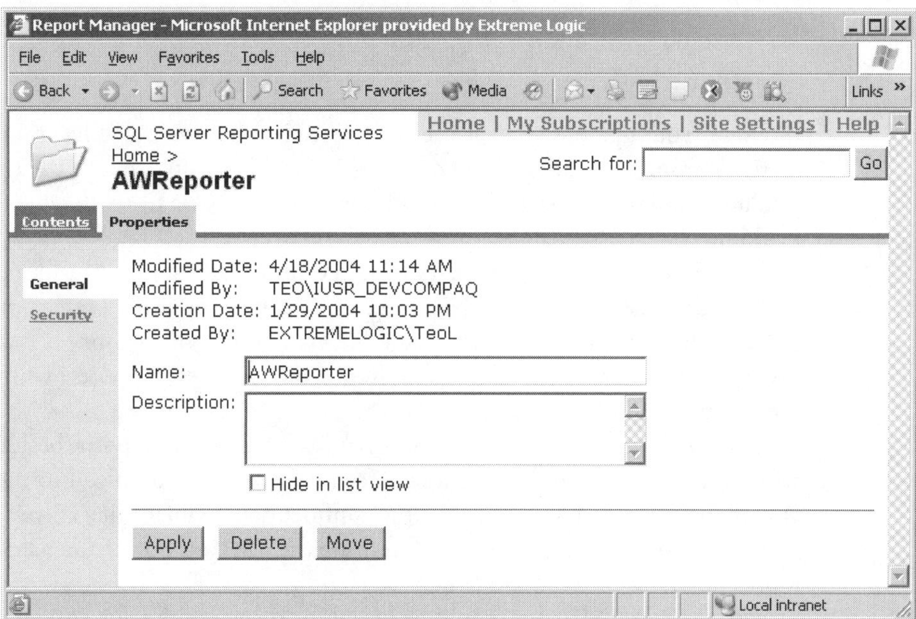

Figure 7.6 Use the folder properties to perform various management tasks, including renaming, deleting, and moving the folder.

Uploading resources

Once the folder structure is established, the administrator can upload report content manually using the Upload File link (see figure 7.2). As we mentioned in chapter 2, if the report author has the appropriate security permissions, the Report Designer will create the project folder straight from the VS.NET IDE when the project is deployed. As a part of the deployment process, the Report Designer links the project folder to the root (Home) folder and names it according to the TargetFolder setting you specified on the project's properties.

The Report Designer doesn't allow you to create additional folders below the root project folder. However, the Report Manager doesn't expose this restriction. You can create as many nested folders as you like.

There are two common situations when uploading files manually may be necessary: when the report author doesn't have the rights to upload the reports directly from the Report Designer and when the report definition file is authored by an outside party.

What resources can be uploaded to a folder? The Report Server doesn't enforce special rules and allows any file to be uploaded to the report catalog. However, in my opinion, it only makes sense to upload the following resources:

- Report definition (*.RDL) files
- Shared data source (*.RDS) files
- Image files
- XSL transformation files (*.XSL)
- HTML pages

But wait, you may say, what if the report needs other types of files, for example, an XML file from which to read some settings? Should you upload it to the Report Server catalog so you don't have to specify the absolute or relative file path when you need to load it in XML DOM using custom code?

The answer is, unfortunately, no. Just like any other resource, the file gets serialized and saved to the Report Server database, so it is not physically present in the Report Server virtual root or elsewhere on the file system. For this reason, it makes sense to upload only external resources that Reporting Services supports, which currently include images, XSLT files, and HTML pages.

For example, for the purposes of the AWReporter sample reports, besides the report definition files and the shared data source files, you need to upload to the report catalog the awc.jpg logo image file and the confidential.jpg image file, as well as the SalesPromotion.xsl file that we used to fine-tune the XML output of the Sales Promotion report in chapter 6.

Uploading HTML pages could be useful for reports with navigational features. For example, you may have a report with hyperlinks that display context-sensitive help for different sections of the report. You can put the help content in HTML pages and upload them with the report.

By the way, the file size limit for external files is 4 MB. The 4-MB limit is a browser upload control limitation. You can post larger resources through the SOAP management API.

Managing folders

How should you partition the folder structure so it is well organized and yet simple to maintain? My advice is to keep it as flat as possible. The advantages of having a flat physical structure are twofold:

- It simplifies the folder maintenance.
- It shortens the report path, which, in turn, makes it easier to request reports programmatically or manually (how do you feel when you have to type in those long URLs in the browser?).

In general, there are two considerations that will affect the folder structure: logical partitioning (for example, you may need to organize your reports in such a way that they reflect organizational hierarchy, client applications, and so on) and security.

There may be other considerations that will affect the folder organization, such as which organizational segment a given Report Server instance serves, how to deal with shared resources, and so forth. Let's look at an example to clarify the last point. To simplify things, we'll assume that our hypothetical company, Adventure Works Cycles, has only one instance of the Report Server installed in its headquarters.

The AWC management has requested the following:

- Reports should be organized logically per department and then per application.
- Cross-department reporting is not permitted.

Given the above requirements, figure 7.7 shows what a possible folder structure might look like.

To meet the logical organization requirements, the administrator could create subfolders for each department. Then, the folder namespace could be further broken down into subfolders per application. As we will see in chapter 8, folders and resources are securable items. To meet the security requirements, the administrator can grant the sales employees permissions to browse the Sales folder but revoke their access to the HR folder.

Subject to security permissions, a report in one folder can reference resources from another folder. For example, the administrator can upload the AWC company logo to the Shared folder. Then, all reports can reference the logo by setting the image item's Value property to /Shared/AWC.JPG.

Those of you who are familiar with web development may think that to reference a parent folder you can use the "../" specifier. RS simplifies folder navigation by allowing you to reference a folder by its relative path to the root Home folder. For example, reports under the App1 folder can reference Resource 2 under the App 2 folder

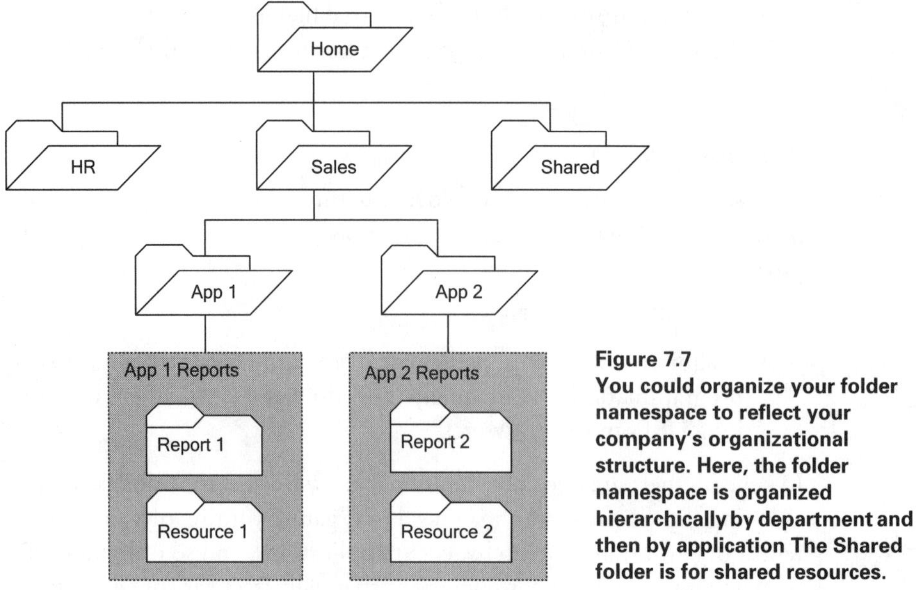

Figure 7.7
You could organize your folder namespace to reflect your company's organizational structure. Here, the folder namespace is organized hierarchically by department and then by application The Shared folder is for shared resources.

as /Sales/App 2/Resource 2. When you are in doubt, make sure that your folder reference matches the value in the Path column of the Catalog table in the Report Server database.

Managing reports

To manage a published (managed) report, you use the report's Properties page, as shown in figure 7.8.

Use the General link to complete the following tasks:

- Change the report name and description.
- Hide the report from the folder view.
- Download or change the report definition (RDL) file by clicking the Edit and Update links, respectively.
- Create a linked report, as we will discuss in section 7.1.5.

To avoid confusion and clutter, the administrator can hide folders or resources by selecting the Hide In List View check box. For example, it is unlikely that you want your users to see shared data source definitions and resources other than the reports in the folder list view. They might confuse these items for reports and attempt to execute them.

There is no special security permission required to see a hidden item. The item is simply excluded from the folder view but the user can see all items by clicking the Show Details button. The Show Details mode also displays the last time the reports were run.

Use the Parameters link to manage the report parameters (figure 7.9).

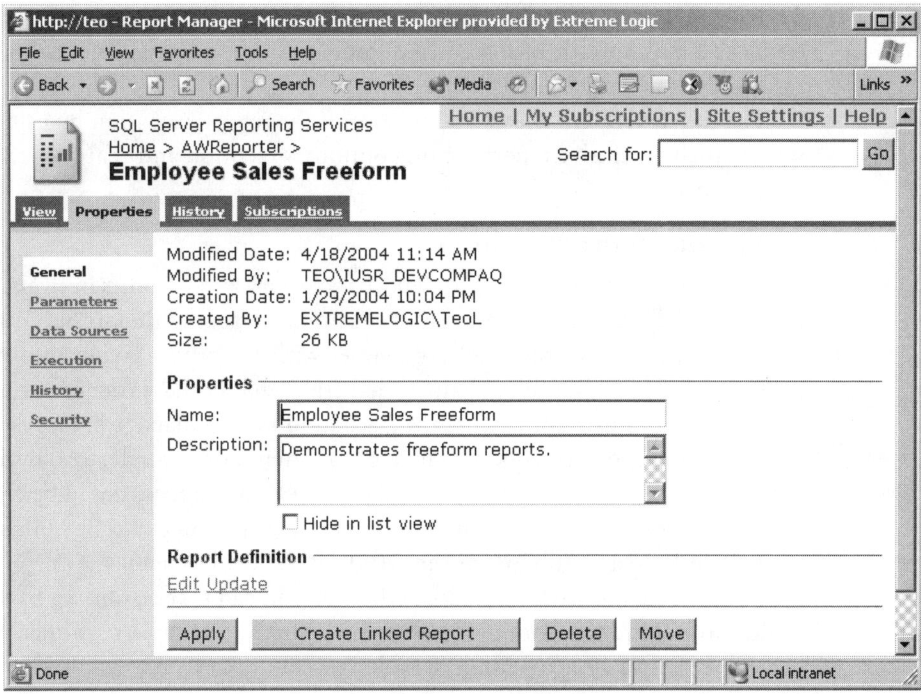

Figure 7.8 Use the report's Properties page to manage the report.

Unfortunately, the Parameters page allows you to maintain existing parameters only. Moreover, the only permitted operations are changing the default values and making the parameter read-only. As we explained in chapter 3, you can make a parameter read-only by clearing the Prompt User check box. When you do this, the Report Server will exclude the parameter from the report toolbar. Moreover, report consumers won't be able to supply a parameter through URL access. RS Service Pack 1 will give you an option to both hide the parameter and allow report consumers to pass the parameter value by URL.

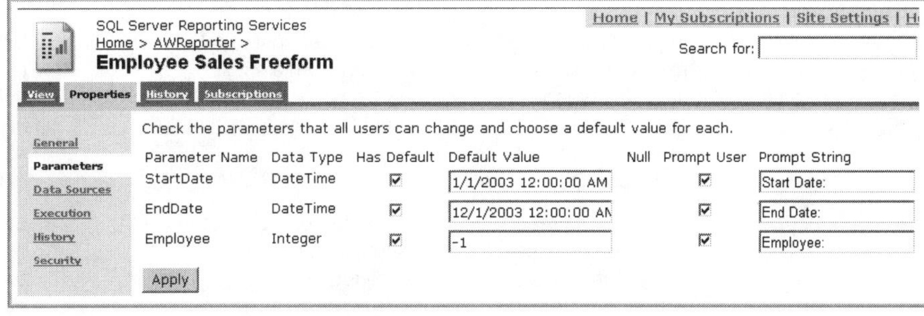

Figure 7.9 Use the Parameters link to manage the report parameters, including the parameter's default value and prompt settings.

The Data Sources link allows you to manage the report's data source, which could be set up as report-specific or shared. We emphasized the advantages of using shared data sources back in chapter 3.

The Execution link allows you to control the report execution by using one of the two mutually exclusive report caching options, execution and snapshot caching, as we discuss next.

7.1.4 Managing report execution

As we explained in chapter 1, the Report Server processes reports in two stages: execution and rendering. During the report execution stage, the Report Server retrieves the report data, combines the resulting dataset with the report layout information, and generates the report's intermediate format (IF), which can be cached for fast retrieval. The report administrator can use the Execution link to manage report caching.

Typically, report data doesn't change that often. For example, to allow client applications to efficiently access the report data, an OLAP database could be created exclusively for reporting purposes. In this scenario, report data could be bulk uploaded on a regular basis (e.g., daily) from the OLTP to the OLAP database.

To make report processing more efficient, you can take advantage of the relatively static nature of report data by caching the report's intermediate format. RS supports three forms of caching, as listed in table 7.4.

Table 7.4 RS supports the report session, execution, and snapshot caching options.

Caching Option	Purpose	How Does It Work?	Default Setting	How To Configure
Report session caching	Ensures data consistency within a configurable time window (report session) by correlating the client with the cached report IF.	RS executes the report each time a request from a different client arrives and caches the report's IF per client in the ChunkData table. For each subsequent request from the same client that includes the session identifier, RS uses the cached IF until the report session expires.	By default, the session duration is 600 seconds.	Cannot be turned completely off. The session duration is controlled by the SessionTimeout setting in the ConfigurationInfo table.
Report execution caching	Improves performance by potentially serving all report requests from the same cached IF instance.	RS serves all requests for the same report from a single cached IF instance stored in the ChunkData table.	Off	Use the report's Execution properties in the Report Manager.
Snapshot caching	Captures the report execution at a specific point of time, usually on a regular basis.	RS stores the report IF in the SnapshotData table and serves all requests from it.	Off	Use the report's Execution properties in the Report Manager.

Please note that all options cache the report's intermediate format (IF), not the final rendered output. Having so many caching options may be confusing, so let's discuss each option in more detail.

Report session caching

It turns out that while the last two caching options are user-configurable and can be turned off (disabled by default), report session caching is not. Judging by the questions posted on the RS discussion list, report session caching is confusing for many people. For this reason, we'll explain why report session caching is needed and how it works.

For non-snapshot reports, the Report Server always caches the report's IF implicitly for the duration of the report session.

DEFINITION A *report session* is a configurable time period within which the Report Server can serve subsequent report requests from the same client and for the same report from the cached report IF. A report session is always associated with exactly one client. In this respect, .NET developers can relate report sessions to ASP.NET sessions. However, the Report Server doesn't use ASP.NET sessions at all.

The premise here is that it is likely that the report's consumer may request the same report again within a certain period of time, for example, to export the report to a different format or for report paging. When a report is processed, the Report Server stores its IF in the ReportServerTempDB database and uses the cached copy until the report session expires, as shown in figure 7.10.

The important observation that you can make by looking at figure 7.10 is that with report session caching, the Report Server caches the report's IF per client and the cached report copy is correlated with the client.

Why do we need report sessions? Report session caching ensures data consistency and improves performance.

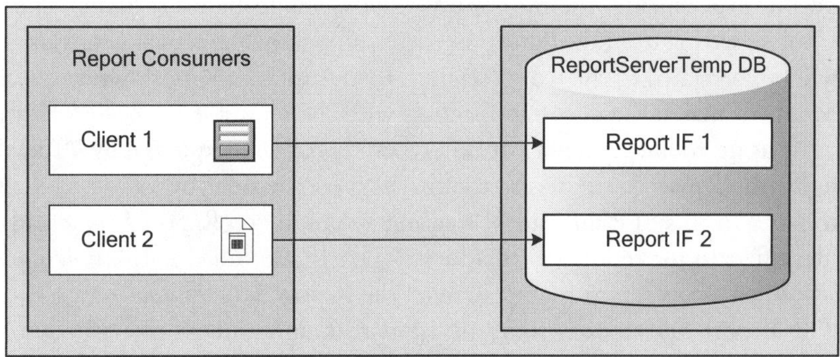

Figure 7.10 With report session caching, the Report Server caches the report's intermediate format as many times as the number of the client applications requesting the same report.

The main reason for having report session caching is to ensure that the report data doesn't change within a given period of time. To understand the need for this, consider the following example. Imagine that you have a presentation and you run a multipage Sales Summary report. Each page displays the sales data for a given company branch. When you navigate from one page to another, the browser asks the server to return the next page of the report. Now, let's imagine that while you are paging from branch A to branch B, the sales data for branch A changes. You navigate back to the page that displays the details for branch A, and all of sudden the report shows different numbers. Not a very compelling presentation, right?

Another unfavorable outcome may happen when you try to export the report and you realize later that the exported copy has different data. To ensure data consistency within a configurable period of time, the Report Server always performs report session caching for non-snapshot reports by saving the report's IF in the ReportServerTempDB database.

Report session caching is also useful for processing reports more efficiently. Let's say you've authored a crosstab report with interactive features such as the Territory Sales Crosstab report we created in chapter 4. The user can expand the report sections to see more data. To process interactive reports more efficiently, the Report Server does not render the whole report at once. Instead, it renders different portions on an as-needed basis.

Finally, because the report session state is stored in the database, it could survive the lifetime of the Report Server application domain. For example, if IIS is restarted, the session state is not lost.

You cannot completely turn off report session caching. However, you can specify the session expiration interval and how the Report Server correlates the report's consumer with the session.

You can manage the report session timeout by changing the value of the SessionTimeout setting in the ConfigurationInfo table in the Report Server database. Based on our experiments, the minimum value seems to be 60 seconds. The UseSessionCookies setting from the same table determines how the report's consumer application will be correlated to the report session. By default, the Report Server will use a session cookie to match the client application with the report session.

If using cookies is not an option when reports are requested by URL, you can configure the Report Server to use cookie-less report sessions by setting UseSessionCookies to false. In this case, instead of sending a cookie, the Report Server adds the session identifiers to the report's URL address. This is also called URL *munging*.

When a new report request arrives, the Report Server looks for a session identifier. The Report Server does some decision making to determine whether to serve the report from the report session, if available, or process the report anew. Specifically, the Report Server checks the following:

- Does the report session match the session identifier included in the report request? We will see how a client application can specify the session identifier in chapter 9.
- Has the report session expired?
- Are the report parameter values the same as the ones passed with previous report requests?

If the Report Server decides to service the report from the same report session, the session expiration timeout is renewed. For this reason, don't be surprised if the report doesn't show the most current data for subsequent requests. This situation may lead to data inaccuracy because data has become outdated ("stale").

NOTE In general, all caching techniques result in outdated data. As a developer and administrator, you have to carefully evaluate how much "staleness" is acceptable.

As I mentioned, the default report session duration is 10 minutes. If the Report Server decides to use the report session, it will serve the report from the cached copy within the report session duration. But is 10 minutes acceptable? If you configure the session duration to expire too soon, you will lose the performance benefits of caching. If the report is cached for too long, data can get stale.

Sometimes, you may want to force the Report Server to abandon the report session and execute the report anew. As a developer, you can do this in a couple of ways, depending on how the report is requested. If the report's consumer requests the report by URL, you can send the rs:ClearSessionID command to the Report Server, as will discuss in chapter 9.

If the report is requested by SOAP, you can programmatically abandon the session by clearing the SessionId property of the SessionHeaderValue proxy class. If the report's consumer doesn't support cookies, the session ID can be explicitly specified in the request URL or as an argument to the `Render` method call, as we will discuss in chapter 9.

From the end-user perspective, if the report includes the standard toolbar, the end user can click the Refresh Report button (or press Ctrl-F5) to clear the session.

Report execution caching

Optionally, the report administrator can turn on report execution caching using the report execution page. To access this page, click the Execution link (see figure 7.8). Report execution caching is another big area of confusion. To make things even more confusing, the pre-release documentation of Reporting Services referred to this form of caching as in-memory caching, which is totally incorrect. When report execution caching is enabled, the report's IF is not cached in memory at all.

Just like report sessions, report execution caching uses the report's IF cached in the ReportServerTempDB database. So what's the difference? While report session caching

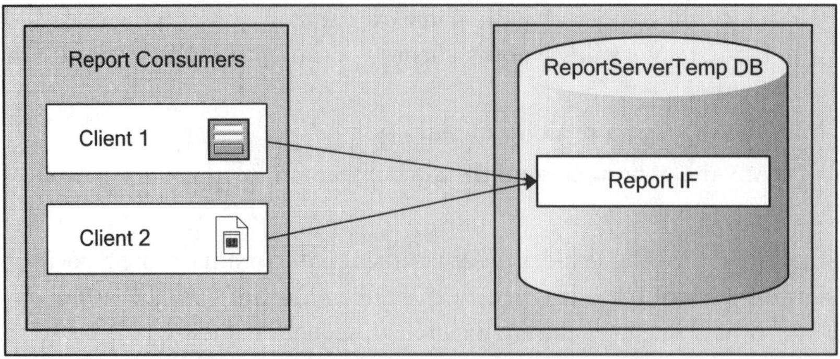

Figure 7.11 With report execution caching, one cached IF instance can be used by more than one client.

is correlated with the client, report execution caching is global. In other words, with the latter form of caching, several client applications (or users, for that matter) may access the same cached instance of a given report, as shown in figure 7.11.

How is report execution caching implemented? As we've just seen, with report session caching, when different clients request the same report the Report Server executes the report for each client and caches as many instances of the report's IF in the ChunkData table as the number of clients. If report execution caching is on, only one instance of the report's IF is cached in the ChunkData table. All subsequent requests will use that instance.

Therefore, while report sessions guarantee data consistency within the duration of the report session, the main goal of report execution caching is better performance. If the report doesn't have parameters, only one instance of the report is cached. Otherwise, several instances of the report are cached, a separate instance for each set of parameters.

The following conditions have to be met to enable report execution caching:

- The report cannot use Windows authentication in expressions or to connect to the database. For example, you cannot use User.UserID in your expressions, nor can you use Windows authentication to log in to the database by impersonating the user (the Windows NT Integrated Security option on the data source properties). However, if the data source connection uses Windows Authentication with stored credentials (the Use As Windows Credentials When Connecting To The Data Source option), then the report can be cached in the execution cache.
- The report doesn't prompt the user for database login credentials.

Let's see an example that will demonstrate the effect that this form of caching has on the report's execution. Suppose that the AWC management has requested a report that shows the territory sales by quarter. The Territory Sales by Quarter report meets this requirement (figure 7.12).

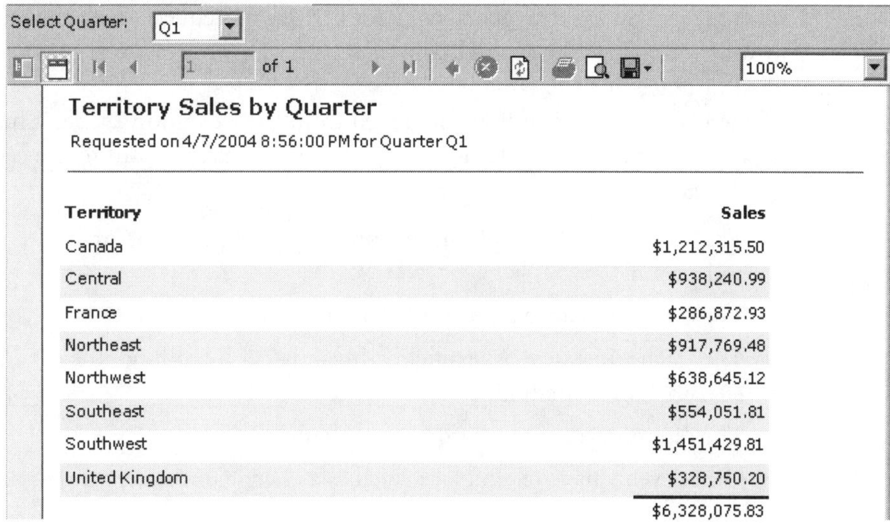

Select Quarter: Q1

1 of 1 100%

Territory Sales by Quarter

Requested on 4/7/2004 8:56:00 PM for Quarter Q1

Territory	Sales
Canada	$1,212,315.50
Central	$938,240.99
France	$286,872.93
Northeast	$917,769.48
Northwest	$638,645.12
Southeast	$554,051.81
Southwest	$1,451,429.81
United Kingdom	$328,750.20
	$6,328,075.83

Figure 7.12 Once report execution caching is enabled, it doesn't get processed by the Report Server when requested with the same parameters.

The report accepts a parameter so that the user can filter the report data by quarter. For simplicity's sake, we restricted the available parameter values to the 2003 quarters only, with Q1 as the default quarter. To demonstrate how execution caching affects the report's execution, the report shows the report's execution time below the title. If the report is not cached, each time you request the report the execution time changes, which means that the Report Server does indeed process the report.

Because it is likely that data for past quarters will be relatively static, let's change the execution options to cache the report in the execution cache for 10 minutes by using the Execution link in the Report Manager, as shown in figure 7.13.

Now, request the report several times for the same quarter. You will notice that the execution time doesn't change, which means the report is effectively cached.

When the report has parameters, a separate copy of the report is cached for each set of parameters. To see this, change the quarter to Q2 and run the report again. Observe that the execution time changes because the Report Server needs to process the report to reflect the new parameter value. If you run the report again for Q2, the

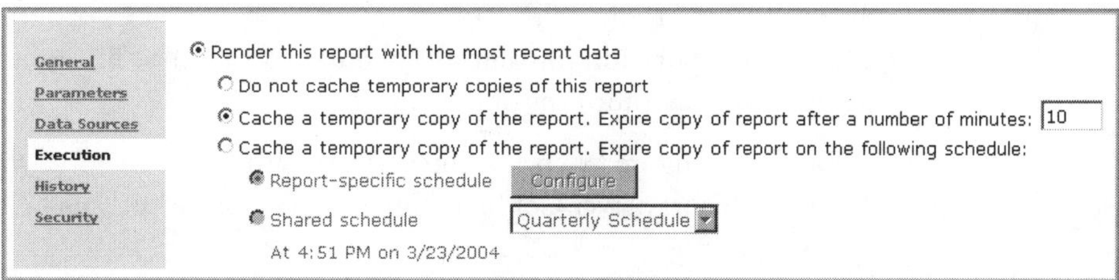

Figure 7.13 Use report execution caching for more efficient report processing.

Report Server will use the cached copy for Q2. If you request to see the report for Q1, you will notice that the cached copy is served. This means that now there are two cached instances for the same report.

When is the cached instance removed from the execution cache? There could be several reasons to cause the Report Server to swap the report out of the cache, including the following:

- The Report Server application domain is restarted, for example, by stopping and starting IIS.
- The cached instance has expired based on the expiration options you specified.
- The cache instance is explicitly invalidated by calling the RS Web service `FlushCache` method.
- The report's execution options have changed.
- Other events have taken place, such as a change to the report definition file and data source.

You can force the Report Server to expire the report's cached instance (if any) on a set schedule. This is useful when you want to ensure that the Report Server will process the report at specified time. Consider again the Territory Sales by Quarter report; the administrator could set the execution cache to expire at the beginning of every quarter by setting the Quarterly Schedule shared schedule. This will ensure that the report requested for the previous quarter reflects the latest changes.

Snapshot caching

The Report Server manages the first two caching options internally, and so you have little control over them. For example, you don't know when the report will be requested for the first time and when the Report Server will start the cache expiration stopwatch. Sometimes, it makes more sense to save report instances at a specific point by configuring the report for snapshot execution. Snapshot caching offers the following advantages:

- It improves the report performance by serving the report from the cached copy in the Report Server database. This could be especially useful for large reports that might take a long time to execute. Such reports can be scheduled to be generated during off-peak hours.
- It allows the report administrator to maintain a snapshot history log and compare different snapshot runs of the report.

When a report is configured to be executed as a snapshot, the Report Server saves the report's IF in the Report Server Configuration database (SnapshotData table), as shown in figure 7.14.

At this point you may wonder how snapshot caching differs from execution caching. Unlike reports configured to use execution caching, snapshots

- *Are usually executed in unattended mode*—Typically, snapshots are generated as a result of a time event. However, the administrator can explicitly create a snapshot using the Report Manager portal, or developers can call the UpdateReportExecutionSnapshot SOAP API to generate it programmatically.
- *Refresh the report cached copy at a specific point of time*—Unlike execution caching, the report administrator can control exactly when the snapshot cache is refreshed.
- Require default parameter values in the case of parameter-driven reports
- *Are not interactive*—Snapshots don't allow the user to change the report parameters if the report is parameter-driven.
- Save the report's IF in the Report Server Configuration database, as opposed to the Report Server Temporary database

Snapshot caching is subject to the same limitations as execution caching. In addition, because the snapshot execution is unattended, the user cannot set the parameter values if the report accepts parameters. For example, if you schedule the Territory Sales by Quarter report for a snapshot execution, you will see that the Quarter parameter is disabled. If the report is parameter-driven, the Report Server will use the parameter default values. In fact, the Report Server will refuse to schedule the report for snapshot execution if default values are not specified for all parameters.

To explain how snapshots can be useful, let's revisit the Territory Sales by Quarter report. Let's assume that once the quarter is up, the data for the previous quarter doesn't change. In addition, we will assume that the users want to run the report to see the sales results for the previous quarter only (users can't specify the quarter interactively).

Given the new set of requirements, we can optimize our report by capturing a snapshot of the report on a quarterly basis. As a prerequisite, we need to default the Quarter parameter to a given quarter, e.g., Q1. Figure 7.15 shows how we can set the snapshot execution using the Report Manager.

Of course, instead of waiting for the current quarter to end, for testing purposes we could see the effect of the snapshot execution sooner by changing the schedule interval

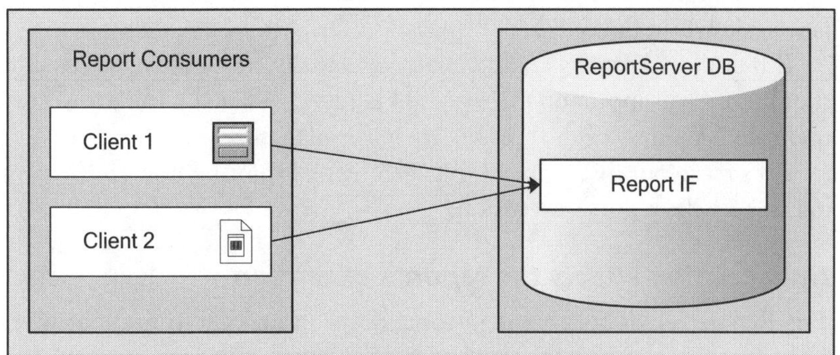

Figure 7.14 With snapshot caching, the Report Server stores the report's IF in the Report Server Configuration database.

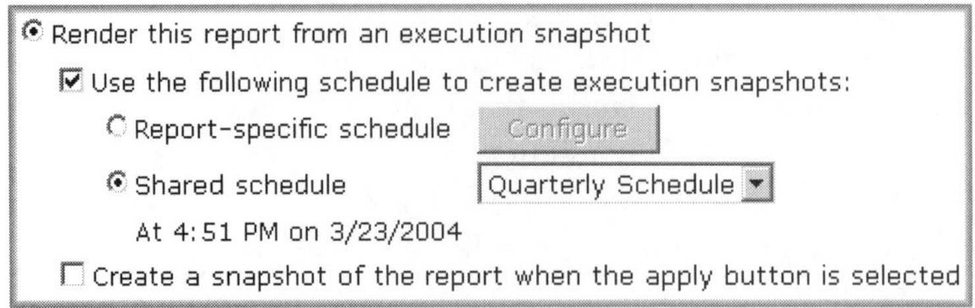

Figure 7.15 You can trigger the snapshot execution from a report-specific or shared schedule.

to a minute or two. Alternatively, we could manually generate the snapshot by selecting the Create a Snapshot of the Report When the Apply Button Is Selected check box on the report's Execution Properties page and clicking the Apply button. This would create the snapshot immediately. If the Store All Report Execution Snapshots in History option is checked on the History tab, we must remember to cancel the snapshot execution after we finish experimenting to prevent filling up the History table.

Once you have finished setting the execution options, run the report. You will notice that the report data is filtered by the default quarter and the parameter is disabled. Similar to execution caching, the report's executing time doesn't change and reflects the time when the snapshot was created.

By default, only one snapshot run is kept in the Report Server Configuration database, and it gets replaced each time a new snapshot is generated. You can keep a historical log of the snapshot executions by enabling the snapshot history. This allows you compare snapshot executions, similar to how Microsoft Project allows you create and compare project baselines.

For example, in our scenario the administrator can decide to keep the snapshot executions for the past four quarters so that management can compare the sales performance from one quarter to the next. You can use the Report History tab (not the Properties tab) to see or delete the snapshot executions.

To change the snapshot history options, click the History link on the Properties tab, as shown in figure 7.16.

If the Allow History To Be Created Manually check box is selected, a New Snapshot button will appear on the report's History tab that you can use to create snapshots manually. The rest of the options are self-explanatory.

Let's recap our discussion about caching by exploring how all three forms of caching impact the report's execution.

How caching affects the report's execution

The Report Server goes through some decision making to find out whether to serve subsequent report requests from the cached report copy or to generate the report anew. Figure 7.17 depicts a simplified diagram that shows how report caching affects the report's execution phase.

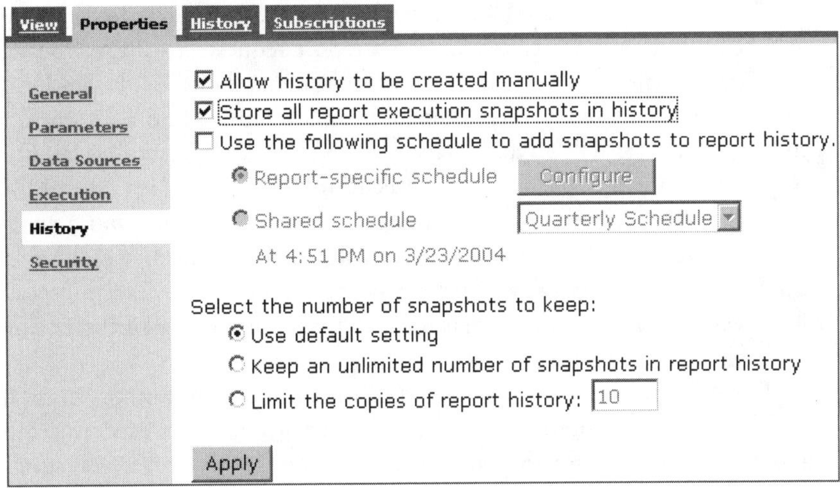

Figure 7.16 Use the History tab to manage the snapshot history.

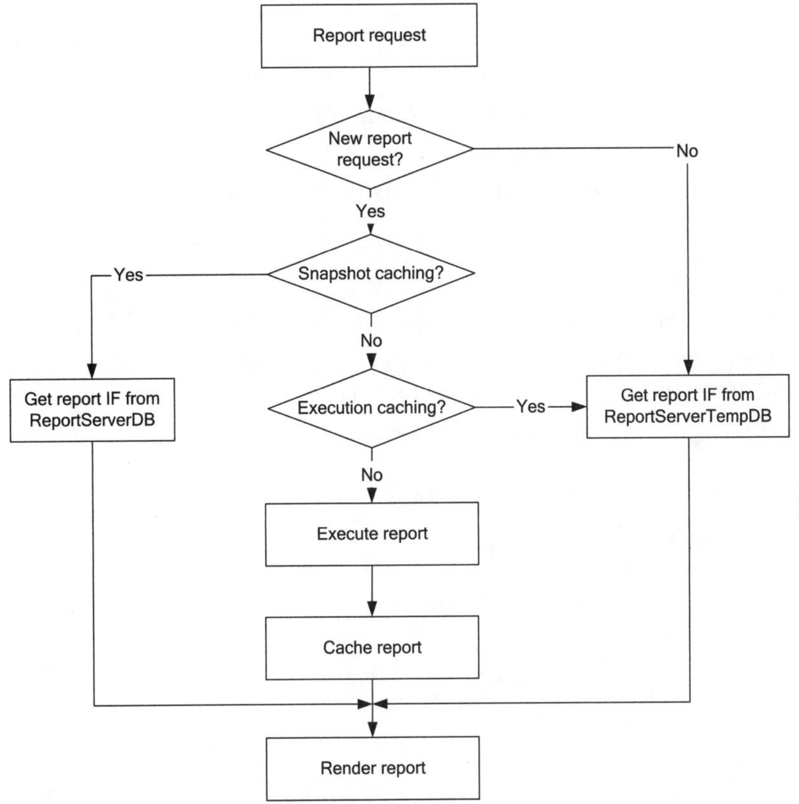

Figure 7.17 RS supports three caching options: report session, execution, and snapshot caching. Report caching may bypass the execution phase completely.

As the diagram in figure 7.17 depicts, the Report Server first checks to see if there is a valid report session associated with the report request. To do so, the Report Server examines the client request for a session identifier and queries the SessionData table in the Report Server Temporary database in an attempt to find a match. If there is one, the Report Server will serve the report from the report session cache. Otherwise, the Report Server will check the report execution options.

If the report is configured to be executed as a snapshot and a snapshot-cached instance is available, the Report Server will use it. If snapshot caching is turned off, the Report Server checks to see if the report is configured for execution caching. If this is the case, the report will serve it from the execution cache (if the execution cache is available and can be used).

Finally, if the report is not cached or the cached copy cannot be used, the Report Server will execute the report and cache it according to its execution settings. If the report is configured for snapshot execution, the Report Server will store the report's IF in the Report Server Configuration database. Otherwise, the Report Server will save the report's IF in the Report Server Temporary database.

To recap, the report can be serviced potentially from one of the following three places:

- *Source database*—If the report is requested for the first time or has been invalidated, for example, the report session has timed out
- *ReportServerTempDB*—If the Report Server decides to reuse the report IF from the report session or execution cache
- *Report Server Configuration database*—For snapshots only, if a snapshot instance has been generated

7.1.5 Managing linked reports

Reporting Services allows you to create "wrappers" on top of existing reports in the form of *linked* reports. You can think of a linked report as a shortcut to another report. Similar to a file shortcut, a linked report is not a copy of the original report. Instead, it simply points to the original report.

Understanding linked reports

Linked reports inherit the following information from the report they are associated with: report definition, report data source, and report datasets. A linked report cannot change these items because they are inherited from the base report. However, a linked report can have different

- Role-based security policy
- Parameters
- Properties
- Catalog location

While the parameter default values can be different, and you can change whether they are prompted or not, you can't add parameters to the report nor can you change their available values.

Why would you ever want to create linked reports? The simple answer is flexibility. Let's see a concrete example to demonstrate how linked reports can be useful.

Implementing linked reports

In the previous section, we set up the Territory Sales by Quarter report for snapshot execution. Although snapshots can be very useful for generating reports according to a schedule, they impose some restrictions, including the fact that the user cannot change the report parameters. But what if we want the best of both worlds? What if some users would like to see the report for an arbitrary quarter, while others want the report to show the data from the previous quarter only?

One approach would be to clone the Territory Sales by Quarter report. But this would present a maintenance issue. Each time we needed to make changes to the report layout, we would have to remember to propagate the changes to the report copy as well. A more elegant approach would be to create a linked report pointing to the original. We can easily accomplish this with the Report Manager by performing a couple of steps:

Step 1 Navigate to the Territory Sales by Quarter Properties page.

Step 2 Click the Create Linked Report button. Enter a name and optionally a description for the linked report, as shown in figure 7.18. You can also change the location of the linked report if you want to place it in a different folder than AWReporter.

By default, the linked report inherits all properties from the original, including the execution properties. To cancel the snapshot execution for the linked report, go to the linked report's Execution tab and select the Render This Report with the Most Recent Data radio button. Once this is done, the users can render the report for any available quarter.

Another practical use for linked reports is security, because the linked report can have a different role-based security policy than the report it is linked to.

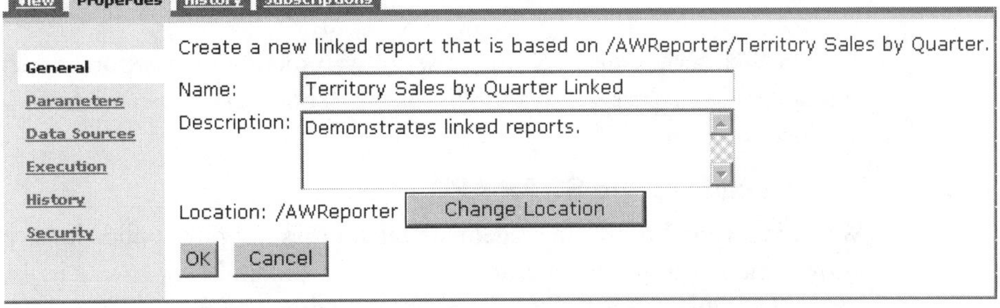

Figure 7.18 You can use a linked report as a shortcut to an existing report.

While in most cases the report administrator will use the Report Manager portal to interactively manage the report environment, some application integration scenarios may require managing RS programmatically. To accomplish this you can use the RS Web service.

7.2 MANAGING RS WITH THE WEB SERVICE

As we explained, the Report Manager is just a presentation façade to the Report Server. Behind the scenes, the RS Web service receives SOAP requests from the Report Manager and forwards them to the Report Server. When the Report Manager is not enough, you can build client applications that call the SOAP management API directly. For example, you can create an ad hoc reporting tool that calls down to the RS Web service to upload the generated report definition file to the report catalog.

7.2.1 Understanding the Web service management API

To allow external applications to manage the report environment, the RS Web service provides a number of web methods, which can be logically grouped in the categories shown in table 7.5.

Table 7.5 The RS Web service API includes many methods for performing various management-related tasks.

Category	Purpose	Web Method Examples
Content Management	Manage site settings, folders, reports and resources	CreateFolder, SetReportDefinition
Role-based Security	Manage tasks, roles, and policies	CreateRole, ListTasks
Data Source	Manage report data sources	CreateDataSource, SetDataSource-Contents
Report Parameters	Manage report parameters	GetReportParameters, SetReport-Parameters
Report History	Manage report history	CreateReportHistorySnapshot, ListReportHistory
Report Scheduling	Manage shared schedules	CreateSchedule, ListSchedules
Subscribed Delivery	Manage subscriptions	CreateSubscription, ListSubscriptions
Linked Reports	Manage linked reports	CreateLinkedReport, ListLinkedReports

The RS Web service also provides a set of web methods for report rendering that we will discuss in chapter 9. For a full list of the Report Server web methods please see the product documentation.

7.2.2 Tracing calls to the SOAP API

When incorporating RS management capabilities in your applications, you may not know which Web service method you need to call and how to call it. In most cases, you will be able to easily find the web method you need to accomplish a given task programmatically just by looking at its name.

When in doubt, you can use the Report Manager as a learning tool. Because the Report Manager calls down to the RS Web service for all management tasks, you can use a tracing utility (such as SOAP Trace or tcpTrace) to intercept the SOAP traffic between the Report Manager and Report Server.

We will show you how to use the SOAP Trace utility to accomplish this. The steps to use tcpTrace are similar. Both utilities work by capturing the HTTP traffic to a virtual port. We provided the download links for both utilities at the end of this chapter.

Using SOAP Trace

For example, let's assume that you need to write a client application that lists all resources located in a given catalog folder. You are not sure which web method to call and which arguments to pass, but you know the Report Manager does this already. You want to find out what happens behind the scenes when you click on a folder in the Report Manager to see the folder content.

As we mentioned, to get started with SOAP Trace, you first need to set up a virtual port to capture the SOAP traffic.

To create a virtual port, change the ReportServerUrl setting in the RSWebApplication.config file to include a virtual port number such as

```
http://<servername>:8080/ReportServer
```

Once this is done, you can open the SOAP Trace utility and create a new formatted trace, as shown in figure 7.19.

The settings shown in figure 7.19 assume that the Report Server is installed locally. If this is not the case, then you must replace localhost with the name of the computer on which the Report Server is installed.

Now, open your browser and request the ReportServerURL, as specified in RSWebApplication.config. At this point, SOAP Trace should capture the SOAP requests that the Report Manager sends to the Report Server. Navigate to the folder in question and explore the SOAP messages captured, as shown in figure 7.20.

Among the captured message calls, you will find a call to the `ListChildren` method that looks promising. A quick look at the documentation confirms that

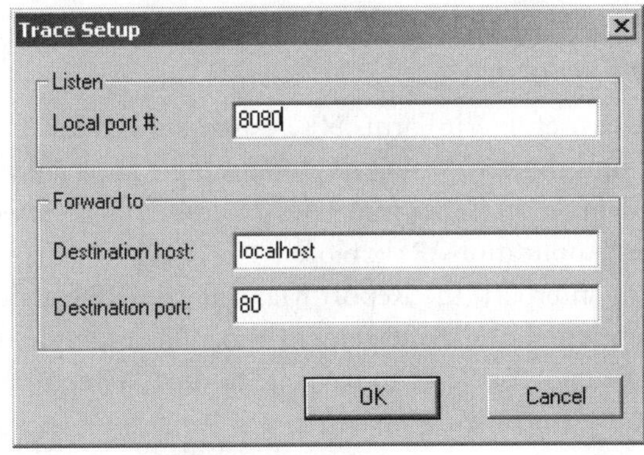

Figure 7.19 Trace the Report Manager to Report Server traffic using the SOAP Trace utility.

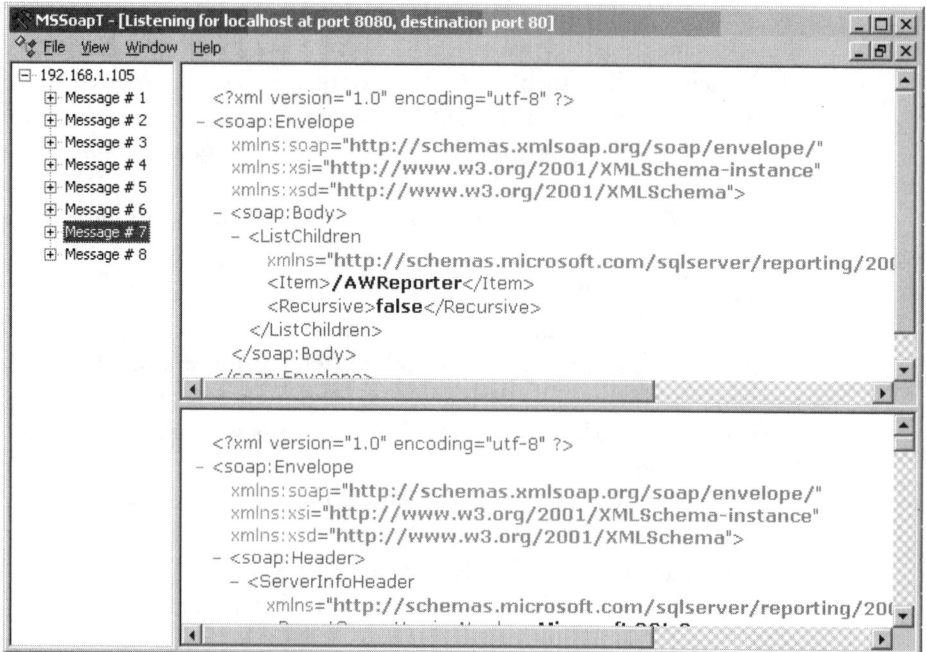

Figure 7.20 Once the Report Manager submits a SOAP request, the SOAP Trace utility will capture it and show the request/response message.

`ListChildren` "gets a list of children of a specified folder." As you can see, in this case `ListChildren` passes the name of the folder to the Item argument and `false` to the Recursive argument to indicate that it needs a "shallow" traversal, where the resources in the subfolders are excluded.

You can use the tracing technique we've just shown you to watch the entire conversation between the Report Manager and the Report Server and mimic it in your applications. If you need a code sample that demonstrates how you can call the SOAP API to manage programmatically the report catalog, have a look at the RS Catalog Explorer application that comes with RS.

Using the RS Catalog Explorer

The RS team has provided a useful WinForm .NET-based application called the RS Catalog Explorer. You can find the RS Catalog Explorer sample application under the Samples folder, which by default is C:\Program Files\Microsoft SQL Server\MSSQL\Reporting Services\Samples\Applications\RSExplorer.

Just like its web-based counterpart, the Report Manager, the RS Catalog Explorer can be used as a report rendering and management tool. For example, figure 7.21 shows that we used the RS Catalog Explorer to navigate to the AWReporter folder and launch the Employee Sales Freeform with Chart report.

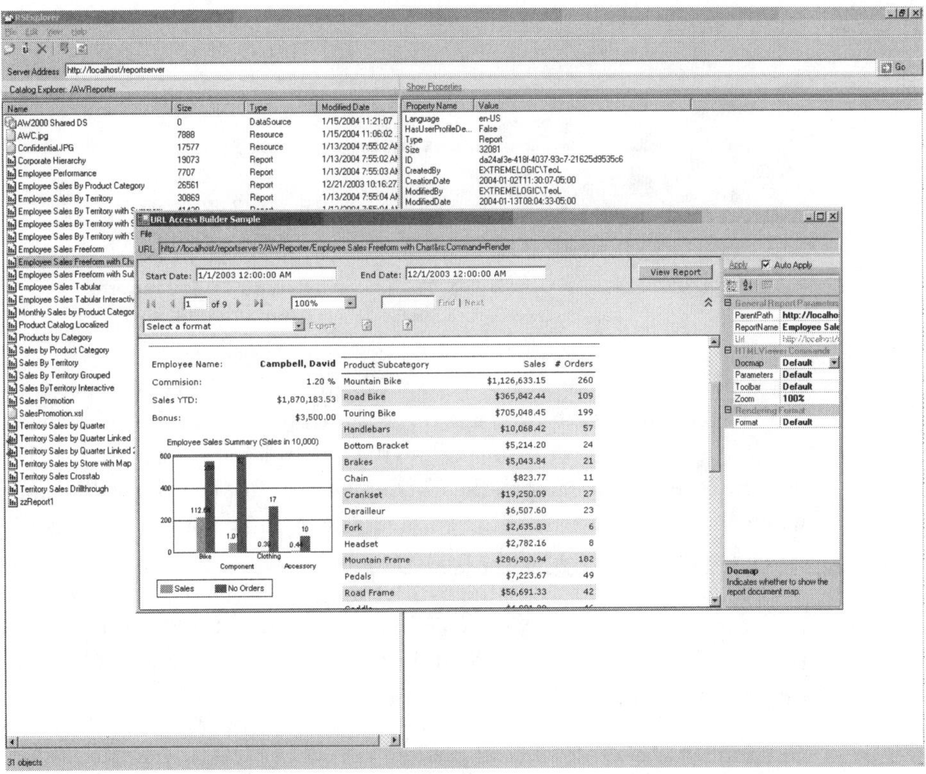

Figure 7.21 You can add management features to your applications, as the RS Catalog Explorer sample demonstrates.

The report properties window on the right displays some report-related properties that you can update, such as the report name. When you do so, RS Catalog Explorer calls the RS SOAP API to propagate the change to the report catalog. The source code is included in both VB.NET and C#. We highly recommend that you carefully examine this sample, especially if you need to integrate RS with WinForms client applications.

Now that you've been introduced to the Report Server management API, let's see how you can use them to perform management tasks.

7.2.3 Deploying reports programmatically

Thanks to the fact that the Report Server exposes its functionality through a series of SOAP APIs, you can easily create client applications to manage the report catalog. Let's write some code to demonstrate how this could be done.

The RDL deployment sample

Back in chapter 2, we saw how to create report definitions programmatically. Now, let's see how easy it is to upload the generated definition to the report catalog in order to create a new report. You can find the sample under the Chapter 7 menu in the

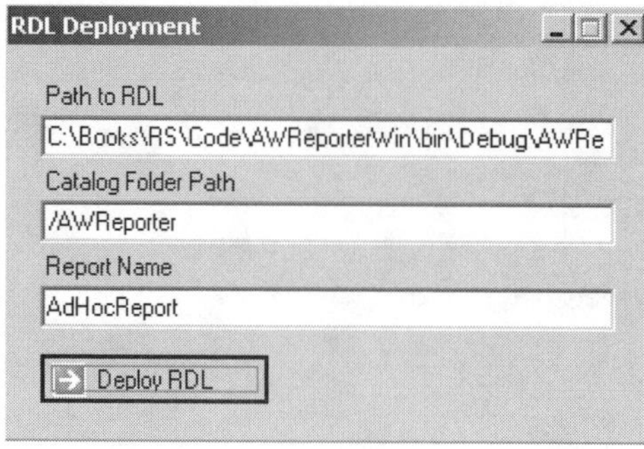

Figure 7.22
The RDL Deployment sample demonstrates how to deploy reports programmatically.

AWReporterWin application that comes with this book's code. Once you click on the RDL Deployment menu, you will be presented with the options shown in figure 7.22.

You need to specify the full path to the report definition language (RDL) file. If you have run the AdHoc sample, the Catalog Folder Path text box will default to the path where the AWReporter.rdl file is located. If you don't want to run the AdHoc sample, you'll have to specify a valid path to any RDL file.

You also need to specify the path of the folder where the report will be uploaded to in the RS report catalog, as well as the report name. Once this is done, you can click the Deploy RDL button to upload the file and create the report. Let's now discuss the implementation details.

Setting up the Web service proxy

When accessing XML Web services in managed code, you typically use a proxy class to let the .NET Framework handle all of the SOAP invocation and plumbing details. Visual Studio .NET makes it easy to create a Web service proxy class by allowing you to create a web reference to the Web service. In our case, this is what we have to do to establish a web reference to the Reporting Web service:

Step 1 Right-click the References node in the Solution Explorer and choose Add Web Reference. The Add Web Reference dialog appears.

Step 2 Specify the RS Web service endpoint (the URL to the ReportService.asmx page) in the URL field, for example, http://<servername>/ReportServer/ReportService.asmx. If the Report Server is deployed on your local machine, you can click the Web Services on the Local Machine hyperlink and choose RS Web Service. VS.NET parses the Web service description and lists all web methods.

Step 3 Specify the Web Reference Name, as shown in figure 7.23. This defines the namespace for the proxy class. For the purposes of the AWReporterWin application, we changed the reference name from localhost to RS. Once you click the Add Reference button, the proxy class will be generated.

To see the proxy class, make sure that the Solution Explorer shows all files (the Show All Files button is activated). Then, you can expand the web reference node. The proxy

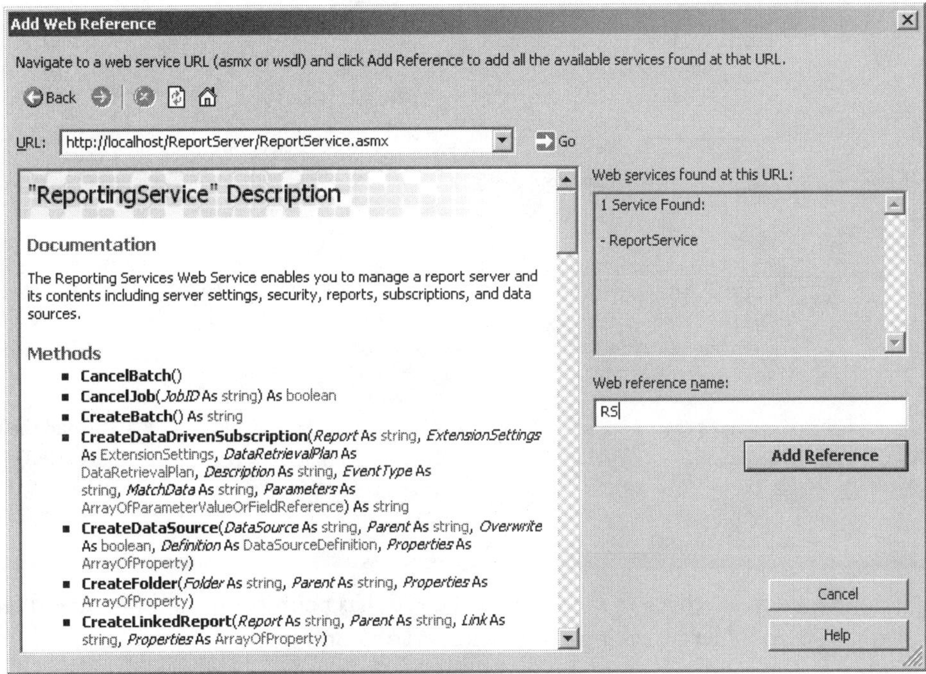

Figure 7.23 Adding a web reference to the Report Server Web service

class name is named Reference.cs if it is a C# project, or Reference.vb in the case of a VB.NET project.

In case you want to trace the SOAP requests going out of the application using a trace utility, you can modify the URL address in the proxy constructor in the proxy class to include a virtual port, for example,

```
this.Url = "http://localhost:8080/ReportServer/ReportService.asmx";
```

Then, you can use tcpTrace or SoapTrace to capture the SOAP traffic, as we discussed previously. Don't forget to take out the virtual port of the URL when you're finished tracing.

Implementing the sample

To centralize the proxy management in one place, we created the RsHelpers wrapper, which encapsulates the proxy instantiation and sets up the authentication credentials. When the application needs the proxy, it gets it from the RsHelpers.Proxy accessor.

The actual report deployment is done in the DeployRDL function. Listing 7.1 shows the abbreviated code.

Listing 7.1 You can use the RS Web service API to deploy the report definition.

```
private void DeployRDL() {
  string[] permissions = {"Create Report"};
  StringBuilder sb = new StringBuilder();
```

```
    Byte[] definition = null;
    Warning[] warnings = null;

    if (!RsHelpers.HasPermissions(PermissionType.Item,
             txtFolderPath.Text, permissions)) {
       MessageBox.Show(String.Format("You don't have sufficient
             rights to …"))
       return;
    }

    FileStream stream = File.OpenRead(txtRDLPath.Text);
    definition = new Byte[stream.Length];
    stream.Read(definition, 0, (int) stream.Length);
    stream.Close();

    ReportingService rs = RsHelpers.Proxy;
    warnings = rs.CreateReport(txtReportName.Text,
             txtFolderPath.Text,true, definition, null);
}
```

❶ **Check whether the user has permissions to create reports in the report catalog**

❷ **Load the report definition**

❸ **Upload the report to the report catalog**

❶ First, we check to see whether the user has permissions to create reports in the specified folder by calling the HasPermissions helper function. This function accepts as arguments the type of the permissions we want to check (item or system), the report item path, and an array of the permissions we want to check. In this case, checking for Create Report rights is sufficient. The HasPermissions wrapper calls the GetPermissions web method, which returns a string array of all permissions that the user has to a given report item. HasPermissions then enumerates through both arrays (requested and granted permissions) and return true only if all requested permissions are successfully matched.

If the user has the rights to create reports, the report definition is uploaded via a call to the CreateReport web method.

❷ Next, we load the report definition to a byte array.

❸ Then, we invoke CreateReport by passing the report name, folder path, and the report definition. We also specify that we want to overwrite the report if it exists. CreateReport optionally takes an array of properties you can pass to the last parameter, for example, the report description.

That's it! Once you execute the code, the report will be uploaded to the report catalog and you can use the Report Manager to navigate to it and run it.

Sometimes, when executing a series of interrelated web methods, you want to ensure that all of them will complete successfully or be rolled back in case of a failure. With RS, this can be achieved by encapsulating the web method calls in a batch.

7.2.4 Batching methods together

The RS Web service supports executing management-related web methods within the scope of a single database transaction with a READ COMMITED isolation level. If any of the batch methods fails, the transaction will be rolled back and all catalog changes will be undone.

For example, let's say that you want to distribute several reports to your customers and these reports are interdependent, such as subreports and related drillthrough reports. You want to make sure that the report deployment is an all-or-nothing operation and you don't leave the catalog database in an inconsistent state.

To achieve this you might take advantage of method batching. You can write a simple application or a script that executes all deployment methods in a transactional batch, as follows:

```
try {
  BatchHeader bh = new BatchHeader();
  bh.BatchID = rs.CreateBatch();
  rs.BatchHeaderValue = bh;
  rs. CreateReport ("Report1", …);
  rs. CreateReport ("Report2", …);
  rs.ExecuteBatch();
}
catch (SoapException ex) {
       rs.CancelBatch();
}
```

Developers experienced in writing transaction code will find the batch semantics familiar. When you group web method calls in a batch, the Report Server logs the methods in a Batch table in the Report Server database but doesn't execute them. When the `ExecuteBatch` method is executed, the Report Server creates an explicit transaction and executes all methods within its scope.

If all methods execute successfully, the Report Server commits the database transaction. If the transaction errors out, you can call `CancelBatch` to delete the batch records from the Batch table.

One final note about batching. After you execute or cancel the batch, you need to clear out the batch header after `ExecuteBatch` (or `CancelBatch`), otherwise the proxy will continue to send the header and you will still be operating under a batch.

Using the RS Web service is not the only way to programmatically manage the report catalog. RS also provides a Windows Management Instrumentation (WMI) provider that can be used to manage the settings of multiple RS installations.

7.3 MANAGING RS WITH THE WMI PROVIDER

As useful as the Report Manager is for administering the report environment, it has its limitations. For example, it allows us to manage only the site settings of one Report Server (the one specified in the Report Manager configuration file).

In a typical enterprise environment, however, there may be multiple installed instances of Report Server. For example, you might have one instance serving the reporting needs of customers on the Web and another for intranet use. Or, to scale out, you can have a web farm of report servers. As an administrator, you might need to manage the server settings from a single location. This is exactly the purpose of the RS WMI provider.

7.3.1 Understanding the WMI provider

The WMI provider is built on top of the Windows Management Instrumentation infrastructure baked into the Windows operating system.

NOTE WMI is a system management infrastructure embedded in the Windows OS. It provides an object-oriented interface that developers can use to interact with system management information and the underlying WMI APIs.

With the WMI provider, developers can write code to programmatically access the configurations settings of a given installation instance of the Report Server and Report Manager in an object-oriented way. Specifically, it offers the MSReportServer_ConfigurationSetting and MSReportServerReportManager_ConfigurationSetting classes.

The first class wraps the Report Server configuration settings stored in the RSReportServer.config file. The second represents the Report Manager configuration settings located in the RSWebApplication.config file. Please consult with the documentation for a detailed coverage of the WMI provider functionality.

Let's demonstrate how the WMI provider can be useful. Because RS doesn't come with a management console snap-in, we wrote a simple RS Console, as shown in figure 7.24. (Version 2.0 of Reporting Services will include a management console integrated with the SQL Server 2005 management tool.)

Empowered with the RS Console, you can manage the settings of an arbitrary Report Server instance installed in your enterprise by specifying the Report Server name. The RS Console shows you the settings for a given Report Server and allows you to make changes. This could be particularly useful when you need to change the

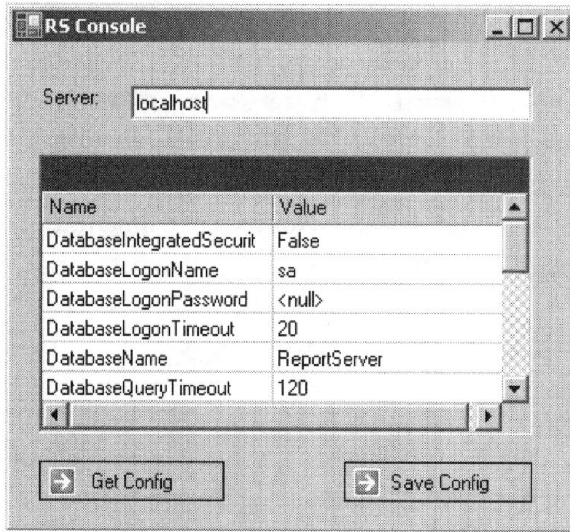

Figure 7.24 Use this sample RS Console to make changes to the RS configuration files of multiple Report Server installations.

Report Server database settings. These settings are stored in encrypted format, as you can see by looking at the RSReportServer.config file.

For this reason, making changes to the Report Server database settings is not an easy task. In fact, the Report Server provides a utility, rsconfig.exe, whose sole purpose is to manage the encrypted database settings. If you are like us, you won't be too excited about working with this command-line utility and messing with switches, which makes the RS Console an even more appealing choice.

7.3.2 Implementing an RS management console

Working with the WMI provider is straightforward. Listing 7.2 shows the abbreviated code of the `GetServerProperties` function, which populates the grid with the configuration settings of the specified server.

Listing 7.2 Getting the server settings

```
private void GetServerProperties()
{
  string WmiNamespace = @"\\" + txtServer.Text +
         @"\root\Microsoft\SqlServer\ReportingServices\v8";
string WmiRSClass = @"\\" + txtServer.Text +
     @"\root\Microsoft\SqlServer\ReportingServices\" +
     "v8:MSReportServer_ConfigurationSetting";
  ManagementClass serverClass;
  ManagementScope scope;
  scope = new ManagementScope(WmiNamespace);

  scope.Connect();
  serverClass = new ManagementClass(WmiRSClass);    <-- 1 Instantiate the WMI provider to read the Report Server configuration settings
  serverClass.Get();
  ManagementObjectCollection instances=serverClass.GetInstances();
  IEnumerator enumerator = instances.GetEnumerator();
  bool result = enumerator.MoveNext();
  m_instance = (ManagementObject)enumerator.Current;

  PropertyDataCollection instProps = m_instance.Properties;
  EntityProperty ds = new EntityProperty ();    <-- 2 Instantiate a .NET type dataset to hold the settings
  ds.Property.RowChanged += new
     DataRowChangeEventHandler(this.grdProperties_ChangedEvent);

  foreach(PropertyData prop in instProps)    <-- 3 Load the dataset
  {
     ds.Property.AddPropertyRow(prop.Name,
     prop.Value!=null?prop.Value.ToString():"<null>");
  }
  ds.AcceptChanges();
  ds.Property.DefaultView.AllowNew = false;
  ds.Property.DefaultView.AllowDelete = false;
  grdProperties.DataSource = ds.Property;    <-- 4 Show the settings to the user by binding the dataset to the grid
}
```

❶ First, we initialize the WMI namespace and class name. Because we are interested in managing the Report Server settings, we use the MSReportServer_ConfigurationSetting class. Then, we instantiate the WMI provider and retrieve all Report Server instances installed on the specified server. For simplicity's sake, we default to the first instance.

NOTE Currently, Reporting Services doesn't support multiple instances on a single server. Microsoft hints that future versions may support this installation option.

❷ Next, we get all settings and load them in a grid. For easier data binding and filtering, we decided to create a typed dataset, EntityProperty, to hold the settings. The dataset defines a table called Property with two columns, Name and Value. After we instantiate the typed dataset, we hook its RowChanged event to an event handler. This event will be triggered when a dataset row is modified, which in turn enables the Save Config button.

❸,❹ Next, we load the dataset with all configuration settings returned by the WMI provider and bind it to the grid control. As you can see in figure 7.24, the provider decrypts the database authentication settings for us.

Once the grid is loaded, the user can change settings at will. Currently, the WMI provider doesn't support deleting existing settings or creating new ones. The `SaveServerProperties` function writes the changes back to the configuration file, as shown below:

```
private void SaveServerProperties() {
  EntityProperty.PropertyDataTable ds = (EntityProperty.PropertiesDataT-
able)grdProperties.DataSource;
  DataView view = new DataView(ds);

  view.RowStateFilter = DataViewRowState.ModifiedCurrent;

  PropertyDataCollection instProps = m_instance.Properties;
  for(int i = 0;i < view.Count ;i++) {
     string name = view[i]["Name"].ToString();
     instProps[name].Value = view[i]["Value"].ToString();
  }
  m_instance.Put();
}
```

Here, we filter out only the changed settings by using a filtered view on top of the typed dataset. Then, we write the changed values back to the WMI provider settings collection. Finally, we call the provider `Put()` method to persist the settings into the configuration file.

Sometimes, writing a full-fledged application to automate maintenance tasks may be overkill. RS provides other options that a savvy administrator can add to his belt of management tools, as we will discuss in the next section.

7.4 OTHER WAYS TO MANAGE REPORTING SERVICES

RS provides two other options for performing management tasks:

- Executing scripts with the RS script host
- Using specialized management utilities

Let's round out our report management discussion with a high-level overview of these options.

7.4.1 Managing RS with the script host

Traditionally, administrators have relied on scripts to perform routine day-to-day chores. Responding to this common need, RS comes with a script host that can be used to run scripts written in VB.NET. Scripting offers several advantages, including the following:

- It doesn't require advanced development skills.
- Scripts can be easily executed from the command line, batch files, or login scripts.
- Scripts can be easily scheduled to run at specific times.

Exploring RS scripting

RS provides a script host utility (rs.exe), which can process and run a script file you pass in. You write RS scripts in VB.NET and you store them as files with the .RSS extension. Inside the script you can call any of the RS Web service methods.

The RS script host automatically connects to the requested Report Server, creates a proxy class, and exposes it as a global variable, *rs*. The host accepts command-line switches, which you can use to specify input parameters, including the Report Server URL, the script file, the user credentials to log on to the Report Server, variables, and so on.

Let's now look at a quick example of how scripting with the RS script host can facilitate the management effort. For a detailed discussion of the RS script host please refer to the product documentation.

Scripting with the RS script host

The RS team has provided two sample scripts that demonstrate how you can use scripting to cancel a given running job and publish reports. These scripts should be enough to get you going. For example, we were able to quickly retrofit the PublishSample-Reports sample and create a useful script to deploy a report. The RDLDeploy script uploads a given report definition file to the report catalog. You can find the DeployRDL.rss in the Chapter 7 folder in the AWReporterWin sample application. To keep things simple, we excluded the role-based security verification.

The bulk of the work is performed by the `PublishReport` function, whose abbreviated code is shown below:

```
Public Sub PublishReport(ByVal reportName As String)
  Dim stream As FileStream = File.OpenRead(filePath)
  definition = New [Byte](stream.Length) {}
  stream.Read(definition, 0, CInt(stream.Length))
  stream.Close()
  warnings = rs.CreateReport(reportName, parentPath, True, _
             definition, Nothing)
End Sub
```

The code should look familiar to you because the RDLDeploy sample we discussed in this chapter serves the same purpose. You can execute the DeployRDL script from the command prompt using the following syntax:

```
rs -i RdlDeploy.rss -s http://servername/reportserver -v file-
Path="C:\Books\RS\Code\AWReporterWin\bin\Debug\AWReporter.rdl" -v folder-
Path="AWReporter" -v reportName="AdHocReport"
```

where

- `-i` specifies the input filename
- `-s` specifies the Report Server URL
- `-v` specifies an input variable

In this case, similarly to the RDLDeploy sample, we upload the AWReporter report definition file to the AWReporter catalog folder and name the new report AdHocReport.

7.4.2 Using other management utilities

Reporting Services provides the additional management utilities shown in table 7.6. Please see the documentation for a more detailed explanation of their purpose and usage.

Table 7.6 RS comes with a few management utilities that report administrators can use to perform specialized tasks.

Utility	Purpose
rsactivate	Activates a Report Server in a web farm or recovers from a hardware failure
rsconfig	Changes the encrypted Report Server database settings
rskeymgmt	Backs up and restores the encryption keys used by the Report Server

One of these utilities deserves more attention. As a first task after installing RS, we would advise all Report Server administrators to use the rskeymgmt utility to extract and back up the public encryption key. The Report Server uses this key to encrypt data in the report server database or catalog.

What is the encryption key good for? Chances are that you may need to change the account that the RS Windows service (ReportingServicesService.exe) runs under. Or, when deploying RS on a web farm environment you may need to set up a new RS installation which points to an existing report catalog. If the encryption key is different, the Report Server will not initialize. Therefore, it is absolutely crucial that you back up and store the encryption key in a safe place.

Analyzing the report execution statistics is an essential task that all report administrators worth their salt will need to perform on a regular basis. To assist report administrators in their effort to analyze and troubleshoot report processing, RS performs detailed logging. Let's see how you can use the RS logs to analyze report execution.

7.5 ANALYZING REPORT EXECUTION

Reporting Services maintains a variety of log files that capture the output from the three RS server-side components: the Report Server, the Report Manager, and the RS Windows service. Table 7.7 summarizes these log files.

Table 7.7 RS maintain a variety of log files to capture the output from the Report Server, the Report Manager, and the RS Windows service.

Log	Purpose
The Report Server execution log	Captures report execution statistics useful for auditing purposes
Trace logs	Stores essential statistics for monitoring and troubleshooting RS
The Microsoft Windows Event log	Records RS events, such as startup and shutdown events
Setup logs	Created by the RS Setup program, these logs can be used to troubleshoot setup issues. For more information about these logs, consult the product documentation.

Let's discuss in more detail the first two logging options, starting with the Report Server execution log.

7.5.1 Analyzing the Report Server execution log

By analyzing the historical log, the administrator should be able to answer such questions as, "Which are the top requested reports by day, month, and user?", "Which reports didn't execute successfully and why?", and "How long does it take on average for a given report to execute?" The Report Server can be set to store report execution statistics in the ExecutionLog table. The execution log is turned on by default and keeps the log data for 60 days. You can modify these settings from the Site Settings menu in the Report Manager.

Retrieving the execution log data

There's really nothing stopping you from querying the ExecutionLog table and its related tables directly. But to save you time and effort, the RS team has provided a useful DTS package called ExecutionLog, which you can find in the Extras folder on the RS setup CD.

When run, the package performs ETL (Extract, Transform, and Load) tasks to extract the execution log data from the Report Server database, transform it into a format suitable for reporting, and load the data into a separate database for reporting purposes. Please read the "Querying and Reporting on Report Execution Log Data" section in the product documentation for the steps needed to install the ExecutionLog DTS package.

Interpreting the execution log data

Once you install and run the package, you are ready to create useful reports and analyze the execution log data. What better way to practice your RS skills than creating RS reports for this purpose? Actually, the RS team has already done this for you and provided the ExecutionLog Business Intelligence project, which you can find in the Extras folder as well.

The project contains several useful reports that you can run right away or customize to fit your specific needs. For example, the ReportsExecutedByDay report (figure 7.25) shows you the report activity and top requested reports per day.

Glancing at the report chart, we can easily see that the Report Server took the most hits on Tuesday during the requested week.

Another report that could help the administrator troubleshoot reports that didn't execute successfully is the Report Status Rates report shown in figure 7.26.

Figure 7.26 reveals that the Employee Sales Freeform report failed to execute due to an invalid parameter. If the administrator needs more details about the failed execution, the next step would be to run the Report Parameters report to find out exactly which parameters have been passed in.

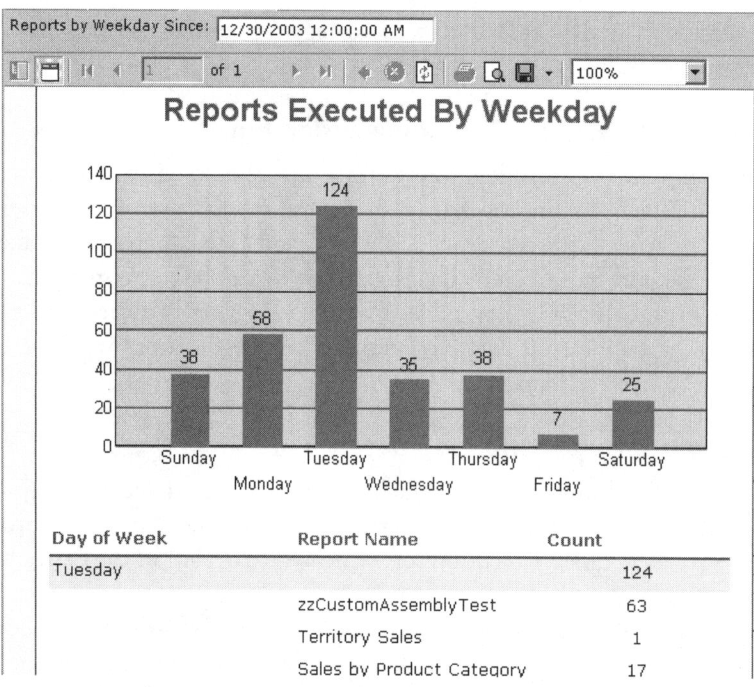

Figure 7.25 Use the ExecutionLog Business Intelligence project to analyze the statistics captured in the Execution Log.

Report Status Rates

Status Code	Total Executions	Status Rate
⊞ rsSuccess	349	96.9%
⊞ rsItemNotFound	3	.8%
⊟ rsInvalidReportParameter	3	.8%
Employee Sales Freeform	1	33.3%
Employee Sales Summary	2	66.7%
⊟ rsProcessingAborted	2	.6%
Sales By Country	2	100.0%
⊞ rsProcessingError	2	.6%
⊟ rrRenderingError	1	.3%
Product Catalog Localized	1	100.0%

Figure 7.26 The Report Status Rates report

7.5.2 Analyzing trace log files

Each of the RS server-side main components—the Report Server, the Report Manager, and the Windows service—maintains its own trace log file. The information captured in these files conveys vital statistics, which are useful for auditing and troubleshooting the report execution.

For example, by examining the log files the administrator can find out who has accessed the Report Server and what action has been requested.

Managing trace log files

The trace log files can be found in the C:\Program Files\Microsoft SQL Server\MSSQL\Reporting Services\LogFiles folder. Table 7.8 outlines their purpose.

Table 7.8 Reporting Services maintain three configuration files, one for each server-side component.

Log Filename	Description
ReportServerService_<timestamp>.log	Trace log for the Report Server Windows service and Web service
ReportServerWebApp_<timestamp>.log	Trace log for Report Manager
ReportServer_<timestamp>.log	Trace log for the Report Server

Reporting Services starts a new log file under two conditions: at the start of a new day and when the server-side component is started. For example, if you restart IIS and then navigate to the Report Manager, new log files will be created to capture the Report Manager and Report Server trace output.

As an administrator, you can specify the level of details for the logged data by adjusting the DefaultTraceSwitch setting in the configuration files. The supported values range from 0 (no tracing) to verbose. In addition, you can instruct the Report Server to purge the old log files by using the KeepForFiles configuration setting.

Examining trace content

The log data is stored in plain text so report administrators can use their favorite text editor to open and search the logs. For example, this is what the log entry looks like after a user has requested the Sales by Territory report:

```
w3wp!runningrequests!7bc!03/24/2004-22:20:17:: v VERBOSE: User
map'<Users><User><Name>"user identity"</Name><Paths><Path>http://localhost/
ReportServer/reportservice.asmx</Path><NrReq>1</NrReq></Paths></User></
Users>'
w3wp!library!7bc!03/24/2004-22:20:17:: i INFO: Call to GetPermissions:/
AWReporter/Sales By Territory
```

Performing runtime tracing

Sometimes, you may want to watch the tracing output in real time, for example, to see the sequence of events before an exception is thrown. Or, you may need to see the tracing output from all three components in one place.

Fortunately, the information captured in the log files is also output to the default trace listener. This allows you to watch the tracing output using tools such as Mark Russinovich's DebugView trace monitor, as shown in figure 7.27.

In this way, not only will you be able to get a consolidated picture of how the different components interact, but you will also be able to watch the tracing statements output by custom code and extensions.

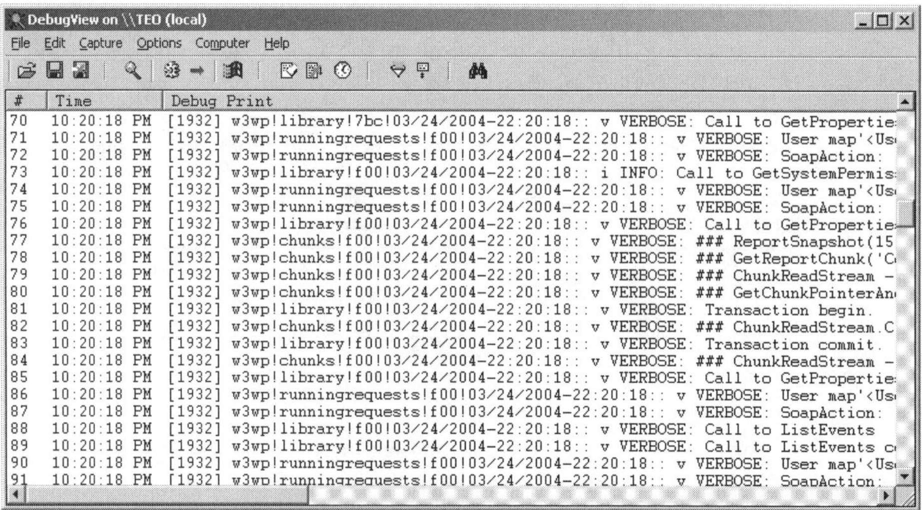

Figure 7.27 Using DebugView to watch the tracing output during runtime

7.6 SUMMARY

In this chapter we have shown how to manage the Report Server environment. Most of the time, you will rely on the Report Manager to perform day-to-day administration activities, such as managing folders, reports, and resources.

We also emphasized the fact that behind the scenes the Report Manager performs management tasks using the RS SOAP APIs. You can call these APIs programmatically in your applications to query and manage the report repository.

If you need to manage multiple Report Servers from a single location, you can use the RS WMI provider. We showed you how this could be done in the RS Console sample.

You can also write script files in VB.NET and execute them with the RS script host. This option doesn't require advanced development skills. Scripts can be easily executed and scheduled to run at specific time.

RS also provides a few management utilities that you can use to perform specific tasks, such as activating a Report Server instance, changing database settings, and saving the encryption keys.

To keep track of report execution, we recommend that you turn on report execution logging and analyze its statistics on a daily basis. To do so, use the ExecutionLog DTS package to import the execution log statistics and the reports in the ExecutionLog Business Intelligence project.

Our report management journey will not be complete if we don't discuss arguably the most important aspect of RS management, which is securing the Report Server environment. Chapter 8 will teach us how to do exactly this.

7.7 RESOURCES

SOAP Toolkit version 3.0 (http://www.microsoft.com/downloads/details.aspx?FamilyID=c943c0dd-ceec-4088-9753-86f052ec8450&DisplayLang=en)
A link to the Microsoft MSDN download center where you can download the SOAP Toolkit, which includes the SOAP Trace utility.

TcpTrace (http://www.pocketsoap.com/tcptrace/)
A great utility that captures the TCP traffic between a client and a server.

How To: Implement Kerberos Delegation for Windows 2000 (http://msdn.microsoft.com/library/default.asp?url=/library/en-us/dnnetsec/html/SecNetHT05.asp)
This article lists the steps required to configure Kerberos authentication.

CHAPTER 8

Securing Reporting Services

Security can no longer be downplayed. Ironically, if you read computer books published in the not-so-distant past, you will usually find the security chapter pushed toward the end of the book, if not in the appendix. Sort of like, "You will probably never need this stuff, but just in case..." Things have certainly changed! The explosion of viruses and hacker attacks in recent years has pushed security concerns to the forefront of development and application design. To address this issue, the Common Language Runtime (CLR) and .NET Framework include classes that enable developers to write secure code easily.

You won't get far with Reporting Services if you don't have a good grasp of how its security works. In this chapter, we will explore the two security models that RS provides: role-based security and code access security.

Administrators can leverage the role-based security model to secure access to report resources, as well as define the permitted actions that a given user is allowed to perform.

Code access security can be used to "sandbox" custom code by taking advantage of the code access security infrastructure baked into the .NET CLR.

We will start our discussion by examining the role-based security model first, followed by code access security. Finally, we will discuss various strategies for securing reports, such as data filtering, dynamic queries, and data hiding.

Because the RS security model is layered on top of the OS and .NET security, understanding security is not easy, and explaining this topic in detail is beyond the scope of this chapter. Therefore, we will assume that you have a basic knowledge about how Windows and ASP.NET security work.

8.1 Exploring Reporting Services role-based security

You will probably find the RS role-based model similar to the security models of other Microsoft and third-party products or homegrown solutions you have come across in the past. In a nutshell, it provides the necessary infrastructure for the following:

- *User authentication*—During the authentication stage the role-based security model determines who the user is by obtaining her identity from a trusted authority. For example, let's say a user called Terri logs in to her machine as AW\Terri (AW is Terri's login domain) and runs a report. If Windows authentication is used, at the end of the authentication phase the Report Server will know that the identity of the user is AW\Terri.
- *User authorization*—Authorization occurs after authentication and determines what the user can do. Given the previous example, during the authorization process the Report Server would verify whether Terri has sufficient rights to run the report by checking the role-based security policy established for her.

In .NET security terminology, the terms *user* and *principal* are used interchangeably. For example, if you want to obtain the security context of the current user when Windows-based authentication is used, you can retrieve the current principal from Thread.CurrentPrincipal. The IPrinicipal object returned from the call implements the IIdentity interface. You can query IIdentity.Name to obtain the user's identity after the user is authenticated.

Once the user's identity is verified, the user can execute tasks or request RS resources subject to the authorization rules set up by the report administrator.

The RS role-based security model serves two purposes:

- It provides the infrastructure to define user roles and assign users to these roles.
- It grants or revokes access to a specific task or resource based on the user's role membership.

A distinguishing feature of RS role-based security is that it is fully customizable. By default, RS relies on Windows authentication to authenticate users. This configuration will probably meet the security needs of most intranet-based applications. For example, Windows authentication allows the report administrator to leverage the pre-established user and group accounts in Active Directory.

When Windows authentication is not an option, developers can replace it with a custom security model in the form of a security extension. For example, using Windows accounts to authenticate web users is often impractical with most Internet-oriented applications. Instead, with this type of application, once the user enters her credentials, the application typically authenticates the user via a database lookup. To add reporting features to such applications, you can write a custom security extension to pass the user's identity to the Report Server. We will see how to do just that in chapter 15. This chapter explains the RS role-based security model in the context of the default authentication mechanism, which once again is Windows authentication.

8.1.1 How Windows authentication works

The Report Server delegates the security-related tasks to a *security extension*. A security extension is a .NET assembly that handles the authentication and authorization of users or groups in RS. When the Report Server needs to authenticate the user or verify that the user is allowed to perform a given task, it asks the extension to do so.

Because the Report Server web application is configured for Integrated Windows authentication, the security extension gets the Windows identity of the user from Internet Information Services (IIS). IIS authenticates the user and passes the Windows access token to the Report Server.

Although IIS provides several authentication mechanisms, RS supports the Basic and Integrated (NTLM or Kerberos) authentication options only.

NOTE Strictly speaking, although you are discouraged from doing so, you can configure the Report Server virtual root to allow anonymous access. This could be useful in situations when you don't care about the identity of the user, for example, when you want to allow any user to access the Report Server with the same level of permissions. The net effect of enabling anonymous access is that you disable the RS role-based security policy. The reason for this is that the Report Server sees all requests as coming under a single Windows account, which by default is IUSR_<computer name>.

Therefore, the role-based security policies cannot be enforced per user, which is a sure recipe for chaos. Please note that you still have to establish a security policy for this Anonymous account (or the Windows groups it is a member of) in the Report Server and map it to a role. Because the Report Server will be unable to differentiate the user requests, to be able to manage the report catalog you will need to grant this account system administrator rights. This means that any user will be able to change the Report Server configuration at will. When anonymous access is mandatory, I strongly suggest that you use custom security authentication performed by the application or a custom security extension.

By default, RS is installed in a locked-down mode, and only members of the Windows local administrators group can manage the report environment and run reports. Similar to the Windows NTFS model, to prevent an accidental lockout, this security policy cannot be removed. As a result, Reporting Services will always allow local administrators on the Report Server machine the right to view items and change security policies, even if they're not explicitly defined in a role-based security policy.

To allow other users to request reports or manage RS, you must create additional security policies and add Windows built-in accounts and/or groups to them. Typically, to simplify the role assignment management, you will organize the Windows user accounts into groups. This will require that you work hand-in-hand with the network administrator to define the appropriate Windows group memberships and create new groups if needed.

To understand how Windows authentication can be used for securing client applications, consider two common integration scenarios:

- Client-to-Report Server
- Client-to-Façade-to-Report Server

NOTE Another common way to describe the above scenarios is to use the "tier" paradigm. Because the Report Server can be viewed as a separate tier, the first scenario could also be named "three-tiered," while the second could be called "multi-tiered." You choose.

Let's discuss how security relates to each of these models, starting with the Client-to-Report Server model.

Exploring the Client-to-Report Server model

The Client-to-Report Server scenario is better suited for intranet-based report consumers. With this model, the report consumer, which could be WinForm or web-based, accesses the Report Server on the client side of the application, and the call goes out under the Windows identity of the user.

Figure 8.1 depicts the Client-to-Report Server integration approach.

By the way, this is the model that the Report Manager uses for report rendering. When the user clicks the report link inside the Report Manager, an HTTP-GET request is made to the Report Server under the identity of the interactive user.

In figure 8.1 Terri is logged in to the AW domain as AW/Terri. Terri then goes to the Report Manager portal to run a report. IIS authenticates Terri as AW/Terri and

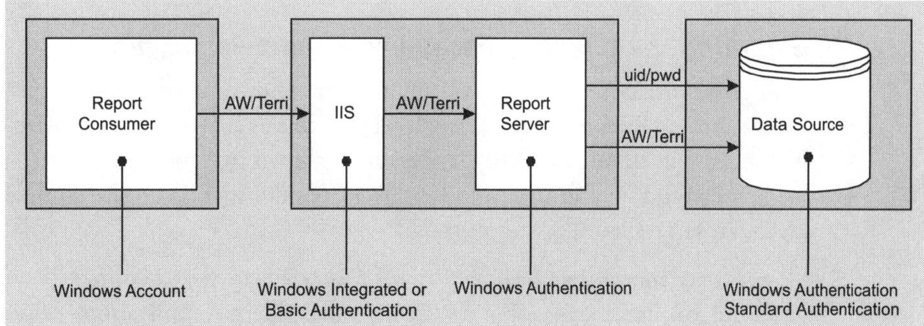

Figure 8.1 The Client-to-Report Server model is most suitable for intranet-based applications and promotes direct access to the Report Server.

passes the security token to the Report Server. Next, the Report Server checks the role-based security policy for Terri and grants or refuses access to the requested report. Let's assume that Terri is granted permissions to run the report, and the report needs to access a data source to display some data. How the database authenticates the request depends on which data source authentication options have been set for this report, as we discussed in chapter 3. The possible outcomes are these:

- *Credentials Stored Securely in the Report Server*—If the Use as Windows Credentials When Connecting to the Data Source option is set, the database will use Windows Integrated authentication to authenticate the call using the Windows account credentials the administrator has set up. Otherwise, the data source will use standard authentication. In both cases, the call to the database will go under a designated account (depicted as uid/pwd on figure 8.1), which facilitates connection pooling.
- *Windows NT Integrated Security*—If the database is installed on the same machine as the Report Server or on another machine with Kerberos delegation enabled, the call to the database will go out under AW/Terri. If the database is on another machine and Kerberos is not enabled, the remote call will use a NULL session and it will fail. As we pointed out in chapter 3, in general you should avoid impersonating the user so you don't lose the benefits of connection pooling.

For the Client-to-Report Server scenario, we recommend the following security configuration:

- Use the default Windows-based authentication coupled with role-based security to enforce restricted access to the Report Server.
- Use the Credentials Stored Securely in the Report Server data source option with Windows or standard authentication for accessing the data source.

Sometimes, this scenario won't be that simple and your integration requirements may rule out the possibility of direct access to the Report Server. In such cases, the Client-to-Façade-to-Report Server model may be a better fit.

Exploring the Client-to-Façade-to-Report Server model

Things get trickier when an additional layer is introduced between the report consumer and the Report Server. We will refer to this as a *façade* to emphasize the fact that it is located in front of the Report Server, as shown in figure 8.2.

Why would you add yet another layer? Besides increasing the complexity, such a layer can serve the following purposes:

- *It may encapsulate the application's business rules.* For example, it may represent the business layer of a WinForm three-tiered application, which could be exposed either as Web services or as a set of .NET remote objects. We will discuss this approach in more detail in chapter 10.

- *It may represent the server-side web layer of the report consumer for both intranet and Internet web-based applications.* For example, the Report Manager can be viewed as a façade to the Report Server. We will look into possible implementation approaches in chapter 11.
- *It may be needed to isolate the report consumer from the Report Server.* For example, in the business-to-business extranet scenario, it is unlikely that an organization will allow direct access to the Report Server. Instead, a Web service façade could be built to expose some of the RS functionality. We will discuss the extranet scenario in more detail in chapter 11.
- *It may enforce custom security rules to extend or replace the Report Server role-based security model when the latter is not enough.* We will see how this could be implemented in chapter 13.

For simplicity's sake, the scenario shown in figure 8.2 assumes that the report consumer runs under the Windows identity of the user. This is the typical case with intranet applications. Things can get more complicated with other implementation approaches. For example, in the extranet scenario, the report consumers can use client certificates for authentication, which can be mapped to Windows accounts. Or, an Internet-based application can use the ASP.NET Forms Authentication model, as we will discuss in chapter 11.

From the Report Server standpoint, how the report consumer is implemented is not important. All the Report Server sees are incoming requests under a given Windows identity. From the report consumer façade standpoint, however, which identity will be passed to the Report Server is very important. Basically, the façade layer has two choices:

- Impersonate the user by passing the user's identity to the Report Server.
- Pass its identity. This model is sometimes referred to as a trusted subsystem.

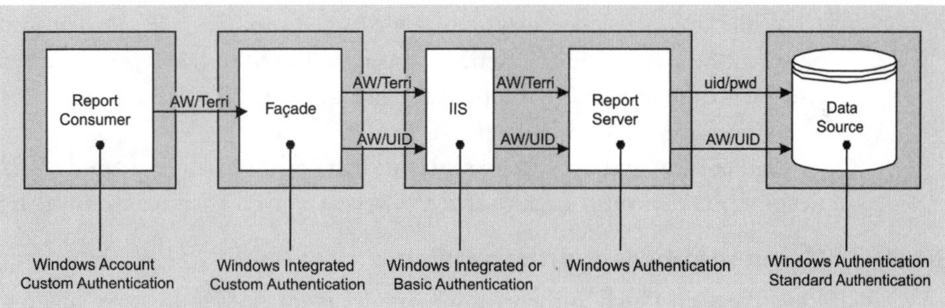

Figure 8.2 In the Client-to-Façade-to-Report Server model, an additional layer is introduced between the report consumer and the Report Server.

Impersonating the user

If the façade decides to impersonate the user, the original user's security context and identity will flow to IIS and then to the Report Server. This is the approach the Report Manager takes for submitting SOAP requests to the Report Server on the server side of the application.

To impersonate the user in ASP.NET applications, you can use the `<impersonate>` element in the web.config configuration file. You can impersonate the user's identity or use a specific Windows account. If the façade and the Report Server are located on separate machines, you must enable Kerberos authentication to flow successfully the user identity between the Façade and the Report Server because NTLM doesn't support delegation. Then the authentication works as we described in the Client-to-Report Server scenario.

Passing the façade identity

Instead of impersonating the user, the façade can pass its own identity. To accomplish this, you would typically change the identity of the ASP.NET worker process to run under a designated domain account. If you decide to use a local computer account, you'll have to clone this account to the Report Server machine to keep the security gods happy.

As figure 8.2 shows, the ASP.NET worker process runs under a domain account AW/UID, which is passed on to the Report Server. If the façade layer runs under IIS 5 (Windows 2000), this will require that you change the `<processModel>` element in machine.config. If IIS 6 is used (Windows 2003), you can change the identity of the application pool to which the application belongs. In addition, you'll need to add the account that you used for the pool identity to the Windows 2003 IIS_WPG group.

Once the façade identity is set up, you must map it to the appropriate role in the Report Server so that it has proper access to RS resources. If the façade will fulfill report-rendering tasks only, you could create a security policy to grant the façade account Browser role permissions.

While the trusted subsystem approach simplifies the authentication process between the façade and the Report Server, you need to take care of authenticating the end users and authorizing them at the façade layer. We will discuss a possible implementation approach in chapter 12.

Authenticating the user represents one half of the security equation. After the authentication, the user must be authorized to access a given resource from the report catalog.

8.1.2 Using role-based authorization

Regardless of which authentication model is used, Windows or custom authentication, Reporting Services authorizes requests based on the membership that the user has in one or more RS roles. RS offers a comprehensive role-based security model to authorize user requests. We will first discuss the theory behind this model and then demonstrate how you can manage the role-based security infrastructure with the Report Manager and the Report Server Web service.

To explain the RS role-based model and how its pieces fit together, we put together the database diagram shown in figure 8.3.

Please note that this diagram doesn't exactly match the Report Server physical database model. You will find only the Users, Roles, and Policies tables in the Report Server database; the rest are fictitious. Where, then, does the Report Server store the rest of the role-based security items? If you examine the actual Policies table, you will notice that it uses proprietary structures to define the role assignment relationship. When the administrator creates a new security policy for a given user to a securable item, a new record is added to the Policies table. This record specifies the item that is secured, the user's Windows account, and the role-based security policy stored as an XML fragment.

Strictly speaking, although not so obvious, tasks in RS are further broken out and consist of entities called *permissions*. However, for simplicity, permissions are not exposed in the Report Manager UI, so you can't see them. The reason for this is that a task is a fixed collection of permissions and can't be changed.

How do you find out what permissions are available with RS? In section 8.1.4 we will author a sample report called Show Security Policy, which will list the permissions associated with a given user and report item. To accomplish this, we will use the `GetPermissions` SOAP API, which returns a collection of permissions, such as Create Data Source, Create Folder, etc.

At this point you may be curious as to how permissions can be used if tasks are fixed entities. RS permissions could be useful if you need to write a custom security extension and you need to deal with permissions, for example, if you want the Report Manager to disable controls according to the security policy associated with the interactive user. We will show how to write a custom security extension in chapter 15.

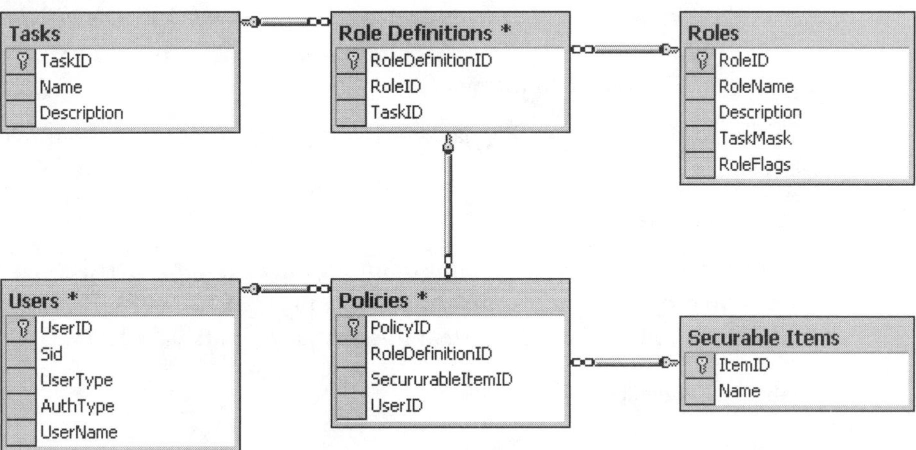

Figure 8.3 Reporting Services comes with a comprehensive role-based security model based on the user's membership in one or more roles.

Understanding tasks

A *task* defines a set of permissions that can be enforced through role-based security. For example, RS defines a task called View Reports, which allows users to run reports. RE defines two types for tasks: system-level tasks and item-level tasks.

System-level tasks represent maintenance actions, such as Define Roles. Item-level tasks define user permissions, such as View Reports, View Folders, and so on. Another way to differentiate between these two types is to note that system-level tasks work on global items (which do not have catalog paths), while item-level tasks work on items with paths.

You can find the full list of predefined tasks under the Site Settings menu. Currently, RS doesn't support custom tasks. For this reason, you will not find a Task table in the Report Server database. In addition, you cannot map users directly to tasks. Instead, to use a task, you need to assign it to a role.

Defining roles

As its name suggests, the role-based security infrastructure in RS uses the concept of *roles* to assign a set of permissions to users with the same security requirements. Simply put, a role is a named set of tasks. Currently, RS doesn't support nested roles. For example, you cannot set up a Content Manager role to include the Browser role.

Because the relationship between roles and tasks is many-to-many, the documentation uses the term *role definition* to represent the tasks-to-role membership. For example, RS includes the predefined item-level Browser and Content Manager roles, and both of them include the View Reports task.

> **NOTE** Strictly speaking, Reporting Services implements the roles-to-tasks relationship by a bit-masked value defined in the TaskMask column in the Roles table. For this reason, the terms *role* and *role definition* are interchangeable. However, I broke it down into two tables to make the concept easier to understand.

Similar to the task types, RS classifies roles in two categories: system roles and item-level roles.

System-level roles

Most applications need an Administrator role that has unrestricted access to the application in order to perform application-wide maintenance tasks. Reporting Services is no exception. It defines two system roles, as shown in table 8.1.

Table 8.1 Predefined system roles

System-Level Role	Rights
System User	View system properties and shared schedules
System Administrator	System User rights plus the rights to view and modify system role assignments and role definitions

System-level roles can include only system-level tasks. When you install RS, the Setup program maps the Windows local administrators group to the System Administrator role.

Item-level roles

Item-level roles contain item-level tasks. Table 8.2 shows the predefined item-level roles.

Table 8.2 Predefined item-level roles

Item-Level Role	Rights
Browser	View folders and reports and subscribe to reports
Content Manager	All item-level permissions
My Reports	Publish reports and linked reports; manage folders, reports, and resources in a user's My Reports folder
Publisher	Publish reports and linked reports to the Report Server

Unlike working with tasks, you can define custom system and item-level roles, as well as modify the predefined roles. Let's say that you don't like the predefined task mapping for the Content Manager role. For example, you don't want members of this role to be able to view reports. You can use the Site Settings menu to either change the role definition or create a new item-level role.

Understanding securable items

Table 8.3 lists the RS resources that can be secured through role-based security.

Table 8.3 RS securable resources

Securable Resource	Description
Folders	Viewing folders and navigating through the folder hierarchy requires the rights to execute the View Folders task. If the user doesn't have the rights to view a folder, the folder is excluded from the folder view. Requesting the folder explicitly through URL access or Web service results in a security exception. Managing folders requires the Manage Folders task.
Reports	In order to view a report, the user must have the rights to execute the View Reports task. To manage the report, the user must have the Manage Reports rights.
Shared data sources	The user needs the Manage Reports rights to change the report data source. After that, no special permissions are required to render reports that use a shared data source. To view the shared data source definition, the user must have the View Data Sources permission. To manage it, the rights to execute the Manage Data Sources tasks are required.
Other catalog items	The View Resources permission is required to view an image item. Similarly, View Resources is required to apply an XSL transformation.

continued on next page

Table 8.3 **RS securable resources** *(continued)*

Securable Resource	Description
Report History	Managing the report snapshot history requires the rights to execute the Manage Report History task.
Subscriptions	Managing user report subscriptions requires the rights to execute the Manage Individual Subscriptions task. Managing report subscriptions of other users requires the rights to execute the Manage All Subscriptions task.

Tasks and roles are useful only when they are associated with users in order to enforce restricted access to the Report Server. To accomplish this, the administrator defines role-based security policies.

Defining policies

A policy defines the relationship among users, roles, and securable items. In other words, a policy determines the permitted tasks that the user can perform on a given securable item, such as a folder or report. The RS role-based security policy is additive, which means that the user is granted the union of the permitted tasks defined in the roles to which the user is mapped.

Let's consider the example shown in figure 8.4.

In this example, David Campbell is assigned to both the Sales Managers and Sales Windows groups of the AW domain. The RS administrator assigned the Sales Managers

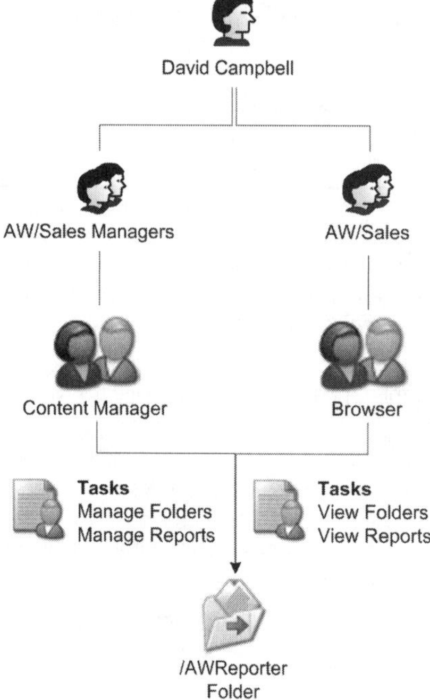

Figure 8.4 The RS role-based security model is additive, and the user is granted the union of the permitted tasks.

group to the Content Manager role when defining the role-based security for the AWReporter folder. The AW Sales group is mapped to the Browser role.

What will be the resultant set of permitted tasks that David Campbell gets? The answer is that he will be able to execute all tasks defined for the Content Manager and Browser roles. If these two roles include the default set of tasks, David will be able to manage the AWReporter folder (create and delete folders, add reports), as well as see all reports in the AWReporter folder.

Overriding security policy inherited from the parent folder

You can enforce role-based security on folders and their content. By default, the security policy propagates through the children of the parent folder, similarly to the way Windows access control list (ACL) permissions are inherited from the parent folder by its descendants. However, the inheritance chain can be overridden if the subfolders or resources must have different permissions than their parent.

For example, considering again the scenario shown in figure 8.4, what if the AWReporter folder contains some sensitive reports that only the members of the Sales Managers group should see? To accomplish this requirement, we can remove the AW/Sales group from the policy list of restricted reports.

What happens when you break the policy inheritance chain at a specific securable item? The Report Server simply assigns a new policy list to this item, which by default gives Content Manager rights to members of the Windows local administrators group.

It is not difficult to understand how the Report Server determines whether the user is permitted to execute a given task on a secured item. First, the Report Server determines whether the item inherits the security policy of its parent. If the security chain is broken at the item level, the Report Server evaluates its policy list to find out which tasks have been assigned to the role(s) the user belongs to. If the security policy is inherited, the Report Server walks recursively up the inheritance chain to find out which of the item ascendants define the security policy.

Simplifying security policy management

To simplify the folder permissions, we suggest that you stick to policy inheritance as much as possible. The approach we recommend is to enforce the minimum set of permissions at the top Home folder. Then, work your way down by adding or taking out permissions on its children on an as-needed basis.

Let's consider a more involved example. Let's say you want to organize your RS folder namespace per department and application, similar to the one shown in figure 8.5.

First, under the Home folder you create department folders, for example, Sales and HR. Then, you create application folders under the department folders, for example, AWReporter for the Sales department to contain all of the sample reports from this book. How can you minimize role-based security maintenance and yet ensure that you

Role	Group
Content Manager	AW/Administrators
Browser	AW/Users

Role	Group	Inherited
Content Manager	AW/Administrators	Y
Content Manager	AW/Sales Managers	
Browser	AW/Sales	

Role	Group	Inherited
Content Manager	AW/Administrators	Y
Content Manager	AW/Sales Managers	Y
Browser	AW/Sales	Y

Figure 8.5
The report administrator can simplify role-based security management by using policy inheritance.

enforce a comprehensive level of security? Let's say you don't want users from other departments to be able to browse the Sales folder and see its contents.

To simplify the security infrastructure, you can take advantage of the inheritance feature of the role-based security policy. You can allow only AW domain administrators to manage the full folder namespace by assigning them to the Content Manager role. You can assign all other domain users to the Browser role so they can browse the Home folder. For the Sales folder you can break the folder's inheritance chain. You can remove the Users group from the Browser role and grant the Sales Managers and Sales groups the Content Manager and Browser roles, respectively. You don't have to perform any extra steps if you want the same permissions to propagate to the AWReporter folder.

When the user doesn't have permissions to view a given securable item, the item is excluded from the results of the Web service method call. For example, if the user clicks on the Home folder to see its subfolders, the Report Server will return only the subfolders to which the user has View permissions. Behind the scenes, the Report Manager invokes the `ListChildren` SOAP API, which excludes restricted resources. This makes developing client applications a lot easier because you don't have to filter out the results to enforce restricted access—one less thing to worry about when writing custom applications that target RS.

Now that we've explained the theory behind the RS role-based security model, let's see how we can manage it using the Report Manager.

8.1.3 Managing role-based security with the Report Manager

It is important to note that when you use the Report Manager to set up a role-based security infrastructure, you are securing not the Report Manager but the Report Server. The policy changes that you make using the Report Manager are persisted in the Report Server database. For this reason, these changes will affect all report consumers that use the same instance of the Report Server.

Managing the role-based security infrastructure with the Report Manager is easy. Let's see whether we can convince you of this by showing what needs to be done to secure the resources in the AWReporter folder. Our fictitious scenario will be similar to the examples we discussed previously. It will include the following actions:

- Creating a few Windows user accounts
- Assigning them to Windows groups
- Assigning the Windows groups to predefined and custom roles
- Enforcing a role-based security policy on the AWReporter folder and its resources

To make our example more realistic, we'll define the new accounts and groups in correspondence with the AWC organizational structure. Back in chapter 5, we created a Corporate Hierarchy report that we can use to get started, as shown in figure 8.6.

Our requirements are as follows:

- Only the members of the Sales Managers and Sales groups can access the AWReporter folder.
- The members of the Sales Managers group have unrestricted access to AWReporter folder.
- The members of the Sales group are able to run reports only.
- The AWC network administrator can manage the AWReporter folder and its resources but cannot view any reports in this folder.

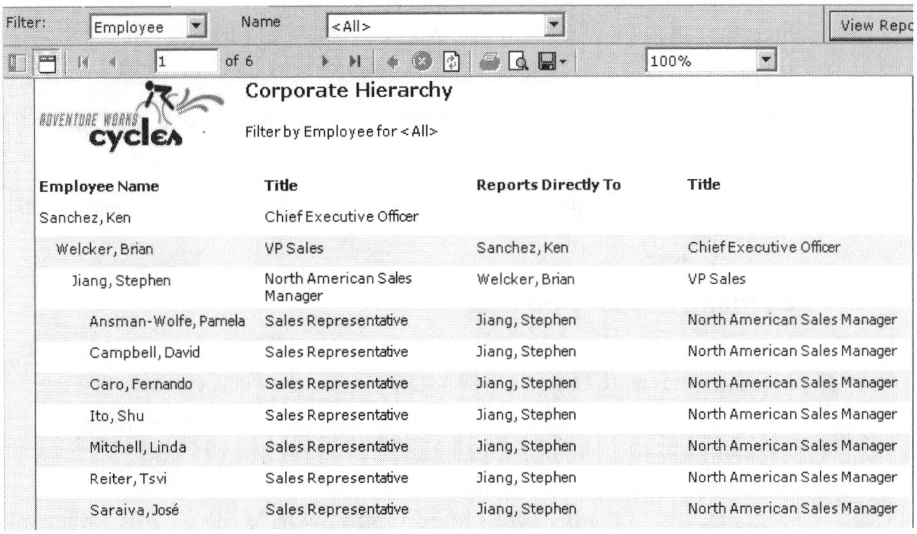

Filter: Employee Name <All> View Repc

1 of 6 100%

Corporate Hierarchy

ADVENTURE WORKS cycles

Filter by Employee for <All>

Employee Name	Title	Reports Directly To	Title
Sanchez, Ken	Chief Executive Officer		
Welcker, Brian	VP Sales	Sanchez, Ken	Chief Executive Officer
Jiang, Stephen	North American Sales Manager	Welcker, Brian	VP Sales
Ansman-Wolfe, Pamela	Sales Representative	Jiang, Stephen	North American Sales Manager
Campbell, David	Sales Representative	Jiang, Stephen	North American Sales Manager
Caro, Fernando	Sales Representative	Jiang, Stephen	North American Sales Manager
Ito, Shu	Sales Representative	Jiang, Stephen	North American Sales Manager
Mitchell, Linda	Sales Representative	Jiang, Stephen	North American Sales Manager
Reiter, Tsvi	Sales Representative	Jiang, Stephen	North American Sales Manager
Saraiva, José	Sales Representative	Jiang, Stephen	North American Sales Manager

Figure 8.6 Use the Corporate Hierarchy report to see the AWC organizational structure.

Creating Windows user accounts and groups

The Employee table in the AdventureWorks2000 database can give us the necessary details to set up the Windows accounts, as shown in table 8.4.

Table 8.4 Test accounts and groups needed to run the role-based security sample

User Name	Login ID	Password	Description	Windows Group
Stephen Jiang	Stephen	Stephen	Sales Manager	AW Sales Managers, Users
David Campbell	David3	David3	Sales Representative	AW Sales, Users
Ashvini Sharma	Ashvini	Ashvini	Network Administrator	AW Sales Admin, Users

To set up these accounts, open the Computer Management console and create the three Windows groups (AW Sales Managers, AW Sales, and AW Sales Admin) listed in table 8.4. In the process of doing so, don't forget to uncheck the User Must Change Password at Next Logon check box. Then, create the three Windows user accounts (Stephen, David3, and Ashvini) and assign them to the appropriate groups.

Creating custom roles

To meet the last of our requirements, we need to create a new role because none of the predefined roles includes only management tasks. We can create a custom role with the Report Manager by following these steps:

Step 1 Click the Site Settings menu.

Step 2 Click the Configure Item-Level Role Definitions link.

Step 3 Click the New Role button. The New Role screen appears (figure 8.7).

Step 4 Name the new role Sales Admin and assign to it all management tasks shown in figure 8.7.

We now have a custom role that we can use to define the role-based security policy for the network administrator.

Defining security policies

Next, we will enforce restricted access to the AWReporter folder. Using the Report Manager, navigate to the AWReporter folder and click the Security tab on the folder's Properties page. If you haven't made any changes to the default security policy, you will see a single button named Edit Item Security. When you click it, you will see the confirmation prompt shown in figure 8.8.

Click OK to confirm your intention to override the security policy inherited from the Home folder. The user interface changes and now shows two buttons (figure 8.9).

The default security policy allows only local administrators to access this folder by granting them permissions to execute all tasks of the Content Manager role. We will now define three additional security policies that will grant different levels of

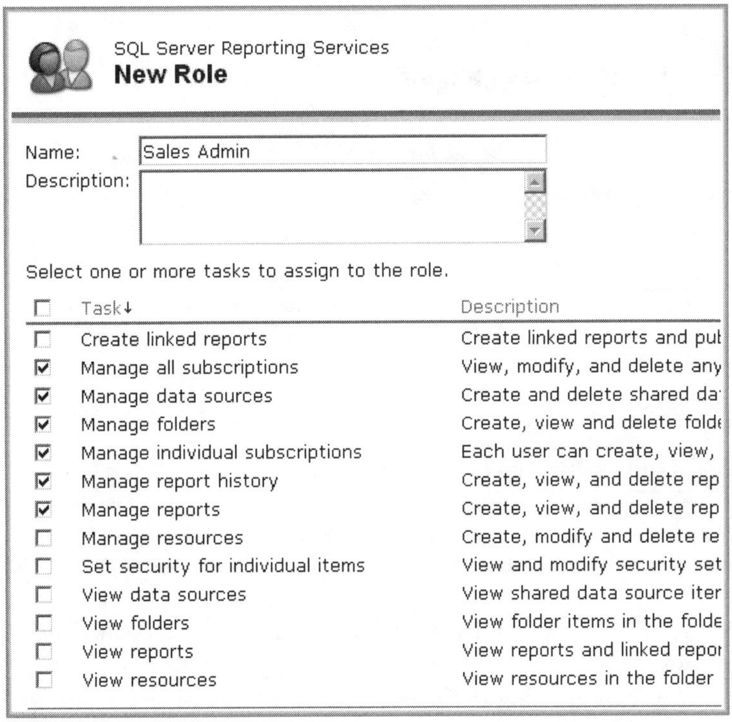

Figure 8.7 With RS you can create a custom role that includes one or more predefined tasks.

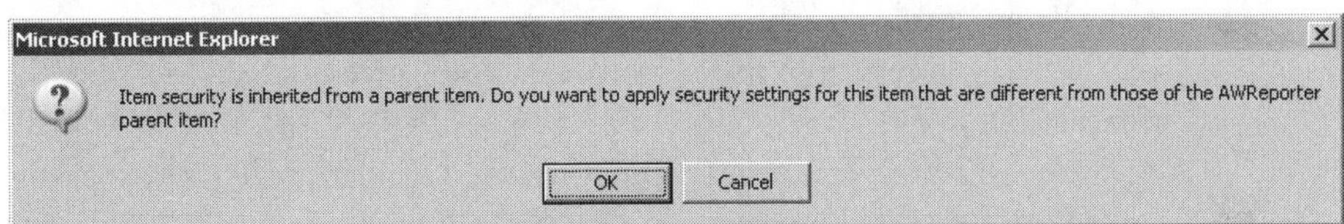

Figure 8.8 When the security policy inherited from the item parent is not a good fit, you can override it.

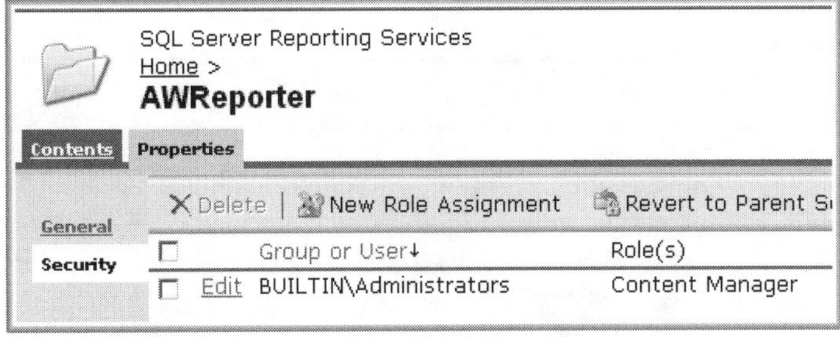

Figure 8.9 Use the report's Security tab to create new role-based security policies.

SQL Server Reporting Services
New Role Assignment

Use this page to define role-based security for AWReporter.

Group or user name: AW Sales Managers

Select one or more roles to assign to the group or user.

	Role	Description
☐	Browser	May view folders, reports and subscribe to r
☑	Content Manager	May manage content in the Report Server.
☐	My Reports	May publish reports and linked reports; manа Reports folder.
☐	Publisher	May publish reports and linked reports to the

OK | Cancel | New Role

Figure 8.10 You create a new role-based security policy by assigning Windows user or group accounts to roles.

access to the AWReporter folder for the Sales Managers, Sales, and Sales Admin Windows groups.

Let's start with granting the members of the Sales Managers group the Content Manager rights to the AWReporter folder. Click the New Role Assignment button to create a new security policy, as shown in figure 8.10.

Create two more role assignments to assign the members of the AW Sales group to the Browser role and the members of the AW Sales Admin group to the Sales Admin role. When you return to the Security tab, your screen should look like the one shown in figure 8.11.

We've finished! You can test the role-based security policies by logging on to Windows as each of the three users. For example, if you log on as Ashvini, you will be able

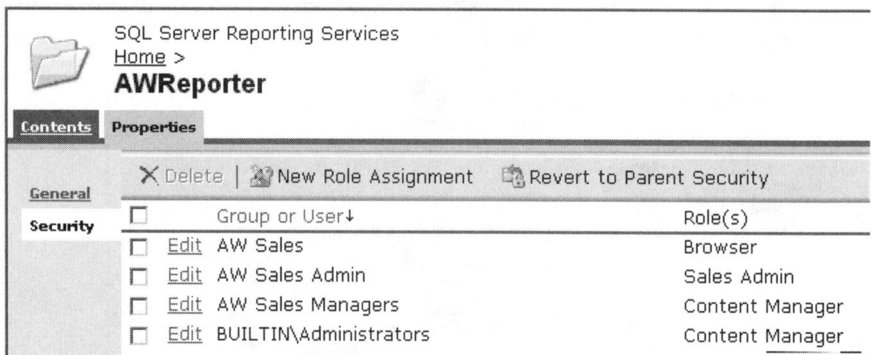

Figure 8.11 Based on your security requirements, you may need to create several security policies to provide restricted access to the report based on the users' role membership.

to manage the AWReporter folder and its resources, but you won't be able to run any of the reports. When you click the report's link, the Report Manager will not render the report. Instead, the report's Properties page will be open.

But wait, you say, what if we need to enforce a more restrictive policy on specific resources? For example, what if we want to prevent the members of the AW Sales group from running the Sales by Territory report? To accomplish this, we can enforce a report-specific security policy by overriding the AWReporter folder policy. To do so, we can click the Edit Item Security button found on the Security tab of the report's Properties page. When we do this, we are presented again with the confirmation prompt shown on figure 8.8 asking us whether we really want to break the security policy inheritance.

Once we confirm our intention, we can delete the AW Sales group from the policy list, which, in turn, will prevent its group members from rendering the report. If we later change our mind, we can always restore the policy inheritance by clicking the Revert to Parent Security button.

As we explained in chapter 7, the Report Manager is just a user-friendly application layer on top of the Report Server. To perform all management tasks, behind the scenes the Report Manager calls down to the RS Web service. In a similar way, you can manage programmatically the RS role-based security in your applications by invoking the Web service's security-related methods, as we will discuss next.

8.1.4 Managing role-based security with the Web service

As we discussed in chapter 7, the RS Web service provides a series of security-related methods that you can use to manage programmatically all aspects of the role-based security infrastructure. When the Report Manager is not enough, you can create custom applications (or reports) that call the security API directly.

For example, as an administrator, you may be interested in authoring a report that lists the permissions that a given user has to all resources within a given folder. Or, you may have defined resource-specific security policies already, and you need a report that shows you where the role assignment takes place.

Determining role-based security policies

Requirements like the ones above go beyond the Report Manager feature set. However, with a little bit of programming effort, you can author such reports easily by directly calling the Web service authorization APIs.

Figure 8.12 shows the Show Security Policy report, which fulfills the above requirements.

The Show Security Policy report takes as parameters the user's Windows login name and password, as well as the Report Server Web service URL. If the Item Name parameter is left NULL, the report will show which permissions the user has to all securable resources. For example, figure 8.12 shows that we wanted the report to indicate which permissions Ashvini has to the resources located in the AWReporter folder.

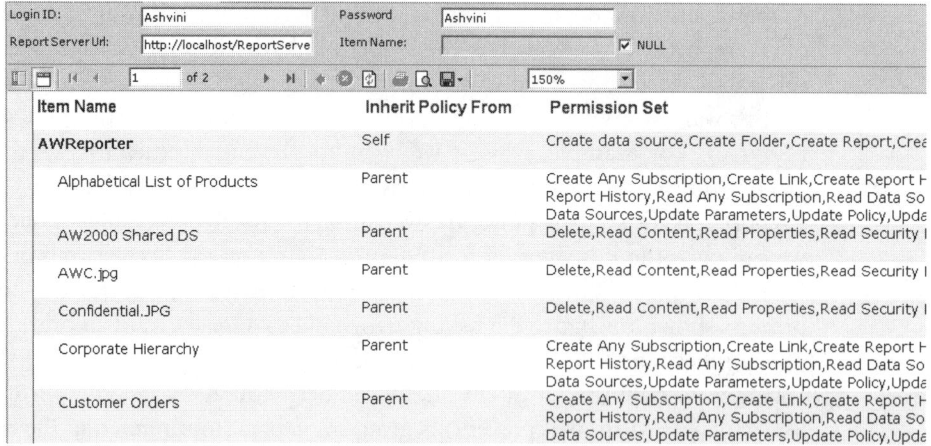

Login ID: Ashvini
Password Ashvini
Report Server Url: http://localhost/ReportServe
Item Name:
NULL
1 of 2
150%
Item Name
Inherit Policy From
Permission Set
AWReporter
Self
Create data source,Create Folder,Create Report,Crea
Alphabetical List of Products
Parent
Create Any Subscription,Create Link,Create Report H
Report History,Read Any Subscription,Read Data So
Data Sources,Update Parameters,Update Policy,Upda
AW2000 Shared DS
Parent
Delete,Read Content,Read Properties,Read Security I
AWC.jpg
Parent
Delete,Read Content,Read Properties,Read Security I
Confidential.JPG
Parent
Delete,Read Content,Read Properties,Read Security I
Corporate Hierarchy
Parent
Create Any Subscription,Create Link,Create Report H
Report History,Read Any Subscription,Read Data So
Data Sources,Update Parameters,Update Policy,Upda
Customer Orders
Parent
Create Any Subscription,Create Link,Create Report H
Report History,Read Any Subscription,Read Data So
Data Sources,Update Parameters,Update Policy,Upda

Figure 8.12 You can query and manage the role-based security infrastructure by calling the RS Web service in your applications and reports.

Alternatively, the administrator can enter the name of a resource (in the Item Name parameter) to filter the report for a single resource in order to see the security policy defined for this item only.

TIP In the real world you will rarely know the user's password. If you don't need the user's permission set but only want to see to the user's roles, then you can use the approach suggested by Tudor Trufinesco, a Microsoft engineer from the RS team. You can use an account with Admin rights to call GetPolicies on all the items in the catalog and find out which ones are not inherited. Then you can display or parse the XML policy in the report.

Let's look at how this report is implemented.

Calling security-related Web service methods

Implementing the Show Security Policy report is straightforward. The report takes advantage of the self-referential integrity defined in the Catalog table in the Report Server database and the RS recursive hierarchy-reporting feature, which we discussed back in chapter 5. The report traverses recursively the Report Server folder namespace and checks the type of the item. If the item is a folder, the item name is shown in bold. For each securable item, the report shows the name of the parent from which the security policy is inherited, as well as the set of permissions that the user has to this item.

To obtain this information, the Show Security Policy report calls down to the AwRsLibrary custom assembly. Specifically, it calls the `PolicyInheritedFrom` method to get the inheritance information and the `GetPermissions` method to get the list of allowed permissions. Listing 8.1 shows the abbreviated custom code.

Listing 8.1 The Show Security Policy custom code

```
public string SetProxy (string uid, string pwd, string rsUrl) {
  m_rs = new ReportingService();
  m_rs.Url = rsUrl;
  m_uid = uid;
  m_pwd = pwd;
  return "None";
}

public string GetPermissions(string itemPath) {
  string result = null;

  m_rs.Credentials = new NetworkCredential(m_uid, m_pwd);
  String[] permissions = m_rs.GetPermissions( itemPath );
  System.Array.Sort(permissions);
  result = String.Join(",", permissions);

 return result;
}

public string PolicyInheritedFrom( string itemPath) {
  bool inheritParent;
  string rolePath = itemPath;
  m_rs.Credentials = System.Net.CredentialCache.DefaultCredentials;

  m_rs.GetPolicies(rolePath, out inheritParent);
  while (inheritParent) {
   rolePath = GetParentPath(rolePath);
   m_rs.GetPolicies(rolePath, out inheritParent);
  }
  return FormatPath(itemPath, rolePath);
}
```

Gets the list of permissions associated with the given resource

Gets the role-based policies recursively for the specified report item

The `GetPermissions` method calls the RS Web service's `GetPermissions` web method under the context of the user whose security policy we need to check. The method returns a string array of the allowed permissions, which we sort and flatten to a string.

The `PolicyInheritedFrom` method invokes the `GetPolicies` web method to find out which ascendant in the catalog hierarchy defines the security policy for each item displayed in the table region. To accomplish this, `PolicyInheritedFrom` calls `GetPolicies` recursively until `inheritParent` is false. Finally, it evaluates the item path and returns one of the following values:

- *Self*—If the item defines its own policy
- *Parent*—If the security policy is inherited from the item parent
- *Home*—If the item inherits the root folder security policy
- In all other cases, the path to the ascendant item that defines the security policy

Implementing "pseudo" report events

Besides showing how you can use the security-related Web service API, this example also demonstrates how you can implement "pseudo" events in your reports. For example, we use an expression for the Body BorderStyle property to initialize the Web service proxy and some class-level variables inside the custom code.

Strictly speaking, we could have made the class stateless by passing the user credentials to the `GetPermissions` method, but we wanted to demonstrate how you can execute custom methods in a specific order. To ensure that the SetProxy method is called only once and before the other two custom methods, we used the following expression for the `BorderStyle` property of the Report Body band:

```
=Code.m_Library.SetProxy(Parameters!Uid.Value, Parameters!Pwd.Value, Param-
eters!Url.Value)
```

This expression will be executed before the expressions in the table region, and it can be safely used to initialize the custom code state. Because we are calling instance methods in the custom assembly, we reference the assembly in the Report Properties dialog, as shown in figure 8.13.

Before testing the report, don't forget to follow the steps for deploying the RsLibrary assembly and elevating its code access security to the Report Designer and Report Server folders, as we discussed in chapter 6.

So far, we've seen how to enforce secured access to the Report Server catalog based on the user's role membership. As we explained in chapter 6, developers can expand the report capabilities by using custom code. When this happens, you, as an administrator, need to know how to properly configure the RS code access security, as we'll discuss next.

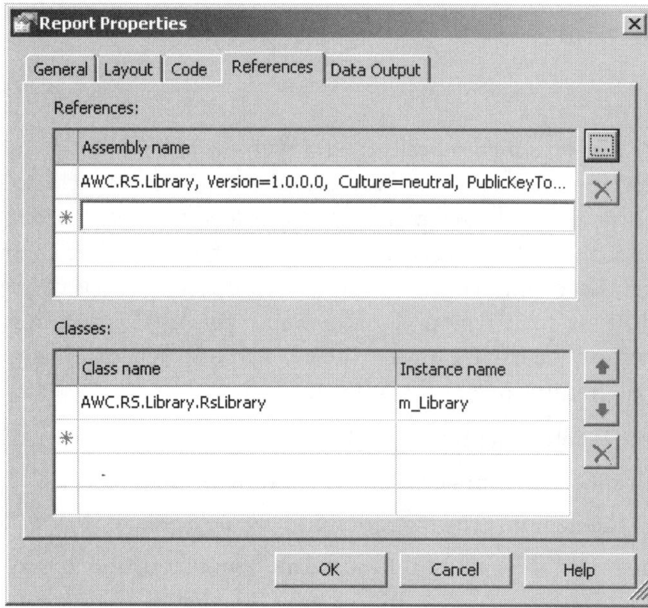

Figure 8.13 Referencing the RsLibrary class

8.2 UNDERSTANDING CODE ACCESS SECURITY

As long as you don't plan to extend RS with custom code, you can live a happy and oblivious life without worrying about RS code access security (CAS). In fact, even if you decide to use custom code, for example, to call code in an external assembly or create a custom data extension, you may find that in most cases the default code access security settings defined in the Report Server configuration files fulfill your needs. If this is the case, the only code access-related management task you need to learn is how to register the custom assemblies with the Report Server and Report Designer.

Sometimes, however, you may need to adjust the default code access policy. Usually, this will happen when the custom assembly needs more rights than the default permissions granted by the Report Server. You will know that this is the case when the Report Server complains with a SecurityException error. As a responsible administrator, you should learn how to solve this issue by giving the failing assembly the minimum set of permissions it needs to execute successfully. If you elevate the code access security too much, you open security holes that could be exploited by malicious code.

In my opinion, CAS is one of the most valuable, and arguably most misunderstood, services that the .NET Common Language Runtime (CLR) provides. In a nutshell, this security model grants permissions to code, not users. This is important because even if the Report Server runs under a highly privileged account, the CLR will sandbox custom code to restrict the actions it can execute. For example, the default RS code access security policy prevents custom code from writing to the Windows file system.

Because RS is written entirely in .NET-managed code, it can take full advantage of the code access security infrastructure built into the .NET CLR. To understand how you can manage the RS code access security model, first you need to learn how it works. By no means will we attempt to provide thorough coverage on this topic, which could easily fill a whole book. If you need more detail, please refer to the resources in section 8.5 at the end of this chapter.

8.2.1 Defining code access terminology

When RS loads an assembly, the .NET CLR goes through some decision making to determine what the assembly can do. As a part of this process, the CLR gathers some information about the assembly, which is called *evidence*. The assembly evidence is then passed to the CLR *code access security policy* for evaluation.

Finally, the assembly is given a set of permissions, as shown in figure 8.14.

Figure 8.14 The CLR code access security policy takes the assembly evidence as input and produces a permission set as output.

Let's now discuss each of these terms in more detail.

Exploring evidence

The assembly evidence provides the code access security policy the following information about the assembly:

- The assembly origin, which tells the CLR where the assembly is loaded from, including the site, URL, zone, and application directory
- For strongly named assemblies, the assembly author information, which includes the assembly's strong name and publisher information

For example, as we saw in chapter 6, the Sales by Product Category report uses custom code located in the AWC.RS.Library.dll assembly. When RS processes the report, it gathers the following evidence about the assembly:

- *Zone*—MyComputer, because the code is loaded from the local file system
- *URL*—file://C:\Program Files\Microsoft SQL Server\MSSQL\Reporting Services\ReportServer\bin\ AWC.RS.Library.dll

Because the assembly is not strongly named, there will be no evidence about its publisher and strong name.

Once the assembly evidence is obtained, it is evaluated based on the security policy configured by the administrator.

Understanding code access security policies

The administrator can set up the security policy at the hierarchical levels listed in table 8.5.

Table 8.5 The code-based security policy is evaluated at four security levels.

Security Level	Purpose
Enterprise	Applies to all machines that are part of an Active Directory installation
Machine	Specifies the machine-wide policy settings
User	Spells out the user-specific policy settings
AppDomain	Includes settings specific to the application host domain. In case of RS, this is the Report Server host domain.

The first three security policy levels are defined in configuration files under the C:\WINDOWS\Microsoft.NET\Framework\<version number>\CONFIG folder. An application can override these setting by using an application-specific configuration file to scope the policy at the application level (more on this in a moment).

The recommended way to make changes to .NET configuration policy files is to use the Caspol utility or the .NET Configuration management console (shown in figure 8.15).

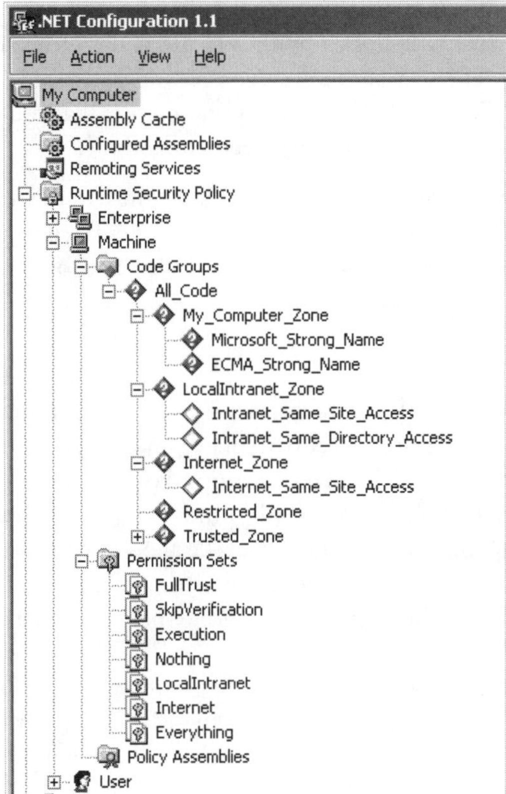

Figure 8.15 To manage the .NET code access security policy, use the .NET Configuration console.

The fourth policy level, AppDomain, is not shown in the .NET Configuration console and it must be set programmatically. An application can use the AppDomain policy level to dynamically sandbox the .NET code by further restricting the set of permissions granted by the other three policy levels.

To use the AppDomain policy level, an application can create a separate application domain and call AppDomain.SetAppDomainPolicy. The security policy configuration file can be loaded via a call to SecurityManager.PolicyLevelFromFile.

Overriding code access security policy

Now you know why the Enterprise, Machine, and User policies don't seem to apply to the RS code access security model. When the Report Server is initialized, it reads the `securityPolicy` element from the Report Server web.config file to determine the name of the configuration file that contains the CAS policies. By using the AppDomain policy level, the Report Server overrides the three levels with the policy settings from this file.

NOTE Although I highly discourage you from doing so, you can entirely bypass the Report Server CAS policy by commenting the `securityPolicy` element. The net effect of doing so is reverting to the code access security policies defined in the .NET configuration files that you can manage using the .NET Configuration management console.

When the CLR evaluates the security policies, it starts from the enterprise-level policy and works its way down to determine the intersection of the permissions grants. Each policy level consists of three elements: a code group hierarchy, a list of predefined permission sets, and a list of fully trusted assemblies at this policy level.

Defining code groups

As figure 8.15 shows, the policy levels can be further broken down into code groups. Most code groups are instances of System.Security.Policy.UnionCodeGroup. The CLR runtime comes with a number of predefined code groups. Four of them—Local Intranet, Internet, Restricted, and Trusted—correspond to Internet Explorer security zones. In fact, one of the easiest ways to elevate (or decrease) the allowed permissions in these zones is to use the Internet Explorer security-related settings. From the RS point of view, the only zone of interest is the MyComputer zone, because all custom code is loaded from the local file system.

To filter out the allowable permissions, each code group has a membership condition. For example, if you look at the properties of the My Computer code group, you will see that it defines a Zone membership condition, which applies the security policy to assemblies from the MyComputer zone only and assigns the FullTrust named permission set to it. As a result, if an assembly is evaluated as belonging to this code group and no further restrictions are imposed, its code can execute unrestricted.

To further restrict the security policy, each code group can contain nested code groups. When the CLR evaluates the code group membership of a given assembly, it traverses the code group hierarchy to find the right match for the assembly.

Using permission sets

Each code group can have a predefined set of permissions, also known as a *named permission set*. You can think of permission sets as equivalent to the role definition concept we discussed in the role-based security section. Similarly, you can relate the code access permissions to role tasks.

For example, figure 8.16 shows the predefined permissions for the Execution permission set. To bring up this dialog, click the Execution permission set in the .NET Configuration console (see figure 8.15); then right-click the Security permission item in the right pane and choose View Permission from the context menu.

As you can see, the only allowable permission here is to execute code. This means that if a custom assembly needs to write to a file under the default Execution permission set, the method call will fail with a security exception.

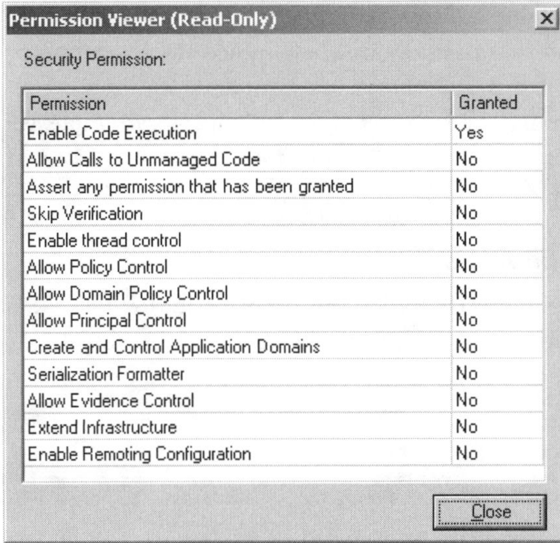

Figure 8.16 By default, the Report Server is configured to grant custom code Execution rights only.

Most permission sets are instances of the System.Security.NamedPermissionSet class. The predefined permission sets cannot be modified. Instead, if they don't meet your security needs, you can create new permission sets. You may find this process similar to working with the RS role-based security model when you create new roles that include different sets of tasks.

8.2.2 Exploring the RS default security policy

How does our code access discussion relate to RS? As we mentioned, any custom code executed under the Report Server and Report Designer (in the Preview window) is subject to code access security restrictions. Not all custom code is created equal, though. To determine which permissions need to be assigned to the executing code, the Report Server categorizes the code by mapping it to a specific code access security policy.

Defining default code access permissions

RS defines default code access security policies for each category of custom code, as shown in table 8.6.

Table 8.6 RS default code access security policies

Code Category	Membership Condition	Permission Set
Report Server native assemblies	Strong Name	Full Trust
Custom extensions	My Computer Zone	Require Full Trust
Expressions	My Computer Zone	Execution
Custom assemblies	My Computer Zone	Execution

For example, looking at table 8.6, we can see that if a report calls external code in a custom assembly, code in this assembly will be assigned the Execution permission set by default. This is fine if this assembly is self-contained and doesn't access external resources that require a more restrictive set of permissions, for example, writing to files, opening database connections, and so on. If it does, then we need to adjust its code access policy accordingly.

Understanding configuration files

The default RS security policy is defined in policy configuration files. RS has three policy configuration files, one per each component, as shown in table 8.7.

Table 8.7 Policy configuration files

Component	Configuration File	Path
Report Server	rssrvpolicy.config	C:\Program Files\Microsoft SQL Server\MSSQL\Reporting Services\ReportServer
Report Manager	rsmgrpolicy.config	C:\Program Files\Microsoft SQL Server\MSSQL\Reporting Services\ReportManager
Report Designer	rspreviewpolicy.config	C:\Program Files\Microsoft SQL Server\80\Tools\Report Designer

Why do we need to enforce code access security policy for the Report Designer? As you would recall from our discussion in chapter 2, the Report Designer gives you the option to run the report in the Preview window. You can use the Preview window to simulate the Report Server environment by cloning its code access settings to the rspreviewpolicy.config configuration file. When you run the report (by pressing F5), the Report Host will read and apply these settings to sandbox the custom code that the report uses.

The Preview window mode allows the author of the report to change the code access security policy locally, and once the custom code executes properly, to propagate the configuration changes to the Report Server policy file. Please note that previewing reports using the Report Designer's Preview tab bypasses the Report Designer's security policy and grants the FullTrust permission set to custom assemblies. Once again, to see the effect of the policy settings from the rspreviewpolicy.config configuration file, preview the report in the Preview window by running the report in Debug mode (F5).

8.2.3 Managing RS code access security

The report administrator can easily adjust the code access security policies by making changes to the appropriate configuration files. For example, let's say our custom assembly, MyAssembly, requires the ability to read from the file C:\MyFile.xml. Because the default code access policy gives custom assemblies only Execution rights, when the assembly attempts to read from the file, it will fail.

As an administrator, you can rectify this situation in two ways. The first one is easier and not recommended. You can modify the Report Server policy file to give all custom assemblies FullTrust execution rights by making the following changes to rssrvpolicy.config (and rspreviewpolicy.config for testing purposes):

```
<CodeGroup class="FirstMatchCodeGroup" version="1"
  PermissionSetName="FullTrust" Description="This code group
  grants MyComputer code Execution permission. ">
```

The important change here is that instead of Execution rights, now all custom code will be given FullTrust rights. Of course, the net effect of doing this will be kissing code access security good-bye for custom code execution. Therefore, you should resist the temptation to take the easy way and open security holes.

Defining custom permission sets and code groups

When you need to elevate the code access security policy, the recommended approach is to grant permissions on an as-needed basis. First, you can define a named permission set that includes the FileIOPermission permission to read from the file, as follows:

```
<PermissionSet class="NamedPermissionSet"
   version="1"
   Name="MyFilePermissionSet"
   Description="Grant access to read from myfile.xml.">
    <IPermission class="FileIOPermission"
       version="1"
       Read="C:\MyFile.xml"/>
</PermissionSet>
```

Once the permission set is defined, you can then create code groups to associate custom assemblies with the named permission set. For example, the code group definition might look like this:

```
<CodeGroup class="UnionCodeGroup"
   version="1"
   PermissionSetName="MyFilePermissionSet"
   Name="MyAssemblyCodeGroup"
   Description="A code group specifically created for
   myassembly.dll">
   <IMembershipCondition class="UrlMembershipCondition"
      version="1"
      Url="C:\Program Files\Microsoft SQL Server\MSSQL\Reporting
      Services\ReportServer\bin\myassembly.dll"/>
</CodeGroup>
```

Please note also that the CAS security is layered on top of the OS security. Therefore, in addition to the CAS settings, you need also to grant the appropriate ACL permissions to any files that the custom assembly needs. In this case, the custom assembly requires at least Read permissions to MyFile.xml. To satisfy this requirement, we need to open the file (or its containing folder) properties and grant the Report Server process account (by default, ASP.NET with IIS5 or Network Service with IIS6) Read permissions to this file.

How do you know which code access permissions a given assembly requires? Well, if the assembly developer has taken the effort to declare the required permissions using attributes, you can use the PermView.NET utility. Most often, though, you will find that this is not the case and you will need to rely on other sources, such as the product documentation or your peers from newsgroups. This entails the trial-and-error approach, which could be painful.

NOTE I struggled quite a bit to find out why the OpenForecast assembly, which we discussed in chapter 6, was failing to execute regardless of the fact that it was given FullTrust permission rights. I went through all possible permutations but to no avail. The strange thing was that neither OpenForecast nor its caller was accessing external resources. I went to the trouble of converting it to C# only to realize that the C# version was executing properly. Finally, I resorted to using System.Diagnostics.Trace.WriteLine to find out at what point the code was failing. Using the DbgView utility I was able to pinpoint the security violation to an overridden implementation of the `toString` method inside the OpenSource DataSet structure. My code was calling this method to output the observed and forecasted values. Removing the tracing calls fixed the problem. The exact reason for the security violation was beyond me, but the moral of my story is this. If giving your custom code FullTrust permissions doesn't help, you should start exploring your code to find out at what point it fails. Once you manage to identify the offending line, the next step will be to find out which code access security permissions it requires. As a last resort, if nothing else works, you could bypass the Report Server CAS policy by commenting out the securityPolicy element in web.config, as I noted before. Before you decide to do this, however, make sure that you have a convincing story when you are asked to stand before the CAS court.

Currently, to the best of my knowledge, there is no tool to help you troubleshoot code access security problems. What I would like to see in future versions of the .NET Framework is more explanatory error descriptions when a security exception is thrown. At least the exception message should spell out name of the failing permission and the offending line of code. My experience is that often this information is missing.

Granting custom assemblies FullTrust rights

Back in chapter 6 we said that AWC.RS.Library and OpenForecast assemblies require full trust permissions to execute successfully. Let's see what changes are required to accomplish this. The assemblies don't require any custom permission sets. To elevate the code access security policy for both assemblies from Execution to FullTrust, we need to add the following lines to the Report Designer (rspreviewpolicy.config) and Report Server (rssrvpolicy.config) security configuration files:

```
<CodeGroup
        class="UnionCodeGroup"
        version="1"
        PermissionSetName="FullTrust"
        Name="SharePoint_Server_Strong_Name"
    />
</CodeGroup>
<CodeGroup class="UnionCodeGroup" version="1"
   PermissionSetName="FullTrust" Name="AWCLibrary">
   <IMembershipCondition class="UrlMembershipCondition" version="1"
   Url="C:\Program Files\Microsoft SQL Server\MSSQL\Reporting
   Services\ReportServer\bin\AWC.RS.Library.dll"/>
</CodeGroup>
<CodeGroup class="UnionCodeGroup" version="1"
   PermissionSetName="FullTrust" Name="OpenForecast">
  <IMembershipCondition class="UrlMembershipCondition" version="1"
  Url="C:\Program Files\Microsoft SQL Server\MSSQL\Reporting
  Services\ReportServer\bin\OpenForecast.dll"/>
</CodeGroup>
```

For reference only

Grant Full Trust to AWC.RS.Library.dll

Grant Full Trust to OpenForecast.dll

It is important to note that when elevating the code access rights for custom code, you need to do so for all custom assemblies where this code resides because CLR will check the entire call stack. This is why we specifically granted full rights to both the AWC.RS.Library and OpenForecast assemblies.

Dealing with unmanaged resources

Sometimes, granting your custom code the FullTrust permission set may not be enough. This may be the case when you need to deal with unmanaged resources.

For example, you could have authored a custom dataset extension that opens a database connection through the .NET System.Data.SqlClient.SqlConnection managed wrapper to a SQL Server database. A database connection is an unmanaged resource, and your custom code requires explicit permissions to execute unmanaged code. Specifically, you need to declare a new permission set, as shown here:

```
<PermissionSet class="NamedPermissionSet"  version="1"
               Unrestricted="true" Name="MyPermission">
  <IPermission
      class="SecurityPermission"
      version="1"
      Flags="UnmanagedCode" />
</PermissionSet>
```

Then you need assert the permission needed in your custom code before accessing the unmanaged resource:

```
SqlClientPermission permission = new
            SqlClientPermission(PermissionState.Unrestricted);
try {
    permission.Assert(); // Assert security permission!
```

```
    SqlConnection con = new SqlConnection("...");
    con.Open();
    //do something with the connection
}
```

When the custom code is called from a report expression, you need to always assert the permission because the code access security checks walk up each stack frame and expect permissions at each level. The default code access security policy grants report expressions Execution rights only, so the security check will fail. `Assert` will short-circuit the stack walk at the current frame.

The MSDN documentation specifically states which permissions are needed by certain method calls. For example, in the case of the SqlConnection class, the documentation says, "SqlConnection makes security demands using the SqlClientPermission object." The `CodeAccessSecurityPermission.Assert` method call instructs CLR to grant your code the requested permission, regardless of the fact that its callers might not have rights to this permission.

For more information about code access security considerations, check out the security chapter in the product documentation.

8.3 Best practices for securing reports

If everything we discussed so far sounds mind-boggling, here is what we would like for you to take with you from this chapter. Your specific application needs will dictate the choice of which authentication options to use. However, as with almost any architecture design, you should carefully weigh the different implementation approaches and make a tradeoff between flexibility and simplicity.

Unless you are architecting an enterprise-wide reporting services infrastructure, don't try to make your security implementation too sophisticated. Try to take advantage as much as possible of the RS role-based security model. Some of the questions that you should ask yourself should be these:

- What is the application architectural model? WinForm or web-based? Intranet, extranet, or intranet?
- How strict are the security requirements? How sensitive is the report information?
- How granular does the security policy level need to be? For example, do you have to enforce restricted access at the report level or do you need a more granular level of security? Do you need to secure some portion of the data inside the report?
- Can you use Windows-based authentication?
- To simplify the role-based security setup with Windows-based authentication, can you group the accounts into Windows groups?

Sometimes, you may find the RS role-based security model too coarse. Such will be the case when you need to secure sensitive data inside the report, or what I refer to as "horizontal security."

Take, for instance, the Employee Sales Freeform report we created in chapter 4. This report shows sensitive data, such as salesperson performance, bonus, and commission. What if we want each salesperson to be restricted to seeing his own sales data without being able to request the report for other sales representatives? Further, what if we want only the members of a certain Windows group, such as Sales Managers, to be able to see the sales data for the sales representatives of whom the manager is in charge?

In such cases, you will need to take extra steps to supplement the role-based security model or, in more extreme cases, to replace it altogether. Let's consider some practical security-related techniques you can use to provide a more granular level of security policy.

8.3.1 Filtering data

The first approach involves filtering the sensitive data at the data source or by using dataset filters. Let's say we want to restrict a salesperson to view his sales performance data only when requesting the Employee Sales Freeform report. Let's assume also that the Employee table in the database defines a column for the user login ID, which is exactly the case with the Employee table in the AdventureWorks2000 database. It defines a LoginID column, which we can use to filter the available values for the Employee parameter. We saved the modified version of the report as Employee Sales Freeform Secured.

In this report, we demonstrate data filtering at the data source. To implement this, we replaced the dataset query of the Employee parameter with the following statement:

```
SELECT      EmployeeID, LastName + N','
            + FirstName AS EmployeeName, LoginID
FROM        dbo.Employee
WHERE      (SalesPersonFlag = 1) AND (LoginID = @LoginID)
ORDER BY    EmployeeName
```

The LoginID parameter is defined as dataset-specific, as shown in figure 8.17.

As we discussed in chapter 5, the User.UserID property returns the Windows login ID if the default Windows-based authentication is used. Therefore, after the lookup dataset is filtered, the user will see his name only in the Employee parameter dropdown. In fact, in this scenario, you can go one step further and take out the Employee parameter entirely.

NOTE The AdventureWorks2000 database uses adventure-works as a domain name in the LoginID column of the Employee table. To test the Employee Sales Freeform Secured report, replace the domain name with your login domain name or your computer name, if the Report Server is installed locally.

For example, assuming that you created the test accounts shown in table 8.4 as local computer accounts and the Report Server is installed locally, make sure that you replace the domain name in the LoginID column with the name of your computer, that is, <mycomputername>\David3. Then, to test the report, you can either log in locally or establish a remote connection to your computer from another box using the test account credentials.

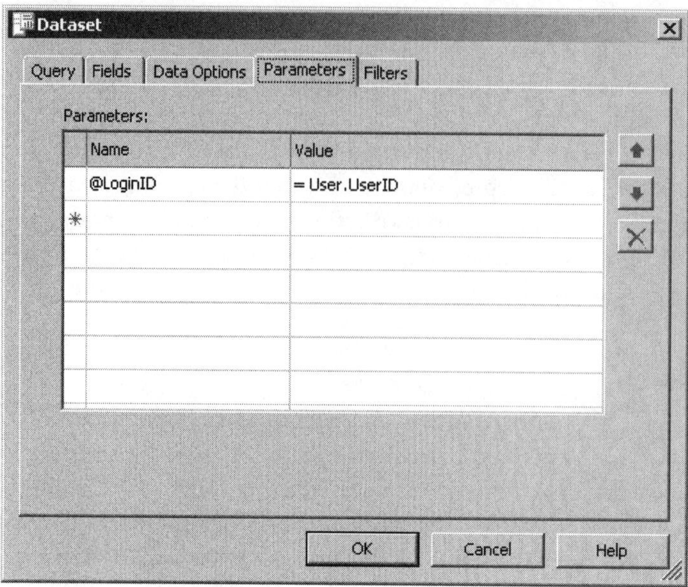

Figure 8.17 Data hiding based on the login ID

8.3.2 Using dynamic dataset queries

Another variation of data filtering is using dynamic queries, where a stored procedure or an expression determines what data will be fetched based on the user's identity.

Let's consider a more complicated scenario than the one we discussed in the above section. This time we want to factor in the user's Windows group membership. For example, we want to allow members of the Sales Managers Windows group to be able to select any salesperson. However, we still want to allow members of the Sales Windows group to be able to see their sales data only.

Determining the user's Windows group membership

With a little bit of embedded custom code, implementing these requirements is straightforward. We could write a simple function to tell us whether the user is a member of a given Windows group. A possible implementation of such a function is the `IsInRole` function.

```
Function IsInRole(ByVal roleName as String) As Boolean
    Dim myPrincipal As WindowsPrincipal =
      New WindowsPrincipal(WindowsIdentity.GetCurrent())

    Return myPrincipal.IsInRole(roleName)
End Function
```

You can find this function as embedded code in the Employee Sales Freeform Secured report sample. The `IsInRole` function calls the `WindowsPrincipal.IsInRole` method and returns true if the user is a member of the passed role, or false otherwise.

Implementing the dataset query

The next step is trivial. We can pass the Boolean flag to the parameter (or report) dataset stored procedure, which can filter the data accordingly. If the user is a sales manager, the stored procedure will return all salespersons, just as the original version of this report (Employee Sales Freeform) does. Otherwise, the Employee parameter will contain only the name of the user.

Of course, if needed, you can call the `GetPolicies` method of the RS Web service to find out to which role(s) this user or Windows group has been mapped. We saw an example of how to call this method in the Show Security Policy report. The `GetPolicies` method returns an array of Policy objects, which represents the security policies associated with a given item, as shown in figure 8.18.

To see the definition of the policy object, step through the `PolicyInherited-From` method in the AwRsLibrary assembly, and once you've invoked the `Get-Policies` SOAP API, display the policies collection in the Object Browser (Ctrl-Alt-J).

Once we know the user's association with a given Windows group, we can find out what role he is mapped to by enumerating the report's security policy.

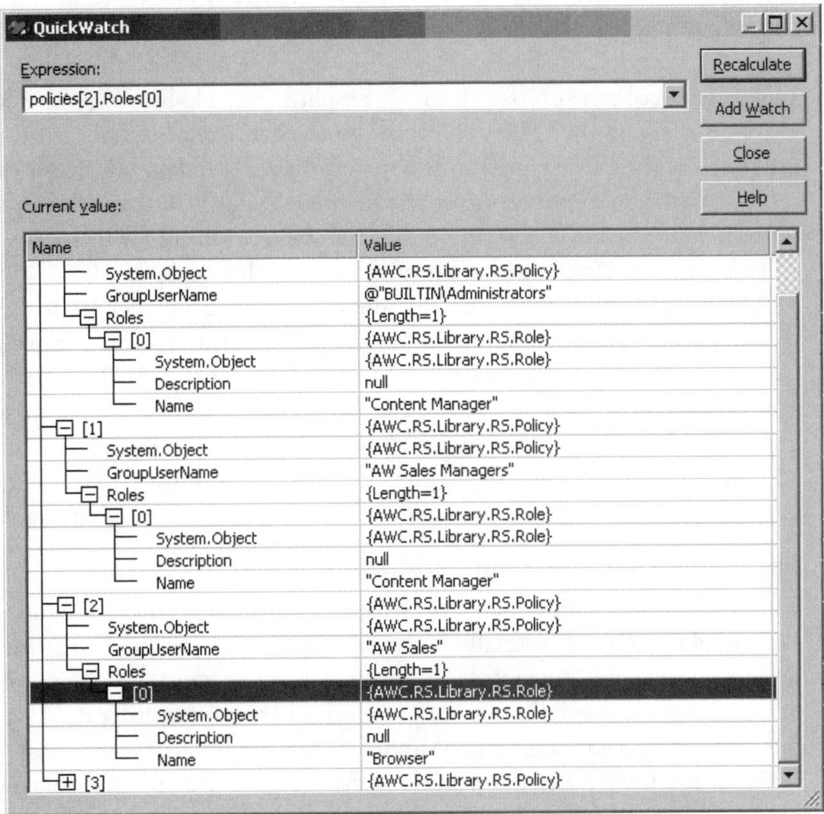

Figure 8.18 The `GetPolicies` SOAP API returns an array of Policy objects.

Hiding data

Sometimes, we might just need to hide some report elements. For example, let's say we have a report that shows the employee's salary and only users of the HR department can see it. Similar to the Dynamic Queries approach, we can determine whether the report user is a member of the HR group.

Then we can use an expression for the salary item's visibility to hide it if the user is not a member, for example:

```
= Not Code.IsInRole("HR")
```

8.3.3 Implementing custom security models

There could be cases when RS role-based security might not be enough and you need to replace the Report Server's role-based security with your own solution. There are two main scenarios that may call for a custom security implementation.

First, the application may need to check some business rules before granting the user the rights to view a report. For example, let's say you have a report that shows the consolidated sales data from all the company's branches. The users can see the report only after all branches have submitted their data. In a typical three-tier model, this rule will be evaluated in the application business layer.

In this scenario, the business layer can serve as a façade to the Report Server. The added benefit of this approach is that it simplifies the role-based security maintenance, as we discussed in the Client-to-Facade-to-Report Server scenario. Instead of impersonating the user, the request to the Report Server could go out under the Windows account of the business layer's process identity. If this is the case, the report administrator is concerned with setting up the appropriate security for this account only. We will see a possible implementation of this approach in chapter 10.

Second, the Report Server security model needs to be integrated with the application security model. The application may already have a custom security implementation in place. For example, the application might use the Windows 2003 Authorization Manager to implement secured access to areas of the application based on predefined roles. Supporting two role-based security models may present a challenge for the report administrator. In this case, the application will be responsible for enforcing restricted access to the Report Server. We will see how this could be done in chapter 13.

8.3.4 Enforcing a secured connection to the Report Server

Sometimes, a report might contain sensitive information, such as a customer's credit card numbers. This is especially true when reports are requested over the Internet. In this case, the report data must be encrypted when it is transmitted between the Report Server and the report consumer to prevent hackers from sniffing the data. For implementing secure data transfer, you can use Secure Sockets Layer (SSL).

With RS, the report administrator can configure which Report Server operations require an SSL connection by using the SecureConnectionLevel setting in the RSReportServer.config file. The allowable range of values is between zero (no SSL required) and three (all access to the Report Server must be encrypted). For example, let's say you want to enforce that all reports must be viewed over an SSL connection. To accomplish this, you can elevate SecureConnectionLevel to two. It is important to note that if a secured connection is enforced, the Report Server will demand that both the HTTP-GET and SOAP types of requests use SSL. Because the RS folders do not correspond to physical folders, you cannot enforce SSL on a per-folder or report basis. It is an all-or-nothing proposition.

Sometimes, you may need to enable SSL selectively. For example, an organization might need an encrypted connection for web reporting only. One possible solution would be to use separate Report Servers—one to serve Internet customers with a secure SSL connection and another for internal reporting needs. For more information about the SecureConnectionLevel setting, please refer to the product documentation.

8.4 SUMMARY

As a report administrator, you shouldn't take report security lightly. Reports often contain sensitive data that must be guarded. You can use the RS role-based security model to restrict user access to RS resources based on the Windows identity of the user. To set up a comprehensive role-based security infrastructure, you define policies that spell out which tasks a given user or group is permitted to execute on a given resource.

The Report Manager makes managing role-based security easy. Alternatively, you can manipulate the role-based model programmatically by calling the Web service security management APIs.

When your reports call custom code or when you need to extend RS with custom extensions, you need to be cognizant of how the CLR code-based security model works. As we recommended, you should grant code access permissions selectively to allow the custom code the minimum set of rights it needs to execute successfully.

Finally, to implement a more granular security level to the report data, you can use several approaches, including data filtering, dynamic queries, and data hiding. When they are not enough, you can implement custom security techniques, some of which we will discuss in subsequent chapters.

After reading chapters 7 and 8, you should feel comfortable managing Reporting Services. Now it is time to learn about the third phase of the report lifecycle: report delivery. In the next chapter, we will see what options developers have to integrate RS with different types of applications.

8.5 RESOURCES

The Microsoft MSDN Security Center
(http://msdn.microsoft.com/security/)
Tons of excellent information to help you secure your applications, including entire books.

"Building Secure ASP.NET Applications: Authentication, Authorization, and Secure Communication"
(http://msdn.microsoft.com/library/default.asp?url=/library/en-us/dnnetsec/html/secnetlpmsdn.asp)
This guide presents a practical, scenario driven approach to designing and building secure ASP.NET applications.

"Code Access Security"
(http://msdn.microsoft.com/library/default.asp?url=/library/en-us/cpguide/html/cpconsecuritypolicymodel.asp?frame=true)
From the *.NET Framework Developer's Guide*

"Code Access Security in SQL Server 2000 Reporting Services"
(http://msdn.microsoft.com/library/?url=/library/en-us/dnsql2k/html/dngrfCodeAccessSecurityInSQLServer2000ReportingServices.asp?frame=true)
This article outlines the new code access security policies of Microsoft® SQL Server™ 2000 Reporting Services.

"The Security Infrastructure of the CLR Provides Evidence, Policy, Permissions, and Enforcement Services"
(http://msdn.microsoft.com/msdnmag/issues/02/09/SecurityinNET/)
In this article, Don Box explains how code access security works in the CLR.

"Security in .NET: Enforce Code Access Rights with the Common Language Runtime"
(http://msdn.microsoft.com/msdnmag/issues/01/02/CAS/)
Keith Brown's article on the same topic.

PART 3

Delivering reports

Often, your reporting requirements will call for integrating Reporting Services with custom applications. The focus of part 3 is the third and final phase of the report lifecycle—report delivery. Here, we will implement various reporting solutions to demonstrate how you can integrate RS with different application scenarios.

We will start by exploring the two access options available with RS: URL and Web service. We will find out how these options compare in the context of different deployment needs, such as intranet, Internet, and extranet applications.

We will implement an end-to-end code sample that demonstrates how you can report-enable a WinForm application. We will also discuss various techniques for requesting RS reports on the client and server sides of a web application. You will learn how to use RS to generate dynamic reports with Analysis Services. You will also find out how you can create a custom enterprise framework that supports multiple report providers.

We will round out this part by exploring the second option that RS offers for distributing reports—through subscriptions.

CHAPTER 9

On-demand report delivery

Once a report is deployed to the report catalog and configured properly, it is ready to fulfill its ultimate purpose, which is to be delivered to the end users. We can accomplish this in one of the following ways:

- On-demand delivery, where the report is explicitly requested by the consumer of the report
- Subscribed delivery, where the report is pushed to recipients

Delivering reports through subscriptions is the subject of chapter 14. In this chapter we will provide an overview of on-demand report delivery. Specifically, this chapter discusses the two access options available to report consumers for submitting report requests to the Report Server:

- URL, where reports are requested via the HTTP-GET protocol
- RS Web service, where reports are requested via SOAP protocol

This chapter covers just the basics of integrating Reporting Services with client applications, but it is important because it lays down the foundation for the next four chapters. In the subsequent chapters, we will apply what we will learn in this chapter to add on-demand reporting capabilities to several different types of report consumers.

9.1 How RS provides on-demand report delivery

Let's say you have authored a set of reports and deployed them to the report catalog. Now you want to provide users with a way to request reports on demand. You could use the Report Manager (we saw how to use the Report Manager as a quick-and-easy report-rendering tool in chapter 7), but that might not always provide the functionality you are looking for. Although useful, the Report Manager will sometimes be insufficient to fully meet your report delivery needs. For example, this may be the case when

- *You need to integrate RS with custom applications*—Many application scenarios call for report-enabling existing or new applications. In most cases, these scenarios rule out using the Report Manager because the application will be responsible for supplying the details of the report request, such as the parameter values, export format, and so on.
- *Your reporting needs go beyond the Report Manager feature set*—For example, you may need to validate the report parameters before the user submits the report request. As we mentioned in chapter 3, the standard report toolbar that the Report Server generates when reports are requested by URL provides limited parameter validation capabilities.

In such cases, a more flexible approach would be integrating the Report Server with your custom applications. The Report Server has two access options to support various integration scenarios:

- *URL access*—Where the request is submitted via the HTTP-GET protocol
- *Web service access*—Where the request is submitted via the SOAP protocol

Figure 9.1 depicts these two integration options.

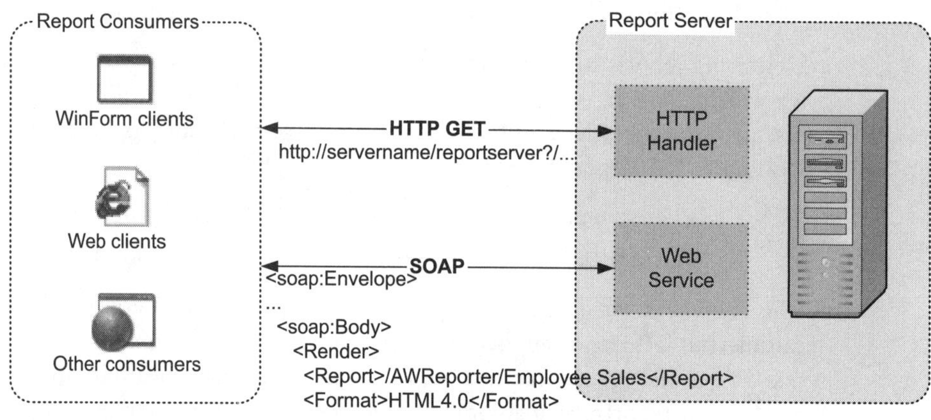

Figure 9.1 The Report Server supports two access options: URL and SOAP.

In the sections that follow, we will explore each access option in more detail and point out its strengths and weaknesses.

9.2 URL-BASED REPORT ACCESS

A report consumer can request a resource from the Report Server by submitting an HTTP-GET request that specifies the resource URL. For example, you can request the Sales by Territory report in the browser by navigating to the following URL:

```
http://localhost/reportserver?/AWReporter/Sales By Territory
```

The Report Server's entry point for HTTP-GET requests is the ReportService-HttpHandler HTTP handler. The handler intercepts HTTP-GET requests, parses them, and forwards them to the Report Server for processing.

> **NOTE** If your reporting requirements rule out URL access, you can set up the Report Server to reject incoming HTTP-GET requests by commenting out the `<httpHandlers>` section in the Report Server web.config file.

As a developer, you can use different techniques in your applications to programmatically request reports by URL. At its simplest, a WinForm-based client could allow the end user to request a report by clicking a hyperlink. For example, a .NET-based Win-Form application could use a LinkLabel control with the report's hyperlink embedded in the control's label. When static hyperlinks cannot be used, a WinForm client can shell out to the browser or use the Microsoft WebBrowser ActiveX control to render the report, as we will demonstrate in section 9.2.6.

The web-based reporting model of RS integrates well with browser-based applications. You have already seen an example of a web-based application that requests reports by URL: the Report Manager. Web developers can use a variety of client and server-side integration techniques to report-enable their applications, as we will discuss in detail in chapter 11.

Finally, both types of applications can leverage other techniques to meet more exotic integration requirements. For example, you may need to implement an application that crawls and parses the report's content similarly to the way web robots and crawlers, such as Google and Yahoo, index web content. To accomplish this requirement, a legacy WinForm client can use the XMLHTTP component on the client side or ServerXMLHTTP on the server side of the application to programmatically submit web requests and "scrape" the received report payload. Both components are included with Internet Explorer. A .NET-based client can accomplish the same thing by using the System.Net.WebRequest object.

Table 9.1 summarizes these techniques.

To report-enable your applications by URL, you need to learn the URL syntax supported by the Report Server.

Table 9.1 Techniques for integrating report consumers with the Report Server by URL

Application Type	Implementation Approaches
WinForm	LinkLabel buttons pointing to the URL address of the report; Microsoft Web Browser ActiveX Control; shell to the browser
Web-based	Client-side report generation: all anchor-capable elements, such as hyperlinks, images, and frames; server-side report generation; HTML fragments; Response.Write
Both	XMLHTTP; ServerXMLHTTP (native code); WebRequest (managed code)

9.2.1 Understanding URL syntax

The URL access option uses a typical HTTP-GET syntax, where additional arguments can be passed as query parameters, as follows:

```
http://<ComputerName>/<ReportServerVroot>?[/<ResourcePath>]&pre-
fix:param=value[&prefix:param=value]...n]
```

Table 9.2 lists the supported URL arguments.

Table 9.2 To request a report by URL, you create an HTTP-GET request that includes URL arguments.

Argument	Description	Example
ComputerName	Specifies the name of the computer hosting the Report Server	localhost
ReportServerVroot	Specifies the Report Server's virtual root name	ReportServer
ResourcePath	Specifies the catalog path to the resource relative to the root (Home) folder. Cannot be longer then 260 characters.	/AWReporter/Sales By Territory
prefix	Specifies the command type. Can be one of the following values: rs—for commands targeting the Report Server rc—for commands targeting the HTML Viewer dsu and dsp—for specifying the user name and password when the "The credentials supplied by the user running the report" data source option is used. blank—a report parameter is assumed	http://localhost/reportserver?/AWReporter/Sales By Territory Interactive&Year=2004&Territory=1&rs:Command=Render
param	Specifies the name of the command or parameter	See the example above, where Year and Territory are report parameters

The URL syntax is not case sensitive. Please note the question mark that prefixes the ResourcePath argument. It is easy to miss (I've done it many times), but if you omit it, the URL request will fail.

You will notice that when you submit URL requests from the browser, the browser URL-escapes the string. For example, "/" is encoded as "%2f." You don't have to do this explicitly when you define static hyperlinks or submit URL requests programmatically, because the browser (or the Web Browser ActiveX control) handles this automatically for you.

Now that you know the URL syntax, let's see how to request RS resources by URL.

9.2.2 Requesting resources by URL

With RS you are not limited to requesting just reports. Instead, you can ask the Report Server to return any resource stored in the report catalog. For example, you may have a web page that needs to show the Adventure Works company logo, which is stored as an image file in the report catalog. To accomplish this, you can set the image source to the URL address of the image item, as shown here:

```
<IMG SRC="http://localhost/ReportServer?/AWReporter/AWC.jpg"/>
```

NOTE Please don't get me wrong. I am far from advocating that you use the report catalog as a document repository. It should be used only to store report-related items.

The response that the Report Server sends back depends on the type of requested resource.

Requesting folders

Just as you would use Windows Explorer to see the files a given folder contains, you may want to see the contents of an RS folder. To see the folder contents using the URL access options, you would use the following syntax:

```
http://<ComputerName>/ReportServer?/<FolderPath>
```

where `<FolderPath>` is the path to the folder in the report catalog.

Optionally, for faster performance, you can tell the Report Server that you mean to view the folder contents by using the ListChildren command. If you don't use this command, the Report Server has to determine the type of the resource being requested and use the default command.

For example, to view the contents of the AWReporter folder, you would use the following syntax:

```
http://localhost/ReportServer?/AWReporter&rs:Command=ListChildren
```

If a folder is requested, the Report Server renders the folder's contents, as shown in figure 9.2.

When you request a folder, the names of the resources contained in that folder appear as hyperlinks. When the link point to another folder, the user can click the hyperlink to drill down further in the folder namespace. Otherwise, the hyperlink will render the resource. As with the Report Manager, the Report Server will show only resources that the user has the rights to view (at least Browser rights are required to view a resource).

Currently, there doesn't seem to be a way to suppress the default Report Server behavior to generate hyperlinks when a folder is requested. It would be useful if a future

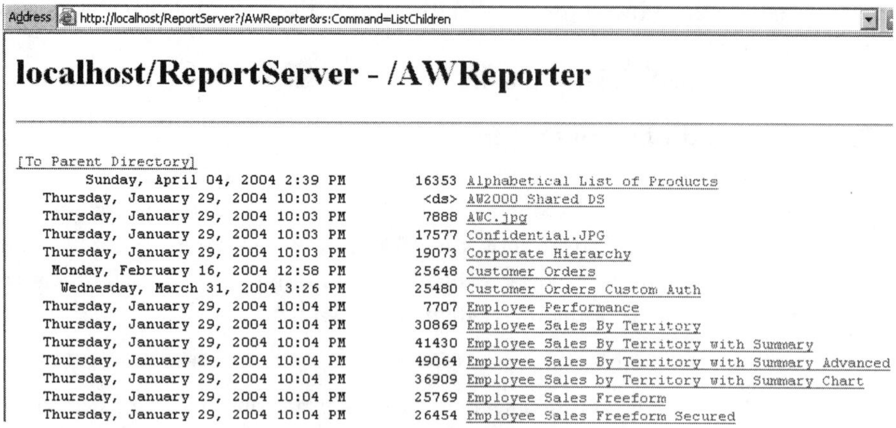

Address http://localhost/ReportServer?/AWReporter&rs:Command=ListChildren

localhost/ReportServer - /AWReporter

```
[To Parent Directory]
       Sunday, April 04, 2004 2:39 PM        16353 Alphabetical List of Products
   Thursday, January 29, 2004 10:03 PM        <ds> AW2000 Shared DS
   Thursday, January 29, 2004 10:03 PM         7888 AWC.jpg
   Thursday, January 29, 2004 10:03 PM        17577 Confidential.JPG
   Thursday, January 29, 2004 10:03 PM        19073 Corporate Hierarchy
    Monday, February 16, 2004 12:58 PM        25648 Customer Orders
     Wednesday, March 31, 2004 3:26 PM        25480 Customer Orders Custom Auth
   Thursday, January 29, 2004 10:04 PM         7707 Employee Performance
   Thursday, January 29, 2004 10:04 PM        30869 Employee Sales By Territory
   Thursday, January 29, 2004 10:04 PM        41430 Employee Sales By Territory with Summary
   Thursday, January 29, 2004 10:04 PM        49064 Employee Sales By Territory with Summary Advanced
   Thursday, January 29, 2004 10:04 PM        36909 Employee Sales by Territory with Summary Chart
   Thursday, January 29, 2004 10:04 PM        25769 Employee Sales Freeform
   Thursday, January 29, 2004 10:04 PM        26454 Employee Sales Freeform Secured
```

Figure 9.2 Requesting the AWReporter folder resources by URL

edition were to introduce a List Folder Contents right, just like the List Folder Contents ACL permission that Windows has. This would allow a user to view only the folder contents without being able to read the resource in case she doesn't have Browser rights.

Requesting data sources

Although we do not recommend this for security reasons, you can allow users to view the definition of a shared data source using the following syntax:

```
http://<ComputerName>/ReportServer?/<FolderPath>/
   <DataSourceName>
```

where `<FolderPath>` is the folder path of the folder where the shared data source resides and `<DataSourceName>` is the name of the shared data source. Optionally, as a performance enhancement technique, you can let the Report Server know that you indeed mean to view the data source definition by using the GetDataSourceContents command, as follows:

```
http://localhost/ReportServer?/AWReporter/AW2000 Shared DS&
rs:Command=GetDataSourceContents
```

This request asks for the contents of the AW2000 Shared DS shared data source. When a shared data source is requested, the Report Server will stream its definition in XML, as shown here:

```
<DataSourceDefinition>
  <Extension>SQL</Extension>
  <ConnectString>data source=.;…</ConnectString>
  <!-The rest of the data source definition-
</DataSourceDefinition>
```

Even though the password is not returned, you should avoid allowing users to see the data source definition for security reasons. To prevent users from doing so, exclude the View Data Sources task from their security policy, as we discussed in chapter 8.

Requesting other resources

If a report is requested, the Report Server renders the report in the specified format. We'll discuss this in detail in section 9.2.3.

If an image is requested, the image will be rendered in the browser. For other resource requests, the Report Server will stream the file content to the browser.

In most cases, your applications will request reports by URL. To custom-tailor the report output, you can use a variety of commands, which we will discuss in section 9.2.4. First, though, let's take a closer look at how to request a report.

9.2.3 Requesting reports by URL

When requesting reports, at minimum you need to specify the report path and the name of the report, for example:

```
http://localhost/reportserver?/AWReporter/Sales By Territory
```

Here, we are requesting the Sales by Territory report located in the AWReporter folder. As we mentioned in section 9.2.1, you can also optionally pass other arguments to control the report processing (see table 9.2).

One of most common uses of the URL arguments is to pass parameter values when requesting parameterized reports.

Passing report parameters

To request a report that takes parameters, you append them to the URL string in the form of query parameters. For example, the URL string to request the Sales by Territory Interactive report for the year 2004 and Northwest is

```
http://localhost/reportserver?/AWReporter/Sales By Territory Interac-
tive&Year=2004&Territory=1
```

There are a few rules worth mentioning when requesting parameterized reports, as follows:

- *Default values*—If the parameter has a default value and you want to use it when requesting the report, you don't have to pass the parameter value explicitly.
- *Parameters with labels and values*—If the parameter is defined with a label and a value, the value must be passed. The previous example adheres to this rule by using the value of the Territory parameter (1), not its label (Northwest).
- *Missing parameter value*—If you don't pass the parameter value in the URL request and the parameter doesn't have a default value, the Report Server will react to this condition differently depending on the export format requested. If HTML is requested and the report toolbar is not suppressed, the Report Server will generate the parameter area of the report toolbar so that the user can enter the report parameters. In all other cases, an exception will be thrown.
- *Parameter validation*—The parameter validation and type casting are performed on the server side. If a parameter doesn't validate successfully, the Report Server throws an exception, for example:

```
"The value provided for the report parameter 'Territory' is not valid
for its type. (rsReportParameterTypeMismatch)".
```

The Report Server doesn't set any specific HTTP response codes when reporting errors. Instead, the error string is shown in the browser. Therefore, you cannot programmatically react to error conditions when requesting reports via URL.

9.2.4 Working with report commands

The Report Server recognizes several commands that you can specify by using the *rs* argument, such as commands for exporting reports and requesting report history snapshots.

For a full list of all supported commands refer to the product documentation.

Rendering commands

For better performance, you can explicitly tell the Report Server that you mean to render a *report* by using the `rs:Command=Render` argument, for example:

```
http://localhost/reportserver?/AWReporter/Sales By Territory&
rs:Command=Render
```

If you don't specify this argument, the Report Server will incur a slight performance hit to find out what type of resource you are requesting.

Exporting commands

Another useful command that you will frequently need is the Format command, in order to export reports in a given format. For example, to export the Sales by Territory report as PDF, you can send the following URL to the Report Server:

```
http://localhost/ReportServer?/AWReporter/Sales By Territory&
rs:Command=Render&rs:Format=PDF
```

When the Report Server receives a request to export a report, it renders the report in the specified format and streams it back to the report consumer. It notifies the consumer about the export format by using the ContentType header. For example, the above request will produce an HTTP response with a content type of application/pdf. If the request is initiated within a browser, the browser will pop up the all-too-familiar prompt to ask the user whether to open or save the streamed content.

If the export format is not explicitly specified, the report is rendered in HTML. If the Report Server can determine the type of browser (if the Accept HTTP header is specified), it renders the report in HTML 4.0 for up-level browsers (for example, Internet Explorer 4.x and later) or HTML 3.2 otherwise.

All export formats support additional parameters that can be passed to control their output. The documentation refers to these parameters as *device settings*. For example, let's say you want to export a report as an image in a format other than the default image format, which happens to be TIFF. You can achieve this by using the OutputFormat device setting, as follows:

```
http://localhost/ReportServer?/AWReporter/Sales By Territory&
rs:Command=Render&rs:Format=IMAGE&rc:OutputFormat=JPEG
```

Another useful device setting is HTMLFragment, which you can use to render a report as an HTML fragment (without the HTML, HEAD, and BODY HTML tags), as follows:

```
http://localhost/ReportServer?/AWReporter/Sales By Territory&
rs:Command=Render&rc:HTMLFragment=true&rc:Toolbar=false
```

Rendering a report as an HTML fragment could be especially useful for web-based reporting, where the report needs to be generated on the server side and "injected" into the page. We will see a practical example of how this can be done in chapter 11.

For a full list of supported device settings, please see the product documentation.

Snapshot history commands

As you will probably recall from chapter 7, a report can be executed and cached as a snapshot on a regular basis. The Report Server can be configured to save the snapshot runs in the snapshot history.

You can use the Snapshot command to request a specific snapshot run from the report history, based on the date it was generated, for example:

```
http://localhost/ReportServer?/AWReporter/Territory Sales
by Quarter&rs:Snapshot=2004-01-16T02:28:01
```

The Snapshot command accepts as a parameter value the date and time when the snapshot was generated. The snapshot time has to be converted to GMT.

Commands for interactive features

One of the most valuable aspects of URL access is that it supports all of the interactive features that we discussed in chapters 4 and 5. There are a few commands that you can use to control these interactive features.

For example, in chapter 4 we authored a report (Employee Sales Tabular Interactive .rdl) that demonstrated visible-on-demand sections. Specifically, the Product Subcategory sections are hidden when the report is initially requested but can be expanded by clicking the plus sign (+).

Instead of hiding all items, sometimes you may need to show a certain section expanded. To accomplish this, you can use the ShowHideToggle command, for example:

```
http://localhost/reportserver?/AWReporter/Employee Sales Tabular
Interactive&StartDate=1/1/2003&EndDate=12/1/2003&Employee=-1
&rs:Format=HTML4.0&rs:Command=Render&rs:ShowHideToggle=29
```

The net effect of using the ShowHideToggle command in this example is that the first Product Subcategory section (the one for Tsoflias, Lynn) will be expanded when the report is requested. As it names suggests, ShowHideToggle toggles the section visibility with each subsequent request (if the item is hidden, it will be expanded, and vice versa).

How do you get the section identifier? Unfortunately, there is currently no way to programmatically find out what the section identifiers are. Instead, you need to look at the source of the rendered report. Each expandable section is assigned an ID number when the report is requested. The section identifiers are formatted as `ID="<section identifier">`.

The inability to determine the section identifiers in advance makes the commands that target interactive features by section identifiers (ShowHideToggle for expandable sections, BookmarkID to jump to a report bookmark, and DocMapID to scroll to a particular document map section) of limited use to developers.

Managing report sessions

As we explained in chapter 7, to ensure data consistency and optimize report performance, the Report Server uses report sessions. When the Report Server creates a session for a given report, it caches the report's intermediate format (IF) in the Report Server Temporary Database (ReportServerTempDB) for a configurable period of time.

By default, to correlate the report consumer with the session, the Report Server uses cookies. If cookies are used to track sessions, you don't have to do anything special from a programming standpoint to manage sessions. The Report Server will automatically generate a cookie for each report session and add it to the HTTP response header. The cookie will then ping-pong between the browser and the Report Server with each subsequent report request.

For example, the following trace excerpt shows the cookie's HTTP header after we requested several reports using the same instance of the browser:

```
Cookie:%2fAWReporter%2fSales+By+Territory+Interactive=
52v13e55bfox0zisan0rsqjy; %2fAWReporter%2fzzTest=
gbsyl4mapuz0m555spbbdsje; %2fAWReporter%2fCorporate+Hierarchy=
gqn5cn5543bjmy45bak5al55;
```

Sometimes the report session caching may get in the way. For example, you may need to view the report with the most recent data. As we explained in chapter 7, you cannot turn off report session caching. However, you can use either of the following approaches to clear the report session so that the report is processed anew:

- If the standard report toolbar is not suppressed, you can click the Refresh Report button (not the browser's Refresh button) or press Ctrl-F5. When you do this, the HTML Viewer intercepts the request and sends the ClearSession command (rs:ClearSession=true) to the Report Server to clear the report session. The Report Server will then process the report again.
- Send the ClearSession command explicitly as a part of the URL request.

Refreshing the report in the browser (by pressing F5) doesn't clear the session. This means that if the report session is valid (hasn't expired, has the same set of parameters, and so on), the Report Server will serve the report from the same report session.

For browsers that are configured not to support cookies, you can use cookie-less report sessions by setting the UseSessionCookies setting in the ConfigurationInfo table in the RS Configuration Database to false. In this case, instead of sending a cookie, the Report Server adds a parameter to the URL to identify the session.

One of the main advantages of requesting reports by URL is the handy report toolbar that the Report Server generates by default, as we will discuss next.

9.2.5 Working with the HTML Viewer

When a report is requested by URL and rendered in HTML, the Report Server generates a useful toolbar, called the HTML Viewer, at the top of the report, as shown in figure 9.3.

You can appreciate the effort that the RS team has done for you by acknowledging the breadth of features that this toolbar provides. It is a mini-application by itself! The RS documentation refers to the HTML framework that hosts the toolbar and the report as the HTML Viewer.

HTML Viewer features

You will find the HTML Viewer very similar to the report toolbar, which the Report Designer generates in report preview mode. Table 9.3 outlines the interactive features supported by the HTML Viewer.

The HTML Viewer is also somewhat customizable. As a part of the URL report request, you can include HTML Viewer–specific commands to customize certain aspects of the HTML Viewer.

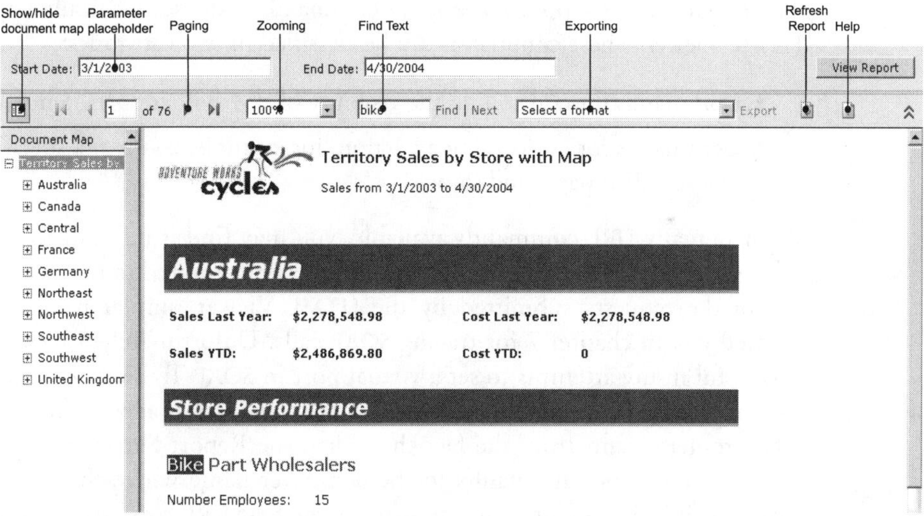

Figure 9.3 When reports are rendered via URL, the Report Server generates the HTML Viewer toolbar.

Table 9.3 The HTML Viewer provides a set of interactive features.

Feature	Description
Show/hide Document Map	Toggles the document map's visibility for reports with document maps.
Parameter placeholders	Generates parameter placeholders for parameterized reports. For example, the screenshot in figure 9.3 shows that the Territory Sales by Store with Map report takes two parameters, Start Date and End Date. If a parameter has a list of available values, the HTML Viewer will automatically generate a drop-down list. If a parameter has a default value, its placeholder will be set accordingly. Only parameters that are set to prompt the user are shown.
Zooming	Zooms the report in or out.
Finding text	For example, as figure 9.3 shows, after I performed a search for the word *Bike*, if a match is found, the browser scrolls and highlights the match. For multipage reports, clicking Next to search subsequent pages causes the HTML Viewer to submit additional requests to the Report Server.
Exporting	Exports the report to all of the formats supported by the Report Server, e.g., PDF.
Refresh Report	Refreshes the report by resubmitting the URL request and clears the report session.
Online help	Navigates to the HTML Viewer online help.

Customizing the HTML Viewer

The Report Server supports a series of commands that are specifically targeted to the HTML Viewer. These commands can be classified in two categories:

- Commands for controlling the visibility of the toolbar or its items
- Commands for performing an action, for example, zoom at a specified level, go to a specified page, and so on

With so many URL commands available, you may find it difficult to construct the right syntax of the URL report request. You may be tempted to try URL request tracing of the requests submitted by the HTML Viewer, similar to the technique I showed you in chapter 7 for tracing SOAP calls. Unfortunately, I haven't been very successful in my attempts to set a virtual port in SOAP Trace or tcpTrace that I can use for tracing URL requests, either from the Report Manager or from the browser. The problem stems from the fact that when the Report Server renders the HTML page for the report, it defaults to the computer name where the Report Server is installed. For this reason, you can capture the first URL request by redirecting it to a virtual port, such as http://servername:8080/reports...., but rendering the report subsequently by pressing the View Report button from the report toolbar will bypass the virtual port.

As you can see by looking at the HTML source of the page, the reason for this is that the action URL of the form that includes the report's rendered presentation doesn't include the port number. As a workaround, you can examine the IIS web logs to find out what URL requests have been sent by the browser. Alternatively, you may find useful the custom HTTP module that we'll implement in chapter 15. It outputs all incoming HTTP-GET and SOAP requests to the default trace listener so that you can use a tool such as DebugView to watch the traffic.

An example of the first category of commands is the Toolbar command. You can use this command to request that the report toolbar won't be rendered at all, as follows:

```
http://localhost/reportserver?/AWReporter/
Sales by Territory&rc:Toolbar=false
```

Or, let's say that you want to instruct the Report Server not to render the toolbar parameter area. This could be useful when you embed the parameters programmatically in the report URL and you don't want the user to see the report parameter area at all. You can accomplish this by using the Parameters command.

For example, the following command will render Sales by Territory report and will exclude the parameter section from the HTML Viewer toolbar:

```
http://localhost/reportserver?/AWReporter/
Sales by Territory Interactive&Year=2004&Territory=1&rc:Parameters=false
```

NOTE Reporting Services Service Pack 1, which will be probably released by the time you read this book, will allow you to pass parameter values in the URL that aren't prompted or displayed in the parameters area of the HTML Viewer. This behavior is different from the read-only parameters (parameters that don't have prompts) that we discussed in chapter 3 because with read-only parameters you cannot pass the parameter value.

In addition, SP1 will introduce the rc:Parameters=collapsed HTML Viewer command, in which the parameters area is accessible but initially hidden.

An example of an action command is Zoom. Use this command to zoom the report in or out before it is rendered. The following URL request zooms the report to its page width:

```
http://localhost/reportserver?/AWReporter/
Sales by Territory Interactive&Year=2004&Territory=1&rc:Zoom=Page Width
```

For a full list of all HTML Viewer–targeted commands, please see the product documentation.

HTML Viewer limitations

The HTML Viewer saves you a lot of effort when integrating applications with RS. It is one of the biggest selling points for choosing the URL access option to render reports. However, it may also be its Achilles' heel. Why? You see, outside the supported commands, the HTML Viewer is not customizable. The area that takes the most criticism and requests for enhancements is the parameters section.

For example, what if you want to implement your custom parameter validation? Or, what if you want to validate the parameters on the client side before the report is submitted? What if you need multi-select parameters? Or multi-value parameters that can be selectively turned on and off based on other parameter values? All of these are valid questions and concerns, but currently they go beyond the HTML Viewer feature set.

Another frequently requested feature is the ability to print reports. Currently, the HTML Viewer doesn't include a print button. If your requirements call for this feature, you may find useful the "Printing Reports Programmatically Using C# and SQL Server 2000 Reporting Services" sample listed under section 9.6.

NOTE Reporting Services Service Pack 1 scheduled for release in June 2005 will allow you to pick a custom style sheet for the HTML Viewer.

You can expect Microsoft to make the HTML Viewer more flexible and customizable in the future. For example, there are plans that the toolbar will support custom validation by the virtue of ASP.NET user controls in the next release. Until that time, however, you have to take the HTML Viewer as it is or provide your own custom application front end to replace it. To demonstrate the latter approach, the next chapter shows how a WinForm application can handle report parameter validation.

Now that we've covered the theory behind URL access, let's see a code sample that demonstrates how a client application can be integrated with the Report Server by URL.

9.2.6 URL access in action

The AccessOptions code sample demonstrates how a WinForm-based report consumer can leverage both access options (URL and SOAP) to request reports. It can be launched from the chapter 9 menu in the AWReporterWin sample application.

AccessOptions demonstrates two possible implementation approaches to integrate a WinForm-based report consumer with Reporting Services by URL:

- Using the Microsoft WebBrowser ActiveX control
- Shelling out to the browser

We kept the code simple on purpose. We will base a more involved example upon this code in chapter 10, where we will implement the Report Wizard sample. For now, our design goals for the AccessOptions example are:

- To show you the minimum steps to access reports using both the URL and Web service access options
- To provide enough implementation details so you can compare both approaches

Figure 9.4 shows the Access Options form.

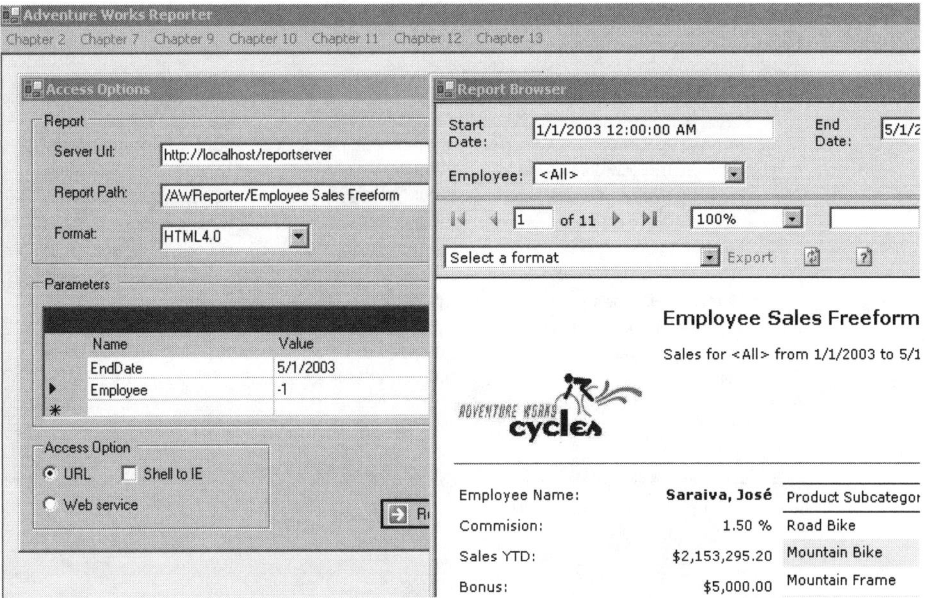

Figure 9.4 The Access Options sample demonstrates how a WinForm application can request reports via URL or the RS Web service (SOAP).

To run a report by URL, the user has to specify the Report Server URL, the report path, and the export format. In the case of parameterized reports, the user must also enter all parameters (name and value) in the Parameters grid. To submit the report request by URL, the user can choose one of two options:

- Using the Microsoft WebBrowser control (the default option if the URL radio button is selected)
- Shelling to the Internet Explorer (the Shell to IE option)

Let's first see how this code sample integrates with the Report Server by URL. Then in section 9.3.1 we will see how we can do this by using the RS Web service.

Using the Microsoft WebBrowser ActiveX control

To request reports by URL, a WinForm application can leverage the Microsoft Web Browser ActiveX control to embed the report inside a form. Once practical scenario where embedding the report can be useful is when your requirements call for implementing a Report Search form. Once the user selects a report, you may want to display the report inside the search form instead of navigating to a new form.

If you haven't used the Microsoft WebBrowser control in the past, you will be happy to find that it allows you to add browsing, document viewing, and data downloading capabilities to your applications. Because the WebBrowser control is COM-based, this approach is also suitable for classic Windows-based applications, for example, Visual Basic 6 clients.

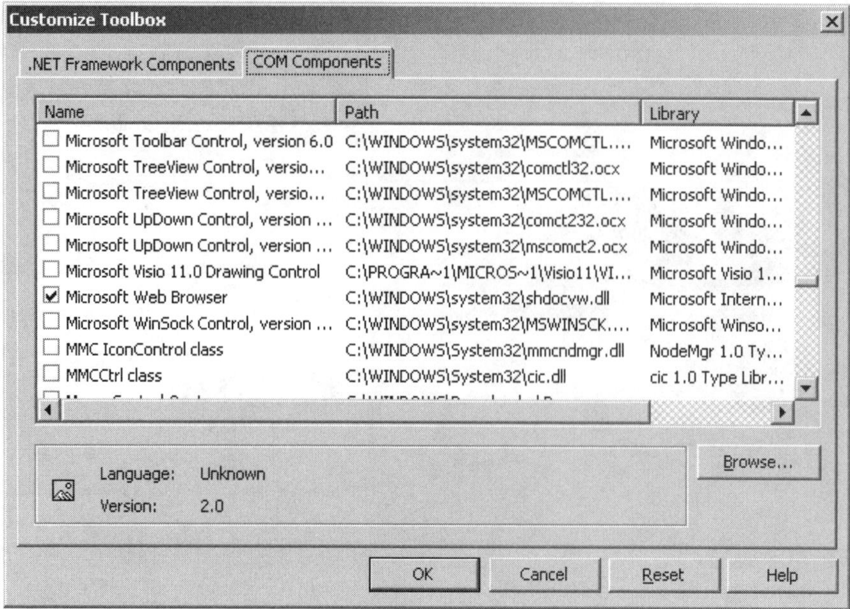

Figure 9.5 Referencing the Microsoft WebBrowser control

To use the WebBrowser control in WinForm .NET applications, you first have to reference it in your project. To do so, follow these steps:

Step 1 Right-click on the toolbox and choose Add/Remove Items.

Step 2 On the Customize Toolbox dialog, flip to the COM Components tab and select the Microsoft Web Browser component, as shown in figure 9.5. The WebBrowser control's library name is shdocvw.dll.

Step 3 Click OK. Visual Studio.NET will add the control's icon to the toolbox. From there, you can drag and drop the control onto your form.

If you need more information about the WebBrowser control, check the resources in section 9.6.

Loading the export formats

When the Access Options form is loaded, the Format drop-down is populated with the rendering formats that the Report Server supports. Instead of hard-coding the drop-down items, a better approach is to call the `ListExtensions` method of the RS Web service. Although the method call incurs a performance hit, the advantage of the latter approach is flexibility, because you don't have to redistribute the application if new rendering extensions have been added. This is the approach that the `LoadFormats` function takes, as shown in listing 9.1.

Listing 9.1 Use the `ListExtensions` SOAP API to populate the drop-down list with export formats.

```
private void LoadFormats()
{
  ReportingService rs = RsHelpers.Proxy;
  Extension[] extensions = null;
  extensions = rs.ListExtensions(ExtensionTypeEnum.Render);

  foreach (Extension extension in extensions) {
     if (extension.Name.ToLower()!="null")
         cmbFormat.Items.Add(extension.Name);
   }
   cmbFormat.SelectedText = "HTML4.0";
}
```

Call the ListExtensions API to get the supported formats

Load the export formats in the drop-down

Skip the NULL rendering extension

Because this method is executed when the form loads, make sure to update the Report Server URL, which defaults to localhost, before running the sample. The `ListExtension` method returns an array of all supported rendering extensions as specified in the RSReportServer.config file. Each rendering extension is exposed as of type `Extension`.

Please note that the code specifically ignores the NULL rendering extension. This extension is not a rendering extension per se because it doesn't render reports in any specific format. Instead, it is useful for prepopulating the report session cache for subscribed report delivery, as we will explain in more detail in chapter 14. Because this is a "dummy" extension and cannot be used for report rendering, we skip it.

For the sake of simplicity, we don't retrieve the list of report parameters from the RS Web service, nor do we validate the parameters in any way. As we mentioned, we will show you a more realistic example in chapter 10. For the purposes of this sample, the user is responsible for setting up the parameters correctly. To show the parameters in the grid, we use a typed dataset, EntityParameter, which we bind to the grid.

Requesting the report

Once the user has filled in the report parameters (if any), we are ready to request the report by calling the `RunByURL` function, whose abbreviated code is shown in listing 9.2:

Listing 9.2 WinForm clients can use the Microsoft WebBrowser control to place the report inside a form.

```
private void RunByURL()
 {
  StringBuilder urlBuilder = new StringBuilder();
  urlBuilder.Append(txtServer.Text);
  urlBuilder.Append ("?");
  urlBuilder.Append (txtReportPath.Text);

  EntityParameter.ParametersDataTable table =
```

Use a StringBuilder object to construct the report URL

Append the report parameters for parameterized reports

```
        EntityParameter.ParametersDataTable)grdParams.DataSource;

    foreach (EntityParameter.ParametersRow row in table.Rows){
      urlBuilder.Append (String.Format("&{0}={1}",
         row.Name, row.Value));
    }
    urlBuilder.Append (@"&rs:Format=" + cmbFormat.Text);
    urlBuilder.Append (@"&rs:Command=Render");

    ReportBrowser reportBrowser = new ReportBrowser();
    reportBrowser.RenderReport(urlBuilder.ToString());
    reportBrowser.Show();
  }
```

Use the ReportBrowser form that includes the WebBrowser control to display the report

First, the code crafts programmatically the report URL according to the URL syntax rules that we discussed in section 9.2. We set up the report path, followed by the report parameters and the specified export format.

Once the URL string is constructed, we instantiate the ReportBrowser form to render the report using the Microsoft WebBrowser control. Inside the ReportBrowser form, we call the Microsoft WebBrowser control's `Navigate` method and pass the report URL:

```
public void RenderReport(string url){
  Object optional = System.Reflection.Missing.Value;
  webBrowser.Navigate(url, ref optional, ref optional,
  ref optional,ref optional);
}
```

At this point the report is displayed. If there are any errors, they will be shown in the WebBrowser control.

Shelling out to the browser

Sometimes, you may just need a quick way to show the report in the browser by navigating to the report's URL address. You can do this by simply shelling out the report request to the browser. To accomplish this task, .NET developers can use the `Process.Start` method to start the application associated with a file extension.

When the Shell to IE option is selected on the Access Options form, once the report URL is ready, displaying the report in the browser takes one line of code:

```
Process.Start ("IExplore", url).
```

When you don't need to embed the report in a form, you should consider shelling out to the browser as a more lightweight implementation approach of requesting a report by URL.

As you've seen, requesting reports by URL is easy. However, there will be cases when URL access is not a viable option. When the URL is not enough, developers can report-enable their applications by calling the RS Web service, as we will discuss next.

9.3 WEB SERVICE-BASED REPORT ACCESS

Requesting reports on demand via SOAP calls to the RS Web service is your second (and final) integration option. The entry point for SOAP requests is the ReportService.asmx page. Here are some application scenarios that may require integration with the RS Web service:

- *When direct access to the Report Server is not an option*—For example, an Intranet-oriented application may rule out direct access to Report Server for security reasons.
- *When a distributed application needs to validate the report request against some business rules before the request is handed out to the Report Server*—This calls for server-side report generation, which rules out the URL access option.
- *When you need to generate one or more reports in unattended mode*—The AWC Campaigner example that we'll look at in section 9.3.4 demonstrates this scenario.
- *When you need to come up with a hybrid approach that encompasses both the URL and Web service access options*—For example, you may need to implement both report rendering and management features in your applications, similar to the feature set supported by the Report Manager. While your application could request reports by URL, only the Web service supports the management API.

The widespread adoption of SOAP facilitates integrating Reporting Services with many types of report consumers and platforms. Because SOAP has been embraced as an industry standard for communication with Web services, most platforms provide programmatic ways for handling SOAP messages and invoking web methods. For example, a web-based application running on UNIX can send a SOAP request to the RS Web service and then generate the report on the server side of the application.

Table 9.4 outlines some common techniques that developers writing Microsoft-centric applications can use to integrate their applications with the RS Web service.

Table 9.4 Techniques to integrate report consumers with the RS Web Service

Client Type	Application Example	Implementation Approaches
WinForm	.NET-based applications Legacy applications written in Visual Basic 6.0	Web service proxy (.NET) Microsoft SOAP Toolkit (legacy applications, e.g., Visual Basic 6.0)
Web-based	.NET-based applications Other web-based applications	Web service proxy (.NET) to submit the report request on the server side Microsoft Web service behavior for Internet Explorer to submit the report request on the client side

Invoking the Report Server SOAP API is easy with .NET clients (both WinForm and web-based) because .NET provides native support for calling Web services. .NET developers are for the most part abstracted from the SOAP message complexities when using Visual Studio .NET. As we saw in chapter 7, in VS.NET you can establish a web reference to the Web service. Once this is done, invoking the RS Web service is not much different than invoking a local object. We will see a code sample that demonstrates requesting report by SOAP in section 9.3.1.

Legacy clients, for example, Visual Basic 6.0 clients, can integrate with the RS Web service by using the Microsoft SOAP toolkit (see section 9.6). Finally, other types of clients can use whatever infrastructure the programming language and platform support for Web service calls.

For example, developers can expand the Internet Explorer capabilities in the form of client-side JavaScript code called a *behavior*. For web-based applications that target Internet Explorer and need to submit request reports on the client side of the application, you can download and use the Microsoft Web service behavior, as we will see in chapter 11.

Next, let's see how a report consumer can request reports with SOAP.

9.3.1 Requesting reports with SOAP

As we saw in chapter 7, the RS Web service provides a series of methods that you can use to query and manage the report catalog. It also provides methods related to report rendering and execution. The pivotal method is the `Render` method, which you can use to render reports on demand. It takes several arguments that you have to set before invoking the method, such as an array of parameters for parameterized reports, the export format, specific device settings, and so on.

If the method succeeds, it returns the report payload as a byte array. In most cases, this means that an extra step is needed on your part, as the developer, to render the report to the user. For example, this may involve saving the byte array to a file and shelling out to it.

Invoking the Render method

To understand how you can call the `Render` method, let's return to the Access Options example we used in section 9.2.6. This time we will see how we can request the report with SOAP. To do so, select the second radio button called Web Service.

When you click the Run Report button, AccessOptions invokes `RunByWS` function, whose abbreviated code is shown in listing 9.3.

Listing 9.3 To request a report by the RS Web service, call the `Render Report` SOAP API.

```
private void RunByWS()
 {
   ReportingService rs = RsHelpers.Proxy;
   rs.Url = txtServer.Text + @"/ReportService.asmx";

   byte[] result = null;
   string reportPath = txtReportPath.Text;
   string historyID = null;
   string format = cmbFormat.Text;
```

```
  string devInfo = null;
  DataSourceCredentials[] credentials = null;
  string showHideToggle = null;
  string encoding;
  string mimeType;
  Warning[] warnings = null;
  ParameterValue[] reportHistoryParameters = null;
  string[] streamIDs = null;
  ParameterValue[] proxyParameters = null;

  EntityParameter.ParametersDataTable userParameters =        ❶
   (EntityParameter.ParametersDataTable)grdParams.DataSource;

  if (userParameters.Rows.Count > 0)  proxyParameters = new
          ParameterValue[userParameters.Rows.Count];

  for (int i = 0; i<userParameters.Rows.Count;i++) {          ❷
     proxyParameters[i] = new ParameterValue();
     proxyParameters[i].Name = userParameters[i].Name;
     proxyParameters[i].Value = userParameters[i].Value;
  }

  result = rs.Render(reportPath, format, historyID, devInfo,  ❸
          proxyParameters, credentials, showHideToggle,
          out encoding, out mimeType,
          out reportHistoryParameters,
          out warnings, out streamIDs);

  string filePath = Util.GetFileForReport(reportPath,
    cmbFormat.Text);                                          ❹
  FileStream stream = File.Create( filePath, result.Length);  ❺
  stream.Write( result, 0, result.Length );
  stream.Close();
  Process.Start(filePath);                                    ❻
}
```

❶ Get the parameters from the data grid
❷ Prepare the parameter array
❸ Call the Web service to render the report
❹ Get the file path where the report payload will be saved
❺ Persist the report payload to a file
❻ Shell out to the application associated with the exported format

One of the benefits of using the RS Web service is that it allows us to request the report in an object-oriented way.

First, we obtain a reference to the Web service proxy by calling the `RsHelpers.Proxy` utility function. This function also takes care of setting the proxy credentials. Next, we set up the Web service URL to the ReportService.asmx end point. Then, we initialize the `Render` arguments to their default values.

The `Render` method is an all-encompassing method for report rendering. For example, by setting appropriate arguments, we can request a cached report from the snapshot history. We will see how this can be done in chapter 10. For now, we will ignore the report history parameters. We will also ignore the device settings.

❶,❷ To specify the report parameters for parameterized reports, we load an array of the ParameterValue structures.

❸ Then, we call the `Render` method to request the report.

Finally, we need to take an extra step for showing the report. When a report is requested by URL, the browser does this automatically for us. However, when requesting reports via SOAP, we are on our own. To display the report, we save the report payload to a file with the appropriate extension. For example, if the report is requested in HTML, the file extension is .HTML; if it is IMAGE, then the extension is .TIF (the default image format), and so on.

❹,❺ We save the report file in the Application Data folder under the user called Document and in the Setting folder. To get the file path and name right, we use a simple `GetFileForReport` helper function that takes the report name and export format and returns the full path to the file.

❻ Once the file is saved, we shell out to it using Process.Start. This will start the application associated with the file extension to load the file and display the report.

Dealing with errors

Unlike with the URL access option, using SOAP allows you deal gracefully with error conditions. The Report Server exposes exceptions as SOAP faults. The Common Language Runtime subsequently maps them to a .NET exception of type `System.Web.Services.Protocols.SoapException`. This allows developers to code defensively using `Try`...`Catch` blocks, as the following example shows:

```
try {
...Invoke a web method
}
catch (SoapException ex){
   // RS exception
   switch (ex.Detail["ErrorCode"].InnerText)
  {
    case "rsReportParameterValueNotSet":
       Util.ShowErrorMessage("The report parameters do not
           match.\n" + ex.Detail.InnerText); return;
    case "rsItemNotFound":
       Util.ShowErrorMessage("Wrong report name."); return;
    default: throw;
 }
}
catch (System.Exception ex)   {
  // something else is wrong
}
```

The bulk of the exception information is exposed as an XML string under the Detail property of the SoapException class. For this reason, you can get to the error code using the SoapException.Detail property and to the error message itself using the

Detail.InnerText or Detail.InnerXml (to get as XML) property. For a full list of the RS error codes, please see the product documentation.

9.3.2 Rendering images

As you have begun to see, requesting reports by SOAP is more involved than the URL option. Another area that requires additional effort on your part is rendering reports that include images. When you export such reports to multistream exporting formats, such as all HTML flavors besides MHTML, the report images and charts are not rendered by default. The reason for this odd behavior is that when the web browser renders an HTML page, it spawns additional requests to the web server to download the images included in the page. This presents an issue for dynamically generated images, such as charts.

To address this dilemma, when generating the report the Report Server serializes the images in the report session cache associated with the report. Unfortunately, in the case of rendering reports by SOAP, the image URLs don't include the session identifier of the report session that the Report Server has created for the report. As a result, the Report Server is unable to match the request with the report session, and the image download request fails. Even if the session identifier were included in the image URL, it would be of little help because direct access to the Report Server is usually not an option when requesting reports by SOAP.

Handling images for exported-to-HTML reports could be quite a hassle. Currently, there are three workarounds for this problem:

- For external images, use the HTMLFragment setting.
- Download the images explicitly using the `RenderStream` method.
- Use cookie-less report sessions. In this case, the image URLs will have the session ID on them.

Let's look at the first two options in more detail.

Rendering external images

As you would recall from chapter 4, you can use the image report item to reference external images by specifying their relative path in the report catalog. This is what we did to display the AWC company logo in our reports. One option to display external images when requesting reports via SOAP, is to render the report as a HTML fragment by setting the HTMLFragment device info setting to true.

When this setting is used, the web server will include the SessionID in the image URL string. Then the HTTP-GET request to the Report Server that the browser will spawn to download the image will succeed. This is as simple as it gets but requires direct HTTP access from the browser to the Report Server. Besides, it doesn't work with chart reports because the Report Server generates the chart images dynamically.

Let's if we can derive to a "universal" image handing solution that works for all types of images and integration scenarios.

Downloading the images explicitly

For intranet-oriented applications you can explicitly download and save the report images using the `RenderStream` web method. This approach involves two implementation steps:

- Setting the StreamRoot device setting to a location where the images will be downloaded
- Enumerating through the image streams and downloading the images explicitly

Rendering images by using the `RenderStream` method is simple. You can set the StreamRoot device setting to a common folder on the user's hard drive, for example, the Documents and Settings folder. This is the approach we demonstrate in the Access Options sample, as shown in listing 9.4:

Listing 9.4 Downloading the images explicitly by using the `RenderStream` API

```
devInf="<DeviceInfo><StreamRoot>" + Application.UserAppDataPath+
        "/</StreamRoot></DeviceInfo>";

result = rs.Render(…) // render the report


// render the images when report is exported to HTML
if ("html" == format.Substring(0, 4).ToLower()){
   foreach (string streamID in streamIDs)    {
     byte [] image = rs.RenderStream(reportPath, format,
      streamID, null, null, proxyParameters,
      out optionalString, out optionalString);

   FileStream stream=File.OpenWrite(Application.UserAppDataPath
        + Path.DirectorySeparatorChar + streamID);
   stream.Write(image, 0, image.Length);
   stream.Close();
  }
}
```

(1) Use the StreamRoot device setting to specify the download location

(2) Handling images explicitly is an issue only when exporting to HTML

(3) Get the image payload by calling `RenderStream`

(4) Download the image to a folder

(1) First, we use the StreamRoot device setting to set the image URLs to point to the user's application folder. Then, we render the report. When the Report Server processes the report, it will see the StreamRoot setting and will adjust the report image URLs accordingly. In the example above, the image URL will be set like so:

```
file:///C:/Documents and Settings/<user>/Application Data/AWC/Win/1.0.0.0/
<streamID>
```

(2) The last argument of the `Render` method takes a StreamIds argument in the form of a string array. When the `Render` method returns, the array will be loaded with the stream identifiers of all report images and charts that the report includes. You may think that the stream identifiers correspond to the report item identifiers as defined

in the Report Server catalog, but such is not the case. The Report Server assigns them during report processing.

> **NOTE** The Report Server prefixes the chart stream identifiers with C_. You can take advantage of this naming convention if you want to render only the chart images.

❸ Next, we loop through all image identifiers and download the images by calling the `RenderStream` web method. One thing that we want to bring to your attention is that you must pass the report parameters when calling the `RenderStream` method for parameterized reports so that the Report Server can correlate the report request with the right report session. If you don't, you will get the "Stream could not be found" exception.

❹ When `RenderStream` returns, we save the image as a binary file to the folder specified by the StreamRoot device setting.

So, as you've seen, using `RenderStream` to render report images is not that difficult. Unfortunately, this approach is often impractical with web-based applications, as we will discuss next.

Proposing a universal image handler approach

Dealing with images gets trickier for web-based applications. In this case, you don't have access to the user's local environment to save the image files. Instead, your only option is to download the images to a globally accessible file store.

For intranet-based applications, you can set the StreamRoot device setting to a network file share. Needless to say, you need to take care of deleting the image files on a regular basis to avoid filling up the server.

What about Internet-based applications? In this case, storing files on a network share is not an option because it won't be accessible to your web users. You may think that you can get around this predicament by setting StreamRoot to a virtual root on your web server. Unfortunately, this doesn't always work. To understand the problem, consider the following example.

Let's say your application's virtual folder is AWReporterWeb and it has a subfolder called temp. If you set StreamRoot to

```
http://<servername>/AwReporterWeb/temp
```

the image URLs will be adjusted to

```
http://<servername>/AwReporterWeb/temp/<streamID>
```

where `streamID` is the image identifier.

All is great, except the fact that the stream identifier doesn't have a file extension, and IIS will have no clue as to how to process this request. Therefore, IIS will complain with a "Page not found" exception.

NOTE Strictly speaking, file extensions in the image URLs are missing only when the Report Server is running on Windows 2003. Reporting Services Service Pack 1, scheduled for release sometime in June 2005, is set to fix this problem, and StreamRoot will work across all supported operating systems. However, even if this is fixed, I still believe that using a server-side image handler page (see chapter 11) could be useful because it can handle the image file bookkeeping chores, such as deleting the image file once it is rendered.

One possible workaround is to implement a server-side image handler page and adjust StreamRoot to point to that page. We will postpone the actual implementation until chapter 11.

There's one last and important consideration about the `RenderStream` method. The `Render` and `RenderStream` calls need to share the same report session. Handling report sessions with SOAP access requires more programming effort on your part, as we will discuss next.

9.3.3 Handing report sessions

Recall our discussion in chapter 7 that when a new non-snapshot report request arrives, the Report Server caches the report's IF in the RS Temporary Database in the form of a report session.

NOTE Ensuring data consistency by using report sessions is more of a concern with URL access than with SOAP. When the report is requested via SOAP, the whole report payload is streamed back to the client. This means that you will get all pages of a multipage report, and no additional requests to the Report Server are necessary when the user pages from one page to the next. On the other hand, when the report is request by URL, only the first page is rendered. Navigating to another page initiates a new URL request. That said, you might still want to consider leveraging report sessions with SOAP as a performance enhancement technique.

Unlike the automatic report session management that the browser provides when the report is rendered by URL, you have to take care of correlating the report sessions yourself when requesting the report by SOAP. The reason for this is that the Web service proxy keeps only one session identifier, so each subsequent report request overrides the report session identifier set by the previous request.

There are two cases when you may need to take care of handing the report sessions by yourself:

- *Rendering the report images via calls to* `RenderStream`—Please note that this is needed only if the session identifier is overridden by another report request. Typically, you will download the report images via calls to `RenderStream` *immediately* after the report is rendered. If this is the case, you don't have to handle report sessions explicitly because the proxy will already have the session identifier associated with the report.

- *Optimizing the Report Server's performance*—As we explained in chapter 7, if the Report Server can correlate the report request with a session, it will bypass the execution phase and use the cached copy. As you will see in chapter 16, report session caching can boost the Report Server's performance considerably. If the report data are not volatile and some data "staleness" is tolerable, we recommend that you leverage report session caching.

To understand how to handle report sessions when requesting reports via SOAP, you need to know how the Web service proxy stores the session identifiers.

How SOAP access handles report sessions

When the report is requested via SOAP, the Report Server exposes the report session–related properties under the SessionHeader proxy class. The SessionId member of this class returns the report session identifier that matches the SessionID primary key in the SessionData table from the ReportServerTempDB database. You can check the IsNewExecution property to find out whether the call to the `Render` method has resulted in a new execution. If IsNewExecution is false, the Report Server has served the report request from an already existing report session.

The Report Server overwrites the SessionID member after each call to the `Render` method. Therefore, if you are not proactive, two subsequent report requests will share the same sessions only if they ask for the same report (assuming that the parameter set is the same).

For example, let's say you run report A, then report B, and then report A again. When report B is rendered, its session identifier will overwrite the previous session identifier, which means that you will lose report A's session identifier. When report A is run again, even if the parameter set is the same, its execution will create a new report session and IsNewExecution will return true.

Therefore, if you need to leverage report sessions, you need to write some code to store the report session identifiers and correlate them with the requested reports. Next we'll discuss a possible implementation approach that does this.

Correlating the report request with a report session

You could keep the reports-to-session association in a collection of some kind. For example, a hashtable collection, as shown in listing 9.5, can do this by storing the report names and session identifiers as name-value pairs.

Listing 9.5 Correlating the report request with the report session

```
Hashtable sessionCollection = new Hashtable();
rs.Render("reportA"....);
sessionCollection.Add("reportA", rs.SessionId);
rs.Render("reportB ");
sessionCollection.Add("reportB ", rs.SessionId);
// need to call report A again
```

```
SessionHeader sessionHeader = new SessionHeader();
sessionHeader.SessionId=sessionCollection["reportA"].ToString();
rs.SessionHeaderValue=sessionHeader;
rs.Render("reportA"....);
```

Each time we render a report we retrieve the session identifier from the Web service proxy and stuff it into the hashtable collection. When the same report needs to be rendered again, we set the proxy's SessionId accordingly.

Now that you've learned the SOAP access basics, we'll look at a practical example that emphasizes its advantages over URL access.

SOAP and report interactive features

One important limitation that you will inevitably discover when requesting reports by SOAP is that most interactive features, such as drilldown, drillthrough, document maps, toggled visibility, and document maps, rely on URL access.

For example, request the Sales by Territory Crosstab report using the Access Options sample. As you would recall from chapter 4, this report allows the end user to drill down by expanding row or column groups. At first glance, when this report is requested by SOAP, it appears that the drilldown interactive feature is unaffected. Don't be fooled, though! This feature relies on direct access to the Report Server by URL.

The way this works is that when the interactive feature is requested by the end user (in this case by clicking the + indicator) the HTML Viewer framework fires an HTTP-GET request to the Report Server to refresh the report. Once again, in order for the request to succeed, the Report Server must be directly accessible by HTTP-GET. In many cases, this will present a problem because you would typically choose SOAP over HTTP-GET when direct access to the Report Server by URL is not an option, for example, to generate reports on the server side of an Internet web-based application.

As a developer, there is really nothing you can do to change this behavior and avoid using HTTP-GET for interactive features. This poses an interesting dilemma, which may further complicate your decision-making process when you are pondering which access option to choose. How important are the report's interactive features to your end users? If interactivity is a must, then your choice is predetermined and it is URL access. Of course, we are not excluding the possibility of a hybrid approach where the report is rendered initially by SOAP but URL access is used to support the interactive features.

But what about security if URL access is the only option? This is an especially valid question for Internet-oriented web applications. The good news is that you can have the best of both worlds: URL access to provide a rich user experience and a comprehensive level of security that doesn't rely on Windows authentication. To accomplish the second objective, you may need to write a custom security extension to replace the default RS Windows-based security mechanism. In chapter 15 we will show you how you can do just this.

At this point you are probably ready to throw SOAP out the window. After all, it is more difficult to implement and cannot be used for reports with interactive features. Not so fast! As you will see next, requesting reports by SOAP can be very useful.

9.3.4 Automating the report generation process

While URL access is more suitable for interactive applications when the user can initiate the report request explicitly, it falls short when the report needs to be generated in an unattended mode, such as for automating the report generation as a result of an event. For example, in the business-to-business scenario, a vendor may need to pull a report on a regular basis to find out the customer's inventory level. If the inventory level falls below a certain threshold, the vendor system can send a notification to the manufacturing department. We will implement a similar example in chapter 11.

Thanks to its object-oriented nature, when reports need to be generated in n unattended mode, SOAP may be a better choice than URL. Let's examine a simple code demo to emphasize this point.

An automation solution: AW Campaigner

Back in chapter 6 we demonstrated how to export the Sales Promotion report to an RSS-compliant XML format. When there is a new campaign, the report's author could run the report by passing the offer identifier, export the report to the XML, and update the RSS blog file manually.

Let's enhance this example by implementing the AW Campaigner solution for automating the whole process. To fulfill the new requirements, our implementation approach will involve the following steps:

Step 1 Create a table trigger that will fire when a campaign record is inserted into the SpecialOffer table and invoke the stored procedure.

Step 2 Create a SQL Server stored procedure that will invoke a custom Web service façade.

Step 3 Create a Web service façade that will run the report and update the RSS file.

Figure 9.6 shows the sequence diagram of our solution.

The AW Campaigner process is initiated when a record is inserted into the SpecialOffer table. This causes the trgSpecialOffer trigger to fire. The trigger calls the spUpdateRssFeed stored procedure. The stored procedure in turn invokes our `StartCampaign` web method of the Campaigner Web service.

The Campaigner Web service then requests the Sales Promotion report via SOAP. It asks the report to be exported as XML. Finally, the Campaigner Web service updates the RSS blog file.

The source code of the Campaigner Web service can be found under the Chapter09 folder in the AWReporterWeb web project, while the stored procedure and trigger script files are included in the Database project.

Next, we'll explain how each component is implemented.

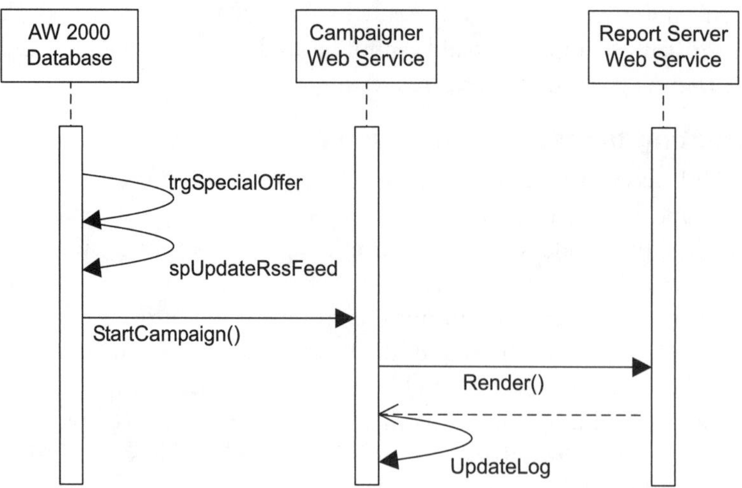

Figure 9.6 The AW Campaigner Web service sequence diagram shows that a table-level trigger initiates the blog file update process.

Triggering the process

The campaign process starts when a new offer record is inserted into the SpecialOffer table. The trgSpecialOffer trigger is implemented as an AFTER INSERT trigger on the SpecialOffer table, as shown in listing 9.6.

Listing 9.6 When a new record is inserted into the SpecialOffer table, the trgSpecialOffer trigger fires.

```
CREATE TRIGGER trgSpecialOffer ON [dbo].[SpecialOffer]
AFTER INSERT
AS

/* Get the new special offer id. */
DECLARE  @SpecialOfferID int
SELECT   @SpecialOfferID = SpecialOfferID
FROM     inserted

DECLARE  @Result varchar(8000)
EXEC     spUpdateRssFeed @SpecialOfferID, @Result OUT
```

The trigger gets the identifier of the record from the inserted table and calls the `spUpdateRssFeed` stored procedure, passing the special offer identifier to it.

One thing to watch for when you work with triggers is that all database operations inside the trigger are performed within the scope of an implicit transaction. This bit me quite badly at first. I wondered why the web method call inside the `spUpdateRssFeed` stored procedure never succeeded. Upon further investigation, I realized that the trigger locks the new record. When the Sales Promotion report tries to read it, the SELECT statement gets deadlocked and the web method call inside spUpdateRssFeed eventually times out.

To solve this issue, I added the NOLOCK table hint in the report query. The NOLOCK table hint permits the report to read "dirty" data that has not yet been committed. For the purposes of the Campaigner scenario, this is fine, because the trigger is defined as AFTER INSERT, which means that the record has been inserted successfully. In other cases, however, you have to take into account the fact that the update operation may fail, in which case the database changes will get rolled back.

Invoking the Campaigner Web service

The main role of the spUpdateRssFeed stored procedure is to invoke the AW Campaigner web service. The abbreviated spUpdateRssFeed stored procedure code (excluding the error-handling logic) is shown in listing 9.7.

Listing 9.7 The spUpdateRssFeed stored procedure uses the XMLHTTP component to invoke the Campaigner Web service.

```
CREATE  PROCEDURE spUpdateRssFeed( @SpecialOfferID  int,
        @Response varchar(8000) out)
AS
DECLARE
  @Url varchar(1000)
 ,@obj  int
 ,@hr  int
 ,@status int
 ,@msg varchar(255)

   set  @Url = 'http://localhost/AWReporterWeb/Chapter9/Campaigner.asmx/
StartCampaign?CampaignID=' + CAST(@SpecialOfferID AS VARCHAR(10))
   exec @hr = sp_OACreate 'MSXML2.ServerXMLHttp', @obj out
   exec @hr = sp_OAMethod @obj, 'Open', NULL, 'GET', @Url, false
   exec @hr = sp_OAMethod @obj, 'send'
   exec @hr = sp_OAGetProperty @obj, 'status', @status OUT
   exec @hr = sp_OAGetProperty @obj, 'responseText', @response OUT
   exec @hr = sp_OADestroy @obj
   return
```

The stored procedure uses the XMLHTTP component included with the Microsoft XML Parser (MSXML) to invoke the Campaigner Web service. (If you need more background information about this technology, please see the resources in section 9.6.) The latest MSXML version as of the time of this writing is 4.0. However, to be on the safe side, we attempt to instantiate version 2.0 of MSXML, which should be installed on your SQL Server box by default. SQL Server 2000 comes bundled with Internet Explorer 5.0, which includes MSXML 2.0.

Once the XMLHTTP object is instantiated, we invoke the `StartCampaign` method of the Campaigner Web service and pass the new record identifier.

Implementing the Campaigner Web service

The `StartCampaign` web method renders the Sales Promotion report as XML for the given special offer identifier. We have already seen how to request a report by SOAP in the Access Options sample.

Next, `StartCampaign` calls the `AddSpecialOffer` method. This method uses XML DOM to load the XML report payload. To do this, we use a memory stream to wrap the payload array and load the XmlDocument from it.

```
MemoryStream stream = new MemoryStream(specialOffer);
XmlDocument specialOfferDoc = new XmlDocument();
specialOfferDoc.Load(stream);
```

Finally, `StartCampaign` updates the RSS blog file (AWCSpecialDeals.xml). This is the file that the RSS newsreaders need to reference when subscribing to the AWC feed. The `StartCampaign` method simply appends the XML definition of the new special offer item to the end of the file. This should be enough to trigger a new item notification in the newsreader.

Securing AW Campaigner

Setting up security for the Campaigner sample warrants more explanation. In real life, it is likely that its three components (SQL Server database, Campaigner Web service, and Report Server) will be located on separate machines. From an implementation standpoint, our sample resembles the Client-to-Facade-to-Report Server scenario that we discussed in chapter 8.

Table 9.5 shows the Windows authentication setup that we used for testing.

Table 9.5 Setting up Windows authentication. All three components of AW Campaigner (database, Campaigner Web service, and Report Server) may be running on separate machines. To integrate them successfully, you need to set up Windows authentication so that the remote calls succeed.

Component	Authentication	Identity
SQL Server	Standard or Windows Integrated	Local system
AWReporterWeb (Campaigner Web service)	Anonymous access (rights to write to AWCSpecialDeals.xml)	Application pool identity changed to a domain account (or member of Users for local machine testing)
Report Server	Windows Integrated	The Campaigner application pool identity mapped to the Browser role for the Sales Promotion report and SalesPromotion.xslt

In our test environment, the SQL Server runs under the context of the Local System account. Because this is a local account, its identity cannot cross the machine boundary when the web method invocation occurs. For this reason, you have at least two choices for authenticating the SQL Server call to the Campaigner Web service:

- Change the SQL Server process identity to a domain account or a local account that is duplicated on the machine where the Campaigner Web service is installed (has the same name and password)
- Set up the AWReporterWeb vroot to allow anonymous access

For testing purposes, we decided to adopt the latter approach. In real life, you should carefully consider the ramifications of using Anonymous access. When Anonymous access is enabled, IIS authenticates all users using a low-privileged Windows account (IUSR_computername by default), which is a member of the Guest Windows group. All requests to access local resources will go under the identity of this account. In our case, the `StartCampaign` method needs to write to the blog file. For this reason, you need to grant the Anonymous account write permissions to this file. Alternatively, you can change the Anonymous identity to an account that has an elevated set of permissions.

Finally, you need to take care of setting the identity of the cross-machine call from the Campaigner Web service to the Report Server. Here, again you have two options:

- *Impersonating the user*—Assuming that Anonymous access is enabled, this means that we will pass the identity of the anonymous account to the Report Server. Again, in order for the cross-machine call to succeed between the Campaigner machine and the Report Server machine, this account has to be a domain account or a duplicated local account, which exists on both machines.
- *Using the trusted subsystem approach by passing the Campaigner Web service identity to the Report Server*—You can change the identity of the ASP.NET worker process on the machine where the Campaigner Web service is running to a domain account.

In both cases, you have to set up a role-based security policy in the Report Server to grant the Campaigner account sufficient rights to view the Sales Promotion report and SalesPromotion.xsl file.

Now that you have a good high-level overview of both access options available for requesting reports, we'll wrap up our discussion by finding out how they stack against each other.

9.4 EVALUATING URL AND WEB SERVICE ACCESS OPTIONS

Choosing the right integration scenario for report-enabling your applications can be challenging. You need to make a careful decision between the ease of use in the case of

URL access and the flexibility offered by the RS Web service. Here are some of the questions that you need to ask yourself:

- *Is this an intranet or Internet-oriented application?* While both access options can be used with intranet-oriented applications, unless you use a custom security extension, Internet reporting in most cases will require requesting reports by SOAP.
- *Can the Report Server be accessed directly by the client application?* If the answer is no (for security, or other reasons), then SOAP is the only choice.
- *Does the report request need to be validated before it is handed out to the Report Server?* If business rules need to be validated before the report request is authorized, SOAP may be the better choice.
- *How will the report parameters be handled?* If the HTML Viewer fits the bill, it would be naïve not to take advantage of URL access.

In general, we recommend that you evaluate URL access first and only if it doesn't meet your integration requirements should you settle on Web service access. As you've seen in this chapter, there are good reasons to keep things simple, and simplicity is the biggest strength of URL access.

Let's enumerate the pros and cons of each option in more detail to help you with the decision-making process.

9.4.1 Evaluating URL access

In general, URL access is best suited for interactive, intranet-oriented applications where the report request can originate on the client side of the application.

Pros of URL access

- *Simplicity*—Compared to requesting reports by SOAP, URL access is far easier. There are no post-processing steps required to render the report payload. The browser handles report sessions automatically. In case of HTML reports, you don't have to worry about downloading the image files. Taking care of the report images and charts could be a hassle, especially for Internet-based reports, as we will discuss in chapter 11.
- *Relatively easy to integrate with client applications*—Due to the venerable history of the HTTP protocol, most development tools and platforms can handle HTTP-GET requests and responses.
- *No client footprint*—Usually, there will be nothing that you need to install to integrate a client application with RS by URL. It could be as easy as embedding the report's URL in a hyperlink. For example, you can have a SharePoint Web part that references a report by URL.
- *Interactive features*—You can leverage URL access to provide a rich user experience by adding interactive features to your reports, such as drilldown, toggled

visibility, document maps, navigational features, and the HTML Viewer. When a report with interactive features is requested in HTML, the Report Server embeds the request-specific details, such as the parameter values, in the report page. When the interactive feature is requested by the end user, for example, to perform a drilldown, the report spawns an HTTP-GET request to the Report Server to refresh itself.

- *Performance*—The performance advantages of URL access are several. First, the report payload is smaller compared to requesting a report by SOAP. When the report is requested by URL, the Report Server doesn't have to serialize the report payload to a byte array before sending it to the consumer. Second, URL access doesn't require any preprocessing by the report consumer to render the report. In contrast, if you request the report from the Web service, in most cases you will need to save the report payload to a disk file and shell out to it so that the user can see it. Finally, report sessions are handled automatically by the browser, which can speed up subsequent requests to render the same report.

Cons of URL access

- *Restricted to report rendering* —You can only render reports using URL access to the Report Server. For all other tasks, you will need to use the RS Web service.
- *Not object-oriented*—Crafting these query parameters can be difficult! However, you can get around it by creating a wrapper, which will generate the right URL syntax for you. For example, the RS Catalog Explorer demonstrates this approach by using a helper class, called URLAccessBuilder. We will use a similar approach in chapter 10 to abstract the URL syntax technicalities.
- *Not suitable for server-side report rendering*—The URL access option is more suitable for interactive applications that generate reports on the client side. For example, you cannot programmatically catch exceptions and react to error conditions. In addition, requesting reports by URL requires direct access to the Report Server. This could be an issue in cases where there is a façade between the consumer and the Report Server and you need to validate business rules validation, provide custom security, or abstract the Report Server.
- *URL length limitations*—Many browsers impose restrictions on the maximum length of the URL address. For example, Internet Explorer has a maximum URL length of 2 KB (2,084 characters). This makes passing large data structures as report parameters impossible. For instance, you won't be able to pass application datasets as a report parameter from a WinForm front end to a report. Although the custom dataset extension, which we are going to create in chapter 15, allows you to report off application datasets, the serialized dataset payload may often exceed 2 KB. As a workaround to this limitation, you can use HTTP-POST, as we will demonstrate in chapter 11.

9.4.2 Evaluating Web service access

On the other hand, the Web service access option may be more suitable for generating reports on the server side of the application.

Pros of Web service access

- *Broad set of features*—Unlike the URL access option, the RS Web service is not limited to report rendering. It exposes the full functionality of the Report Server as a series of web methods.
- *An industry standard for exchanging messages between heterogeneous platforms*—This increases the RS client base to applications running on other platforms.
- *Object-oriented access*—Requesting a report via SOAP is as easy as instantiating the Web service proxy and calling its methods. In addition, the Report Server exposes exceptions as SOAP faults, which allows developers to code defensively.
- *Flexible invocation*—As we've seen, interfacing with the Web service doesn't require user interaction.

Cons of Web service access

- *HTML Viewer not available*—Unlike the URL option, a report rendered via SOAP doesn't include the HTML Viewer toolbar. For this reason, development effort will typically be required upfront for interactive client applications, for example, to get the report parameters, export format, and so on.
- *Interactive features rely on URL access*—In general, you will find that requesting reports from the Web service will give you a reduced interactive feature set. For example, although interactive features, such as drilldown, hyperlinks, and document maps, are available when reports are rendered via SOAP, they rely on URL access to the Report Server. This could be a problem if the Report Server is behind a façade and direct HTTP-GET access to the Report Server is impossible.
- *More involved report rendering*—Extra steps are required for report rendering and maintaining report sessions.
- *Slower performance*—Report serialization results in an increased report payload. The percentage of increase varies based on the export format and the report itself, but experiments show an added overhead of about 20–30 percent. This could be an issue with low-speed connections between the client and the Report Server.

9.4.3 Choosing an integration approach

So, where does this chapter's discussion leave us in terms of integrating client applications with Reporting Services? We saw that there are two options available when adding on-demand reporting capabilities to client applications: URL and SOAP. How would you choose between them? In some cases, the application requirements will dictate the access option and you won't have much choice. For example, as we have seen, the AW Campaigner requirements mandate the use of the RS Web service for report rendering in unattended mode.

In other cases, you have to carefully weigh the pros and cons of each option before deciding which one will be better suited for your particular situation. Once again, we recommend that you consider the URL access option first. It supports all interactive features, plus it is easier to integrate with client applications.

The main advantages of using the Web service are its flexible invocation options and extensive set of web methods. However, introducing additional layers and using SOAP for report rendering will often necessitate extra development effort and compromises in the interactive feature set.

One excellent approach would be to take the best of both worlds by using URL for report rendering and SOAP for everything else. There may be other factors that might influence your decision, including the type of the application (WinForm or web-based) and restrictions that the application's requirements might impose. For this reason, we will revisit this topic in subsequent chapters and make more specific recommendations as we discuss different application scenarios.

9.5 SUMMARY

In this chapter we laid out the foundation for the next four chapters. We discussed the two options that the Report Server offers for integrating with client applications.

First, we discussed the URL access option. We explored its syntax and discussed the HTML Viewer, which is available only with this option. Then we saw a practical example, the AccessOptions code sample, which demonstrated how a WinForm-based application could submit a report request by URL.

Second, we discussed the RS Web service integration option. We saw how we can address some of its complexities, such as handling report sessions and images. Again, we looked at the AccessOptions sample to find out how a client application could leverage this option to request reports by SOAP.

Finally, we rounded up our discussion by comparing both integration options. We pointed out that URL access is the fastest and easiest way to request reports and that it supports all of a report's interactive features. For these reasons, we recommended that you consider URL access first when choosing an integration approach for report-enabling your applications.

However, URL access may not be a good fit with more involved integration scenarios, such as when you need to generate reports in an unattended mode, as we demonstrated in the AW Campaigner code sample. In this case, you should consider integrating your applications with the RS Web service by SOAP.

Let's now apply what we've learned in this chapter by discussing how we can integrate Windows Forms applications with RS.

9.6 RESOURCES

WebBrowser Control Overviews and Tutorials (http://msdn.microsoft.com/library/default.asp?url=/workshop/browser/webbrowser/browser_control_ovw_entry.asp)

Provides an overview and tutorial articles for the Microsoft WebBrowser control.

Microsoft XML Parser (MSXML)

(http://msdn.microsoft.com/library/default.asp?url=/library/en-us/xmlsdk/html/xmmscXMLOverview.asp)

The MSXML 4.0 Software Development Kit (SDK) provides conceptual and reference information for developers using MSXML.

Printing Reports Programmatically Using C# and SQL Server 2000 Reporting Services

(http://blogs.msdn.com/bryanke/articles/71491.aspx)

Learn a technique for printing reports programmatically using the Reporting Services XML Web service and C#.

CHAPTER 10

Reporting for Windows Forms applications

Reporting is an integral part of every complete Windows-based application. Yet, providing comprehensive reporting capabilities in these applications has often proved to be a tedious chore. Microsoft Reporting Services helps developers to report-enable their Windows Forms (WinForm) applications.

In this chapter, we will discuss practical techniques that can help you integrate your WinForm applications with RS. Our discussion will include the following topics:

- Report-enabling rich clients
- Client-to-Report Server reporting
- Client-to-Façade-to-Report Server reporting
- Techniques for enhancing an application's performance

To show you how these pieces fit together, this chapter provides a complete end-to-end example: the AWC Report Wizard. This tool empowers the employees of our fictitious company, Adventure Works Cycle, to generate standard reports.

10.1 RICH CLIENT WANTED

Windows Forms applications are often referred to as "rich" clients. This term emphasizes the fact that this type of application enjoys the full feature set of the operating system on which it runs. The main characteristics of a rich client are as follows:

- Feature-rich UI, including drag and drop, toolbars and menus, animation, and so on
- Easier to implement than its web-based counterpart—Implementing rich client features in web-based applications could be difficult if not impossible.
- Unrestricted security permissions—When installed locally, WinForm applications enjoy unrestricted permissions, while web-based applications and downloaded controls are usually "sandboxed."
- Access to all hardware resources and peripherals, such as drives, printers, scanners, and ports

NOTE Although locally installed WinForm .NET applications are granted unrestricted permissions by default, the administrator can control the permitted operations granted to their code by using code access security policies, as we explained in chapter 8.

Based on my experience, however, many organizations shy away from designing homegrown solutions as WinForm applications. Instead, they usually opt for web-based designs. Why is that, considering all the advantages that the rich client model has to offer? There are a few good reasons, but the top one I hear is the difficult deployment model. WinForm applications usually have binary dependencies to other system or third-party libraries. For this reason, they need to be explicitly installed on the client machine.

In the past, this has led to many problems, including the notorious "DLL Hell" phenomenon, where a rogue installation program replaces system files, which in turn, causes one or more existing applications to stop working. To further complicate the matter, after the application is rolled out to the end users, some infrastructure has to be set up to handle the application updates, such as bug fixes and new versions.

The Microsoft .NET Framework introduces several new features aimed at simplifying the WinForm application deployment, such as web-based deployment, versioning, and side-by-side execution. Expect these features to improve in the next versions of Windows and .NET. For example, the forthcoming release of Visual Studio .NET, code-named Whidbey, will feature the "ClickOnce" deployment model. It will allow us to create rich clients that can automatically update themselves from a central web location. For this reason, I predict that the pendulum will start swinging back in the near future and the rich client will take the place it deserves.

10.1.1 Report-enabling rich clients

Let's now see how what we learned in chapter 9 applies to report-enabling WinForm clients. As you would recall, in chapter 9 we said that RS offers two options for requesting reports. First, you can requests reports by URL. This is the simplest and easiest way to request reports. Second, when URL access is impractical, you can request reports by SOAP. The main characteristic of the second access option is the increased feature set accessible via a wide spectrum of SOAP APIs that goes beyond requesting reports only.

These two access options map to the two application design models that we discussed in chapter 8 in the following ways:

- *Client-to-Report Server*—With this model, the client application requests reports by URL via direct access to the Report Server.
- *Client-to-Façade-to-Report Server*—With this model, an additional layer, which we will call a *façade*, is introduced between the client and the Report Server. The façade submits report requests on the server side of the application by calling the RS Web service.

When evaluating both patterns, I recommend that you consider the Client-to-Report Server model first. In hindsight, if there is one thing that my consulting career has taught me, it is to keep things simple, unless there is a good reason to deviate from the KIS principle (Keep It Simple). Translated to WinForm reporting this means that you should

- Request reports by URL whenever possible
- Take advantage of the Report Server role-based security model whenever possible

My advice is to avoid the temptation to make your reporting architecture too flexible and sophisticated. As usual, there is a delicate balance between flexibility and complexity. If you focus on the side of flexibility, you may end up with an over-engineered solution with a reduced reporting feature set.

Let's now examine how the Client-to-Report Server reporting model can be applied to WinForm applications.

10.1.2 Using the Client-to-Report Server model

The Client-to-Report Server model can be used with both client/server and distributed application designs. Yes, the latter case doesn't necessarily invalidate requesting reports by URL.

For example, if the client needs to evaluate some business rules before the report is submitted, it could ask the business layer to do so and, if the validation is successful, request the report on the client side, as shown in figure 10.1.

There are good reasons to keep things simple and favor the Client-to-Report Server model, including the following:

- *Easy integration with RS*—You don't need to take extra steps to handle report images, report sessions, and presenting the report to the end user.
- *The HTML Viewer*—As we mentioned in the previous chapter, when reports are requested by URL, they are rendered inside the HTML Viewer, which sponsors

the handy report toolbar. The HTML Viewer can simplify some mundane reporting tasks, such as handling parameters, exporting to different formats, zooming, and so on.

- *Support of all interactive features*—URL access preserves all interactive report features when reports are exported to HTML because most of the interactive features, such as expandable sections, document maps, and toggled visibility, require additional HTTP-GET requests.
- *Faster performance*—No additional overhead is incurred to serialize the report payload to a binary array and render the report on the client side.

In terms of security, the Client-to-Report Server design fits naturally into the role-based security model of the Report Server. If restricted report access is required, the administrator can assign the Windows user accounts and groups to RS roles and establish security policies to secure items in the report catalog. We discussed the role-based security model in detail in chapter 8.

One thing that you should be cautious about is performing security checks inside the presentation layer. An adept user could figure out the report's URL and request the report directly in the browser, bypassing the presentation layer. Instead, for applications with stringent security requirements, you should consider the following approaches:

- Using the security techniques based on user identity, such as the ones we discussed in chapter 8—For example, your report can pass the interactive user identity obtained from the User.UserID property to the data source to filter data per user
- Using custom code in your reports to access the application business logic layer for business rules validation, as shown in figure 10.1
- Migrating to the Client-to-Façade-to-Report Server model

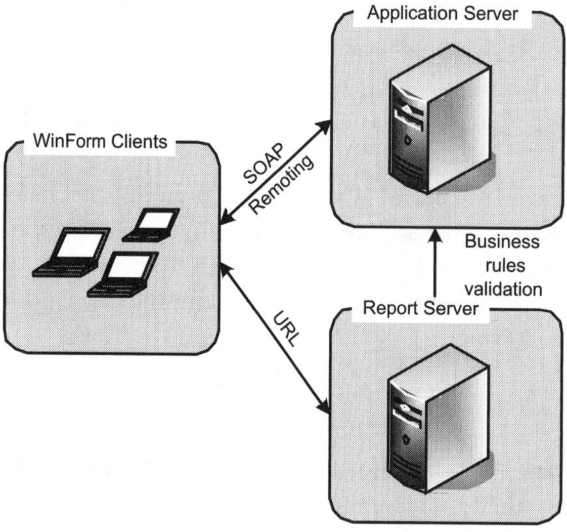

Figure 10.1 The WinForm version of the Client-to-Report Server model promotes requesting reports by URL.

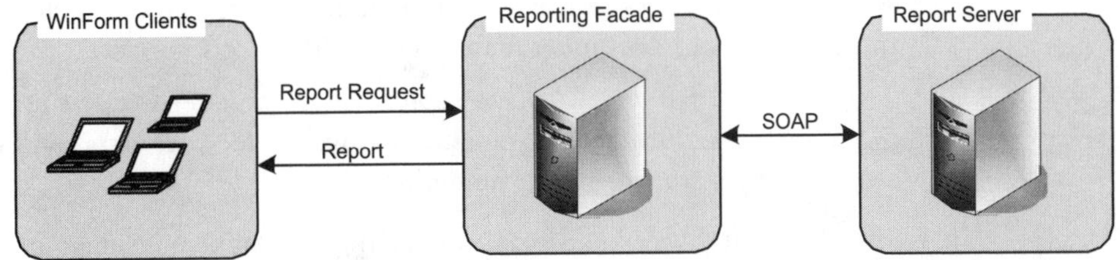

Figure 10.2 In the Client-to-Façade-to-Report Server model a façade layer is introduced between the client and the Report Server for business rules validation, security, and other reasons.

Sometimes, things are more complicated, and the Client-to-Report Server model may not be a good fit. If this is the case, you can use the Client-to-Façade-to-Report Server model with WinForm clients.

10.1.3 Using the Client-to-Façade-to-Report Server model

Consider using the Client-to-Façade-to-Report Server model in these situations:

- *When a level of indirection is required between the client and the Report Server*—For example, an additional layer may be needed to support multiple report providers, including RS, as we will discuss in chapter 13.
- *When server-side reporting is needed*—For example, with distributed applications, reports may need to be generated off application datasets available on the server side. For instance, you may want to generate a report in the business layer from a dataset retrieved from the application data layer using the custom dataset extension, which we will create in chapter 15.
- *When the role-based security model is not a good fit*—For example, the report request needs to pass some business rules validation, or a custom security authentication is required.

Figure 10.2 depicts the Client-to-Façade-to-Report Server model.

We use the term *façade* broadly to denote the layer that sits between the client and the Report Server. This façade may represent the application business layer or may be implemented as a designated service layer that "wraps" the Report Server. The WinForm client submits a report request to the Reporting Façade, which, in turn, requests the report via SOAP from the Report Server.

While the main advantage of this model is flexibility, it introduces some challenges, including the following:

- *Additional development effort*—Because reports generated by SOAP don't include the HTML Viewer, the application is responsible for taking care of all chores associated with requesting reports, such as collecting and validating parameters, handling report images and export formats, and so on.

- *Reduced interactive feature set*—All interactive report features, such as drilldown, drillthrough, and document maps rely on URL access.
- *Less efficient than the Client-to-Report Server model*—Requesting reports by SOAP incurs performance degradation, as well as requires extra steps on the presentation layer side for report rendering.

In terms of security, we would recommend that you take advantage of the Report Server role-based security to simplify user authentication and authorization if possible. To accomplish this, the Reporting Façade could impersonate the user and pass the user's identity to the Report Server. When using RS role-based security is not possible, the façade could be responsible for user authentication and authorization. In this case, the Report Server could be configured to grant the façade's identity a restricted set of permissions, such as report viewing only.

In most cases, the application's requirements will dictate the choice of the reporting model. In some cases, however, it may be more practical to support both models. This is the approach that our sample application, the AWC Report Wizard, will take. It defaults to requesting reports following the Client-to-Report Server model, but it allows the administrator to selectively configure reports to be generated following the Client-to-Façade-to-Report Server pattern.

10.2 INTRODUCING THE ADVENTURE WORKS REPORT WIZARD

Here is our hypothetical scenario for this chapter. You have been tasked to report-enable the next version of one of the Adventure Works line-of-business WinForm applications. To make our report-integration task more interesting, we will assume that this application is implemented as a typical distributed application, with presentation, business, and data layers. For the sake of simplicity, we will not be interested in the application specifics. Instead, we will scope our work to enhancing the application to generate the sample reports we authored in chapter 4.

After evaluating the user's requirements, you've proposed a reporting solution based on, you guessed it, Reporting Services. Here are the RS features that the Adventure Works Report Wizard sample demonstrates:

- Retrieving a list of reports from the report catalog
- Determining the report execution options-live or snapshot reports
- Working with custom properties
- Requesting snapshot reports and working with snapshot history
- Obtaining the report parameters
- Authoring reports with multi-value parameters
- Retrieving the supported export formats by the Report Server
- Requesting reports by URL and RS Web service

10.2.1 Designing the Report Wizard

The Report Wizard demo can be launched from the Chapter10 main menu in the AWReporterWin project. As a prerequisite for running the Report Wizard, you need to upload the book's sample reports to the Report Server. As usual, before discussing the actual implementation of our sample, we will start with defining the user requirements and high-level design goals.

Defining application requirements

Our hypothetical application is based on the following high-level reporting requirements:

- Provide an intuitive, user-friendly tool for generating standard reports on demand.
- Implement the tool as a "wizard," which will walk the user through a series of steps to collect the details of the report request and generate the report.
- Support both client-side (Client-to-Report Server) and server-side (Client-to-Façade-to-Report Server) report request options. By default, the reports will be requested and rendered on the client side by URL. However, some reports may require business rules validation that needs to be performed on the server side. In this case, the report administrator should be able to configure the report to be generated on the server-side of the application by SOAP.
- Allow the user to generate both snapshots and live reports.
- Wherever needed, customize the RS report parameter features to provide additional functionality, such as client-side parameter validation and multi-select parameters.
- Leverage the existing Active Directory user and group setup to enforce restricted access using the Report Server role-based security model.
- Process report requests efficiently by taking advantage of performance enhancement techniques, such as caching and multithreading.

Undestanding the workflow of the application

As you've seen, RS provides a plethora of report execution and rendering options. For example, reports can be cached as snapshots. They could accept parameters and could be exported to different formats that support various device settings.

While the rich feature set of RS is great in terms of flexibility, it may present additional challenges for application developers. How would you tell the user that the report is configured to be executed as a snapshot? How would you handle report parameters? What if you need to check some business rules on the server side of the application before submitting the report request? How would you generate larger reports more efficiently? The challenge is to implement a user-friendly and flexible application layer that will allow the end users to select the right report options and submit report requests easily.

For these reasons, we decided to implement the Report Wizard. Instead of providing the users with intimidating choices, the Report Wizard will be "smart" enough to evaluate the user's selection and branch the program logic to the right step accordingly.

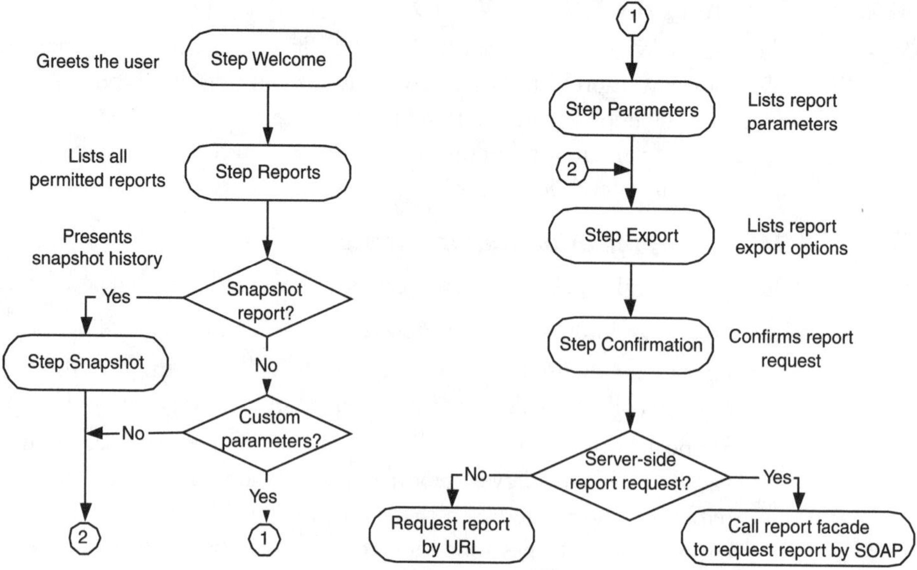

Figure 10.3 The Report Wizard walks the user through a series of steps to generate the report.

Figure 10.3 shows the workflow that the Report Wizard follows to request a report.

The Report Wizard workflow encompasses the following steps:

Step 1 WELCOME Greets the end user.

Step 2 REPORTS Allows the user to select a report to run.

Step 3 SNAPSHOT For snapshot reports, gives the user an option to run the report as a snapshot or pick a specific version from the snapshot history.

Step 4 PARAMETERS If the report is configured for custom parameters, handles the report parameters.

Step 5 EXPORT Allows the user to specify the report export format and additional device settings.

Step 6 CONFIRMATION Asks the user to confirm the report request. If the report is configured for server-side execution, gives the user an option to submit the report request asynchronously.

Now, let's discuss the purpose of each step and how it fits in the workflow process shown in figure 10.3.

10.2.2 The Report Wizard step-by-step

As with many wizard-like applications, the Report Wizard sponsors an easy-to-navigate user interface that allows the user to advance to the next step or move backwards to the previous step.

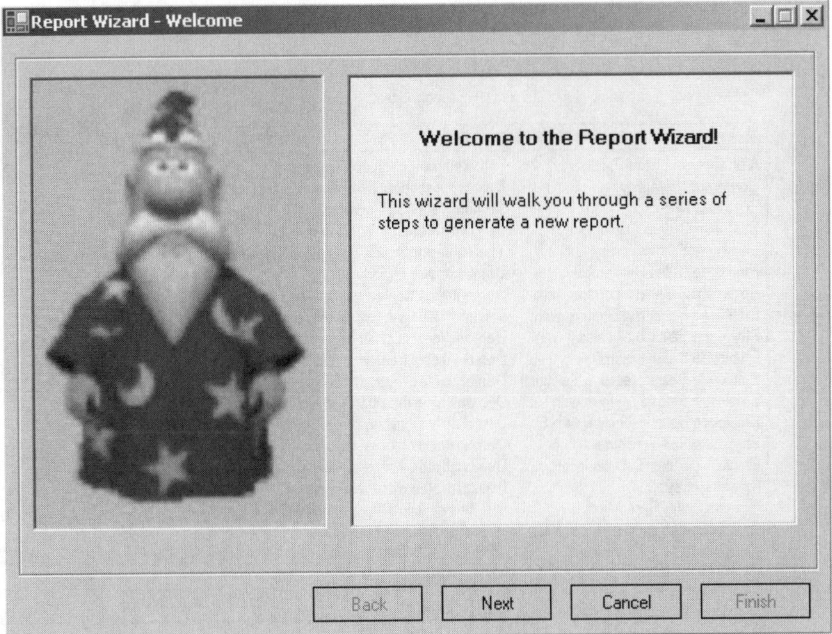

Figure 10.4 Step Welcome greets the user.

Step Welcome

This step is the familiar greeting step, as shown in figure 10.4.

From an implementation standpoint, this is by far the easiest step! No, Merlin is not animated.

Step Reports

This step lists all reports that the user is permitted to request based on the predefined Report Server role-based security policy, as shown in figure 10.5.

The successful outcome of this step is the selection of a single report. The Report Wizard then evaluates the selected report to determine whether it is configured for a snapshot or for live execution. In the former case, Step Snapshot is shown. In the latter case, the Report Wizard checks to see whether the report requires custom parameters. If so, Step Parameters is shown; otherwise, the Report Wizard advances to Step Export.

Step Snapshot

If the report is configured for snapshot execution, this step allows the user to specify the snapshot execution options, as shown in figure 10.6.

If the snapshot history is enabled, the user can request a specific history to be run from the Snapshot History grid. Alternatively, the user can select the Run the Report as a Snapshot option to request the latest snapshot cached copy of the report.

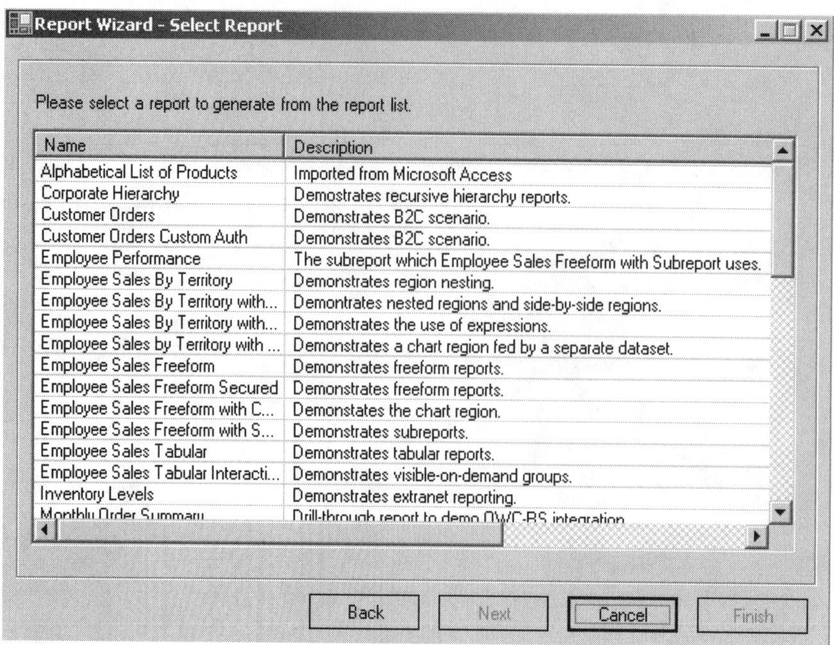

Figure 10.5 Step Reports prompts the user to select a report.

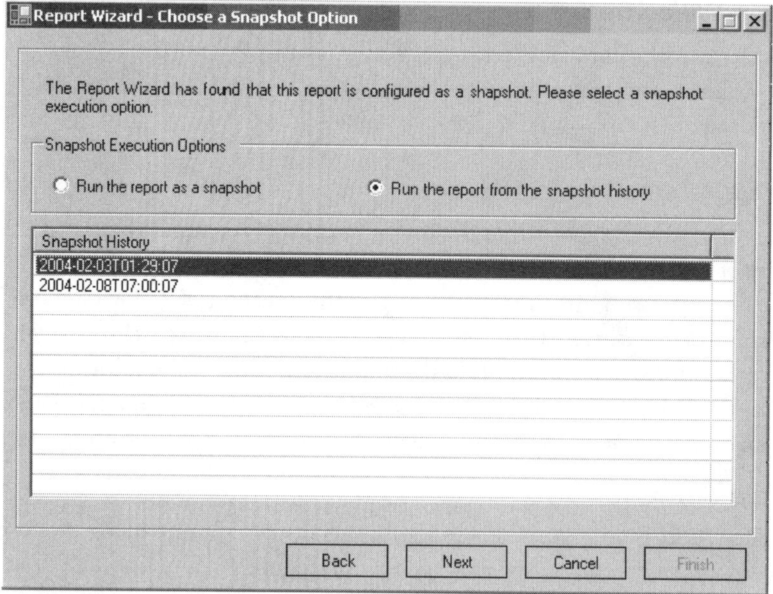

Figure 10.6 If the report is configured for snapshot execution, Step Snapshot allows the user to select a specific history run.

Step Parameters

As we said in chapter 9, sometimes the HTML Viewer toolbar may fall short in handling more involved report parameter requirements. The trivial workaround is to delegate this responsibility to the application. In our case, the Report Wizard will handle the report parameters in these situations:

- *When the report is configured explicitly to require custom parameters*—For example, one of the report parameters may be a multi-select parameter. In other cases, client-side parameter validation may be required.
- *When the report is configured to be requested on the server side of the application, for example, from the business layer*—Because in this case the report will be requested via SOAP, the HTML Viewer won't be available. Therefore, the application has to take care of gathering and validating the report parameters.

The Report Wizard handles the report parameters in Step Parameters (shown in figure 10.7).

Step Parameters supports custom parameter data types, such as multi-select, as well as optional client-side validation. For example, as figure 10.7 shows, the report in this case takes an Employee multi-select parameter, which is a feature that is currently not supported by the HTML Viewer.

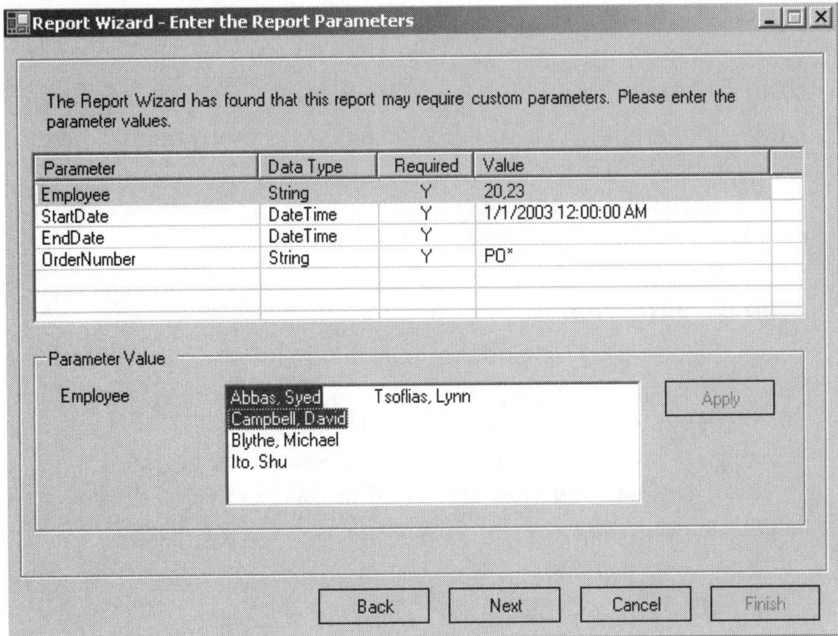

Figure 10.7 Step Parameters handles the report parameters when the HTML Viewer is not enough.

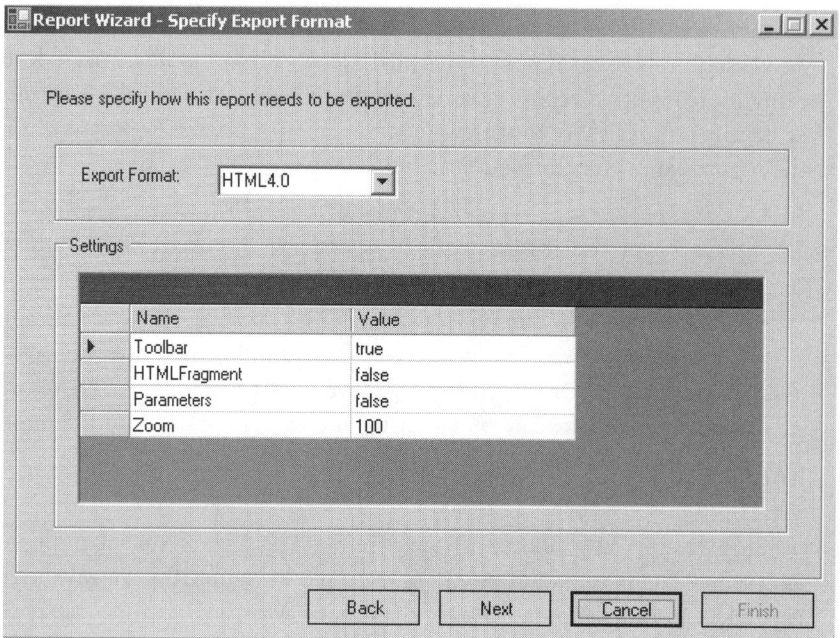

Figure 10.8 Step Export prompts the user to specify the export format and device settings.

Step Export

During this step, the user specifies the report's export format and device settings, as shown in figure 10.8.

We discussed the available export format and device settings in chapters 6 and 9, respectively.

Step Confirmation

Once the report request is ready, the only thing left to do is to ask the user to confirm it before it is handed out to the Report Server by showing Step Confirmation (figure 10.9).

If the report is configured to be requested on the server side of the application, the Report Wizard gives the user an option to request the report to be generated asynchronously.

Now that we've seen how the Adventure Works Report Wizard works, let's look behind the scenes to see how it is implemented.

10.3 BEHIND THE SCENES OF THE ADVENTURE WORKS REPORT WIZARD

We thought that many of you might appreciate a behind-the-scenes tour, especially if your reporting requirements call for a similar implementation approach.

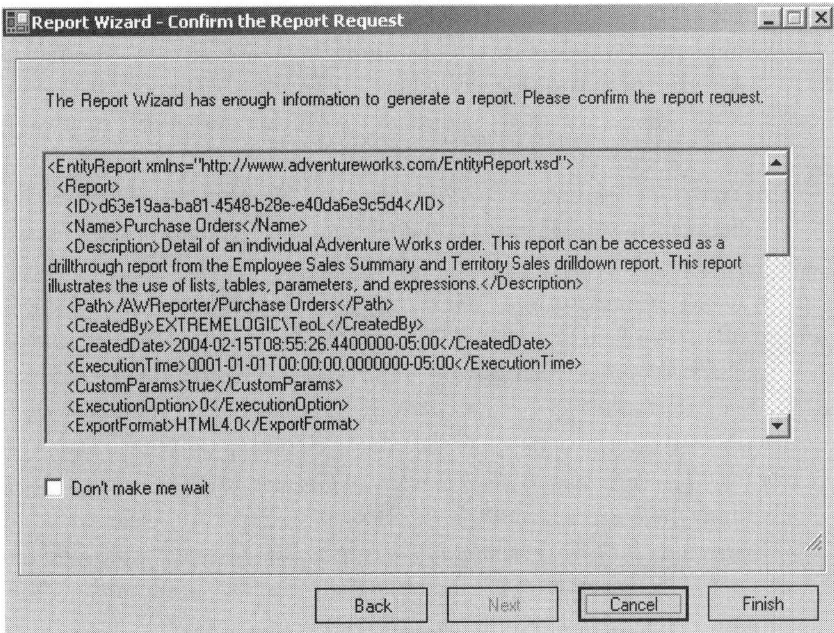

Figure 10.9 Confirming the report request

As an added bonus, we hope you will find some useful programming techniques that you can add to your programming arsenal, such as form inheritance, CodeDom code generation, dynamic control creation, caching, multithreading, and more.

10.3.1 Implementing the application framework

As with any real-life application, it is always a good idea to spend some time up front and design a framework layer to take care of essential programming aspects, including storing and passing data among the application tiers and encapsulating common programming logic in a set of reusable classes.

Let's see how the Report Wizard framework handles these programming tasks.

Choosing the data entity

The Report Wizard stores the report request details in an application-defined structure called ReportEntity that is located under the Entities folder in the AWReporterWin project. We use this entity for two purposes: to maintain state by capturing the user choices as the user navigates from one step to another and to encapsulate the report request details when submitting the request to the report façade in the case of reports generated on the server side of the application.

As with any custom structure, we have several implementation options. You have probably used several of them in the past, including custom classes, arrays, XML, datasets, and so forth. We decided to use a typed dataset for the following reasons:

- *Typed datasets are based on XML schemas.* This could be useful if you need to implement a report façade on top of RS. Using an XML schema allows you to advertise to the outside world how the façade needs to be called. In this case, the XML schema serves as a contract to which external callers must adhere when submitting report requests.
- *Typed datasets are serializable structures.* When a typed dataset is transmitted between two application domains, the .NET Framework serializes it automatically to XML.
- *Unlike the plain-vanilla datasets, typed datasets are strongly typed structures.* This offers two benefits. First, calls to the typed dataset methods and properties are checked and verified during the code-compilation phase. Second, developers can access the typed dataset members in an object-oriented way, for example, Report.Path, as opposed to ds.Tables["Report"].Columns["Path"].
- *Typed datasets support all of the dataset functionality.* Because typed datasets inherit from the System.Data.DataSet class, they support all dataset features, including searching for rows, tracking row changes, data relations, nulls, and so on. In addition, typed datasets can be bound to controls that support data binding.

NOTE During one of my project assignments, there was a fierce discussion about which approach reigns supreme when it comes to passing data between the application tiers: custom-defined entity classes or typed datasets. By the time I joined the project, the jury had already sentenced typed datasets for execution and had decided in favor of custom classes.

Subsequently, the client realized the complexities surrounding custom entity implementation, for example, handing of nulls, serialization, data binding, and so on, and admitted that they were well on their way to reinvent the typed dataset wheel. Some bridges were burned but, in the end, the architect's decision was reversed and typed datasets were reinstated. The moral of this story is that you should evaluate typed datasets as a medium to pass data between the application tiers before you decide on homegrown solutions.

Typed datasets are not perfect and are subject to several limitations, including these:

- *Typed datasets are regenerated when the schema is saved.* Each time you change and save the schema, VS.NET regenerates the typed dataset. This makes it impractical to add extra members and methods to the typed dataset because they will be wiped out if someone inadvertently updates the schema. One workaround is to subclass the typed dataset class, but this has its own complexities too.
- *You have little control over the typed dataset generation process.* For example, a typed dataset defines the table columns as internal, which makes them inaccessible if the typed dataset is defined in an external assembly.

Let's now see how the Report Wizard uses typed datasets to capture the report request details.

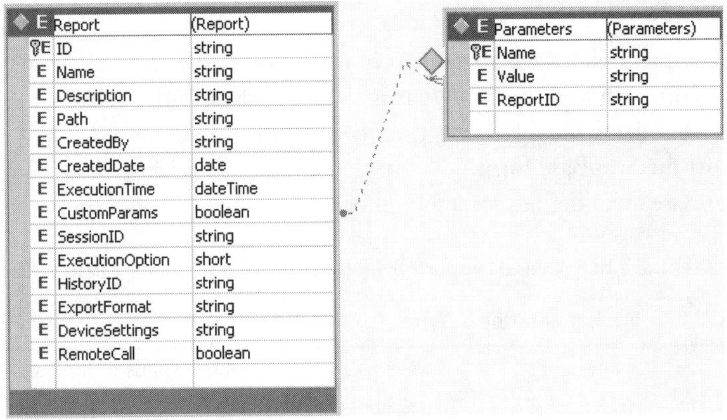

Figure 10.10 The report request details are captured in a ReportEntity type dataset.

Implementing the report entity

Figure 10.10 shows the ReportEntity XML schema, which we generated using the VS.NET XML Schema Editor.

The schema consists of two elements: Report and Parameters. The Report element has the same attributes as the Report Server CatalogItem structure that the `ListChildren` web method returns. We defined some extra attributes for the Report Wizard's purposes, as shown in table 10.1.

Table 10.1 ReportEntity exposes a series of properties to capture the report request details.

Name	Type	Description
CustomParams	Boolean	Defines whether the report requires custom parameters
SessionID	String	Stores the report session ID, when the report is requested via SOAP
ExecutionOption	Short	Corresponds to the RS ExecutionSettingEnum enumeration and stores the report execution option (0-live, 1-snapshot)
HistoryID	String	Stores the history ID if the user has selected to run a snapshot history (snapshot reports only)
ExportFormat	String	Stores the requested export format, e.g., HTML4.0
DeviceSettings	String	Captures the user-specified device settings, e.g., Toolbar=true, Parameters=false, etc.
RemoteCall	Boolean	False, if the report is configured for client-side generation; true, if the report is configured for server-side generation

The second schema element, Parameters, captures the report parameters. The relation defines the one-to-many relation between the Reports element and the Parameters element.

Once we decided on a data entity strategy, the next step was to refactor some common programming logic that all Report Wizard steps need.

The StepBase form

Because all steps of the wizard share a common look and features, it makes sense to refactor the common logic and move it into a base class. Indeed, each step of the wizard, which we collectively refer to as the *step forms*, is implemented as a WinForm that inherits from the StepBase form.

The StepBase form defines several members, including the ones shown in table 10.2.

Table 10.2 StepBase has several properties (accessors) that all steps will inherit.

Member	Implementation	Type	Description
IsValid	Property	Boolean	Returns the status of the step validation. True, if the step is valid. Some steps require validation. For example, if a report defines custom parameters, validation is required to ensure that all required parameters have been filled in. Before the Report Wizard loads a new step, it calls IsValid to find out whether the step is valid.
Result	Property	Object	Returns the step results. A step may return some data to the ReportWizard form. For example, Step Reports return the selected report.
WizForm	Property	ReportWizard	Returns a reference to the ReportWizard form. Used by the step forms to invoke the Report Wizard's members.
OnStatusChanged	Event		Raised by the step forms. The Report Wizard uses this event to configure its UI, e.g., to enable or disable the navigation buttons.

The StepBase form is implemented as a borderless form (FormBorderStyle=None) so that its descendants can be seamlessly "docked" to the GroupBox control (grpStep) placed on the ReportWizard form.

When the user advances to the next step by clicking the Next button, the Report Wizard calls the `LoadStep` function (shown in listing 10.1), located inside the ReportWizard form.

Listing 10.1 Using the factory design pattern to load the steps of the wizard.

```
private void LoadStep () {
 StepBase frm = null;
 switch (m_nextStep)  {
   case WizStep.Welcome   : frm = new StepWelcome(); break;
   case WizStep.Reports   : frm = new StepReports();break;
   case WizStep.Snapshots   : frm = new StepSnapshot();break;
   case WizStep.Parameters   : frm = new StepParameters();break;
   case WizStep.Export   : frm = new StepExport();break;
   case WizStep.Confirmation:frm = new StepConfirmation();break;
```

```
    }
                                          Sites the
                                          step form
    frm.TopLevel = false;
    frm.Parent = this.grpStep;
    frm.Location = new Point (2, 10);
    frm.Show();
    // unload the previous step                     Unloads the
    if (grpStep.Controls.Count>1)  {                previous step
      StepBase oldStep = (StepBase) grpStep.Controls[0];
      oldStep.Close();
    }
  }
```

Because all step forms inherit from StepBase, the Report Wizard instantiates the steps through a reference to the StepBase base class. Then, the Report Wizard sites the form by hooking it to the group box container located inside StepBase and sets the group box as the form parent. Next, the Report Wizard positions the form within the GroupBox control. Finally, it unloads the previous step.

The ReportWizard form

The Report Wizard follows the factory design pattern for loading and executing the report-generation steps. You can think of it as a controller that orchestrates the report request's workflow. The Report Wizard supports backward and forward step navigation. For navigating backwards, the Report Wizard maintains the step chain history in the form of a stack collection. When the user advances to the next step, the Report Wizard follows this process:

Step 1 Calls the StepBase virtual `IsValid` method, which the step can override to provide a step-specific validation.

Step 2 Retrieves and stores the step results.

Step 3 Determines the next step to be executed.

Step 4 Loads the next step.

For the developer's convenience, the Report Wizard exposes the ReportEntity object through a series of public properties, shown in table 10.3.

Table 10.3 The Report Wizard forms public properties that the step forms can query.

Member	Type	Description
Reports	EntityReport	Returns a list of reports. Once Step Reports is executed, the Report Wizard stores the report list in a instance of the ReportEntity object.
SelectedReport	EntityReport.ReportRow	Returns a reference to the report selected by the user in Step Reports.
ReportRequest	EntityReport	Clones and returns the selected report.

Each step form can reference these properties to access the data it needs from the ReportEntity object. For example, a step can call SelectedReport to obtain a reference to the report selected in Step Reports.

10.3.2 Selecting reports

Step Reports presents the user with a list of reports. The user has to select exactly one report to advance to the next step. The abbreviated form code to retrieve the report list is shown in listing 10.2.

Listing 10.2 Step Reports retrieves the reports that the user has the rights to run by calling the RS `ListChildren` API.

```
private void GetReports()
{
  ReportingService rs = RsHelpers.Proxy;
  CatalogItem[] items = null;
  EntityReport entityReports = WizForm.Reports;

  items = rs.ListChildren(reportPath, false);        <-- (1) Retrieves the catalog resources in the specified folder

  foreach (CatalogItem item in items){      <-- (2) Populates the report entity with the reports
    if (item.Type == ItemTypeEnum.Report)
      entityReports.Report.AddReportRow(item.ID, item.Name, item.Descrip-
tion,
      item.Path, item.CreatedBy, item.CreationDate,
      item.ExecutionDate, false, null, -1, null, null, null, false);
    }

  // pass the reports to the Report Wizard form         (3) Loads the reports in the ListView control
  WizForm.Reports = entityReports;
  foreach (EntityReport.ReportRow reportRow in entityReports.Report){  <--
    ListViewItem reportItem = new ListViewItem();
    reportItem.Text = reportRow.Name;
    reportItem.SubItems.Add(reportRow.Description);
    reportItem.SubItems.Add(reportRow.CreatedBy);
    reportItem.SubItems.Add(reportRow.CreatedDate.ToString());
    reportItem.Tag = reportRow.ID;
    lstReports.Items.Add (reportItem);
  }
}
```

We'll discuss a few implementation areas of Step Reports in more detail in the next few sections.

Retrieving the report list

(1) The list of reports is retrieved in the `GetReports` function via a call to the Report Server `ListChildren()` web method. As we mentioned back in chapter 8, the `ListChildren` method factors in the Report Server role-based security policy.

Therefore, if the user is not permitted to view a given report, the report will be excluded from the results. The `ListChildren` method returns all catalog items associated with the specified folder as a collection of CatalogItem objects. Each catalog item exposes a number of reserved properties, such as the item name, path, and so on.

❷ Next, we filter out only the report items from the CatalogItem collection and store them in an instance of the ReportEntity object.

❸ Finally, we populate the ListView control with the reports to show them to the user.

NOTE Why did I choose the ListView control over the Windows Forms DataGrid control? In the latter case, I could have just bound the typed dataset to the grid instead of iterating through the report items again. At first, this was the approach I intended to take. All went well until I wanted to disallow the default multirow selection. It turns out that this wasn't easy and required subclassing the grid control and overriding the mouse events. At this point, I thought that this would be overkill for the purposes of my demo and decided to switch to the plain-old ListView control. If you use a third-party grid control, which doesn't have the Windows grid limitations, by all means use data binding to simplify the presentation logic.

The rest of the code logic in this form is straightforward. The form validation rules consist of checking whether a report item is selected in the grid. Finally, the step returns the report identifier of the selected report.

Once the user clicks the Next button, the control returns to the Report Wizard form.

Retrieving the report details

Now that the user has selected the report, the Report Wizard needs to retrieve the report details to find out which form to display next. Listing 10.3 shows the abbreviated code from the "Next" programming logic applicable to Step Reports.

Listing 10.3 Evaluating the report selection

```
m_selectedReport = (EntityReport.ReportRow)
m_entityReports.Report.Rows.Find((string) result);
                                              Retrieves the report
GetReportProperties(m_selectedReport.ID);  <-- custom properties

if (m_selectedReport.ExecutionOption==-1) {  <-- Is this a snapshot report?
  executionOption = GetReportExecutionOption(m_selectedReport.Path);
  m_selectedReport.ExecutionOption = (short) executionOption;
  m_selectedReport.AcceptChanges();
}

switch (executionOption) {
  case ExecutionSettingEnum.Snapshot  : m_nextStep = WizStep.Snapshots;
break;
```

```
  case ExecutionSettingEnum.Live     : {
    if (HasCustomParameters())
      m_nextStep = WizStep.Parameters;
    else
      m_nextStep = WizStep.Export;
    break;
  }

private void GetReportProperties (string reportID){
  // Set the item namespace header to be GUID-based
  m_reportService.ItemNamespaceHeaderValue = new ItemNamespaceHeader();
  m_reportService.ItemNamespaceHeaderValue.ItemNamespace =
        ItemNamespaceEnum.GUIDBased;
  Property[] properties = null;
  Property[] props = new Property[2];
  props[0] = new Property();
  props[0].Name = CUSTOM_PARAMS;
  props[1] = new Property();
  props[1].Name = REMOTE_CALL;

  properties = m_reportService.GetProperties(reportID, props);

  if (properties.Length > 0) {
   foreach (Property property in properties) {
      switch (property.Name) {
        case CUSTOM_PARAMS: m_selectedReport.CustomParams = true; break;
        case REMOTE_CALL :
         if (property.Value.ToLower() == "true")    {
           m_selectedReport.RemoteCall = Boolean.Parse(property.Value);
           break;
        }
      } // end switch
   } // end foreach
  } // end if
  else m_selectedReport.CustomParams = m_selectedReport.RemoteCall = false;

  m_selectedReport.AcceptChanges();
}

private ExecutionSettingEnum GetReportExecutionOption (string report) {
  ScheduleDefinitionOrReference scheduleDefinition = null;
  ExecutionSettingEnum result = ExecutionSettingEnum.Live;

  result =  m_reportService.GetExecutionOptions(report,
            out scheduleDefinition);
  return result;
}
```

The Report Wizard defines two custom Boolean properties, custom parameters and remote invocation

Retrieves the report's execution options from the Report Server

The code starts by filtering out the selected report in the ReportEntity object. Next, we need to determine which properties have been defined for this report.

Using custom properties

After the Report Wizard gets the selected report, it calls the `GetReportProperties` function to find out whether the report has custom properties defined in the Report Server catalog. RS allows you to define custom properties on a per–catalog item basis. If you open the Catalog table in the RS Configuration Database (ReportServer), you will notice that there is a column named Property that you can use to associate any user-defined properties you need with a given catalog item.

NOTE You can use the Web service proxy `ItemNamespaceHeaderValue` property to retrieve the item's properties by either its identifier (primary key) or path. For some obscure reason, the `GetProperties` method is the only method available to support the `ItemNamespaceHeaderValue` proxy property. The rest of the web methods identify catalog items by their path only.

There are two restrictions to which user-defined properties are subject. First, because the properties are defined as an XML snippet, they have to conform to the rules of a well-formed XML document. Second, each property must be entered as a name-value pair. Nested properties are not supported.

The Report Server offers a pair of methods that you can use to manipulate the catalog item properties, as follows:

- *`GetProperties`*—Returns both reserved and user-defined properties. The reserved properties correspond to the properties of the CatalogItem class, which is returned from a call to `GetChildren`. Similarly to using a SQL WHERE clause to filter out the data at a database level, you can optionally pass a filter to the Report Server to get only a subset of the user-defined properties.
- *`SetProperties`*—Updates the catalog item properties.

Of course, you can update the Property column manually at your own risk. To do so, you need to scroll down in the Property cell for the given report and enter the new property element, abiding by the XML syntax rules. If you make errors in the property syntax, the call to the `GetProperties` method will fail. Once again, the recommended approach to making changes to the report catalog is through the SOAP API, which in this case is `SetProperties`.

For the purposes of the Report Wizard demo, we use a couple of custom properties, as shown in table 10.4.

Table 10.4 Reporting Services allows developers to associate custom properties with catalog items.

Property	Type	Purpose	Example
CustomParameters	Boolean	If CustomParameters is true, the Report Wizard will handle the report parameters.	<CustomParameters>True </CustomParameters>

continued on next page

Table 10.4 Reporting Services allows developers to associate custom properties with catalog items. ***(continued)***

Property	Type	Purpose	Example
RemoteCall	Boolean	If true, the report request process will follow the Client-to-Façade-to-Report Server pattern.	<RemoteCall>True</RemoteCall>

So, this is easy. If you need the Report Wizard to handle the report parameters for you, you can add a new `CustomParameters` property to the list of properties and set its value to True.

Similarly, if a given report needs to be generated by SOAP, you can add a `RemoteCall` property and set its value to true.

Once again, these are user-defined properties, so don't expect to find them in the product documentation or when you install the sample reports. Instead, you have to manually add them to the Property column of the report you need to test.

To help you configure the Report Wizard sample, we provided a script file (SetProperties.rss.), which you can find under the Chapter10 folder in the AWReporterWin project. To run the script, go to the command prompt and navigate to the folder where SetProperties.rss is located. Then, assuming that the Report Server is installed locally and the folder where the sample reports are located is called AWReporter, type the following command:

```
rs -i SetProperties.rss -s http://localhost/reportserver
-v folderPath="AWReporter"
```

The SetProperties script file calls the `SetProperties` SOAP API to configure the custom properties for two reports: `CustomParameters=True` for the Purchase Orders report and `RemoteCall=True` for the Employee Sales Freeform report.

The Report Wizard's `GetReportProperties` method calls the RS `GetProperties` SOAP API to find out if these properties are defined. If this is the case, it updates two flags in the Report Entity object. We will see in a moment how the Report Wizard utilizes these user-defined properties.

Determining the report's execution options

As we said in chapter 7, you can configure a report to be executed as a snapshot, in which case the Report Server saves the report's intermediate format (IF) in the RS Configuration Database and serves all subsequent requests using the cached instance. Because a snapshot represents a static capture of the report at a specific point in time, the Report Server doesn't allow you to pass report parameters because the snapshot already includes the parameterized data.

To determine the next step after Step Reports, the Report Wizard queries the Report Server to find out how the report is configured to be executed. Then, it saves the execution option in the ExecutionOption field of the ReportEntity object. If the report is configured for snapshot execution, the Report Wizard advances to Step Snapshot. If this is not the case and the report requires custom parameters, the Report Wizard proceeds with Step Parameters. If custom parameters are not required, for example, the HTML Viewer will be used, Step Parameters is bypassed and Step Export is shown.

Let's assume that the selected report is configured for snapshot execution. In this case, the Report Wizard will display Step Snapshot.

10.3.3 Dealing with snapshot reports

Step Snapshot allows the user to execute the report as a snapshot or to request a specific snapshot history run, if the report administrator has enabled the snapshot history option. In the latter case, the snapshot is retrieved via a call to the `ListReportHistory` SOAP API, as shown in listing 10.4.

Listing 10.4 If a report is configured for snapshot execution, the snapshot history can be obtained by calling the `ListReportHistory` API.

```
private void GetSnapshotHistory()  {
  ReportHistorySnapshot[] items = null;
  items = rs.ListReportHistory(WizForm.SelectedReport.Path);

  foreach (ReportHistorySnapshot item in items) {
   ListViewItem reportItem = new ListViewItem();
   reportItem.Text = item.HistoryID;
   lstSnapshotHistory.Items.Add (reportItem);
  }
}
```

Retrieves the snapshot history runs

Displays the snapshot history

The snapshot history is obtained via a call to the `ListReportHistory` web method and loaded in a ListView control. If the user selects a history snapshot, the Report Wizard saves the history identifier in the HistoryID field of the ReportEntity object.

Because a snapshot report can have only fixed parameter values, when the user clicks Next, the Report Wizard advances to Step Export.

If the report is not configured to be executed as a snapshot, which step will be shown next depends on whether the report is configured for custom parameters. If this is the case, Step Parameters is shown.

10.3.4 Handling report parameters

Handling report parameters on your own could be a tricky business. If your application design follows the Client-to-Report Server pattern and requests reports via URL, you should try whenever possible to delegate this responsibility to the HTML Viewer.

Your application will typically need to handle parameters by itself in the following scenarios:

- *The report is requested by SOAP*—As you know by now, when the report is requested by SOAP, the HTML Viewer is not rendered at all.

- *The HTML Viewer is not enough*—For example, when you need to handle multivalue parameters.
- The parameters need to be validated before the request is submitted

A good approach would be to use the HTML Viewer by default and treat the reports that require custom parameters as exceptions to the rule. This is the approach that the Report Wizard takes. Let's look at an example of a report that requires a multivalue parameter and therefore needs special attention.

Dealing with multivalue parameters

Let's say that the AWC Sales department has requested a report that shows the purchase orders by salesperson, date range, and order number. Figure 10.11 illustrates the Purchase Orders report.

The report itself is nothing to brag about. What makes it special is that it sponsors a multivalue Employee parameter. This allows the end user to type a comma-separated list of Employee identifiers to see the purchase orders submitted by multiple salespersons.

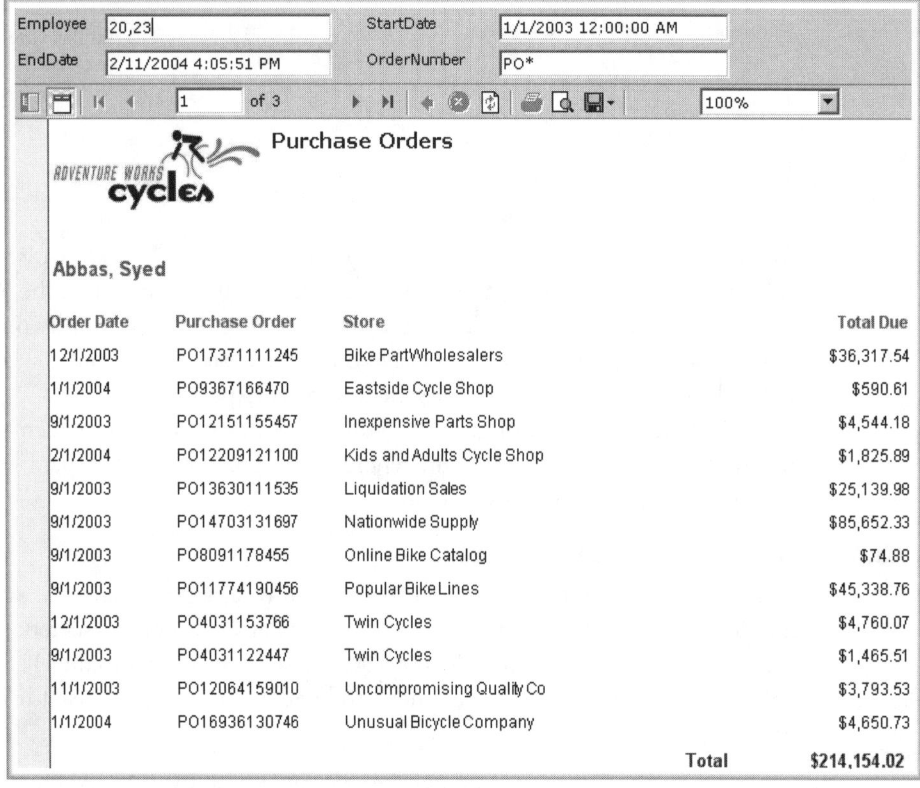

Order Date	Purchase Order	Store	Total Due
12/1/2003	PO17371111245	Bike PartWholesalers	$36,317.54
1/1/2004	PO9367166470	Eastside Cycle Shop	$590.61
9/1/2003	PO12151155457	Inexpensive Parts Shop	$4,544.18
2/1/2004	PO12209121100	Kids and Adults Cycle Shop	$1,825.89
9/1/2003	PO13630111535	Liquidation Sales	$25,139.98
9/1/2003	PO14703131697	Nationwide Supply	$85,652.33
9/1/2003	PO8091178455	Online Bike Catalog	$74.88
9/1/2003	PO11774190456	Popular Bike Lines	$45,338.76
12/1/2003	PO4031153766	Twin Cycles	$4,760.07
9/1/2003	PO4031122447	Twin Cycles	$1,465.51
11/1/2003	PO12064159010	Uncompromising Quality Co	$3,793.53
1/1/2004	PO16936130746	Unusual Bicycle Company	$4,650.73
		Total	$214,154.02

Figure 10.11 Handling custom parameters

To implement the multivalue Employee parameter, we need to base the report query on the following expression:

```
SELECT   Employee.EmployeeID, …
FROM     SalesOrderHeader LEFT OUTER JOIN Employee ON …
WHERE    EmployeeID IN (" & Parameters!Employee.Value & ")
AND      OrderDate BETWEEN '" & Parameters!StartDate.Value
         & "' AND '" & Parameters!EndDate.Value & "'
AND      PurchaseOrderNumber LIKE '" &
         Parameters!OrderNumber.Value.Replace("*", "%") & "'"
```

As you can see, we used the SQL IN operator to construct a `WHERE` criteria to filter the purchase orders for multiple salespersons. In addition, we used the SQL LIKE operator in the `WHERE` clause to support wildcards for the purchase order number.

The users can run this report as it is, but you will probably agree that the Employee parameter is not very intuitive. Users usually don't memorize employee identifiers. Instead, they may prefer the Employee parameter to show the salesperson's name. From an implementation standpoint, what is really needed is a lookup table for the Employee parameter to resolve the employee name to the employee identifier.

This is exactly where Step Parameters comes in because it can handle multivalue parameters. You can delegate the task of handing parameters to the Report Wizard by setting the CustomParameters property to true for a given report.

```
<Properties>
  <Language>en-US</Language>
  <!--other properties may appear here-->
  <CustomParameters>True</CustomParameters>
</Properties>
```

As we discussed before, the Report Wizard will query the report catalog for this property and, if found, will show Step Parameters.

There could be several approaches that you can use to handle custom parameters inside your applications. Which one will be most suitable will depend on your specific reporting requirements. I thought that it might be useful to share with you one possible design I have used in the past.

Using a database-driven approach to handle parameters

In this case, the parameter metadata is stored in the database. Figure 10.12 depicts what the database schema may look like.

The design goals of the database-driven approach are as follows:

- Store the parameter metadata in a database.
- Define custom parameter data types.
- Allow the client application's user interface to self-configure based on the parameter metadata.

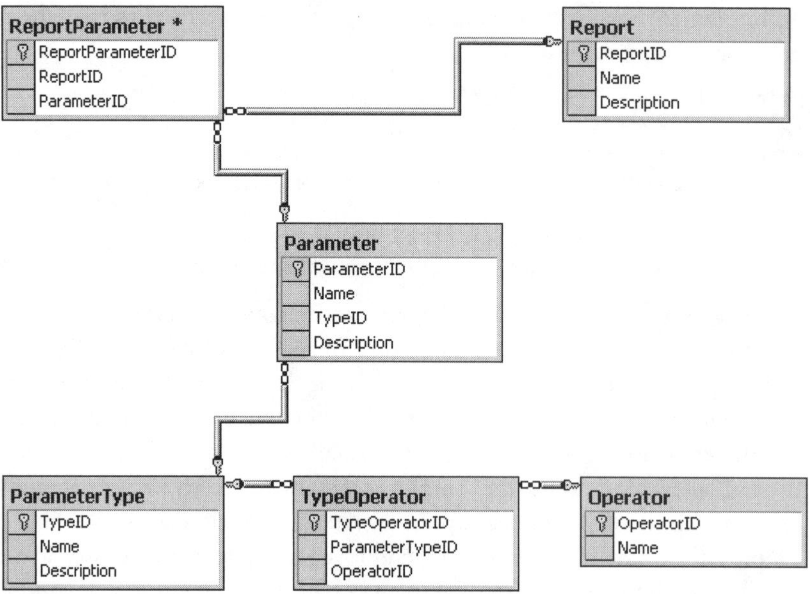

Figure 10.12 One approach to handling parameters in your applications is to store the parameter configuration in the database.

The idea behind the database-driven approach is simple. We want to allow the report administrator to be able to define custom parameter data types. For example, the Purchase Orders report requires a multi-select parameter. Given the model shown in figure 10.12, the report administrator could define a new data type called MultiSelect. Optionally, the administrator could define parameter operators that will be evaluated during the parameter validation. For example, if the parameter data type is DateTime, the report administrator could define a `BETWEEN` operator to enforce a business rule stating that the date entered by the user has to fall within a certain date range.

Once the parameter infrastructure is set, the client reporting application could adjust its user interface to handle the custom parameter types. For example, if the parameter is of the type MultiSelect, the front end might display a listbox control prepopulated with the available parameter values. Or, if the parameter type is DateTime, the application might display a DateTimePicker control.

The Report Wizard approach

For the purposes of the Report Wizard demo, we chose a lightweight version of the database-driven approach. To simplify the demo setup, we decided to use an XML configuration file (Parameters.xml) to store the custom parameters. Listing 10.5 shows what the configuration file might look like in the case of the employee multiselect parameter.

Listing 10.5 The Report Wizard parameter configuration file

```
<?xml version="1.0" encoding="utf-8" ?>
<reports>
  <report id="4b90f039-32db-464a-b6b6-97ba89856191">    <-- Links the parameters to a given report
    <customparameters>
      <parameter name="Employee" type="100">   <-- Defines a custom parameter type
        <availablevalues>
          <availablevalue value="20" label="Abbas, Syed"/>
          <availablevalue value="23" label="Campbell, David"/>
          <availablevalue value="38" label="Blythe, Michael"/>
          <availablevalue value="26" label="Ito, Shu"/>
          <availablevalue value="36" label="Tsoflias, Lynn"/>
        </availablevalues>
      </parameter>
    </customparameters>
    <validationCode>   <-- Defines the parameter validation rules
public static bool EvalParameters(System.Data.DataTable
                           parameters) {
 bool result = true;
 System.Data.DataRow row=parameters.Rows.Find("StartDate");
 DateTime startDate=Convert.ToDateTime(row["Value"].ToString());
 row = parameters.Rows.Find("EndDate");
 DateTime endDate = Convert.ToDateTime(row["Value"].ToString());
 if (startDate>endDate) {
     MessageBox.Show("The start date cannot ….");
     result = false;
 }
 return result;
}
    </validationCode>
  </report>
</reports>
```

RS defines an enumeration called ParameterTypeEnum that defines integer values for the five supported parameter types (System.String=4, System.DateTime=1, and so on). To integrate our custom-defined parameter types with the RS predefined types, we decided to define integer type identifiers starting with 100.

You may be tempted to use the available parameter values that you can set up using the Report Designer Report Parameters menu to populate the list of allowed choices for custom multivalue parameters. This approach could have been a good fit for lookup tables because the `GetReportParameters` web method returns both the parameter label and value fields. Unfortunately, it won't work because with version 1.0 of RS there is no way to disable the available values validation that the Report Server performs to match the parameter against the list of the available values. Let's explain this limitation in more detail.

Let's say you base the available values of the Employee parameter on a database query that returns EmployeeID and Name. Assuming that your application supports multivalue parameters, the request to render a report for a single salesperson will succeed because the Report Server will find a match for the employee identifier among the available values. However, a request for multiple employees (for example, "21, 23") will fail because an exact match does not exist. We hope the next version of RS will allow turning the validation off. For the time being, your application needs to take care of populating the lookup table, for example, by asking the business layer to supply the list. To simplify things, we hard-coded the lookup list inside the configuration file.

Configuring the user interface to handle custom parameters

The Report Wizard retrieves the report parameters by calling the `GetReport-Parameters` SOAP API of the RS Web service. Considering the limitations of parameter available values we just mentioned, in case you have configured the available values for a given parameter and if you want to use them, you can set the For-Rendering argument to true to get these values. `GetReportParameters` returns an array of ReportParameter objects. ReportParameter exposes a series of public properties you can query to determine how the parameters are configured. For the purposes of the Report Wizard, we are interested only in the parameter name, type, default value, and whether it is required.

Because we've decided that the HTML Viewer is getting in our way, our application needs to take its place and provide some sort of user interface that will self-adjust based on the parameter type. When the user selects a parameter, the Report Wizard configures the user interface in accordance with the parameter type, as shown in listing 10.6.

Listing 10.6 Configuring the user interface

```
private void ConfigureParameterPanel() {
  ListViewItem selectedParam = lstParameters.SelectedItems[0];
  System.Windows.Forms.Control control = null;
  lblParamName.Text = selectedParam.Text;

  short paramType = (short)GetParameterType(
     WizForm.SelectedReport.ID, selectedParam.Text);     <-- 1

  switch (paramType) {
   case (short) ParameterTypeEnum.DateTime:   {     <-- 2
    control = new DateTimePicker();
    //...
   }
   case PARAM_TYPE_MULTISELECT:     {     <-- 3
    // create a new ListView control to allow multi-select
    control = new ListView();
    ((ListView)control).View = View.List;
    ReportParameter reportParameter = GetParameter
                                  (selectedParam.Text);
    // Get the parameter valid values
```

1 Determines the parameter type

2 For the date type, we use the DateTimePicker control

3 For multivalue parameters, we use the ListView control

```
    ValidValue[] validValues = GetMultiParameterValues(
         WizForm.SelectedReport.ID, selectedParam.Text);

    //load the list view with the parameter valid values
    foreach(ValidValue validValue in validValues) {…}
   }
   default:    {     <-4 For all other data types, we use the TextBox control
    control = new TextBox();
    //…
    break;
}
  }

  pnlCustomParam.Controls.Clear();       <-5 Creates the control
  control.Parent = pnlCustomParam;           dynamically and positions
  //…                                        it on the panel
}
```

❶ First, we determine the parameter type by calling the `GetParameterType` function.

❷ If the parameter type is DateTime, we will present the user with the DateTimePicker control to enter the parameter value.

❸ If the parameter is a multi-value parameter, we load the parameter lookup values in a ListView control that allows multi-selection.

❹ For all other parameter types, we use a TextBox control.

❺ Finally, we create the control, place it on the pnlCustomParam, and size it appropriately.

At this point, the user interface is configured and the user can set the parameter value. Once the Apply button is clicked, the code needs to validate the parameter's value.

Validating parameters with custom validation rules

An essential chore when working with custom parameters is validating their values. While the HTML Viewer is limited to checking only the parameter data type before the report request is submitted, the Report Wizard can validate just about any business rule. For example, if you consider again the Purchase Orders report, you may need to ensure that the end date is greater than the start date.

The Report Wizard design goals applicable to custom parameter validation are as follows:

- Allow the report administrator to add ad hoc parameter validation rules.
- Store the rule logic in an external storage medium.
- Dynamically execute and evaluate the business rules.
- Do not require recompilation of the client application when new rules are added or existing rules have changed.

- Provide a flexible rule validation; for example, the rule may need to perform cross-parameter validation, call external assemblies, or in general perform all possible tasks that .NET code can do.

But where would you put the validation logic? Ideally, you would want to associate the validation rule with the parameter so that the Report Wizard could check the rule when evaluating the parameter's value. If you decide to follow the database-driven approach for the custom parameter configuration, you could store the validation logic as a code snippet inside the Parameters table. Then, your application could execute the code dynamically.

In the pre-.NET era, one way for extending the application's capabilities ad hoc was by scripting. For example, you could use the JavaScript `Eval` function to execute script code dynamically. However, for the purposes of the Report Wizard demo, we decided to use the CodeDom technology available in .NET for dynamic code compilation and execution. For more information, please check the resources in section 10.6 for a link to Dino Esposito's excellent article, "Using an Eval Function in Web Services." I was able to retrofit Dino's approach easily and allow the Report Wizard to execute parameter-specific business rules. Let's see how this is done.

The Report Wizard validation process first checks to see whether all required parameters have values. Next, the Report Wizard checks to see if the parameter has a custom business rule associated with it. If you look back at listing 10.6, you can see that the Employee parameter has a business rule associated with it, which is implemented as a C# function called `EvalParameters`. The .NET Framework includes code generators and code compilers for C#, JScript, and VB.NET, so we could have written this function in any of these languages. If the parameter has a custom validation rule, the Report Wizard invokes the `Eval` function, passing the code of the rule and the list of the report parameters, as shown in listing 10.7.

Listing 10.7 Evaluating custom business rules

```
public bool Eval(string csCode, System.Data.DataTable parameters)
{
CSharpCodeProvider c = new CSharpCodeProvider();
ICodeCompiler icc = c.CreateCompiler();
CompilerParameters cp = new CompilerParameters();
cp.ReferencedAssemblies.Add("system.dll");
cp.ReferencedAssemblies.Add("system.xml.dll");
cp.ReferencedAssemblies.Add("system.data.dll");
cp.ReferencedAssemblies.Add("system.windows.forms.dll");

cp.CompilerOptions = "/t:library";
cp.GenerateInMemory = true;
StringBuilder sb = new StringBuilder("");
sb.Append("using System;");
sb.Append("using System.Xml;");
sb.Append("using System.Data;");
sb.Append("using System.Windows.Forms;");
```

❶ **Adds references to external assemblies**

❷ **Stores the compiled code in memory**

❸ **Adds namespaces**

```
sb.Append("namespace AWC.Reporter.Win { class ParameterValidator {");
sb.Append(csCode);
sb.Append("}}");
CompilerResults cr = icc.CompileAssemblyFromSource(cp, sb.ToString());
System.Reflection.Assembly a = cr.CompiledAssembly;
Object o;
MethodInfo mi;
o = a.CreateInstance("AWC.Reporter.Win.ParameterValidator");
Type t = o.GetType();
mi = t.GetMethod("EvalParameters");
bool result;
object[] arguments = new object[]{parameters};
result = (bool) mi.Invoke(o, arguments);
return result;
}
```

Defines the validator class ❹

❺ **Instantiates the class**

❻ **Reflects on the class type and invokes the EvalParameters method**

When working with dynamic code, you may want to minimize trial-and-error headaches by first testing your validation functions as static code in a VS.NET project before trying to execute it dynamically.

In this case, we are passing a list of all report parameters so that we can perform cross-parameter validation, for example, how the start date compares to the end date.

First, we instantiate the C# code compiler. Then, we load the validation code in an instance of a StringBuilder class.

❶ Next, we add the referenced assemblies, as you would typically do when working with code projects inside the VS.NET IDE.

❷ Then, we instruct the code compiler to put the dynamically generated assembly in memory as opposed to on the disk

❸ Next, we include the namespaces we need for the purposes of the parameter validation logic.

❹ In order for the .NET Common Language Runtime to be able to execute a piece of code, it must be defined inside a type. For this reason, we create a class called ParameterValidator and define it inside a namespace called `AWC.Reporter.Win`.

Then, we compile the code and store its intermediate language in memory.

❺ Next, we instantiate the temporary assembly.

❻ We reflect on it to execute the `EvalParameters` function.

The `EvalParameters` function returns a Boolean value that represents the validation outcome: true, if the validation has succeeded, or false otherwise. For example, if you enter a start date that is greater than the end date, the `EvalParameters` function displays an error message and returns false.

As you can see, dynamic code execution adds a lot of flexibility when you need to add ad hoc custom business rules to your applications.

Once the report parameters have been taken care of, we can advance to Step Export, where the user can specify the report's export format and device settings.

10.3.5 Specifying the export format

Step Export shows the export formats that RS supports as well as device settings associated with the selected format. The export formats are retrieved via a call to the `ListExtensions` API, as you saw when we discussed the AccessOptions sample in chapter 9.

Strangely, the RS Web service doesn't include a SOAP API that returns a list of the supported device settings for a given export format. As a workaround, we created our own configuration file (DeviceSettings.xml) to define the relationship between export formats and device settings.

We also defined some business rules in this step to disallow some combinations. Specifically, if the report is configured to take custom parameters, we default the Parameters device setting to false so that the Parameters section of the HTML Viewer toolbar is hidden.

Also, we set the Toolbar setting to false if the report is configured for Client-to-Façade-to-Report Server execution, because reports rendered via SOAP don't include the HTML Viewer.

10.3.6 Confirming the report request

Finally, the user is presented with Step Confirmation to validate the report request before it is submitted to the Report Server. The step invokes the ReportRequest accessor of the Report Wizard form to get the report request details. Because the ReportEntity object contains all reports from Step Reports, ReportRequest filters and clones only the selected report and its associated parameters.

```
m_reportRequest = new EntityReport();
System.Data.DataRow[] rows = new
    System.Data.DataRow[]{m_selectedReport};
m_reportRequest.Merge(rows);
rows = m_selectedReport.GetChildRows("ReportParameters");
m_reportRequest.Merge(rows);
return m_reportRequest;
```

Next, Step Confirmation shows the XML representation of the report request to the user so it could be verified. If all is well, the user clicks the Finish button to request the report. At this point, control is returned to the Report Wizard, which generates the report via the Client-to-Report Server or the Client-to-Façade-to-Report Server model.

Let's see how each of these models is implemented.

Client-to-Report Server report generation

If the report is not configured for remote execution, the Report Wizard generates it by URL.

To facilitate building the URL report request string, we created a helper function called `BuildURL`, which is defined as a static method in the RsHelpers class. This function takes the report request entity as a parameter and returns the report's URL. Once you have the report's URL ready, requesting the report is a matter of shelling out to the browser, as you saw back in chapter 9.

```
Process.Start ("IExplore", reportURL);
```

Client-to-Façade-to-Report Server report generation

As we mentioned, by default the Report Wizard generates reports by URL. You can configure a report to be requested on the server side of the application by adding the `RemoteCall` custom property to the Property column in the Catalog table. For example, to request the Employee Sales Freeform report in this way, add the following XML element to the report properties:

```
<RemoteCall>True</RemoteCall>
```

Once this is done, the Report Wizard will send the report request to the Reporting Façade. To simulate a distributed application, we created a Web service façade (ReportFacade.asmx), which you can find under the Chapter10 folder in the AWReporterWeb application.

NOTE Some of you may be curious about why I decided to implement the façade as a Web service instead of choosing .NET Remoting as a cross-machine communication mechanism. Indeed, I was initially planning to use .NET Remoting until I realized that Microsoft has deprecated this technology in the long term.

The next version of Windows, code-named "Longhorn," promotes the use of SOAP for communicating with service-oriented applications. For this reason, developers are advised to use .NET Remoting sparingly. For more information about building service-oriented applications, please see section 10.6.

The ReportFacade Web service exposes the `RenderReport` method:

```
[WebMethod]
public byte[] RenderReport(ReportRequest reportRequest,
              out string sessionId){
  string optionalString = null;
  byte[] reportPayload = RsAdapter.RenderReport(reportRequest,
                         out optionalString);
  sessionId = optionalString;
  return reportPayload;
}
```

This method delegates the responsibility of requesting the report to the `RsAdapter`. If you wonder why we have chosen to name the class "RsAdapter", wait until chapter 12 when we explain the "adapter" concept in detail. `RenderReport` method, which generates the report via SOAP, as we saw in chapter 9. There are several points worth mentioning about the inner workings of this method.

The first one has to do with security. By default, the call to the Report Server will go out under the process identity of the Web application. This means that if you don't take extra steps to change the ASP.NET process identity (or the application pool's identity in IIS 6), the call will fail. Please refer to chapter 8 to learn more about how to properly set up the Windows authentication in this scenario. If you want the Report Server to see the report request coming under the identity of the interactive user (the user who has started the AWReporterWin application), you can impersonate the user by using the identity element in the application's web.config configuration file, as follows:

```
<identity impersonate="true"/>
```

Alternatively, you can explicitly set the identity of the call by setting up the Report Server proxy credentials in the RsHelpers.Proxy accessor, as follows:

```
rsProxy.Credentials=new System.Net.NetworkCredential("username",
      "password");
```

Second, as we mentioned in chapter 9, when requesting reports by SOAP, you have to take an extra step to display the report's images by saving the image streams to a shared location (one to which the interactive user has read permissions). The Reporting Façade does this by configuring the StreamRootPath device setting to point to a temp folder before calling the Report Server `Render` method. Then, the Reporting Façade downloads the images explicitly to this folder. Needless to say, you have to take care of cleaning up this folder, for example, by scheduling a job that deletes the files in this folder on a regular basis.

Finally, if you want to leverage report session caching to process report more efficiently, you should take care of saving the report session identifier and passing it back to the Report Server when requesting the same report. The Reporting Façade does this by returning the session identifier through the sessionId output argument of the `RenderReport` method. After the call is completed, the Report Wizard updates the SessionID property of the ReportEntity object and sends it back when the same report is requested.

Now that we've seen how a WinForm client can provide an application front end to facilitate the report-generation process, let's see how we can make it more efficient by discussing some performance-enhancement techniques, including caching and multithreading.

10.4 ENHANCING APPLICATION PERFORMANCE

Writing efficient and responsive code is an essential design goal for any successful reporting application. As a developer, you can use various techniques to improve the user's experience and streamline report processing.

One of the easiest ways to provide fast access to application resources is by caching them in memory.

10.4.1 Using in-memory caching

Whenever possible, you should abundantly use in-memory caching to speed up the data retrieval in your applications. Because data stored in the computer' memory can be retrieved extremely fast, serving its cached instance is very efficient.

For this reason, we recommend that you take advantage of in-memory caching whenever possible. For example, you can cache in memory the returned data from the calls to the Report Server web methods.

Microsoft Application Blocks

Microsoft has released a number of Application Blocks that implement common design patterns for .NET applications. If you haven't heard about them, I strongly urge you to explore their features and consider using them instead of reinventing the wheel. The Application Blocks have saved me a lot of time and effort in some of my projects.

One of the blocks is specifically designed to facilitate in-memory caching. The Report Wizard takes advantage of the Caching Framework Application Block to cache in memory the list of reports returned from Step Reports. The premise here is that because the Report Server catalog data is not volatile, it is unlikely that it will be changed for a certain duration. The cache duration is specified in the application's configuration file.

Implementing in-memory caching

The Reports accessor (shown in listing 10.8) is called from the Step Reports Form_Load event to return the report list. Here, we need to check to see whether the report list is cached, and if it is, return the cached copy so that Step Reports can bypass the ListChildren call.

Listing 10.8 The Report Wizard caches the list of reports in memory as a performance-enhancement technique.

```
public EntityReport Reports {
  get {
    m_entityReports = (EntityReport)
            CacheManager.GetCacheManager().GetData("reports");
    if (m_entityReports == null)      <-❶ Is the report list cached?
         m_entityReports = new EntityReport();   // not cached

    return m_entityReports;
  }
  set {
    m_entityReports = value;                  ❷ Caches the
    ICacheItemExpiration[] exp = new       <-  report list
           AbsoluteTime(DateTime.Now.AddMinutes(10));
    CacheManager.GetCacheManager().Add(CONFIG_REPORT_CACHE_KEY,
```

```
            m_entityReports, exp, CacheItemPriority.Low, null);
    }
}
```

❶ We ask the CacheManager to return the cached report list if it exists. If the report list is cached, the Report Wizard returns the cached instance. Otherwise, Step Reports makes a call to the `ListChildren` web method to retrieve the reports from the report catalog.

❷ Once the ListChildren call is made, Step Reports calls the Reports accessor to pass the reports to the Report Wizard. At this point, the Report Wizard caches the reports for the specified duration in the application's configuration file.

10.4.2 Using multithreading

Another technique that you can use to make your reporting applications more responsive is multithreading. Traditionally, creating multithreaded classic applications has always required advanced programming skills. The .NET Framework makes this almost child's play. In many cases, you don't even have to create and manage threads by yourself. Instead, you can draw a thread from the application thread pool, do something with it, and when you have finished, the .NET runtime will recycle the thread and return it to pool. For example, in .NET, any method can be called asynchronously using an asynchronous delegate, which executes the method on a thread from the application pool.

The advantage of using multithreading is that you don't block the main application thread. This allows the user to continue working with the application instead of just sitting there and waiting for a long-running task to finish. For example, a report may take a long time to be processed by the Report Server. If you request the report via SOAP, the call to the `Render` method will block until the report is ready. This will freeze the main application thread and your application will become unresponsive. Instead, a better approach would be to return control to the user as soon as the request is submitted by invoking the `Render` method asynchronously.

The Report Wizard follows this design pattern when executing reports in the Client-to-Façade-to-Report Server scenario if the Don't Make Me Wait check box on Step Confirmation is selected.

NOTE There is no need to use multithreading when requesting reports via URL using Process.Start because the call to Process.Start is nonblocking and returns immediately.

With .NET, calling a web method asynchronously is a three-step process, as shown in listing 10.9.

Listing 10.9 Requesting a report asynchronously

```
private void GenerateReportBySOAP(EntityReport reportRequest,
                                  bool async){
  if (!async) {
```

```
    byte[] reportPayload=m_reportFacade.RenderReport(
              facadeRequest, out sessionID);
    UpdateSession(sessionID);
    ShowReport (reportPayload, filePath, sessionID);
  }
  else
    m_reportFacade.BeginRenderReport(facadeRequest,       ◁─ ❶ Invokes the web method asynchronously
          AsyncCallback(ReportReady), filePath);

private void UpdateSession(string sessionID) {
  // save the report session id
  this.SelectedReport.SessionID = sessionID;
  this.SelectedReport.AcceptChanges();
}

void ReportReady(IAsyncResult res)     {   ◁─ ❷ Creates a callback function
try {
       string filePath = (string)res.AsyncState;
       string sessionId = null;
       ShowReport(m_reportFacade.EndRenderReport(res,     ◁─ ❸ Retrieves the call results
                  out sessionId), filePath,sessionId);
}
catch( WebException ex ) {
  Util.ShowErrorMessage(ex);
}
}

private void ShowReport(byte[] reportPayload, string filePath,
                        string sessionId) {
  if (this.InvokeRequired == false) {
    this.SelectedReport.SessionID = sessionId;
    this.SelectedReport.AcceptChanges();

    FileStream stream = File.Create(filePath,
                        reportPayload.Length );
    stream.Write( reportPayload, 0, reportPayload.Length );
    stream.Close();
    Process.Start(filePath);
  }
  else {
    ShowReportDelegate showReport = new
                        ShowReportDelegate(ShowReport);
    this.BeginInvoke(showReport, new object[] {reportPayload,
       filePath, sessionId});
  }

}
```

Let's discuss each of these steps in more detail.

Submitting the report request asynchronously

The .NET Framework has built-in support for invoking web methods asynchronously. When VS.NET generates a web reference to a Web service, it also emits in the proxy code a couple of `BeginXxx/EndXxx` methods for each web method. For example, if you examine the source code of the RS Web service proxy inside the AWReporterWin project, you will see that it includes the `BeginRender` and `EndRender` method pairs, which allows us to invoke the `Render` method asynchronously.

❶ *Invoking the web method asynchronously*—Given that, the first step to request asynchronously is to call the `BeginRender` method. This method takes three arguments. The first one is the report request entity that the `Render` method takes. The session identifier is excluded from the argument list because it is declared as out of parameter.

The second argument is an instance of an AsyncCallback delegate that points to the `ReportReady` callback function. The `ReportReady` function will be called when the web method calls completes.

The third argument is of the type AsyncState. This is an open-ended argument that you can use to pass anything you want. In our case, we pass the file path where the report payload will be saved if the `Render` method is executed successfully. Once we call `BeginInvoke`, .NET will dispatch a background thread from the application thread pool to invoke the `Render` method and will return the control immediately to our application.

❷ *Receiving the report payload*—The second step involves writing the callback function. The function's signature must match the AsyncCallback delegate, which has a single argument of the type IAsyncResult.

This function is called when the Web service call returns something. To get the results, we must call the `EndRender` method. If the web method has been executed successfully, we are ready to show the report. If, on the other hand, the call has been terminated abnormally, `EndRender` will throw a WebException, which is why we wrap the call in a `try-catch` statement.

The most important point to observe here is that this function will be executed on the thread that services the web method call, which will always be different than the primary UI thread.

❸ *Displaying the report*—Finally, we are ready to show the report to the user. When creating multithreaded WinForm applications, you must take the necessary steps to ensure thread safety. Specifically, you must abide by the most important threading rule, which states that you should access UI resources on the thread on which they are created. In most cases, the UI resources will be created on the primary UI thread and, for this reason, this is the only thread that's allowed to access the form object and its controls. Applied to the Report Wizard demo, this means that we need to marshal the web method results to the primary UI thread.

NOTE Strictly speaking, in our case, we don't have to do this because we are not accessing controls created on the primary UI thread. Instead, we just need to update the report's session identifier in the RequestEntity object and save the report's payload to a file. However, I decided to demonstrate how you can implement safe threading with WinForms in case you need it. For example, in real life, you may want to show the outstanding report requests in a window so that the user knows when a given report request has finished executing. In this case, you must access this window through the primary UI thread.

The .NET Form object exposes a Boolean property called `InvokeRequired`, which you can use to find out whether the call is executed on the primary UI thread. In our case, if the `ShowReport` function is called on a background thread as a result of the web method's asynchronous execution, we will use `BeginInvoke` to serialize and marshal the function call on the primary UI thread. Now we can safely access windows created on the primary thread. For more information about creating multithreaded rich clients, please refer to the resources in section 10.6.

10.5 SUMMARY

This chapter has been quite a "brain crunch." We have explored a code-intensive, end-to-end example and discussed possible strategies and techniques for integrating WinForm applications with Reporting Services. Traditionally, report-enabling WinForm applications has been a difficult task that has required third-party tools or homegrown solutions. As you have seen, RS fills in this space elegantly and allows you to add on-demand reporting capabilities to both client/server and distributed applications.

In this chapter, we discussed the advantages of the rich client for building intranet-reporting applications. The Report Wizard code sample demonstrated how we can report-enable WinForm applications using the Client-to-Report Server and Client-to-Façade-to-Report Server design patterns.

To enhance the application performance, consider using in-memory caching and executing tasks on a background thread.

After reading chapter 9, you should have enough background information to know how to programmatically request reports using either URL or SOAP. More important, you know how to choose between these two options based on your application's requirements.

Next, we'll see how we can integrate RS with the second most popular type of application—web-based.

10.6 RESOURCES

"Introducing Client Application Deployment with ClickOnce'"
(http://msdn.microsoft.com/vbasic/whidbey/default.aspx?pull=/library/en-us/dnwinforms/html/clickonce.asp)
Discusses the forthcoming new deployment model for WinForm applications in the next version of Visual Studio.NET.

"Using an Eval Function in Web Services"
(http://msdn.microsoft.com/msdnmag/issues/02/09/CuttingEdge/)
Demonstrates how the CodeDom technology can be used to compile and execute code dynamically.

"Safe, Simple Multithreading in Windows Forms"
(http://msdn.microsoft.com/library/default.asp?url=/library/en-us/dnforms/html/winforms01232003.asp)
A three-part article that shows how to use multithreading in WinForm applications.

Microsoft patterns and practices for Application Architecture and Design
(http://msdn.microsoft.com/library/default.asp?url=/library/en-us/dnanchor/html/Anch_EntDevAppArchPatPrac.asp)
An essential read on the best practices for Microsoft-centered application development. Includes the documentation of the Microsoft Application Blocks.

CHAPTER 11

Reporting for web-based applications

Nowadays everyone wants to be on the Web. In a response to this trend, many organizations have built web-based solutions to reach a broad audience of users. While the tools to create such applications have matured, web reporting often boils down to tabular reports in the form of HTML tables. Many reporting vendors have attempted to fill in this gap with a certain degree of success, but only a few offer complete solutions to address the full spectrum of web reporting needs. For example, exposing reports as Web services has been traditionally difficult if not impossible with third-party products.

Microsoft Reporting Services can be easily integrated with different types of web applications. Organizations can use RS to make data easily accessible to internal users, customers, and partners by integrating this reporting platform with their intranet, Internet, and extranet applications.

In this chapter, we will discuss different techniques for report-enabling your web applications. We will start by seeing how to request reports on the client side of the application, including

- Static and application-generated hyperlinks
- Submitting report requests through HTTP-POST

- Write-back reports
- Requesting reports via SOAP

Then, we will discuss various ways for generating server-side reports, including

- The ReportViewer sample control that comes with the RS samples
- The enhanced version of the ReportViewer control that will support generating reports on the server side of the web application
- Reporting off application datasets
- Business-to-consumer (B2C) reporting and business-to-business (B2B) reporting

Let's start by laying out the theory first, and then we'll discuss different report integration scenarios for web-based applications.

11.1 UNDERSTANDING WEB REPORTING

Thanks to its web-enabled and open architecture, RS integrates well with web-based applications. As we saw in chapter 9, RS provides two options that developers can use to request reports: URL access that relies on HTTP-GET and Web service access that uses SOAP.

These options fit nicely into the web-based model because most web-based applications support HTTP-GET or SOAP. However, report-enabling web-based applications may bring additional challenges, the first and foremost being security.

From the deployment standpoint, most web applications can be categorized as intranet, Internet, and extranet applications.

11.1.1 Reporting for intranet applications

Intranet applications are deployed and used in an isolated and secured intranet environment. Access to this type of application is restricted to a limited group of authorized users (such as employees who belong to a domain).

In terms of reporting, intranet web-based applications could follow an identical implementation approach to their WinForm counterparts.

Applying the Client-to-Report Server model

As you would probably recall in our discussion from chapter 10, we recommended the Client-to-Report Server model for intranet-oriented applications. Figure 11.1 depicts this model.

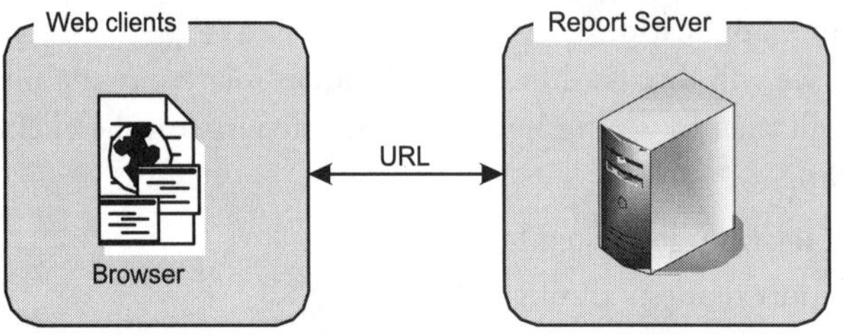

Figure 11.1 Intranet applications typically follow the Client-to-Report Server pattern, where reports are requested by URL.

The report consumer, which in this case is the web browser, directly accesses the Report Server to request reports by URL on the client side of the application. At its simplest implementation, using your favorite browser to request a report by typing the report's URL follows the Client-to-Report Server model.

As we explained in chapter 9, there are several advantages of requesting reports via URL, such as its simplicity, its interactive feature support, and its native RS security support.

Security considerations

As with the WinForm scenario, you have to be cognizant of the potential security risk when reports are requested on the client side of the application. This is especially true with web-based applications because the client-side scripting environment is generally not secured. A hacker could easily intercept the URL request and exploit it for her own malicious purposes. This is especially a concern when a report is requested in HTML because the report's URL address and parameters get embedded into the HTML page.

If exposing the URL address is an issue, you can leverage various client-side techniques to hide the URL address from prying eyes, as we will discuss in section 11.2.1. In the case of more stringent security requirements, this model could be replaced with the Client-to-Façade-to-Report Server model, where the report request is validated and the report generated entirely on the server side of the application, as we discussed in chapter 8.

11.1.2 Reporting for Internet applications

While intranet-oriented applications have the luxury of executing reports in a secure and well-controlled environment, this is not the case with Internet reporting, where you will face additional challenges. For example, directly accessing the Report Server and requesting reports by URL is usually not an option with Internet reporting because of the stringent security requirements that are frequently enforced upon this type of application. In addition, Windows authentication is rarely a feasible option, because creating and maintaining Windows accounts for hundreds and often thousands of users presents a maintenance challenge.

Given the latter limitation, here are two possible approaches for report-enabling Internet-oriented web applications in terms of security:

- The Client-to-Façade-to-Report Server model in which secured access is enforced on the server side of the application.
- Client-to-Report Server model with custom security—As discussed in chapter 8, developers can replace the RS security model with a custom security extension. We will see how this could be done in chapter 15.

Either way, validating the user request requires you to write additional code to enforce secure access to the Report Server.

Now, let's discuss each of these deployment models in more detail to find out how they could be applicable for the Internet scenario.

Web reporting with the Client-to-Façade-to-Report Server model

With this model, the user request is checked before it is handed out to the Report Server. This calls for introducing a Reporting Façade to isolate the Report Server from the clients, as shown in figure 11.2.

The main characteristics of using this model with Internet-oriented web applications are as follows:

- The presentation layer communicates with the façade using HTTP-GET or HTTP-POST.
- The Reporting Façade layer requests reports via SOAP.
- The details of the report request are never revealed to the end user.

The façade's role in web-based applications is usually a responsibility of server-side code logic encapsulated in web pages or business layer components. For example, this is what a typical report request flow might look like for an Internet-oriented application:

Step 1 The user accesses the reporting page.

Step 2 The user fills in the report request details, such as the report name, parameters, export format, etc.

Step 3 The user submits the page.

Step 4 When the page is submitted to the web server, the user request is validated.

Step 5 The page invokes the Render SOAP API to generate the report on the server side of the application.

In terms of security, we recommend the following setup:

- An application-based mechanism to authenticate the users, for example, Forms Authentication
- Passing the façade's identity to the Report Server using the trusted subsystem approach we discussed in chapter 8

Authenticating web users with the Client-to-Façade-to-Report Server model is the responsibility of the Reporting Façade, as you have undoubtedly noticed with most

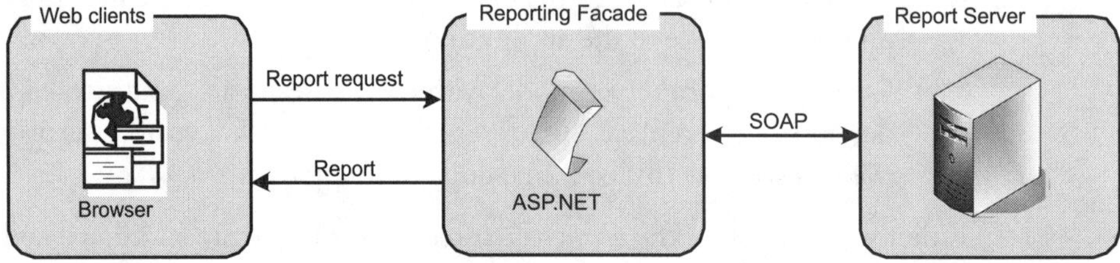

Figure 11.2 Typically, Internet-oriented applications generate reports on the server side of the application following the Client-to-Façade-to-Report Server model.

commercial web sites. For example, an ASP.NET application can use Forms Authentication to validate the user credentials against the database store. We will see a B2C example that uses Forms Authentication shortly in this chapter.

Once the user is authenticated, the façade submits the report request under its own identity. For example, you can grant a minimum set of permissions to the Windows account that the façade runs under, such as Browser role permissions. In this scenario, the Report Server will see all report requests coming under the Reporting Façade's identity. The disadvantage of this approach is that your application has to validate the users before the report request is made to the Report Server.

When the application requirements call for strict security, the Client-to-Façade-to-Report Server model will be our recommended approach.

Web reporting with the Client-to-Report Server model

Sometimes, your reporting requirements may call for granting web users direct access to the Report Server, as was the case with the intranet-reporting model we discussed in section 11.1.1. For example, you may want to give your users a better experience by allowing them to request reports with interactive features by URL.

NOTE RS allows you to expose the Report Server for Internet access so that users outside the Report Server domain can request reports by URL. In general, you should carefully evaluate this approach because of the security vulnerabilities it entails, such as denial of service attacks.

Here is how you can configure the Report Server for Internet access. Let's say the Report Server computer name is myreportserver and its fully qualified Internet-addressable name is myreportserver.adventure-works.com. To make the Report Server accessible via the Internet you add a **ReportServerExternalURL** setting in the RSReportServer.config configuration file. In our case this setting should be set as follows:

```
<ReportServerExternalURL>http://myreportserver.adventure-
works.com/</ReportServerExternalURL>.
```

Because using Windows-based authentication with Internet-oriented applications is often impractical, to apply the Client-to-Report Server model with this type of application you can write a custom security extension to authenticate the user against a data store before the request reaches the Report Server. The advantages of this approach compared to the Client-to-Façade-to-Report Server model are as follows:

- *Requesting reports by URL*—We've emphasized on a few occasions the benefits of URL access, including full support of all interactive features, simplicity, and so on.
- *Discriminating web users*—Similarly to way the Windows authentication works, with custom security the user's identity is passed to the Report Server. This means that you can use role-based security to enforce secured access to the report catalog based on the user's identity or role membership.

On the downside, this approach requires upfront development to write a custom security extension. In addition, depending on how strict your security requirements are, giving web users direct access to the Report Server may present a risk.

We will postpone implementing the custom security extension to chapter 15, where we will see a practical example of how custom authentication could be useful with Internet-oriented applications.

11.1.3 Reporting for extranet applications

Many B2B integration solutions are implemented as *extranet* applications. Extranets allows business partnerships to streamline their internal processes by electronically exchanging information. To accomplish this, an organization makes select information available to third parties while still maintaining complete security over its core data.

For example, Adventure Works Cycles may want to expose its product inventory data to its vendors in a form of a XML report. This will allow the company's vendors to automate their supply chain processes. A vendor could create a system to pull the report on a regular basis in unattended mode. When the inventory level of a certain product falls below the threshold value, the vendor system could initiate an automated product delivery to Adventure Works. We will see a scaled-down example of this scenario in section 11.3.5.

Figure 11.3 depicts the high-level deployment view of the extranet-reporting scenario.

The implementation approach shown in figure 11.3 promotes the Client-to-Façade-to-Report Server model. While you could allow direct access to the Report Server from extranet consumers, in reality, you may want to "wrap" it by introducing a Reporting Façade layer. In the extranet scenario, such a level could be useful to provide the following features:

- *Authenticate the external consumers*
- *Expose a limited subset of reporting features*—For instance, in the previous scenario, Adventure Works may use a façade to disallow exporting the report in formats other than XML.
- *Provide the input/output schema definitions*—These definitions could serve as a contract to which the consumers must adhere when submitting report requests.

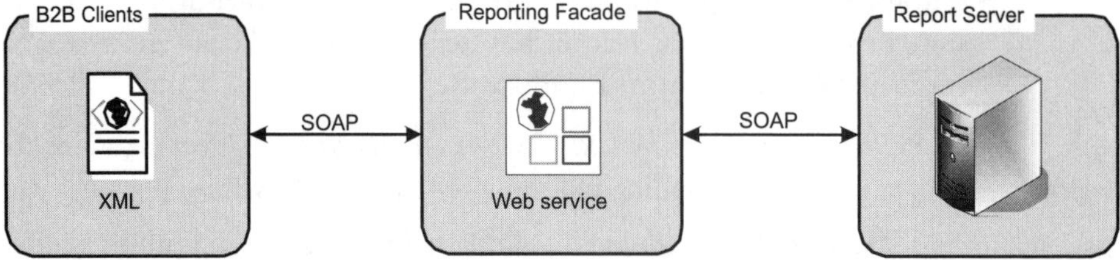

Figure 11.3 In the extranet scenario, a façade layer could provide selective access to the Report Server in the form of a Web service.

For maximum interoperability, the façade layer is typically implemented as a Web service. In terms of security, there are several well-known approaches that you can use to authenticate incoming requests to the façade, including these:

- *IP address filtering*—Access to the façade is restricted to a limited set of IP addresses.
- *Windows authentication*—The external clients can be authenticated with Windows user accounts.
- *Client certificates*—Each external vendor could be given a certificate. Client certificates can be mapped to Windows users.
- *Application-based security*—For example, you can use the Microsoft Web Services Extension toolkit to implement an application authentication model that follows the WS-Security specification.

For more information about different strategies for securing extranet applications, please see the resources in section 11.5.

Now that we've discussed at a high level how we can report-enable the three web-based application types, let's examine some practical web-reporting techniques. We will refer collectively to our web samples as the Adventure Works Web Reporter, or AWReporterWeb for short.

11.1.4 Introducing the Adventure Works Web Reporter

Once you've authored your report in RS, there are myriad ways to get it to your web-based users. From an implementation standpoint, we can organize the web reporting techniques into two categories: client-side reporting techniques and server-side reporting techniques. This breakdown reflects the location from which the report request originates.

In the case of client-side reporting, the report request is initiated on the client side of the application, for example, by clicking a hyperlink on a page rendered in the browser. Most of the techniques in this category follow the Client-to-Report Server pattern and request reports by URL.

In the latter case, the report is requested and rendered on the server side of the application, for example, by using ASP.NET server-side code. In general, the techniques under this category follow to the Client-to-Façade-to-Report Server approach and request reports by SOAP.

The AWReporterWeb code examples can be found under the Chapter11 folder in the AWReporterWeb project. Once you request the default.aspx page, you will be presented with the drop-down main menu, as shown in figure 11.4.

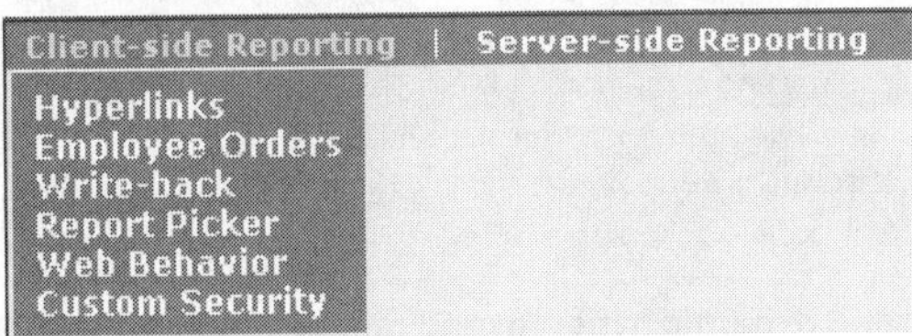

Figure 11.4
The main menu of the AWReporterWeb project displays two menus: one for the client-side reporting samples and one for the server-side reporting samples. To see the server-side menu items, hover your mouse cursor on top of the Server-side Reporting menu.

The main menu is implemented as a drop-down menu. The client-side reporting samples can be initiated from the Client-side Reporting menu, while the server-side reporting samples can be launched from the Server-side Reporting menu.

NOTE I used Peter Bromberg's excellent ASP.NET menu sample to easily integrate his menu control with my web application. The menu items are specified in the menu.xml file. The menu control loads the menu definition and applies XSLT transformation to render the menu in DHTML.

For more implementation details about the menu control, check the resources in section 11.5.

Let's now discuss the AWReporterWeb client-side reporting samples in the order in which they appear on the menu.

11.2 CLIENT-SIDE REPORTING TECHNIQUES

Requesting reports on the client side may be a good fit for intranet-based applications where the reports are rendered in a secured environment. Whenever possible, when report-enabling this type of application try to take advantage of URL access and leveraging the RS role-based security model.

Let's start by discussing the easiest and quickest ways to render reports and then move to more advanced techniques.

11.2.1 Requesting reports from hyperlinks

One way to get a report on the web is to request it by clicking on a hyperlink. The Requesting Reports with Hyperlinks (Hyperlinks.aspx) page of the AWReporterWeb project shown in figure 11.5 demonstrates the following common hyperlink techniques: static, dynamic, and server-side generated.

In its simplest implementation, you can use *static* hyperlinks to run reports. By static, we mean a hyperlink that includes the report's URL address.

Alternatively, you can use *dynamic* hyperlinks to run reports. By the term *dynamic* hear we mean hyperlinks that are constructed on the client side of the application so they don't contain fixed URL report addresses.

Finally, you can also use *server-side generated* hyperlinks in which the hyperlinks are generated on the server side of the web application.

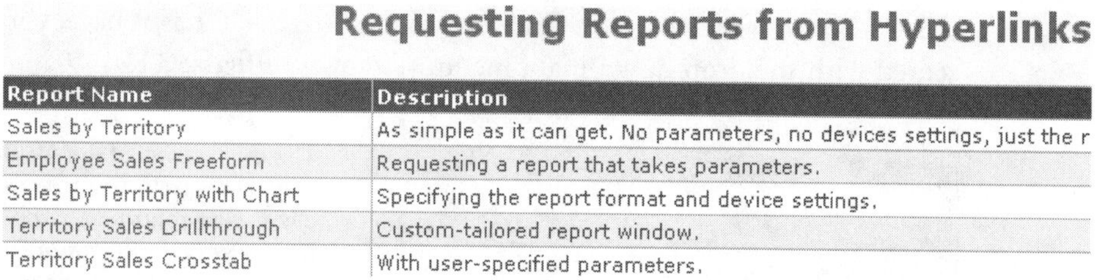

Requesting Reports from Hyperlinks

Report Name	Description
Sales by Territory	As simple as it can get. No parameters, no devices settings, just the r
Employee Sales Freeform	Requesting a report that takes parameters.
Sales by Territory with Chart	Specifying the report format and device settings.
Territory Sales Drillthrough	Custom-tailored report window.
Territory Sales Crosstab	With user-specified parameters.

Figure 11.5 You can use static and dynamic hyperlinks to requests reports by URL.

Using static hyperlinks

By using static hyperlinks you can easily integrate your reports with other web-based applications. For example, a SharePoint-based web portal can have web parts that use static hyperlinks to render reports of interest.

The Requesting Reports with Hyperlinks page of the AWReporterWeb project lists several reports that you navigate to based on a static hyperlink. These hyperlinks also demonstrate how to use the URL syntax we discussed in chapter 9.

The Sales by Territory report's URL demonstrates a static hyperlink at its simplest:

```
http://localhost/reportserver?/AWReporter/Sales by Territory
```

This hyperlink will generate the Sales by Territory report in the default format, which is HTML4.0 for up-level browsers or HTML3.2 for down-level browsers.

The Employee Sales Freeform report's URL demonstrates how to request a parameterized report from a hyperlink:

```
http://localhost/reportserver?/AWReporter/Employee Sales Freeform&Start-
Date=1/1/2003 12:00:00 AM&
EndDate=12/1/2003 12:00:00 AM&Employee=-1
```

The Sales by Territory with Chart report's URL demonstrates how to embed Report Server commands and device settings into a static hyperlink:

```
http://localhost/reportserver?/AWReporter/Employee Sales
Freeform with Chart&StartDate=1/1/2003 12:00:00 AM&
EndDate=12/1/2003 12:00:00 AM&rs:Format=PDF&rs:Command=Render
```

Although the static hyperlink approach excels in simplicity, it falls short in terms of customization and security. For example, when using static hyperlinks, you have little control over the appearance of the browser window. At most, you can request the report to be rendered in a new instance of the browser or a particular frame by setting the hyperlink's target property to _blank. Using static hyperlinks may also present a security risk because the user can see and change the report's URL at will to request another report or modify the report's parameters.

Fortunately, with RS you are not restricted to static report hyperlinks only. Often, your application requirements may rule out hard-coding the report's URL address in the hyperlink. In such cases, you can dynamically construct the link on the client or server side of the application.

Using dynamic hyperlinks

Dynamic hyperlinks can be useful when you need to custom-tailor the browser window and hide the report request's details by using familiar client-side web techniques.

For example, the Territory Sales Drillthrough report's URL demonstrates how you can use JavaScript code to customize the browser window:

```
<A onclick='window.open("http://localhost/reportserver?/
AWReporter/Territory Sales Drillthrough&
```

```
StartDate=1/1/2003 12:00:00 AM&
EndDate=12/1/2003 12:00:00 AM&
rs:Command=Render", "_blank", "location=no,tool-
bar=no,left=100,top=100,height=600,width=800")'>
```

The `onclick` JavaScript handler displays the report in a customized browser window, as shown in figure 11.6.

To hide the report's URL from the end user, the window doesn't have a toolbar or address bar. In addition, the JavaScript code sizes and positions the window explicitly. This approach may offer a good compromise between simplicity and security for intranet-based applications.

The Territory Sales Crosstab report's URL extends the dynamic hyperlink technique by allowing the user to enter the report's parameters and encapsulates the report request in a client-side JavaScript function, as shown in figure 11.7.

In this example, the `onclick` event handler attached to the hyperlink toggles the visibility of the parameter section. Once the parameters are entered, the user can request the report by clicking the Run Report button.

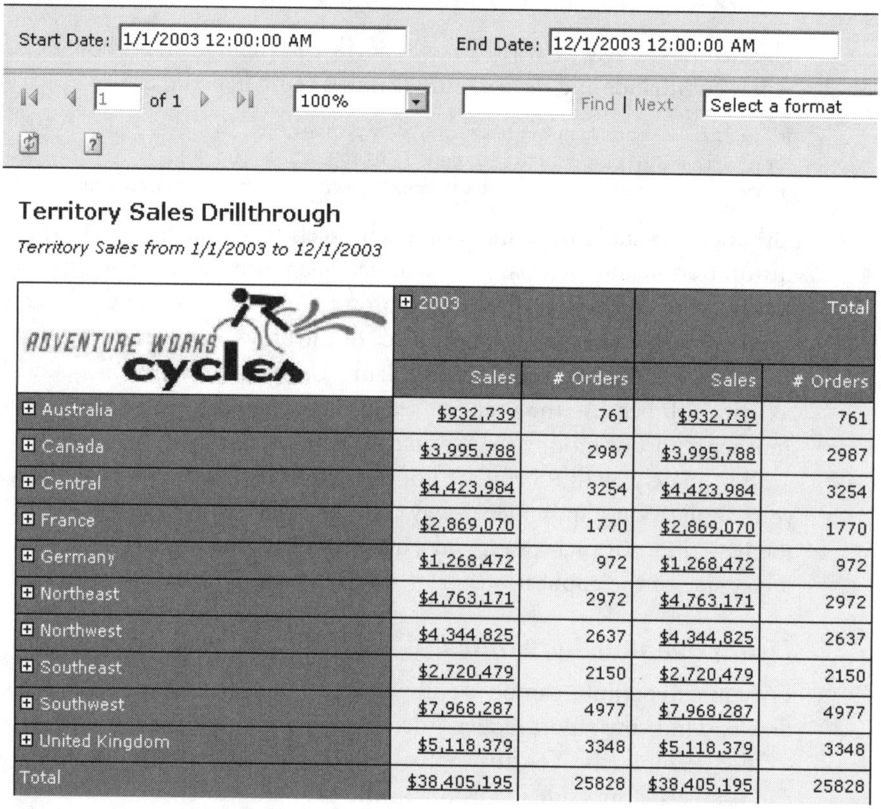

Start Date: 1/1/2003 12:00:00 AM End Date: 12/1/2003 12:00:00 AM

1 of 1 100% Find | Next Select a format

Territory Sales Drillthrough

Territory Sales from 1/1/2003 to 12/1/2003

ADVENTURE WORKS cycles	2003		Total	
	Sales	# Orders	Sales	# Orders
Australia	$932,739	761	$932,739	761
Canada	$3,995,788	2987	$3,995,788	2987
Central	$4,423,984	3254	$4,423,984	3254
France	$2,869,070	1770	$2,869,070	1770
Germany	$1,268,472	972	$1,268,472	972
Northeast	$4,763,171	2972	$4,763,171	2972
Northwest	$4,344,825	2637	$4,344,825	2637
Southeast	$2,720,479	2150	$2,720,479	2150
Southwest	$7,968,287	4977	$7,968,287	4977
United Kingdom	$5,118,379	3348	$5,118,379	3348
Total	$38,405,195	25828	$38,405,195	25828

Figure 11.6 Use dynamic hyperlinks when you need to customize the browser window.

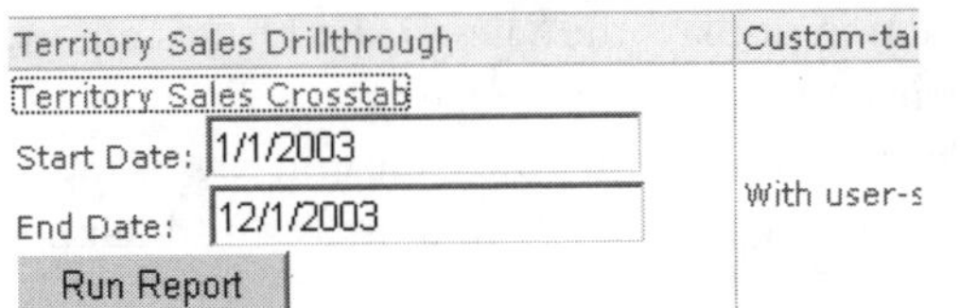

Figure 11.7 You can use client-side JavaScript to generate the report's hyperlink.

The button event handler invokes the `requestReport` client-side function and passes the start and end date parameters as arguments:

```
function requestReport(startDate, endDate) {
  window.open("http://localhost/reportserver?/
      AWReporter/Territory Sales
      Crosstab&StartDate=" + startDate + "&EndDate=" + endDate+
      "&rs:Command=Render", "_blank", "location=no,toolbar=no,
       left=100, top=100, height=600,width=800")
}
```

The `reportRequest` function renders the report in a customized browser window, as we saw in the previous example.

Using server-side generated hyperlinks

Most web-based applications require some server-side preprocessing before the page is rendered. For example, it is a common requirement to generate HTML tables on the server side of the application that include clickable hyperlinks to bring the user to another page or report that shows more details.

To see how to integrate a report's hyperlinks with a server-side-generated ASP.NET grid, click the Employee Orders link from the main menu of the AW Web Reporter. The Salesperson Orders (EmployeeOrders.aspx) page is shown in figure 11.8.

The EmployeeOrders.aspx page retrieves the sales order information from the Adventure Works database using a data reader. The user can click the Details hyperlink

Salesperson Orders

Salesperson: Abbas Syed

Order Date	Order #	Store	Sub Total	Details
9/1/2003	SO5812	Nationwide Supply	$77,513.42	Details
9/1/2003	SO6038	Liquidation Sales	$22,751.11	Details
9/1/2003	SO6245	Popular Bike Lines	$41,030.55	Details
9/1/2003	SO7604	Inexpensive Parts Shop	$4,112.38	Details
9/1/2003	SO7703	Online Bike Catalog	$67.76	Details
9/1/2003	SO7714	Twin Cycles	$1,326.26	Details
11/1/2003	SO6116	Uncompromising Quality Co	$3,433.06	Details
12/1/2003	SO5421	Bike Part Wholesalers	$32,866.56	Details
12/1/2003	SO7546	Twin Cycles	$4,307.75	Details

Figure 11.8 Report hyperlinks can be generated on the server side.

to see the order details. This action displays the Sales Order Details report, which happens to be one of the Reporting Services sample reports.

The hyperlink passes the order number from the same grid row as the report parameter. This is accomplished by defining the Details column as a grid template column:

```
<asp:TemplateColumn HeaderText="Details">
  <ItemTemplate>
   <a href="#" onclick="javascript:requestReport
     ('<%#DataBinder.Eval(Container.DataItem,"SalesOrderNumber")
    %>');">Details</a>
  </ItemTemplate>
</asp:TemplateColumn>
```

For those of you not familiar with the ASP.NET data binding model, the odd-looking DataBinder expression retrieves the SalesOrderNumber field from the underlying data reader row and injects it into the page. As a result, when the page is rendered, the `onclick` event for the first record will be set to something like this:

```
onclick="javascript:requestReport('SO5812');"
```

The `requestReport` JavaScript client-side function submits the report request as we've just seen.

11.2.2 Creating write-back reports

By "write-back" reports, we will mean reports that allow the users to update the report's data and post back the changes to the report's database, very much like the way server-side web pages work. This sounds like a cool thing, doesn't it? The only caveat is that RS (or any other reporting tool that we know of) doesn't support write-back reports. However, as a workaround, you can leverage the RS navigation features to integrate your reports with server-side pages. Let's see how this could be done.

As you saw in chapter 5, your reports can include navigational features in the form of hyperlinks. Hyperlinks don't have to request RS reports only. Instead, you can "reverse" their purpose and use hyperlinks inside your reports to perform some custom action.

Let's say the AWC sales management has realized that sometimes the sales order data is entered erroneously. The management has requested that you enhance the Sales Order report to meet the following requirements:

- The sales administrator can request a report for a given salesperson and date range.
- If wrong sales order data is entered, the sales administrator must be able to change the order's details.
- The changes have to be persisted back to the data source.

At first look, you may think that these requirements call for application-based reporting because RS doesn't currently support write-back reports. However, you can get around this limitation by using hyperlinks in your reports that request server-side pages.

To see how to implement this type of functionality, click the Write-back link from the main menu of the AW Web Reporter. The Write-back menu item renders the Sales Order Writeback report, as shown in figure 11.9.

The navigation action for the Sales Order report item is set to the following hyperlink:

```
="http://localhost/AWReporterWeb/Chapter11/Client/
   Writeback.aspx?SO=" & Fields!SalesOrderNumber.Value
```

As a result, when the user clicks on a sales order number, the hyperlink requests the Writeback Demo (Writeback.aspx) page (figure 11.10), passing the Sales Order Number as a query parameter.

The report will open the page in a new browser window by default. However, you can use the LinkTarget device setting in the report request's URL to instruct the report to load the page in a specific frame, for example, rc:LinkTarget=myFrameName.

Writeback.aspx queries the database and populates the Sales Person drop-down with the list of all salespersons. Next, it retrieves the sales order details. The user can change the order data and click the Update Order hyperlink to submit the page and propagate the changes to the database. In our case, to simplify things, we just output the field values back to the page.

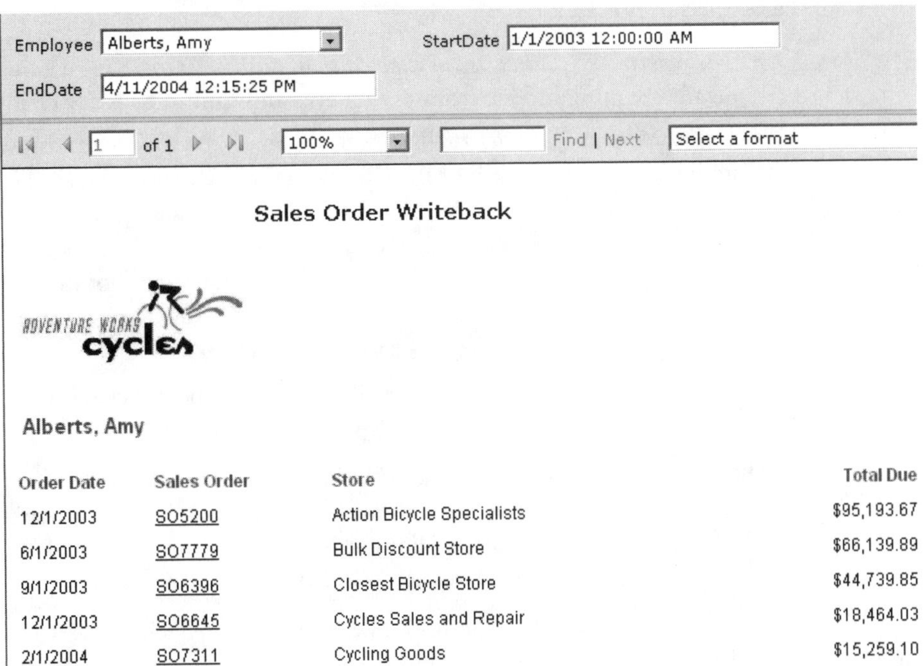

Figure 11.9 You can use RS navigational features to implement write-back reports.

Writeback Demo

Report Name	Description
Sales Order Number	SO5200
Sales Person	Alberts Amy
Order Date	12/20/2003
Update Order	

Order Updated
Sales Order Number: SO5200
Order Date: 12/20/2003
Sales Person: Alberts Amy

Figure 11.10 Report links can point to any URL-addressable resource including ASP.NET pages to implement write-back features.

11.2.3 Using HTTP-POST

All of the examples so far in this chapter have used HTTP-GET to submit the report request to the Report Server on the client side of the application. Sometimes, using HTTP-POST as a web protocol may be a better choice because of the following advantages it has over HTTP-GET:

- *The report URL address is less exposed than with HTTP-GET*—The report request details are more hidden from prying eyes and cannot be easily changed.
- *Unlimited parameter length*—As we said in chapter 9, many browsers impose limitations on the length of the URL string in the case of the HTTP-GET protocol. In contrast, with HTTP-POST, the length of the request parameters (report parameters, commands, and device settings) is unlimited, because the name/value pairs are transferred in the request's HTTP header, not in the URL.

Submitting the report request via HTTP-POST

To view a report requested by HTTP-POST, click the Report Picker link from the main menu of the AW Web Reporter. The Report Picker page is shown in figure 11.11.

> **NOTE** Because the Report Picker and the samples that follow use the credentials of the interactive user to invoke the RS SOAP API, make sure that the AWReporterWeb application is configured for Integrated Windows security and Anonymous access is disabled.

The Reports and Export Format drop-downs are populated with server-side code, which is similar to the Report Wizard sample code that we discussed in chapter 10. The Reports drop-down is set to post back the page automatically. When the report selection changes, the page posts back to itself to retrieve and display the report parameters.

The page gets the report parameters on the server side by invoking the `GetReportParameters` RS web method. Then, the page loops through the report

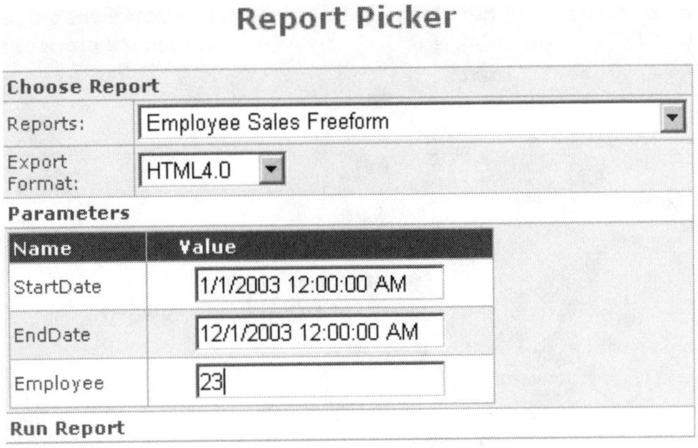

Figure 11.11 Use HTTP-POST to hide the URL address details and unlimited parameter length.

parameters and loads them into a DataTable object. Finally, the page binds the parameter table to the Parameter grid control. The grid's Value column is implemented as a template column similar to that in the Sales Orders sample report.

To request the report via HTTP-POST on the client side of the application, the page defines a second form that includes a few hidden fields to capture the report request's details and post them back to the Report Server:

```
<FORM id="frmRender" action="http://localhost/reportserver?"
         method="post" target="report">
  <INPUT type="hidden" value="Render" name="rs:Command">
  <INPUT type="hidden" value="HTML4.0" name="rs:Format">
  <INPUT type="hidden" value="_blank" name="rc:LinkTarget">
</FORM>
```

The hidden fields serve as placeholders for Report Server commands and device settings.

Handling parameters

As part of submitting the report request via HTTP-POST, we need to send the parameter values. Handling the report parameters is tricky because a report could have an arbitrary number of parameters. For this reason, we need to generate the parameters' placeholders dynamically. This is done inside the `runReport` client-side JavaScript function, as shown in listing 11.1.

Listing 11.1 Submitting a report via HTTP-POST

```
var reportServerUrl = null;
function runReport()  {
  frmRender.action = reportServerUrl +              ❶
       frmReports.drpReports.value;
  frmRender.Format.value = frmReports.drpExport.value;

  var parameters = frmReports.txtParameter;          ❷
  var paramUrl ="";
```

❶ Generates the action target of the form

❷ Gets a reference to the parameter textboxes

```
  var oldParameters = frmRender.Parameter;           <-3 Removes the old parameters
  if (oldParameters!=undefined) {                       from the previous run
   var count = parameters.length
   for (i=0;i<count;i++) {
    oldParameter = oldParameters[i];
    frmRender.removeChild(oldParameter);
    i--;count--;
   } // end for
  } // end if
                                              4 Generates as many hidden fields
  if (parameters.length>0) {           <-       as the report has parameters
    for (i=0;i<parameters.length;i++) {
      var newParam = document.createElement("INPUT");
      newParam.type = "hidden";
      newParam.id = "Parameter";
      newParam.name = parameters[i].name;
      newParam.value = parameters[i].value;
     frmRender.appendChild(newParam);
   } // end for
  } // end if

  window.open("about:blank", "report",
    "location=yes,toolbar=no,left=100,
    top=100,height=600,width=800")

  frmRender.submit();         <-5 Submits the form
}                                 via HTTP-POST
```

The `runReport` function is invoked from the `onclick` event of the Run Report hyperlink.

❶ First, we set the form's action to the report's URL. Next, we set the Format hidden field to the selected export format.

❷,❸ Next, we remove the parameters from the previous report run.

❹ Then, we loop through all parameter textbox controls in the grid. For each parameter, we create a new hidden input element and set its name and value. To render the report, we create a new named browser window.

❺ Finally, we submit frmRender to the Report Server and display the report in a custom-tailored browser window.

11.2.4 Calling the RS Web service on the client side

To round up the client-side web-reporting techniques, we would like to show you a way to submit the report request via SOAP on the client side of the application. There are at least two good reasons for generating reports via SOAP with web-based applications:

- *URL access to the Report Server is not allowed*—For example, security requirements may force the report administrator to disallow requesting reports via

HTTP-GET or POST. As we mentioned in chapter 9, you can do this by taking out removing the ReportServiceHttpHandler declaration from the Report Server's web.config file.

- *"Pseudo" web-based rich clients*—The web application can be designed to behave like a WinForm stateful application, where the data retrieval and rendering are done entirely on the client side, for example, by using XSL transformations. This approach has been popular with "fat" DHTML clients that don't post their pages back to the web server.

To submit the report request via SOAP on the client side of a web-based application, you can use the Microsoft WebService behavior.

Using the Microsoft WebService behavior

If your target browser is Internet Explorer, you can use the Microsoft WebService behavior to call web methods on the client side of the application using your favorite scripting language. To learn more about the WebService behavior, please see the resources in section 11.5.

The Web Behavior sample builds upon the Report Picker sample to demonstrate how reports can be requested via SOAP. At first look, the WebBehavior.aspx page appears identical to the ReportPicker.aspx page. However, the client-side reporting model is very different. Now, when the report request is submitted, the page doesn't post to itself. Instead, it invokes the RS Web service to request the report via SOAP and render it on the client side of the application.

Once we downloaded the WebService behavior file (webservice.htc) from the Microsoft web site, we configured it as follows. First, we created a DIV element to expose the WebService behavior as a DHTML element:

```
<div id="proxy" style="BEHAVIOR: url(webservice.htc)"></div>
```

Next, we changed the page body element to invoke the JavaScript `init()` function so that we could initialize the behavior to point to the RS Web service by calling the `useService` method:

```
<body onload="init()">
function init() {
   proxy.useService("http://localhost/reportserver/
      reportservice.asmx?WSDL","RS");
}
```

The second argument of the `useService` method allows you to specify a friendly name for the Web service.

Requesting reports

Requesting a report using the WebService behavior resembles the asynchronous report generation pattern that we discussed in chapter 9. Listing 11.2 shows the implementation details.

Listing 11.2 Requesting a report by SOAP using the Microsoft WebService behavior

```
function runReport() {
  var optional;   <-1 Prepares the report request
  var objCall = proxy.createCallOptions();
  objCall.funcName = "Render";
  objCall.params = new Array();
  objCall.params.Report = frmReports.drpReports.value;
  objCall.params.Format = "XML";
  objCall.params.HistoryID = optional;
  var parameters = frmReports.txtParameter;
  if (parameters.length>0)   <-2 Sets the report parameters
    objCall.params.Parameters = getParameters(parameters)

  proxy.RS.callService (fnHandler, objCall);
}

function parameter()   {   <-3 The report parameter definition
  this.Name = null;
  this.Value = null;
  return true;
}

function getParameters(parameters)  {   <-4 Enumerates the report parameters
  reportParams = new Array();
  for (i=0;i<parameters.length;i++) {
    var newParam = new parameter();
    newParam.Name = parameters[i].name;
    newParam.Value = parameters[i].value;
    reportParams[i] = newParam;
  }
  return reportParams;
}

function fnHandler(res)  {   <-5 The resultant callback function
  if (!res.error) {
    var decodedResult = decode(res.value.Result);
    OpenReport (decodedResult);
  }
  else alert(res.errorDetail.string);
}
```

Clicking the Run Report hyperlink triggers a call to the `runReport` JavaScript function.

❶ We start by defining our report request to the `Render` web method. We decided to hard-code the report format as XML so that we could save the report's payload as a disk file. To accomplish this, we use the FileSystemObject object, which currently doesn't provide the ability to save binary data to a file.

NOTE You may need to adjust the browser's security settings to prevent client-side JavaScript errors when using FileSystemObject.

❷ Next we populate the report parameters ❹ by calling the `getParameters` function, which loops through the parameter elements on the page and adds them to an array object.

❸ Because the `Render` method defines the parameter argument as of the ParameterValue type, we need to define a JavaScript structure that matches the ParameterValue layout. This is exactly what the `parameter()` function does.

❺ Next, we call the `Render` method asynchronously and pass a pointer to the `fnHandler` callback function, which will be called automatically when the web method returns something. If the call completes successfully, we decode the results from Base64 encoding. Finally, we call the `OpenReport` function to save the report's payload to a text file and shell out to the browser so we can see the file's contents.

While intranet-based applications could enjoy the simplicity and the rich feature set of the Client-to-Report Server reporting model, other scenarios may require server-side report generation by following the Client-to-Façade-to-Report Server pattern. The next section shows you how you can do just that.

11.3 SERVER-SIDE REPORTING TECHNIQUES

While client-side reporting is simple, many web applications include dynamically generated content in the form of server-side web pages. From the reporting perspective, there will be cases when you need to perform certain aspects of the report-generation process on the server side, ranging from validating the report's parameters to generating the report entirely on the server side.

There are at least a couple of ways to integrate RS with server-side web pages:

- Use the ReportViewer sample control
- Generate the report on the server side of the application.

First, in this section we will discuss how the ReportViewer control can be used as a server-side reporting technique.

Then, we will supercharge it to achieve "true" server-side report generation. We will also see how the enhanced version can help us to report off application datasets, which is a common application requirement for B2C applications.

Finally, we will discuss how reports can be integrated in the B2B scenario.

11.3.1 Using the ReportViewer control

To facilitate integrating RS on the server side of the application, Microsoft has provided an interesting sample called ReportViewer. As the documentation says, "ReportViewer is an ASP.NET server control developed using Visual Studio .NET. The server control is based on a real-world scenario and it demonstrates how to develop a custom control that you can use to integrate Reporting Services reports in a Web application. ReportViewer server control uses Reporting Services URL access functionality to render and navigate reports in a Web browser."

We highly recommend that you explore the ReportViewer source code even if you don't plan to use it in your applications. You can learn a lot from it, especially if you are new to developing ASP.NET web server controls.

Understanding ReportViewer

The ReportViewer control sample is implemented as a .NET web control library and, as such, it can be used only with ASP.NET applications. Both VB.NET and C# source code is included with the sample.

Follow these steps to reference the ReportViewer control in your ASP.NET applications:

Step 1 Compile the source code of the control. If you have accepted the default installation settings, the ReportViewer source code can be found under C:\Program Files\Microsoft SQL Server\MSSQL\Reporting Services\Samples\Applications\ReportViewer.

Step 2 Right-click the VS.NET toolbox and choose Add/Remove Items.

Step 3 In the Customize Toolbox dialog, make sure that the .NET Components tab is selected. Click the Browse button and navigate to the ReportViewer binary file (ReportViewer.dll). After you confirm the selection, the ReportViewer control should be added to the toolbox.

Step 4 Now you can drag and drop the control onto your web form, just as you would do with other controls on the toolbox.

ReportViewer allows you to configure the following report request details in an object-oriented way during the application design or runtime:

- General report parameters, including the report path, i.e., /AWReporter/Employee Sales Freeform, and the Report Server URL, i.e., http://localhost/ReportServer
- HTML Viewer commands, including the visibility of the toolbar (rs:Toolbar) and parameters (rs:Parameters), as well as zooming
- Rendering format, i.e., HTML4.0

For the rest of the report request's details, such as the report's parameter values, the control relies on the HTML Viewer toolbar, which is rendered by default when the report is requested by URL.

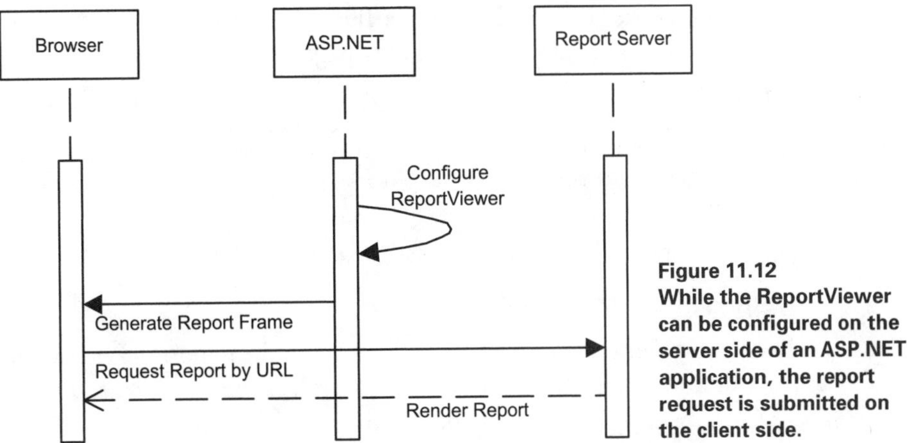

Figure 11.12
While the ReportViewer can be configured on the server side of an ASP.NET application, the report request is submitted on the client side.

The ReportViewer control allows you to add "pseudo" server-side reporting capabilities to your applications. What we mean by this is that, while the control allows you to configure the report request on the server side, the request itself is submitted on the client side of the application.

The sequence diagram shown in figure 11.12 should make this clear.

This is what happens during the application runtime when an ASP.NET page renders the control:

1 ReportViewer generates a report placeholder that will host the rendered report, by injecting an IFRAME HTML element into the hosting page. The SRC property of the frame will be set to the report's URL string, per the ReportViewer property values set by the developer.
2 When the page is rendered in the browser, the IFRAME element requests the report by URL.
3 The rendered report is displayed in the IFRAME element.

For example, let's say you've set up the ReportViewer control during design time with the settings listed in table 11.1.

Table 11.1 Based on the settings you enter, ReportViewer generates an IFRAME element and sets its URL accordingly.

Setting	Value
ServerUrl	http://localhost/reportserver
ReportPath	/AWReporter/ Corporate Hierarchy
Toolbar	True
Format	HTML4.0
Zoom	100%

Given the above settings, here is the IFRAME element definition that the ReportViewer control will inject in the hosting page:

```
<iframe src="http://localhost/reportserver?/AWReporter/Corporate Hierar-
chy&rs:Command=Render&rc:parameters=true&rc:toolbar=true&
rs:Format=HTML4.0" width="800px" height="100%" style="border: 1
solid #C0C0C0" border="0" frameborder="0">
</iframe>
```

Let's see a practical example that uses the ReportViewer control.

Using ReportViewer

The ReportViewerDemo.aspx page builds upon the ReportPicker example we saw earlier, but now it uses the ReportViewer control, as shown in figure 11.13.

Once the user picks a report, specifies the export format, and clicks the Run Report link, the page posts back to itself. Then, on the server side, we set the ReportViewer.ReportPath property to the selected report and the Format property to the desired export format. Once the page is rendered, the report will be displayed in the generated IFRAME.

The most important point about ReportViewer is that the report is requested by URL on the client side of the application. Therefore, in our opinion, the ReportViewer control will be a good fit for intranet-based applications or Internet-oriented applications that are configured for custom security. As we stressed on numerous occasions, URL access should be your preferred choice because of the advantages that we discussed in detail in chapter 9. In such an environment, the ReportViewer hybrid design allows developers to have the best of both worlds:

- Server-side control configuration—For example, the application can configure the control on the server side in an object-oriented way and shield the developer from the URL syntax technicalities.
- Client-side URL-based report generation with all the advantages it has to offer.

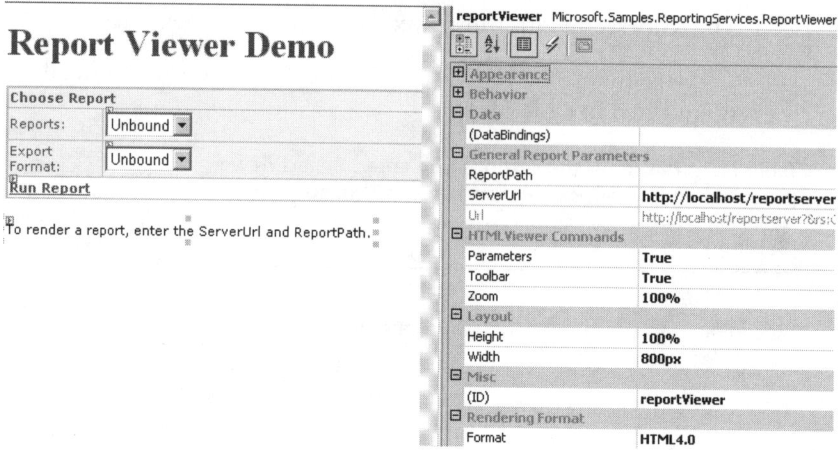

Figure 11.13 The Report Viewer Demo page

Let's now see how we can enhance the ReportViewer control to support server-side report generation.

11.3.2 Using the Adventure Works ReportViewer control

Depending on your reporting requirements, the ReportViewer control may not be a good fit because it is subject to the following limitations and restrictions:

- Direct access to the Report Server may not be an option.
- ReportViewer doesn't support server-side report generation.
- ReportViewer relies on the RS HTML Viewer control to handle report parameters.

The last limitation presents a problem if you need to report off data available only on the server side of the applications, such as ADO.NET datasets.

When report-enabling Internet-oriented applications, what you may need is an enhanced version of ReportViewer that is capable of generating reports entirely on the server side. For this reason, we decided to supercharge the ReportViewer control. Enter the Adventure Works Report Viewer, or AWReportViewer for short.

The AWReportViewer design goals

The main design goals for the AWReportViewer control are as follows:

- *Support both client-side and server-side report generation*—We left the client-side report-generation logic the same to make the new version compatible with the ReportViewer implementation. If the server-side option is set, the control renders the report as an HTML fragment if the requested export format is HTML. For export formats different than HTML, the control downloads the report to the client.
- *Expose the control functionality as a set of properties and methods*—Similar to its cousin the ReportViewer control, AWReportViewer allows the developer to set the report's properties in an object-oriented way during application design time and runtime.
- *Facilitate reporting off application datasets*—The control has a DataSource property, which the developer can set to an instance of an ADO.NET dataset. For this option, the control relies on the custom dataset data extension that we'll discuss in detail in chapter 15.
- *Implement the control as a web server control*—This allows developers to drag and drop the control on the page canvas and easily manipulate its position, layout, and report-related properties during design time.

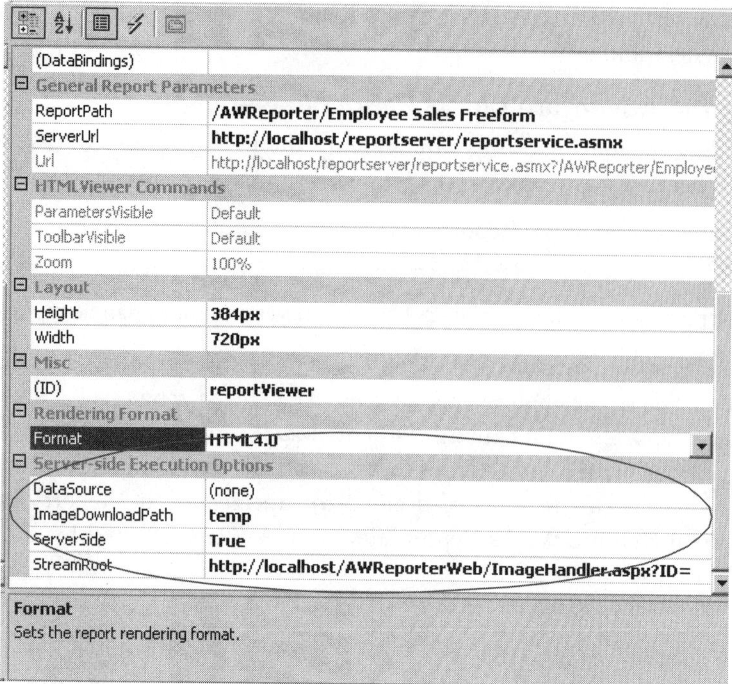

Figure 11.14 The AWReportViewer includes properties for server-side report generation.

Configuring AWReportViewer

You can find the AWReportViewer C# source code under the Code/AWReportViewer folder. To use the control in your web applications, reference it similarly to the way you did the ReportViewer control.

Once you drag and drop the control onto an ASP.NET page, you will see some extra properties grouped under the Server-side Execution Options category, as shown in figure 11.14.

The purpose of these properties is shown in table 11.2.

Table 11.2 The AWReportViewer server-side properties

Property	Type	Availability	Purpose
DataSource	System.Data.DataSet	Runtime only	Set to an instance of an ADO.NET dataset for reporting off application datasets.
ServerSide	Boolean	Design time/runtime	Set to true to generate the report on the server side.

continued on next page

Table 11.2 The AWReportViewer server-side properties *(continued)*

Property	Type	Availability	Purpose
ImageDownloadPath	String	Design time/runtime	Specifies the location where the report images will be downloaded. The path is relative to the application's root path.
StreamRoot	String	Design time/runtime	Specifies the URL location of the image handler page.

In addition, the control exposes a publicly accessible method called `AddParameter`, which you can use to configure programmatically the report's parameters.

As we said, the control can be used for both client-side and server-side report generation. When the ServerSide property is set to true, the client-side properties, such as ParametersVisible, ToolbarVisible, and so on, are irrelevant and are disabled. When ServerSide is set to false, the server-side properties are not accessible.

AWReportViewer in action

Let's now look at an example to demonstrate how the AWReportViewer control can be useful for Internet-based reporting.

Imagine that the AWC management has decided to enhance their Internet portal by allowing users to generate some reports. The new requirements are as follows:

- The users can export the reports in any of the supported formats.
- Due to security restrictions, the reports must be generated on the server side.

To meet these requirements, the AWReportViewerDemo.aspx page takes advantage of the server-side report-generation capabilities of the Adventure Works ReportViewer control. From an implementation standpoint, the sample page is similar to the ReportPicker example.

The AWReportViewer control is configured as shown in figure 11.14. After the user has specified the report, export format, and report parameters, the page posts back to itself. Then, the RunReport `OnClick` event handler calls the `SetParameters` function to configure the report's parameters:

```
private void SetReportParameters() {
  ParameterValue[] parameters = null;
  if (grdParams.Items.Count>0) {
    parameters = new ParameterValue[grdParams.Items.Count];

    foreach (TableRow row in grdParams.Items) {
      reportViewer.AddParameter(row.Cells[0].Text,
        (TextBox)row.Cells[1].FindControl("txtParameter")).Text);
    }
  }
}
```

To retrieve the user-specified parameters from the ASP.NET grid, we loop through the grid rows to get to the parameter label and value. For each parameter, we call the AWReportViewer public method `AddParameter` to add the parameter to a collection of the report's parameters. Next, the page overrides the ReportPath and Format AWReportViewer properties as per the user selection.

During the page-rendering phase, the page asks the AWReportViewer to render itself. When the control is configured for server-side reporting, the AWReportViewer requests the report via SOAP. If the export format is one of the HTML flavors, the control embeds the report inside the page as an HTML fragment, as shown in figure 11.15.

If the report is requested in another format, the report's payload is streamed back to the browser. As you can see, the client is not aware of, and therefore cannot spoof, the report request because the whole report-generation process is server-oriented.

Now that you've seen how the AWReportViewer can be used, let's take a behind-the-scenes tour to find out how it is implemented.

Adventure Works Report Viewer Demo

Choose Report

Reports:	Employee Sales Freeform
Export Format:	HTML4.0

Parameters

Name	Value
StartDate	1/1/2003 12:00:00 AM
EndDate	12/1/2003 12:00:00 AM
Employee	23

Run Report

Employee Sales Freeform

Sales for Campbell, David from 1/1/2003 to 12/1/2003

Employee Name:	**Campbell, David**
Commision:	1.20 %
Sales YTD:	$1,870,183.53
Bonus:	$3,500.00

Product Subcategory	Sales	# Orders
Mountain Bike	$1,126,633.15	260
Touring Bike	$705,048.45	199
Road Bike	$365,842.44	109
Mountain Frame	$286,903.94	182
Touring Frame	$127,463.41	81

Figure 11.15 Rendering a report with the AWReportViewer control

Setting design goals

Granted, we could generate reports on the server side without the help of a server-side control. However, we liked the control implementation approach because of the following advantages it offers:

- *Code encapsulation*—All code logic is implemented in the web control.
- *Reuse*—The control can be easily reused by another ASP.NET application.
- *Object-oriented access*—AWReportViewer exposes a set of public properties and methods.
- *Easy configuration*—The AWReportViewer properties can be set during both design time and runtime.
- *Handling report images for HTML reports*—The control takes care of displaying the report images when the report is generated on the server side of the application.

We found enhancing the ReportViewer control for generating server-side reports to be straightforward. The area that had to undergo the most changes was the control's `Render` method. The hosting ASP.NET page asks the control to render itself on two occasions:

- When the control needs to be redrawn during design time—For example, when you drag and drop the control on the page canvas, the page asks the control to show its "face."
- During runtime, when the page asks each of its child controls to render itself

Let's now see how AWReportViewer generates the report on the server side by calling the RS Web service.

Rendering reports

Listing 11.3 shows the server-side report-generation logic.

Listing 11.3 Server-side report rendering

```
byte[] result = RenderReport();      <-❶ Requests the report via SOAP
if (IsHtmlReport)  {      <-❷ For HTML reports renders the report as an HTML fragment
  string res = Encoding.UTF8.GetString(result);
  output.Write(res);
}                       For other export formats streams
else {    <-❸ the report to the browser
  HttpResponse response=System.Web.HttpContext.Current.Response;
  response.ClearContent();
  response.ClearHeaders();
  string fileName = GetFileName(this.ReportPath, this.Format);
  response.ContentType =
         GetContentType(Path.GetExtension(fileName));
  response.AddHeader ("content-disposition", "attachment;
           filename=\"" + fileName + "\"");
```

```
    response.BinaryWrite(result);
    response.Flush();
    response.Close();
}
```

❶ First, we generate the report by SOAP. The process is similar to the examples we looked at in chapter 9, so we won't be discussing it here. Once the report is generated, we need to display it on the page.

❷ If the requested format is one of the HTML flavors, such as HTML4.0, HTML3.2, or HTMLOWC, the report is rendered as an HTML fragment by turning on the HTMLFragment device setting. This setting instructs the Report Server to remove the HTML, HEAD, and BODY elements from the HTML representation for the report. Then the report output is embedded in the hosting page, at the location where the AWReportViewer control is placed on the page.

❸ In the case where the export format is other than HTML, AWReportViewer streams the report's payload to the browser. To accomplish this, we first clear the response buffer. Then, we let the browser know the type of the response stream, for example, application/pdf in the case of Adobe PDF. We also need to specify the filename, which we default to the report name with an appropriate file extension as per the specified export format.

For example, if the user has requested the Employee Sales Freeform report in PDF, the filename will be Employee Sales Freeform.pdf. Finally, we stream the report to the browser using the `Response.BinaryWrite` method. This will force the browser to display the familiar download confirmation dialog, just as it does when we export a report using the HTML Viewer.

Handling images

As we said in chapter 9, when you generate an HTML-based report via SOAP, you have to take care of the report's images. While for intranet-based applications you can download the image streams to a network file share, Internet-oriented applications make this option impractical.

Because the AWReportViewer control could be used in both scenarios, we decided to implement a flexible image-handling mechanism that works for both types of applications. The design goals of our image handler were

- Create a server-side image handler page to render the images
- Download the report images to a configurable image store
- Allow developers to easily configure the location of the image store, as well as the image handler end point

To make the image handler easily configurable, the AWReportViewer control exposes a couple of properties. You can use ImageDownloadPath to specify the image's download location. The default value is /temp, meaning that by default the report images will be downloaded to the AWReporterWeb/temp folder. In our implementation, the folder has to be relative to the application's root folder. However, if this is not convenient for you, you can modify the code to handle an alternative location. Please note that because the image handler page (more on this in a moment) takes care of streaming the images, the image store doesn't have to be accessible by the interactive users.

The second property, StreamRoot, corresponds to the StreamRoot device info setting. If left blank, it defaults to the ImageDownloadPath property. You will typically set StreamRoot to point to the image handler page's URL using the following syntax:

```
http://<webservername>/<applicationroot>/ImageHandler.aspx?ID=
```

When the report is processed, the Report Server will parse the StreamRoot setting and adjust the image's URLs accordingly. Specifically, it will append the image stream's identifier to the end of the URL string. When the report is rendered on the client side, the browser will invoke the image handler page and pass the stream's identifier as a query parameter.

We implemented the image handler page as an ASP.NET page (ImageHandler.aspx), which can be found under the AWReporterWeb project's root. The page attempts to load the image from a location specified in the application's configuration file. Because AWReportViewer and the image handler may reside in different web applications, you need to ensure that both are configured to use the same image store.

Next, the page converts the image to a byte array and streams it back to the browser. The added advantage of the image hanlder approach is that you don't have to take care of the image's housekeeping chores because page deletes the image once it is done with it.

Implementing control properties

The last area that deserves more attention is the control property synchronization. As we mentioned, the control has built-in logic that determines which properties will be available for server-side and client-side modes. To accomplish this, we had to implement the `ICustomTypeDescriptor` interface and override the property descriptor. If you look at the custom properties declaration inside the control's source code, you will see that they are decorated with attributes, as in the following example:

```
[Browsable(true), ReadOnly(true),
  Category("Server-side Execution Options"),
Description("Set this to an instance....")]
public System.Data.DataSet DataSource {}
```

You can use property attributes such as these to let the VS.NET Designer get more insight about your custom properties so it can configure the Properties window accordingly. For example, the DataSource property is decorated with the Browsable attribute set to true, which means that we want this property to appear in the VS.NET Properties window. It is also marked with a ReadOnly attribute, so the property appears disabled.

To override the design time property configuration, you need to implement the ICustomTypeDescriptor interface as we did with the AWReportViewer control.

The ICustomTypeDescriptor interface has many methods but, with the exception of GetProperties (shown in listing 11.4), all are implemented as simple pass-through methods.

Listing 11.4 To override the web control properties, you need to implement ICustomTypeDescriptor.

```
public PropertyDescriptorCollection
   GetProperties(System.Attribute[] attributes)     {

 PropertyDescriptorCollection filteredProperties = new
    PropertyDescriptorCollection(null);
 PropertyDescriptorCollection existingProperties;
 PropertyDescriptor tempProperty = null;

existingProperties = TypeDescriptor.GetProperties(this.GetType(),
    attributes);    <-- Gets a list of all of the AWReportViewer properties
 foreach (PropertyDescriptor pd in existingProperties)
    filteredProperties.Add(pd);    <-- Copies the properties to a new collection

 tempProperty = filteredProperties["ToolbarVisible"];    <-- Configures them according to the report-generation mode
 if (tempProperty !=null)  {
   filteredProperties.Remove(tempProperty);
   tempProperty = TypeDescriptor.CreateProperty
   (tempProperty.ComponentType,
   tempProperty, new System.Attribute[] {this.ServerSide ==
   multiState.True?ReadOnlyAttribute.Yes:ReadOnlyAttribute.No});
   filteredProperties.Add(tempProperty);
 }
  // configure more properties here…
}
```

Our GetProperties implementation filters the existing properties by adding them to a new collection called filteredProperties.

Then, we configure the properties according to the report-generation option. For example, if ServerSide is true, we disable the ToolBarVisible property because the HTML Viewer is not available with reports requested via SOAP.

Debugging AWReportViewer

To understand how the AWReportViewer works, you may want to step through its code using the VS.NET debugger. We have found that the easiest way to debug the control during runtime, that is, when the page is rendered, is to set the web control library's debug mode to URL, as shown in figure 11.16.

The Start URL property points to the hosting ASP.NET page, which in our case is AWReportViewerDemo.aspx. With this setup, when you press F5, VS.NET will load

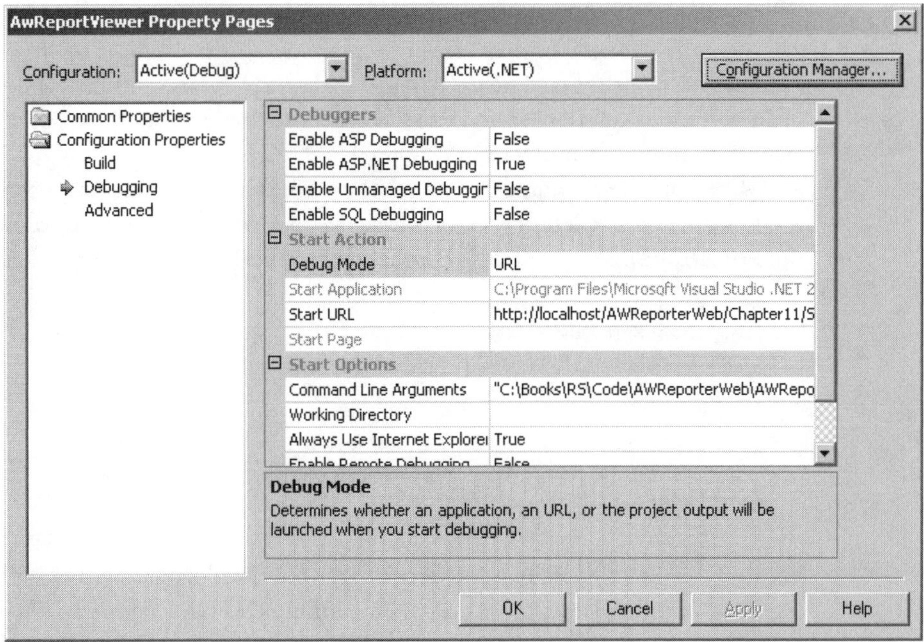

Figure 11.16 To debug the AWReportViewer control, set its mode to URL and its Start URL setting to the ASP.NET page that hosts the control.

the hosting page, which, in turn, will call the control's `Render` method. Now, the VS.NET debugger should stop at your breakpoints inside this method.

As we mentioned, VS.NET will ask the control to render itself during design time as well. If you want to debug the control code during design time, you can set the Debug Mode property to Program. In addition, you will need to set the Start Application setting to the full path of the Visual Studio 2003 executable, which by default is C:\Program Files\Microsoft Visual Studio .NET 2003\Common7\IDE\devenv.exe. Finally, you will need to set the Command Line Arguments to the full path of the AWReporterWeb project, for example, C:\Books\RS\Code\AWReporterWeb\AWReporterWeb.csproj.

With this setup, putting the AWReportViewer in debug mode will result in a new instance of VS.NET that will load the AWReporterWeb project. This will allow you to open the control's hosting page inside the second instance of VS.NET, which will fire the control's `Render` method when the page asks the control to render itself.

One interesting feature supported by the AWReportViewer control is reporting off ADO.NET datasets, as we will discuss next.

11.3.3 Reporting off application datasets

We can't resist the temptation to fast-forward a bit and show you how you can use the AWReportViewer control to report off application datasets.

The ApplicationDataset.aspx page does just this. It uses AWReportViewer to render the Salesperson Summary report, shown in figure 11.17. This report is special because it accepts a DataSource parameter that can be used to pass a serialized copy of an ADO.NET dataset. To report off datasets, the report uses the custom dataset data extension, discussed in detail in chapter 15.

Once you have authored a report that uses the custom dataset extension, rendering the report with AWReportViewer is easy, as you would probably agree by looking at the `RenderReport` method found in the ApplicationDataset.aspx page:

```
private void RenderReport()    {
  salespersonSummary = new
     AWC.Reporter.Web.Entities.SalespersonSummary();
  sqlDataAdapter.Fill(salespersonSummary);

  // bind the dataset to the report viewer
  reportViewer.DataSource = salespersonSummary;
  reportViewer.Visible = true;
}
```

For the purposes of this demo we decided to use a typed dataset, although there's nothing from stopping you from using plain-vanilla ADO.NET datasets. The salespersonSummary variable is set to an instance of the typed dataset. In real life, the ASP.NET

Salesperson Summary

Employee Name:	Campbell, David
Title:	Sales Representative
Hire Date:	5/2/2003

Year	Month	Sales	No Orders
2003	1	$220,228.99	71
2003	2	$112,937.13	74
2003	3	$46,550.00	50
2003	4	$247,247.44	122
2003	5	$128,473.37	90
2003	6	$41,874.56	51

Figure 11.17 Use the AWReportViewer control to report off ADO.NET datasets by setting its DataSource property to a "plain-vanilla" or typed dataset.

front end will most likely get the dataset from the application data layer. In our case, we populate the dataset with the results of a SQL statement. Finally, we bind the AWReportViewer control to the dataset.

To pass the dataset as a parameter to the Salesperson Summary report we need to serialize it first. If you use the AWReportViewer control, you can skip this part because the control's DataSet property does this for you, as shown in listing 11.5.

Listing 11.5 The implementation of the DataSet accessor serializes the passed dataset and passes it under a DataSource report parameter.

```
public System.Data.DataSet DataSource    {
  get {return null;}
  set {
    if (_parameterValues["DataSource"]!=null)
      _parameterValues.Remove("DataSource");

    StringBuilder stringBuilder = new StringBuilder();
    StringWriter stringWriter = new StringWriter(stringBuilder);
    value.WriteXml(stringWriter, XmlWriteMode.WriteSchema);
    _parameterValues.Add("DataSource",stringBuilder.ToString());
    stringWriter.Close();
  }
}
```

The DataSource property implementation serializes the dataset content and schema to an instance of StringBuilder. Then, for the developer's convenience, it creates a new report parameter to pass the serialized dataset copy to the report.

Now that we've covered various web-reporting techniques, let's see how we can use some of them to implement a more realistic business-to-consumer (B2C) Internet-oriented reporting example.

11.3.4 Business-to-consumer reporting

Most popular commercial web sites allow customers to view their order history. Following this trend, imagine that the AWC management has requested that you enhance the company's web portal to support a similar feature, which we will call My Orders. Our design goals for the My Orders sample are as follows:

- Authenticate web users using ASP.NET Forms Authentication
- Show a report that lists the orders submitted by the customer

Figure 11.18 shows what the My Orders page looks like. The page lists the customer's order history, including the item details.

The source files for the My Orders sample are located under the Chapter11/B2C folder inside the AWReporterWeb project.

Let's start by implementing the first requirement, which calls for a comprehensive security model for authenticating web users.

ADVENTURE WORKS cycles

Customer Orders for 529

Product #	Product Name	Order Qty	Unit Price	Discount	Total
Order: SO6775	8/1/2002				**$9,494.00**
BK-R89R-52	Road-250 Red, 52	1	$1,759.21	0.00 %	$1,759.21
BK-R50B-48	Road-650 Black, 48	2	$563.75	0.00 %	$1,127.51
BK-R64Y-42	Road-550-W Yellow, 42	1	$720.32	0.00 %	$720.32
BK-R50B-62	Road-650 Black, 62	2	$563.75	0.00 %	$1,127.51
FR-R92B-44	HL Road Frame - Black, 44	1	$963.01	0.00 %	$963.01
FR-R38B-60	LL Road Frame - Black, 60	4	$226.86	0.00 %	$907.43
FR-R92B-48	HL Road Frame - Black, 48	1	$963.01	0.00 %	$963.01
FR-R92R-48	HL Road Frame - Red, 48	2	$963.01	0.00 %	$1,926.02
Order: SO6809	11/1/2002				**$12,383.31**

Figure 11.18 The Customer Orders report demonstrates the My Orders feature.

Authenticating web users

As we said at the beginning of this chapter, most ASP.NET-based Internet applications authenticate the users using application-based authentication. To implement this we can take advantage of the ASP.NET Forms Authentication security model baked into the .NET Framework.

To configure the AWReporterWeb application for Forms Authentication, you need to change the AWReporterWeb web.config file as follows:

- Comment out the `<authentication mode="Windows">` element.
- Enable the `<authentication mode="Forms">` element.

Once this is done, run the B2B sample from the B2C Demo menu found under the Server-side Reporting menu. At this point, the application should pop up the Login Form shown in figure 11.19 to prompt the user for login credentials.

For detailed coverage of ASP.NET Forms Authentication, please check the VS.NET product documentation. In essence, if the user needs to be authenticated, ASP.NET redirects the request to a page that you have specified in the application's configuration file. In our case, the loginUrl attribute dictates that the web form used to authenticate the user be Chapter11/B2C/Login.aspx.

Login Form

Customer ID: 529

Log in

Figure 11.19 With ASP.NET Internet applications you can use Forms Authentication to authenticate the user.

To specify which resources require authenticated access, we used another web.config file located in the B2C folder. If you inspect this file, you will see that it includes the following section:

```
<location path="MyOrders.aspx">
  <system.web>
   <authorization>
     <deny users="?" />
   </authorization>
  </system.web>
</location>
```

What this means is that unauthorized users will not be permitted to access the MyOrders.aspx page. Instead, they will be redirected to the Login.aspx page. To keep things simple, the Login web form takes only the customer identifier. We authenticate the user on the server side of the page, as follows:

```
string customerID = txtCustomerId.Text;
if (IsAuthentic(customerID))
  FormsAuthentication.RedirectFromLoginPage(customerID, false);
else
  lblStatus.Text = "Login Failed!";
```

We pass the identifier that the user has entered to the `IsAuthentic` function, which queries the Customer table in the AdventureWorks2000 database. If a match is found, we call the `FormsAuthentication.RedirectFromLoginPage` method. This method serves two purposes:

- Issue an authentication ticket in a form of a cookie to the browser
- Redirect the user to the originally requested page

In our case, we request that the cookie will be created as a session cookie by passing false to the method's second argument. The browser will pass the cookie with each subsequent request to the AWReporterWeb site. The Forms Authentication mechanism will parse each request in an attempt to find this cookie to determine whether the user has been authenticated or not. For this reason, only the first request to the My Orders page will pop up the Login Form for the duration of the browser session.

Implementing the My Orders page

Implementing the MyOrders.aspx page is nothing we haven't seen so far. To facilitate generating the report on the server side, we use the AWReportViewer control, which is preset with the following properties:

- *ReportPath*—/AWReporter/Customer Orders
- *Format*—HTML4.0
- *ServerSide*—True

With this configuration, the AWReportViewer control will generate the Customer Orders report on the server side as an HTML fragment that will be injected into the page output.

The only thing left is to take care of the CustomerID parameter that the Customer Orders report takes. The following line of code passes this parameter to the AWReport-Viewer control inside the MyOrders Page_Load event:

```
reportViewer.AddParameter("CustomerID", User.Identity.Name);
```

User.Identity.Name matches the first argument of the `FormsAuthentication.RedirectFromLoginPage` method call, which, in our case, is the customer identifier.

Another popular web reporting scenario that you may need to support is business-to-business reporting. Let's finish this chapter by seeing how RS can be used with B2B applications.

11.3.5 Business-to-business reporting

Our sample will implement the hypothetical scenario that we described in section 11.1.3. We will build a solution that will expose the Adventure Works Cycles product inventory levels to their outside partners. The AWC vendors will be able to request the product inventory report in XML in order to automate the vendor-to-AWC supply chain. To implement this fictitious scenario we will create the following components:

- An Inventory Levels report to expose the inventory information about the vendor's products in XML
- A Web service façade to authenticate the vendor request and return the Inventory Levels report
- A simple WinForm client to test the façade

Implementing the Inventory Levels report

The Inventory Levels report takes the vendor's identifier as a parameter, queries the product inventory data, and produces the output shown in figure 11.20.

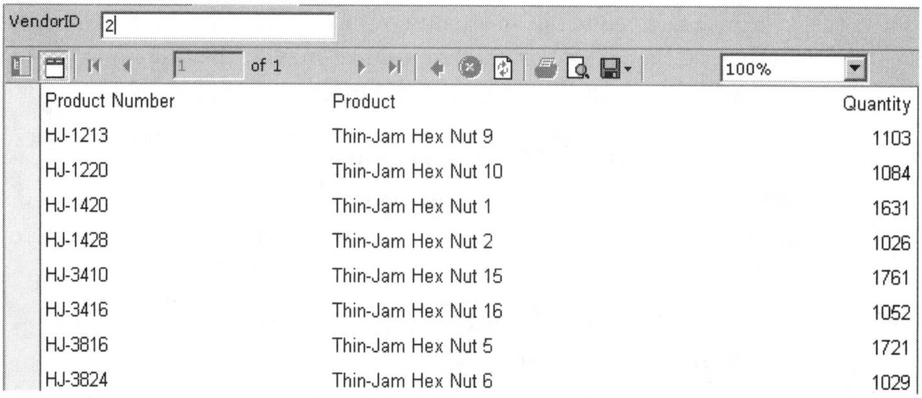

VendorID 2

1 of 1 100%

Product Number	Product	Quantity
HJ-1213	Thin-Jam Hex Nut 9	1103
HJ-1220	Thin-Jam Hex Nut 10	1084
HJ-1420	Thin-Jam Hex Nut 1	1631
HJ-1428	Thin-Jam Hex Nut 2	1026
HJ-3410	Thin-Jam Hex Nut 15	1761
HJ-3416	Thin-Jam Hex Nut 16	1052
HJ-3816	Thin-Jam Hex Nut 5	1721
HJ-3824	Thin-Jam Hex Nut 6	1029

Figure 11.20 Vendors will request the Inventory Levels report in XML to find out their product inventory levels.

Granted, the report layout has left much to be desired, but remember that this report is not intended to be displayed interactively. Instead, the façade will export the report as XML and pass the XML report's payload to the caller. We used the Data Output property tab of several report items to customize the report's XML output until it conformed to the schema we wanted.

Implementing the façade

The Inventory Levels façade can be found under the B2B folder in the AWReporterWeb project. To test the façade successfully, please make sure that the application is set to use Windows Authentication in the web.config file.

NOTE If using Windows Authentication with your real-life extranet applications is impractical, you can use other techniques to secure access to the Web service façade, as we explained in section 11.1.3. For the purposes of our demo, we use Windows Authentication because we set the web service proxy to use DefaultCredentials in order to pass the credentials of the interactive user to the Report Server.

The façade exposes a web method called `GetProductInventory` that has the following signature:

```
[WebMethod]
public EntityInventory GetProductInventory(int vendorID)
```

The AWC vendors will call this method to get the inventory data for their products. For this reason, `GetProductInventory` takes the vendor's identifier as an argument.

As you can see, this method returns the inventory data as an object of an `EntityInventory` type, which happens to be implemented as a typed dataset. While we could have returned the XML report's payload as a plain string, you should avoid doing so because the façade's consumers won't be able to determine beforehand what the response schema looks like. In our case, the `EntityInventory` XML schema matches the report's output. The easiest way to define the schema is to derive it from the report's XML output using VS.NET by following these steps:

Step 1 Export the Inventory Levels façade in XML and save it as a file.

Step 2 Open the file in VS.NET. Right-click anywhere inside the file and choose Create Schema. This will produce the XML Schema file with an .xsd extension.

Step 3 Fine-tune the schema, for example, change the data type of the attributes.

Step 4 Right-click on the schema and choose Generate Dataset to get the typed dataset class.

Using XML schemas allows the façade's callers to find out the response definition by querying the `EntityInventory` schema as follows:

```
http://<servername>/AWReporterWeb/Chapter11/B2B/
        InventoryLevel.asmx?schema=EntityInventory
```

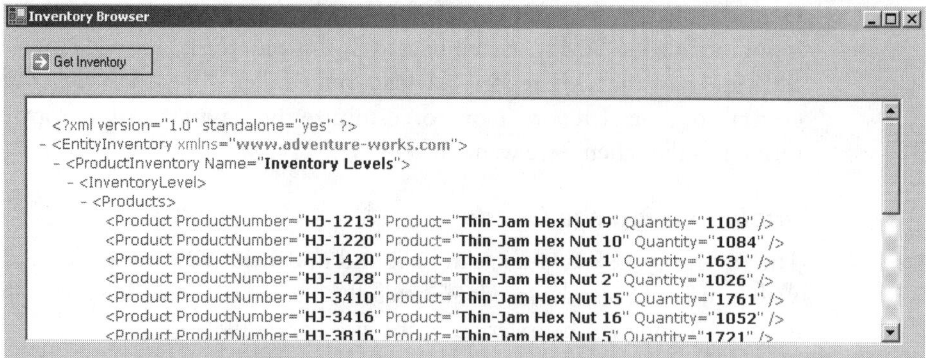

Figure 11.21 Use the Inventory Browser WinForm client to test the B2B sample.

This will allow the AWC partners to create strongly typed objects on their side to hold the method results similar to the `EntityInventory` typed dataset.

The façade requests the Inventory Levels report via SOAP. Once the façade obtains the report's payload in XML, it loads it into an instance of the EntityInventory typed dataset:

```
MemoryStream stream = new MemoryStream(result);
stream.Position = 0;
stream.Seek(0,SeekOrigin.Begin);
inventory = new EntityInventory();
inventory.ReadXml (stream);
```

Here, we push the report's payload into memory so that we can load the typed dataset.

Tesing the B2B solution

To test the sample, we created a simple WinForm client, Inventory Browser, shown in figure 11.21, which you can find under the Chapter11 folder in the AWReporterWin project.

Inventory Browser calls down to the façade and saves the report to a disk file. Then, it uses the WebBrowser control to display the file's contents. As we said before, in real life, the façade's consumers could parse the report's payload and pass the data to other systems. For example, the Inventory Browser could pass the inventory data to a BizTalk schedule, which could orchestrate the supply chain application's integration.

11.4 SUMMARY

As you have seen in this chapter, RS allows you to get your reports on the web in many ways. The implementation approach you choose will vary based on the application type. You may find that integrating RS with intranet-based applications is similar to doing so with their WinForm counterparts. In this case, URL access may prove to be the easiest and richest way to report-enable your intranet application.

Internet-based applications often call for server-side report generation. To facilitate this, you can build a web control similar to the Adventure Works Report Viewer that we implemented in this chapter. Besides rendering the report on the server side of the application, such a control can facilitate reporting off data sources not natively supported by RS, such as external datasets.

Finally, extranet applications often follow the Client-to-Façade-to-Report Server design pattern. Thanks to RS's flexible exporting options, you can custom-tailor the report's XML output to meet your integration needs.

Sometimes the user requirements will demand more flexible reporting options than generating standard reports. The next chapter shows you how you can achieve this goal by integrating RS with OLAP applications.

11.5 RESOURCES

Building Secure ASP.NET Applications: Authentication, Authorization, and Secure Communication
(http://msdn.microsoft.com/library/default.asp?url=/library/en-us/dnnetsec/html/secnetlpmsdn.asp)
This guide presents a practical, scenario-driven approach to designing and building secure ASP.NET applications.

Web Services Enhancements (WSE) 1.0 SP1 for Microsoft .NET
http://www.microsoft.com/downloads/details.aspx?FamilyId=06255A94-2635-4D29-A90C-28B282993A41&displaylang=en
Web Services Enhancements for Microsoft .NET (WSE) is an add-on to Microsoft Visual Studio .NET and the Microsoft .NET Framework, providing developers the latest advanced Web services capabilities to keep pace with the evolving Web services protocol specifications, such as WS-Security, WS-Routing, WS-Attachments, and DIME specifications.

Generic ASP.NET XML/XSL DHTML Menu ServerControl
http://www.gotdotnet.com/Community/UserSamples/Details.aspx?SampleGuid=175796d4-d08b-4130-8bbf-8d1a7fa94d85
Generic ServerControl takes your custom XML, XSL, JavaScript, and CSS files and renders your DHTML drop-down or other menu. A sample implementation is included along with the article and documentation.

About the WebService Behavior
http://msdn.microsoft.com/library/default.asp?url=/workshop/author/webservice/overview.asp
The WebService behavior enables client-side script to invoke remote methods exposed by Web services, or other web servers, that support the SOAP and Web Services Description Language (WSDL) 1.1.

C H A P T E R 1 2

Reporting for OLAP applications

Many organizations have realized the benefits of data warehousing and Online Analytical Processing (OLAP) technologies for analyzing vast amounts of data efficiently. In this chapter, we will see how Reporting Services can be integrated with OLAP applications to create versatile reporting solutions. Our discussion will center on the following topics:

- Overview of data warehousing and OLAP
- Using Microsoft Analysis Services cubes as data sources for standard reports
- Dynamic reporting using Microsoft Office Web Components
- Creating solutions with standard and dynamic reporting features

To see a practical application, we will build a scaled-down OLAP-based solution to address the reporting needs of the Adventure Works business analysts. Powered with the Adventure Works Data Miner, our users will be able to analyze data from different angles for discovering trends and decision-making purposes.

12.1 UNDERSTANDING OLAP

The terms *OLAP* and *data warehouse* are often used interchangeably, although an important distinction exists. As its name suggests, a *data warehouse* can be simply described as a place that stores vast volumes of data. The term *OLAP*, on the other hand, represents the tools used to make the warehouse data available for fast retrieval and analysis. OLAP solutions facilitate data mining and reporting because they are designed to meet the following characteristics:

- Deliver a great user experience by allowing the users to easily slice and dice warehouse data
- Provide a central repository of consistent data
- Answer complex queries quickly
- Provide a variety of powerful analytical and reporting tools

If you are currently reporting off OLTP databases, you may wonder at what point you need to consider switching to OLAP. The next section should make this clear.

12.1.1 OLTP vs. OLAP

While the process of generating reports from OLTP databases may be fine for small applications, it can quickly become inefficient and cumbersome as data grows both in size and complexity. In fact, there is a contradiction between OLTP systems that are designed for transactional efficiency and OLAP systems that are designed for efficient queries. Table 12.1 contrasts the design characteristics of these technologies.

Table 12.1 OLTP vs. OLAP

OLTP Database	Warehouse Database
Designed for real-time business operations	Designed for data analysis
Optimized for heavy transaction loads	Optimized for data retrieval and reporting
Volatile data	Usually read-only data. New data is appended on a regular basis.
Usually small in size	May contain large volumes of data, often in the range of gigabytes or even terabytes
Frequently supports many concurrent users	Supports few concurrent users

Because the OLTP and OLAP design characteristics are conflicting, an organization can use a data warehouse to offload the transactional data as it accumulates in the OLTP system and store it in a format optimized for data analysis and reporting.

For example, while an OLTP database stores data in a normalized form, it is perfectly fine for an OLAP database to denormalize the data, even if this results in redundant information. Moving the historical data to a central data warehouse database allows the OLTP system to operate at maximum efficiency because high volumes of analytical and reporting queries are handled by OLAP servers retrieving data from the data warehouse without impacting the performance of OLTP.

Besides performance, another valid reason for using OLAP with warehousing is data consolidation. While an OLTP system usually has all of its data located in one database, a warehouse typically consolidates data from several OLTP databases. For example, Adventure Works Cycles may have a SQL Server–based online sales ordering system, an Oracle-based HR system, and an IBM AS/400 mainframe–based invoicing system.

While OLAP systems offer distinct advantages in terms of reporting, you need to consider also the following pitfalls before you decide to jump on the OLAP bandwagon:

- *Increased complexity*—Implementing a well-designed OLAP solution is not a simple undertaking and requires careful planning and significant development effort.
- *Data dependency*—Data warehouses are dependent on other OLTP systems. If the OLTP data needs to be updated, the changes have to be propagated to the warehouse as well. Given the fact that data is usually transformed using sophisticated algorithms and massaging techniques before it enters the warehouse, synchronizing the warehouse data with the OLTP source may be rather involved.

The Microsoft OLAP offering is a product called Analysis Services. Just like Reporting Services, Analysis Services is an add-on to SQL Server 2000. Those of you who have used or built Microsoft-centric OLAP solutions may wonder how the products compare. After all, both products are designed to be used for data analysis and reporting. The next section should make this clear.

12.1.2 How Reporting Services and Analysis Services compare

You shouldn't view these products as competing with each other. Instead, they are complementary technologies that address different user needs, as shown in figure 12.1.

Figure 12.1 shows that a small percentage of users will use Analysis Services compared to the larger population of users who will use RS to meet their reporting needs.

According to Microsoft, in today's enterprise environment, a relatively small number of users need advanced reporting features. These users will access vast volumes of a company's historical data to analyze the company's performance and reach business decisions. An OLAP data warehouse solution based on Analysis Services could meet the complex requirements posed by this type of user. OLAP technology enables data warehouses to be used effectively for online analysis, providing rapid responses to sophisticated analytical queries.

For example, queries asked often by data analysts include the following:

- Show me the top-selling products.
- Show me product sales grouped by year and quarter on columns and product categories on rows.
- What is the company's sales performance for the past year broken down by quarter and month?

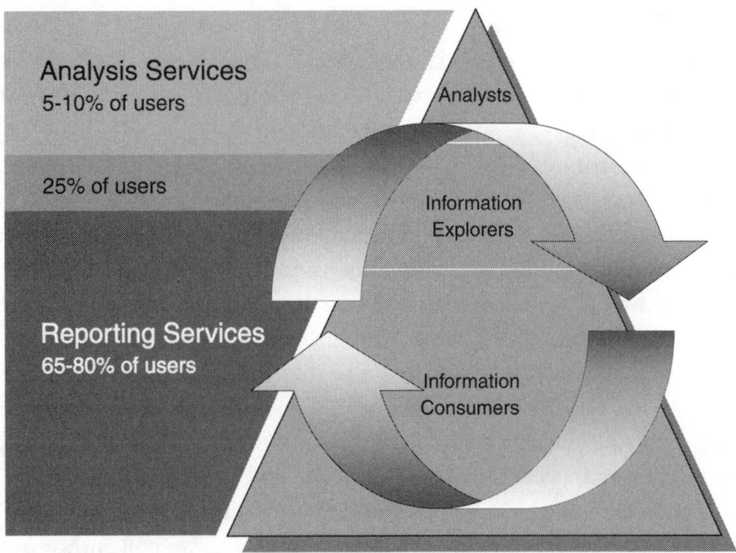

Figure 12.1 Reporting Services is positioned to meet the reporting needs of 65–80 percent of information workers.

Answering questions like these typically requires processing vast volumes of data, which is what OLAP technologies are designed for.

Most users of the data warehouse are information consumers, who will regularly use standard reports that others have developed. This is where RS could be useful. It provides a set of tools and applications that you can use to author, publish, and manage such reports.

Thus, Reporting Services and Analysis Services are not competing products but rather complementary technologies that can be used together to provide synergistic data analysis capabilities. In fact, you can architect a business intelligence solution that takes the best of both worlds by integrating these two platforms, as we will see shortly.

At this point, the OLAP concept may look appealing to you, and you may wonder how OLAP works. The next section should make this clear.

12.1.3 Understanding the OLAP storage model

As we explained in section 12.1.1, OLAP is a great technology that your users can leverage to access vast volumes of data efficiently. But as the character Spider-Man will conclude wisely, with great power comes great responsibility. Because OLAP solutions are not simple to implement, they require careful and responsible planning and architecting.

We'll now cover a few essential data warehouse concepts that will help you to implement the Adventure Works Data Miner solution.

OLAP cubes

The pivotal storage entity in the data warehouse model is the *OLAP cube*. You can conceptualize the cube as a hybrid between a table and a view in the relational database model. Similarly to a view, each cube has its schema defined as a set of joined data warehouse tables from which the cube draws its source data. Similarly to tables, cubes represent the most granular OLAP data storage entity.

Unlike the relational database entities, however, cubes are not limited to storing and displaying information in a two-dimensional format. Instead, cubes can be and often are multidimensional. For this reason, we consider the term *cube* to be a misnomer because it implies only three dimensions, while a data warehouse cube can include (and usually has) many dimensions. The multidimensional nature of the cube storage model lets OLAP users analyze the information from many angles. Smart OLAP front-end reporting systems know how to manipulate and present the cube model in a user-friendly way to facilitate data drilldown and trend analysis.

One way to explain the cube terminology is to look at a crosstab report produced with RS, such as the Territory Sales OLAP report, which we will author in this chapter. Figure 12.2 shows the report.

This report draws its data from the Sales cube, which we will implement shortly. The report labels, which the Dimension lines point to, are called cube *dimensions*. The grid cells, which the Measures lines point to, are the cube *measures*.

Territory Sales OLAP

Dimensions | Measures

ADVENTURE WORKS cycles		2001				2002	
		Quarter 3		Quarter 4			
		Sales	# Units	Sales	# Units	Sales	# Units
Europe						$6,206,505	15369
Internet		$2,912,084	1044	$3,625,702	1130	$13,122,405	5970
North America		$7,688,094	8770	$11,722,108	12900	$55,925,518	106236
	(Abbas, Syed data)						
	Tsoflias, Lynn						
	(Alberts, Amy data)						
	Pak, Jae					$3,056,216	7561
	Valdez, Rachel						
	Varkey Chudukatil, Ranjit						
	Ansman-Wolfe, Pamela	$229,829	240	$499,829	443	$1,111,361	1777
	Blythe, Michael	$366,080	504	$537,159	741	$3,781,831	7789
	Campbell, David	$244,284	200	$364,276	323	$1,775,580	3158
	Caro, Fernando	$548,297	803	$951,814	1159	$4,633,554	8203

Figure 12.2 The pivotal OLAP storage medium is the OLAP cube, and it consists of dimensions and measures.

Measures and fact tables

Measures represent the numerical values that you need to monitor your business. For example, the Sales cube defines the Sales Dollars and Sales Units measures. A Call Center cube may define measures such as Calls Received, Calls Handled, Call Time, and so on. The data warehouse measures are physically stored in *fact tables.* These tables are usually narrow (have few columns) but can have thousands to millions of rows of historical data.

Dimensions, levels, and dimension tables

Dimensions represent the various categories into which the cube measures can be organized. The Sales cube has several dimensions, including the three used by the Territory Sales OLAP report: Territory, Employee, and Time. Dimensions allow analysts to see the cube data from different angles.

Dimensions can be further broken down into *levels.* For example, the Time dimension in the Sales cube has Year, Quarter, and Month levels (the Month level is not used in the Territory Sales OLAP report).

The cube dimensions are stored in *dimension tables,* which are linked to the fact table similarly to the way lookup tables are linked to other tables in a typical relational database.

Aggregations

Granted, the previous report can be produced from relational database tables, which is what we did to author the Territory Sales Crosstab report in chapter 4. "Then," you may ask, "why do we need a cube?"

The main purpose of having a cube is to retrieve and store the aggregation results efficiently. For example, the mathematical operations of `count` and `sum` are the most frequent functions performed on warehouse data. They are called *aggregations.* If you look back at figure 12.2, you will notice that the report measures are summarized in each of the dimension intersections. For example, the sales total for Europe for 2002 is $6,206,505, while the Internet Users total for Quarter 4 of 2001 is $3,625,702.

While in this case the matrix region does the heavy lifting of summarizing the information, performing aggregations on vast volumes of data, especially with dynamic reports, can tax the performance of the relational database. When cubes are used, aggregations are precalculated in the cube when the cube is processed, which occurs before the end users access the cube. Once this is done, queries are answered using the aggregated values.

Remember, warehouse data is typically appended on a regular basis, meaning that data aggregations can be precalculated as soon as new data is added. Generally, aggregations are calculated immediately after the cube is initially populated or there is a change in the cube's content.

12.1.4 Designing OLAP solutions

Once the warehouse storage model is designed, the next step is to populate it and analyze the warehouse data on a regular basis.

Figure 12.3 depicts the high-level data process flow in a typical OLAP solution.

The diagram shows the distinct stages of the data flow from its source to the end user. Each of these stages could be the subject of a separate book and, in fact, there are such books available, as you could see by looking at the resource in section 12.4.

Because this book discusses Microsoft technologies, you should know that the Microsoft Business Intelligence platform provides a complete set of tools to help you implement each stage of your data warehouse project. One of the most attractive aspects of using Microsoft technologies is that most of the tools are bundled with SQL Server and, therefore, will not incur any additional licensing costs.

Loading data in the warehouse

First, we have extraction, transformation, and loading (ETL) processes, which import the data from the OLTP source database to the warehouse on a regular basis. This phase will probably be the most difficult and time-consuming part of your OLAP system

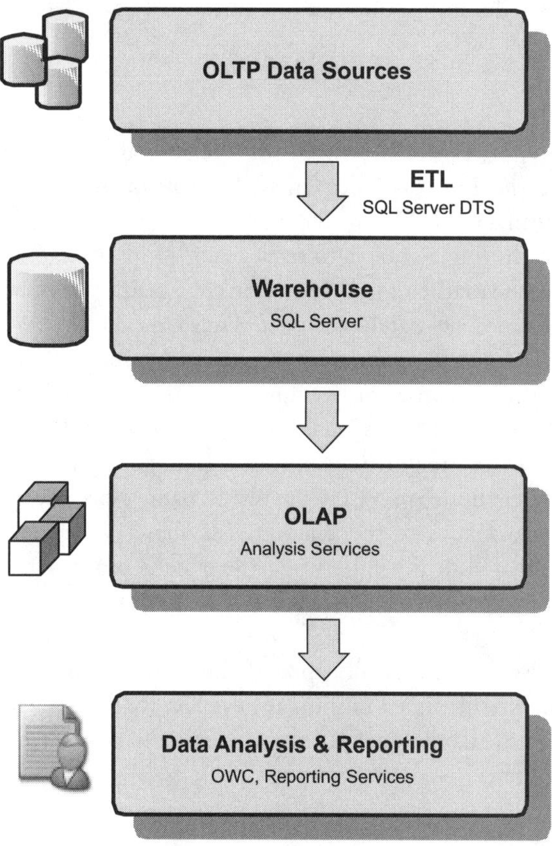

Figure 12.3 Implementing an OLAP solution involves setting up the warehouse schema, loading the warehouse, loading aggregates in cubes, and implementing data analysis and reporting solutions.

implementation. Often, to fully meet the user's reporting requirements, you will need to extract data from several OLTP systems that may not be easily accessible. For example, direct access to mainframe systems is usually not an option. In this case, data has to be exported on a regular basis from the OLTP system to flat files and then uploaded to the warehouse.

One of the most important decisions that you have to make when architecting a warehouse is the level of data consolidation. Because the main purpose of a warehouse is to show historical patterns for trend analysis, it rarely makes sense to import the OLTP data at its most granular level. Instead, the data warehouse measures are typically grouped around coarser time periods, such as days or months. Storing data at levels that are too granular may unnecessarily increase the size of the warehouse and impact its performance. Consolidating data too much may not address more detailed queries posed by the warehouse users.

During the ETL stage, you will also need to take care of resolving the data inconsistencies by scrubbing and transforming the source data. For instance, during one of my OLAP projects, I found out that all the OLTP source systems had a different way of storing the employee information. As a result, matching employee data from one database to another presented a challenge. To handle cases like this, you would probably need a staging database as an intermediate "cleansing" store where you could perform several passes of data scrubbing and massaging before the data is loaded into the warehouse database.

For ETL tasks, you can use the Microsoft Data Transformation Services (DTS). DTS sponsors a graphical designer that you can use to define various tasks to extract, transform, and consolidate data from disparate sources. If you have installed the Execution Log sample that we discussed in chapter 7, you have seen how DTS can be used to import data.

For data warehouse hosting, you can use the SQL Server relational database. In my opinion, SQL Server is one of the best products Microsoft has ever invented. SQL Server has been holding the top TPC (Transaction Processing Council) benchmarks in the price/performance category, as you could see online at http://www.tpc.org.

Processing OLAP cubes

The next stage of data lifecycle is loading the OLAP cubes with the calculated data aggregations. To accomplish this, you need to "process" the cube. During the processing phase, the cube reads and updates the dimension tables, reads the fact table, calculates specified aggregations, and stores the results.

As we've already mentioned, the Microsoft OLAP product is called Analysis Services. We will see Analysis Services in action in section 12.2.

Once the new data is uploaded into the cube, the cube is available for querying and reporting.

Data analysis and reporting

Finally, after a cube is processed, data is ready to travel to its final destination—reports. You can author reports that query the cube data and display it in the form of standard or dynamic reports, as we will see shortly in this chapter.

For data analysis and reporting, you can use Microsoft Reporting Services or Microsoft Office to report off Analysis Services cubes.

Now that we've taken a whirlwind tour of OLAP, let's see how we can put our knowledge into practice by implementing an OLAP solution to meet the needs of the Adventure Works business analysts.

12.2 Implementing an OLAP solution: AW Data Miner

Here is our hypothetical scenario that will drive the Adventure Works Data Miner solution. Despite the sluggish economy in the recent years, Adventure Works Cycles has been enjoying phenomenal business growth. However, the company's expansion has brought its own challenges, first and foremost of which is the most common data-related problem—that there is always too much of it. After analyzing the current situation, you have identified the following problem areas:

- *Historical data is not available.* To keep an OLTP system's performance at its peak, the database administrator periodically truncates the sales data. This makes it impossible for business analysts to analyze historical data and discover trends.
- *Data sources are disparate.* Data is captured and stored in several OLTP systems. Relating and consolidating data from these systems is very difficult.
- *Performance is slow.* Business analysts complain that ad hoc data-mining queries take a long time to execute and sometimes result in errors. Upon further investigation, you have found out that the source of these problems is related to the database locks imposed by the queries in the OLTP database.
- *Standard reports don't address all reporting needs.* Although the standard reports produced by RS meet the requirements of most information workers, they don't fully address the needs of the company's business analysts and decision makers. They have requested an OLAP system that will allow them to easily view the data from different angles.

To solve the above problems, you propose a Microsoft-centric OLAP solution based on the following approach:

- *A data warehouse will be implemented.* DTS processes will extract sales data on a monthly basis, consolidate it, and upload it to a central data warehouse database.
- *An OLAP cube will be created.* An Analysis Services cube (Sales cube) will be designed and loaded with the data warehouse data to provide fast response times to data-mining queries.

- *Standard RS-based reports will be authored to report off the OLAP cube.*
- *A user-friendly application front end will be provided for dynamic reporting.* We will implement the Adventure Works Data Miner (AW Data Miner) WinForm application to provide dynamic reports produced by Microsoft Office PivotTable and ChartSpace components linked to the OLAP cubes. In cases where reports need to show information not available in the data warehouse, the OLAP solution will generate standard "canned" reports produced by Microsoft Reporting Services.

Table 12.2 shows the list of tasks that we need to accomplish to implement the Adventure Works Data Miner solution.

As the task map indicates, we will start by implementing the data warehouse model.

Table 12.2 The task map for implementing the Adventure Works Data Miner solution

Phase	Task	Description
Implementing the data warehouse	Create the data warehouse storage model	Create the physical database model
	Define measures	Define SalesDollars and SalesUnits measures
	Define dimensions	Define Customers, Territory, Product, and Employee dimensions
	Load the data warehouse	Execute ETL tasks to load the data warehouse with data from the AdventureWorks2000 OLTP database
Implementing the OLAP cube	Create the cube	Create the Sales cube
	Create the fact table	Choose the Sales data warehouse table as the cube's fact table
	Create the cube dimensions	Set up the Customers, Territory, Product, Employee, and Time dimensions
	Fine-tune the cube schema	Optimize the cube's schema for performance and reporting
	Process the cube	Process the cube to make it available for querying and reporting
Data analysis and reporting	Author an OLAP-based report	Use RS to create an OLAP-based report to query the Sales cube using an MDX statement
	Author dynamic reports	Use Microsoft Office Web Components (OWC) to create dynamic pivot and chart reports
	Integrate OWC and RS	Demonstrate how a standard RS-based report can be launched from Office Web Components

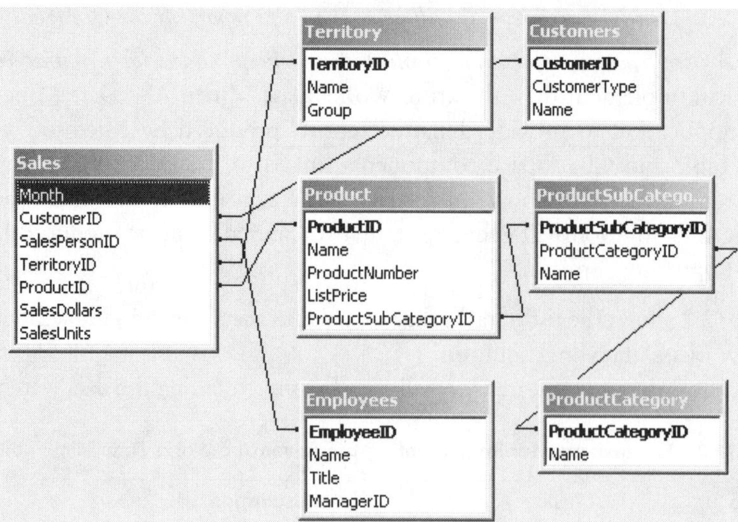

Figure 12.4 The Data Miner warehouse schema consists of one fact table (Sales) and several dimension tables.

12.2.1 Implementing the data warehouse

For simplicity and portability reasons, we used a Microsoft Access–based database called AdventureWorks.mdb to capture the warehouse data. This database will serve as a source for the Sales cube that we will build using Analysis Services. Needless to say, in the real world you should use a more powerful database server to host the data warehouse database, such as Microsoft SQL Server.

You can find the AdventureWorks database (AdventureWorks.mdb) under the Code/Database folder. Our warehouse dimensional model is shown in figure 12.4.

The model consists of a single fact table, Sales, and six dimension tables. The data in the fact table represents the consolidated monthly sales data from the AdventureWorks2000 relational database.

The consolidated historical data spans three years and includes more than 100,000 records.

Defining measures

The Adventure Works warehouse database has two measures defined in the Sales table:

- *SalesDollars*—Which represents the sales dollar amount
- *SalesUnits*—Which captures the number of products sold

Defining dimensions

We'll use the dimension tables in our sample data warehouse to form the following dimensions:

- *Customer*—The Customer dimension has two levels: Customer Type, such as Store, Individual, or Retail, and Customer Name.
- *Territory*—This dimension has also two levels: Territory Group, such as North America, and Name, such as Southeast.
- *Product*—The Product dimension has three levels: Product Category, Subcategory, and Product Name.
- *Employee*—The Employees table will be used to form a recursive cube dimension demonstrating a typical HR hierarchy, where each employee is linked to a manager.

Loading the data warehouse

While in real life, you would typically use Microsoft DTS to transform and upload data, to keep things simple, we loaded the warehouse database from a set of database views referencing the appropriate tables in the AdventureWorks2000 database. You can find the views in the views.sql script in the Database.dbp project under the Code/Database folder. The SQL views are included for your reference only because the data is already uploaded to the Access database.

The Sales view serves as a data source for populating the Sales table. It also consolidates sales data by grouping it by month. The other views facilitate loading the warehouse dimensions.

12.2.2 Implementing the OLAP cube

Once the warehouse database (AdventureWorks.mdb) is loaded, it is time to design the Analysis Services cube. Unfortunately, the current version of Analysis Services doesn't support exporting cubes. As a result, we were left with two implementation choices to make the cube model available to you:

- We could walk you through the steps needed to create the cube with Analysis Services.
- We could export the cube using Microsoft Query so you could bind the Data Miner application to the local version of the cube.

For the purposes of the demo, we decided to show you the "real thing" by walking you through the process of creating the Sales cube with Analysis Services.

Creating the Sales cube

A prerequisite task for creating a cube is setting the database connection to the data warehouse database. Follow these steps to set up a database connection to the AdventureWorks2000 database in Analysis Services:

Step 1 Open the Analysis Manager and connect to a computer running Analysis Services. Right-click on the computer name and choose New Database to create a new database definition. Name the database **AdventureWorks** and click OK.

Step 2 Just like a report can draw data from more than one data source, an Analysis Services cube can have more than one data source. For the purposes of our demo we need only one data source that points to the MS Access AdventureWorks.mdb database. To create the data source definition, expand the AdventureWorks database node. Right-click the Data Sources node and choose New Data Source.

Step 3 Choose Microsoft Jet 4.0 OLE DB Provider and browse to the location of the AdventureWorks.mdb database.

Once the database connection is ready, we can create the Sales cube by right-clicking the Cubes node inside the Analysis Services console and choosing New Cube → Wizard. We will use the Cube Wizard to help us set up the cube model.

Setting up the fact table

In this section, we need to specify the name of the table from the data warehouse database that will serve as the cube's fact table. A cube can have only one fact table. Follow these steps to set up the fact table:

Step 1 From the Select a Fact Table from a Data Source screen, choose the Sales table, as shown in figure 12.5.

Step 2 On the next screen, the wizard prompts you to select the columns from the Sales table that will represent the cube measures. In our case, we have only two measures: Sales Units and Sales Dollars. Select both, as shown in figure 12.6, and click Next to continue.

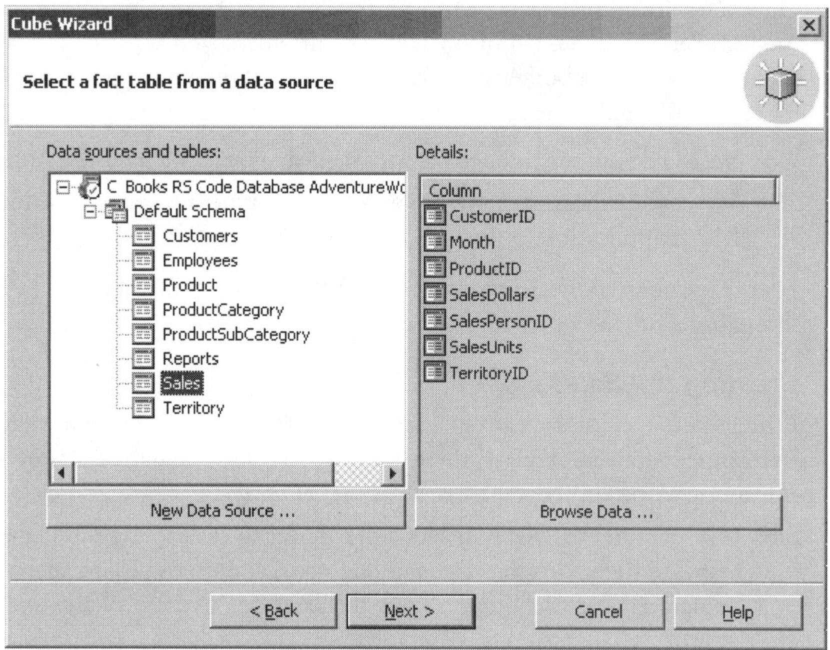

Figure 12.5 Select the Sales table as the cube's fact table.

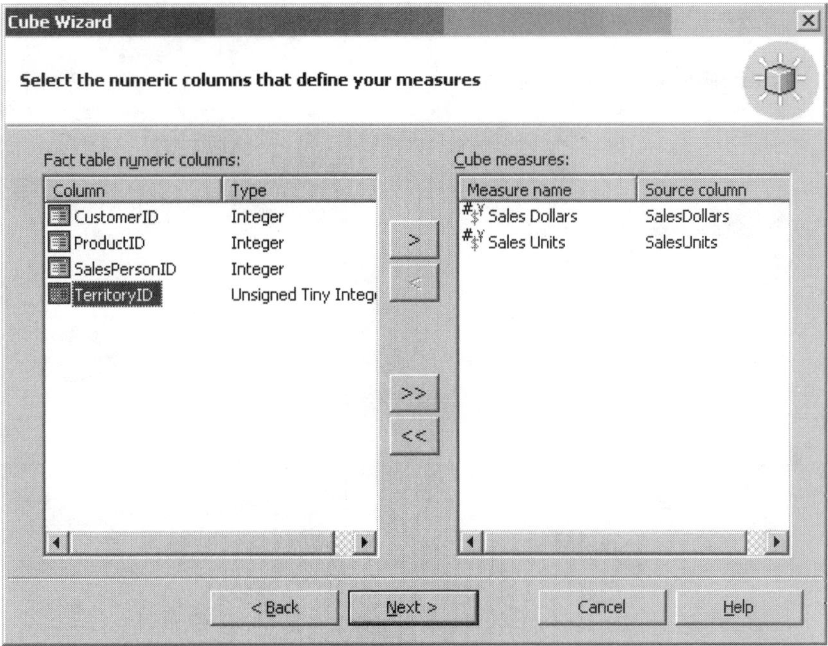

Figure 12.6 Select Sales Dollars and Sales Units as cube measures.

The next step of the wizard is about setting the cube dimensions. You can create the cube dimensions as private or shared. A private dimension can be used only within the cube that defines it. A shared dimension can be reused across cubes, similarly to the way a shared report data source can be used by more than one report. Shared dimensions allow us to standardize metrics across multiple cubes and link cubes in queries, very much like the way we can link relational tables by using joins. For the purposes of our demo, we will create all dimensions as shared.

Back in the Cube Wizard, click the New Dimension button. The Dimension Wizard appears. We will create several different types of dimensions, starting with the Customer dimension.

Setting up the Customer dimension

The Customer dimension will allow OLAP users to drill down into the sales data by customer type and name. Follow these steps to set up the Customer dimension:

Step 1 Choose the Star Schema radio button to create the Customer dimension from a single table.

Step 2 On the next screen, select the Customers table and click Next.

Step 3 Because this dimension has two levels, on the next screen select both Customer Type and Name in that order, as shown in figure 12.7.

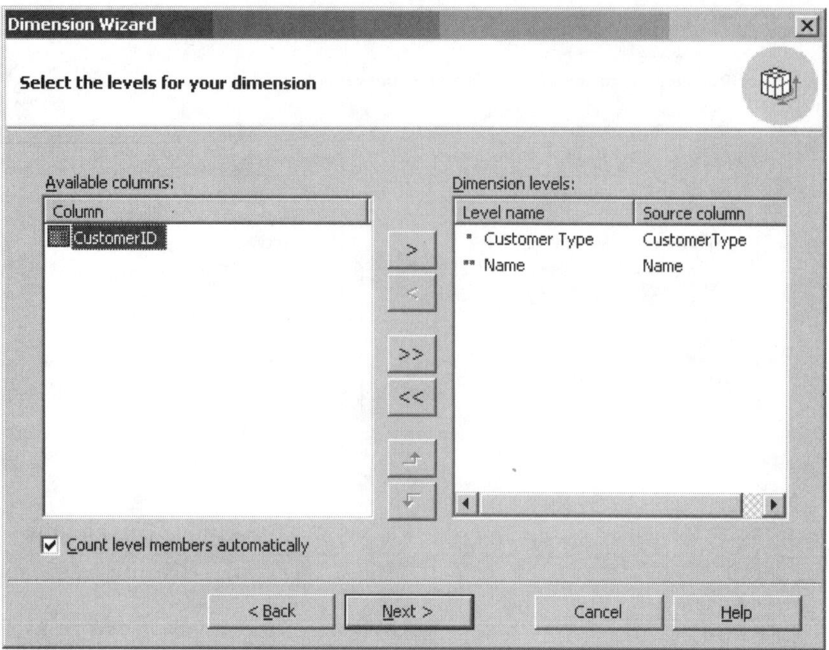

Figure 12.7 Set up the Customer dimension so that we can query the sales data by customer.

Step 4 Accept the default settings on the next two screens and name this dimension **Customer**. Make sure that the Share This Dimension with Other Cubes check box is selected.

Setting up the Employee dimension

The Employee dimension is going to be a recursive dimension because it will allow us to drill down recursively in the employee hierarchy. Here are the steps to create the Employee dimension:

Step 1 Use the Dimension Wizard to create the Employee dimension as a parent-child dimension.

Step 2 On the next screen, select the Employees table.

Step 3 Set the Employee dimension as shown in figure 12.8.

Step 4 Here, we are instructing Analysis Services to create a hierarchy by linking the ManagerID column to the EmployeeID column. Skip the next two screens and name the new dimension **Employee**.

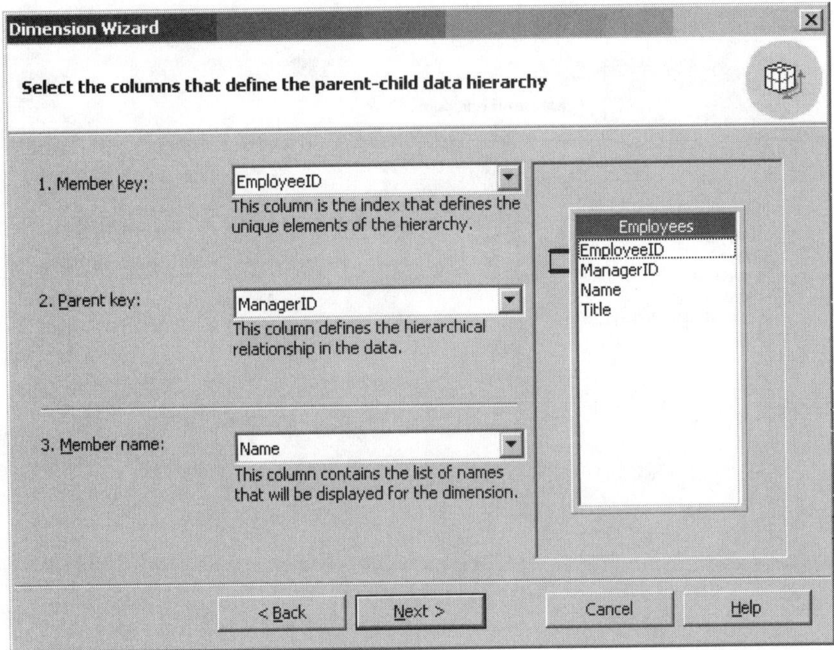

Figure 12.8 Set up the Employee dimension so we can query the cube by salesperson.

Setting up the Product dimension

This will be a typical three-level dimension, consisting of Product Category, Subcategory, and Product Name. Follow these steps to set up the Product dimension:

Step 1 Click the New Dimension button to restart the Dimension Wizard. This time, choose the Snowflake Schema option because this dimension will encompass more than one table.

Step 2 On the next screen, choose the Product, Product Subcategory, and Product Category tables.

Step 3 On the Create and Edit Joins screen, remove the default table relations that the wizard suggests and link the tables by dragging and dropping columns, as shown in figure 12.9. Click Next to continue.

Step 4 On the Select the Levels for Your Dimension screen, select the ProductCategory.Name, ProductSubcategory.Name and Product.Name columns in that order, as shown in figure 12.10.

Because all three of these columns are named the same, the wizard adds sequential numbers to differentiate them. We will fix this issue later.

Step 5 Finally, name the new dimension **Product**.

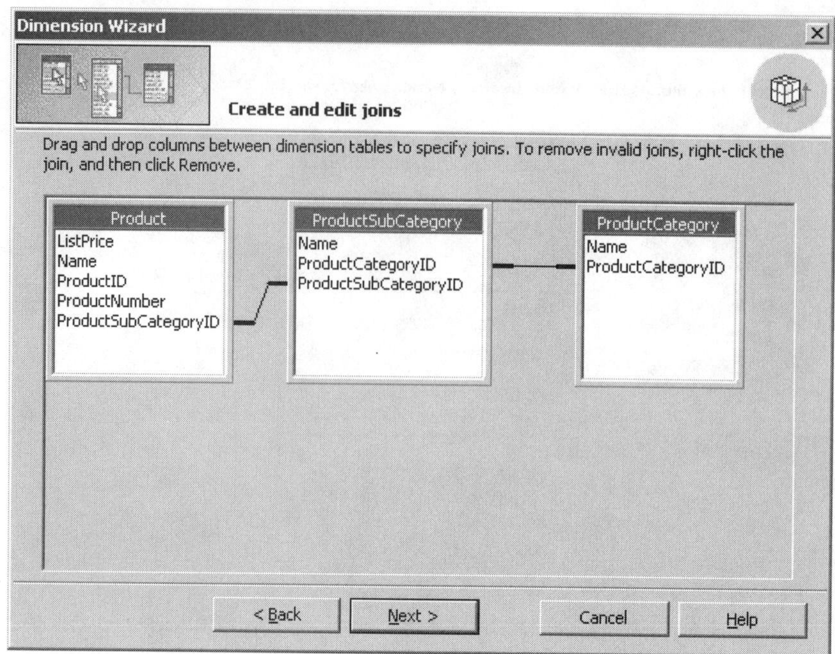

Figure 12.9 Set up the Product dimension so that we can query the cube by product.

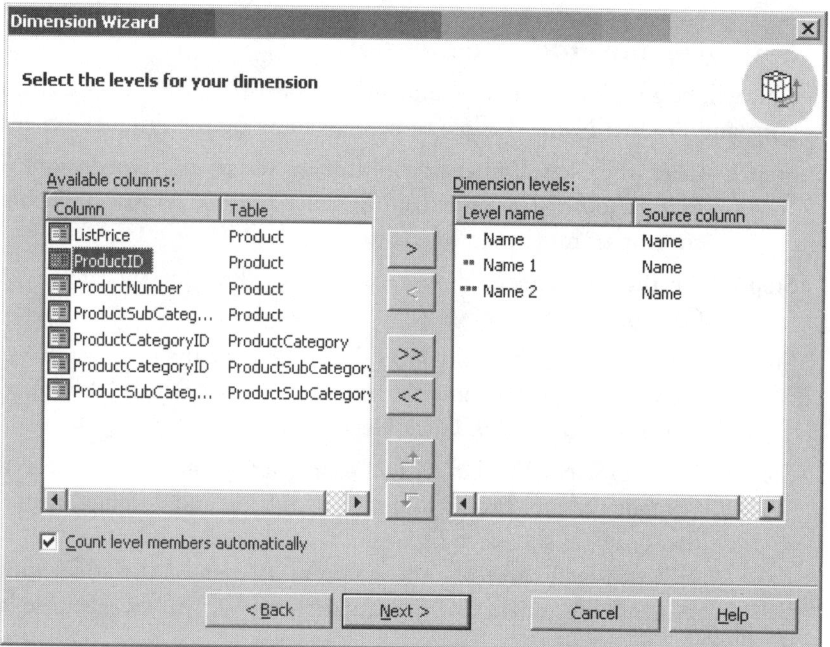

Figure 12.10 The Product dimension consists of Product Category, Subcategory, and Product Name.

Setting up the Territory dimension

The Territory dimension allows the users to drill down by sales territory and region. The process of setting it up is identical to creating the Customer dimension, as follows:

Step 1 Base this dimension on the star schema.

Step 2 Select the Territory table.

Step 3 To specify the dimension levels, select the Group and Name columns in that order, as shown in figure 12.11.

Step 4 Finally, name the new dimension **Territory.**

Setting up the Time dimension

Almost all cubes will require a Time dimension. Analysis Services knows how to create time dimensions based on the type of date columns, which means that you don't need a separate dimension table. In real life, however, you should create a separate time dimension table for flexibility and performance reasons. First, a separate time dimension table allows you to add additional columns, which you can use as custom members when querying cubes. For example, you may need to define a column called Holiday to track non-workdays. Second, such a table could have a primary integer key, which takes less space than the date type. This minimizes storage space with large fact tables.

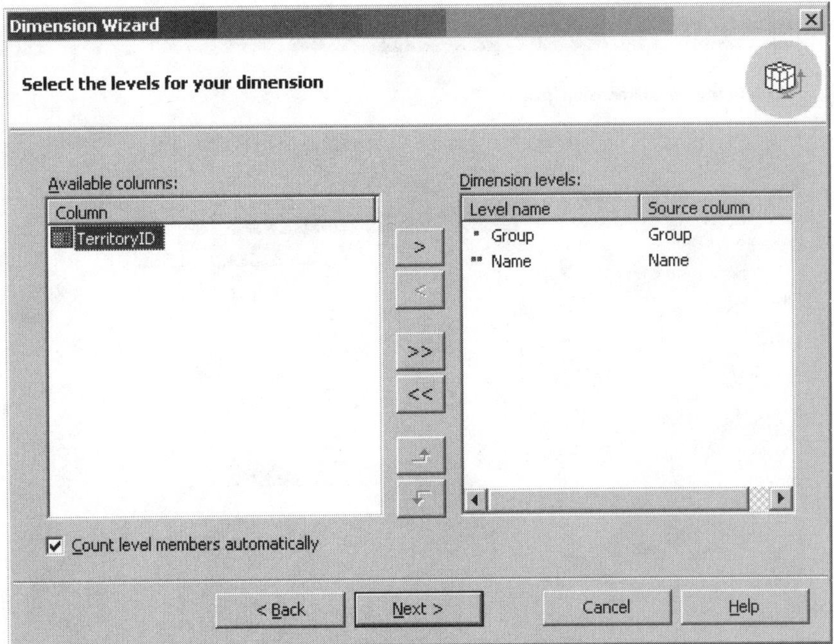

Figure 12.11 Set up the Territory dimension so that we can query the cube by territory.

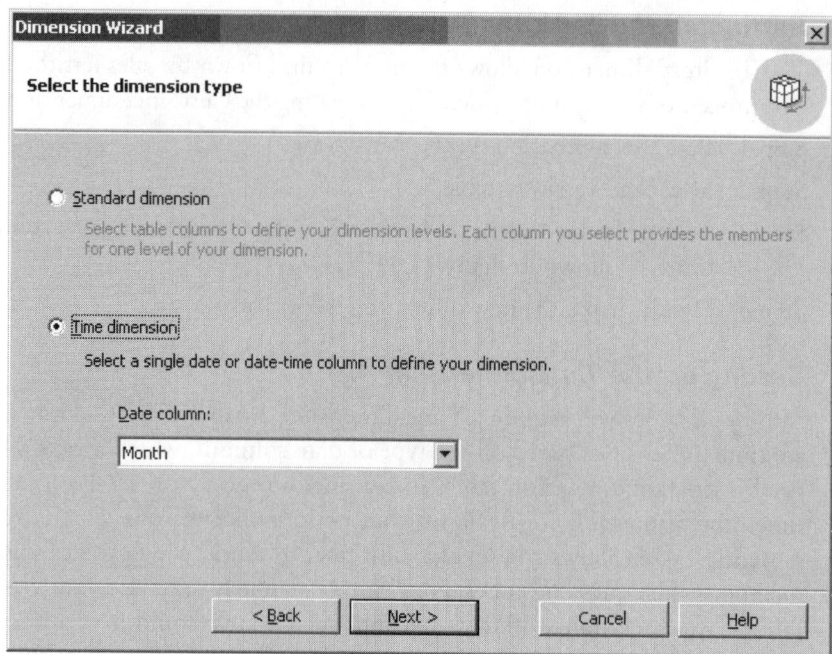

Figure 12.12 Set up the Time dimension from the fact table.

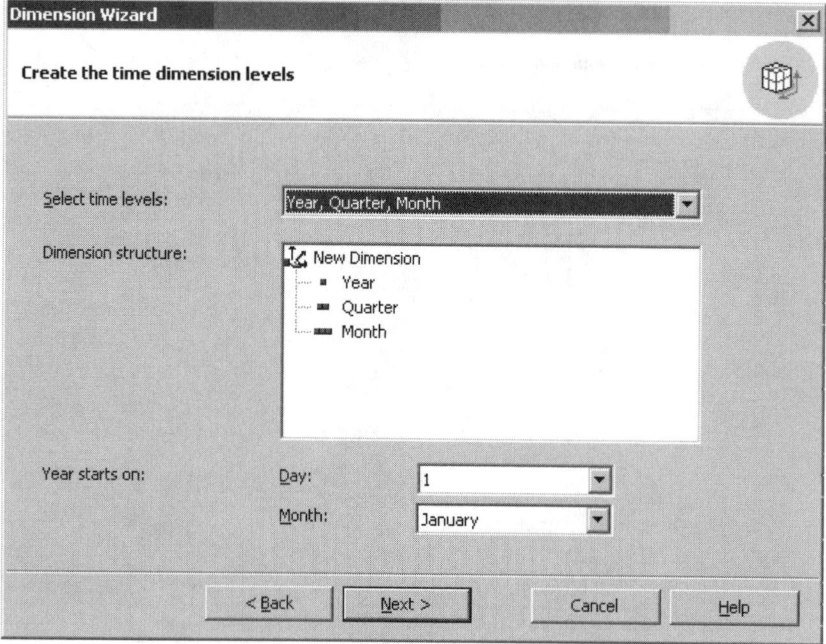

Figure 12.13 The Time dimension will consolidate data per year, quarter, and month.

For the purposes of this demo, we will create the Time dimension off the OrderDate column, as shown in the following steps:

Step 1 Create a new dimension based on the star schema.

Step 2 Choose the fact table named Sales as a dimension source table.

Step 3 On the Select the Dimension Type screen, choose Time Dimension. The wizard will correctly default the Date column drop-down to the only date column in this table: Month, as shown in figure 12.12.

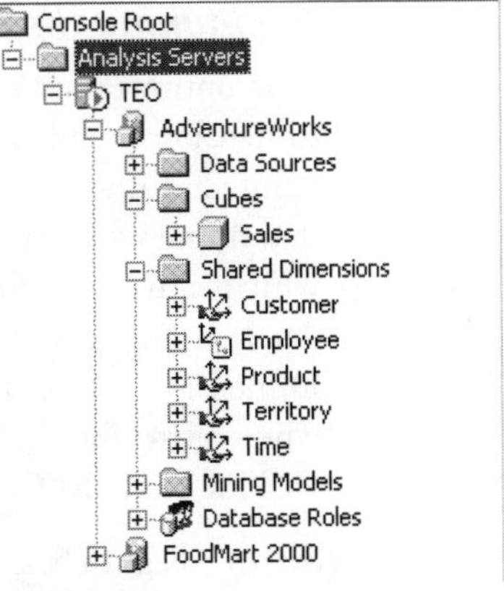

Figure 12.14 The Sales cube structure

Step 4 Because sales data in the warehouse database is grouped by month, on the next screen choose the Year, Quarter, Month dimension structure, as shown in figure 12.13.

Step 5 Name the new dimension **Time**.

We have finished setting up the cube dimensions. Name the cube **Sales** and exit the wizard. Figure 12.14 shows what the cube structure should look like when you return to the Analysis Manager console.

> **NOTE** One of the activities that the Dimension Wizard performs behind the scenes is creating joins between the dimensions and fact tables. To accomplish this, the Dimension Wizard tries to find matching column names between the dimension and the fact table. Of course, as you could imagine, this will succeed if the columns are named the same. If they are not, upon exiting the Dimension Wizard you may get an error message, "Unable to find an automatic join between the cube's fact table and the following dimension tables…." Then, the wizard will open the Cube Editor to give you chance to define the missing relationship(s). To "help" the wizard, in the Cube Editor drag and drop the column from the dimension table onto the corresponding column from the fact table.

The cube schema is almost done. We can use the cube as it is now, but let's add a few touches to finalize the cube schema. We will use the Analysis Services Dimension Editor to make the changes.

Fine-tuning the Customer dimension

One optimization technique that we want to take advantage of is to set up unique dimension member keys for better performance. If you select the Optimize Schema command under the Tools menu, Analysis Services will evaluate each dimension to determine whether it can be optimized. If the dimension member keys are unique, which is the case when the Member Key Column property references a primary key, Analysis Services will use the foreign key in the fact table instead of the key in the Dimension table. Therefore, Analysis Services will not use the Dimension table when retrieving the data. Fewer joins lead to faster cube processing.

Fine-tune the Customer dimension by following these steps:

Step 1 Right-click the Customer dimension and choose Edit. Expand the dimension properties by clicking the Properties button on the bottom of the Dimension Editor's left pane.

Step 2 Select the Customer level. Switch to the Advanced property tab and change the All Caption property from All Customer to All Customers.

Step 3 Select the Name level and click the Basic property tab. Change the Member Key Column property to "Customers"."CustomerID", as shown in figure 12.15.

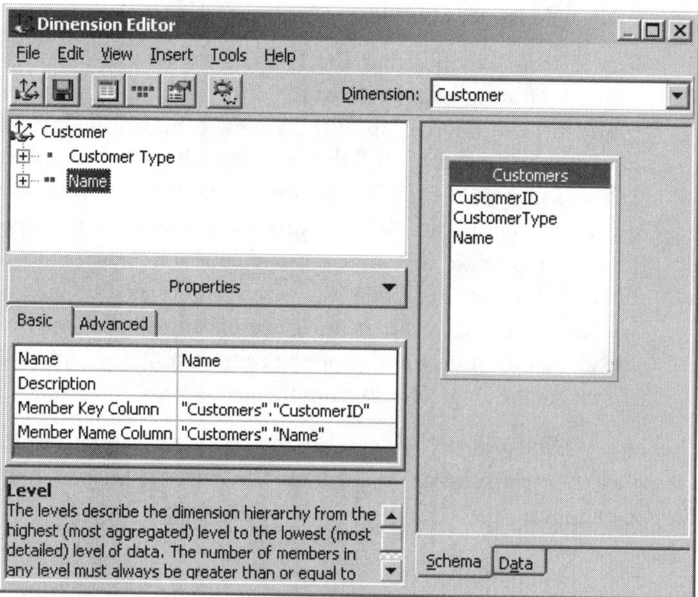

Figure 12.15 Use unique member keys for better performance.

Step 4 While the Name level is selected, switch to the Advanced tab and change the Member Keys Unique property to True. Click the Save button on the toolbar to persist your changes to the Customer dimension.

Fine-tuning the Employee dimension

The Employee dimension is a recursive dimension. By default, Analysis Services will name each hierarchical level sequentially, for example, Level01 for the top manager, Level02 for her subordinates, and so on. Let's come up with better captions for the levels, by following these steps:

Step 1 Open the Employee dimension and select the Employee level. Switch to the Advanced tab and set the All Level property to No to prevent Analysis Services from showing the All Dimension member. Next, set the Member With Data property to Non-leaf Data Visible. This is needed because the Employee dimension is hierarchical and not all of its members will have associated data in the fact table.

Step 2 Select the Employee Id level. Switch to the Advanced tab. The Level Naming Template property is blank by default. Set up the Level Naming Template property as shown in figure 12.16.

Step 3 Back on the Advanced tab, change the Root Member If property to Parent Is Blank, Self, or Missing. This prevents Analysis Services from repeating the parent name in case the employee hierarchy is unbalanced.

Fine-tuning the Product dimension

It may be confusing for the user to have Product Category, Subcategory, and Product Name all named the same. Let's assign unique names to all levels of the Product dimension by taking these steps:

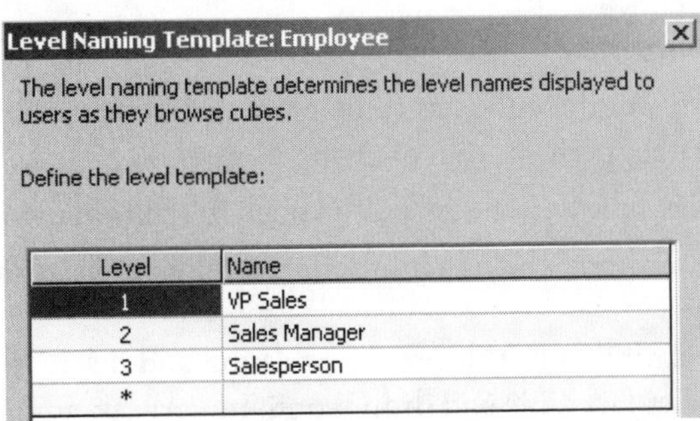

Figure 12.16
Use the Level Naming Template to define names for recursive hierarchies.

Step 1 Select the Name level and change its Name property to Category.

Step 2 Select the Name 1 level and change its Name property to Subcategory.

Step 3 Select the Name 2 level and change its Name property to Product. On the Basic tab, change the Member Key Column property to "Product"."ProductID". On the Advanced tab, change the Members Keys Unique property to True.

Fine-tuning the Territory dimension

Again, let's choose more descriptive names for the levels for the Territory dimension:

Step 1 Select the Group level and change its Name property to Territory Group.

Step 2 Select the Name level and change its Name property to Region. Change the Member Key Column property to "Territory"."TerritoryID".

Fine-tuning the Time dimension

Let's start by changing the name of the All member of the Time dimension:

Step 1 In the Dimension Editor click on the root node called Time.

Step 2 Switch to the Advanced tab and set the All Caption property to All Periods.

By default, Analysis Services displays the full name of the month. Besides being too verbose, this will make integrating our RS reports with the PivotTable component more difficult. To change the Month member name, follow these steps:

Step 1 Select the Month level of the Time dimension.

Step 2 On the Basic tab change its Member Name Column property to DatePart ('m',"Sales"."Month"). Preview the Data tab and verify that the Month level of the Time dimension now shows the months as numbers.

The cube schema is ready! Finally, we need to process the cube.

Adjusting the cube schema

Once the cube model is set up, the cube has to be processed before it is available for querying. To process the cube, perform the following steps:

Step 1 Right-click the Sales cube and choose Edit to open the cube in the Cube Editor.

Step 2 In the right pane, on the Schema tab, set the table relations as shown in figure 12.17.

To fix a table relation, select the existing relation and delete it. Then, drag a field from the Sales fact table and drop it onto its corresponding field in the dimension table. For example, to link the Sales table with the Employees table, drag the SalesPersonID field from the Sales fact table and drop it onto the EmployeeID field of the Employees dimension table.

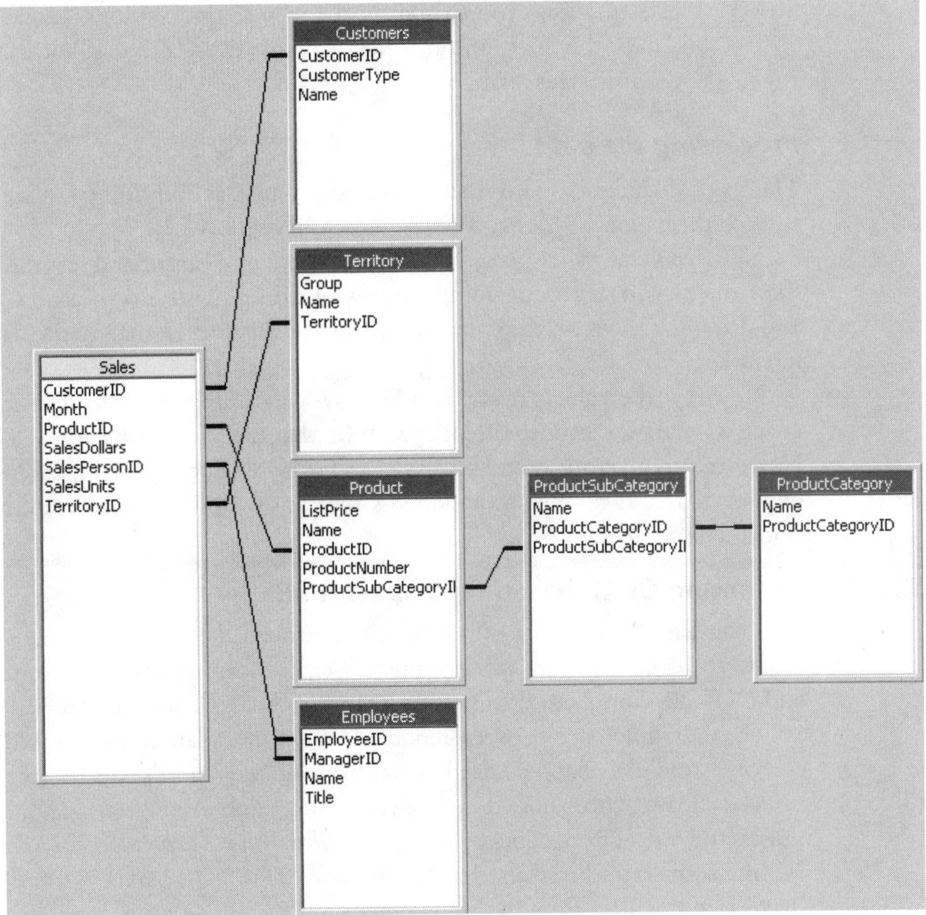

Figure 12.17 Use the Data tab to set up the table relations.

Choosing a cube storage model

Before we can process the Sales cube, we need to set up its storage configuration. With Analysis Services, you have complete control over the storage location and size of the cube aggregations. The easiest way to set the cube's storage options and process the cube is to use the Storage Design Wizard by following these steps:

Step 1 In the Cube Editor, select the Design Storage option from the Tools menu. The Storage Design Wizard appears.

Step 2 Explore the various data storage options. Leave the default setting, which is MOLAP.

Step 3 This step allows you to specify the aggregation settings. Leave the defaults and click the Start button. Click Next to advance to the Process Cube screen and initiate this task.

Processing the cube

The Storage Design Wizard then processes the cube. If everything is okay, you should see a confirmation of your success, as shown in figure 12.18.

Now, you can switch to the Data tab in the Cube Editor and test the cube's data. Experiment with different combinations of dimensions and measures by dragging and dropping them on the columns or rows of the grid to analyze the data from different angles.

Now that the cube is ready, let's see how we can report off its data. First, we will create a standard ("canned") report with RS that use the OLAP cube as a data source. Next, we can give our users the ability to create ad hoc reports by taking advantage of the smart Office Web Components that know how to manipulate multidimensional data sources.

12.2.3 Authoring OLAP-based reports with RS

Can you use RS to report off OLAP cubes? You bet! As we discussed in chapter 3, thanks to its flexible data architecture, RS reports can retrieve data from any ODBC and OLE DB–compliant data source, including Analysis Services cubes.

The only difference between reports drawing their data from an OLAP-based data source instead of a relational database is setting up the report's data source. Unlike relational databases, cubes hosted in Analysis Services don't understand SQL. Instead, you must retrieve data from cubes by using ***Multidimensional expressions***, or MDX for short.

Microsoft introduced the MDX extensions with SQL Server 7 OLAP Services to make accessing data from multiple dimensions easier and more intuitive. Although it

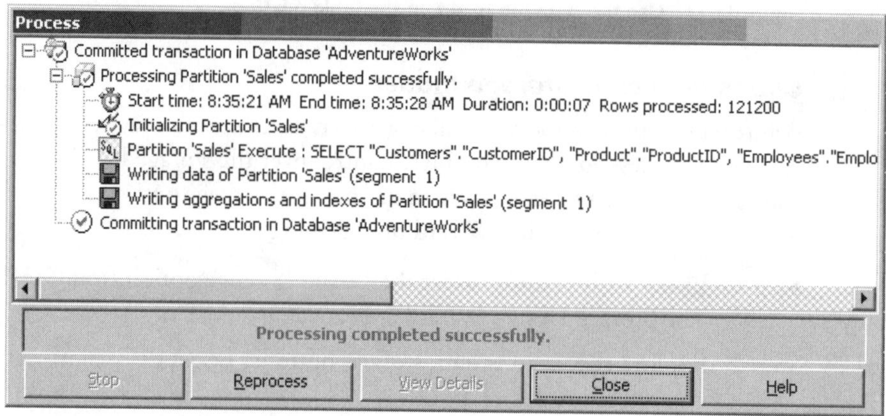

Figure 12.18 When the cube schema is ready, you must process the cube to make it available for querying.

is technically an extension to SQL and is similar to SQL in syntax, MDX is a separate and more difficult language. If you are new to MDX, you may find the MDX resources, which are listed in section 12.4, useful.

NOTE I was initially planning in this chapter to focus more on MDX queries until I come across the excellent "Integrating Analysis Services with Reporting Services" white paper (see section 12.4) from Microsoft. After reading this document, I realized that I don't have much to say about writing MDX queries to access Analysis Services cubes. This is where I thought that the concept of "dynamic reporting" with Microsoft Office Web Components would nicely complement the article to round out how RS can be integrated with Analysis Services.

You will probably find the RS matrix region very useful when authoring OLAP standard reports. Thanks to its drilldown capabilities, it naturally fits into the multidimensional nature of OLAP data.

Let's see how we can convert the Territory Sales Crosstab report to draw its data from the Sales cube instead of the relational database. We already mentioned the new version of this report in section 12.1.3.

Let's start by copying the Territory Sales Crosstab report and changing the name of the new report to Territory Sales OLAP.

Setting up the report's data source

The first step of modifying the Territory Sales OLAP report to meet the new requirements is to change its data source by switching to the Microsoft OLE DB Provider for OLAP Services 8.0, as shown in figure 12.19.

Also, we need to set the initial catalog to the name of the Analysis Services database we created in section 12.2.2 to host the Sales cube, which in our case is AdventureWorks.

Creating the report's dataset

To reproduce the Territory Sales Crosstab report, we need to craft an MDX statement to retrieve the data we need in three dimensions. This is what the final version of our query looks like:

```
SELECT {[Measures].[Sales Dollars], [Measures].[Sales Units]}
  ON COLUMNS,
  {CrossJoin([Territory].Children, [Employee].Members)} ON ROWS,
  {Descendants([Time].[All Periods], [Time].[Quarter])} ON PAGES
FROM Sales
```

Even if you don't have a good grasp of MDX, you will probably be able to deduce what is going on here. We retrieve the two measures, Sales Dollars and Sales Units, on the COLUMNS dimension, which will be used to populate the matrix's data cells.

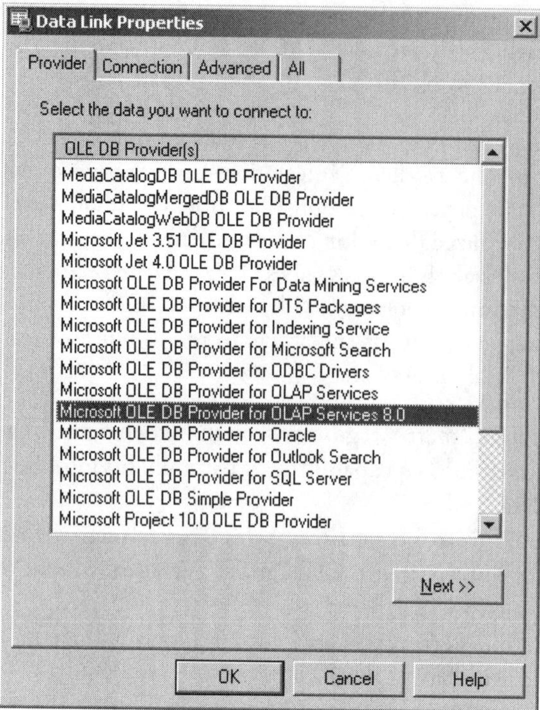

Figure 12.19 To report off Analysis Services cubes, use Microsoft OLE DB Provider for OLAP Services 8.0.

Because we want to show both the Territory and Salesperson dimensions as matrix row groups, we use the MDX `CrossJoin` function, which returns an MDX set on the ROWS dimension. The [Employee].Members statement returns all items of the Employee dimension. We use the Children statement to retrieve only the items at the Territory group level.

Finally, to set the matrix's column groups, we need to fetch the members of both the year and quarter levels of the Time dimension. We accomplish this by using the Descendants statement. This statement retrieves the dimension members between two specified levels.

NOTE You may need to pass parameters to your MDX queries. Unfortunately, in SQL Server 2000, Analysis Services doesn't support parameterized MDX. As a workaround, you need to base your query on an expression and concatenate the parameter values. For practical examples about how to do this, you may find useful the OLAP Sample Reports download that the Reporting Services team has published on MSDN. For more information, please see section 12.4.

Once the query is crafted, there are only a few final touches left. First, let's change the dataset's field names to abbreviated captions, so we can reference these fields easier, for example, Year as opposed to [Time].[Year].[MEMBER_CAPTION]. We can accomplish this by using the Fields toolbox window or accessing the dataset properties (Fields tab). Next, we need to go through all the matrix region textboxes and groups and adjust their underlying field names accordingly to match the dataset fields.

While standard OLAP-based reports could be useful, the powerful data-analysis capabilities of OLAP could be better realized when cubes are integrated with smart client applications. We'll see how to do this next by leveraging the Microsoft Office Web Components.

12.2.4 Implementing AW Data Miner

By now you probably see RS as a powerful platform for creating, managing, and distributing standard reports. As we said in section 12.1.2, in a typical enterprise environment, this type of report will usually meet the reporting needs of 60–80 percent of the users. However, a relatively small group of information workers representing the company's business analysts, statisticians, information explorers, and decision makers may need more dynamic and interactive report features.

To respond to this need, we will create a WinForm application (AW Data Miner) that has the following high-level design goals:

- Allow the Adventure Works business analysts to easily create dynamic reports ad hoc from the OLAP Sales cube.
- Support crosstab and chart reports.
- Support preconfigured standard and user-defined reports. Users can save their personalized version of the reports, very much like the My Reports feature in RS.
- Allow users to drill through the sales data to see the daily sales orders. Because the Sales data warehouse consolidates data per month, we will accomplish this by integrating the Monthly Order Summary RS report with the PivotTable component.

The concept of dynamic reporting may be new to you, so we'll discuss it in more detail in the next section.

Understanding dynamic reporting

To understand what we mean by *dynamic* reporting, let's revisit the crosstab reports that we can create with RS by using the matrix region. Granted, the matrix region provides a certain level of interactivity. It allows the report users to drill down the data by expanding groups, which happens to be of the most popular interactive feature requested by business analysts. However, the matrix region has one important limitation. It can operate only within the underlying query's data. This makes it impossible to see the data from dimensions other than the ones the query fetches.

Let's take for example the Territory Sales OLAP report we just authored. It allows the users to drill down into the sales data by year, territory, and salesperson. But what if we want to see a breakdown of sales by product and year? Or, what if we need the report to show how many products have been sold by each store? How about the top-selling products? There are countless angles from which a business analyst may want to see the data. Well, we have two options for solving this dilemma. One approach is to create some additional standard reports. However, by taking this route, it is unlikely that we will be able to answer in full the plethora of questions that may be posed by information explorers. Besides, it can quickly become counterproductive from the standpoints of both maintenance and development effort.

What we really need is some kind of a smart ad hoc reporting tool that can empower our users to create dynamic reports on the fly. By the term *dynamic*, we mean fully interactive reports, where changing dimensions, sorting, grouping, and querying data in different ways is just a click away. Ideally, such a tool would abstract both report authors and consumers from the MDX technicalities by allowing them to submit the correct MDX query behind the scenes when the user interface changes. Enter Microsoft Office Web Components!

Understanding Microsoft Office Web Components

Microsoft Office Web Components (OWC) is a marvelous piece of technology that we highly recommend you consider for building OLAP-based solutions. OWC was first introduced with Microsoft Office 2000 as a collection of COM (ActiveX) controls, covering spreadsheet, charting, and pivot (crosstab) functions. Therefore, these controls are typically used with rich web or WinForm-based clients, where OWC is preinstalled on the client side. In terms of licensing, each user needs a valid Office license to be able to use OWC interactively.

The latest version of OWC included with the Microsoft Office 2003 suite is version 11. It is also available as a separate download from the Microsoft web site, as detailed in the section 12.4. However, to use OWC from .NET-based applications, you will also need the OWC Primary Interop Assemblies (PIAs).

To facilitate integrating Office 2003 with .NET applications, Microsoft has released a series of interop assemblies called Office 2003 Primary Interop Assemblies. A primary interop assembly is a specialized .NET assembly that contains definitions (as metadata) of types implemented with COM. Currently, Office 2003 PIAs are distributed only on the Microsoft Office 2003 Setup CD.

There are two OWC components that report authors may find particularly attractive for creating dynamic reports: PivotTable and ChartSpace.

Understanding OWC PivotTable reports

The PivotTable component is a mini-application by itself, as figure 12.20 shows.

You can think of the PivotTable component as a matrix region on steroids. Similarly to the matrix region, you can use PivotTable to create crosstab drilldown reports. However, it also supports changing dimensions and measures at will. For example, the user can drag and drop a dimension on the row or column area. If you don't need the

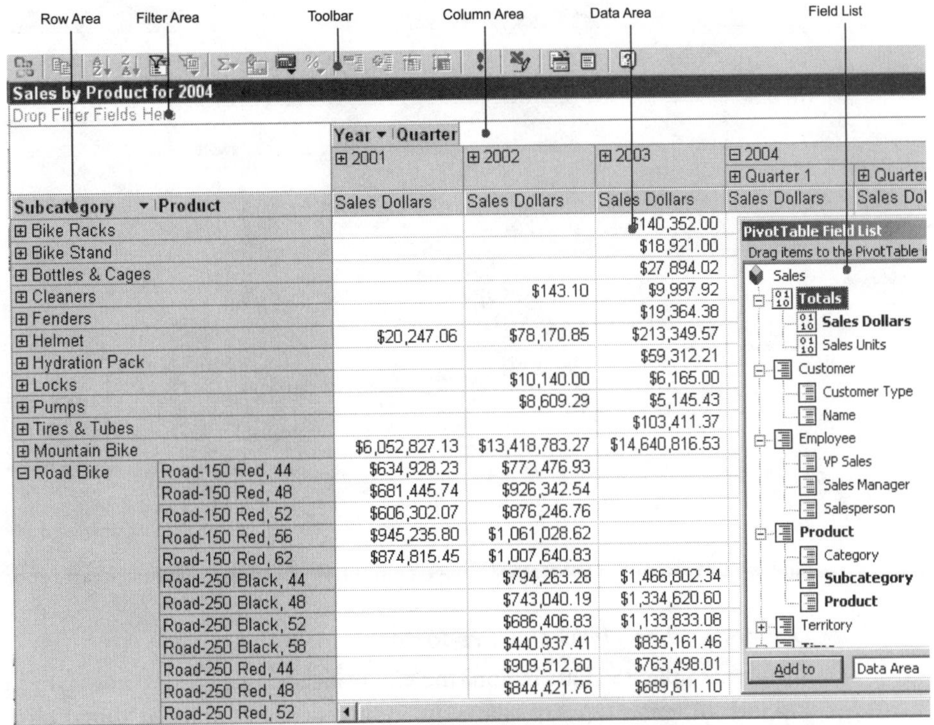

Figure 12.20 Use the OWC PivotTable component to add dynamic reporting features to your WinForm or web-based applications.

dimension anymore (or one of its levels), you can remove it by dragging and dropping it outside the component area.

It addition, PivotTable sponsors a handy toolbar, packed with features, including:

- Dimension member filtering and sorting
- *Top/bottom filtering*—For example, you can select the Product Name column and instruct PivotTable to show you only the five top-selling products.
- Calculated fields
- Exporting to Excel

PivotTable can retrieve its data from the following data sources:

- Tabular data sources, such as a relational database
- Multidimensional data sources, such as an OLAP cube
- XML, by using the same data provider (Microsoft Persistence provider) that reports that have been exported to HTML OWC RS use

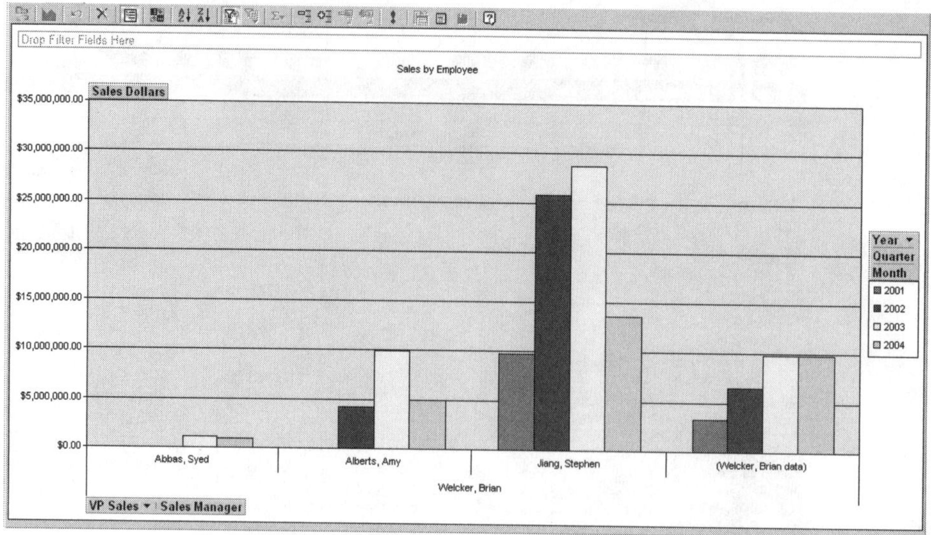

Figure 12.21 Use the OWC ChartSpace component to create dynamic chart reports.

Understanding OWC chart reports

Similarly to the RS chart region, the ChartSpace component (shown on figure 12.21) supports different types of charts, including area, column, pie, doughnut, and so on.

As with the PivotTable component, you can interact with ChartSpace by using the familiar drag-and-drop technique to add or remove dimensions and measures. The ChartSpace component can draw its data from the cube it is connected to, or it can be synchronized with a PivotTable component, as the Data Miner sample will demonstrate shortly in this chapter.

How Do Office Web Components Work?

The interaction between OWC and OLAP servers follows the client/server model, as shown in figure 12.22.

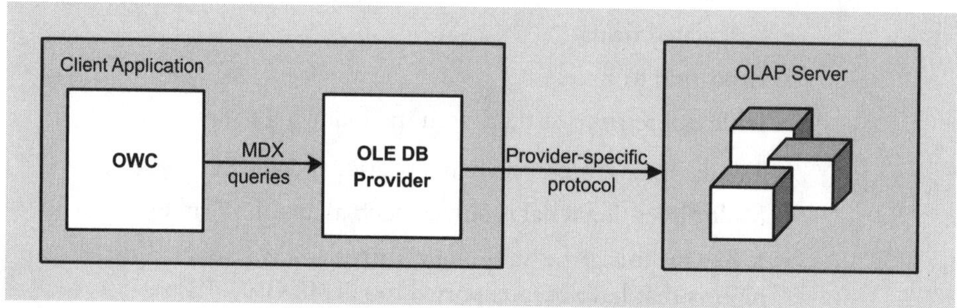

Figure 12.22 When the user interacts with an OWC component, it creates and sends MDX queries through the OLE DB providers to the OLAP server.

The OWC components communicate with the OLAP server via an OLE DB provider. For example, in the case of Analysis Services, OWC uses Microsoft OLE DB Provider for OLAP. Once the component is connected to the server, it populates the Field List window with the available measures and dimensions from the cube.

As the user interacts with an OWC component, for example, drags and drops dimensions and measures, the component creates and sends MDX queries behind the scenes to the OLE DB provider, which in turn communicates with the server to fetch the data. As most of you who have used MDX before would agree, this is one of the most appealing aspects of OWC. You can build a complete OLAP reporting solution without having to write a single MDX query statement, because OWC does this for you.

If you are concerned with performance issues that the OWC client-server may exhibit, please note that the data payload between OWC and the server is actually quite small, because OWC sends the query string and gets only the aggregated values from the OLAP server.

Setting up Microsoft Office Web Components

You will probably face two predicaments when building OWC-centered solutions. The first one has to do with the lack of quality programming documentation. .NET developers will be the most unconvinced, because all of the documentation samples use scripting languages. It seems to me that the Microsoft OWC team is the last holdout of legacy technologies within Microsoft. This is probably related to the fact that in the past many organizations have shied away from using WinForm clients because of the deployment issues we described in chapter 8.

The second issue again concerns .NET developers and is related to the convoluted setup process required to configure OWC with Visual Studio .NET. For the purposes of the Data Miner demo, migrating some web-based OWC code from one of my applications to .NET took a substantial number of hours to work around all the setup issues. To avoid setup headaches, we'll show you what needs to be done to configure OWC for .NET development.

First, you need to make sure that you install the OWC Primary Interop Assemblies on your development machine, as well as on all clients that will run your application. As we mentioned before, the OWC PIAs are available only on the Office 2003 Setup CD, and they are not installed by default. To install them, you have to run the Office Setup and select the .NET Programmability Support component from the Office 2003 Web Components section, as shown in figure 12.23.

The Setup program will install the PIAs in the .NET Global Assembly Cache (GAC). Once you have installed the OWC PIAs, you can add the components to your toolbox in Visual Studio .NET. The PivotTable control is listed as the Microsoft Office PivotTable 11.0 control under the Customize Toolbox COM tab, while the ChartSpace control's name is Microsoft Office Chart 11.0. Once you reference the controls, check the VS.NET references. There should be a reference to the OWC11

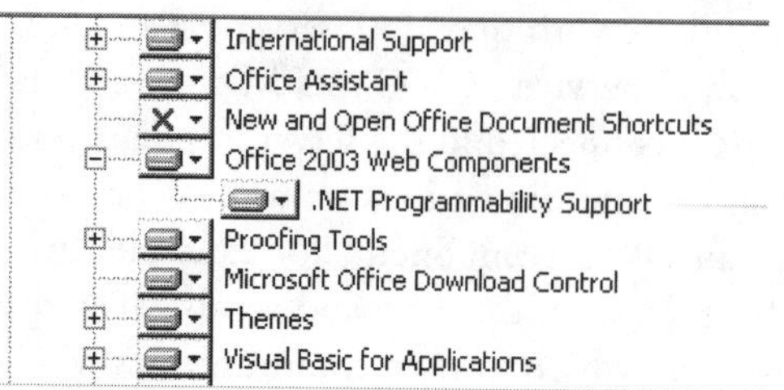

Figure 12.23 To integrate OWC with .NET applications you have to install the OWC PIAs.

library that should point to the .NET Global Assembly Cache folder. If it doesn't, either PIAs are not installed or you will have to refresh the reference.

You will also notice that VS.NET has helpfully created an interop assembly called AxOWC11. The purpose of this assembly is to host the OWC class wrappers. Unfortunately, this assembly won't allow you to sink many of the OWC events, as documented in Knowledge Base Article 328275. The article outlines the steps to regenerate the wrapper assembly for OWC version 10, which are also applicable for version 11.

Because you need to reference PIAs, and getting them from the GAC is like performing brain surgery, we included the AxOWC11 source code and binary in the AWReporterWin\OWC11 folder. You'll need to remove the autogenerated reference to AxOWC11 inside VS.NET and replace it with a reference to our version so you can handle events successfully. You don't have to do this for the Data Miner demo because its project file already has the correct reference.

Now that you have a good understanding of how the Office Web Components work, let's see how we can leverage them for the purposes of the Adventure Works Data Miner demo.

Implementing the AW Data Miner presentation layer

Let's start by taking a quick walk-through of the AW Data Miner user experience. Figure 12.24 shows the AW Data Miner UI. This sample can be launched from the Chapter12 menu in the AWReporterWin project.

As figure 12.24 shows, we selected the Sales by Territory and Product Category for 2004 report from the My Reports drop-down. The Pivot tab is selected and shows the pivot version of this report, which displays some data from the Sales cube we authored in section 12.2.2.

We can drag measures and dimensions from the PivotTable Field List and drop them onto rows or columns to see the data from different angles. Once we're happy with the new version of the report, we can save it as our personal report. We can also switch to the Chart tab to see a chart report that uses the same data as the pivot report.

As you would probably agree, this sample is packed with features. However, it took us only a few hours to implement it thanks to the Office Web Components.

Let's now take a behind-the-scenes tour of the Adventure Works Data Miner, starting with the My Reports feature.

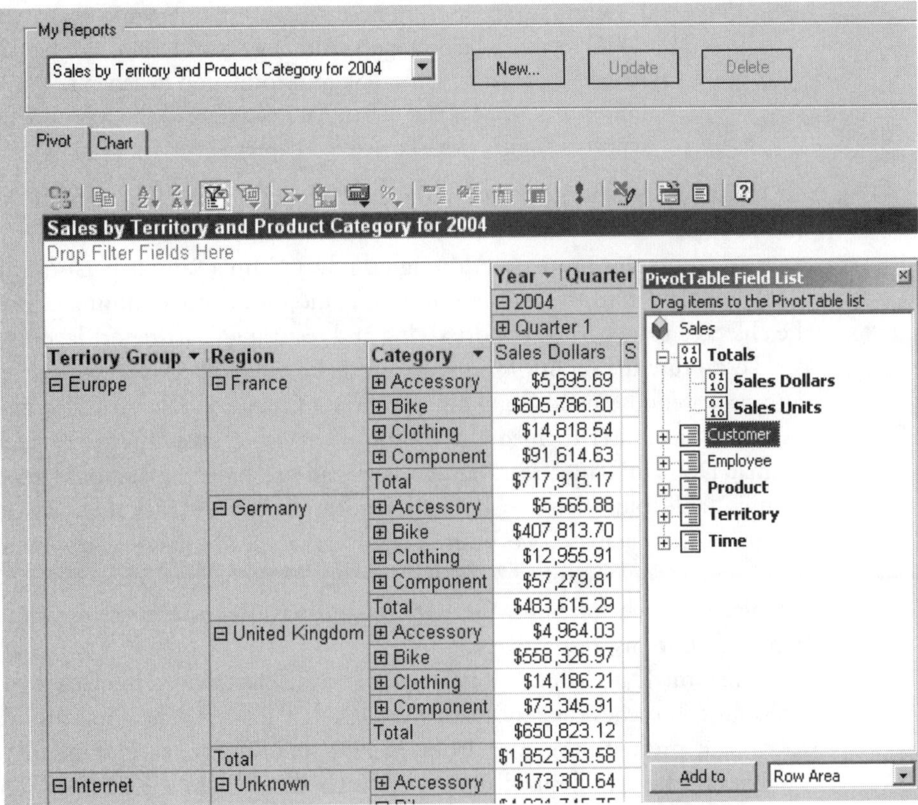

Figure 12.24 The Adventure Works Data Miner solution uses Office Web Components to allow the user to create ad hoc reports.

Implementing the My Reports feature

Once we figured out the setup issues, implementing the Data Miner demo was straightforward. The Data Miner sample follows a design pattern similar to the one demonstrated by Dave Stearns in his book *Programming Microsoft Office 2000 Web Components*. This approach has proven very successful in some of my real-life applications. In its simplest implementation, you may find that one screen, the one shown in figure 12.24, may be able to satisfy most of your users' dynamic reporting requirements.

Most of the implementation effort of the Data Miner demo went into implementing the My Reports feature. It allows the users to retrieve preconfigured reports, personalize them any way they want, and save them for future retrieval. To accomplish this, we used the XMLData property, which represents in XML the current report definition (excluding the data) of the OWC PivotTable or ChartSpace component. In this respect, you can relate XMLData to the RDL report definition in RS.

TIP Here is a tip in case you need to convert a dynamic report generated with OWC to an RS-based report. Although XMLData is not based on the RDL schema, you can write an XSL transformation to generate the RS report definition from XMLData. Then, you can upload the report definition to the report catalog, as we showed in chapter 7.

XMLData is a read/write property and can be used to save and restore the report layout. All three of the UI Office Web Components—PivotTable, ChartSpace, and Spreadsheet—expose this property. Although the Data Miner sample persists only the PivotTable report definition, with a minimum amount of programming effort you should be able to enhance it to support saving and restoring chart report layouts as well.

To capture the report layouts, we created a table called Reports in the AdventureWorks warehouse database. This table has a Category field that classifies the report as standard or user-defined. In addition, the table saves the user's identity in the format DomainName/UserName. Users can see only the standard reports defined in this table plus the user-defined reports they have authored. To facilitate the access to the database, we built a web service façade, MyReports, which you can find under the Chapter12 folder in the AWReporterWeb project. The façade exposes two web methods, GetReports and SaveReports, to retrieve or change the report definitions, respectively.

When the Data Miner application starts, it calls down to the façade to retrieve the report list. It caches the reports in an ADO.NET dataset. The application's user interface logic prevents the user from making modifications to standard reports. All changes to the user-defined reports are cached locally in the dataset. When the user clicks the Update My Reports button, the modified user-defined reports are sent to the façade, which in turn propagates the changes to the database.

Implementing dynamic chart reports

To generate the chart report when the Chart tab is clicked, we bind the ChartSpace component to the PivotTable control, as shown in listing 12.1.

Listing 12.1 Creating chart reports bound to the PivotTable control

```
private void LoadChart() {
  ChChart chart;
  PivotView pview = pivotTable.ActiveView;
  chartSpace.DataSource = (msdatasrc.DataSource)
            pivotTable.GetOcx();
  chartSpace.DisplayFieldList = true;
  chartSpace.AllowUISelection = true;

    if (chartSpace.Charts.Count == 0)
    chart = chartSpace.Charts.Add(0);
  else
    chart = chartSpace.Charts[0];
```

Binds the chart to the PivotTable component

Gets the chart or creates one if needed

```
    chart.HasTitle = true;
  chart.Title.Caption = pview.TitleBar.Caption;
}
```

If you use the PivotTable component on the same form, the easiest way to configure the chart is to synchronize it with the PivotTable control itself. Once this is done, the chart series will be automatically bound to the Pivot Column field and the chart categories to the Pivot Row field.

Next, we set up some chart properties to allow users to drag dimensions and measures from the Field List and select chart elements. The ChartSpace control can have more than one chart associated with it. In our case, we need only one chart. Once the chart is created, we set its title to match the title of the pivot report.

Implementing drillthrough reporting

One of the most useful OLAP features is drilling down through data from one dimension level to the next. Eventually the user will reach the lowest level in the dimension hierarchy. A common requirement is to allow the users to drill through data. For example, the Sales data warehouse that we built in this chapter consolidates data per month. However, a business analyst may question the accuracy of the current month's sales figures and would like to see a daily breakdown of the sales orders. Unfortunately, this level of data is not available in the data warehouse.

However, provided that daily sales data is available in another data source, such as the OLTP system or the staging database, we could allow the business analyst to generate a standard report by double-clicking the pivot cell or selecting the report's name from a context menu. In this way, we can integrate the dynamic pivot-based reports with a standard report generated by RS.

The most challenging aspect of implementing this is to ensure that the intersected dimensions of the user's selection give us enough information to set the standard report's parameters. For example, in the above scenario, the user must have the Time dimension expanded all the way down to the Month level so that we can determine the selected month.

Determining the user's selection

The PivotTable component exposes the user's selection under its Selection property. Each time the user selects a new item, the SelectionChanged event fires. We used this event to output the row and column dimension members for demonstration purposes. When the user double-clicks on a cell or right-clicks to access the context menu, we validate the user's selection in the `IsSelectionValid` function, which is shown in listing 12.2.

Listing 12.2 Determining the user's selection

```
private bool IsSelectionValid() {
  string selection = pivotTable.SelectionType;
  PivotAggregates aggregates = null;
  PivotAggregate aggregate = null;
  bool valid = false;
  string uniqueName = null;

  if (selection != "PivotAggregates")  return false;     <-- Is a data cell selected?
  aggregates = (PivotAggregates)pivotTable.Selection;
  aggregate =  aggregates[0];
  if (aggregate.Value == System.DBNull.Value) return false;   <-- No data in the data cell
                                         Reference the time dimension
  uniqueName = aggregate.Cell.ColumnMember.UniqueName;   <--
  valid = IsDateDimensionExpanded(uniqueName);   <-- Is the time dimension expanded to the Month level?
  if (!valid) {
    uniqueName = aggregate.Cell.RowMember.UniqueName;
    valid =  IsDateDimensionExpanded(uniqueName);
  }
  return valid;
}
```

At different times, the user may select different PivotTable areas. We are interested only in the case when a data cell is selected. If this is true, the Selection property will return PivotAggregates.

Next the code checks to see whether the cell is empty. Then it tries to find the Time dimension in both rows and columns. Finally, we call the `IsDateDimensionExpanded` function to find out whether the dimension is expanded all the way to the Month level. If this is the case, we consider the selection to be valid because we can retrieve the corresponding year and month to construct the report's parameters.

Implementing custom actions

OWC allows you to easily change the context menu and add your own items. Before the context menu is expanded, the PivotTable component fires the BeforeContextMenu event. If the user's selection is valid, we can use this event to add the Show Monthly Orders Summary Report command, as shown in figure 12.25.

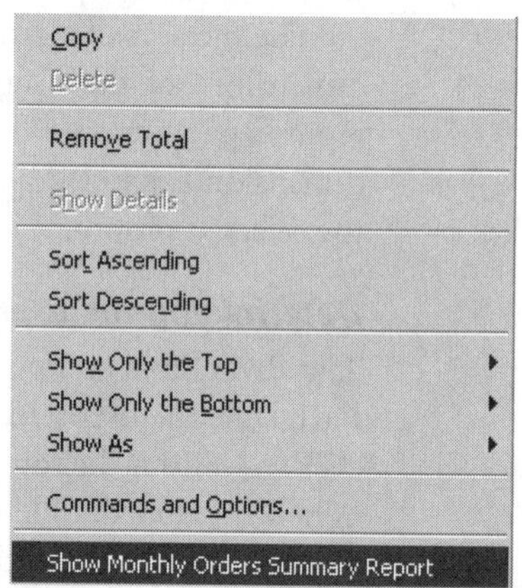

Figure 12.25 Office Web Components allows developers to define custom actions that can be launched from the context menu.

When the user clicks a context menu item, the PivotTable control fires the CommandExecute event. The CommandExecute event

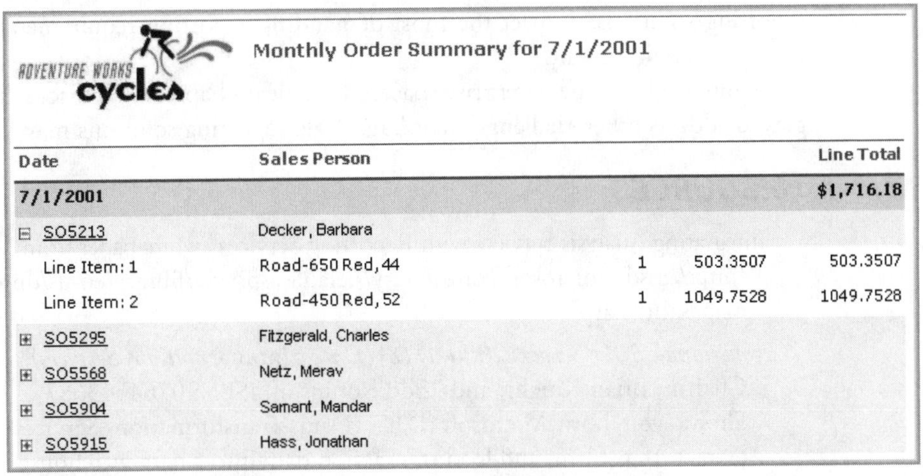

Monthly Order Summary for 7/1/2001

Date	Sales Person			Line Total
7/1/2001				$1,716.18
⊟ SO5213	Decker, Barbara			
Line Item: 1	Road-650 Red, 44	1	503.3507	503.3507
Line Item: 2	Road-450 Red, 52	1	1049.7528	1049.7528
⊞ SO5295	Fitzgerald, Charles			
⊞ SO5568	Netz, Merav			
⊞ SO5904	Samant, Mandar			
⊞ SO5915	Hass, Jonathan			

Figure 12.26 The Monthly Order Summary report will be requested via a drillthrough custom action from an OWC PivotTable report.

handler requests the Monthly Order Summary report, which we authored with Reporting Services. Figure 12.26 shows this report.

The Data Miner sample requests this report by URL. The report takes a single parameter, Date, which we set to the selected date in the Time dimension of the PivotTable control.

As you can see, OWC components give you a lot of flexibility to perform various custom actions. Another useful practical application of this could be to request a server-side web page to write back data, similar to the write-back sample we discussed in chapter 11. Finally, Analysis Services also support custom actions, including shelling out to an executable and requesting a page by URL. For more information, check out the "Creating Actions" topic in the Analysis Services documentation.

12.3 SUMMARY

The chapter has been a whirlwind tour of OLAP tools and technologies and how they can be used for business intelligence reporting. By now, you should understand how the various pieces of the Microsoft Business Intelligence stack fit together to form a comprehensive reporting framework.

We hope the last few chapters have helped you realize the benefits of Reporting Services for generating standard reports. In many cases, you will probably find that by integrating your applications with RS, you will be able to satisfy the reporting needs of the majority of the information workers in your organization.

However, sometimes a small group of users may require more advanced reporting features, such as multidimensional queries and dynamic reporting. In this chapter, we have shown how you can use OLAP technologies coupled with RS to create all-encompassing reporting solutions to meet the most demanding reporting requirements in today's enterprise environment.

Before we leave the enterprise space, in the next chapter we'll discuss some strategies to address other challenges that large-scale reporting solutions may face.

12.4 RESOURCES

"Integrating Analysis Services with Reporting Services" white paper from Microsoft (http://msdn.microsoft.com/library/default.asp?url=/library/en-us/dnsql2k/html/olapasandrs.asp)

Professional SQL Server 2000 DTS (Data Transformation Services), by Mark Chaffin, Brian Knight, and Todd Robinson, ISBN: 0764543687
Shows you how Microsoft DTS (Data Transformation Services) helps you extract, transform, and load transaction data into a data warehouse.

Microsoft SQL Server 2000 Analysis Services Step by Step, by OLAP Train and Reed Jacobson, ISBN: 0735609047
A good introduction to implementing OLAP solutions with Microsoft Analysis Services.

Programming Microsoft Office 2000 Web Components, by Dave Stern, ASIN: 073560794X
A great starting point for getting into Office Web Components.

MDX Solutions: With Microsoft SQL Server Analysis Services, by George Spofford, ISBN: 0471400467
A detailed reference guide for using Multidimensional Expressions (MDX) to query Microsoft Analysis Services.

"Manipulate and Query OLAP Data using ADOMD and Multidimensional Expressions" (http://www.microsoft.com/msj/0899/mdx/mdx.aspx)
An excellent introductory article to MDX and ADOMD.

Reporting Services 2000 - OLAP Sample Reports (http://www.microsoft.com/downloads/details.aspx?FamilyID=f9b6e945-1f4c-4b7c-9c83-c6801f0576ff&DisplayLang=en)
Contains a couple of sample reports illustrating how to use Analysis Services cubes as a data source.

he OWC 2003 download URL (http://www.microsoft.com/downloads/details.aspx?FamilyID=7287252c-402e-4f72-97a5-e0fd290d4b76&DisplayLang=en)

"Introducing the Office Web Components" (http://msdn.microsoft.com/library/default.asp?url=/library/en-us/dno2kta/html/ofintrowbcom.asp)
Excerpted from *Programming Microsoft Office 2000 Web Components*.

Microsoft Office XP Web Component Toolpack
(http://www.microsoft.com/downloads/details.aspx?FamilyID=beb5d477-2100-4586-a13c-50e56f101720&DisplayLang=en)
The toolpack contains valuable samples and walkthroughs of the Office XP Web Components, which for the most part are compatible with Office 2003 Web Components.

CHAPTER 13

Enterprise reporting

Today's enterprise reporting requirements are more complex and diverse than ever before. They present a new set of challenges, including

- Delivering a flexible solution that can grow with the evolving needs of the user
- Supporting multiple report providers to prevent vendor lock-in to a proprietary infrastructure or tool
- Facilitating the report management by centralizing the report configuration in one place
- Protecting the company data by integrating the report solution with existing enterprise security frameworks

In many cases, the optimal approach to address the above needs is to implement a custom reporting framework. In this chapter we will show how the sample framework that we will build, the Adventure Works Enterprise Reporter, can help you to implement some of these requirements.

13.1 UNDERSTANDING ENTERPRISE REPORTING

Just as with any enterprise-oriented solutions, implementing an enterprise reporting framework is not a trivial undertaking. For example, in one of my real-world projects, we had to derive to a solution that met the following requirements:

- New providers had to be plugged seamlessly with the reporting framework. Our system had to support both homegrown reporting providers as well as third-party products, such as Reporting Services, Crystal Reports, and so on.
- The reporting framework had to be able to integrate easily with different types of applications. To meet this requirement we implemented a Web service communication façade so that client applications could submit SOAP-based report requests.
- The report-to-report provider relationship had to be transparent to clients. In other words, the client would not be aware of which reporting provider would handle a given report. To meet this requirement, we had to implement a report catalog that stored the report configuration.
- The framework had to handle core architectural services, such as security, caching, report serialization, and so on.

Do some implementation aspects of our framework look familiar to you? In a nutshell, we reinvented Reporting Services with a twist so that it could support multiple reporting providers. As you would imagine, the development effort required to implement our homegrown framework wasn't trivial. For this reason, before you embark on a similar endeavor, it may make sense to consider other less-involved design patterns that may offer a reasonable compromise between flexibility and simplicity.

Our advice is to tackle this dilemma from the standpoint of simplicity, as opposed to trying to implement full-blown flexible solutions. A famous novelist was once asked how he knew when his novel was complete, to which he answered, "When there is nothing left to take out." We would suggest that you adopt this design paradigm when architecting your enterprise reporting solution as well.

13.1.1 Evaluating enterprise reporting

To better understand why we advocate simplicity, let's look at some tradeoffs that you will need to consider as you design a custom enterprise reporting solution.

Increased complexity

The report request may need to traverse several layers before reaching the report provider. For example, once the client initiates the report request, it may need to go to be validated by the application business layer. Next, the business layer will submit the request to the communication layer of the reporting framework. Here, we will need to validate the request again, parse it, invoke the report adapter, and so on.

Compare this invocation pattern with directly accessing the Report Server by URL in the case of Reporting Services, and you will start to understand the price of flexibility.

Reduced feature set

You may find that when dealing with heterogeneous report providers you need to use the least-common-denominator approach, such as supporting only the on-demand report delivery model. For example, with RS you can deliver reports to subscribed users. However, Microsoft Access doesn't offer this feature.

This leaves you with two implementation options if you need to support both RS and Access. First, you may decide not to support the subscribed report delivery feature at all. Or, you can opt to support this feature only for RS reports. The latter option will entail more complicated logic to build a provider-specific report request.

Reinventing the wheel

In your quest to abstract report providers, you may find that you have to reimplement a subset of the provider features that you need. For example, as we have seen, RS supports different forms of caching. To make your reporting solution vendor-neutral, you may decide to design your own middle-tier caching mechanism.

Given the above tradeoffs, sometimes your reporting requirements may call for a sophisticated and flexible reporting framework as opposed to integrating your applications with a single reporting provider, such as with RS only. Let's look at a framework example, the Adventure Works Enterprise Reporter, to see how it addresses some of the enterprise challenges you may face in real life.

13.1.2 Introducing the Adventure Works Enterprise Reporter

Let's put ourselves in a hypothetical situation that many enterprise architects will probably be able relate to. While moving to RS is a long-term management objective in Adventure Works, in the short term replacing all disparate reporting providers to RS is not feasible. Instead, we've been tasked with consolidating the most popular report providers under a single layer, which we will call the Reporting Façade. The end result of this vision is a common reporting model where developers don't have to worry about provider specifics. Instead, to report-enable their applications, they need to integrate them with the Reporting Façade.

Here are the specific requirements that will drive the Adventure Works Enterprise Reporter implementation:

- *Isolate the provider implementation details from the report consumers*—To prevent tight coupling between the report provider and the client, we will introduce a Reporting Façade layer. This layer will abstract the report provider's implementation details. The Reporting Façade takes the report request as input and produces the report's payload as output.
- *Support multiple report providers*—Our reporting framework should provide seamless integration with multiple report providers.
- *Enforce a trustworthy reporting environment*—Different report providers may support different security mechanisms to authenticate and authorize users. For this

reason, one of the main goals for our framework is to act as a gatekeeper that validates report requests before handing them to the provider for processing.

- *Implement a centralized report configuration store*—While some providers, such as RS, offer centralized report management, others don't. For this reason, it makes sense to centralize the report metadata in one place.

Here, we use the term "metadata" to refer to the information describing the reports. An example of report metadata is the definition of parameters that the report takes, as well as the provider which will be responsible for generating the report. In this respect, our configuration store is similar to the RS catalog: it isolates the client from the report-specific details. At best, the only information that the client will need in order to request a report is the report's identifier, the available export formats, and the parameter list.

Supporting multiple report providers

Perhaps the most important feature of the above design goals is supporting multiple report providers. In a typical enterprise environment, you will often witness a hodgepodge of technologies. While by now you are probably convinced that RS has many appealing features, upgrading the existing report providers to RS won't happen overnight, or it may not be an option at all. Therefore, our solution needs to deal with today's enterprise realities where RS may have to coexist with other reporting tools.

To support multiple providers, we will introduce the concept of *adapters*. Most of you have probably built database-driven applications that interface with data stores via ODBC or OLE DB drivers. Similarly, our enterprise façade will interface with the report providers using adapters. Thanks to the adapter design pattern, plugging a new provider into our framework will be a matter of creating and registering a new adapter.

Now that we've described our envisioned reporting framework, we'll discuss how to implement it.

High-level architectural view

Based on our design goals, figure 13.1 shows the high-level architectural view of our solution.

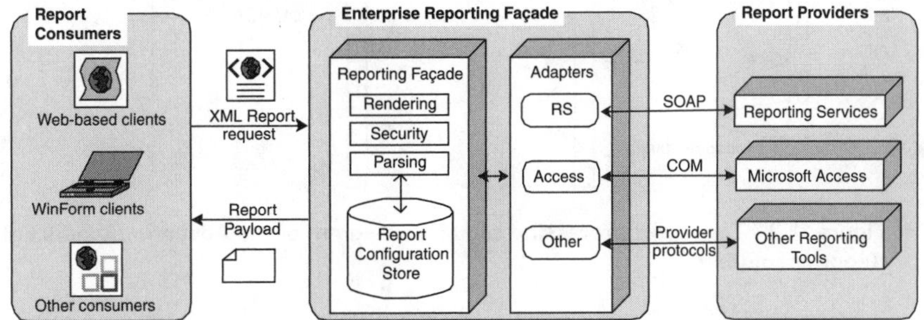

Figure 13.1 At the heart of the AW Enterprise Reporter is the Enterprise Reporting Façade, which intercepts the report requests from the report consumers and forwards them to the appropriate report providers.

At a high level, our reporting framework will be implemented as a server-based layer that could be accessed by different types of consumers, such as WinForm or web-based client applications. At the heart of it is the Reporting Façade, which accepts incoming report requests submitted by the consumer, sends the requests to the report providers, and returns the generated reports.

As we explained, the Reporting Façade communicates with the report providers via adapters. For example, as figure 13.1 shows, to generate an RS-based report, the Reporting Façade will use a Reporting Services adapter; to generate a Microsoft Access–based report, it will use a Microsoft Access adapter, and so forth.

To understand how the Adventure Works Enterprise Reporter works, let's look at the report processing flow among the different layers and find out how they work together.

Report processing flow

Figure 13.2 shows the sequence diagram of the report processing flow in the Adventure Works Enterprise Reporter.

Let's discuss the purpose of the main components shown in the diagram, starting with the report consumer's role.

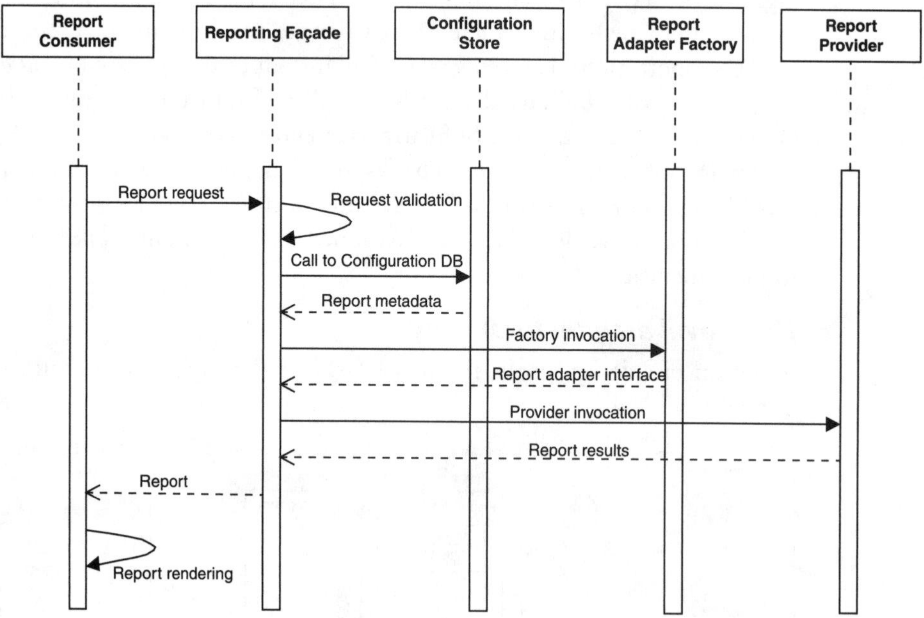

Figure 13.2 The report processing sequence diagram of the Adventure Works Enterprise Reporter solution

The report consumer

The report consumer initiates the report request. The report request is described in XML and contains the minimum set of consumer-related input details that the façade needs to generate the report, including the following:

- *The report identifier*—A unique identifier that corresponds to the primary key of the report in the Report Configuration Store. As we said, the main goal of the Report Configuration Store is to centralize the report configuration details in a single report repository.
- *The report parameters*—For parameterized reports, the report consumer needs to specify the parameter values.
- *The export format*—The format that the report will be rendered to, such as HTML, PDF, and so on.

Once the report consumer creates the report request, it submits the request to the Reporting Façade.

The Reporting Façade

The Reporting Façade provides the following services:

- Validates the report request against an application-defined security policy
- Queries the Report Configuration Store to retrieve the report details in order to find out which adapter is associated with this report
- Instantiates the adapter and forwards the report request to it

Report adapters and providers

Based on the incoming generic request, the adapter formulates a provider-specific report request and forwards it to the report provider. The report provider generates the report.

Once the report is ready, the adapter serializes the report's payload and sends it back through the call chain. The report consumer receives the result, deserializes the report's payload, and either renders the report on the screen or processes it in unattended mode.

Let's now take a behind-the-scenes tour of Adventure Works Enterprise Reporter to find out how it is implemented.

13.2 BEHIND THE SCENES OF THE ADVENTURE WORKS ENTERPRISE REPORTER

We will now direct our attention to the implementation details by tracing the call from the client to the report provider. Our discussion will focus on the following architectural topics:

- The Report Configuration Store schema.
- Submitting report requests
- The Reporting Façade layer
- Implementing provider-specific adapters to generate RS and Microsoft Access reports

Let's start by looking at the Report Configuration Store.

13.2.1 Implementing the Report Configuration Store

One of the most common requirements imposed on enterprise reporting solutions is that they should provide a centralized report repository. The purpose of the Report Configuration Store is to hold the report's metadata. To be available for querying by report consumers, the Report Configuration Store could be located in either a relational database or Windows Active Directory. In the Adventure Works Enterprise Reporter sample, the Report Configuration Store fulfils the following tasks:

- Defines the report export formats
- Describes the report parameters
- Defines the report-to-adapter relationship

Figure 13.3 depicts the database schema of our Report Configuration Store.

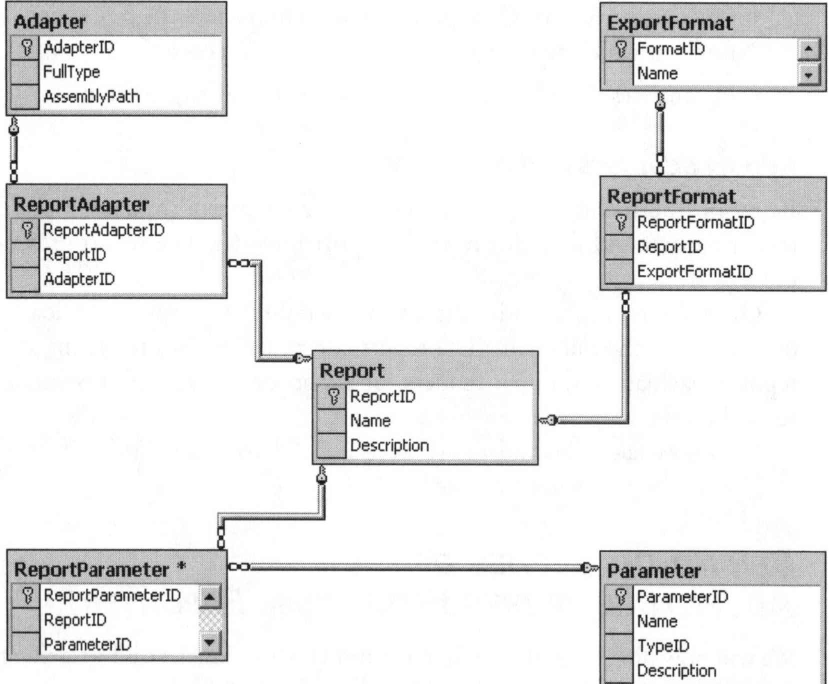

Figure 13.3 Use the AW Enterprise Reporter client to test the Reporting Façade.

You will probably notice that we built this diagram upon the report parameter schema (not shown here) that we discussed back in chapter 10. Table 13.1 explains the role of the new tables.

Table 13.1 The Configuration Store tables

Table	Purpose
Report	Stores all reports
ExportFormat	Defines the report export formats, e.g., PDF, Excel, Access Snapshot, etc.
ReportFormat	Defines the relationship between reports and export formats
Adapter	Defines the report adapter details, such as the adapter type and assembly path
ReportAdapter	Defines the relationship between reports and adapters

In real life, report consumers will retrieve the list of reports and export formats from the Reporting Facade. Similar to RS, the façade could apply application-defined security policies and return only the reports that the user is permitted to run.

To keep things simple, for the purposes of the Enterprise Reporter demo, we simulate the configuration store by using name-value settings defined in the AWReporterWeb web.config configuration file in the format

```
<add key="report identifier" value="adapter class name",
     "assembly name"/>
```

These settings define the report-adapter relationship. For example, to describe that a report with an identifier of 1 is serviced by the RS adapter, we can add the following configuration setting:

```
<add key="1" value="AWC.Reporter.Web.Adapters.RsAdapter,
AWC.Reporter.Web, Version=1.0.0.0, Culture=neutral,
PublicKeyToken=null"/>
```

The preconfigured settings in the web.config file define four reports; two define RS reports and the other two define Microsoft Access reports.

13.2.2 Implementing the presentation layer

To simulate a report consumer requesting reports from the Reporting Façade, we developed a simple WinForm client, as shown in figure 13.4. You can launch it from the Chapter13 menu in the AWReporterWin project.

Figure 13.4 Similar to the RS configuration database, the Report Configuration Store stores the report's metadata in a central repository.

For simplicity's sake, we didn't implement the following features:

- Retrieving the report list
- Retrieving the export formats supported by the report provider
- Handling the report parameters

As we mentioned, in the real world, the report consumer could fulfill the above tasks by calling the Reporting Façade. As you would expect, various report providers may differ substantially in their supported feature set. For example, the subset of the available export formats between RS and Access is limited to HTML and Excel.

For the purposes of the demo, we decided to use the least-common-denominator approach and restrict the list of available formats to these two formats only. To make your applications more flexible, you should enhance our implementation and query the façade to get the report formats supported by a given report provider. This will allow you to use provider-specific formats. For example, when using Microsoft Access, you may want to request the report in a Microsoft Snapshot format to get a full-fidelity copy of the report.

To handle the report's parameter list, you could follow the approach we discussed in chapter 10. As you will probably recall, it promotes storing the parameter's metadata in a custom database and dynamically configuring the presentation layer to handle different parameter types.

Submitting report requests

Once the user is ready with the report selection, we can generate a report request and submit it to the Reporting Façade. We have a number of request serialization options to choose from, as we mentioned in chapter 10. For the purposes of the Enterprise Reporter demo, we decided to reuse the Report Request entity that we created in the Report Wizard sample. The Report Request entity is based on a typed dataset and its definition is included in the AWReporterWeb project.

If you look at the façade communication layer (the EnterpriseReporting.asmx Web service) you will notice that its `RenderReport` method takes a single parameter of type ReportRequest. Given that, generating the report request on the consumer side is easy, as shown listing 13.1.

Listing 13.1 Requesting a report

```
private void RunReport()  {
  byte[] reportPayload = null;
  ReportRequest reportRequest = new ReportRequest();        // 1 Creates a report request
  reportRequest.Report.AddReportRow(cmbReport.SelectedValue,
       cmbReport.Text, String.Empty, String.Empty,
       GetUserIdentity(), DateTime.Now, DateTime.Now,
       false, null, 0, null, cmbFormat.Text, null, false);

  ReportingFacade facade = GetFacadeProxy();
  reportPayload = facade.RenderReport(reportRequest);       // 2 Invokes the façade's RenderReport method
```

```
    string filePath = Util.GetFileForReport(cmbReport.Text,
        cmbFormat.Text);
    FileStream stream = File.Create(filePath,reportPayload.Length);
    stream.Write( reportPayload, 0, reportPayload.Length );      <-❸ Deserializes the report's payload to disk
    stream.Close();
    Process.Start(filePath);
}
```

❶ First, the code creates a new instance of the ReportRequest entity. You may wonder how we can reference the ReportRequest entity because it is physically located in the Reporting Façade assembly. To obtain its proxy code, we established a web reference to the Reporting Façade Web service. This caused Visual Studio .NET to generate the signature of the ReportRequest entity in the proxy source code. Strictly speaking, we don't need all columns of ReportRequest, because we will pass to the façade only the report's identifier, export format, and parameters (if any). The Reporting Façade will query the Report Configuration Store to get the rest of the report's details.

The code also stores the Windows identity of the user in the format Domain\UserName inside the request entity to pass it to the façade. Passing the user's identity could be useful when the Reporting Façade doesn't support or cannot retrieve the Windows identity of the user. Our implementation of the façade ignores this argument because it is configured to use Windows authentication and can retrieve the user's identity on its own.

NOTE If you need to delegate the user's credentials to the report provider configured for Windows authentication, you will need to enable Kerberos so that the user's credentials flow from the Reporting Façade and the report provider, as we discussed in chapters 7 and 8.

❷ Next, we call down to the façade to generate the report.

❸ Once we receive the report from the facade, we deserialize the report's content to a physical file and render it by shelling out to the application associated with the file extension. This is very similar to the way the Report Wizard demo renders reports, as we saw in chapter 10.

Securing the presentation layer

Something that may not be obvious is that the report consumer configures the user interface according to the application-based security model (discussed in detail in section 13.3).

Although all configured reports are loaded into the Report drop-down list, the WinForm client prevents the user from requesting a report that the user is not permitted to run. To accomplish this, the client retrieves the list of the permitted reports from the façade using the following code:

```
public static void ConfigureSecurity() {
  ReportingFacade facade = AWER.GetFacadeProxy();
```

```
    user = facade.GetApplicationUser();
    user.Operations.PrimaryKey =
        new DataColumn[]{user.Operations.IdColumn};
}
```

The `GetApplicationUser` façade method returns an entity of type UserEntity. This entity contains all application-defined operations that the interactive user is allowed to perform.

We also define a primary key on the ID column in the typed dataset so that we can easily search on it. When the user changes the report selection in the drop-down, the event handler determines whether the report identifier of the selected report is among the permitted reports. If this is not the case, the code logic disables the Run Report button.

A better implementation from a security standpoint would be to enhance the façade to filter out the report list before it is returned to the client. As we saw in chapter 10, this is exactly how the RS `ListChildren` method works. However, we decided to enforce the security policy on the client side to showcase how the client can configure the application user interface because this is a common application requirement.

Once the report request is ready, it is submitted to the Reporting Façade.

13.2.3 Implementing the Enterprise Reporting Façade

For maximum interoperability, the Reporting Façade is implemented as a Web service. Let's now look at the following implementation sketches of the Reporting Façade layer:

- Processing report requests
- Handling multiple report providers
- Generating Microsoft Access reports
- Validating report requests using Windows Authorization Manager

Processing report requests

To submit report requests, report consumers call down to the Reporting Façade Web service communication layer. Specifically, the report consumers call the `RenderReport` web method (listing 13.2).

Listing 13.2 Rendering reports

```
[WebMethod]
public byte[] RenderReport(ReportRequest reportRequest)  {
  string reportId = reportRequest.Report[0].ID;     <-❶ Retrieves the
                                                        report identifier
  if (!SecurityManager.IsOperationPermitted(Int32.Parse(reportId)))  <-
      throw new System.Security.SecurityException(...);        Authorizes
                                                               the request ❷
  string reportAdapterFullTypeName =
```

```
    ConfigurationSettings.AppSettings[reportId];        <-3 Queries the configuration
                                                           store to get the adapter
  IReportAdapter reportAdapter = (IReportAdapter)          metadata
    GenericFactory.Create(reportAdapterFullTypeName);   <-4 Instantiates
                                                            the adapter
  byte[] reportPayload = reportAdapter.RenderReport(reportRequest);  <-
  return reportPayload;                                 Renders the report 5
}
```

❶ First, the code inside the RenderReport method retrieves the report identifier from the report request entity.

❷ Next, it calls down to a custom class called Security Manager to authorize the report request. Although the presentation layer enforces security checks, the façade duplicates them on the server side. This is done to prevent a scenario where some malicious code could bypass the client security and access the façade directly.

❸ Next, the code queries the configuration store to determine which adapter is responsible for servicing the report request.

❹ Then, it instantiates the adapter and binds to it.

❺ Finally, the RenderReport method sends the report's payload to the report consumer.

Using report adapters

The Enterprise Reporting Façade supports multiple report providers. Because this book is about Microsoft technologies, we decided to restrict the list of supported providers to the two most popular Microsoft reporting tools: Reporting Services and Access. To add another report provider to the Enterprise Reporter, you will have to write an adapter for that provider.

The only rule that the façade enforces on the adapter is that it must implement the IReportAdapter interface. If you are new to interface-based programming, you may take a little detour to the first section of chapter 15 to find out how it works.

The IReportAdapter interface has the following signature:

```
public interface IReportAdapter {
  byte[] RenderReport(ReportRequest reportRequest);
}
```

Because each adapter will implement this interface, the adapter must implement the RenderReport method. This method accepts the report request of a ReportRequest-type entity and returns the report serialized as a byte array.

Once the façade authorizes the report request, it queries the configuration store to find out which adapter will handle the report request. Then, it invokes the GenericFactory.Create method to instantiate the report adapter.

Loading report adapters

This implementation of the dynamic adapter loading and binding was built on the approach demonstrated in the Microsoft Configuration Application Block (see the resources in section 13.5). This implementation uses the factory design pattern to load the adapter assembly and late-bind to it using the .NET Activator class, as shown in listing 13.3.

Listing 13.3 Using the factory design pattern to load the adapter

```
public static object Create( string assemblyName, string typeName,
       object[] constructorArguments ) {

 Assembly assemblyInstance    = null;
 Type typeInstance       = null;

 if (assemblyName.IndexOf(Path.DirectorySeparatorChar)>0)
   assemblyInstance = Assembly.LoadFrom(assemblyName.Trim());
 else
    assemblyInstance =
        Assembly.Load(assemblyName.Trim() );

 typeInstance = assemblyInstance.GetType( typeName.Trim(),
    true, false );

 if( constructorArguments != null )
    return Activator.CreateInstance( typeInstance,
         constructorArguments);
  else
    return Activator.CreateInstance( typeInstance );
}
```

Loads the adapter assembly from a specific location

Loads the adapter assembly from the application domain base path

Instantiates the adapter type by late binding to it

For maximum flexibility, our implementation of the generic factory supports loading the adapter assembly from both the application binary folder as well as an arbitrary location. In the first case, we use the `AssemblyLoad` method, which probes the application domain's base path to find the assembly. To try the second scenario, change the application's configuration file and define the adapter assembly location; for example:

```
<add key="1" value="AWC.Reporter.Web.Adapters.RsAdapter,
     c:\somepath\AWC.Reporter.Web.dll"/>
```

Please note that in our case the adapters are part of the AWReporterWeb code-behind assembly because their source is located inside the AWReporterWeb project. In real life, you will probably want to move the adapter implementation to a separate assembly. This approach will allow you to change the adapter implementation and add new adapters without recompiling the application.

Once the adapter assembly is loaded, we reflect on it to get to the adapter type, which is passed as one of the `Create` method arguments. Finally, we instantiate the adapter and return the reference to the façade layer.

```
IReportAdapter reportAdapter = (IReportAdapter)
 GenericFactory.Create(reportAdapterFullTypeName);
byte[] reportPayload = reportAdapter.RenderReport(reportRequest);
```

Because all adapters implement a common interface, the façade can cast the reference to `IReportAdapter` and call the `Render` method to invoke the adapter-specific report-rendering implementation.

Generating Microsoft Access reports

While requesting RS reports by SOAP is nothing we haven't seen before, generating Access reports deserves more explanation. To accomplish this, the Reporting Façade uses the AccessAdapter adapter. Listing 13.4 shows how this adapter generates Access-based reports.

Listing 13.4 Generating Microsoft Access reports

```
public byte[] RenderReport(ReportRequest reportRequest) {
  MsAccess.Application oAccess = null;
  byte[] reportPayload = null;

  AWC.Reporter.Web.Entities.ReportRequest.ReportRow rptRst =
      reportRequest.Report[0];

  string fileName = Path.GetTempFileName();          <-1 Creates a temporary file to save the report's payload

  oAccess = new MsAccess.Application();              <-2 Instantiates Access through OLE automation
  oAccess.OpenCurrentDatabase('...', false, null);   <-3 Opens the Access reporting database
  oAccess.DoCmd.OpenReport(rptRst.Name,
      MsAccess.AcView.acViewPreview,
      null, null, MsAccess.AcWindowMode.acWindowNormal, null);   <-4 Renders the report
  oAccess.DoCmd.OutputTo(AcOutputObjectType.acOutputReport,
    String.Empty, GetAccessReportFormat(rptRst.ExportFormat),
    fileName, null, null, null);                     <-5 Exports the report to the temp file
  reportPayload = ConvertPayload (fileName);         <-6 Serializes the report payload to a byte array
  File.Delete(fileName);

  return reportPayload;
}
```

1. First, the code generates a temporary file to which we will export the report.

2. Next, it instantiates an object of type `MsAccess.Application` via Object Linking and Embedding (OLE) automation.

NOTE In the real world you should avoid using Microsoft Access with high-volume reporting applications. Microsoft Access was designed as a desktop application and was never intended to be used in a multithreaded server environment. Here, we use Microsoft Access for demonstration purposes only. If you need to use Access as a report provider, consider serializing the report requests in a queue of some sort, as we explain in section 13.2.4.

For the purposes of our demo, we use Microsoft Access 2003 to generate reports. To facilitate integrating .NET code with the Office 2003 suite, Microsoft includes a set of .NET assemblies called Office Primary Interop Assemblies (PIAs) on the Office 2003 Setup CD. Once the PIAs are installed, you can create a reference to the Microsoft Access 11.0 Object Library found on the COM tab of the Reference dialog. Because the Office Setup program installs PIAs in the Global Assembly Cache (GAC), you can verify that the Access reference is correct by checking to see if it points to the GAC.

❸ Next, the code opens the Access database by getting its location from the application's configuration file.

❹,❺ Next, we generate the report and export it in the requested format.

❻ Once the report is saved, we call the `ConvertPayload` helper function to serialize the report's payload to a byte array. Finally, we delete the temporary file.

13.2.4 Designing for scalability

Scalability is an important requirement for every enterprise system. Our Reporting Façade may need to handle a large number of report requests. While Microsoft Reporting Services is designed to scale well under an increased load, other report providers may not.

For example, Microsoft Access is a file-based database and doesn't perform well with many concurrent users. Therefore, in the real world you may need to architect your enterprise reporting framework in such a way that it performs equally well with heterogeneous report providers.

Let's discuss one common design pattern that you can use to make the Reporting Façade more scalable. I used a similar design pattern successfully during one of my projects a few years ago when I had to implement a Report Server–type application.

Using the asynchronous design pattern

Good design is the foundation of a highly scalable enterprise reporting framework. One excellent way to make the application more scalable is by performing operations in an asynchronous manner, as shown in figure 13.5.

The basic idea behind the asynchronous design pattern is simple. Instead of processing the report requests synchronously, we will log them in a queue and process them on a first-in first-out (FIFO) basis. This architecture will require introducing a new component whose main goal is to read the messages from the queue. We will call this component the *Queue Listener Service.*

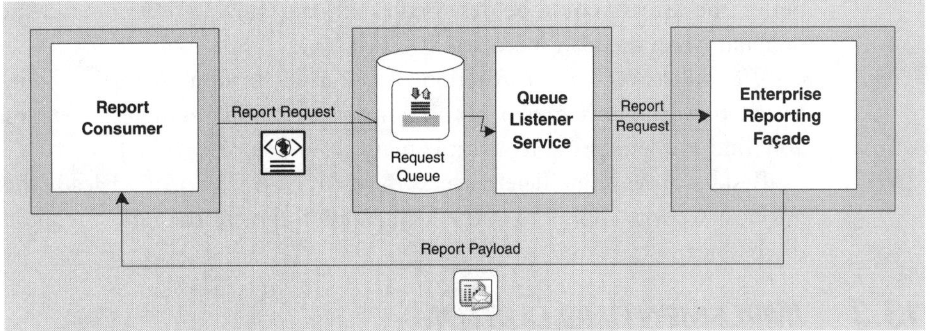

Figure 13.5 Use the asynchronous design pattern to make the Reporting Façade scale better by queuing the report request in an MSMQ message queue.

While you can log the messages to the database, you may want to consider integrating your application with a product specifically designed for message queuing. If the Reporting Façade is running on a Windows 2000 or later operating system, consider using Microsoft Message Queuing (MSMQ), which is baked into the Windows operating system.

For more information about building solutions with MSMQ, please see the resources in section 13.5.

Generating reports asynchronously

This is what the report request-response sequence may look like with the asynchronous pattern:

Step 1 The report consumer prepares the report request as it typically would.

Step 2 Instead of submitting the report request to the façade, the report consumer submits the request to a publicly available queue. This is important because the client is not forced to wait for the report request to complete. Instead, similarly to the multithreaded design we discussed in chapter 9, the client can continue its work immediately after submitting the request asynchronously.

Step 3 On the server side, the Queue Listener Service waits for the message's arrival. Once it has been notified by the queue, it retrieves the message and sends the report request to the façade.

Step 4 The façade processes the report request as it normally would.

Step 5 The façade sends the report payload asynchronously, for example, by e-mail, to the report consumer.

The Queue Listener Service doesn't have to process the report request in a sequential manner. In the real world, you could implement a sophisticated multithreaded queue listener service capable of processing the report requests on background threads. Even better, the listener could be designed as self-tuning, where it could create threads on demand when the load increases.

We will leave the construction of the asynchronous reporting solution to you. Developers who have previously used message queuing in their applications will probably find implementing it a simple matter.

Besides providing efficient access to reports, our Reporting Façade should provide a robust security model to authenticate and authorize the report requests, as we will discuss next.

13.3 IMPLEMENTING CUSTOM APPLICATION AUTHORIZATION

While RS provides a comprehensive role-based authorization model, other report providers may not. A common requirement for many enterprise-wide applications is integrating them with security frameworks that are already in place. Such frameworks will typically enforce application security policies to control access to application resources, including windows, reports, and privileged operations.

Typically, the application will configure the user interface based on the role membership that the logged-on user has. For instance, it may disable or hide certain menu items and buttons, configure screens in read-only mode, and employ other techniques to hide data or prevent data changes. In addition, a well-written distributed enterprise application will implement the same security checks in the business layer to enforce an even greater level of application security.

In the past, you may have used homegrown solutions to implement custom authorization features in your applications. For the purposes of our Enterprise Reporting framework, we will design a security layer that uses the Windows 2003 Authorization Manager (AzMan). For an excellent introduction to AzMan, please read Keith Brown's article listed in the resources in section 13.5.

13.3.1 Understanding the Windows Authorization Manager

You will probably find the Authorization Manager's security model similar in many aspects to the RS role-based security model. Table 13.2 lists the security entity equivalents of both models.

Table 13.2 AzMan model vs. RS role-based security model

Authorization Manager Entity	RS Role-Based Equivalent
Operation	Permission
Task	Task
Role	Role
Group	N/A
Role Assignment	Role Assignment

As you can see, the security models are very similar. However, as you will soon find out, the AzMan model is much more flexible. Armed with the Authorization Manager, we can easily fulfill the following security requirements:

- Implement a role-based security infrastructure similar to the RS role-based model.
- Support application-defined operations, tasks, and groups.
- Provide a user-friendly interface that the security administrator can use to configure the custom security infrastructure.

While discussing the Authorization Manager in detail is beyond the scope of this chapter, we will walk you through the process of defining a custom authorization security policy for the needs of our Reporting Façade. The steps to accomplish this goal are as follows:

Step 1 Create an authorization store that will hold the role-based security infrastructure.

Step 2 Define two application groups: Sales Managers and Sales Representatives.

Step 3 Assign the appropriate Windows user accounts to these groups.

Step 4 Configure the Sales Representatives group to have rights to run Access reports.

Step 5 Set up the Sales Managers group to include all of the Sales Representatives' rights plus the ability to run RS reports.

Just as RS stores the security setup in the configuration database, the Authorization Manager saves the authorization infrastructure in an authorization store.

Creating the authorization store

One of our favorite AzMan features is its user-friendly Microsoft Management Console, which makes setting up the security infrastructure a breeze.

> **NOTE** Unfortunately, while the AzMan runtime is supported on Windows 2000 (please see section 13.5 for a link to a Windows 2000 AzMan download), its console is available only on Windows 2003.

To create the authorization store, open the Authorization Manager console (choose Start → Run and type **azman.msc**). Switch to Developer mode by right-clicking the Authorization Manager node and choosing Options.

Authorization Manager supports two options for the location of the authorization store:

- *XML file*—Opting for an XML authorization store gives you ease of use and portability. This is also the only option if you don't have Active Directory installed or you don't have write permissions to it.
- *Windows Active Directory*—Choosing Active Directory as an authorization store offers an added level of security and a centralized location for your application security definitions.

We recommend that you use XML as an authorization store during application development and then switch to Active Directory during deployment. For the purposes of our demo, we will use an XML-based file store, which we have already created for you. Instead of hard-coding the URL to an XML file in your code, we recommend that you specify it in the application configuration file, as we have done in the Enterprise Reporter sample.

To open the authorization store, perform the following steps:

Step 1 Right-click the Authorization Manager node and choose the Open Authorization Store option.

Step 2 Browse to the location of the AWReporterWeb installation folder. The authorization store's filename is AWReporter.xml, and it is located under the Chapter13/Security subfolder. Don't forget to adjust the azManConfigurationStore setting in the AWReporterWeb web.config file to reflect the correct location of this file. In addition, if you need to make changes to the authorization store, make sure that the file is not marked as read-only to avoid errors when AzMan writes to the authorization store.

Step 3 Open AWReporter.xml in the AzMan console, as shown in figure 13.6.

The security entities are shown in the left pane. One configuration store can hold the security settings of more than one application. In our case, we've defined only one application, called AWReporter. When you click on a security entity, its details are shown in the right pane.

Setting up the application groups

Unlike the RS role-based mode, with Authorization Manager you are not restricted to creating role assignments based only on Windows groups. Instead, you can set up

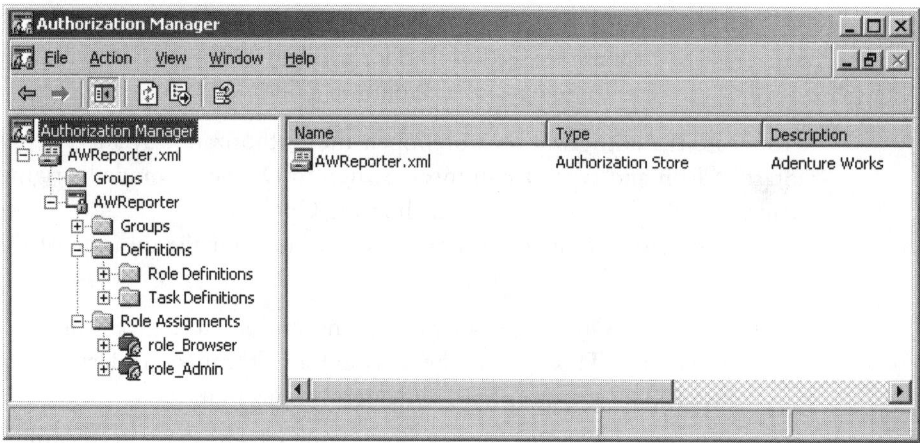

Figure 13.6 The Microsoft Windows Authorization Manager sponsors a user-friendly console that you can use to configure the authorization store.

application-defined groups. This is great because you don't have to chase down the network administrator to create new Windows groups in Active Directory for the purposes of your application's security infrastructure.

To meet the Adventure Works Enterprise Reporter's security needs, we defined two application groups, Sales Managers and Sales Representatives, as shown in figure 13.7.

Of course, instead of creating application groups, we could have taken advantage of predefined Active Directory Windows groups and completely skipped this step.

In this case, we assigned the local Administrators group to the Sales Managers application group and the local Users groups to the Sales Representatives application group. You will need to delete our assignments and re-create them because the security identifiers (SIDs) of our Windows accounts won't match yours.

Defining operations

Next, we need to define the elements that we need to secure. With AzMan, an operation is a logical concept and can represent anything you want, such as "Run ABC report," "Process order," "Update Customer," and so on. The Authorization Manager could care less about how the application will use the operations.

Because we need to enforce secured access to all the four configured reports, we defined four operations. Operations op_rpt_EmployeeSalesFreeform and op_rpt_TerritorySalesCrosstab represent the Employee Sales Freeform and Territory Sales Crosstab RS reports, respectively. Operations op_rpt_SalesByCategory and op_rpt_Catalog represent the Sales by Category and Catalog Access reports, which you can find in the Northwind.mdb sample database included with Microsoft Office.

In the process of creating a new operation, you will need to assign it a unique integer identifier. While the name of the operation is insignificant, the operation's identifier is important because this is how your application can query AzMan to find out whether a certain operation is permitted for a given user.

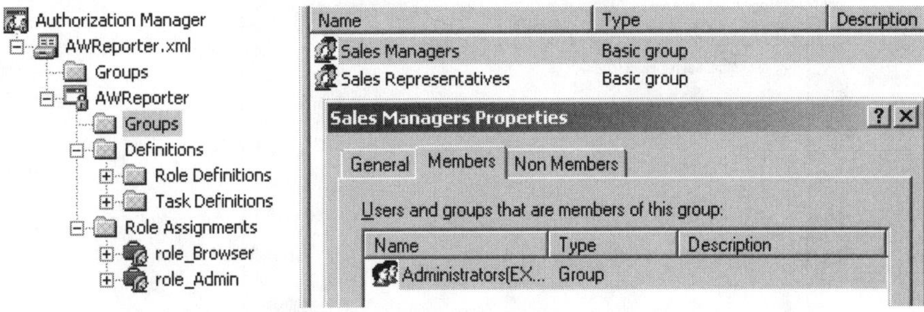

Figure 13.7 With AzMan you can define application groups.

Defining tasks

Just as you can group tasks into roles with RS, you can group operations into tasks with AzMan to create more granular security assignments. Unlike RS, however, the Authorization Manager doesn't force you to use tasks. Instead, you can define security policies using operations and/or tasks.

An example of a practical use of tasks is a workflow application. Each workflow can consist of a number of steps. You can define the workflow steps (screens) as operations and then define the workflows as tasks. During the application runtime, the application can hide a workflow from the list of the available workflows if the user doesn't have access to it. If she does have access, the application can start the workflow and further restrict the user's access to the individual steps. For example, if the user doesn't have access to a certain step, this step can be skipped or displayed in a read-only mode. Of course, as we said, you can forgo the task concept altogether and define only operations.

To demonstrate how tasks can be used with AzMan, we defined two tasks. The task_SalesRepReports task defines the operations (reports) that the sales representatives can execute. With AzMan, tasks can be nested. The second task, task_SalesManagerReports, encompasses the first task plus the operations permitted for the Sales Manager group, that is, the RS reports, as shown in figure 13.8. Alternatively, instead of nesting tasks, we could have assigned all four operations to task_SalesManagerReports.

You may be curious about the purpose of the Authorization Script button. The Authorization Manager allows you to fine-tune the security checks by using business

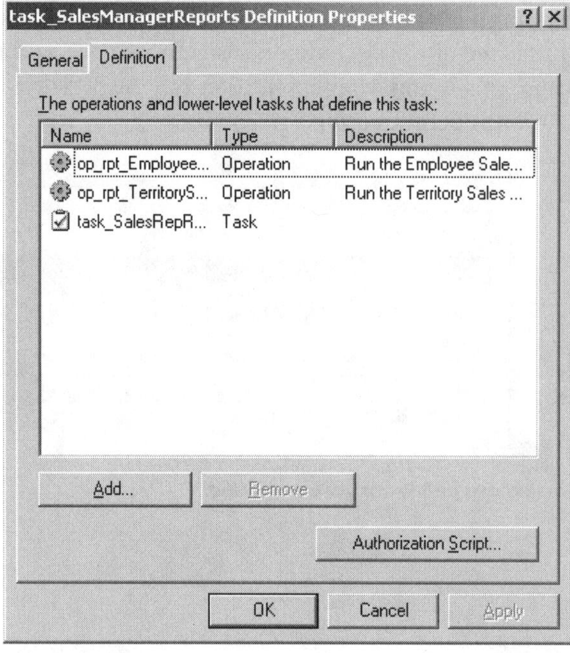

Figure 13.8 Unlike RS, the Authorization Manager allows you to define your own tasks.

rules implemented as scripts. The application developer can attach a VBScript or JScript authorization script to a task. The script will be executed at the time of the access request. This allows you to use information available only at runtime, such as "current time" or "order total" to make an authorization decision.

For more information about authorization scripts, please check the "Using Dynamic Business Rules in Windows Server 2003 Authorization Manager" article listed in section 13.5.

Defining roles

Once we've defined operations and tasks, we are ready to assign them to roles. Just as with RS, tasks and operations are useful only if they assigned to roles. We created two role definitions that you may find similar to the RS Browser and Manager predefined roles.

First, we created a role called role_Browser and assigned the task_SalesRepReports task to it. As a result, all role assignments including this role will have rights to run the Microsoft Access reports.

Next, we created a role called role_Admin. Similarly to tasks, AzMan allows you to nest roles to simplify the operations to role assignments. In our case, role_Admin includes role_Browser, as well as task_SalesManagerReports, as shown in figure 13.9.

As a result, all role assignments that include the role_Admin role will have permissions to run both Access and RS reports.

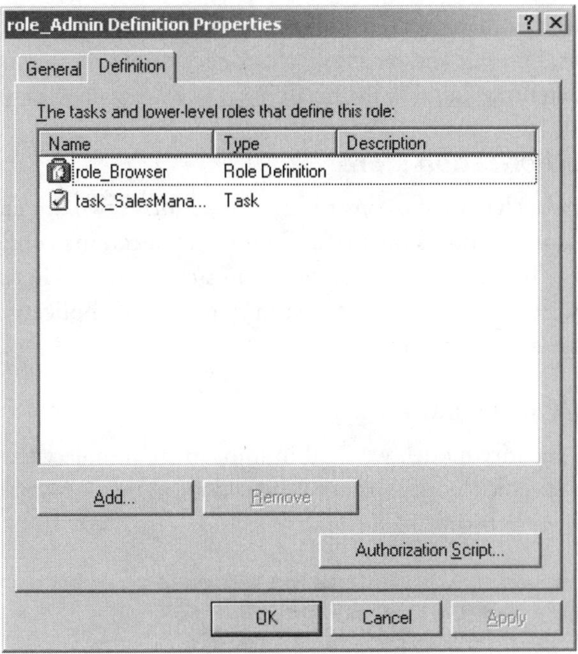

Figure 13.9 With the Authorization Manager you can assign tasks and operations to roles.

Defining role assignments

Now that we have set up the security entities, it is time to define the security policy by assigning roles to users. A role assignment can include Windows groups, individual Windows user accounts, as well as application groups. We used the application groups that we defined previously to create the following role assignments:

- role_Browser, which has the Sales Representatives application group assigned to it
- role_Admin, which has the Sales Managers application group assigned to it

We have finished configuring the Enterprise Reporting Façade authorization store! Now it is time to write some code to enforce authorization checks in the Reporting Façade layer. To implement this we will create a Security Manager class that will wrap the AzMan API.

13.3.2 Securing the AW Enterprise Reporter

This is how the Reporting Façade uses the Security Manager layer at a high level:

Step 1 The facade calls `SecurityManager.GetApplicationUser` to get a User entity object. This object contains only the operations (reports) that the user is permitted to run.

Step 2 The façade then passes the serialized copy of the User object to the report consumer.

Step 3 The consumer can then proceed with configuring the application's security elements (menus, buttons, and so on) by checking whether the appropriate operations are among those found in the User object, as we explained in section 13.2.2.

Initializing the authorization store

The SecurityManager class has a static constructor that performs two initialization tasks. First, it retrieves the authorization store's URL from the application's configuration file and initializes the store. In our case, the authorization store is the AWReporter.xml file we created previously. Second, because a store can span several applications, the code instructs AzMan to open the application we need.

Creating a security principal

Similarly to the .NET security model, we need to implement an object to represent the user and hold the user-specific security settings. This is done in the `GetApplication-User` method, as shown in listing 13.5.

Listing 13.5 The `GetApplicationUser` method creates an UserEntity object that encapsulates the user-specific details.

```
public UserEntity GetApplicationUser() {
   UserEntity user = new UserEntity();
   user.User.AddUserRow (GetUserIdentity().Name, null);
```

```
    // retrieve permitted operations for this user from AzMan
  GetUserOperations(user);
  user.AcceptChanges();

  return user;
}
```

The `GetApplicationUser` method returns a typed dataset entity called User-Entity, whose schema is shown in figure 13.10.

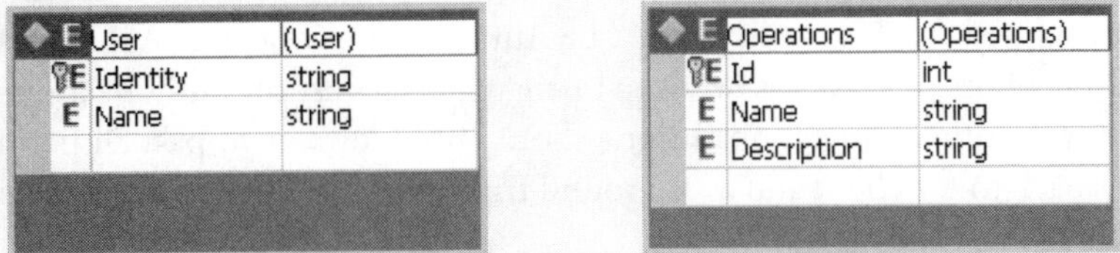

Figure 13.10 AW Enterprise Reporter uses the UserEntity typed dataset to store the user details.

In the real world, the UserEntity object could capture some useful information about the interactive user. For example, besides storing the user's identity, you could enhance the Security Manager to query the Windows Active Directory and retrieve the user's full name and e-mail address.

The Operations element represents the permitted operations. The actual relationship between the User and Operations elements is one-to-many. However, it is not defined in the typed dataset schema because there will always be only one user (one user row in the typed dataset).

To load the permitted operations we call the AzMan API.

Getting permitted operations

This is where the crux of the Authorization Manager logic is. Listing 13.6 shows the `GetUserOperations` code.

Listing 13.6 Retrieving permitted operations

```
private void GetUserOperations(UserEntity user)  {
  HybridDictionary applicationOperations =
                  GetApplicationOperations();    <-- Retrieves all application-
  int index = 0;                                     defined operations

  object[] operations = new object[applicationOperations.Count];
  foreach (DictionaryEntry o in applicationOperations) {
      operations[index] = ((Operation)o.Value)._id;
      index++;                                       Filters out only
  }                                                  the permitted
  object[] results = GetAuthorizedOperations(operations);  <-- operations
```

```
  for (int i = 0; i < results.Length; i++)
   Operation appOperation = (Operation)
       applicationOperations[operations[i]];

     if ((int)results[i] == 0)
       user.Operations.AddOperationsRow(appOperation._id,
       appOperation._name, appOperation._description);
  }
}
```

Loads the user entity object with permitted operations

First, the code calls `GetApplicationOperations` to retrieve the list of all operations defined for this application. The Authorization Manager API allows you to pass an array of operations that needs to be matched against the authorization store. In our case, we verify all operations in one shot. This allows us to pass all permitted operations back to the client and avoid round trips when the client needs to check the user's access to a given operation.

For better performance, `GetApplicationOperations` caches the collection of application operations in the ASP.NET Cache object. If there is a cached copy, `GetApplicationOperations` returns it; otherwise, it enumerates the operations in the AzMan authorization store and builds the Operations collection. The Operations collection is a collection of Operation types, where each operation has the following properties: ID, Name, and Description. These correspond to the operation properties we defined using the Authorization Manager console.

Then, the code calls to the `GetAuthorizedOperations` method to filter out only the operations permitted for this user. `GetAuthorizedOperations` does this by retrieving the Windows token of the application's user and calling the AccessCheck Authorization Manager API.

```
clientContext = _application.InitializeClientContextFromToken
(ulong)Security.GetUserIdentity().Token, null);
object[] results = (object[])clientContext.AccessCheck(_applicationName,
scopes, operations, null, null, null, null, null);
```

The result of this call is an array that has as many elements as the passed operations array, with values of zero in case the operation is permitted or one otherwise. `GetUserOperations` proceeds by filtering out only the permitted operations and adding them to the UserEntity object.

The Security Manager also defines the `IsOperationPermitted` method, which checks the user's access to a single operation using the AzMan API. As we have seen before, the façade calls this method to double-check whether the user has rights to run the requested reports.

13.4 SUMMARY

Microsoft Reporting Services is a full-feature reporting tool designed to meet the reporting needs of today's enterprise. Sometimes, you may need to build large-scale reporting solutions using both RS and other third-party or homegrown reporting tools. Such hybrid systems usually pose tough requirements and demand scalable, secure, and flexible architectures. Armed with the techniques we discussed in this chapter, you are well prepared to face these challenges and build sophisticated enterprise reporting frameworks.

In this chapter, we walked through the process of designing and implementing a custom enterprise reporting framework. First, we emphasized the tradeoffs surrounding the design and implementation of all-encompassing reporting solutions, such as increased complexity, reduced features set, and reinventing functionality already available in third-party reporting platforms, such as RS.

Thanks to the rich capabilities of the Microsoft .NET platform, we can easily add enterprise features to our applications. For example, we discussed how MSMQ could be used to process report requests asynchronously. In addition, we showed how the Microsoft Authorization Manager can help us implement a custom authorization security model.

With the completion of this chapter, we've covered what you need to know to add on-demand reporting capabilities to your applications by integrating them with RS. Let's now explore the second report delivery option that RS offers: subscribed report delivery.

13.5 RESOURCES

"Use Role-Based Security in Your Middle Tier .NET Apps with Authorization Manager," by Keith Brown
(http://msdn.microsoft.com/msdnmag/issues/03/11/AuthorizationManager/default.aspx)
A great introductory article to the Windows 2003 Authorization Manager for implementing a custom authorization framework.

Authorization Manager Runtime Download for Windows 2000
(http://www.microsoft.com/downloads/details.aspx?FamilyID=7edde11f-bcea-4773-a292-84525f23baf7&DisplayLang=en)

"Using Dynamic Business Rules in Windows Server 2003 Authorization Manager"
(http://msdn.microsoft.com/library/default.asp?url=/library/en-us/dnnetserv/html/AzManBizRules.asp)

"Building Distributed Applications with .NET"
(http://msdn.microsoft.com/library/default.asp?url=/library/en-us/dnbda/html/bdadotnetasync2.asp)
Discusses how to use recoverable messages, transactions, and acknowledgements with MSMQ and the Microsoft .NET Framework.

Microsoft patterns & practices for Application Architecture and Design (http://msdn.microsoft.com/library/default.asp?url=/library/en-us/dnbda/html/cmab.asp)
Includes reference architectures and application blocks.

C H A P T E R 1 4

Subscribed report delivery

In this fast-paced information age, we all know the value of having access to accurate, relevant, and up-to-the-minute data. Most of us enjoy various subscription-based services, such as magazine or e-mail subscribed delivery. Regardless of the type of information being delivered, these services share a common model. The subscriber imitates the subscription service for a given period of time. The service provider delivers the service either on a regular basis or as a result of an event.

In chapter 9, we provided an overview of how RS provides on-demand delivery, and in chapters 10–13, we showed how to implement on-demand reporting features for various types of client applications. With on-demand report delivery, the interactive user explicitly initiates the report request.

In this chapter, we will discuss the second report delivery scenario supported by Reporting Services, where the reports are "pushed" to the user automatically by the Report Server. As you will see, RS offers a flexible and extensible subscription-based reporting model, suitable for both Internet and intranet-based reporting solutions.

Our discussion will cover the following main topics:

- Overview of the subscribed report delivery process
- Creating standard subscriptions
- Creating data-driven subscriptions
- Triggering the subscribed report delivery process programmatically

14.1 UNDERSTANDING SUBSCRIBED REPORT DELIVERY

I love subscription-based information delivery! As I type this chapter, there are several subscription-based applications running on my computer. Microsoft Outlook lets me know when a new e-mail arrives. My favorite RSS aggregator, IntraVNews, notifies me when my feeds are updated. The Microsoft Messenger Alerts service interrupts me every now and then to tell me how much value my favorite stocks have lost during the course of the day's trading session.

The subscription-based delivery model is great because I don't have to poll the information sources to find out when data has changed. Instead, as long as I am subscribed, information is delivered to me. This saves me a lot of time and, as the famous adage says, time is money.

How does all this translate to reporting? There are many reporting scenarios that may call for delivering reports via subscription, as we will discuss next.

14.1.1 Subscription-based reporting scenarios

You can use subscribed report delivery to meet various reporting requirements, including the following:

- *"Pushing" reports to users on a regular basis*—There could be many valid reasons why an organization might want to implement automatic report delivery. For example, a sales manager may want to subscribe his subordinates to receive an employee performance report on a quarterly basis. The company's CEO may require that the company sales report be sent to the top managers periodically. A financial institution may want to distribute the monthly statement report to its customers.
- *Generating reports when the underlying data changes*—For example, an organization may want to e-mail the updated product catalog report when a new product is introduced.
- *Offloading long-running reports*—Some reports may take substantial time and resources to be processed. Such reports could be scheduled to be generated during off-peak hours.
- *Report archiving*—The report administrator may need to periodically archive reports to a network share for auditing purposes.

Now that we've seen some popular subscription scenarios, let's discuss how the RS subscribed delivery process works.

14.1.2 The subscriber-publisher design pattern

The RS subscribed delivery model follows the subscriber-publisher (also called *observer*) design pattern. This pattern is very popular with many modern programming frameworks. For example, one of the main reasons for the immense success of Microsoft Windows is its event-driven architecture.

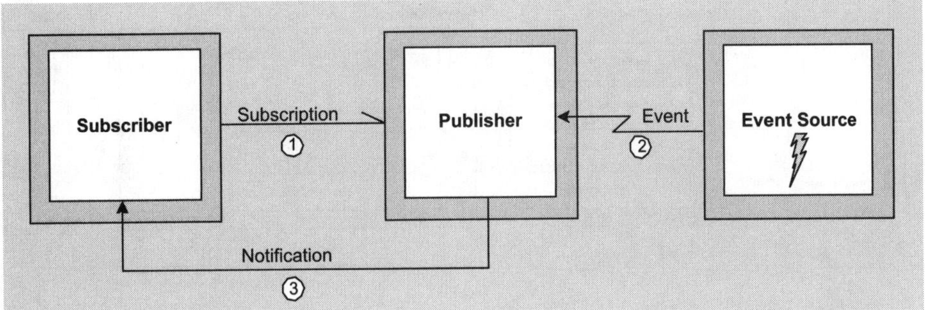

Figure 14.1 In the subscriber-publisher model, the client (subscriber) subscribes to one or more events. When the event occurs, the publisher notifies the subscriber.

Figure 14.1 shows how you can use the subscriber-publisher programming model in your applications.

The process is initiated by the *subscriber* (1) when it informs the *publisher* of its intent to be notified when a certain *event* of interest takes place.

When the event occurs (2), the publisher notifies (3) the subscriber about the event's occurrence.

The publisher typically runs in unattended mode, such as a background service listening to incoming events. For example, as I type on my laptop keyboard, each keystroke generates a hardware interrupt request. The CPU intercepts the request and generates a software interrupt. The event traverses the operating system and application layers to output the character on the screen. In this example, you can view the keystroke as an event source, the CPU as a publisher, and the OS and application layers as subscribers.

Let's now see how the subscriber-publisher pattern applies to the RS subscription-based delivery mechanism.

14.1.3 How the Reporting Services subscription-based model works

In a nutshell, when a report is scheduled for subscribed delivery, report processing is triggered as a result of an event, such as a timing event from a schedule. The generated report is then delivered asynchronously to its subscribers, as shown in figure 14.2.

With RS, here's how the subscriber-publisher pattern applies: the subscriber is typically the report's end user who subscribes herself or other users on their behalf. For example, a manager could subscribe herself and her subordinates to receive a report. The publisher is the Report Server, and the event source is the SQL Server Agent.

To better understand the process flow, we could break down subscribed report delivery into two phases:

- Creating the report subscription interactively by the user
- Processing and delivering the report asynchronously

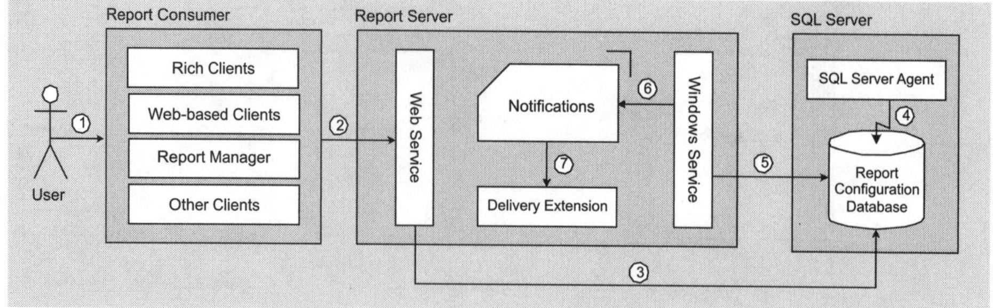

Figure 14.2 With the subscription-based report delivery model, the report processing is triggered by an event and the generated report is delivered asynchronously to its subscribers.

In the sections that follow, we'll refer back to figure 14.2 to explain each phase.

Creating report subscriptions

While we are not excluding the possibility of more sophisticated ways to generate subscriptions, such as by applications running in unattended mode, typically the user will create the subscription interactively by using a client application, which we will call a report consumer. For example, the user could access ① the Report Manager to initiate the subscription process.

Once user has entered the subscription details, the report consumer invokes ② one of the `CreateSubscriptionXXX` RS Web service SOAP APIs to save ③ the subscription details in the Report Catalog and schedule the subscription.

NOTE Some of you may need to create subscriptions programmatically using the SOAP API. The documentation has good examples of how this could be done for both subscription types supported by RS. For this reason, I decided not to include a code sample to demonstrate this concept. If the documentation samples are not enough, you can use the tracing technique I showed you in chapter 7 to find out how the Report Manager uses the Web service API to create and schedule subscriptions.

At this point, the Report Server has saved the subscription details in the Subscriptions table in the report catalog, and control is returned to the report consumer. This step concludes the interactive, synchronous part of the subscription process.

Executing report subscriptions

RS supports two kinds of events that can trigger the subscribed delivery:

- Time-based events, such as events generated by a subscription-specific or shared schedule
- Snapshot refreshes (for snapshot reports only), where the subscription processing is initiated when the snapshot data is updated

Going back to figure 14.2, here is a simplified version of the process flow for executing subscriptions. Once the subscription event is up, the SQL Agent job inserts ④ a record into the Event table. As we saw in chapter 7, the Reporting Services Windows Service (ReportingServicesService.exe) scans this table on a regular basis to see if any new events have been published. As you will probably recall, the polling interval can be configured by adjusting the PollingInterval setting in the RSReportServer.config configuration file.

In case there is a new event, the Reporting Services Windows Service picks it up ⑤ and handles the event. Specifically, for a time-based subscription this means creating a notification record in the Notifications table. The Windows Service polls the Notifications table periodically. When it discovers a new entry, the Windows Service creates ⑥ a *notification object*. If the subscription is data-driven (more on this in section 14.2.2), the Windows Service creates as many notifications as the number of recipients.

Next, the Report Server instantiates the *delivery extension* associated with the subscription and passes ⑦ the notification object to it.

DEFINITION *Delivery extensions* are .NET assemblies that implement the Reporting Services delivery extension API. Delivery extensions are able to receive notifications from the Report Server and distribute reports to various destinations. Out of the box, RS comes with two delivery extensions for e-mail and file share delivery. Developers can write custom delivery extensions to distribute reports to other destinations, as we will demonstrate in chapter 15.

Finally, the delivery extension distributes the report to its final destination, for example, by sending an e-mail to the recipient in the case of e-mail delivery or saving the report's payload to a network share for file share delivery.

As you've just seen, the second phase of subscribed report delivery is executed entirely in unattended mode. Therefore, subscribed reports are subject to the same limitations as report snapshots, which we discussed in chapter 7. Specifically, these limitations are as follows:

- The identity of the interactive user is not available during the report's processing stage.
- Report parameter values must be specified when the subscription is created.
- Stored data source credentials must be used for database authentication.

Let's explain each of these limitations in more detail.

First, the user-specific information is not available when reports are delivered via subscriptions. Specifically, this means that it is not possible to access the properties of the User global collection, for example, to get the user's identity or the language identifier. Failure to abide by this rule results in the following error message when an attempt is made to create a new subscription:

```
Subscriptions cannot be created because the credentials used to
run the report are not stored, the report is using user-defined
parameter values, or if a linked report, the link is no longer
valid.
```

Second, because the report is generated in unattended mode, the report parameter values have to be known by the time the report is processed. If you look at the signatures of both subscription-related web methods, `CreateSubscription` and `CreateDataDrivenSubscription`, you will notice that they take a Parameters array of type `ParameterValue`, which you can use to fill in and pass the report parameters. If you use the Report Manager to create the subscription, you will notice that it generates parameter placeholders for each parameter on the Subscriptions page.

NOTE If a user creates a subscription with a certain parameter, and then the administrator sets the report to snapshot execution but chooses a new parameter value, if the subscription is run, then it will be deactivated. Deactivating the subscription provides an indication that the report has been modified. To reactivate the subscription, the user needs to open and then save the subscription.

If the parameter has a default value, you can use it if you don't want to specify the value explicitly.

Finally, stored credentials must be used for authenticating against the data source, because subscriptions are processed in an unattended mode and it is not possible to supply the credentials interactively.

Having discussed subscribed report delivery at a high level, let's now see how the end user can configure and manage subscriptions using the Report Manager.

14.2 CONFIGURING SUBSCRIBED REPORT DELIVERY

Subject to security permissions, with RS each end user can use the Report Manager web application to subscribe to a report of interest. For example, a sales manager can subscribe to receive the Territory Sales Crosstab report that we authored in chapter 4 on a regular basis, for example, each quarter.

To create a new subscription, the user must specify the following:

- The report that the subscription will be attached to—A subscription is always associated with exactly one user and one report.
- The subscription type, for example, standard or data-driven—We will discuss the supported subscription types in section 14.2.2.
- The delivery extension type, for example, e-mail or file share delivery
- The event that will trigger the subscription, such as a timing event based on a schedule
- The report parameter values for parameterized non-snapshot reports

Although the process of creating subscriptions looks involved, the Report Manager makes it easy, as we will discuss next.

14.2.1 Creating a new subscription

In the typical scenario, the enterprise users will access the Report Manager portal to create and manage the subscriptions they own, as shown in figure 14.3.

To create a new standard subscription with the Report Manager, the end user performs the following steps:

Step 1 Navigate to the report the user wants to subscribe to.

Step 2 Click the New Subscription button found on the View and Subscriptions tabs.

Step 3 Enter the subscription details.

These steps require Manage Individual Subscriptions rights. The report administrator sets up these permissions as mentioned in chapter 8.

Some delivery extensions may call for a more involved setup process. For example, most organizations will be cautious about letting users send reports via e-mail to an arbitrary list of recipients. For this reason, the Report Server is set up by default to require a two-phase setup process for configuring e-mail subscriptions, as follows:

- *Creating the subscription*—This phase can be performed by individual users and requires only Manage Individual Subscription rights. During this phase the Report Manager prevents the user from entering the recipients' addresses by disabling the To field and hiding the Cc (Carbon copy) and Bcc (Blind carbon copy) fields.
- *Finalizing the subscription*—By default, only users with rights to execute the Manage All Subscriptions task can enter the recipients' addresses.

NOTE The availability of the e-mail address fields (To, Cc, and Bcc) is controlled by the SendEmailToUserAlias setting in the Report Server configuration file (RSReportServer.config). If this setting is True (the default), only users who have the Manage All Subscriptions right can change these fields. If the setting is False, these fields are enabled for any user who has the Manage Individual Subscriptions right. For better security, I suggest that you leave this setting set to True so that the report administrator can control the e-mail recipient list.

Let's now discuss what types of subscriptions are natively supported by Reporting Services.

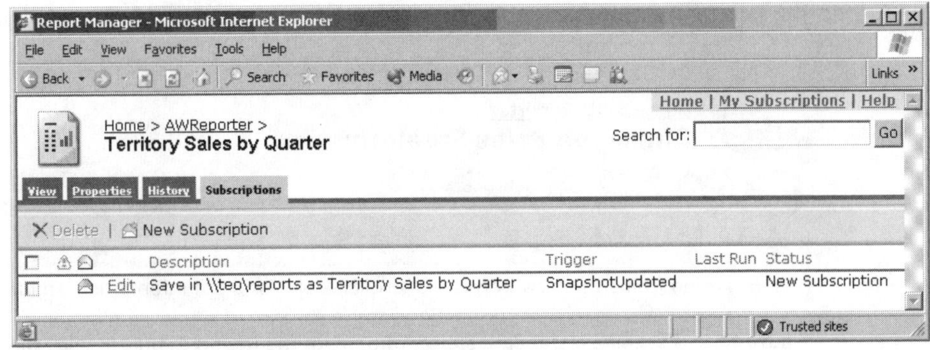

Figure 14.3 End users can use the Report Manager to create subscriptions.

14.2.2 Choosing the subscription type

With RS you can create two types of subscriptions:

- *Standard subscriptions*—With this type of subscription, the subscription configuration details are fixed and must be known at the time the subscription is set up.
- *Data-driven subscriptions*—With data-driven subscriptions, many aspects of the subscription can be dynamic. For example, a data-driven e-mail subscription can retrieve the list of recipients from a database. The Report Server will retrieve them from a data store when the subscription is processed.

These two types correspond to the `CreateSubscription` and `CreateDataDrivenSubscription` SOAP APIs, respectively. Let's find out how we can create and manage both types of subscriptions.

Setting up standard subscriptions

The configuration details of standard subscriptions, such as the report's export format, list of recipients, and so forth, are static. For example, with standard e-mail subscriptions the report administrator enters a fixed list of e-mail recipients by specifying each recipient's e-mail address.

As we said, standard subscriptions require only Manage Individual Subscriptions rights, which the predefined Browser role already includes.

To create a standard subscription using the Report Manager, the end user will follow these steps:

Step 1 Navigate to the report of interest.

Step 2 Click the Subscriptions tab, as shown in figure 14.4.

Step 3 Click the New Subscription button.

Clicking the New Subscription button opens the Report Delivery Options screen. The options on this screen may vary depending on the selected delivery extension, as we will discuss by example in section 14.3.

You use standard subscriptions when the subscription details for all recipients are the same. For example, you may want to push a report by e-mail to a small list of recip-

Figure 14.4 To create a standard subscription with the Report Manager, click the New Subscription button found on the report's Subscriptions tab.

ients. All recipients will receive the report in a single format, such as PDF. No personalization is necessary; e.g. you don't have to greet the recipient by first name. In this case, a standard e-mail subscription is a good choice.

Sometimes your requirements may call for more flexible subscription options, such as when you want to allow the recipients to specify their preferred report format. In this case, you can use data-driven subscriptions.

Setting up data-driven subscriptions

As its name suggests, data-driven subscriptions permit certain subscription properties to be retrieved from the database during runtime, including

- The list of recipients
- The report rendering format
- The report parameters
- Extension-specific properties, such as Priority and Subject for reports delivered via e-mail

As you could probably imagine, data-driven subscriptions give you a lot of flexibility by allowing you to customize the report's content and destination. Here are some scenarios where data-driven subscriptions could be useful:

- An organization can e-mail the product catalog report to its customers who have placed orders in the past six months.
- Reports can be personalized by synchronizing the report parameters with the results from the subscription query. For instance, an Order History report could greet the user by his name.
- An organization could permit the report's users to customize certain aspects of the report delivery during the subscription process. For example, a customer could be given an option to specify the preferred report format, such as MHTML or PDF, during the subscription process.

Data-driven subscriptions mandate having Manage All Subscriptions rights. If the role-based security policy of the interactive user includes this task, then the New Data-driven Subscription button is visible in the Report Manager interface, as shown in figure 14.4.

Data-driven subscriptions require a data store that holds the subscriber's data. As a part of setting up a data-driven subscription, you need to specify a database query to retrieve the recipient list. This query could be one of the following:

- A nonparameterized SQL SELECT statement that retrieves the recipient list from a database table or view, for example:

  ```
  select * from recipients where type='individual'
  ```

- A stored procedure call prefixed with EXEC, for example:

  ```
  EXEC spGetRecipients parameter1, parameter2,…
  ```

The statement must produce a rowset with as many rows as the number of recipients. The Report Manager Subscription Wizard facilitates the query setup process, as shown in figure 14.5.

In this case, we omitted the EXEC command from the stored procedure call, which resulted in an error when the Validate button was clicked. The validation logic checks to determine whether the query is syntactically correct by parsing and sending the query to the data source. It doesn't validate whether the returned data is semantically correct or if the call has resulted in an empty dataset.

The Subscription Wizard is kind enough to list the delivery extension's publicly available properties. You can use fields from the query to set these properties, as we will see in a data-driven subscription example in section 14.3.3. During runtime, the Report Server will execute the query to get the list of recipients. For each recipient row,

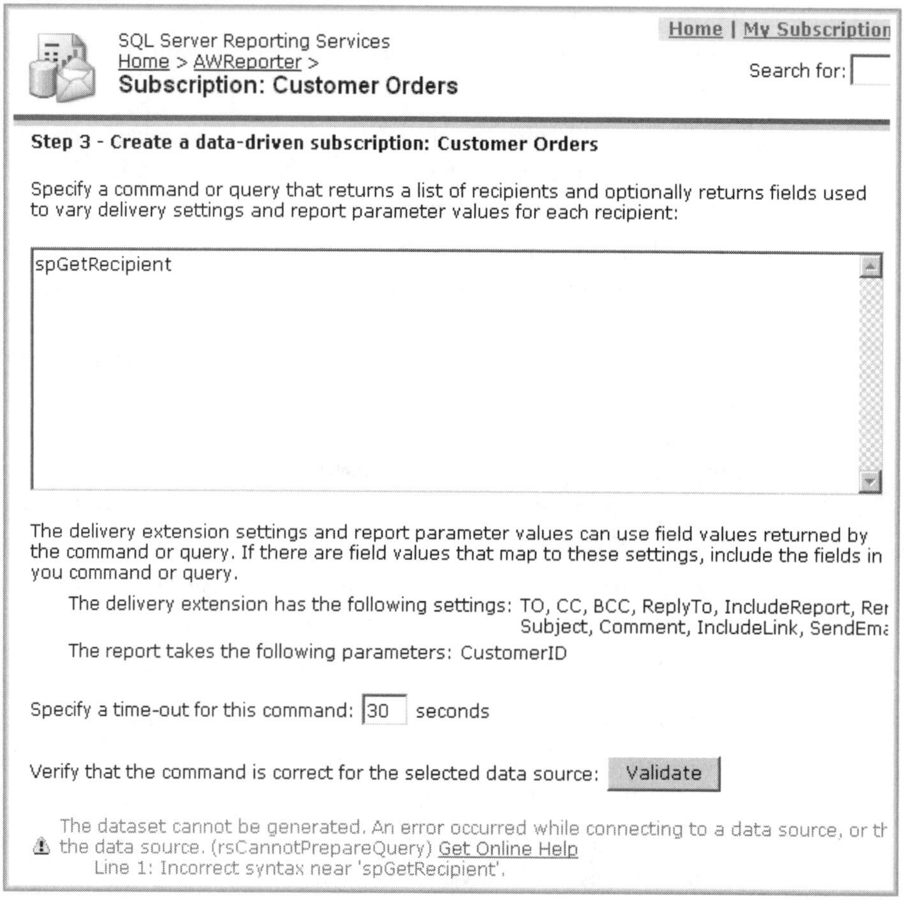

Figure 14.5 The Report Manager Subscription Wizard makes setting up the subscription query easy.

the Report Server will set the data-driven properties of the delivery extension and ask the extension to distribute the report.

Developers writing custom delivery extensions will appreciate the data-driven subscription model because querying the database and setting up the subscription properties are responsibilities of the Report Server, not the extension. This allows the developer to focus only on implementing the delivery logic by shifting the task of generating the list of recipients to the Report Server. Once the delivery extension is ready, it can be used as both a standard and a data-driven extension. We will see how this can be done in chapter 15.

14.2.3 Configuring delivery extensions

As a part of the subscription configuration process, you need to select the extension responsible for delivering the report to its final destination. If you use the Report Manager, you will define the subscription-delivery extension association using the Report Delivery Options page (see figure 14.7), which is the first page shown after you click the New Subscription or New Data-driven Subscription button.

Out of the box, RS comes with two extensions to address two of the most common delivery scenarios:

- *E-mail delivery extension*—Sends reports to one or more recipients via e-mail
- *File share delivery extension*—Persists reports as disk files to a target folder, such as a network share

When these two extensions are not enough, you can extend RS by plugging in custom extensions. We will see how to accomplish this by creating a Web service delivery extension in chapter 15, which can be used to send reports to a Web service.

When you set up your subscription you may wonder why none of the HTML-based export flavors appears in the Format drop-down. This could be explained by the fact that all HTML formats except MHTML are multistream rendering formats and require additional trips to the Report Server to fetch the report's images.

While a delivery extension can render the report's image streams on the server, "shredding" the report in this way may be unacceptable. For example, in the case of e-mail report delivery, using an HTML-based format may result in several mail attachments, one for the report body and one for each report image. Therefore, if you need to send reports in HTML format, consider the MHTML export option, which embeds the images inside the report's payload.

Configuring the e-mail delivery extension

Delivering reports successfully via the e-mail delivery extension requires a preconfigured and functioning mail server.

NOTE Windows 2000 and 2003 include SMTP services that you can use to send e-mail. Windows 2003 also comes with a POP3 service that you can leverage to receive e-mail in your applications if they need this functionality. For more information about how to set up these services, please refer to the resources in section 14.5.

Once the e-mail server is ready, you need to configure the Report Server to use it for e-mail delivery. To accomplish this, you need to change the e-mail extension settings found under the `<Report Server Email>` element in the RSReportServer.config configuration file. The RS documentation explains the role of these settings in detail, so we won't discuss them here.

TIP Many organizations use Microsoft Exchange Server as an e-mail server. If you want to use an existing Exchange Server for e-mail report delivery, here is how to configure the Report Server. First, you need to find the fully qualified domain name (FQDN) of the Exchange server. One of way to accomplish this, besides harassing the network administrator, is to look at the message header of any of the e-mail messages received in your Outlook Inbox. To do this, open a received e-mail and from the View menu select Options. In the Internet Headers textbox you will see something like this:

```
Microsoft Mail Internet Headers Version 2.0
Received: from <exchange server FQDN> ([xxx.xx.xxx.xxx]) by
<exchange Server FQDN > with Microsoft SMTPSVC(xxx.xx.xxx.xxx);
   Sat, 13 Mar 2004 11:44:49 -0600
```

In my case, the first Exchange Server FQDN gave me the fully qualified name of the Exchange Server responsible for servicing the outgoing e-mail in my domain.

Sometimes the FQDN of the Exchange Server that you will get from the message headers may point to an incoming mail server that may not necessarily be the server responsible for outbound mail messages. Check with your network administrator to verify if this is the case. In addition, an outbound Exchange server may require authentication to avoid relaying.

NOTE Once you get the name of the Exchange Server, you can change the SMTPServer setting in RSReportServer.config to point to that Exchange Server. In my case, changing this setting and setting the "From" e-mail account were sufficient to send reports via e-mail successfully.

It is important to note that the RS e-mail extension doesn't verify the status of the e-mail delivery. For example, the Report Server has no way of knowing whether the e-mail delivery to a given recipient address has failed. Developers who have written code in the past to send e-mail programmatically should be able to relate to this limitation easily.

As far as the Report Server is concerned, the execution of the subscribed delivery task is successful as long as the e-mail is relayed successfully to the mail server. Therefore, you need to work with the mail server's administrator to ensure that the report has indeed been delivered successfully to all subscribers.

Configuring the file share delivery extension

Configuring file share delivery is easy. As a part of the subscription process, you need to specify the file share location and credentials in order to access the file share.

The file share path must be specified in Uniform Naming Convention (UNC) format. The UNC format requires the following syntax:

```
\\<computername>\<sharename>
```

Make sure that the shared folder exists because the file delivery extension doesn't create the folder, so the delivery process will fail otherwise.

You also need to enter the credentials (user name and password) of the Windows account that will be used to access the file share.

Once the subscription is configured, it can be managed via the Report Manager UI.

14.2.4 Managing subscriptions

The report administrator configures the role-based security policies that dictate which rights a given user has for managing report subscriptions. For example, typically the end users will have rights to manage the subscriptions they own, while the report administrator will be responsible for managing all subscriptions.

Using My Subscriptions

End users who have Manage Individual Subscriptions rights can view and use the options on the Report Manager's My Subscriptions page. This page lists the subscriptions they own, as shown in figure 14.6.

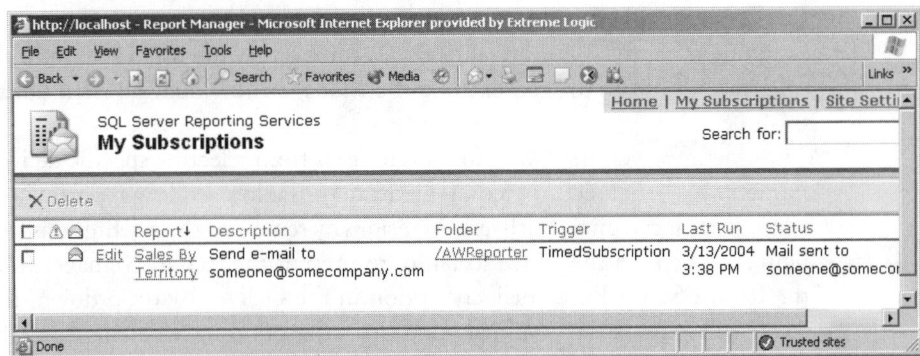

Figure 14.6 Users can use the My Subscriptions page to manage the subscriptions they own. Here, the user is subscribed to the Sales by Territory report.

The My Subscriptions page is similar to the screen linked to the Subscriptions tab, but it doesn't give the user an option to create new subscriptions. Using My Subscriptions or the Subscriptions tab from the report properties allow users to

- Make changes to an existing subscription
- See the last date and time when the subscription was run
- Verify the subscription status
- Delete the subscription

Managing all subscriptions

Users with Manage All Subscriptions rights can manage the subscriptions they own plus those of other users. The Report Manager doesn't include a screen that shows a single view of all subscriptions. Instead, you need to drill down to individual reports to see the subscriptions associated with each report.

For example, to see all time-based subscriptions, the administrator would follow these steps:

Step 1 Click the Manage Shared Schedules link from the Site Settings menu.

Step 2 Select the schedule of interest.

Step 3 View the reports linked to that schedule.

Step 4 Click the Subscriptions tab for each report to get to the subscriptions associated with that report.

As a workaround, if you want to see all subscriptions, you can create a database view that links the Subscriptions, Catalog, and Users tables to return the report and user names.

The administrator can prevent individual users from creating subscriptions by setting up a new role that doesn't include the Manage Individual Subscriptions task and assign users to this role. Alternatively, assuming that the users belong to the Browser role, the administrator can exclude the Manage Individual Subscriptions task from this role.

Sometimes, you may want to prevent users from selecting specific delivery options. For example, strict security requirements may disallow sending reports via e-mail. The administrator can disable delivery extensions by removing their definitions from the configuration files. In the above scenario, to prevent the Report Manager from showing the Report Server Email delivery option in the Deliver By drop-down, the administrator can remove or comment out the corresponding element from the RSWebApplication.config configuration file.

NOTE Removing a delivery extension from the RSWebApplication.config file will only prevent this extension from showing in the Report Manager UI. You can still use the SOAP subscription-related APIs to create subscriptions associated with the excluded extension. If you want to prevent users from creating subscriptions with a given delivery extension, you will need to remove it from the RSReportServer.config file.

Now that we've covered the theory behind subscribed report delivery, let's put it into action to address some common subscription-based needs.

14.3 SUBSCRIBED REPORT DELIVERY IN ACTION

In this section, we will implement the following examples:

- A standard e-mail subscription
- A standard file-based subscription
- A data-driven e-mail subscription
- Triggering a subscription programmatically

14.3.1 "Pushing" reports via standard e-mail subscriptions

In our fictitious scenario, the AWC North American Sales Manager, Stephen Jiang, will subscribe his subordinates to receive the Employee Sales Freeform with Chart report, which we created in chapter 4. We will assume that Stephen has rights to execute the Manage Individual Subscriptions task included by default in the Browser role. To simulate this scenario, we could reuse Stephen's Windows account that we created in chapter 8. If you decide to do so, please remember to grant this account Browser permissions to the AWReporter folder.

To make the things more interesting, we will also assume that Stephen doesn't have the Manage All Subscriptions rights and that SendEmailToUserAlias is set to True (the default value). As a result, the e-mail address fields (To, Cc, and Bcc) will appear disabled for Stephen. Therefore, the report administrator will need to finalize the subscription that was initiated by Stephen by entering the recipients' e-mail addresses.

Creating a standard e-mail subscription

Start by logging in to Windows with Stephen's login credentials. Next, perform the following steps:

Step 1 Use your favorite browser to open the Report Manager web application.

Step 2 Navigate to the Employee Sales Freeform with Chart report.

Step 3 Select New Subscription from the View or Subscriptions tab. This will initiate the process of creating a new subscription, as shown in figure 14.7.

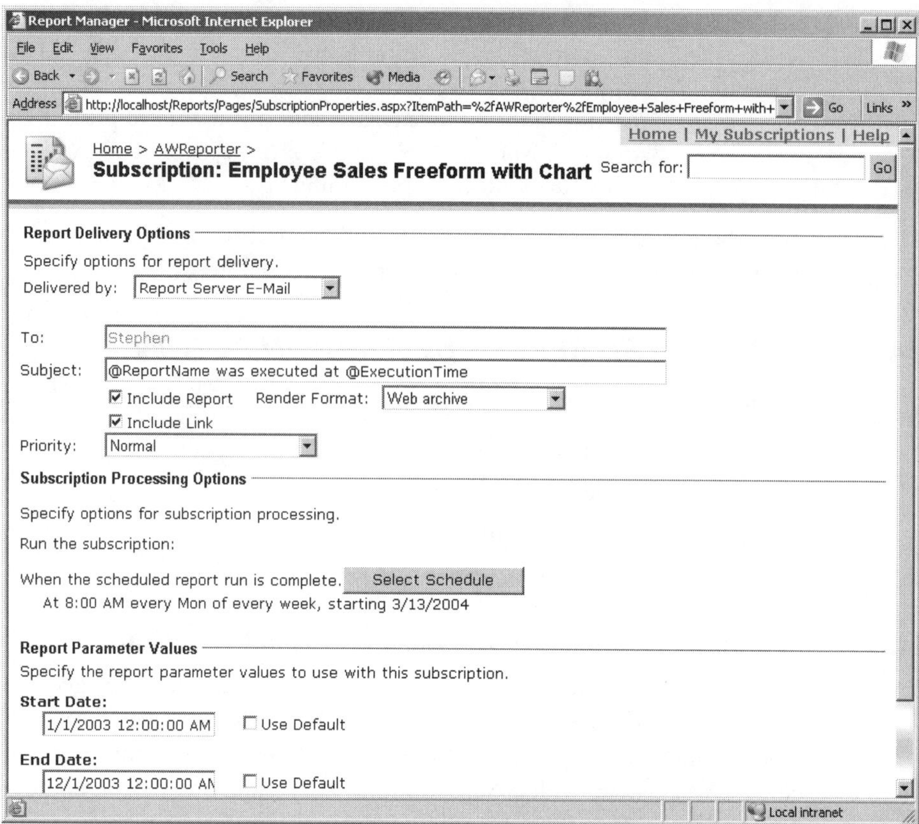

Figure 14.7 Using the Report Manager to create an individual e-mail subscription

As you can see, the Report Manager adjusts the user interface to reflect the fact that Stephen doesn't have rights to execute the Manage All Subscriptions task. Specifically, the following changes are made:

- The To field is disabled, so Stephen can't enter the recipients' e-mail addresses.
- The Cc, Bcc, and Reply-To fields are missing.
- The screen doesn't give the user an option to run the subscription on a shared schedule.

Some of the available fields deserve more attention. The default Subject field has two predefined variable placeholders, @ReportName and @ExecutionTime. During runtime, the Report Server will replace them with their counterparts from the Global object collection, ReportName and ExecutionTime. While you may think that you can use the rest of the Global variables, for example, TotalPages or ReportServerUrl, this is not the case. Why? I don't know. A good case could be made to support parameter values, results from a call to custom code, and so on. Unfortunately, the Report Server is currently wired to support only these two variables.

Checking the Include Report check box will embed the report in the e-mail when the export format is a Web archive (MHTML) or enclose it as an e-mail attachment otherwise.

If selected, the Include Link check box will add the report's URL to the body of the e-mail. This could be useful when you want to let the user conveniently request the report to see the latest data.

The Priority field reflects the status under which the e-mail will be sent. For example, if the subscription is created with a high priority, Microsoft Outlook will show an exclamation mark in the Importance field.

Finally, for parameter-driven reports, the Report Manager generates placeholders for each report parameter. For non-snapshot reports, the user can enter the parameter values or opt to use the default values.

While Stephen can create a subscription-specific schedule to trigger the subscribed delivery, he won't get very far. The e-mail server will error out when trying to resolve the recipients' addresses. In short, the security-conscious user interface of Report Manager is good enough to log the subscription request but not to execute it successfully. Doing so will require intervention by the report administrator.

Finalizing the e-mail subscription

We will now assume that Stephen has notified the report administrator of his intention to distribute the report to a fixed number of sales representatives.

Next, the report administrator will navigate to the report and override Stephen's subscription, as shown in figure 14.8.

In our scenario, the report administrator would enter the e-mail addresses of Stephen's subordinates.

> **TIP** You will probably recall that in chapter 5 we authored the Corporate Hierarchy report. You can create similar reports to find out who reports to whom.

The e-mail addresses shown in figure 14.8 are taken from the AdventuresWorks2000 database and are fictitious. To test the example successfully, you may want to enter valid e-mail addresses in the To field. In addition, you may want to change the schedule duration to a shorter interval, such as every five minutes. Don't forget to stop the schedule or dissociate the report from it when you have finished experimenting to prevent filling up your e-mail box!

That's it! At this point the standard e-mail subscription is scheduled and ready for execution. When the schedule is up, the Report Server will generate the Employee Sales Freeform with Chart report and mail it to the specified recipients.

14.3.2 Archiving reports to a file share

In this scenario, we will archive the Territory Sales by Quarter report that we authored in chapter 7 each time its underlying data is refreshed. As you will probably recall, we

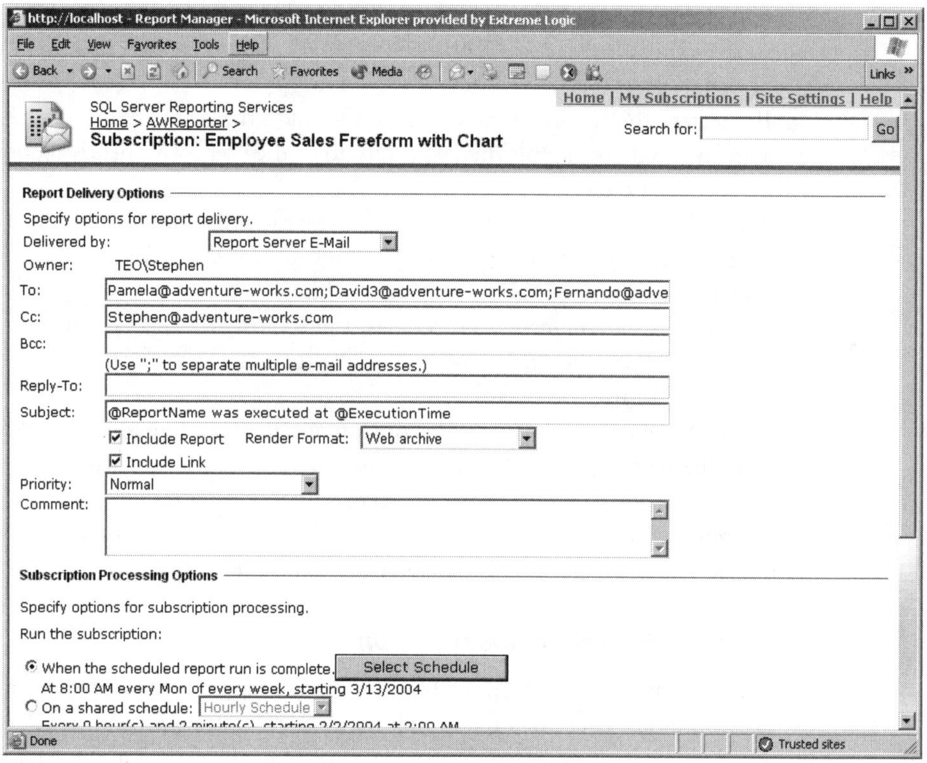

Figure 14.8 The report administrator can finalize the report subscription by entering the recipients' addresses.

configured this report to be executed as a snapshot that will be refreshed on a quarterly basis. We set the snapshot execution process to be triggered by a shared schedule.

This time we will extend our example by creating a subscription that will run each time the snapshot is refreshed. The subscription will export the report in PDF and use the file share delivery extension to save the report as a file to a network share.

Setting up the target folder

Start by choosing the target folder where the report archive will be created. The file share delivery extension doesn't create the specified folder if it doesn't exist, so we need to specify an existing folder. For the purposes of this demo, we've chosen to export the report to the C:\Reports folder. In real life, you will probably want to use a globally accessible network share. As we've discussed, the target folder must be specified in the Uniform Naming Convention (UNC) format that includes the computer's network name. In our example, the UNC format for C:\Reports is \\<computer-name>\C$\Reports.

NOTE In our case we use an administrative share (indicated by the $ sign). In real life, you should use network shares that are off the root of the server, for example, <computername>\Reports.

As we've said, to create file share subscriptions, the user must have Manage Individual Subscriptions rights. Unlike working with e-mail subscriptions, however, the Report Manager doesn't enforce any additional security rules. Therefore, users with Manage Individual Subscriptions rights will be able to configure execution-ready file share subscriptions.

You may wonder why file share subscriptions are more relaxed in terms of security. In my opinion, the reason for this laissez-faire approach is that file share delivery is naturally more restricted than e-mail delivery because the report cannot be exported outside the organization's boundaries. In addition, access to UNC shares can be controlled by other means, such as using Windows Access Control Lists (ACL).

Configuring file-share delivery

Once you've decided on the target folder, follow these steps to configure the Territory Sales by Quarter report for file-share delivery.

Step 1 Using the Report Manager, navigate to the Territory Sales by Quarter report.

Step 2 Verify that the report is scheduled for a snapshot execution by checking the Execution tab's properties. If it isn't, follow the directions in chapter 7 to configure the report for snapshot execution that is triggered by the shared Quarterly Schedule.

Step 3 Click the New Subscription button from the View or Subscriptions tab. Configure the file share delivery as shown in figure 14.9.

To export the report to a target folder, we use the Report Server File Share delivery option, which will delegate the report distribution to the file share extension. To append the export format extension we select the Add a File Extension When the File Is Created check box. This will allow the user to double-click on the file and load the report in the application that is associated with the file extension, for example, Adobe Acrobat for files with the .PDF extension.

In my case, the share UNC path is \\teo\c$\reports because my computer name is named teo. The export format is set to Adobe Acrobat (PDF). The file share extension requires you to specify the credentials of a Windows account that has write access to the target folder. The overwrite options are self-explanatory.

To trigger the subscription when the report snapshot is refreshed, we choose the When the Report Content Is Refreshed option. This option is available only for snapshot reports.

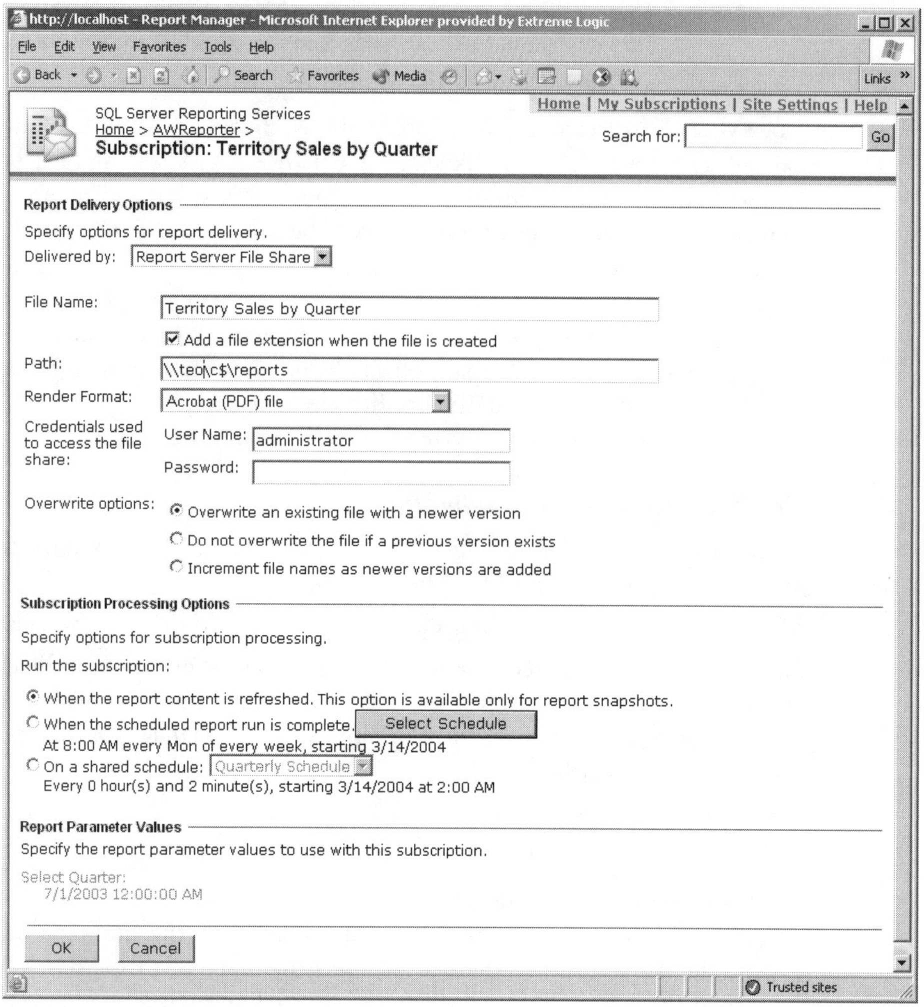

Figure 14.9 To configure a file share subscription for report archiving, specify the file share path in UNC and the account credentials.

Parameter limitations

Finally, please note that the parameter placeholders are disabled. As we discussed in chapter 7, once the snapshot parameter values have been defined, they cannot be changed prior to the report's execution. In our case, this means that the report will filter the report data for the third quarter.

The administrator has to remember to change the parameter value on the report's Parameters tab before the next quarterly execution. Of course, this could be avoided by changing the report to filter the underlying data using the system date instead of using a report parameter.

Observing the subscription results

Once we've defined the file share subscription, we are ready to put it in action.

Instead of waiting for the next quarter, let's change the Quarterly shared schedule interval to five minutes. Then, switch to the Territory Sales by Quarter report's Subscription tab, as shown in figure 14.10.

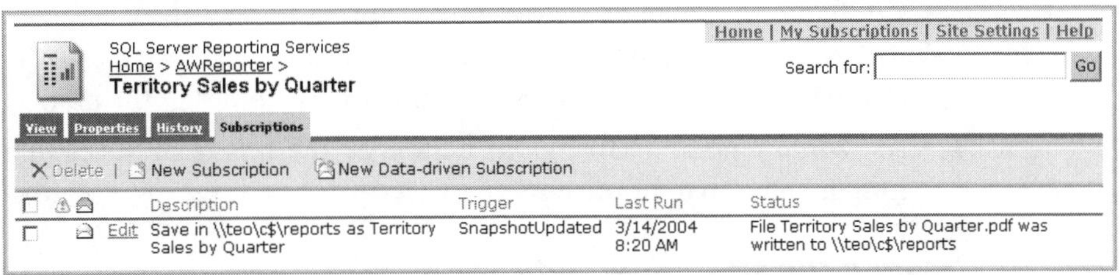

Figure 14.10 Using the Subscription tab to observe the subscription run

Please note that the Trigger column shows SnapshotUpdated to signify that the subscription will be triggered by a snapshot refresh.

Once the schedule is up, the Report Server will process the report and will ask the file share extension to deliver the report. As a result, the report will be saved to the specified target folder.

14.3.3 Sending reports to a data-driven list of recipients

While distributing reports to a fixed list of recipients may be useful for intranet-oriented reports, it may be impractical when reports need to be delivered to web-based subscribers. For example, imagine that Adventure Works would like to send the Product Catalog report to its web customers on a regular basis. Hard-coding hundreds and thousands of customers' e-mail addresses would present a maintenance challenge.

In addition, a common requirement for Internet-oriented applications is to support report personalization features and custom-tailor the report to meet the specific requirements of the user. For example, it is unlikely that all customers would like to receive the Product Catalog report exported in the same format. Instead, a better approach would be to allow the subscribers to specify the export format, such as PDF, HTML, and so forth. All of these requirements call for a more flexible subscribed delivery option.

On the provider side, many organizations may want to implement custom delivery rules to filter out the list of recipients who will receive the report. For example, to fight the recent proliferation of spam e-mail, government regulations in the U.S. dictate that all commercial e-mail must allow the subscribers to be able to opt out at will from e-mail distribution lists.

Another common scenario that requires validating business rules is when an organization wants to deliver reports only to recipients who meet specific criteria. For example, Adventure Works may want to distribute the product catalog report only to subscribers who have placed orders in the past six months.

To address needs such as these, RS supports data-driven subscriptions. In this section, we will implement a data-driven e-mail subscription to meet the following design goals:

- Create a data store to capture the subscribers' data. In real life, the AWC customers will typically use a web-based front end to opt in for subscribed report delivery. The data store could also save the customers' subscription preferences.
- Configure an e-mail data-driven subscription to send the Customer Order History report to all subscribers. As you'll probably recall, we created this report in chapter 11 to show the orders placed by the customer in the past.
- Allow the report's recipients to customize the report by specifying the export format and e-mail priority.

Creating the subscriber data store

The AdventureWorks2000 database model supports several types of customers, including individuals, stores, and retail. The individuals' profile data is captured in the Individual table. If you look at the definition of this table you will see that among other things it stores the customers' names and e-mail addresses, which makes this table suitable for a recipient data store. Unfortunately, the AdventureWorks2000 data is not consistent. Specifically, the orders placed by individuals don't have matching records in the Individual table.

To fix this, you need to add customer records into the Individual table with identifiers matching the CustomerID column in the SalesOrderHeader table. To make your life easier, we've provided a SQL script that you can run to insert a few customer records. The script is called Recipients.sql and it is located in the Database.dbp project. If you want to test the e-mail delivery end to end, make sure to change the customers' e-mail addresses to valid e-mail addresses.

To simulate an opt-in distribution list, we created a database view, called Recipients, which you can find in the Views.sql script located in the same project. The view simply filters out data in the Individual table to return only the customers whom we've added using the Recipients.sql script. In real life, instead of a view, you may want to use a stored procedure to implement additional business rules.

Figure 14.11 shows what the subscriber data looks like as returned by the view.

To implement the view we decided to reuse the CreditCardNumber and EmailPromotion columns from the Individual table to store the report format and e-mail priority data, respectively. We did so to avoid adding columns to the Individual table.

CustomerID	FirstName	LastName	EmailAddress	Format	Priority
21768	Ryan	Lewis	rlewis@adventure-works.com	MHTML	LOW
28389	Miguel	Thomas	mthomas@adventure-works.com	PDF	NORMAL
25863	Nicholas	Thompson	nthompson@adventure-works.com	IMAGE	HIGH
14501	Ariana	Ramirez	aramirez@adventure-works.com	PDF	LOW
11003	Maya	Hill	mhill@adventure-works.com	MHTML	NORMAL

Figure 14.11 Creating a view to serve as a subscriber data source

Once you've created the view, don't forget to grant permissions to it for the database login that the AW2000 Shared DS data source uses to log in to the AdventureWorks2000 database.

Configuring the e-mail data-driven extension

Now it is time to create the subscription. Open the Report Manager portal and navigate to the Customer Orders report. Click the Subscriptions tab and choose New Data-driven Subscription.

Step 1: Specifying the delivery option

The Data-driven Subscription Wizard starts, as shown in figure 14.12.

Here, we've chosen to distribute the report via e-mail. In addition, we've indicated that the subscriber data store will be queried using a shared data source, which we will specify in the next step. Click Next to advance to the second step.

Step 2: Selecting the data source

If you have selected to use the shared data source option in Step 1, you need to tell the Subscription Wizard where it is located, as shown in figure 14.13.

In our case, we've selected the AW2000 Shared DS data source because the Recipient view is located in the AdventureWorks2000 database.

Step 3: Setting up the recipient query

Next, we need to set up the query that will return the list of recipients, as shown in figure 14.14.

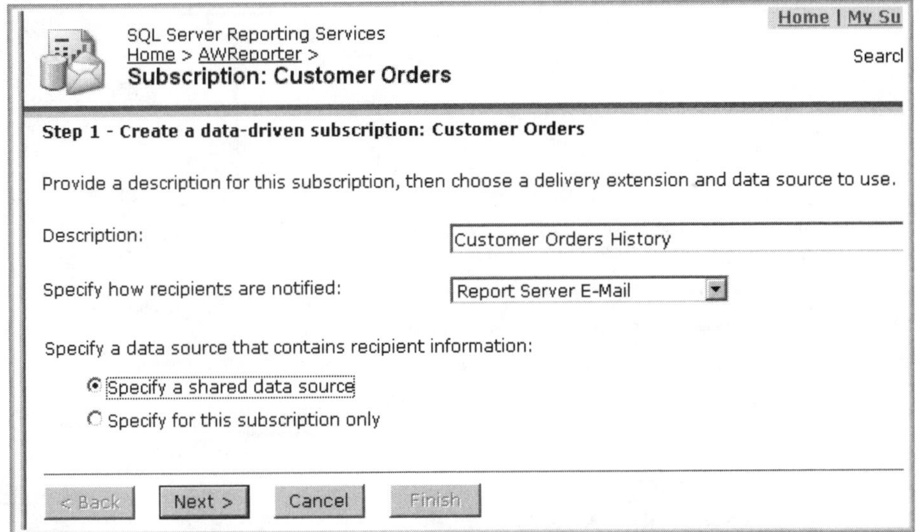

Figure 14.12 In Step 1 of the Subscription Wizard, choose the delivery extension.

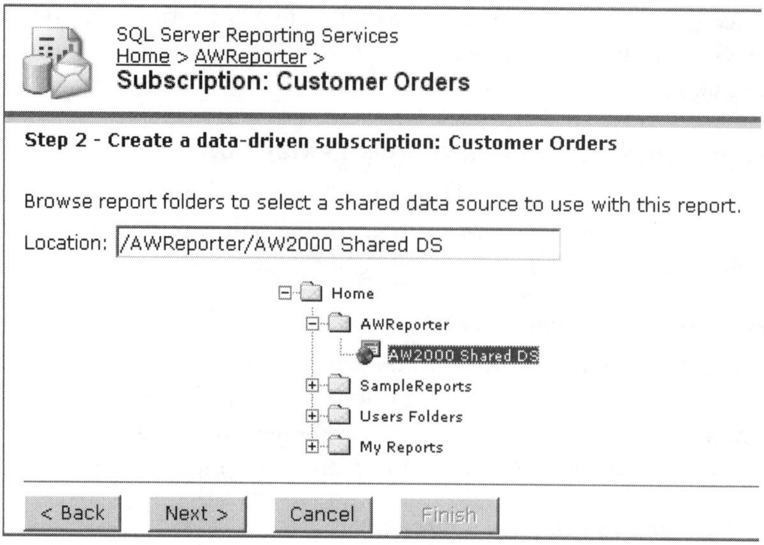

SQL Server Reporting Services
Home > AWReporter >
Subscription: Customer Orders

Step 2 - Create a data-driven subscription: Customer Orders

Browse report folders to select a shared data source to use with this report.

Location: /AWReporter/AW2000 Shared DS

Home
AWReporter
AW2000 Shared DS
SampleReports
Users Folders
My Reports

< Back | Next > | Cancel | Finish

Figure 14.13 In Step 2 specify the data source that will be used to get the subscriber data.

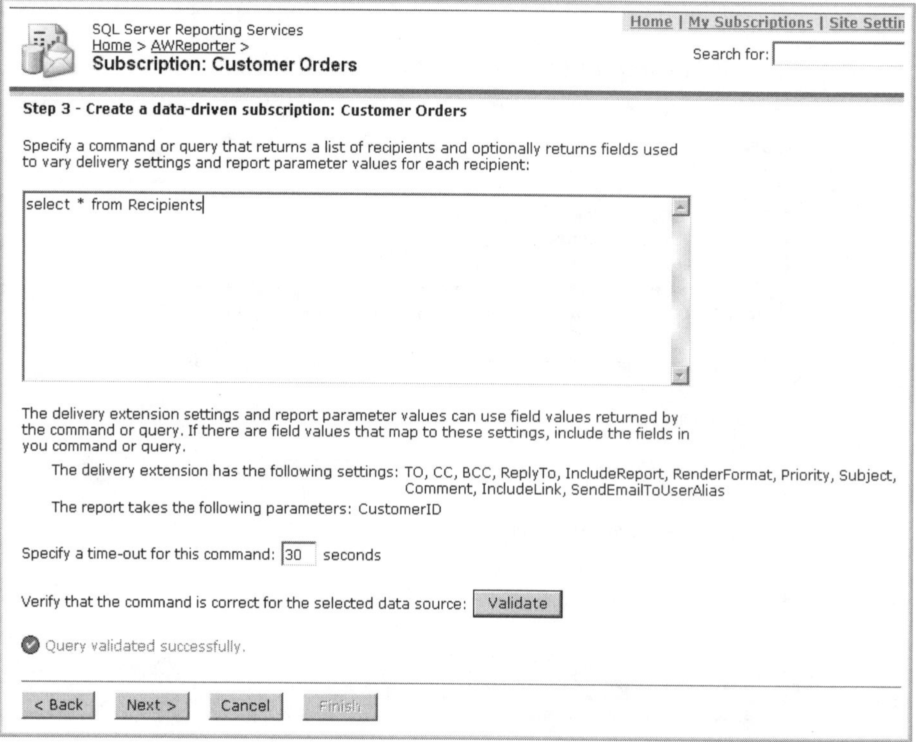

Figure 14.14 In Step 3 specify the query statement used to return the recipient list.

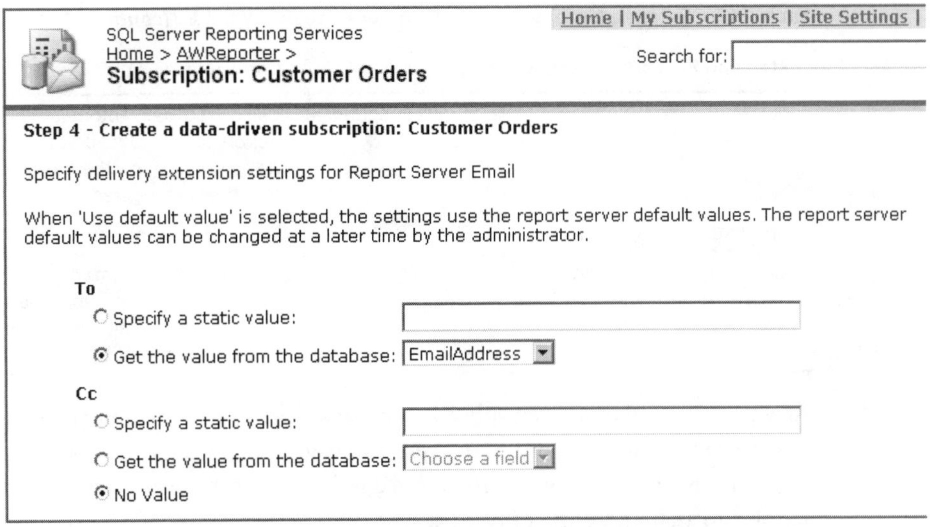

SQL Server Reporting Services
Home > AWReporter >
Subscription: Customer Orders

Home | My Subscriptions | Site Settings |

Search for:

Step 4 - Create a data-driven subscription: Customer Orders

Specify delivery extension settings for Report Server Email

When 'Use default value' is selected, the settings use the report server default values. The report server default values can be changed at a later time by the administrator.

To

Specify a static value:

Get the value from the database: EmailAddress

Cc

Specify a static value:

Get the value from the database: Choose a field

No Value

Figure 14.15 In Step 4 specify the delivery extension settings.

Here, we are selecting all records from the Recipient view.

Step 4: Specifying the delivery extension settings

The next step is the most important step of setting up the data-driven subscription. Here, we will need to map the recipients' addresses and optionally other extension-specific properties to the query fields, as shown in figure 14.15.

Set the extension properties as shown in table 14.1.

Table 14.1 Extension properties can be mapped to query fields.

Extension Property	Setting	Comment
To	EmailAddress (database field)	Data-driven from the recipient query
Cc	No Value	We won't cc the e-mail to another recipient
Bcc	No Value	We won't bcc the e-mail to another recipient
Reply-To	No Value	No need to specify an explicit return address
Include Report	True	The report will be embedded when the report format is MHTML or attached otherwise
Render Format	Format (database field)	Data-driven from the recipient query
Priority	Priority (database field)	Data-driven from the recipient query

continued on next page

Table 14.1 Extension properties can be mapped to query fields. *(continued)*

Extension Property	Setting	Comment
Subject	@ReportName was executed at @ExecutionTime	Will be replaced automatically by the Report Server to read "Customer Orders was executed at <the time when the schedule is triggered>"
Comment	No Value	No need for comments
Include Link	False	Web-based recipients won't normally have URL access to the Report Server, so there is no need to give them an option to request the report by URL

As you can see, data-driven subscriptions give you a lot of flexibility to customize the report's execution. Any of the delivery extension properties can be set to get its value from the recipients' rowset. In our scenario, our web customers could specify the report's format and e-mail priority.

Step 5: Configuring report parameters

During the next step, we need to take care of the report parameters, as shown in figure 14.16.

The Customer Orders report takes a single parameter, CustomerID. To synchronize the report with the recipients' rowset, we need to link this parameter to the CustomerID column returned by the query.

Step 6: Setting up the subscription event

Finally, let's set this subscription to be triggered on a quarterly basis by using the predefined Quarterly Schedule, as shown in figure 14.17.

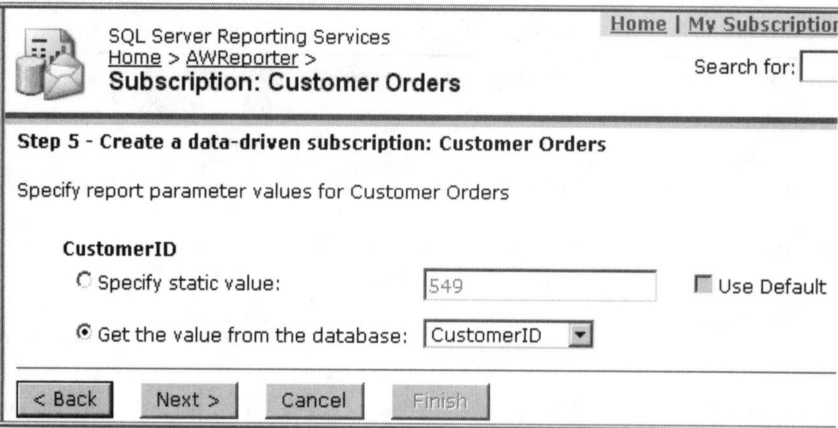

Figure 14.16 In Step 5 we need to filter the customer orders per recipient. We do this by setting the CustomerID report parameter to the CustomerID column from the recipients' rowset.

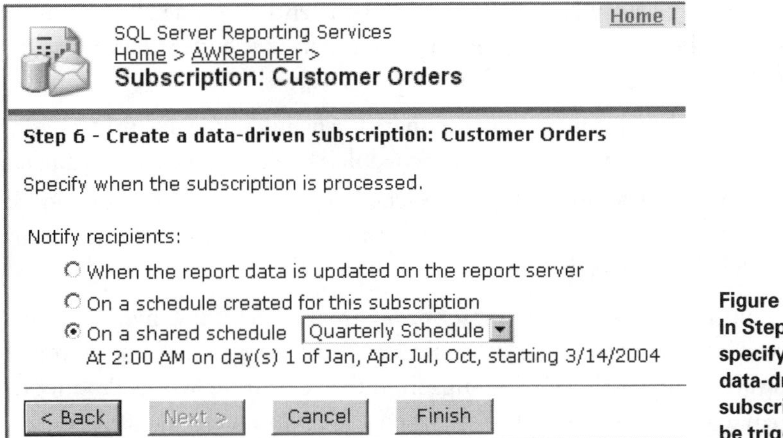

Figure 14.17 In Step 6 we specify how the data-driven subscription will be triggered.

That's it! We managed to set up an automated data-driven report delivery in six easy steps. We can apply a similar approach to implement an e-mail campaigner service to send the product catalog by e-mail to a list of subscribers when there is a new product promotion. Or, a spam service? Just kidding to see if you are still here! You can further enhance this scenario to add more personalization features. For example, you could easily modify the Customer Orders report to greet the user by name.

You can use any delivery extension with data-driven subscriptions. For example, with file share subscriptions, the recipient's data source could keep the target folders where the reports need to be saved.

With RS you are not limited to triggering your subscriptions on a fixed schedule. Instead, you can programmatically fire subscriptions, as we will discuss next.

14.3.4 Triggering subscriptions programmatically

While running subscriptions at a reoccurring scheduled interval can be very useful, sometimes you may need to programmatically trigger the subscribed delivery process.

For example, say you have scheduled an e-mail delivery of the Adventure Works product catalog to a list of subscribers on a quarterly basis. However, the company management has requested the report to also be distributed when a new product is added to the catalog. How would you implement this?

Publishing events programatically

One option to trigger a subscription programmatically is to reset the subscription schedule to run when a new product is added. While this will work, it requires manual intervention. Ideally, what we need is the ability to automate the process by being able to pragmatically fire the subscription event. Can we do this with RS? You bet.

The RS Web service already includes a web method for this task. It is called `FireEvent`, and it has the following signature:

```
public void FireEvent(string EventType,  string EventData);
```

It is one of the event types listed under the EventProcessing element in the RSReportServer.config configuration file. The event data is the identifier of the item that triggered the event and can be of the following values:

- For subscriptions based on shared schedules, the EventData is the schedule identifier, as specified in the ScheduleID column in the Schedule table.
- For subscriptions with private schedules, the EventData corresponds to the subscription identifier, which is the value of the SubscriptionID column from the Subscriptions table.

In a nutshell, triggering the subscription programmatically involves inserting an event record into the Event table in the Report Server database. While there's nothing stopping you from writing a table trigger on the Adventure Works Product table to insert a new record in the Event table when a new product has been added, the recommended way is to use the `FireEvent` API.

TIP If you decide to log the event directly into the Event table, you may wonder how to get the event type and data. One way to obtain them is to wait for the subscription schedule to run and then query the Event table in the Report Server catalog. To avoid racing with the Reporting Services Windows Service to determine who will get to the logged event first, you can stop the Reporting Services Windows Service.

Among other things, when the `FireEvent` API is used, the Report Server could verify that the call is permitted as configured by the administrator's role-based security policy. Only callers who have rights to execute the Generate Events system-level task are trusted to fire events programmatically, as shown in figure 14.18.

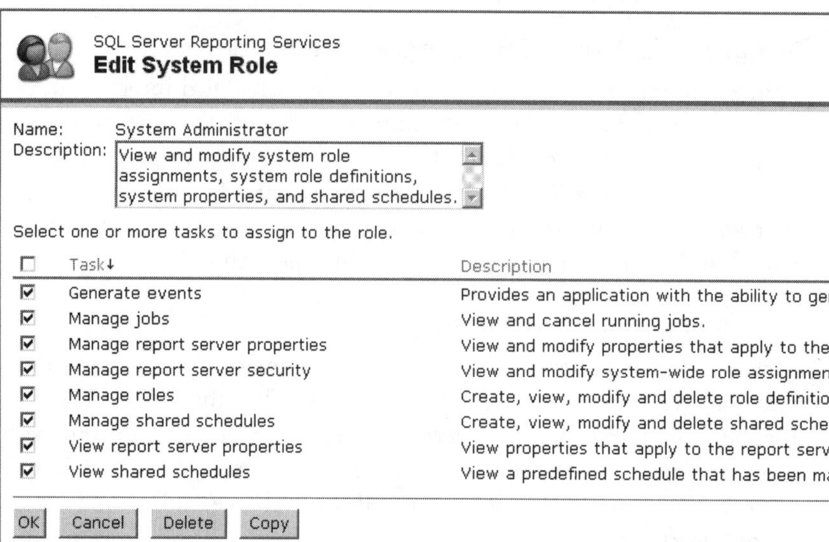

Figure 14.18 Calling FireEvents requires Generate Events rights.

Interestingly, by default the System Administrator role doesn't include this task. Therefore, as a prerequisite for running our sample successfully, you need to grant the `FireEvent` caller Generate Events rights.

Implementing the solution

Once the security policy is set up, we are ready to implement the code sample. Table 14.2 lists the task map of our solution.

Table 14.2 The task map for programmatically firing a subscription

Component	Task	Description
Table Trigger	Create INSERT table trigger	Write an ON INSERT table trigger attached to the Product table that will fire when a new product is added.
	Call web method FireSubscription	Inside the trigger, call a custom web method called FireSubscription. Pass the report and user identity with which the subscription is associated.
Web method FireSubscription	Call ListSubscriptions	Get the list of subscriptions associated with the report-user combination.
	Call GetDataDrivenSubscription-Properties	Retrieve the subscription properties to get to the event details.
	Call FireEvent	Call FireEvent to publish the event programmatically.

Similarly to the Campaigner example we discussed in chapter 9, we will use a table trigger to call a web method, which in turn calls the `FireEvent` API. Why don't we call the `FireEvent` method directly from the trigger? If we do this, it will require hard-coding the event type and data inside the trigger, which is something that we would like to avoid. Instead, we will write a new web method, called `FireSubscription`, which you can find in the Campaigner Web service source code under the Chapter09 folder in the AWReporterWeb project.

The `FireSubscription` source code is shown in listing 14.1.

Listing 14.1 Triggering a subscription programmatically using the `FireEvent` API

```
[WebMethod]
public void FireSubscription(string reportPath, string userName)  {
  ReportingService rs = new ReportingService();
  rs.Credentials=System.Net.CredentialCache.DefaultCredentials;

  DataRetrievalPlan dataRetrievalPlan = null;
  ExtensionSettings extSettings;
  string desc;
  ActiveState active;
  string status;
```

```
  string eventType;
  string matchData;                         Gets the list of subscriptions for the
  Subscription[] subscriptions = null;        requested report and user name
  ParameterValueOrFieldReference[] extensionParams = null;

  subscriptions = rs.ListSubscriptions(reportPath, userName);  <-

  if ( subscriptions != null )  {   <-- Gets the subscription properties
rs.GetDataDrivenSubscriptionProperties(
  subscriptions[0].SubscriptionID,
  out extSettings,  out dataRetrievalPlan, out desc, out active,
  out status, out eventType, out matchData,
  out extensionParams );

      rs.FireEvent(eventType, matchData);    <-  Fires the
  }                                              event
}
```

To make the FireSubscription method more generic, we pass the report path of the report that needs to be delivered as well as the owner's name in the format DOMAIN\USERNAME. The latter argument is needed because, as you will probably recall, a subscription is associated with exactly one user and one report.

The call to the ListSubscription web method returns a list of subscriptions associated with the requested report-user combination. For the sake of simplicity, we default to the first subscription. If you need to support reports that have more than one subscription per given user, you may want to pass the subscription identifier as a third argument to FireSubscription.

Next, we need to get the subscription properties by calling the GetDataDriven-SubscriptionProperties web method. This is needed to get the event type and data before the call to FireEvent. Because there are two types of subscriptions, standard and data-driven, the RS Web service API includes two web methods, GetSub-scriptionProperties and GetDataDrivenSubscriptionProperties.

In our case, we assume that we need to trigger a data-driven subscription. Once the GetDataDrivenSubscriptionProperties call executes successfully, the event type and data are exposed under the eventType and matchData arguments respectively. Finally, we call the FireEvent method to log the event that will trigger the subscription processing.

The only piece left to implement is the INSERT trigger attached to the Products table. This trigger will invoke the FireSubscription method when a new product is added to the Products table in the AdventureWorks2000 database. It will be very similar to the trgSpecialOffer trigger discussed in chapter 9, so we will leave its implementation details to you.

14.4 SUMMARY

In this chapter we explored the second option for distributing reports with Reporting Services—via subscriptions. Coupled with requesting reports on demand, subscribed report delivery should address the most common distribution requirements for making the reports available to your users.

Once you've read this chapter along with chapter 7, you should know when and how to use both delivery options appropriately. When the report's requirements call for immediate synchronous access to the report, the on-demand option could be a better fit. Alternatively, when a report needs to be executed on a regular basis in unattended mode, it can be scheduled and "pushed" to recipients via subscribed delivery.

With subscribed report delivery, users can subscribe to reports that are distributed to them or other destinations as a result of an event. RS supports standard and data-driven subscriptions. Standard subscription options are fixed, while data-driven subscription options can be set during runtime when the subscription is executed.

We put these concepts into practice by implementing various examples. We showed how we can create standard e-mail and file share delivery subscriptions. Then, we demonstrated how data-driven subscriptions work to deliver reports to a data-driven list of recipients. Finally, we looked at how developers can programmatically trigger subscriptions using the `FireEvent` API.

By now, you would probably agree that RS gives you a lot of flexibility in all three phases of the report's lifecycle: authoring, management, and delivery. But, as flexible as it is, there will be cases when RS may not fit all reporting needs out of the box.

In such cases, you will probably appreciate the extensible nature of the RS architecture that allows developers to plug in programming logic in the form of custom extensions, as we will discuss in chapter 15.

14.5 RESOURCES

"E-mail Services" topic from the Windows 2003 product documentation
Learn how to configure an e-mail server using the Windows 2003 SMTP and POP3 services.

PART 4

Advanced reporting

One of the most appealing features of Reporting Services is that it can be easily extended by writing custom add-ons in the form of extensions. Part 4 discusses the implementation details of three custom extensions that you can use to extend the RS features.

You will see how you can author a dataset data extension to report off ADO.NET datasets. You will learn how to distribute reports to web services by means of a custom delivery extension. You will find out how to replace the RS Windows-based security model with a custom security extension.

Besides being feature-rich, your reporting solutions must also perform and scale well under increased user loads. To ensure that these objectives are met, you need to learn how to evaluate the Report Server performance and capacity before "going live" in a production environment. You will learn how to establish performance goals, how to create test scripts with Application Center Test, and how to stress-load your Report Server installation.

CHAPTER 15

Extending Reporting Services

An important characteristic of every enterprise-oriented framework, such as Reporting Services, is that it has to be easily extensible. Simply put, *extensibility* relates to the system's ability to accommodate new features that are built out of old ones. When a software platform is extensible, it allows developers to custom-tailor it to meet their specific needs. For example, when your reporting requirements rule out Windows-based security, RS allows you to replace it with custom security models.

One of the most prominent and appealing aspects of RS is its modular architecture, which is designed for extensibility. We've already witnessed this in chapter 6 when we saw how we could supercharge our reports by writing custom code. In this chapter, we will explore additional ways to take advantage of the unique extensibility model of RS by writing custom extensions. Specifically, we will develop the following extensions:

- A dataset data extension to report off ADO.NET datasets
- A Web service delivery extension to distribute reports to Web services

- A security extension to implement custom authentication and authorization
- An HTTP module for tracing requests

By the time you finish reading this chapter, you should have enough knowledge to develop, install, and manage custom extensions. First, though, let's discuss the essential concepts that you need to know to effectively leverage the extensibility features of RS.

15.1 UNDERSTANDING REPORTING SERVICES EXTENSIBILITY

You can extend RS by plugging in custom extensions written in .NET code. In order to do that, you need to be familiar with the concept of *interface-based* programming. Based on my experience, many developers find working with interfaces difficult to grasp.

For this reason, we would like to make a little detour at the beginning of this chapter and explain the basic concepts and benefits of this style of programming. By no means will our discussion attempt to provide exhaustive coverage of this topic. If you need more information, refer to the .NET product documentation, which includes many technical articles on object-oriented programming.

15.1.1 Understanding interface-based programming

Suppose that you are an architect on the RS team and you are responsible for designing a flexible model for plugging in delivery extensions. As we saw in chapter 14, RS comes with two extensions out of the box: e-mail and file share extensions. As useful as these extensions are, it is unlikely that they will meet all subscription-based distribution requirements. For example, what if an organization wants to automate the report-printing process by sending reports directly to a printer? Instead of enduring the Herculean effort of creating and supporting all possible delivery scenarios out there, you prudently decide to let customers author and plug in their own extensions.

What implementation pattern will you choose? Obviously, you need to establish some standardization to which other developers will need to conform. Once you've come up with an easy-to-follow standard pattern, you could use generic code logic to load and execute custom extensions. As a seasoned architect, you set the following high-level design goals for the envisioned extensibility model:

- It must allow developers to write and plug in their own extensions.
- The extensibility model shouldn't require an intimate knowledge of how the extension is implemented or what it does for that matter. In other words, as long as the extension adheres to the standard, it can be treated as a "black box."
- The extensibility model should be as robust as possible. For example, it should be able to determine at runtime whether a given custom extension follows the standard design pattern and, if it doesn't, the Report Server will not attempt to load it.

Let's now discuss how we can implement the above requirements. To enforce a common standard for report delivery, you can lay out the following rules:

- Each custom extension type must expose a method that the Report Server will invoke to distribute the report.
- This method must have at least one argument that the Report Server will use to pass the report notification object.

Given the above specifications, figure 15.1 shows how two custom delivery extensions could be implemented.

Let's say that the first extension supports report delivery to a printer similarly to the sample that comes with RS, while the second can be used to distribute reports to a Web service. In the first case, you've decided to encapsulate the delivery logic in a method called `Deliver`, while in the latter, in a method called `Distribute`.

Once the custom extensions are registered with the Report Server, you can define subscriptions that use these extensions, as we discussed in chapter 14. During runtime, the Report Server will instantiate the appropriate extension and delegate the report delivery to it. Everything looks great! Or does it?

15.1.2 Working with interface inheritance

Upon further inspection, several issues surface. First, the Report Server has to know beforehand not only the type name of the extension but also the name of the method responsible for the report delivery. One possible workaround would be to save the method name in the configuration file too, but this will present a maintenance issue. Another solution would be to change the specification and stipulate that all delivery methods must have the same name, for example, `Deliver`. However, this approach

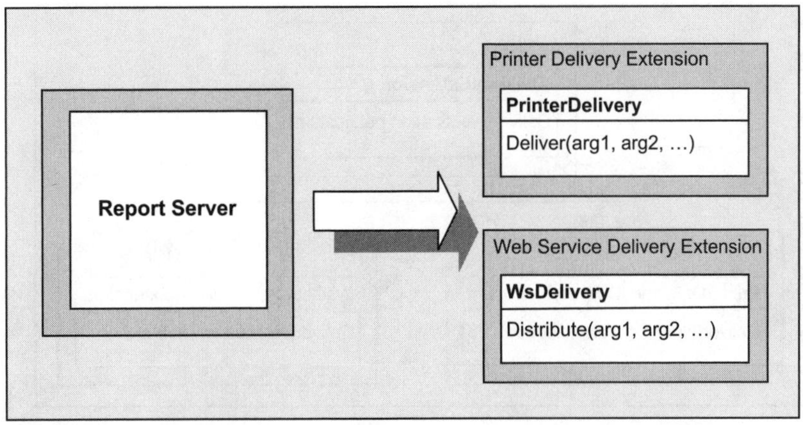

Figure 15.1 Without interfaces, it is difficult to achieve standardization. For example, this figure shows two possible implementation approaches to implement custom delivery extensions. Because they don't follow a single standard, it is difficult for the Report Server to integrate them.

is not easily enforceable, especially by people who are as opinionated and strong-willed as developers tend to be.

Second, the Report Server won't be able to easily inspect the signature of the delivery method in advance to check to see if it follows the specification. For example, what if the developer has neglected to specify an argument for the notification object? This will certainly result in a runtime exception. Finally, there is no easy way for the Report Server to invoke the delivery method.

Interface inheritance

The above issues can be easily overcome by using interface inheritance. At this point, you may be curious as to what an *interface* really is. We can loosely define an interface as a set of methods, properties, and events that define an object's characteristics and behavior. You define an interface similarly to the way you define a class. For example, in the above scenario, this is what the delivery extension interface may look like in C#:

```
interface IDeliveryExtension {
  void Deliver (Notification notification);
}
```

By convention, the interface name is prefixed with a capital *I*. Please note that an interface contains only the method's signatures, not their implementation. In addition, unlike working with objects, an interface cannot be instantiated. In fact, the whole purpose of having an interface is to inherit from it, as shown in figure 15.2.

Now both extension classes inherit from the `IDeliveryExtension` interface, which in C# is denoted by the colon (:). When a class inherits from an interface, we say that the class *implements* this interface.

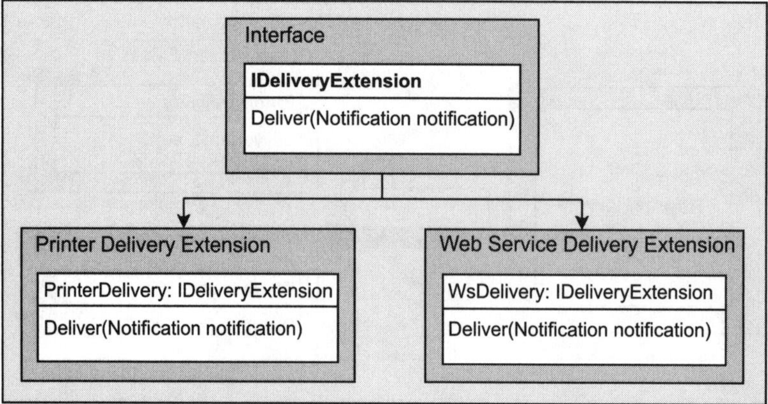

Figure 15.2 Using interface inheritance to enforce a specification. Now both extensions follow the same standard. The Report Server can load them by using the factory design pattern.

Interface inheritance offers the following benefits:

- Standardization
- Dynamic type discovery
- Polymorphism
- Multiple inheritance

Achieving standardization by using interfaces

Once a class inherits from an interface, it must implement all methods included in the interface definition. In addition, the implementation of the method names and signatures must match those defined in the interface. The compiler enforces these rules during code compilation.

Therefore, to enforce a common standard, we can change our specification to stipulate that all custom extensions must inherit from the `IDelivery` interface. This means that all custom extensions will expose a method called `Deliver`, which takes exactly one parameter of the type Notification, as required by the definition of the interface.

Dynamic type discovery

But what if the developer forgets to inherit the custom extension class from our interface? After all, a standard is only good when it is followed. You see, the second advantage of using interface inheritance, as well as object inheritance for that matter, is that the caller can easily discover whether an object implements a given interface during runtime. For example, we can write the following code in the Report Server to find out if the custom extension indeed adheres to our specification:

```
// instantiate the custom extension using Factory design pattern.
if (typeof(customExtension) is IDeliveryExtension)
  // do something with the extension
else
  throw new Exception("This custom extension doesn't
       implement IDeliveryInterface");
```

Here, we use the C# type of operator (the VB.NET equivalent is TypeOf) to check to see whether the extension class implements the required interface after the custom extension object is instantiated. If this is not the case, we can react to this condition by throwing an exception.

Polymorphism

Interface inheritance allows us to use another powerful object-oriented technique called *polymorphism*. It allows the caller to treat different objects in the same way. We already used this technique in chapter 13. First, we implemented two pluggable report adapters that inherited from a common `IReportAdapter` interface. Then, we used the factory design pattern to instantiate the requested adapter and cast its reference to `IReportAdapter`.

In our scenario, polymorphism helps to expand the above example and work with the custom extension objects in this way:

```
// instantiate the custom extension using Factory design pattern.
if (typeof(customExtension) is IDeliveryExtension)
  // cast to IDeliveryExtension to call Deliver
  ((IDeliveryExtension) customExtension).Deliver(notification);
else
  throw new Exception("This custom extension doesn't
    implement IDeliveryInterface");
```

Once we make sure that the extension object is of the right type, we can cast to its base interface and call the `Deliver` method. As you can see, by using the interface inheritance, the caller can easily discover the type of the object during runtime and treat all objects that implement the required interface in the same way.

Implementing multiple interfaces

Finally, unlike class inheritance, with interface inheritance you can implement as many interfaces as you'd like. For example, to introduce a common standard that all custom delivery extensions will follow to retrieve the configuration information, we could come up with the following interface:

```
interface IExtension  {
  void SetConfiguration(string);
}
```

Once a custom extension implements the `IExtension` interface, the Report Server can call its `SetConfiguration` method to pass the extension's configuration settings that can be defined in the Report Server configuration file. This looks like a cool feature, so let's enhance our printer delivery extension to implement both the `IDeliveryExtension` and `IExtension` interfaces, as follows:

```
public class WebServiceDeliveryProvider : IDeliveryExtension, IExtension {
    public void Deliver (Notification notification)  {…}
    public void SetConfiguration (string configSettings)  {…}
}
```

Please note that, in most cases, the Report Server makes multiple interface inheritance unnecessary because the more "specialized" interfaces inherit from the `IExtension` interface. This means that all custom extensions indirectly inherit from `IExtension`.

Extending RS with interface inheritance

Now that you have a good grasp of interface inheritance, you are ready to extend the RS features by writing custom data, delivery, rendering, and security extensions. To make your life easier, Microsoft has encapsulated all RS-related interface definitions into a single Microsoft.ReportingServices.Interfaces library.

Figure 15.3 shows the publicly available type definitions included in this library.

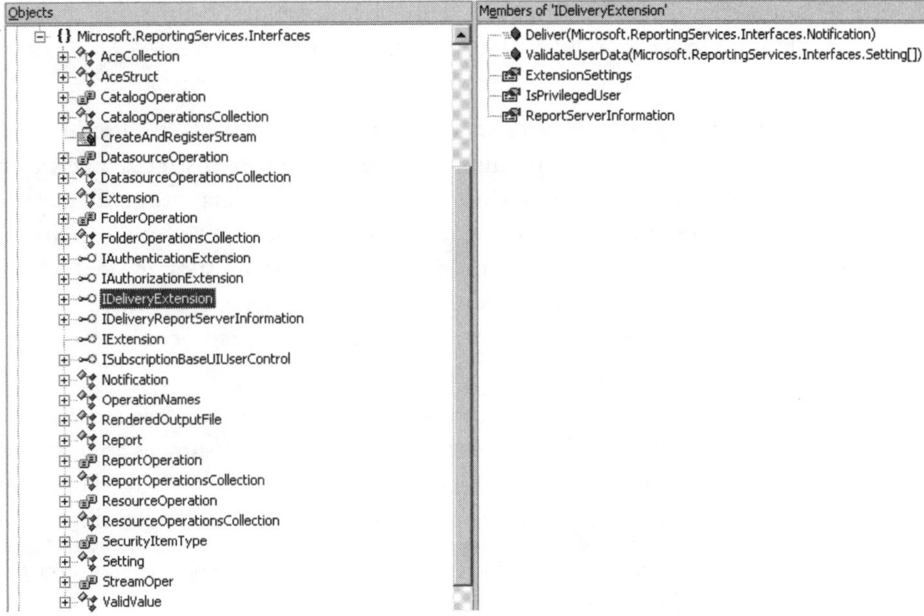

Figure 15.3 The Microsoft.ReportingServices.Interfaces library includes all interface definitions.

Therefore, as a prerequisite for writing a custom extension, in your project you need to set up a reference to this library, which can be found in both the Report Server binary folder (C:\Program Files\Microsoft SQL Server\MSSQL\Reporting Services\ReportServer\bin) and the Report Manager binary folder (C:\Program Files\Microsoft SQL Server\MSSQL\ReportManager\bin).

For your convenience, we have encapsulated all custom extensions that we will discuss in this chapter in a single project called AWC.RS.Extensions. This setup also simplifies configuring the code access security for the custom extensions because you need to grant full trust permission to this assembly only. This project also includes our versions of both the Report Server and Report Manager configuration files to help you configure the sample extensions properly.

Now, let's put interface-based programming into action by creating our first custom extension.

15.2 REPORTING OFF ADO.NET DATASETS WITH A CUSTOM DATASET DATA EXTENSION

Why would you want to write a custom data extension because, with RS, a report can draw its data from virtually any database? One good reason would be to report off custom data structures, such as ADO.NET datasets and XML documents. For example, version 1.0 of Reporting Services doesn't support natively binding and reporting off application ADO.NET datasets. However, developers can write a custom data extension to expose an ADO.NET dataset as a report's data source.

There are at least two approaches to implement this process:

- *The custom extension calls an external .NET assembly to get the dataset.* This is the approach that the product documentation demonstrates. The advantage of this approach is better performance because the dataset doesn't have to cross process boundaries. However, this comes at the expense of flexibility. For example, this approach cannot be easily retrofitted to support the scenario where a three-tier application needs to report off datasets returned from the data tier layer. In addition, the application cannot preprocess the dataset before the report is generated.
- *The application passes the copy of the dataset that has been serialized to XML to the Report Server.* This approach allows a report consumer's application to obtain a dataset during runtime, for example, from a data layer, and "bind" it to a report. This is the design pattern that our dataset extension will follow.

Figure 15.4 depicts a typical integration scenario for requesting a report that uses the custom dataset extension.

The report consumer will typically obtain the dataset from the application data layer. Then, the report consumer will serialize the dataset to XML and request the report by passing the serialized dataset copy as a report parameter. Assuming that the report is configured to use the custom dataset extension, the Report Server will ask the extension to provide the report data. To do this, the extension reconstructs the dataset and exposes its data through a well-defined set of interfaces. During the report-processing phase, the report draws its data from the dataset. Finally, the generated report is sent back to the report consumer.

As noted before, an alternative usage scenario could be reporting off datasets that are persisted as XML files. In this case, the application will be responsible for saving the dataset to a file and passing the file's location as a report parameter.

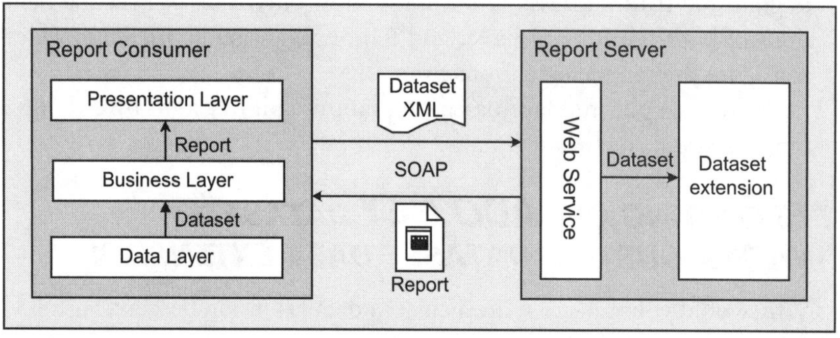

Figure 15.4 A report consumer can use a custom dataset extension to report off application datasets.

15.2.1 Design goals and tradeoffs

The high-level design goals for our custom dataset data extension are as follows:

- *The custom dataset extension should be integrated seamlessly with the RS data architecture.* From report design point of view, the use of datasets should be transparent to the report's author.
- *Dataset table columns will be exposed as fields in the Report Designer to facilitate the familiar drag-and-drop technique for laying out the report.* For this reason, the custom dataset extension promotes the use of XML schemas and typed datasets during the report's design phase.
- *The dataset data extension will support reporting off an arbitrary table from a multitable dataset.*
- *The dataset data extension will support reporting from serialized datasets, as well as datasets saved to XML files.* The latter option could be useful for reports with interactive features.

NOTE Adding interactive features to dataset-bound reports presents an unusual challenge. As we explained in chapter 11, these features rely on HTTP-GET, which cannot be used with large parameters. As a workaround, consider saving the dataset as an XML file and passing the file path as a report parameter.

Our implementation of the custom extension will be subject to the following tradeoffs:

- *Performance overhead is incurred from serializing and marshaling the dataset between the application and the Report Server.* When a .NET dataset crosses the application's domain boundary, the .NET Framework automatically serializes it to XML. The dataset is subsequently deserialized into the receiving application's domain (the Report Server process).
- *Data relations are not supported.* An ADO.NET dataset can include several tables joined with data relations. Unfortunately, ADO.NET datasets currently don't support SQL-like SELECT statements to fetch data from joined tables. As a result, supporting queries from multiple tables linked with data relationships could become rather involved. If this is a definite requirement, you may try to extend the sample by implementing row filtering, for example, by using the `GetChildRows` method of the DataRow object. That said, please note that the report's author can configure our extension and specify which table from a multitable dataset will be used for reporting.
- *Requesting a dataset-bound report via HTTP-GET is impractical.* Due to the query parameter's size limitation of the HTTP-GET protocol, the report consumer would typically use SOAP for passing the serialized dataset copy to the Report Server. If URL access is the preferred option, you have two choices. First, you could use HTTP-POST to pass the ADO.NET dataset. As we mentioned in chapter 11, HTTP-POST enjoys almost unlimited parameter length because the

parameter name/value pairs are transferred in the request's HTTP header instead of in the form of a URL query string. The Report Picker code sample that we discussed in chapter 11 demonstrated how a web application can leverage HTTP-POST to request reports. Another option for getting around the HTTP-GET request limitations would be to save the dataset to a file on the server side of the application and pass the file path as a report parameter.

Now, let's see how we can use the custom dataset extension to report off application datasets. Inside the AWReporter BI project, you will find the TestDS report that we will use to demonstrate how to create dataset-bound reports.

15.2.2 Authoring dataset-bound reports

Before using the custom dataset extension to create dataset-bound reports, we need to configure it properly. We included detailed setup instructions in the readme file found under the DataExtensions\Dataset folder in the AWC.RS.Extensions project.

Once the extension is set up, you can follow the task map shown in table 15.1 to author a dataset-bound report.

Table 15.1 The task map for creating a dataset-bound report

Phase	Task
Create the dataset schema.	Create a typed dataset. Or, infer the schema from a persisted-to-file dataset.
Set up the report dataset.	Create a private data source. Set up the query parameters. Retrieve the dataset fields. Configure the DataSource report-level parameter.
Lay out the report.	Use the Report Designer's Layout tab to drag and drop dataset fields.
Test the report.	Use the Report Designer's Preview tab to test the report.
Deploy the report.	Use VS.NET or the Report Manager to deploy the report to the Report Server.
Request the report.	Request the report programmatically on demand via SOAP.

As noted in the table, the first task for creating a dataset-bound report is to define the schema.

Creating the dataset schema

While there's nothing stopping you from hard-coding the dataset field names inside report items, a better approach would be to expose the dataset schema in the Report Designer. Once this is done, the report's author can drag and drop dataset fields to the report canvas, as she would do when working with extensions natively supported by RS.

With the custom dataset extension, you can expose the dataset schema in one of the following ways:

- *Create a typed dataset*—With Visual Studio .NET, you can create typed datasets easily. The end result is a file with the .xsd extension. The Test Harness application includes a typed dataset called EntitySalesOrder.xsd. It was created by using the SQL Data Adapter component found on the Data tab of the VS.NET toolbox.
- *Infer the schema from a persisted dataset*—The custom extension can be configured to infer the dataset schema from a dataset that has been saved to a file. For example, the Test Harness application includes the DatasetSalesOrder.xml file, which contains the XML presentation of a dataset. The file could include only the schema, only the data, or both the dataset schema and the data. The custom extension uses DataSet.ReadXml to load the dataset and infer its schema.

Now that we have the dataset schema, we are ready to author the dataset-bound report.

Setting the report dataset

Let's start by setting up a new private data source that points to the dataset schema file. Begin by creating a new report. Flip to the Report Designer Data tab and create a new dataset.

Creating a private data source

From the Dataset properties dialog, click the button next to the Data Source dropdown to create a new data source, as shown in figure 15.5.

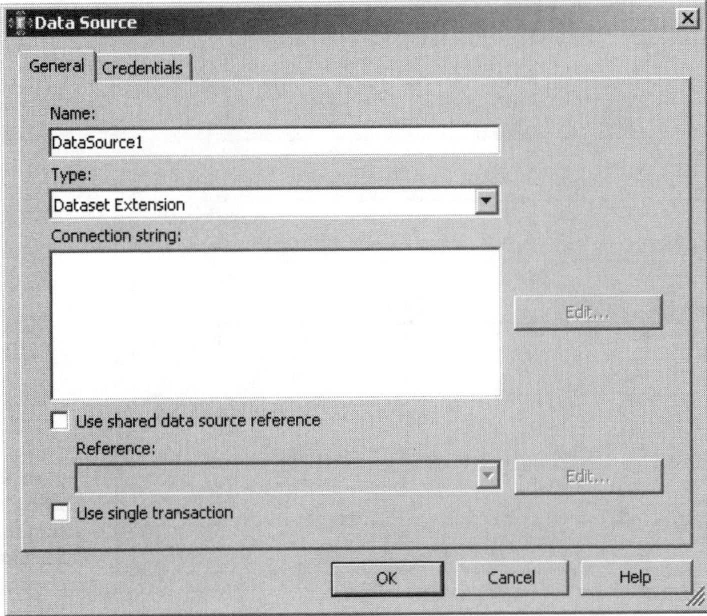

Figure 15.5 Using the dataset extension to set up the report's data source

If the dataset extension is configured properly, it will be listed in the Type drop-down. Set the data source type to Dataset Extension.

NOTE If you are creating a new dataset and the standard UDL dialog pops up instead of the Data Source dialog shown in figure 15.5, you can set up the dataset data source using any of the OLE DB providers, such as the Microsoft OLE DB provider for SQL Server. Once the data source is configured, access the dataset properties and click the "…" button next to the Data Source drop-down on the Query tab. This should bring you to the dialog shown in figure 15.5, from which you can change the extension type to Dataset Extension.

Leave the Connection String blank because the dataset extension doesn't establish a database connection. Remember, the report's data will be encapsulated inside the dataset that will be passed as a report parameter. The Credentials tab is also not applicable in our case because the extension doesn't establish a database connection. To move past the Report Wizard validation, choose the Windows Authentication (Integrated Security) option from the Credentials tab.

Back in the Dataset properties dialog, in the Query String text area, enter the name of the dataset table off which you want to report, as shown in figure 15.6.

A dataset can have multiple tables. In case there is only one table or you want to default to the first table, you can enter **Nothing** as a query string. Initially, we were planning to default to the first table in case the query text was left blank, but the Report Designer insisted that we specify a query string. For the purposes of the TestDS report, enter **SalesOrderHeader** (or **Nothing**) as query text because this is the name of the first (and only) dataset table.

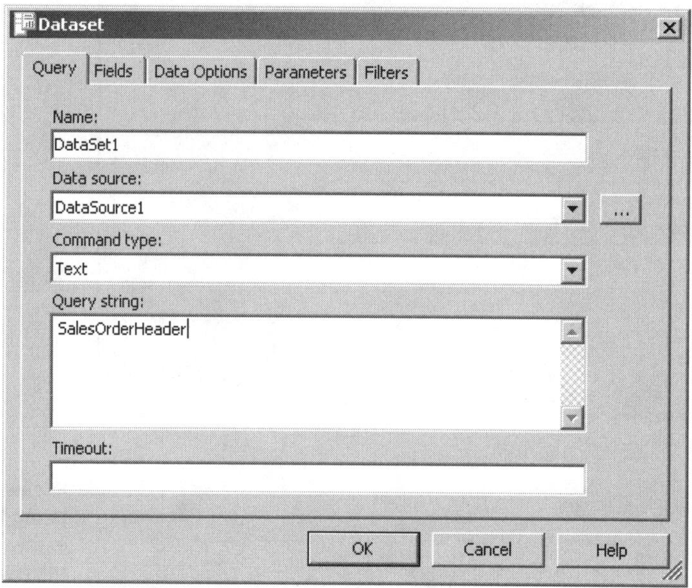

Figure 15.6 Setting the query string to the dataset table used for reporting

Setting up the query parameters

Now, we are ready to set up the query parameters. Because the query string we just entered is not a valid SQL statement, we need to switch to the Generic Query Designer. Now, run the query by clicking the Exclamation button. The Generic Query Designer will ask the data extension to parse the query text and return a list of the query parameters.

The custom dataset extension is wired to prompt for a parameter named DataSource. When designing the report, you need to set this parameter to the path pointing to the dataset schema file. During runtime, you will use this parameter to pass the serialized copy of the dataset or the path to the persisted dataset file.

Figure 15.7 shows that we entered the full path to the EntitySalesOrder.xsd typed dataset file as a parameter value.

Retrieving the dataset fields

Now, click OK so that the data extension can parse the dataset schema and return the fields of the requested table, as shown in figure 15.8.

TIP You may wonder why the Generic Query Designer doesn't show any data after you click the Exclamation button. The reason for this is that a typed dataset schema contains only the dataset's definition, not its data. However, if you use a dataset that has been saved to a file instead of only its schema, then the Generic Query Designer will show the table records in the query pane.

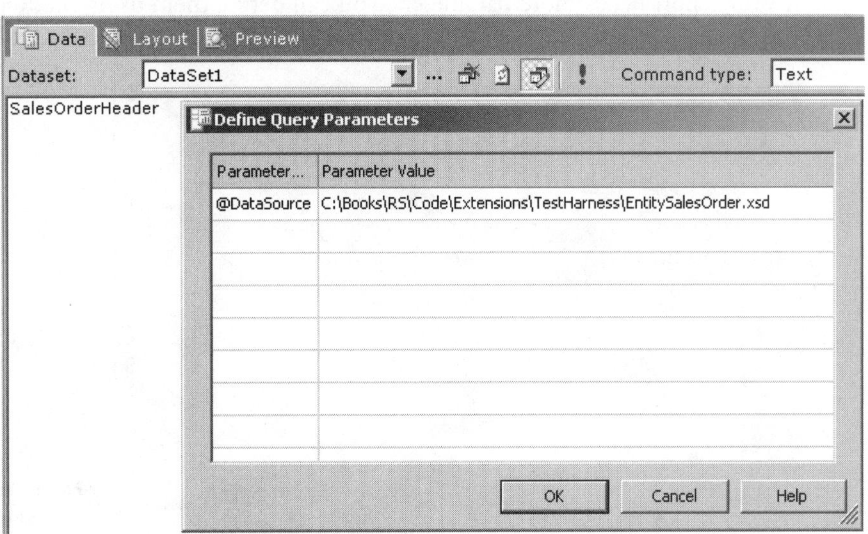

Figure 15.7 Setting up the DataSource parameter to the dataset schema file

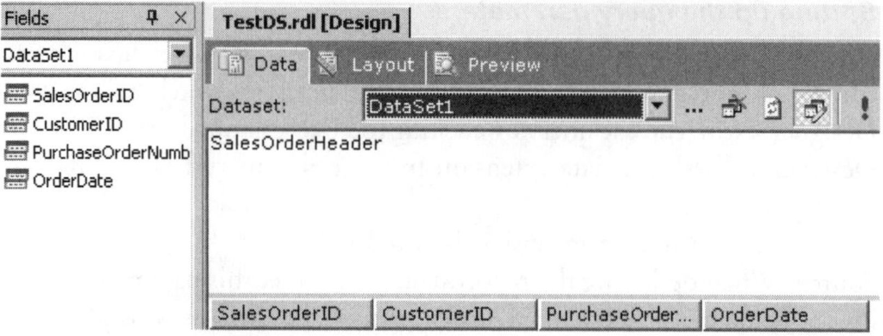

Figure 15.8 Retrieving the list of table fields

At this point, the Fields toolbar should show all table columns, as defined in the dataset schema. In addition, the Parameter tab of dataset properties should include the DataSource parameter.

Configuring the DataSource report-level parameter

Next, you need to verify that the DataSource parameter is linked to the DataSource report-level parameter, as shown in figure 15.9.

This is perhaps the most crucial step of the dataset-driven report-authoring process. As we noted before, during runtime the report consumer will pass the dataset as a report-level parameter. By linking the DataSource report-level parameter to its query counterpart, we ensure that the dataset will indeed be passed to the dataset extension. If your report needs more parameters, you can define them using the Report Parameters dialog.

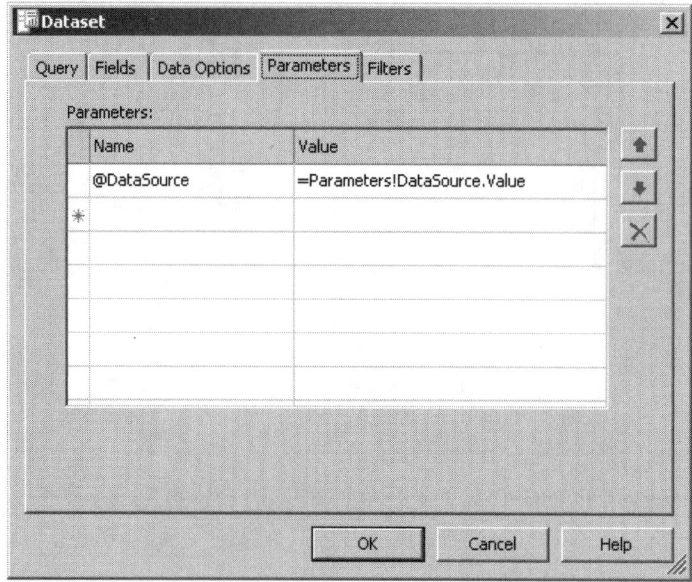

Figure 15.9 Verifying that the DataSource parameter is linked to the DataSource report-level parameter

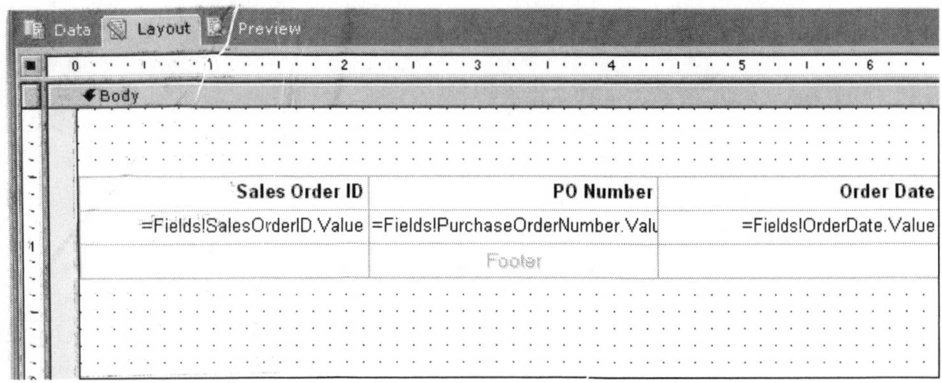

Figure 15.10 Using the Report Designer's Layout tab to lay out the report

Laying out the report

Now that the report dataset is set up, we can proceed to laying out the report itself using the familiar drag-and-drop approach. Switch to the Report Designer's Layout tab and lay out the report as you normally would.

For example, figure 15.10 shows that we used a table region to create a tabular report. Then we dragged and dropped some dataset fields into the table region.

Testing the report

To successfully preview the report in the Report Designer, you have to feed it data by setting the report's DataSource parameter. During design time, you may find it more convenient to use one of the following techniques:

- Copy and paste an XML snippet from the dataset's serialized copy.
- Specify the path to the dataset that was saved to disk.

For example, figure 15.11 shows that we used the first approach and entered the following string as the DataSource value:

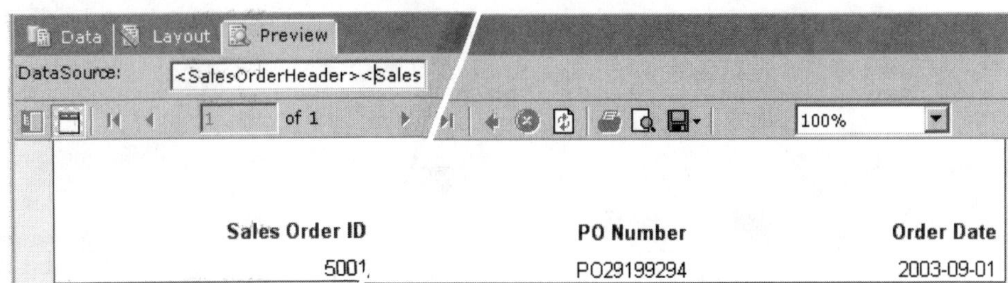

Figure 15.11 Using an XML snippet as a report's data source during design time

```
<SalesOrderHeader>
  <SalesOrderID>5001</SalesOrderID>
  <CustomerID>304</CustomerID>
  <PurchaseOrderNumber>PO29199294</PurchaseOrderNumber>
  <OrderDate>2003-09-01</OrderDate>
</SalesOrderHeader>
```

Deploying the report

Once you have finished with the report, you can deploy it to the Report Server, so that it is available for delivery.

As you know by now, the easiest way to do this (if you have Content Manager permissions to the Report Server repository) is to deploy it straight from the Visual Studio IDE by right-clicking the report file and choosing the Deploy command from the context menu.

Alternatively, you can deploy the report manually by uploading its report definition file using the Report Manager web application.

Requesting the report

When requesting a dataset-bound report, the client application must set the DataSource parameter as follows:

- If the report is accessed by SOAP, the application can pass the serialized dataset or the path to the dataset file (if the application has persisted the dataset beforehand).
- Due to the size limitations of the HTTP-GET query string, passing a large dataset as a query parameter is not possible. For this reason, this protocol will seldom be used to request dataset-bound reports. As noted before, if the URL method must be used, the report consumer can save the dataset to a file and pass the file path to the DataSource parameter. Alternatively, the report consumer can leverage HTTP-POST.

The implementation pattern that a client application will typically follow when requesting a dataset-bound report by SOAP is shown in listing 15.1.

Listing 15.1 Passing a dataset to Reporting Services

```
ReportingService rs = new ReportingService();
// Set the Render method arguments
ParameterValue[] proxyParameters = new ParameterValue[1];   ❶ Create a parameter placeholder

DataSet ds = new DataSet();   ❷ Get the dataset
sqlDataAdapter.Fill(ds);
proxyParameters[0] = new ParameterValue();
proxyParameters[0].Name = "DataSource";
proxyParameters[0].Value = entitySalesOrder.GetXml();   ❸ Pass the dataset's serialized-to-XML copy
result = rs.Render(...);
```

❶ First, we create at least one parameter placeholder for the DataSource parameter.

❷ In this case, the application uses a plain-vanilla dataset. However, there's nothing stopping you from using typed datasets if your application's design supports them.

❸ Next, the application serializes the dataset to XML and passes the serialized copy under the DataSource parameter.

To facilitate the TestDS report testing, we enclosed a simple WinForm-based client that takes the Report Server's URL and report path and uses similar code to request the report by SOAP.

Now that you've seen how to use the custom dataset extension to create dataset-bound reports, let's discuss its implementation.

15.2.3 Implementing the custom dataset extension

Armed with the FsiDataExtension source code (included with the RS samples) and the RS product documentation, we found the process of implementing the custom dataset extension straightforward.

Custom dataset extension types

Table 15.2 lists the types used to implement the custom dataset extension.

Table 15.2 To plug into the Report Server data architecture, the custom dataset extension has several classes that implement standard interfaces.

Type	Inherit From	Purpose	Implemented?
DsConnectionWrapper	IDbConnection, IDbConnection-Extension, IExtension	Responsible for establishing a database connection	No
DsTransaction	IDbTransaction	Enlists the database commands in the data source transaction	No
DsCommand	IDbCommand, IDbCommandAnalysis	Responsible for handling the report query string	Yes
DsDataParameter	IDataParameter	Represents a query parameter	Yes
DsDataParameter-Collection	ArrayList, IData-ParameterCollection	Holds a collection of query parameters	Yes
DsDataReader	IDataReader	Handles the access to the dataset data	Yes

At first look, you may find dealing with so many interfaces mind boggling, but you may find that your requirements call for implementing many interface methods as simple passthroughs.

Runtime conversation map

Figure 15.12 shows a simplified version of the conversation map between the Report Server and the custom extension during runtime.

First, the Report Server instructs the dataset extension to establish a database connection by passing the connection string to it. Then, the Report Server asks the Connection object to return a reference of type `IDbCommand`.

Next, the Report Server calls the `IDbCommand.CreateParameter` method as many times as the number of parameters the report query has. The Command object responds by returning an object of type `IDataParameter` for each parameter.

NOTE It is important to note that the Report Server will pass only the query parameter to the data extension and not the report-level parameters. If a report-level parameter is not linked to the query parameter, it won't be passed. An important consequence of this rule is that you can't get a reference to the report-level parameters inside the dataset extension if they are not linked to the query parameters.

Because each parameter is of a common base type, the Report Server knows how to set it up. After the parameter is initialized, the Report Server invokes the `IDataParameter-Collection.Add` method so that you could append this parameter to the parameter collection. Once the parameters have been taken care of, the Report Server calls the `ExecuteReader` method of the Command object to get a reference to an object of type `IDataReader`.

For each report dataset field, the Report Server calls the `IDataReader.Get-Ordinal` to get the positional index of each field in the reader's field collection. This is needed because later the Report Server will ask for the value of the field by its positional

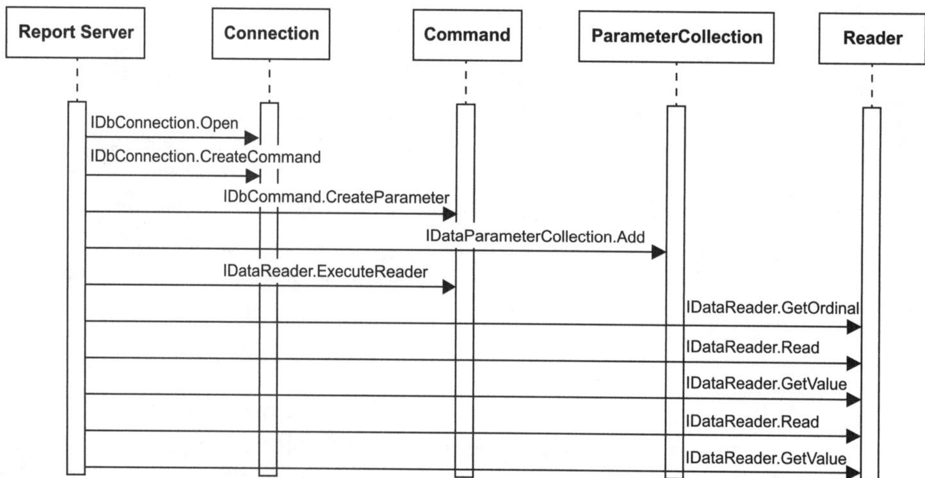

Figure 15.12 A sequence diagram of custom dataset extension processing. The Report Server calls the implemented interface methods to configure the extension and retrieve the data.

index. Once the fields are matched, the Report Server asks the reader repeatedly to advance to the next row of the rowset until the end of the rowset is reached. For each field, the Report Server calls the `IDataReader.GetValue` method to retrieve the field's value.

You may be curious to know how the Report Designer discovers the report query's parameters during design time in order to prompt the user for their values. To support this feature, the developer of the extension can implement the `IDbCommandAnalysis` interface in the Command object. This interface exposes a single method, `GetParameters`. When you click the exclamation mark to run the report query, the Report Designer probes the extension to find out if it implements this interface, and if this is the case, it calls the `GetParameters` method. This method is responsible for parsing the query string and returning a collection with the parameter's placeholders.

Now that we've discussed the high-level interaction between the Report Server and the extension, let's talk about some implementation sketches.

Implementing IDbConnection

You can relate the `IDbConnection` interface to the ADO.NET connection wrappers, for example, SqlConnection. The main purpose of this object is to establish a database connection to the data source, if this is needed. As noted before, in our case we have nothing to connect to because all data is either passed as a dataset during runtime or is retrieved from a dataset file.

In cases where you do need to connect to a data source, you use the `IDbConnection.Open` method to establish a database connection. Prior to calling this method, the Report Server will call the `IDbConnectionExtension` public properties to pass the user's credentials that you set on the Data Source Credentials property. Strictly speaking, in our case, we didn't have to implement the `IDbConnectionExtension` interface at all, but we decided to do this so that you could see the sequence of events when you step through the extension code.

Implementing IDbCommand

The main tasks of the object that implements the `IDbCommand` interface are to populate the query parameters and to execute the report query and then return a reference to a data reader object that allows the caller to process the results.

In this respect, you can relate the `IDbCommand` interface to the ADO.NET Command objects, such as SqlCommand. The Report Server passes the query text prior to executing the `ExecuteReader` method. In our case, the query text represents the name of the table off which we want to report. Then, `ExecuteReader` instantiates the reader object and calls `LoadDataset` to retrieve the rowset.

Implementing IDataReader

This is where the crux of the data retrieval and processing logic is. Similarly to the ADO.NET `IDataReader`, an object that implements this interface is responsible for providing a means to read the rowset in a forward-only fashion. The bulk of the data retrieval and manipulation logic (exception handling excluded) is shown in listing 15.2.

Listing 15.2 Retrieving the rowset

```
internal void LoadDataset()   {
  string dataSource = null;
  DsDataParameter parameter = m_parameters.GetByName(Util.DATA_SOURCE)
                              as DsDataParameter;     <-1 Gets the DataSource
  dataSource = parameter.Value.ToString();                parameter

  m_dataset = GetDataSet(dataSource);

  if (m_cmdText.Trim().ToLower()=="nothing")     <-4 References the requested
    m_datatable = m_dataset.Tables[0];               table inside the dataset
  else {
    m_datatable = m_dataset.Tables[m_cmdText];
  }

  m_ie = m_datatable.Rows.GetEnumerator();      <-5 Sets up the row
}                                                   enumerator

private DataSet GetDataSet(string dataSource)    {
  DataSet dataset = new DataSet();                        2 A serialized
                                                            copy of the
  if (dataSource.IndexOf("<")>=0) {                         dataset has
    StringReader reader = new StringReader(dataSource);  <- been passed
    dataset.ReadXml(reader);
  }                                          3 A path to a persisted-
  else {                                       to-file dataset has
    FileIOPermission permission = new    <-    been passed
    FileIOPermission(FileIOPermissionAccess.Read, dataSource);
    permission.Assert();
    dataset.ReadXml(dataSource);
  }

  return dataset;
}
```

1 First, we attempt to find a parameter named DataSource. As you will probably recall, the value passed to this parameter can be one of the following: the serialized-to-XML dataset copy or a file path to the persisted-to-file dataset. `GetDataSet` determines what the value of the DataSource represents by inspecting its payload.

2 In the first case, we deserialize the dataset from its XML payload.

3 In the latter, we read the dataset's content from the file. Note that we are specifically demanding a read permission to the physical file. Regardless of the fact that the code

access policy of the dataset extension assembly is configured for Full Trust rights, CAS is layered on top of the OS security. For this reason, if you decide to use persisted datasets, make sure you grant the ASP.NET workers' process identity at least read permissions to their files.

❹ Once the dataset is successfully deserialized, we reference the table specified by the query text.

❺ Finally, we save the row enumerator to a class-level variable to save its state between subsequent calls to `IDataReader.Read`.

15.2.4 Debugging dataset extensions

You will probably find that the easiest way to step through a custom dataset extension is to follows these steps:

Step 1 Add the custom dataset extension project to your Business Intelligence solution in VS.NET.

Step 2 Set the StartItem setting of your Business Intelligence project to the name of the report that uses the extension.

Step 3 Set breakpoints in the data extension code.

Step 4 Run the report in Debug mode (F5). Once you click the ViewReport button, your breakpoints should be hit.

As you'll probably agree, authoring custom data extensions is not that difficult. Once you get used to interface-based programming, you will probably find writing different types of extensions similar. Let's now see how we can create custom delivery extensions.

15.3 DISTRIBUTING REPORTS TO WEB SERVICES USING CUSTOM DELIVERY EXTENSIONS

As you will probably recall, in chapter 11 we discussed how RS could be used in the B2B scenario. Back then, we exposed the Inventory Level report as a Web service that the Adventure Works partners could use to request the report on demand. Instead of "pulling" the report, let's now implement a mechanism that will allow Adventure Works to "push" the report to the vendor's Web service on a regular basis through subscribed report delivery.

Figure 15.13 depicts the high-level architectural view of our solution.

In our hypothetical scenario, the report's administrator could configure one or more reports for subscribed delivery to the vendor's Web service that we created in chapter 14. As part of the subscription setup process, the report's administrator will specify the following Web service particulars:

- The end point URL
- The Web service name (type name)
- The web method name responsible for receiving the report's payload

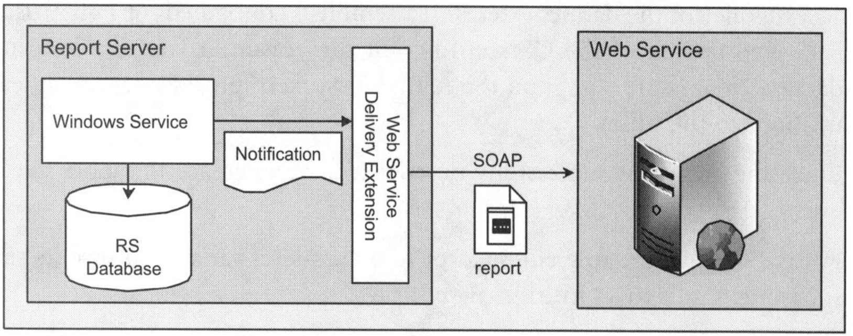

Figure 15.13 Using a custom delivery extension to distribute reports to a Web service

As figure 15.13 depicts, once the subscription is triggered, the Report Server will instantiate our extension and pass the notification object to it. Next, the custom delivery extension will ask the Report Server to render the report and will serialize the report's payload to an XML document. Finally, the custom extension will dynamically invoke the Web service and pass the report's payload to the web method.

15.3.1 Design goals and tradeoffs

The high-level design goals for our custom delivery extension are as follows:

- *The custom delivery extension should plug seamlessly into the presentation layer of the Report Manager.* To accomplish this requirement, the extension will implement an intuitive user interface to help the end user configure the extension.
- *The custom delivery extension must validate the user's input on the client and server sides.*
- *Because the custom extension can send the report to an arbitrary Web service, it should support dynamic binding to the Web service by constructing the web service proxy during runtime.*

Our implementation of the custom delivery extension will be subject to the following tradeoffs:

- *The custom extension will pass the report's payload (exported as XML) to the first argument of the web method.* Therefore, the target web method must be parameterized, and the first argument must be a string data type. Enhancing the custom delivery extension to fit your specific Web service requirements should be simple.
- *Currently, the extension doesn't provide a user interface for configuring the export format; it renders the report as XML before passing it to the Web service.* Enhancing the custom delivery extension to let the user choose the export format should be easy. For example, similarly to the e-mail and file share extensions, the custom extension web control could include a drop-down that is populated with the results from a call to the `ListExtensions` SOAP API, as we saw in chapter 9.

Now that you have a high-level understanding of what the custom delivery extension does, let's see how we can put it into action.

15.3.2 Using the custom delivery extension

Before using the custom delivery extension to distribute reports to Web services, we need to configure it properly. We included detailed setup instructions in the readme file found under the DeliveryExtensions\WebService folder in the AWC.RS.Extensions project.

Once the custom delivery extension is configured, we can use the Report Manager to create a report subscription that uses the extension. We've already shown how to do this in chapter 14, so we'll discuss only the custom delivery extension specifics.

After we've decided on the subscription type, either a standard or data-driven subscription, we need to choose a delivery extension, as shown in figure 15.14.

If the custom delivery extension is registered properly, it will appear in the Delivered By drop-down as Web Service Delivery. In case you are wondering where this name comes from, it is returned by our implementation of the `IExtension.LocalizedName` property inside the extension's source code. As its names suggests, this property lets the developer localize the extension name based on the user's language settings.

The user interface of the custom delivery extension consists of three text placeholders for the Web service description language URL, its type, and its method name. The default settings are retrieved from the RSReportServer.config configuration file but can be overwritten by the user.

SQL Server Reporting Services
Home > AWReporter >
Subscription: Sales By Territory

Report Delivery Options

Specify options for report delivery.

Delivered by: Web Service Delivery

WSDL URL: http://localhost/AWReporterWeb/Chapter15/Reporter.asmx?WSDL

Type Name: Reporter

Method Name: SendReport

Subscription Processing Options

Specify options for subscription processing.

Run the subscription:

(•) When the scheduled report run is complete. [Select Schedule]
At 8:00 AM every Mon of every week, starting 3/21/2004

( ) On a shared schedule: Quarterly Schedule
At 11:09 AM on 3/21/2004

Figure 15.14 To use the custom Web service delivery extension, select it from the Delivered By drop-down in the Report Manager UI.

15.3.3 Implementing the custom delivery extension

Once we stepped through the printer delivery extension that comes with the RS samples and understood its inner workings, retrofitting its code to meet our requirements was easy. To understand how the custom Web service extension works, it may be beneficial to break its functionality in two stages:

- Design time, when the extension is hosted in the Report Manager and used for setting up the subscription
- Runtime, when the Report Server asks the extension to deliver the report

To mirror the above stages, we separated the extension login into two source files: WebServiceDeliveryUIControl, which encapsulates the extension UI, and WebServiceDeliveryProvider, to host the runtime functionality.

Implementing the user interface

As we've seen, the Report Manager will ask our extension to render itself as a part of the subscription setup process. From an implementation standpoint, this requires writing a custom web control that is implemented in the WebServiceDeliveryUIControl class.

This control implements the `ISubscriptionBaseUIUserControl` interface, which, in turn, inherits from `IExtension`. Figure 15.15 shows a simplified version of the conversation map between the Report Manager and the custom delivery extension during design time.

When the Web service delivery extension is selected on the Subscription setup page, the Report Manager instantiates the WebServiceDeliveryUIControl web control and calls the `IExtension.SetConfiguration` method first. When you register

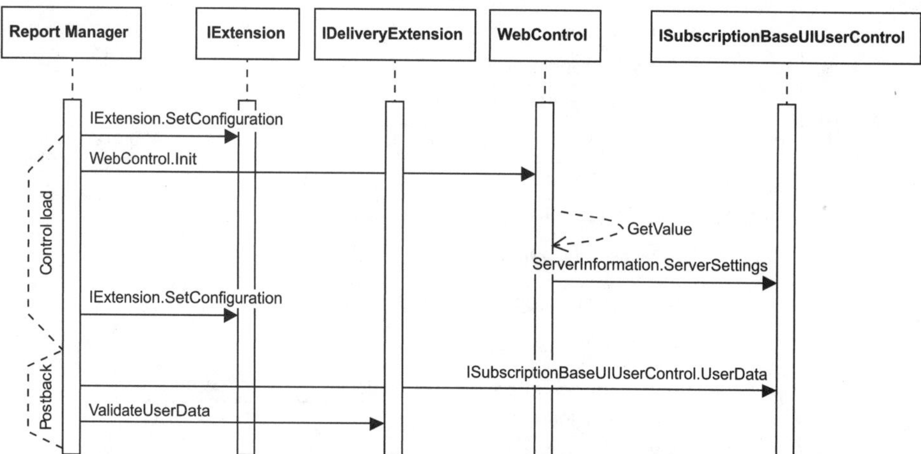

Figure 15.15 The conversation map between the Report Manager and the custom delivery extension

a custom delivery extension, you can optionally specify configuration settings in both the Report Server and Report Manager configuration files. As noted before, we use the Report Server settings to specify the default Web service specifics. You can also use the Report Manager's configuration file to define any UI-related settings. In our case, the custom delivery extension doesn't need any UI-specific settings. For this reason, the `SetConfiguration` call passes an empty string.

Next, the Report Manager sites the control that invokes the control's `Init` method. At this point, the web control is supposed to render itself. In our case, this boils down to creating three textbox controls and some validation controls to validate the user-entered values on the client side. Because the web control has access to all of the ASP.NET functionality, you can use any ASP.NET-compatible control for the user interface. For example, if you decide to expand the extension to allow the user to specify the report's format, you can use a drop-down control that contains the supported export formats.

Each control gets its default value by calling the `GetValue` private member. To retrieve the configuration settings defined in RSReportServer.config, `GetValue` accesses the `ISubscriptionBaseUIUserControl.ReportServerInformation.ServerSettings`. This call triggers the invocation of `IExtension.SetConfiguration` by the Report Manager to pass the server-side configuration settings in XML. The ServerSide property exposes them as an array of Settings [] objects. The code iterates through this array to find the setting that corresponds to the textbox. At this point, the web control is rendered on the screen.

Once the user posts the page back to the server, the Report Manager calls the `ISubscriptionBaseUIUserControl.UserData` property to pass the user-entered values. Finally, the Report Manager calls `IDeliveryExtension.ValidateUserData` to give the control a chance to inspect the user-entered values and throw an exception in case they are not valid.

If everything is fine, the Report Manager calls to the Report Server Web service API to persist the subscription configuration in the Report Server database.

Implementing the runtime functionality

The runtime interaction is much simpler. When the subscription is triggered, the Report Server first calls `IExtension.SetConfiguration` to pass the user-entered extension-specific values. Then, the Report Server prepares a notification object and invokes the method.

In the case of a data-driven subscription, the Report Server invokes `IDeliveryExtension.Deliver` for each recipient. The notification object encapsulates everything the extension needs to deliver the reports and notify the Report Server about the delivery status.

First, the code retrieves the user-entered values from the `Notification.UserData` property. Then, it calls the `DeliverReport` method, which is where the bulk of the custom delivery logic resides, as shown in listing 15.3.

Listing 15.3 Implementing the report delivery

```
private void DeliverReport(Notification notification,
              SubscriptionData data) {
  StringWriter stringWriter = null;
  m_files = notification.Report.Render("XML", @"<DeviceInfo/>");

  if (m_files[0].Data.Length > 0) {
   byte[] reportPayload = new byte[m_files[0].Data.Length];
   m_files[0].Data.Position = 0;
   m_files[0].Data.Read(reportPayload, 0, reportPayload.Length);
   m_files[0].Data.Flush();

   string payload = Convert.ToBase64String(reportPayload);
   StringBuilder stringBuilder = new StringBuilder();
   stringWriter = new StringWriter(stringBuilder);
   XmlTextWriter writer = new XmlTextWriter(stringWriter);
   writer.Formatting = Formatting.Indented;
   writer.WriteStartElement("Report");
   writer.WriteElementString("ReportPayload", payload);
   writer.WriteEndElement();

   DynamicWebServiceProxy ws = new DynamicWebServiceProxy();
   ws.WSDL = data.WSDL;
   ws.TypeName = data.typeName;
   ws.MethodName = data.methodName;
   ws.AddParameter(stringBuilder.ToString());
   string result = ws.InvokeCall() as string;

   if (result==null) throw new Exception(...);
  }

  notification.Status=String.Format("Report delivered to {0}",
                 data.WSDL);
  }
```

Annotations: ❶ Renders the report; ❷ Gets the first stream; ❸ Processes the report's payload; ❹ Sends the report's payload to the Web service; Notifies the Report Server about the delivery status

❶ First, the code instructs the Report Server to render the report in XML. As listing 15.3 shows, rendering the report is as simple as calling the `Notification.Report.Render` method. It really can't be simpler!

❷ Once the report is rendered, its payload is exposed as one or more streams. As we noted in chapter 14, if you request the report in one of the HTML multistream rendering formats (all HTML formats except MHTML), the first stream will include the report's payload, while the subsequent streams will include the report's images. Single-stream rendering formats will always produce only one stream with the images embedded in it. Because we are rendering the report in XML, we can get the entire report results from the first stream.

❸ Next, we create a simple XML document to contain the Base64-encoded version of the report's payload, so that it can be sent over the web to the target Web service.

❹ Finally, we send the XML payload to the target Web service.

Delivering the report to a Web service

Now for the fun part! As we've mentioned, our custom delivery extension supports sending the report's payload to an arbitrary Web service. This presents an implementation challenge, though. Because the Web service's end point is not known until runtime, we cannot "early bind" to it by establishing a web reference. Instead, we need to generate the Web service proxy dynamically.

How should we go about implementing this? Before I decided to write my own dynamic Web service invocation using CodeDom, it dawned on me that someone else might have already done this. Indeed, a quick Google search confirmed my hypothesis.

It turned out that there is already a great Dynamic Web Service invocation library, DynWSLib, written by Christian Weyer (see the resources in section 15.8). As the author says, "Given the URL to the Web Service WSDL file, the type and method name, DynWSLib uses CodeDom to generate the proxy. For better performance, DynWSLib caches the generated proxy library as a file in the system temp folder." A quick DynWSLib test convinced me that this is exactly what I needed to dynamically invoke an arbitrary web method.

As you can see in listing 15.3, we instantiate DynWSLib and pass the user-entered WSDL URL, type, and method name. Next, we pass the report's payload as a parameter to the proxy. Finally, we invoke the web method. Under the Chapter15 folder in the AWReporterWeb project, you will find a simple Web service, Reporter.asmx, which the default extension configuration settings point to. It simply gets the report's payload and outputs it using Trace.WriteLine.

Please note that you won't get far testing the custom extension if you don't adjust the code access security policy for both the AWC.RS.Extensions and DynWSLibrary assemblies to full trust. In addition, you need to grant full rights to the cached Web service proxy library. This presents a challenge because DynWSLib generates a unique name for the temporary file for each Web service. You need to grant full trust rights to all assemblies in that folder, as the setup instructions for the custom delivery extension explain.

NOTE For some obscure reason that I wasn't able to figure out, the system Temp folder appears to be treated differently by the RS code access security policy. Despite the fact that I assigned Full Trust rights to folder and its contents (by using the * wildcard), I wasn't able to get past code access security. I was getting a target invocation exception. Strangely, switching to another folder seemed to keep the CAS gods happy. Therefore, as a workaround, you may want to change the DynWSLib source code to save the temporary file to another folder, for example, C:\Temp. Let me know if you find a way to get CAS working with the system Temp folder.

15.3.4 Debugging custom delivery extensions

Debugging a custom delivery extension is tricky because it isn't loaded when the report is generated, so using the dataset extension debugging approach won't work. Because a custom delivery extension could be invoked from both the Report Manager and the Report Server Windows Service, the debug instructions vary.

Design time debugging

During design time, the Report Manager process invokes the custom extension. To be able to debug your custom extension, change its project's Debug mode to Wait to Attach to an External Process. Then, start the Report Manager and manually attach to its process from the Debug → Processes menu in VS.NET, as shown in figure 15.16.

In our case, we used Windows 2003 as the operating system, so we attached to the w3wp.exe IIS worker process. If you use Windows 2000, you'll need to attach to the ASP.NET worker process, aspnet_wp.exe. Finally, set the When Debugging Is Stopped option to Detach from This Process to keep the Report Manager process running once you stop the debugger session. Terminating the aspnet_wp.exe or w3wp.exe process will affect all ASP.NET applications running on the server, which is something you wouldn't normally want to do. To step through the extension code, create a new sub-

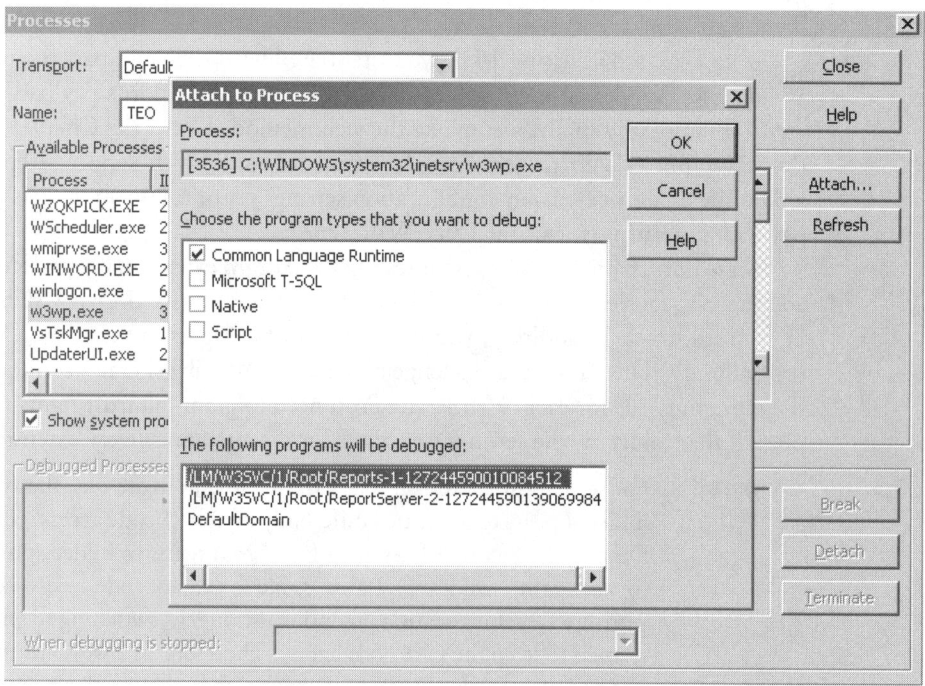

Figure 15.16 To debug your custom extension during design time, attach to the Report Manager process.

scription in the Report Manager that uses your extension or edit an existing one. At this point, your breakpoints should be hit.

Runtime debugging

To debug a custom delivery extension during runtime, for instance, when the subscription is triggered by a schedule, follow the design time debugging steps shown previously, but this time attach to the Report Server's Windows Service process (ReportingServicesService.exe), as shown in figure 15.17.

This should come as no surprise to you, if you recall that it is the Report Server's Windows Service that monitors the report catalog for the event's occurrence and initiates the subscribed report delivery. For this reason, the delivery extension is loaded during runtime in the ReportingServicesService process.

TIP I've found that the easiest way to trigger the subscription execution for debugging purposes is to base the subscription on a schedule that's configured to run once. To use this approach, stop the ReportingServicesService Windows Service and wait until the event record is inserted into the Event table in the Report Server database. Then, start the Windows Service and attach your extension to its process, as explained previously. To trigger the subscription's execution, paste the event record in the Event table. The next time the Windows Service polls this table, it will pick up the event and run your extension.

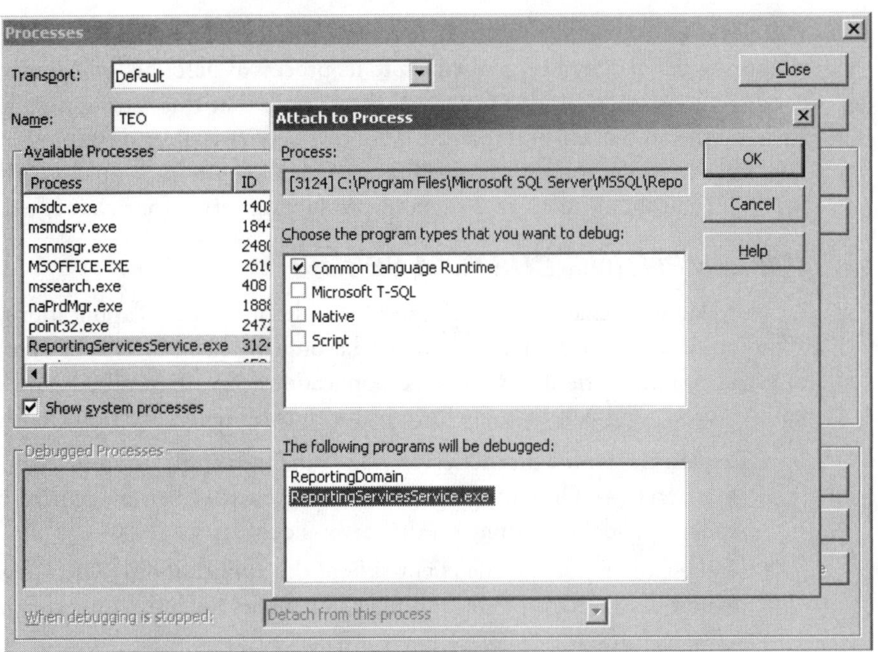

Figure 15.17 To debug a custom delivery extension during runtime, attach to the ReportingServicesService Windows Service process.

There are two debugging issues associated with debugging custom delivery extensions. The first one is that to successfully call the `Notification.Render` method to render the report, you need to be logged in to your login domain controller. If you are logged in using a disconnected session, the call results in the following exception:

```
Report Server has encountered a configuration error;
more details in the log files, AuthzInitializeContextFromSid:
Win32 error: 1053
```

The feedback we got from the Microsoft RS team is that this behavior is by design because the Report Server needs to access the domain controller to check permissions for the subscription owner. This may change in a future version and may include a way to disable subscription checks.

Second, by default, the Windows Service will time out the debugging session after a minute even if you are stepping through the code. Not only does this prevent longer debugging sessions, but it also terminates the Windows Service process. To prevent this from happening, you need to create a Registry key, as shown in table 15.3.

Table 15.3 Create the UnderDebugger Registry setting to prevent the RS Windows Service from timing out the debug session.

Parent Key	Name	Value
HKLM\Software\Microsoft\Microsoft SQL Server\80\Reporting Services	UnderDebugger	1

Once you have created this Registry key, you must restart the RS Windows Service (ReportingServicesService) and attach to its process as described previously. Now your debugging session shouldn't time out. Please note that this setting disables the management thread that ensures that the Windows Service is up and running correctly. For this reason, while you can leave this permanently set to 1 on your development machine, you should set it to 0 on your production server (or delete it entirely).

15.4 IMPLEMENTING CUSTOM SECURITY

As we explained in chapter 8 and chapter 11, with some types of applications, the default Windows-based security model of RS may become impractical. This will typically be the case with Internet-oriented web-based applications serving hundreds and often thousands of users. This will typically leave you with two implementation choices:

- Request the report on the server-side of the web application by calling to the RS Web service—The advantage of this approach is better security because the report is rendered entirely on the server-side.
- Request the report on the client-side of the application by URL—As you know by now, URL access offers a number of benefits, including support for all interactive features, the HTML Viewer toolbar, etc.

Requesting reports by URL with Internet-oriented application almost always will require replacing the default RS Windows-based security model. Fortunately, the extensible RS architecture allows developers to replace the default security model with custom security extensions. This scenario allows you to configure the Report Server for Anonymous access and route the authentication and authorization checks through the custom security extension. I personally don't know of many other products that support pluggable authentication and authorization modules.

If you haven't done this already, before going any further, please read the "Using Forms Authentication in Reporting Services" white paper listed in the resources in section 15.8. This article, as well as the accompanying code sample, will give you the essential knowledge that every developer must have before implementing custom security extensions with RS.

Using custom security with Internet-oriented applications can be a good option for these reasons:

- *The application can request reports by URL on the client side by directly accessing the Report Server.* For example, a web page can include a View My Reports hyperlink with the URL address of the report.
- *The Report Server can discriminate among web users.* For example, an online hotel portal can assign users to Silver, Gold, and Platinum roles and give users different levels of access based on their user membership. In this respect, custom security is no different than the default Windows-based security model.

Figure 15.18 depicts how your applications can leverage a custom security extension to implement your own authentication and authorization rules.

Although the RS custom security architecture is most suitable for and works best with web-based applications, any type of application can leverage it, including WinForm clients and Web services.

NOTE Bending the custom security model to work with non-web clients boils down to writing additional code for storing the session cookie returned by the `LogonUser` method and sending it back with each request to the Report Server. This requires that you overwrite the RS Web service proxy. For more information, please check the LogonUser documentation.

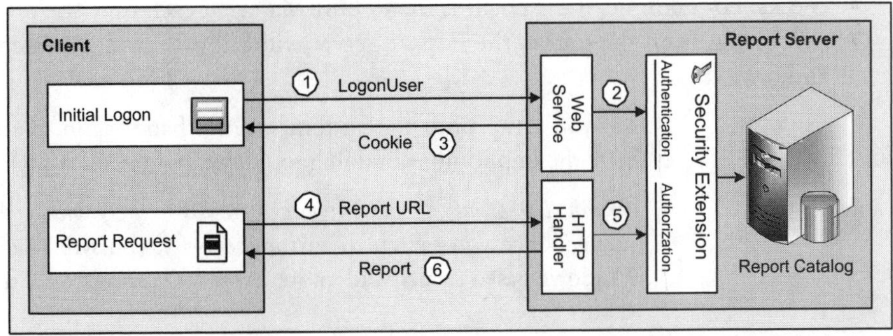

Figure 15.18 You can use a security extension for custom authentication and authorization.

.NET developers familiar with the ASP.NET Forms Authentication will probably find the RS custom security model similar. Here is the sequence flow (shown in figure 15.18) between the client and the Report Server, configured to use a custom security extension:

1. The client application displays a login form to prompt the user for credentials, such as the user name and password. In the case of ASP.NET applications, Forms Authentication can be used to redirect the user to the login form automatically.
2. Once the user's credentials are collected, the application invokes ① the `LogonUser` RS web method to log the user on to RS. For example, a web application that leverages Forms Authentication can call the `LogonUser` SOAP API once the user is authenticated in the logon page.
3. Next, the Report Server asks ② the custom security extension to authenticate the user. How the custom security extension does this is of no concern to the Report Server. Typically, with a large number of users, a database store will be used to store the user's profile and credentials.
4. If the user is successfully authenticated, the `LogonUser` method returns ③ a ticket in the form of a session cookie, which the Report Server expects to find in subsequent calls from the client. When a browser is used as a client, the session cookie will be automatically passed back when a URL request is made to render a report. When other types of clients are used, you will need to take an extra step to pass the cookie explicitly with the call to the Report Server.
5. The client submits ④ the report request by URL to the Report Server.
6. The Report Server asks ⑤ the custom security extension to authorize the user request.
7. If the request is successfully authorized, the Report Server generates the report and sends ⑥ it back to the client.

Although the scenario depicted in figure 15.18 specifically refers to requesting reports, any type of action against the report catalog will be subject to custom authorization checks. For example, if the client is the Report Manager, each time the user initiates a new action from the portal, the Report Server will call the custom authentication to authorize it.

NOTE Before you jump onto the custom security bandwagon, please carefully evaluate the implications of doing so, including the following:

- *Version 1.0 of RS doesn't support a mixed-security mode.* As a consequence, once you switch to custom security, you won't be able to use Windows-based security anymore, even for administrator access to the Report Server.
- *You may need to implement features that you take for granted when Windows authentication is used.* For example, if you need to assign users to

groups for easier maintenance, you will have to roll off your own group membership infrastructure. You may consider using the Microsoft Authorization Manager, which we discussed in chapter 13, when your requirements call for a more involved application security model.

- *Because the report consumers will access the Report Server directly, you may need to secure the connection to the Report Server using SSL.* This is especially important for Internet-oriented applications. If you don't, a hacker may sniff the network traffic and intercept the login credentials.
- *Configuring RS for custom security is an involved process that requires a number of steps to set up the Report Server and Report Manager.* Going back to Windows-based security and "undoing" all steps could be quite a hassle, so make sure that you know what you're getting yourself into.

Because in most cases the main purpose of using custom security is to allow reports to be request by URL, you may need to take extra steps to protect the data. For example, you will need to ensure that a customer can see only her order history data by filtering the orders at the data source.

There may be other tradeoffs applicable to your particular situation.

Now that we've seen at a high level how custom security works, let's examine its implementation details.

15.4.1 Design goals and tradeoffs

Here is our hypothetical scenario. In chapter 11, we discussed a possible approach that Adventure Works Cycles can follow to implement the My Orders feature. As you will probably recall, this feature allows AWC web-based customers to view their order history. The implementation approach in chapter 11 relied on the AWReportViewer control for rendering the Customer Orders report via SOAP on the server side. Let's now change our implementation approach by allowing the customers to request the report by URL on the client side of the application.

This approach has a number of advantages, including simplicity and a rich user experience. Because the report is now requested by URL, we can add interactive features to the report, such as toggling visibility, drilldown, and so on. While we can reap the benefits that URL access has to offer, we shouldn't compromise the application's security in doing so. To ensure secure access to the Report Server, we will use a custom security extension to authenticate and authorize the report requests.

Here are the high-level requirements for our solution:

- Allow customers to access reports by URL.
- Enforce restricted access to the Report Server by implementing a custom security extension.
- Authenticate users against a user profile store. In our case, the profile store will be represented by the Individuals table in the AdventureWorks2000 database.

- Implement horizontal data filtering at the data source based on the user's identity to ensure that a customer can see only her own orders.
- Implement the necessary infrastructure to provide administrator-level access to the Report Server using a designated admin account.
- Support assigning customers to groups for easier maintenance. Creating role-based security policies for hundreds and thousands of web customers is impractical. Instead, a better approach would be to assign customers to groups, for example, Individual or Store groups, to reflect the existing customer types in the AdventureWorks2000 database.

Our implementation will be a subject to the following tradeoffs:

- *To keep the solution as lightweight as possible, we won't require the customer to enter a password.* Needless to say, in real life, you should provide as robust authentication as possible. The Microsoft custom security sample shows you some practical techniques for using strong passwords. Once again, consider using SSL to secure the connection to the Report Server.
- *For the sake of simplicity, we won't provide the database infrastructure needed to support organizing customers in groups.* Instead, we will use the customer's identifier as a user name and a hard-coded group name called Individual. During the authorization stage, we will check the name and, if it is a valid number, we will assume that the customer belongs to the Individual group. In real life, your authorization logic will typically make a database call to determine the level of access the user has based on his group membership.
- *Unlike the Microsoft custom security sample, we won't be implementing a login form to log the user to the Report Server in case the session has expired or the user has bypassed the application authentication.* In our opinion, having too many login screens may be confusing for the user and may present a security risk. Instead, our design pattern promotes a single logon to both the application and the Report Server, which will be the responsibility of the application. In cases where the user requests an RS resource without being authenticated or the RS cookie session has expired, we will display an error page and prompt the user to log in again to the web application.

Now, let's see how our solution works from an end-user perspective.

15.4.2 Intranet reporting with custom security

We will assume that the Adventure Works customers have been already registered and their profile data is captured in the Individual table. The first step that the report administrator needs to do is grant the users access to view the appropriate reports.

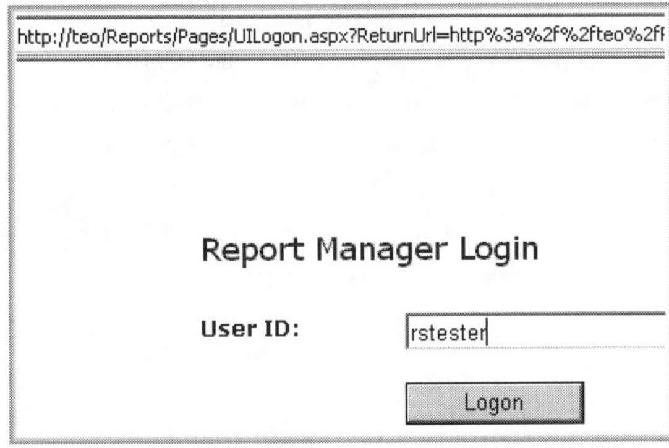

Figure 15.19 Enforcing secured access to the Report Manager portal

Setting up role-based security policies

This step should look familiar to you. The report administrator will use the Report Manager portal to create role-based security policies for the AWC customers. In real life, the Report Manager portal won't be configured for Internet access, and only a few privileged users will be assigned as administrators. Ideally, you should be able to configure the Report Manager with Windows-based security for user authentication, while the Report Server could be configured with custom security.

However, as we've mentioned, currently RS doesn't support a mixed security model. For this reason, once we switch to custom security, we need to take care of authenticating the user's access to the Report Manager, as well as the Report Server. Therefore, once the user accesses the Report Manager, the authentication screen shown in figure 15.19 is displayed.

If you have followed the setup instructions, there will be predefined admin account, rstester, which you can use to log in to the Report Manager portal.

Next, we need to grant rights to those web customers who will be able to access the Customer Orders Custom Auth report. Our custom security extension supports creating role-based security policies using individual and group accounts. For the purposes of our demo, let's grant Browser role rights for the Home and AWReporter folders to the accounts shown in figure 15.20.

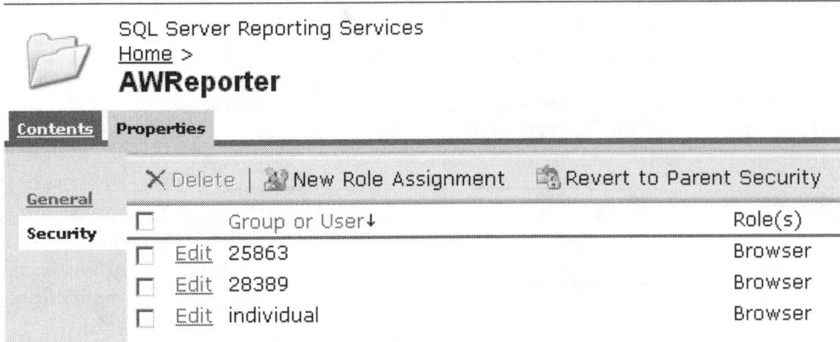

Figure 15.20 Creating individual and group security policies

Here we created one group-based security policy (the Individual group) and two individual security policies that correspond to two of the customer identifiers created by the Recipients.sql script (please see the readme file for setup instructions). The Individual-based security policies are for demonstration only. Even if we don't set them up, all customers listed in the Individual table will be authenticated successfully because they belong to the Individual group. When creating a new security policy, the Report Server asks the custom security extension to validate the user, so make sure that the customer identifiers you use exist in the Individual table.

Requesting reports

Once the security policies have been set up, customers can request reports using the AWReporterWeb web application by navigating to the default page. To simulate this, expand the client-side Reporting menu and choose Custom Security. If the application is set up correctly to use Forms Authentication, at this point you should see the Adventure Works Portal Login form, as shown in figure 15.21.

The Custom Security menu points to the MyOrders page located under the Chapter15 folder. Because this page is defined in the application's configuration file as secured, the ASP.NET Forms Authentication security framework automatically navigates to the designated login page, Login.aspx. Once the customer posts to the page, it calls the `LogonUser` method to pass the customer's credentials to the Report Server.

Next, the MyOrders page is displayed. Unlike its chapter 11 implementation, this time the page sponsors a URL link to the Customer Orders Custom Auth report. Using the link, the user can see her order history by requesting the report by URL, as shown in figure 15.22.

To emphasize the difference between this implementation of the report and the one discussed in chapter 11, we changed the Customer Orders report to include interactive features as well as the HTML Viewer toolbar. When examining this report, please note that we changed the report query to filter the data based on the identity of the user. In our case, we set the user's identity to match the customer's identifier. In this way, we enforce at the data source the security-related business rule that a customer can see only her own orders.

Having seen how our demo works, let's delve into the technical details to find out how it is implemented.

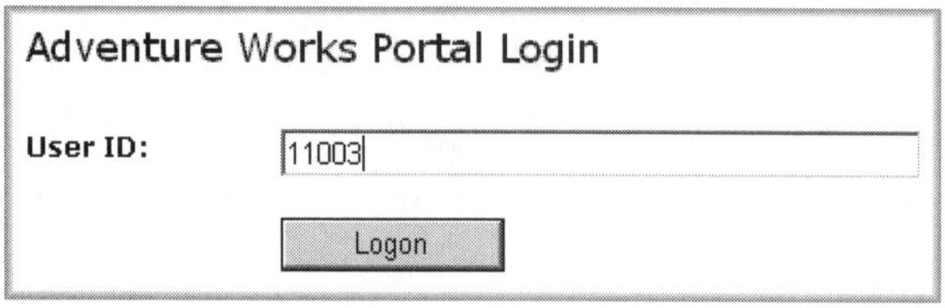

Figure 15.21
To request a report, the customer has to be authenticated by the application.

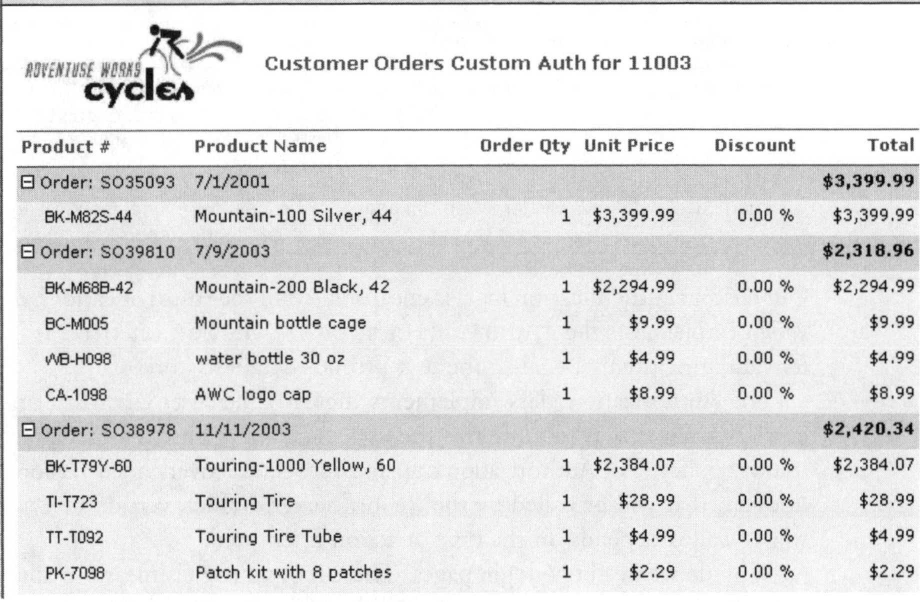

Product #	Product Name	Order Qty	Unit Price	Discount	Total
⊟ Order: SO35093	7/1/2001				**$3,399.99**
BK-M82S-44	Mountain-100 Silver, 44	1	$3,399.99	0.00 %	$3,399.99
⊟ Order: SO39810	7/9/2003				**$2,318.96**
BK-M68B-42	Mountain-200 Black, 42	1	$2,294.99	0.00 %	$2,294.99
BC-M005	Mountain bottle cage	1	$9.99	0.00 %	$9.99
WB-H098	water bottle 30 oz	1	$4.99	0.00 %	$4.99
CA-1098	AWC logo cap	1	$8.99	0.00 %	$8.99
⊟ Order: SO38978	11/11/2003				**$2,420.34**
BK-T79Y-60	Touring-1000 Yellow, 60	1	$2,384.07	0.00 %	$2,384.07
TI-T723	Touring Tire	1	$28.99	0.00 %	$28.99
TT-T092	Touring Tire Tube	1	$4.99	0.00 %	$4.99
PK-7098	Patch kit with 8 patches	1	$2.29	0.00 %	$2.29

Figure 15.22 With custom security, web users can request reports by URL.

15.4.3 Implementing the custom security extension

You can find the custom security extension code under the SecurityExtensions folder in the AWC.RS.Extensions project. Detailed setup instructions can be found in the readme file located in this folder. Because setting up the custom extension requires changing almost all configuration files, we copied our version of the Report Server and Report Manager configuration files to the ConfigurationFiles/CustomSecurity folder.

The custom security extension was built upon the Microsoft sample extension. Once again, read that white paper if you feel that you need more background information.

Custom security extension types

Table 15.4 lists the most significant security extension components and their purpose.

Table 15.4 The custom security extension implements several interfaces for plugging into the Report Server security architecture.

Source File	Inherit From	Purpose
AuthenticationExtension	IAuthenticationExtension	Include custom authentication implementation
Authorization	IAuthorizationExtension	Include custom authorization implementation

continued on next page

Table 15.4 The custom security extension implements several interfaces for plugging into the Report Server security architecture. *(continued)*

Source File	Inherit From	Purpose
Logon Page	System.Web.UI.Page	The login page for authenticating the user if direct browsing of the report catalog is permitted. Our implementation simply returns an error message.
UILogon Page	System.Web.UI.Page	The login page for authenticating the user for access to the Report Manager

Our custom authentication logic is encapsulated in the AuthenticationExtension class, which implements the `IAuthenticationExtension` interface. It includes code for validating the user against the user profile's database store.

The Authorization class implements the `IAuthorizationExtension` interface. Its main task is to authorize the user's actions against the predefined role-based security policy. The Authorization class includes several overloaded versions of `CheckAccess` that will be called by the Report Server. Which version of `CheckAccess` will be called depends on the type of action attempted.

Why do we need two login pages? The UILogon page is meant to authenticate the user when the user tries to access the Report Manager portal, as shown in figure 15.19. The second login screen, Logon, is used to authenticate the user when she tries to browse the report catalog. As we've said, in our case, we don't allow bypassing the application's authentication and hitting the Report Server directly, so the implementation of this page is very simple. It prompts the user to log in again by clicking a hyperlink that will bring her to the application's login screen.

Let's now see how the custom security extension works by looking at the processes of authentication and authorization in detail.

Runtime conversation map

As we explained in chapter 8, when implementing custom security models, we need to differentiate between the processes of authentication and authorization. During the authentication phase, we determine the identity of the user, while the authorization phase is concerned with verifying the user's rights to the requested resource. Figure 15.23 shows the simplified sequence of events for both phases.

As figure 15.23 depicts, authentication must take place before the request is authorized. After a successful authentication handshake, the Report Server sends the application a ticket in the form of a session cookie. The Report Server automatically checks this cookie during subsequent requests to the Report Server catalog. If the cookie is not found or it is invalidated, the Report Server will display the Logon page.

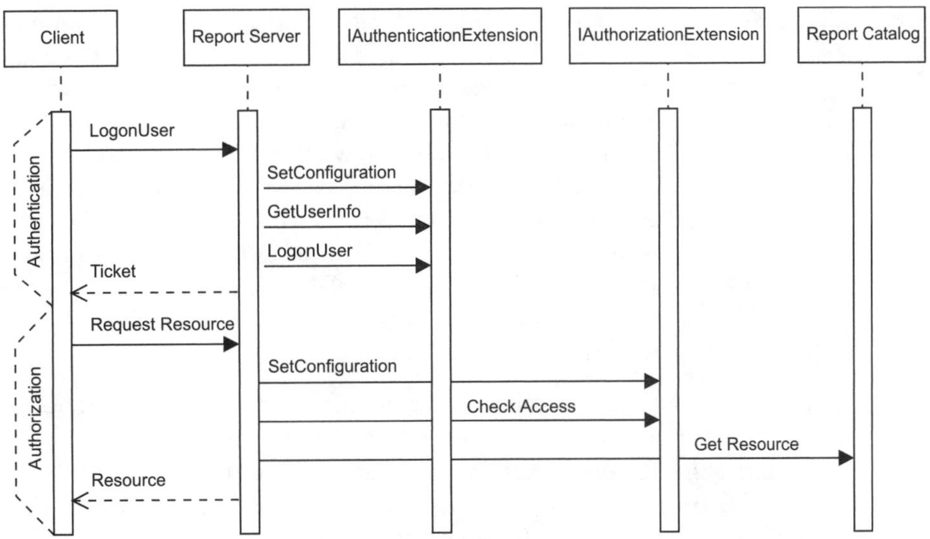

Figure 15.23 The runtime conversation map of the custom security extension events

> **NOTE** Although you can use the same settings in the Report Server web.config file to configure the cookie (name, expiration, and so on) as you would when using ASP.NET Forms Authentication, the two cookies are not compatible. In other words, if you have a web application that needs to support both ASP.NET Forms Authentication and custom security, you will end up with two cookies—one generated by the ASP.NET Forms Authentication APIs and another generated by the Report Server when the `LogonUser` API is called. As a consequence, you will typically need to synchronize both cookies to expire at the same time by using the same timeout setting in the configuration files.

If the cookie is valid, authorization takes place. Here, the request is validated against the predefined role-based security policy set up by the report administrator. Your custom authorization logic has the final say when the request is authorized successfully. This adds a lot of flexibility because developers can implement custom rules to validate the request, as we will see shortly.

Implementing custom authentication

From client perspective, the first task that the application has to do to grant the user access to the Report Server is to call the RS `LogonUser` web method and pass the user's credentials.

NOTE The RS documentation erroneously states that the LogonUser method must be called over a secured (SSL) connection. While you must definitely consider securing the connection to the Report Server with your real-life applications, you don't need SSL when calling this method.

Another consideration to watch for, which bit me at the beginning, is that when using the Report Manager with custom security, you need to enter the portal's URL exactly as specified under the ReportServerUrl element in the RSWebApplication.config Report Manager configuration file. If you don't do this, for example, if you use localhost as a server name, you will get an exception and custom security won't work. However, you can request reports using localhost.

After the LogonUser call, the Report Server invokes the IAuthenticationExtension methods in the sequence shown in figure 15.23.

First, the Report Server invokes the IAuthenticationExtension.SetConfiguration method to give the authentication extension a chance to configure itself by passing the Configuration XML fragment from the RSReportServer.config configuration file. In our case, the configuration section includes the connection string to the user's profile store as well as the credentials that the report administrator can use to log in to the Report Manager. The premise here is that, in real life, you will typically keep the administrator's credentials and the user's profile store separate. Of course, there's nothing stopping you from putting the administrator's credentials in the user's profile store if your application's design calls for it.

Once the extension is initialized, the Report Server calls GetUserInfo to obtain the user's identity. This method is also called with each request to the Report Server. In our case, we set the user identity as follows:

```
userIdentity = HttpContext.Current.User.Identity;
```

When the user is not yet authenticated (IAuthenticationExtension.LogonUser is not yet called), the Report Server will set the user's identity to a temporary user. The userIdentity object passed as an out argument to GetUserInfo is of the type System.Security.Principal.IIdentity interface, so it can be set to any valid object that implements this interface.

NOTE I was initially tempted to implement the user-to-group membership assignment in GetUserInfo. My envisioned approach was to check the user's profile store and assign the user to one or multiple roles as you could do when using ASP.NET Forms Authentication, for example:

```
// check the group membership and assign user to the Individual
role
HttpContext.Current.User = new GenericPrincipal (userIdentity,
          new string[] { "Invididual" });
```

Then, my plan called for verifying the user group in CheckAccess by using the IPrincipal.IsInRole() method and authorizing the user based on the group membership. Unfortunately, while this approach will work, GetUserInfo is called repeatedly within a single request, and performing a database lookup each time may very well hinder the application's performance. For this reason, I abandoned my original plan in favor of performing the database lookup in the CheckAccess overloads, as suggested by Bryan Keller, a Microsoft engineer from the RS group.

After several SetConfiguration and GetUserInfo calls, eventually the Report Server will call the LogonUser method to ask you to validate the user's credentials. The Report Server will conveniently pass the user name and password that were sent in the LogonUser web method call. Our implementation of LogonUser performs a database lookup against the Individual table in an attempt to find a customer identifier that matches the user name. If this is the case, we will consider the user valid and set the method's return value to true.

Please note that the Report Server will call IAuthentication.LogonUser only once during the lifetime of the user's session as a result of the call to the LogonUser web method. As we've noted before, if the user is authenticated successfully, the Report Server will issue a ticket in the form of a cookie that will be checked automatically with each request to determine if authentication has already taken place. The cookie's details are specified in the Report Server's web.config configuration file. In our case, we set the cookie to expire after one hour, as shown below:

```
<authentication mode="Forms">
  <forms loginUrl="logon.aspx" name="sqlAuthCookie"
     timeout="60" slidingExpiration="true" path="/">
  </forms>
</authentication>
```

ASP.NET developers familiar with the ASP.NET Forms Authentication model will find this syntax familiar. For example, you can use the same declaration attributes to configure the RS custom authentication.

You may wonder how the Report Server validates the user name when the administrator creates a new role-based security policy using the Report Manager portal. When an attempt is made to change the role-based security policy of a given item in the report catalog, the Report Server calls IAuthenticationExtension.IsValidPrincipalName (not shown in the sequence diagram). The Report Server will pass only the user name (not the password) and ask your authentication extension to verify that the user name is valid.

You can view the call to IsValidPrincipalName as a safeguard against the possibility that some malicious code could try to exploit the RS role-based security policy to gain access to the report catalog. Interestingly, the Report Server calls IAuthenticationExtension.IsValidPrincipalName for each user or group assigned to the catalog item. If a match is not found, an exception is raised and the attempt to change the role-based security policy won't succeed.

Implementing custom authorization

Once authenticated, our custom authorization model needs to verify that the user has adequate rights to perform the attempted action. How involved this will get will depend on your security requirements. In the simplest case, you won't have to change the authorization code included in the Microsoft sample at all. Its authorization implementation checks to see whether the user has permissions to perform the requested action. If you don't need to support assigning users to groups, the sample authorization implementation will most likely suffice for your needs.

Similarly to the authentication model, the authorization process starts when the Report Server calls `IAuthorizationExtension.SetConfiguration` to give your custom authorization extension a chance to configure itself using the setting in the configuration file. In our case, the configuration section includes only the administrator's name. This is needed because we want to bypass the authorization check if the user has admin rights.

Depending on the type of attempted action, the Report Server will call different `CheckAccess` overloads. For example, in the case when a report is requested, the Report Server will call the following overload:

```
public bool CheckAccess(string userName, IntPtr userToken,
            byte[] secDesc, ReportOperation requiredOperation)
```

If the report includes images, the Report Server will also call the `CheckAccess` overload that takes ResourceOperation as the last argument:

```
// Overload for Report operations
public bool CheckAccess( string userName, IntPtr userToken,
        byte[] secDesc, ReportOperation requiredOperation) {

   if (0 == String.Compare(userName, m_adminUserName, true,
         CultureInfo.CurrentCulture)) return true;

   IPrincipal user = HttpContext.Current.User;
   if (Util.IsNumeric(userName)) userName = "individual";

   AceCollection acl = DeserializeAcl(secDesc);
   foreach(AceStruct ace in acl)    {
     if (0 == String.Compare(userName, ace.PrincipalName,
             true, CultureInfo.CurrentCulture) { )
       foreach(ReportOperation aclOp in   ace.ReportOperations)
          if (aclOp == requiredOperation) return true;
     }
   }
   return false;
}
```

Allows unrestricted access for the administrator

Assigns the user to a group

Traverses the role-based security policy to determine the user's access to this resource

All `CheckAccess` variations take as an argument the security descriptor of the requested item in the form of a serialized array. In your `CheckAccess` implementation, you can deserialize the item's security descriptor in the form of an AceCollection class to find out which role-based security policies have been defined for this item. The Report Server passes all role-based security policies defined for the requested catalog item, not just the ones defined for the interactive user. It simply tells you, "Here are all role-based policies defined in the report catalog for this item." This is great because it can greatly simplify your authorization implementation, as you will see in the next section. It is important to note that your authentication extension can take the stand and have a final say before the Report Server grants or revokes access to the requested resource. Our default implementation is to loop through the role-based policies and find out whether the user has been associated at all with the requested resource. If this is the case, the code verifies whether the user indeed has rights to the requested operation.

NOTE If you change the CheckAccess overloads you may need to change also the implementation of the IAuthorizationExtension.GetPermissions method. GetPermissions returns the list of permissions available to a given user and it is only called by the Report Manager. Although the sequence diagram on Figure 15.23 doesn't show it, the Report Manager calls AuthorizationExtension.GetPermissions to adjust its UI based on the security policy defined for the logged on user.

Assigning users to groups

But wait, you may say! Do I have to create a role-based policy for each user? Just imagine the nightmare that will follow if the report administrator needs to maintain hundreds and thousands of role-based security policies with large sites that support many registered users, such as Adventure Works. In such cases, groups provide a practical solution for implementing more granular security assignments because rights are granted to groups, not individual users.

Can groups be used with custom security? You bet, provided that you are willing to write some code. Currently, the Report Server doesn't have any notion about assigning users into application groups. While you may implement a custom infrastructure to support assigning users to one or more application groups, for example, database-driven or based on the Authorization Manager (see chapter 12), the Report Server doesn't have the means to differentiate users and groups. However, because it will pass all security policies defined to the requested item to the `CheckAccess` overloads, you can easily perform additional lookups to resolve the user-role relationship. For example, if the user is not explicitly granted permissions to request reports, you can find out which roles she belongs to and iterate through the AceCollection collection to find out whether these roles have been given the rights to do so.

There are at least two approaches that we can think of for supporting group assignments. As we mentioned before, assigning the user to groups in `GetUserInfo` is impractical because it is called many times within each request. One approach would be to use a custom HTTP handler, similar to the one we will discuss shortly, to perform the database lookup based on the user's identity, create a new GenericPrincipal object, and assign the groups (roles) to that user. The advantage of this approach is that it centralizes the group assignments in one place. In addition, it allows the developer to use `IPrincipal.IsInRole` to simplify the authorization checks. The disadvantage is that it requires a custom HTTP handler. Microsoft doesn't officially support using HTTP handlers to extend RS.

Another approach would be to use the `CheckAccess` overloads for additional authorization rules, such as group membership. This is the approach we decided to implement for both report and resource authorization checks. We kept our implementation simple on purpose. The code checks only to see if the user name is a valid number, because the custom identifiers are numeric. If this is the case, we reset the user name to Individual. In other words, we assume that the user can belong to only one group. Then, we leave the rest of the authorization logic to find out if a principal named Individual has been assigned the rights to request the resource.

If you want, you could extend our sample by allowing accounts defined in the Store table to log in to the Adventure Works portal. In this case, you could assign these accounts to a group called Store, which may have a different level of access to the report catalog. Your application requirements may call for assigning users to multiple groups. Thanks to the fact that the authorization checks are performed in the custom security extension, you can make them as flexible and sophisticated as needed.

15.4.4 Debugging the custom security extension

Debugging the custom security extension is easy when you follow these steps:

Step 1 Request the MyOrders.aspx page from the AWReporterWeb application. This will start the aspnet_wp (w3wp in IIS6) process. Alternatively, you can open the Internet Information Services (IIS) management console and browse the ReportService.asmx page.

Step 2 Open the AWC.RS.Extensions project.

Step 3 From the Debug menu in VS.NET select Processes, find the aspnet_wp (w3wp) process, and attach to it. When the Attach to Process dialog opens, make sure that the Common Language Runtime program type is selected.

Step 4 Log in using the Login form in AWReporterWeb. At this point, the call to the `LogonUser` web method will be made, and the breakpoints in your custom authentication extension should be hit.

Step 5 Click the My Order History link found in the MyOrders.aspx page. This will request the Customer Orders report. At this point, the breakpoints in your custom authorization extension should be hit.

15.5 USING CUSTOM HTTP MODULES

Finally, we would like to show you how you can extend RS with custom HTTP modules. Those of you who are experienced in ASP.NET development will probably recall that the ASP.NET processing pipeline supports plugging in custom HTTP modules.

You can think of HTTP modules as filters that can inspect and possibly change the contents of the HTTP request and response messages as they pass through the pipeline. The HTTP modules are the modern equivalents of the legacy pre-.NET ISAPI filters. However, while ISAPI filters can be implemented only in C++, ASP.NET HTTP modules can be coded in any of the supported .NET languages.

NOTE There is one setback worth mentioning about the HTTP modules and RS. Currently, RS does not officially support HTTP module extensibility. This may change in subsequent releases, but with version 1.0 you are on your own.

15.5.1 The HTTP module design goals and tradeoffs

The original scenario that I intended to demonstrate with a custom HTTP module was defaulting the user's language settings to a specific culture. This could be especially useful for Internet-based reporting where the reports can be requested by a variety of international users. In such a case, while an organization may want to take advantage of the culture-neutral formatting supported by RS, it may want to limit the number of supported cultures. If a report request originates from a user with an unsupported culture, the HTTP module will revert to the default culture. From an implementation standpoint, this could have been accomplished by changing the thread culture before the request reached the RS runtime. Unfortunately, my plans were upset when I realized that RS uses the accept-language header to determine the user's culture. And, of course, the HTTP header collection is read-only and cannot be changed by the HTTP module.

At this point, I was running out of ideas as to what my HTTP module could do because we can extend RS in almost all possible aspects by using extensions. As we mentioned section 15.4, HTTP modules are typically used to implement custom security management, for example, by assigning users to application groups to simplify the role-based security maintenance. For the purposes of my demo, however, I decided to use an HTTP module as a tracing tool to output incoming URL and SOAP calls. As we noted in chapter 9, tracing URL requests from the HTML Viewer or Report Manager is tricky because they bypass the virtual port settings of the trace tools. The custom HTTP module makes tracing easier by writing the requests to the default trace listener. This allows you to use Mark Russinovich's excellent DbgView tool to monitor all incoming RS traffic.

15.5.2 Implementing the custom HTTP module

You can find the custom HTTP module source code and setup instructions under the HttpModules/AWRsHttpModule folder in the AWC.RS.Extensions project.

You will probably appreciate the heavy lifting that the ASP.NET pipeline model does behind the scenes to plug in custom HTTP handlers and shield the developer from the plumbing details. For example, implementing the tracing logic requires only a few lines of code:

```
public class AwRsHttpModule : IHttpModule {

    public void Init(HttpApplication app) {     ◁─┘ ❶ Hooking the OnBeginRequest event
```

```
    app.BeginRequest += new EventHandler(this.OnBeginRequest);
  }

public void OnBeginRequest(object obj, EventArgs ea) {
  bool soapRequest = false;
  HttpApplication app = (HttpApplication) obj;
  HttpContext ctx = app.Context;          <-2 Getting to the current
                                              request context
  soapRequest = (ctx.Request.Headers["SOAPAction"]!=null);

  if (!soapRequest)  {     <-3 In case of a URL request, output the request's URL
    Trace.WriteLine("AwRsHttpModule - URL request: "
+ ctx.Request.Url);
  }
  else  {     <-4 In case of a SOAP request, output the SOAP action
    stream = ctx.Request.InputStream;
    byte[] requestBody = new byte[stream.Length];
    stream.Read(requestBody,0,requestBody.Length);
    ctx.Request.InputStream.Position = 0;
    string request =
      System.Text.ASCIIEncoding.ASCII.GetString(requestBody);
    Trace.WriteLine("AwRsHttpModule - SOAP request: " +
       ctx.Request.Headers["SOAPAction"]);
    Trace.WriteLine("AwRsHttpModule - SOAP payload:"+request);
    Trace.WriteLine("AwRsHttpModule - SOAP request: "
+ ctx.Request.Headers["SOAPAction"]);
    }
}
```

Every HTTP module must implement the `IHttpModule` interface. This interface has only two methods: `Init` and `Dispose`.

1. We use the `Init` method to hook the `OnBeginRequest` event, which fires when a new HTTP request arrives.
2. Inside `OnBeginRequest`, the code obtains a reference to the ASP.NET context.
3. Then the code examines the value of the SOAPAction header to determine whether this is a URL or SOAP request.
4. In the case of a SOAP request, we save the request's body stream to an array to convert it to a string.

Once you deploy the HTTP module, you can fire DbgView to watch the traffic, as shown in figure 15.24.

Depending on your particular needs, you may have other reasons to use custom HTTP modules. For example, you may need to verify the request by inspecting the report request and rejecting it under some conditions. The commented code in `OnBeginRequest` shows how you can properly terminate the current request and return an error to the browser if certain conditions are not met.

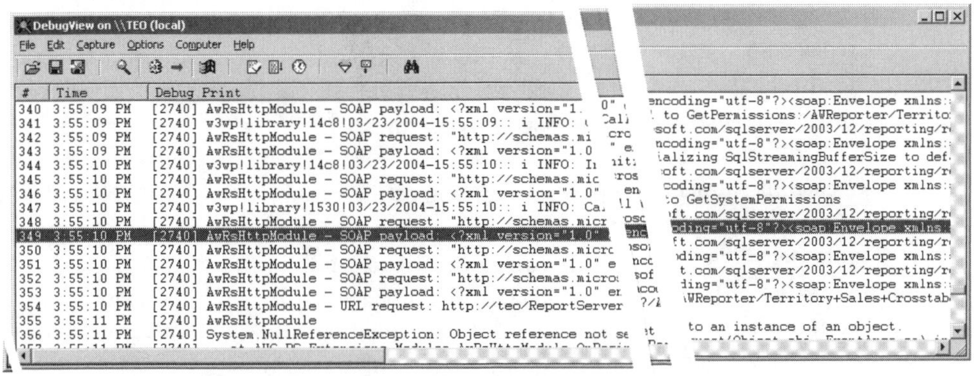

Figure 15.24 Use the custom HTTP module to watch the traffic coming into the Report Server.

15.6 CONSIDERATIONS FOR CUSTOM RENDERING EXTENSIONS

But wait! What about a custom rendering extension sample?

Unfortunately, although I was initially planning to write one, I had to scope it out for several reasons. First, at the time of this writing, the custom rendering extensions are not documented. Based on the feedback I got from Microsoft's RS team, a documentation refresh has been slated for one of the public SQL Server 2005 betas.

Second, given the flexible XML exporting capabilities of RS, there aren't many formatting gaps left that would require you to write a custom extension. Granted, exporting to Microsoft Word could be useful, but this would require significant effort well beyond the scope of this book. As you could imagine, writing custom rendering extensions is not easy.

You can expect a proliferation of rendering extensions from third-party vendors in the near future. For example, if you want to create reports with Microsoft Word or earlier versions of Excel within RS, then consider the SoftArtisans OfficeWriter, which will be integrated with RS in the third quarter of 2004. While RS supports only Office XP or later and Office Web Components, the OfficeWriter helps fill in the missing format gaps by providing Microsoft Word and native Excel Binary Interchange File Formats (BIFF) from versions 97 through 2003. See the resources in section 15.8 for a link to the SoftArtisans web site.

15.7 SUMMARY

Having read this chapter, you should view Reporting Services as a reporting framework that you can use to create versatile reporting solutions. In my opinion, no matter how hard Microsoft works to enhance RS, it will not be able to meet all possible integration requirements. In cases such as these, you need to take the road less traveled and custom-tailor RS to meet your particular needs.

Thanks to the extensible architecture of RS, .NET developers can easily extend or replace RS's "canned" features by writing add-ons in the form of custom extensions. In this chapter, we showed you how you can do just that by enhancing the RS data processing, delivery, and security features.

To demonstrate how you can extend the RS data processing features, we authored a custom dataset extension that you can use to report off ADO.NET datasets.

To showcase how you can distribute your reports in flexible ways, we created a custom delivery extension. You can use it to send reports to Web services.

When Windows-based security is not a good fit, you can replace it by writing a custom security extension. We did exactly this to show how custom security extensions can be leveraged in the Internet reporting scenario.

If you need to perform some preprocessing tasks before the report request reaches the Report Server, you can write custom HTTP modules.

Finally, although we didn't demonstrate it, to export reports to formats not supported by RS, you can write custom rendering extensions.

Another important and often-neglected requirement posed to enterprise-oriented applications is that they need to perform and scale well under heavy loads. The next chapter discusses practical techniques you can leverage to ensure that your report-enabled solutions are well prepared to meet the anticipated request loads.

15.8 RESOURCES

Custom Dataset Data Extension for Microsoft Reporting Services
(http://www.gotdotnet.com/Community/UserSamples/Details.aspx?SampleGuid=B8468707-56EF-4864-AC51-D83FC3273FE5)
My custom dataset extension uploaded to the gotdotnet site.

Christian Weyer's Dynamic XML Web Services Invocation sample
(http://www.gotdotnet.com/Community/UserSamples/Details.aspx?SampleGuid=e9c2f46f-449b-4344-b796-7d8b63a2f954)
Dynamically creates a proxy from the Web service WSDL file.

"Using Forms Authentication in Reporting Services" white paper on MSDN
(http://msdn.microsoft.com/library/?url=/library/en-us/dnsql2k/html/ufairs.asp?frame=true)
A must read for implementing custom security extensions.

"Securely Implement Request Processing, Filtering, and Content Redirection with HTTP Pipelines in ASP.NET"
(http://msdn.microsoft.com/msdnmag/issues/02/09/httppipelines/)
A great article by Tim Ewald and Keith Brown to introduce you to the architecture of the ASP.NET pipeline and show you how to create your own HTTP modules and handlers.

The SoftArtisians OfficeWriter

(http://officewriter.softartisans.com/officewriter-250.aspx)

In the third quarter of 2004, the SoftArtisans OfficeWriter will fully support and integrate with Microsoft SQL Server Reporting Services, making the distribution of Excel and Word reports over the Web easier than ever.

CHAPTER 16

Performance and scalability

To realize the full potential of a report-enabled application, developers must meet the users' demands, which typically consist of quality of service, quality of content, and efficient access to the application's resources. So far, this book has shown you how applications integrated with RS can meet the first two objectives.

Let's discuss in this chapter how we can ensure that our reporting solutions also perform and scale well to meet increased user loads. To ensure that these objectives are met, you need to learn how to evaluate the application's performance and capacity before "going live" in a production environment. The specific areas that are the focus of this chapter are as follows:

- Explaining the capacity planning process
- Establishing a performance goal
- Stress-testing the Report Server
- Identifying performance bottlenecks
- Optimizing the application's performance

Although this chapter specifically targets evaluating the Report Server's performance and scalability, you can use the same principles to plan the capacity requirements of other web-based applications.

16.1 UNDERSTANDING CAPACITY PLANNING

Reading the messages posted on the Reporting Services discussion list, I frequently come across questions related to RS scalability and performance. Usually people ask, "Is Reporting Services capable of supporting X number of users?" or "What are the recommended hardware and software specifications to handle high loads?"

Answering questions like these is not easy. It is hard to predict how variables in application design, database schema, user behavior, and architecture will combine to affect the application's performance. Because no exact formulas can be given, the burden of ensuring that your reporting solutions will meet the anticipated load is shifted to you. Microsoft has done their job by giving you a platform that can scale up and out. Your job is to prove that your homegrown reporting solutions meet your specific performance and capacity requirements.

16.1.1 Capacity planning fundamentals

Conducting a capacity planning study is not difficult. While discussing this subject in detail is beyond the scope of this book, we will give you the essential knowledge and techniques needed to get you started. If you need more information, please refer to the resources in section 16.4.

We'll start by explaining some essential capacity planning concepts.

Performance vs. scalability

The terms *performance* and *scalability* are often used interchangeably, but an important distinction exists. Performance usually measures how fast the application's code executes. On the other hand, scalability is concerned with how the application responds under increased user loads.

An application that scales well usually performs well. The reverse is not necessarily true. An application may exhibit excellent performance with a small number of users but may grind to a halt in a high-volume environment. Take, for example, Microsoft Access database applications. When serving a handful of clients, this type of application performs well. However, due to the desktop file-based nature of the Access Jet engine database, the application's performance deteriorates quickly as the number of users increases. In this respect, the application is not scalable.

When conducting a capacity planning study of Reporting Services, you are trying to understand how the Report Server responds at various user load levels. In general, you want to measure the *latency*, *throughput*, and *utilization* of the Report Server by simulating simultaneous report requests by virtual users. Ideally, at the end of your study, you will find out that your Report Server site exhibits low latency, high throughput, and low utilization.

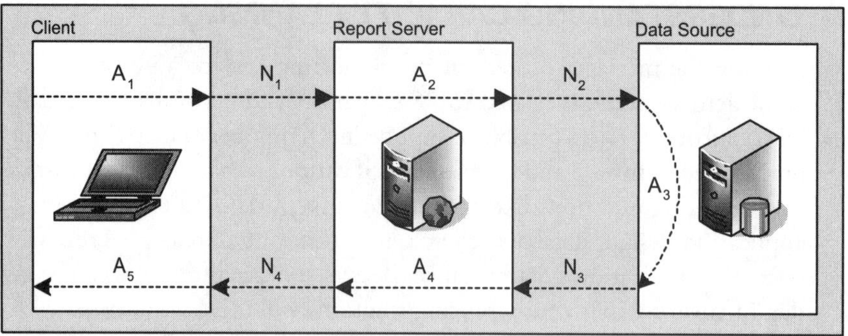

Figure 16.1 The report's request-response trip incurs network and application latencies.

Understanding latency

Latency is the delay experienced between the time when the client makes a report request and the Report Server receives the report's payload. Latency is typically measured in terms of seconds or milliseconds. Some stress-testing tools, such as the Visual Studio .NET Application Center Test, use the *time to last byte* (TTLB) metric to represent latency. The request-response trip delay depends on two major latency factors: network and application latencies. Network latency characterizes the time spent to move data through the wire. Application latency, on the other hand, refers to the delay incurred to process the report request on the server side.

Figure 16.1 depicts how the application and network latencies impact the overall report request's round trip in a typical on-demand reporting solution.

As shown on figure 16.1, the total latency time from the point of requesting the report to rendering it on the screen can be calculated with the following formula: `Total latency (response time) = (A1+A2+A3+A4+A5) + (N1+N2+N3+N4)`, where `An` represents application latencies and `Nn` stands for network latencies, as explained in table 16.1.

Table 16.1 The report request's round trip incurs application and network latencies. To improve the performance and scalability of your reporting environment, you need to find ways to minimize these latencies.

Latency	Reason
A1	Prepare the report request on the client, e.g., validate the report request, prepare the report parameters, etc.
A2	Process the report request
A3	Process the report query
A4	Generate the report

continued on next page

Table 16.1 The report request's round trip incurs application and network latencies. To improve the performance and scalability of your reporting environment, you need to find ways to minimize these latencies. ***(continued)***

Latency	Reason
A5	Render the report, e.g., in the case of a SOAP call save the report's payload to a file and shell out to it
N1, N4	Network delays between the client and the Report Server
N2, N3	Network delays between the Report Server and the database server

How much the network delays impact the report request's total latency depends to a great extent on the type of the reporting application and your deployment scenario. For example, with intranet-based reporting applications deployed on a 100Mb corporate network, network latency may not be an issue at all. However, it may become a constraining factor with Internet-oriented solutions, where slow dial-up connections are still prevalent.

One way to reduce the network delays on the trip from the Report Server back to the client is to minimize the network traffic by requesting reports by URL instead of SOAP. As we discussed in chapter 9, the latter access option adds about 20–30 percent overhead for serializing the report's payload to a binary array.

Minimizing the application's latencies is often more of an art than a science. With custom applications, you would typically use code profilers to determine which code sections take up the most time and seek ways to optimize them. Of course, with RS, this is not an option because you don't have access to its source code. Instead, you need to focus on optimization techniques within your reach. For example, as we discussed in chapter 7, you can use several report-caching techniques to minimize the report's processing time. If caching doesn't conflict with your particular reporting requirements, we recommend that you use it abundantly. For example, the easiest way to reduce the time spent on the Report Server to generate a report is not to generate it at all but to serve it from a cached copy.

Another potential area that may negatively affect the latency of the server-side application is the time required to process the report query. If you determine that the database is a constraining factor, you can use query profilers, such as the Microsoft SQL Server Query Analyzer, to find out how you can optimize your report queries. Alternatively, you can use the report's execution log (see section 16.2.1) to determine how much time the Report Server has spent on processing the query and executing and rendering the report.

"How can I get a latency breakdown of the request-response round trip?" I hear you ask. I've used a third-party tool, Compuware Application Expert, to a great degree of success to address similar questions with my performance-related projects. To use this tool, you first need to capture the network traffic of the request-response round trip using network-tracing tools, such as the Microsoft Network Monitor. For the best results, you may want to obtain network traces from all nodes involved in your reporting solution, such as the client application, the Report Server, and the database server where the report data resides.

Once you have captured the network traffic, you can import it into the Application Expert to get a conversation map showing you the network and application latencies. This tool supports also what-if analysis. Let's say you need to find out how a 56K dial-up connection will impact the report's response time. Application Expert includes a predictor component that uses sophisticated algorithms to extrapolate the latency map to factor in various network connection speeds.

Understanding throughput

For the purposes of planning the capacity of your RS environment, by the term *throughput* we mean the number of report requests that the Report Server can process within a given unit of time.

No matter how scalable a given application is, its throughput-versus-load graph will eventually reach its peak, as shown in figure 16.2.

In this respect, you can visualize your reporting application as a highway. When traffic is light, vehicles move quickly. However, as most big city dwellers can relate, once all highway lines are saturated, traffic jams follow and throughput decreases. Therefore, when we evaluate the capacity of a given RS installation, we apply increasing loads to the Report Server to find out the point of maximum throughput.

How do we measure the application's throughput? Often, people want to know how many concurrent users a given web application, in our case the Report Server, can handle. In our opinion, trying to quantify the application's throughput using concurrent users could be highly inaccurate. First, it is not clear within what time frame the users are considered to be concurrent. Second, "concurrent users" is an ambiguous term that may mean different things to different people. For example, many people use this term to refer to the number of users logged on to the application. But should a user who has logged on to the Report Manager to request five reports and then has gone on a one-hour lunch break be considered a concurrent user?

Instead, we typically measure throughput in *requests per second* (RPS) or *pages per second* (PPS). What's the difference between the two? Readers experienced with web

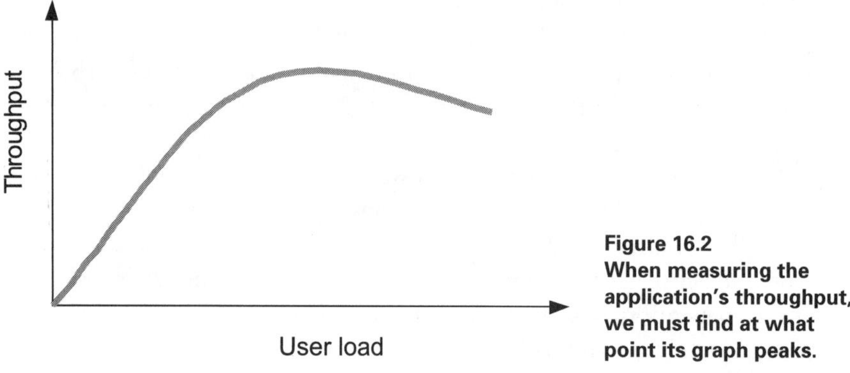

Figure 16.2
When measuring the application's throughput, we must find at what point its graph peaks.

development will probably recall that rendering one page in a browser can result in several round trips to the server. For example, when you request a report that includes images in HTML, the browser will spawn additional requests to fetch the images. Therefore, a page is more granular than a request because one page (report) may require several requests.

NOTE For the purposes of stress-testing the Report Server, we need to differentiate between requests and pages only when the report is requested in a multistream format. The multistream formats supported natively by the Report Server are all HTML options except MHTML. Because browsers tend to cache images, you may find it easier to ignore the image requests, especially with high-speed networks.

But wait, all reports are not created equal, right? While some may take seconds to render, others may need significant processing resources. What, then, does a request really mean, and how can we use it to represent various reports? These are excellent questions that deserve more attention. The short answer is that there isn't an exact rule to correlate requests with the actual reports. Let's go back to our highway example to clarify this.

Imagine that you need to measure the highway throughput for a given period of time. One way to do this is to count how many vehicles of different types, such as tractor-trailers, minivans, cars, and so on, have gone down the highway during the time period in question. The advantage of this approach is its accuracy. On the negative side, it is more involved because it is difficult to work with multiple units. For example, how many cars can be substituted for a tractor-trailer? What car models are we talking about? As they say, the devil is in the details. To simplify things, you can introduce an abstraction metric called a "vehicle" that you would use to represent an average vehicle on the highway. This simplifies your task considerably because now you are not concerned with the type of vehicles. In fact, you can use automatic counting equipment to count the vehicles for you.

In a similar way, you can use requests per second to represent the number of successfully completed report requests that the Report Server can handle within a second. Instead of requests per second, you may prefer to use other metrics. For example, another common stress-testing metric is the number of virtual users that the application can handle before its utilization exceeds the specific threshold values. Please note, though, that this approach is more involved to set up because you need to simulate the users' request patterns. For instance, once the user has requested the report, she will typically analyze it or print it before requesting another report. When using virtual users, you need to examine the report's execution history and factor in the user's think time. Another disadvantage of this method is that it may require a significant number of test client machines to "saturate" the web server.

If you want, you can conduct two sets of tests to use both approaches—requests per second and virtual users. Ideally, in this case, your test findings should match.

Understanding utilization

While determining the maximum load that the Report Server can handle is useful, often we need to find out how our report-enabled applications can scale better to meet our performance goal. In other words, an essential objective of every capacity planning study is to find what performance bottlenecks cause the throughput graph to decline, as shown in figure 16.2.

You can determine resource constraints by examining the *utilization* of your system. You typically do this by monitoring a set of performance counters. Specifically, you need to monitor the utilization of the following resources at minimum:

- CPU
- Memory
- Database server

Table 16.2 lists the most frequently used Windows performance counters to track the utilization of these resources.

Table 16.2 Windows performance counters that you can use to monitor the Report Server's usage

Resource	Performance Counter	Purpose
CPU	Processor(_Total)\% Processor Time	Represents the average CPU utilization. The average CPU utilization on any processor should not exceed 60–70%.
CPU	Process(aspnet_wp)\% Processor Time (or Process(w3wp)\% Processor Time for Windows 2003)	The percentage of the CPU utilization spent in the ASP.NET worker thread
SQL Server	Process(sqlservr)\% Processor Time	The percentage of the CPU utilization consumed by SQL Server
Memory	Memory\Available Bytes	The amount of available RAM memory in bytes

RS comes with its own performance counters that you can use to track the utilization of the RS Web service and Windows Service. For more information about the RS-related counters, please see the product documentation.

16.1.2 The capacity planning process

A successful capacity planning study necessitates a guided process that shouldn't be much different than the software development methodology in general. The capacity planning process consists of several stages, as shown in figure 16.3.

As you can see, the capacity planning process is an iterative one. At the end of each iteration, we compare the performance results against preestablished performance goals. If our objectives are not met, we need to find the reasons why and think of ways to improve the system's scalability.

Let's discuss each of the stages in more detail.

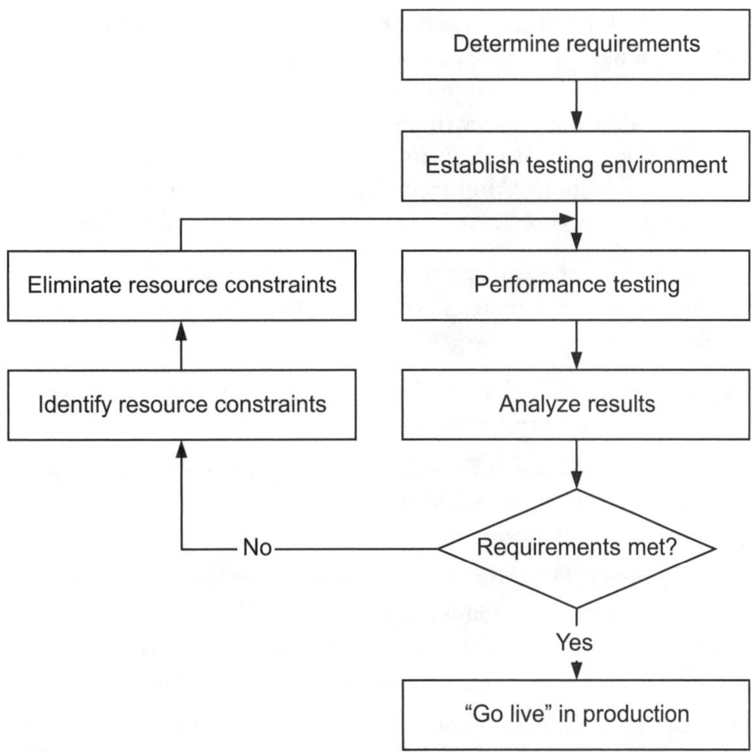

Figure 16.3 The capacity planning process consists of several stages and may include more than one iteration until the performance goals are met.

Determining requirements

This is arguably the most important phase of the capacity planning effort. As with any software project, you shouldn't underestimate the importance of getting and documenting the application's performance requirements. My overall impression is that developers tend to ignore establishing performance goals for their applications. In most cases, the result of this optimistic approach is poor scalability, which necessitates total redesign of the application.

NOTE I was once involved in a large-scale web-based project. My first task was to find out why the application was performing poorly. After stress-testing the system, I found out that it couldn't handle more than one request per second! For a web-based application this was clearly unacceptable. After a long and painstaking process of running tests against each application tier, I found several performance bottlenecks. The most significant were related to the poor throughput when requesting data from the mainframe database. In addition, I discovered that, enamored with XML, the application developers had abundantly used XML DOM manipulations and XSL transformations in each tier of the application. The application was moving ever-growing

XML payloads between the web server and the browser. XSL transformations were used on the client side to render the presentation screens.

"Fixing" the application to scale better wasn't easy. It had to be totally redesigned and rewritten in ASP.NET. After several iterations, the application finally met the performance goals and was deployed to the high-volume production environment. The moral of this story is that you must plan for performance as early as possible in the application's lifecycle.

After you determine the application's performance requirements, you need to quantify them in performance metrics. For applications integrated with RS, these metrics could include

- *Requests per second*—This is the total number of report requests that the web server (or cluster) can handle.
- *Utilization counters*—For example, the average CPU utilization of any of the web server's processors should stay below 70 percent, the memory consumption shouldn't top 80 percent, and so on.
- *Response time*—The industry standard response time for web-based applications is no more than 10 seconds measured from the time the request is made until the page is rendered to the browser or the response is received from the web server. This is a reasonable latency time for report rendering as well.
- *Application availability*—For example, your reporting requirements may call for 99.9 percent availability. Aside from scalability, this is one of the main reasons to use a cluster or web servers, as we will discuss in section 16.2.6.

While the last three of the above-mentioned metrics are easy to formulate, establishing a throughput benchmark may require more effort. Basically, to accomplish this you can use the following two approaches:

- *Empirical*—If RS is deployed and running in a production environment, this will be our preferred method because it is more realistic and accurate. This method involves analyzing the report's execution log to gather some statistics about the application's usage. This is the method that we will demonstrate shortly.
- *Theoretical*—If production data is not available, you can derive the throughput metrics by calculating the envisioned load. For example, let's say you determine that your user base will consist of 5,000 users and each user may request up to 100 reports per day. Assuming that the report requests are distributed evenly throughout the day, this means that the Report Server needs to handle about six requests per second (`(5,000 x 100)/(24 x 3600) = 6 requests/sec.`).

The performance goal you establish at the end of the "Determining requirements" phase will serve as a benchmark against which you will measure the actual performance and determine whether additional performance optimization work is required.

Establishing a testing environment

This phase typically involves the following steps:

Step 1 *Understanding the application architecture*—In general, you need to have an intimate knowledge about the architecture of the reporting application. This necessitates working hand-in-hand with the application's developers and report authors throughout the entire capacity-planning effort.

Step 2 *Setting up the testing environment*—You should get a dedicated test server with hardware and software specifications matching as closely as possible the production server setup. Otherwise, your test results will be skewed.

Step 3 *Creating test use cases*—In a typical web application, you should create test use cases that you will later script and stress test. For example, you may come up with a use case called User Login that involves two web pages: the home page and the login page. For reporting applications, you could identify a representative set of reports that need to be tested. You can analyze the RS Execution Log to find out the most requested reports.

Step 4 *Preparing test scripts*—This is where you will put on your developer's hat and create test scripts using your favorite stress-testing tool. You will use the scripts to apply an ever-increasing load to the Report Server to determine its maximum throughput.

Once the test environment is set up, it is time to find out whether your specific RS installation can stand up to the test and deliver what is expected of it.

Performance testing

This is my favorite sit-and-watch step. Most stress tools are designed to simulate multiple users submitting requests via HTTP-GET or HTTP-POST. For example, ACT can be used to generate customizable loads and offers a rich set of reporting features for analyzing performance data.

The main objective of this phase is to produce the graph shown previously in figure 16.2. My favorite method to accomplish this is to increase the number of the Application Center Test's virtual users (connections) by a factor of two, for example, one, two, four, eight, and so on. Eventually, the web server utilization will max out. At this point, you will know the maximum throughout that your particular RS installation can handle expressed in requests per second.

Next, you compare these results against the previously established performance benchmark. If the results meet or exceed your expectations, you can congratulate yourself. Otherwise, you need to cancel your vacation and go back to the drawing board and identify the performance bottlenecks.

Identifying performance bottlenecks

A bottleneck is a resource constraint, either hardware or software, that prevents performance from increasing. As noted previously, you determine the performance bottlenecks at a high level by examining the performance counters. Identifying performance bottlenecks is not always easy, but here are some tips you may find useful:

- Often, with web-based applications such as Reporting Services, the web server processor will become the first resource constraint. The Processor: % Processor Time/Total is the best counter for viewing processor saturation. If the processors are running between 90 and 100 percent, then they are most likely the bottleneck.
- If there is heavy disk activity, then the memory is likely to be the bottleneck. The Memory: Available Bytes performance counter can tell you how much physical memory is remaining and available for use.
- If the database server's processor is highly utilized, then this is an indication that the database may be a resource constraint. In the case of the SQL Server, check the Process(sqlservr)\% Processor Time counter to find out whether this is the case.
- If the ASP.NET Applications/Requests Queued counter fluctuates considerably during the test run, and the processor utilization remains low, this is an indication that the report is most likely calling custom code that is receiving more calls than it can handle.
- If none of these resources is a problem, yet the requests/second still do not increase despite the increased load, then the network card bandwidth should be examined. The best counter to use to examine the network card saturation bottlenecks is Network Interface: Bytes Total/sec. The bytes/sec should be less than 40 percent of the total available bandwidth.

Once you identify the resource contention area, you can focus on finding ways to eliminate it.

Eliminating performance bottlenecks

There are a number of performance-enhancing techniques you can try based on your particular situation. For example, if the CPU utilization is high, you may want to consider using report execution or session caching. As we discussed in chapter 9, when reports are requested via URL, report sessions are handled automatically. With SOAP access, you have to go an extra step to correlate the report with the session.

Another potential area that may lead to a high CPU utilization is if your reports use resource-intensive custom code. If you suspect this to be the case, you can use third-party profilers, such as the Compuware DevPartner to find which portions of your code are the most processor-intensive.

If your report queries process vast volumes of data, you may want to explore options to decrease the amount of data displayed. For example, you may want to consider implementing web-style paging to display one page of a report at a time with a handful of records. Finally, when performance-optimization techniques don't yield results, you can add more processing power by scaling RS up and out.

Now that we have covered the fundamentals of the capacity-planning process, let's see how we can apply them in practice.

16.2 CAPACITY PLANNING WITH REPORTING SERVICES IN ACTION

Here is our hypothetical scenario that will drive the capacity-planning effort for Adventure Works. As we've mentioned on several occasions throughout this book, Adventure Works is blessed with success. The company is expanding by acquiring some of their competitors. As a part of this process, the IT management needs to plan for growth. You've been tasked to find out whether the reporting infrastructure can handle an increased load that is expected to be 10 times greater than before. To estimate the impact, you decide to perform a capacity-planning study by following the steps we just discussed.

You can find the ACT scripts we used in this chapter included in the book's source code under the Performance Testing folder.

16.2.1 Determining requirements

As noted before, in this stage we need to determine the capacity planning requirements and establish a performance goal. The bulk of the effort will be spent on quantifying the anticipated load in requests per second (reports per second). In our hypothetical scenario, RS has already been deployed and is running in production. Therefore, as a first step, we need to analyze the RS Execution Log to find out the following:

- How many report requests has the Report Server handled for a given period?
- How were these requests distributed?

Once we answer these questions, we can easily extrapolate the increased load.

Determining the number of report requests

By far, the easiest way to find out how many reports the Report Server has handled within a given period of time is to analyze the report's execution log.

NOTE If you are evaluating web-based applications other than Report Server, you can determine the number of report requests by examining the web server logs. There are many third-party commercial and free tools you can use to analyze web server log files. For example, for my real-world projects I have used the Analog log analyzer to a great degree of success. Among the several analyzers that I've tried in the past, I've found the Analog's output to be the most accurate. The tool is also free of charge. If you need glitzier and more convincing presentation formats than those produced by Analog, you may want to try another free tool, ReportMagic. See the resources in section 16.4 to find out how to obtain Analog and ReportMagic.

As we discussed in chapter 7, RS stores important execution statistics in the ExecutionLog table in the RS Configuration Database (ReportServer). We also said that to convert the statistics to a format that is easy to understand, you can use the Execution Log DTS package (RSExecutionLog_Update.dts) included with the RS Setup CD. This package extracts the report's execution log data, transforms it, and uploads it to a separate SQL Server 2000 database called RSExecutionLog.

The data captured in the RSExecutionLog database includes a wealth of information associated with the report's execution, as well as vital performance-related metrics. For example, the ExecutionLogs table in the RSExecutionLog database includes report response times as well as times spent in retrieving data (TimeDataRetrieval column) and in executing (TimeProcessing column) and rendering (TimeRendering column) the report. For this reason, the report's execution log should be your first resource when troubleshooting performance issues with your reports.

Finding out the number of reports handled by the Report Server from the report's execution log is a matter of running the following simple query against the ExecutionLogs table:

```
SELECT COUNT(*) AS ReportCount
FROM   ExecutionLogs INNER JOIN
       Reports ON ExecutionLogs.ReportKey = Reports.ReportKey
WHERE  ReportType = 2 /*reports only*/
AND    TimeStart BETWEEN <start date> AND <end date>
```

where `<start date>` and `<end date>` specify the time period we are interested in.

If you are running the Report Server in a web farm environment and you need to find out how many reports a particular node in the cluster has handled, you can filter the query further by the MachineKey column.

To derive the number of requests per second, a weekly time period should be sufficient. Let's say that after you run this query you determine that for a given week your Report Server handled 2,000 reports. This number includes both on-demand (user) and subscribed (system) report requests.

We need to account for the extra load incurred by the web server to handle images for multistream rending formats, Report Manager pages, and so on. To be on the safe side, let's increase this number by 50 percent. As a result, we come up with the estimate that, for that week, the Report Server handled about 3,000 report requests. If the web server where RS is installed hosts other web applications, we need to account for their load as well. As you've already guessed, determining the Report Server's load, as well as that of any other type of application, is not an exact science but rather an educated guess.

Determing request distribution statistics

One more thing we need to account for is the fact that it is unlikely that all requests were distributed evenly during the day. For example, typically more requests are submitted within normal working hours. To find out the request distribution statistics, I authored the ReportsExecutedByHour chart report, which you can find included with the book's source code (in the Performance Testing folder). I based this report on the ReportsExecutedByDay sample report, which happens to be one of the reports included in the ExecutionLog Business Intelligence project. As mentioned in chapter 7, you can find the ExecutionLog sample reports on the RS Setup CD.

The Reports Executed By Hour chart report accepts a start date parameter and breaks down the report's execution statistics per hour for all report requests handled after that date, as shown in figure 16.4.

Examining the distribution chart shown in figure 16.4, we determined that all of the activity for the given week occurred within the period 7 a.m.–10 p.m.

NOTE As attentive readers will probably point out, the report count shown in the chart report doesn't total to our hypothetical metric of 2,000 report requests. This is because I ran the report against my local report execution log, which, of course, doesn't represent a real-world production environment.

Therefore, within that week, the web report server has handled about 0.07 requests per second (`3,000/(13 hrs. x 3600 sec.`). As you can tell, my web server hasn't been very busy, but your production load will likely be many times that number.

As the new capacity requirements state, our web server is expected to handle a tenfold increase in load in the future. This means that the anticipated load will be about 0.7 requests per second (`0.07 requests per sec. x 10`). Finally, let's account for the unexpected, such as holiday seasons, end-of-quarter activity, and so on, by tossing in another 50 percent increase. This means that our throughput performance goal will be about *one request per second.*

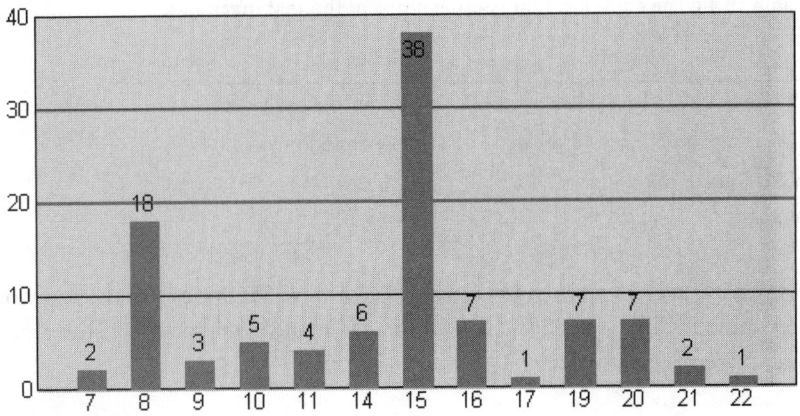

Figure 16.4 To account for the load distribution pattern, use the Reports Executed By Hour sample report.

As we've discussed before, besides throughput, there are other important performance metrics to consider. Table 16.3 lists all performance goals for the Adventure Works scenario.

Table 16.3 Performance goals for the Adventure Works scenario

Metric	Goal
Latency	Less than 10 seconds to render a report
Throughput	1 request/sec.
Utilization (CPU)	Less than 70% on average
Utilization (memory)	Less than 80%

Now that we have established our performance goals, we can continue with the next phase of the capacity planning effort: setting up the testing environment.

16.2.2 Setting up the testing environment

The prerequisite for successfully executing this phase is setting up the machines used for testing. You should have dedicated machines for the client and the test server. You will use the client machine to run the ACT tests, while the server will host RS. Once again, the server configuration should match the production server setup as closely as possible to avoid skewing the results. On the other hand, you don't need a beefed-up client because it will spend most of its time waiting for the server to respond.

Table 16.4 lists the configuration details of the client and server machines that we used for testing. Both the Report Server and SQL Server 2000 were installed on the server machine.

Table 16.4 The configuration specifications of the test machines

	Client	Server
Make	Dell Dimension 4550	Compaq Evo N610c
OS	Windows Server 2003	Windows Server 2003
CPU Speed	2.5 GHz	2.5 GHz
RAM	512MB	1GB

As you can see, my server configuration is somewhat modest. In the real world, I would recommend that you consider a more powerful server machine, for example, a two-way server with several gigabytes of RAM.

Creating use cases

Creating use cases for testing reports usually boils down to identifying a good representative set of reports that will be stress-tested. Again, the easiest way to accomplish this is to examine the RS Execution Log. While there isn't a precise formula for determining a good representative set, scripting the top 10 reports will be sufficient in most cases. To find out the most popular reports, you can create a query that retrieves this information from the Execution Logs and Reports table, as shown below:

```
SELECT    TOP 10 COUNT(Reports.Name) AS ReportCount,
          Reports.Name AS ReportName
FROM      ExecutionLogs INNER JOIN
          Reports ON ExecutionLogs.ReportKey=Reports.ReportKey
WHERE     Reports.ReportType = 2
GROUP BY Reports.Name, Reports.ReportType
ORDER BY COUNT(Reports.Name) DESC
```

For the sake of simplicity and for the purposes of our hypothetical capacity-planning study, we will limit the number of scripted reports to three, as follows:

- Employee Sales Summary
- Territory Sales Drillthrough
- Purchase Orders

In addition, we will assume that the types of the requests for these reports are divided equally between URL and SOAP access.

TIP If you need to do so, you can account for disproportional request access distributions (URL vs. SOAP) programmatically in your test scripts. One reason why you may want to do so is to simulate as close as possible your production environment, for example, to account for the increased size of the report's payload in the case of SOAP. Unfortunately, the report's execution log doesn't capture the type of request access. However, you can examine the IIS log files to find out the URL-to-SOAP access ratio. For example, let's say that after analyzing the IIS logs you find that only 10 percent of the report requests have been submitted via the RS Web service (SOAP) and the rest via URL (HTTP-GET). You can simulate these distribution statistics by adding scripting logic to fire a SOAP request after nine HTTP-GET requests.

Having identified the reports to be tested, it is time to use your favorite stress-testing tool to craft a script that will be used to simulate the request load.

Creating test scripts

To stress test the report server, I created an ACT script that you can find in the AWReporter.act Application Center Test project. Although ACT doesn't have ambitions to be a high-level stress-testing package, it is my tool of choice because of the following advantages it has to offer:

- *Flexibility*—I've used ACT on several real-life projects and found it to be very flexible. Because you can write tests using your preferred scripting language, you can do with ACT anything that can be done with scripting, such as manipulating files using the File System Object, reading environment variables, logging, and so on.

- *Ease of use*—Many stress-testing tools require that you use C++ or proprietary language derivatives for scripting. Most Visual Basic or Java programmers will find themselves instantly at home using VBScript or JScript languages.
- *Excellent reporting capabilities*
- *Cost*—ACT is bundled with Visual Studio .NET.

Of course, ACT is far from perfect. One feature that I hope a future release will bring is tighter integration with the VS.NET IDE environment for easier debugging. Another welcome addition would be the ability to write scripts in managed code instead of using script languages.

The best way to get started creating scripts is to use the New Test Wizard's auto-record feature. This starts an instance of the Internet Explorer browser so that you can request the desired report by URL. Then, you can examine the produced script and custom-tailor it to meet your particular needs.

Most Visual Basic programmers will find my report-testing script easy to understand. The only area that deserves more attention is generating SOAP requests, as shown in listing 16.1.

Listing 16.1 Generating SOAP report requests with the Application Center Test project

```
Sub SendRequestSoap(payloadFile)
  Set oRequest = Test.CreateRequest
  oRequest.Path = "/ReportServer/ReportService.asmx"    <-- Sets the path to point to the Reporting Services Web service
  oRequest.Verb = "POST"
  oRequest.HTTPVersion = "HTTP/1.1"
  set oHeaders = oRequest.Headers
  oHeaders.RemoveAll
  oHeaders.Add "Accept", "image/gif, image/x-xbitmap, …"
  oHeaders.Add "Accept-Language", "en-us"
  oHeaders.Add "User-Agent", "…"
  oHeaders.Add "Host", "(automatic)"
  oHeaders.Add "Content-Length", "(automatic)"
  oHeaders.Add "Content-Type", "text/xml; charset=utf-8"    <-- Sets the request content type to text/xml
  RemoveCookies()    <-- Removes all browser cookies
  oHeaders.Add "SOAPAction", _
       "http://schemas/.../reportingservices/Render"    <-- Sets the SOAP action to the Render web method
  oRequest.Body = GetXMLRequest(payloadFile)    <-- Gets the report's payload from the file

  Set oResponse = g_oConnection.Send(oRequest)
  CheckResponse oResponse, payloadFile
End Sub
```

SOAP requests can become rather verbose, so embedding them in the script page may be impractical. Instead, you can follow these steps to facilitate submitting report requests to the RS Web service:

Step 1 Use the Access Options sample (chapter 9) and your favorite tracing tool to capture the SOAP report request's payload.

Step 2 Save the payload to a disk file.

Step 3 To submit a report request, read the contents of the file using the File System object and set the request body.

This is exactly the design pattern that `SendRequestSoap` follows. It accepts the full path to the report request file. First, the code creates a report request using the ACT object model. Next, it sets the request path to point to the RS Web service end point. Because the Report Server relies on Windows authentication, we need to change the HTTP version from the default 1.0 to 1.1. When this is done, ACT will handle the authentication handshake between the browser and the server automatically.

Next, we need to set the required HTTP headers. We start by clearing the browser's cookies collection. For URL requests, this is done to prevent the automatic report session caching that the Report Server automatically performs behind the scenes. While, in real life, you should use caching techniques abundantly, we wanted to avoid report sessions so they won't skew up the results. As we've said, when requesting reports via SOAP, this is not required because you have to set explicitly the session identifier anyway.

The code continues by defining the SOAP action attribute, which is mandatory for SOAP-based calls. Then, we call the `GetXmlRequest` helper function to read the report's payload from the file and set the request body accordingly. Once the request is submitted, we check the response code to find out whether the request has resulted in an exception and, if so, log the exception accordingly.

TIP Dealing with SOAP exceptions is easy if you follow this tip. When a SOAP exception is thrown, the Report Server will set the response code to indicate that an error condition has occurred. However, the actual exception message is in the SOAP response's payload and it won't be logged by default. To find out more about what went wrong, you can intercept the ACT request using a tracing tool, such as MSSoapT or tcpTrace. To redirect the request to the virtual port, you will need to change the RS_PORT constant in the ACT script accordingly, for example, to 8080. Now, you can run the script to fire a single request and look at the SOAP response's payload to get to the exception message. Alternatively, you can use DebugView to trace the Report Server's output.

Once the script is ready, you can run it and verify that it runs successfully. In our script, we have implemented a logging feature that you can use to examine the status of the request by setting the g_iDebugMode variable to 1. When you have finished debugging the script, don't forget to reset it to zero to avoid additional performance overhead and filling up your hard drive.

16.2.3 Performance testing

Let's put our test script into action to find out how scalable our web server is. As we've discussed before, to accomplish this, we need to apply an ever-increasing load to the web server until its throughput graph peaks. Let's start by defining only one virtual user using the script properties, as shown in figure 16.5.

Don't forget to specify some time for warming up the web server. After a certain period of inactivity, the Report Server's web application will time out and shut down. By warming up the web server, you ensure that the initialization tasks don't skew your results.

Now comes the fun part! Run the script and enjoy the show, as figure 16.6 depicts.

> **NOTE** ACT runs scripts under a designated Windows user account called ACTUser. Based on my experience, the default permissions assigned to this account are insufficient to execute scripts successfully. You will know that this is the case when you receive an "Access Denied" error when you start the script. If this happens, elevate the ACTUser account's permissions, for example, by assigning it to the local Administrators group.

You may want to configure the script to run for at least five minutes to get stable statistics. When a script is run, ACT displays valuable metrics in the Status area. The most interesting measure of these is perhaps the Requests Per Second (RPS) indicator, which

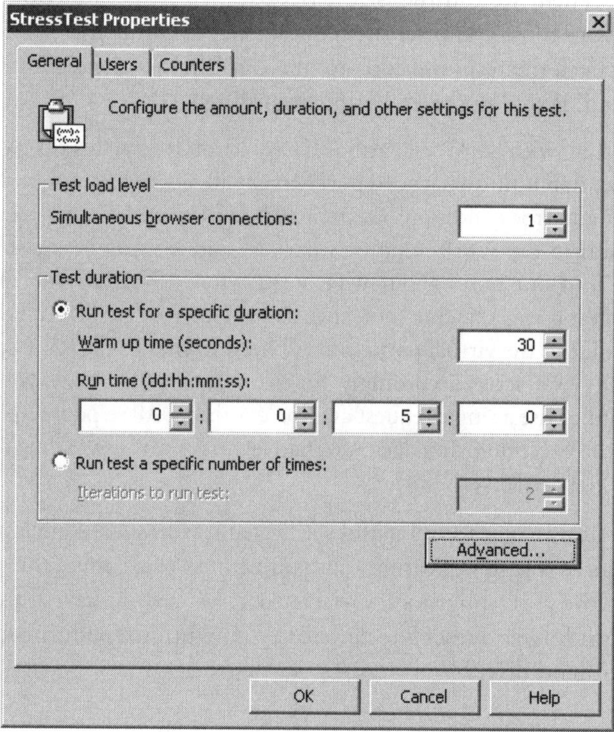

Figure 16.5 Finding out the throughput graph's peak requires that you gradually apply an ever-increasing load to the web server by incrementing the number of simultaneous browser connections.

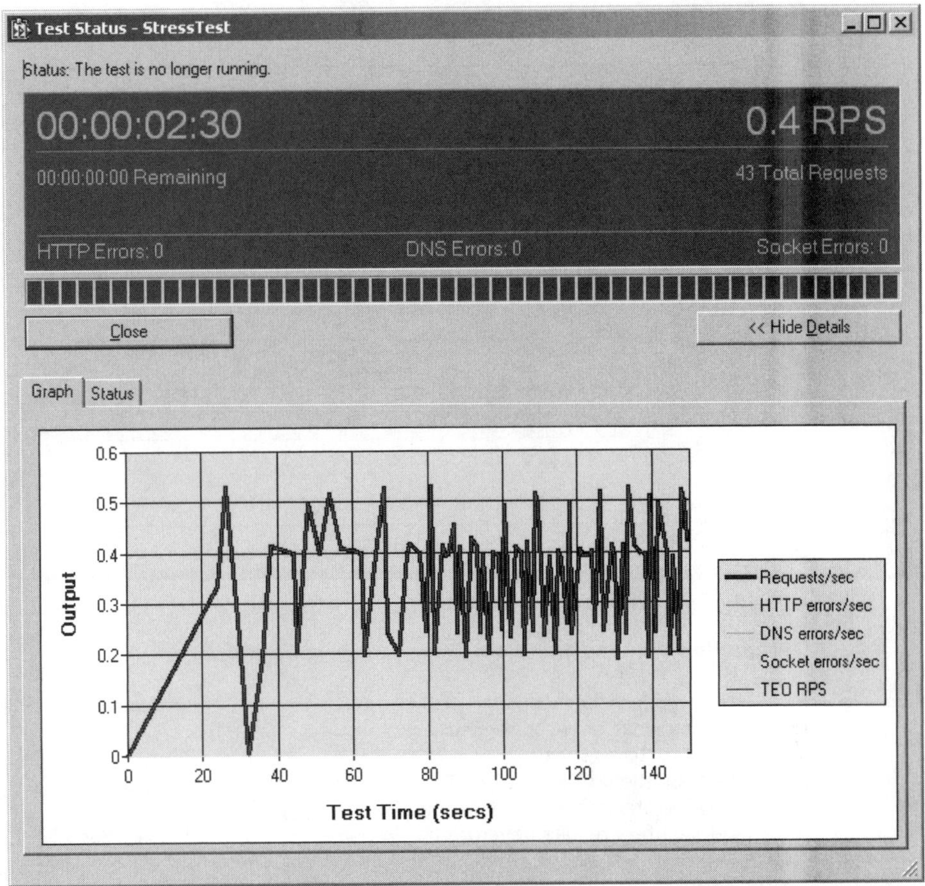

Figure 16.6 While the script is running, ACT displays performance metrics in the Test Status window.

reflects the throughput capacity. Please note, though, that this indicator is updated on a regular basis, and it may not reflect the final RPS result.

16.2.4 Analyzing performance results

Once the script is run, you may want to analyze its execution by examining the ACT Overview Summary report, as shown in figure 16.7.

Analyzing figure 16.7, we can see that the web server has processed 40 requests and the RPS ratio is 0.67 with one virtual user. In addition, the Average Time to Last Byte (TTLB) metric tells us that ACT has received the complete report payload within about 1.5 seconds.

Another interesting report is the Requests: Summary report shown in figure 16.8.

Using this report, we can see how both report access options, SOAP and URL, stack against each other. For example, when requesting the Employee Sales Freeform report,

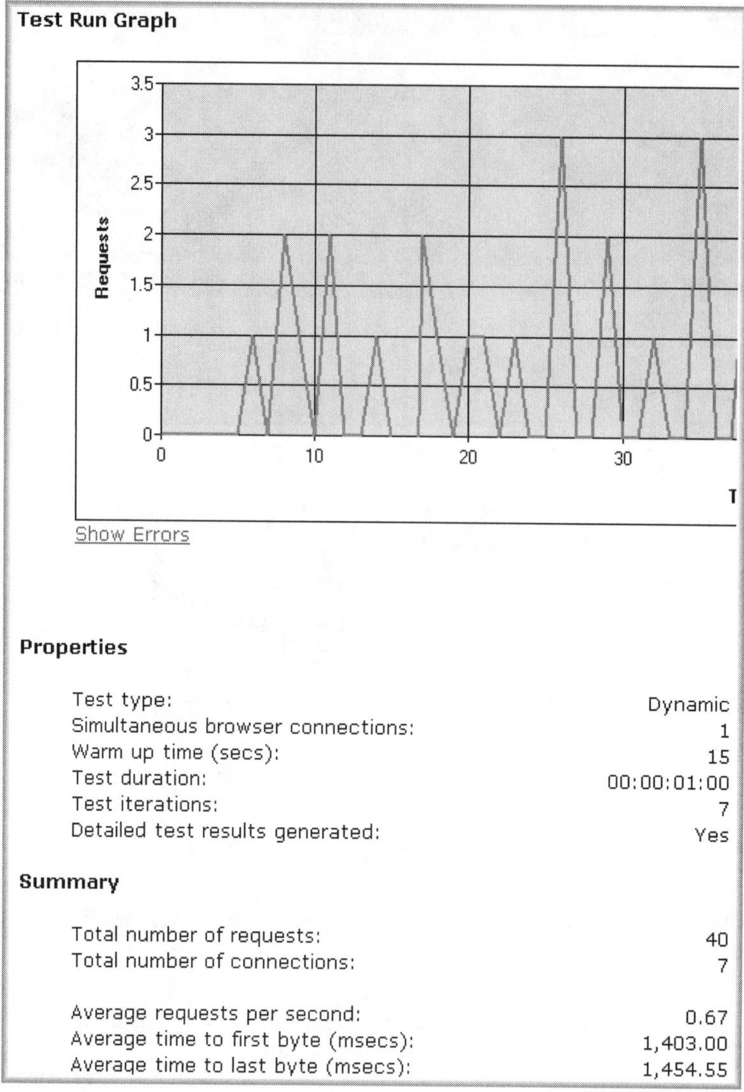

Figure 16.7 Analyzing the script results with the Overview Summary report.

we can see that accessing the report via SOAP adds about 20 percent more overhead to the report's payload. This stems from the fact that when a report is requested by SOAP, the report's payload is serialized to a binary array.

Surprisingly, despite the increased payload, requesting reports via SOAP is somewhat faster than URL access, as you can see by looking at the Time to Last Byte (TTLB) column. For high-speed 100Mbit networks, such as my LAN, the SOAP overhead

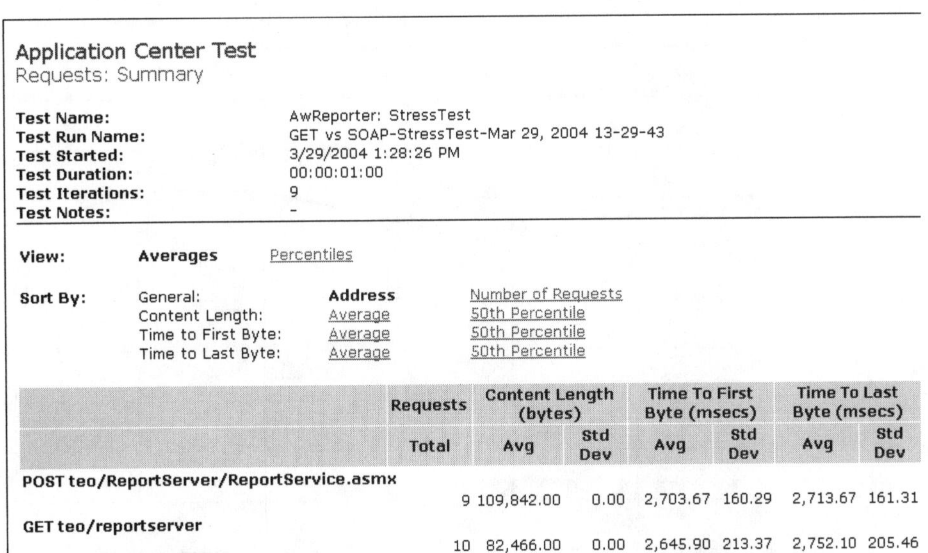

Application Center Test
Requests: Summary

Test Name:	AwReporter: StressTest
Test Run Name:	GET vs SOAP-StressTest-Mar 29, 2004 13-29-43
Test Started:	3/29/2004 1:28:26 PM
Test Duration:	00:00:01:00
Test Iterations:	9
Test Notes:	-

View: **Averages** Percentiles

Sort By:		
General:	**Address**	Number of Requests
Content Length:	Average	50th Percentile
Time to First Byte:	Average	50th Percentile
Time to Last Byte:	Average	50th Percentile

	Requests	Content Length (bytes)		Time To First Byte (msecs)		Time To Last Byte (msecs)	
	Total	Avg	Std Dev	Avg	Std Dev	Avg	Std Dev
POST teo/ReportServer/ReportService.asmx	9	109,842.00	0.00	2,703.67	160.29	2,713.67	161.31
GET teo/reportserver	10	82,466.00	0.00	2,645.90	213.37	2,752.10	205.46

Figure 16.8 To compare SOAP vs. URL access statistics, use the Requests: Summary report.

should be negligible. However, it may be a constraining factor for low-speed networks, such as 56K dial-up connections.

Now, run a few more iterations by increasing the number of connections by a factor of two. When you do this, ACT creates additional threads to simulate concurrent users. ACT may not create as many threads as the number of connections. Instead, it is intelligent enough to adjust the thread pool on an as-needed basis. For example, if the web server doesn't return responses quickly, new threads won't be created.

You don't have to plot the throughput graph manually because ACT does this for you. In our case, for the six report requests we scripted, the server throughput graph maxed out with about five simultaneous users, as shown in figure 16.9.

Before you jump to quick conclusions, please note that the point of this chapter is not to show how scalable (or not scalable, for that matter) Reporting Services is. Instead, its goal is to teach you how to conduct a comprehensive capacity-planning study to determine whether your particular reporting environment meets the anticipated load. As we've said, there are many hardware- and software-related factors that will affect the server throughput, so your results may be completely different than ours.

Analyzing the throughput graph, we conclude that the results don't meet our performance goal. Specifically, the maximum requests/sec. ratio of 0.7 is less than the benchmark—one request/sec. Therefore, we need to identify the source of the performance bottleneck.

16.2.5 Identifying resource constraints

We can use the ACT Performance Counters report, shown in figure 16.10, to identify the resource constraints at a high level.

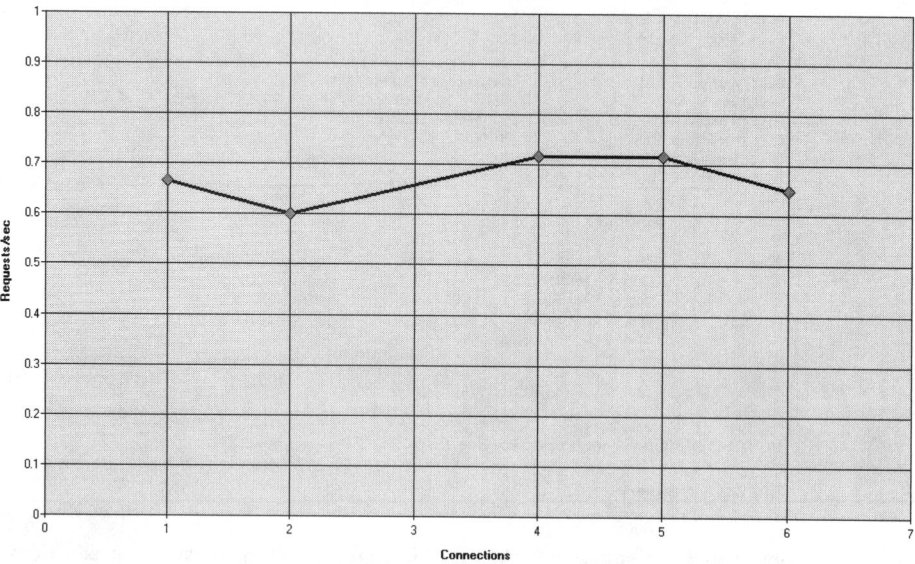

Figure 16.9 The throughput graph depicting requests/sec vs. browser connections

Application Center Test

Overview: Performance Counters

Test Name:	AwReporter: StressTest
Test Run Name:	report-StressTest-Mar 28, 2004 17-35-22
Test Started:	3/28/2004 5:34:04 PM
Test Duration:	00:00:01:00
Test Iterations:	7
Test Notes:	-

\\TEO\Process\% Processor Time\w3wp

Minimum:	39.68
Maximum:	46.76
Average:	42.88
25th Percentile	42.53
50th Percentile	42.58
75th Percentile	45.02

\\TEO\Processor\% Processor Time_Total

Minimum:	70.59
Maximum:	77.39
Average:	73.61
25th Percentile	73.45
50th Percentile	73.61
75th Percentile	75.67

Figure 16.10 Using the ACT Performance Counters report to identify high-level performance bottlenecks

A quick look at this report reveals the following:

- Even with one connection, the average CPU utilization of 75 percent is above the targeted threshold of 70 percent.
- The memory is not a constraint.
- The processor time spent on carrying out SQL Server activities (not shown in figure 16.10) is low; therefore, the database is not a constraint, either.

As we expected, due to the processor-intensive report-generation activities, CPU utilization is a major resource constraint. Analyzing the results from the successive runs reveals that the CPU utilization reaches 85 percent when the throughput graph peaks at five concurrent users. Therefore, we need to continue our study by finding ways to eliminate this performance bottleneck.

16.2.6 Eliminating resource constraints

When CPU utilization is a constraining factor, you basically have two ways to increase the web server's throughput: optimize report performance and add more processing power by scaling up or out.

These two approaches are not mutually exclusive. In my opinion, the best approach will be to optimize the application's performance before scaling up or out.

Optimizing report performance

With custom applications, determining the code bottlenecks requires meticulous and painstaking profiling using code profilers. When doing so, a useful approach is to follow the method of the biggest returns. In a nutshell, this entails identifying the 10 slowest code areas and seeking ways to optimize them. However, with off-the-shelf applications such as Reporting Services, this is not an option, unless your reports make extensive use of custom code. Instead, you can try other ways to take some of the burden off the CPU, such as using different forms for report caching.

Let's see how report execution caching affects server utilization by changing the execution options for all three scripted reports. As we discussed back in chapter 7, this option causes the Report Server to cache the report's intermediate format in the database and to serve subsequent requests from the cached copy. Figure 16.11 shows what the new throughput graph looks like when we reran the tests after turning on report execution caching.

Not bad, I would say, for a few seconds of work! All of a sudden, we can now scale to 15 requests per second. But please don't get me wrong. I am not trying to advocate that you fire the Report Manager and turn on report execution caching for all reports. For example, if a report needs to display the most recent data, it may not be a good candidate for caching. But definitely do consider all three forms of report caching—report execution caching, snapshots, and report sessions—as performance-enhancement techniques.

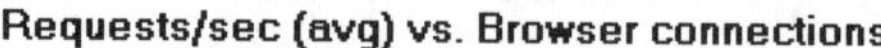

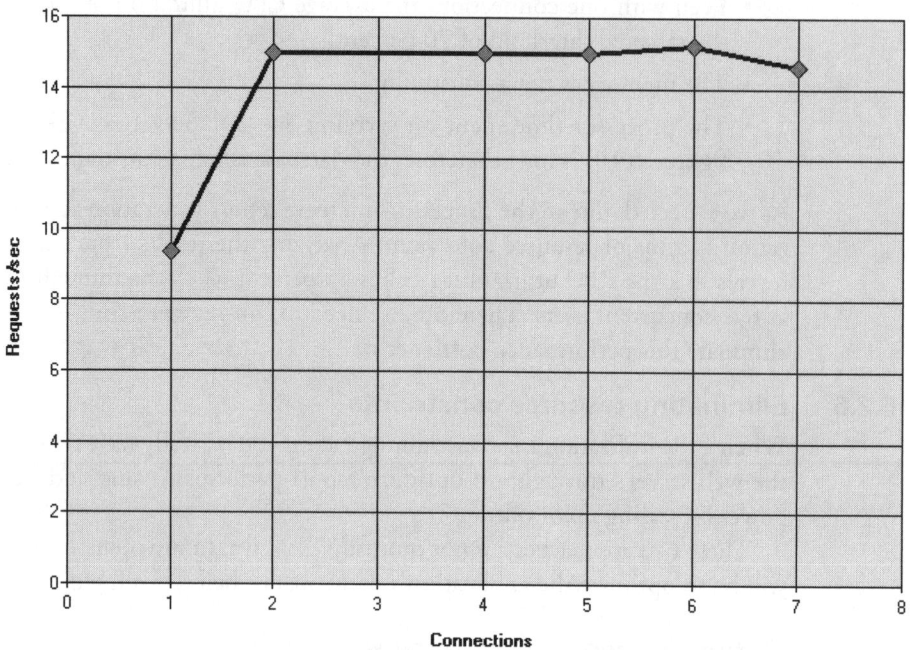

Figure 16.11 Using report caching is the easiest way to increase the Report Server's scalability.

Scaling up

Sometimes, there may not be much you can do to improve the web server's performance. If this is the case, you can scale Reporting Services up (vertical scalability) and out (horizontal scalability).

NOTE By the time you read this book, the Microsoft RS team will probably have released a white paper about RS performance and scalability. The white paper will include performance tests comparing scaling up and out approaches. The document is meant to help customers understand the scalability characteristics of RS and determine hardware and software requirements needed to support planned deployments.

You scale RS up by beefing up your server hardware, that is, by adding memory or CPU power. The memory capacity recommended by Microsoft for a production report server is 4GB of RAM.

When scaling up by adding more processors, note that you shouldn't expect linear scalability. For example, adding a second CPU may result in a 60 percent increase in performance, while adding a third CPU, only 30 percent more.

When scaling up becomes counterproductive, you can scale out RS by deploying it in a web farm environment.

Scaling out

You scale out RS by distributing the processing load across multiple report servers. Scaling out offers the following advantages:

- Allows you to incrementally add (or remove) resources as needed
- Makes it possible to balance heavy workloads across multiple servers configured in a web farm environment
- Offers fault tolerance because even if one of the clustered servers fails, the rest of the cluster is unaffected

Figure 16.12 depicts a typical scale-out scenario where the Report Server is deployed in a web farm environment.

Scaling out works well because it results in almost linear scalability to the point where another resource is pushed past its limits, such as database, memory, or network utilization. In general, even if only one web server meets your performance objectives, we suggest that you pair it with a second server for fault-tolerance reasons.

The Reporting Services Enterprise and Developer editions support scaling out. When you scale out RS, multiple report servers share a single Report Server database (or a cluster of Report Server databases). When the RS Setup program detects that the Report Server database already exists, it assumes a web farm deployment and doesn't create the Report Server database.

For more information about setting up RS, please read appendix A. For more information about configuring RS in a clustered web farm environment, read the "SQL Server 2000 Reporting Services Deployment Guide" document and the "Installing Reporting Services" section of the RS product documentation (see section 16.4).

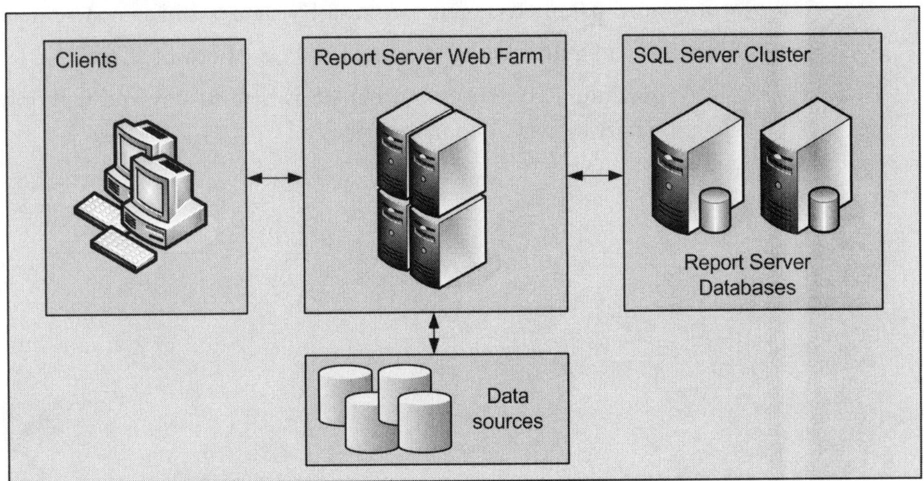

Figure 16.12 A typical enterprise deployment model using a cluster of Report Servers and clustered Report Server databases

16.3 SUMMARY

Thanks to its web-oriented stateless architecture, RS is well positioned to meet the high-volume reporting requirements of today's enterprises. This chapter has given you the necessary skills to find out whether your specific reporting infrastructure will meet your capacity needs.

Specifically, we discussed the capacity-planning process and learned how to establish performance goals.

Next, we showed how we can stress test the Report Server with the Visual Studio .NET Application Center Test.

Finally, we looked at ways to identify performance bottlenecks and increase the Report Server's capacity by scaling up and out.

Well, we are at the end of the RS (code-named Rosetta) journey! We've traveled a long and, hopefully, enjoyable road to see how Reporting Services can help us author, manage, and integrate reports with our applications. We hope you have found this product to be a well-rounded, comprehensive reporting platform.

Having barely rolled out the first release, Microsoft is hard at work on its next major version of Reporting Services, which will coincide with the Microsoft SQL Server 2005 release. Among other features, the new release is expected to include the following:

- Graphical Query Generator for Analysis Services data sources
- Management through the new Windows-based SQL Server management tool
- New embeddable WinForm and ASP.NET controls to allow standalone reporting without the need for a separate report server
- Custom report items and the ability to add server-side controls
- Multivalued parameters (generation of IN clauses and so on)
- Auto-sort and auto-filter report features (a la Microsoft Excel)
- All of this should convince you that RS is here to stay and will only get better. Happy reporting with Reporting Services!

16.4 RESOURCES

Performance Testing Microsoft .NET Web Applications
(http://www.amazon.com/exec/obidos/tg/detail/-/0735615381/qid=1080272077/sr=8-1/ref=sr_8_xs_ap_i1_xgl14/104-6183135-6491931?v=glance&s=books&n=507846)
Direct from a Microsoft team that has analyzed hundreds of web-based and .NET-based applications, this book shows developers how to plan and execute performance tests, configure profile tools, analyze data from Microsoft Internet Information Services, analyze transaction costs, and more.

The "Performance" chapter from the Visual Studio .NET documentation
(http://msdn.microsoft.com/library/default.asp?url=/library/en-us/vsent7/html/vxconperformanceoverview.asp)
Discusses how to write efficient and scalable .NET applications.

The Compuware Application Expert tool
(http://www.compuware.com/products/vantage/appexpert.htm)
An excellent tool that you can use to find out how changes in network bandwidth, latency, load, and TCP window size affect the application's response time.

The Analog analyzer
(http://www.analog.cx/)
Analog is a tool that you can use to measure the usage on your web server. It tells you which pages are most popular, from which countries people are visiting, from which sites they tried to follow broken links, and all sorts of other useful information.

ReportMagic for Analog
(http://www.reportmagic.org/)
By harnessing the power of Analog and building readable, compelling reports, Report Magic can help you and the rest of your organization understand how your web site is used.

"SQL Server 2000 Reporting Services Deployment Guide"
http://www.microsoft.com/technet/prodtechnol/sql/2000/deploy/rsdepgd.mspx

"Installing Reporting Services" section from RS Books Online
(http://msdn.microsoft.com/library/default.asp?url=/library/en-us/RSINSTALL/htm/gs_installingrs_v1_8jom.asp)

APPENDIX

Installing Reporting Services

Before you run the Reporting Services Setup CD, it may make sense to take the "think before you leap" approach and spend some time planning your deployment. To help you in this process, Microsoft has provided the excellent "SQL Server 2000 Reporting Services Deployment Guide" (see the resources in section A.9). As the document says, the "guide provides a high-level overview of Reporting Services components, describes the hardware and software requirements for deploying Reporting Services, and offers installation and configuration instructions. It is meant to provide you with sufficient guidelines to install and configure Reporting Services."

Another document that you may need to review is the "Installing Reporting Services" section from RS Books Online (see the resources in section A.9). It discusses the RS editions, as well as deploying RS in a web farm environment.

Here are some lessons learned from trenches that could make your setup experience smoother:

- RS installs only on the default web site. However, it is okay if the default web site has been redirected to point to a folder other than the default (C:\Inetpub\wwwroot).

- RS will not install on a computer with Terminal Services installed. The setup process will fail with the error "SQL Setup failed to connect to the database service for server configuration" when configuring the Report Server database. As a workaround, uninstall Terminal Services, reboot, install RS, and then reinstall Terminal Services.
- Make sure that IIS is functioning properly and that you can browse pages. This sounds like a no-brainer, but you will be surprised at how often people forget to check that darn Bypass Proxy Server for Local Addresses check box on the IE Connections settings when a web proxy server is used. If the setup fails at the end with the mysterious warning message "Setup cannot initialize report server," remember this tip before you spend hours uninstalling and installing IIS over and over again.
- If you are deploying RS on a web farm environment, the new instance will not be activated at the end of the Setup program. Don't panic if you see the "RS Report Server Not Activated" error message when you open the Report Manager web application. To activate the new RS instance, run the rsactivate utility. Please see the "Activating a Report Server" topic in the product documentation about how to use the rsactivate utility.
- If you need to reinstall RS, note that uninstalling it doesn't remove the Report Server database. Consequently, when installing RS again and pointing to the same SQL server, the Setup program assumes web farm deployment. To avoid this, before installing RS make sure you delete the Report Server databases (ReportServer and ReportServerTempDB).
- The setup program uses Windows integrated security to log on to the SQL Server where the Report Server databases need to be installed and it doesn't support standard security. For this reason, make sure that your Windows logon has admin rights to that SQL Server.

With these tips in mind, go ahead and insert the RS Setup CD into your CD-ROM drive. If your computer has been set up with the CD Autoplay feature, the RS Setup program starts automatically. Otherwise, run setup.exe manually from the CD.

A.1 CHOOSING COMPONENTS TO INSTALL

After the familiar licensing agreement step, the Setup program checks to see if the computer on which you are installing RS meets the minimum hardware and software requirements. If all is well, you will see the Feature Selection screen (figure A.1).

Which components you need to install depends on your deployment scenario, as table A.1 shows.

Table A.1 The components required per your deployment needs

Deployment Need	Components
Evaluate RS by installing it on your local computer.	Install both server and client components.
Install on a production or testing server.	Install only the server components.
Author reports or extend RS programmatically. Report Server is installed on another machine.	Install only the client components. Visual Studio .NET 2003 is required.

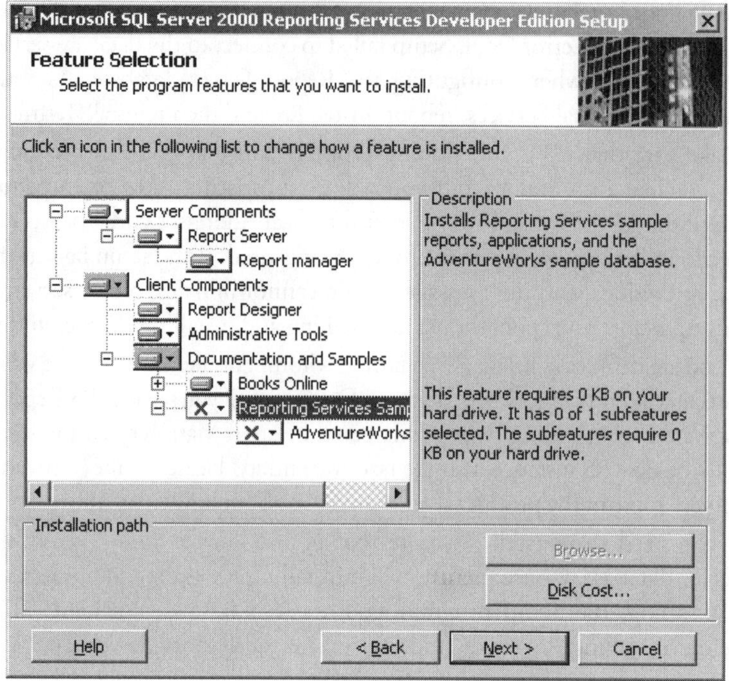

Figure A.1 In the Feature Selection step you select the RS components that you want to install.

As shown in figure A.1, by default the Setup program doesn't install the Reporting Services sample reports and AdventureWorks2000 database. If you are new to RS, we highly recommend that you install and explore the RS samples. Because this book's sample reports use the AdventureWorks2000 database, make sure that the appropriate installation option is selected. The next steps assume that you are installing all RS components.

Click Next. The Setup program now shows the Service Account screen.

A.2 SELECTING THE SERVICE ACCOUNT

In the Service Account screen (figure A.2), you need to specify which account the RS Windows Service (ReportingServicesService.exe) will run under. Please note that there is an error at the bottom of the screen. It is not the Report Server Web service that we are configuring here but the Report Server Windows Service.

Among other things, the RS Windows Service executes tasks in unattended mode, for example, scheduled report delivery and snapshot reports.

Your account options are

- Local built-in account
- Domain user account

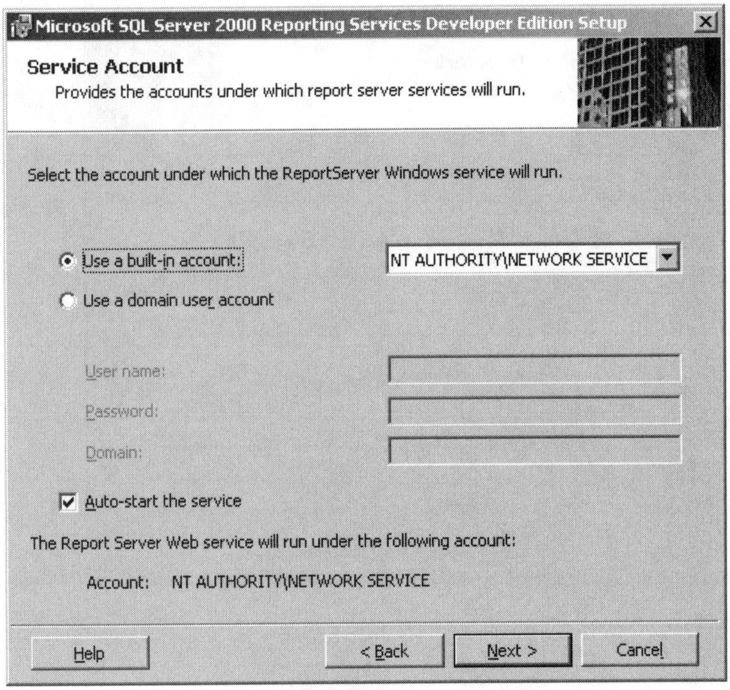

Figure A.2 In the Service Account step you specify the account under which the RS Windows Service will run.

I strongly suggest you consider using a domain account, especially if you are planning to use data-driven report subscriptions. This type of subscription allows you to distribute ("push") reports to a data-driven list of recipients. If the recipient's data store is located on another machine and you want to use Windows authentication between the RS Windows Service and the database server, don't use a local built-in account, such as the default NETWORK SERVICE account. The reason for this is that you must set the corresponding account on the database server with the same password in order for Windows authentication to succeed on both machines.

You can always change the account the RS Windows Service runs under using the Services applet. Make sure that the Auto-start the Service check box is selected so that Windows automatically starts the RS Window Service when the computer is rebooted. Click Next.

A.3 SPECIFYING RS VIRTUAL FOLDERS

If you are installing the RS server components, you need to specify the virtual directories (vroots) of the Report Server and Report Manager, as shown in figure A.3.

The Report Server web application hosts the web communication facades (URL and RS Web service) that the client applications will use to integrate with the Report

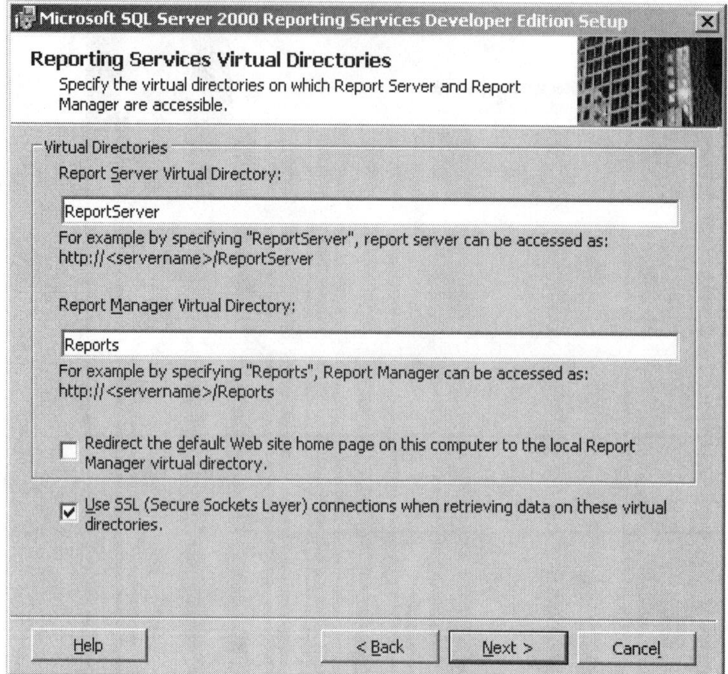

Figure A.3 In the RS Virtual Directories step you specify the Report Server and Report Manager virtual directories.

Server. The default virtual folder is ReportServer. If you later (after the setup is complete) change your mind and decide to use a different virtual root name, be sure to update both the Report Manager RSWebApplication.config and Report Server RSReportServer.config files to reflect the new URL.

If you opted to install the Report Manager in the Feature Selection step, specify the virtual root of the Report Manager in the second textbox. Optionally, you can select the "Redirect…" check box to change the home page on the server to automatically redirect to the Report Manager web application. For example, if this check box is selected, and the user types http://<computername>/, she will be redirected to the Report Manager web application.

One thing that can get you in trouble is the "Use SSL…" check box, which is selected by default. Chances are that you won't have SSL configured (server certificate installed) on your local or intranet IIS server. If this is the case, deselect this check box. If you leave it selected, you won't be able to access the Report Server if IIS is not configured for SSL. That's said, you should definitely consider securing the connection between clients and the Report Server, especially for Internet reporting.

Click Next to advance to the Report Server Database screen.

A.4 CONFIGURING THE REPORT SERVER DATABASE

As a part of the setup process, RS creates the Report Server Database, which consists of two SQL Server 2000 databases:

- *ReportServer*—This is the Report Server Configuration Database that will host the report catalog.
- *ReportServerTempDB*—The Report Server uses this database for caching purposes.

The Report Server Database screen is shown in figure A.4.

In this step you specify the following:

- The SQL Server 2000 instance where these two databases will be installed
- The name of the Report Server Configuration Database
- The login credentials that the Report Server and RS Windows Service will use to connect to the Report Server Database to perform ongoing operations

If the database already exists on the specified SQL Server instance, the Setup program assumes that you will deploy RS on a web farm environment, where multiple report servers share the same Report Server Database.

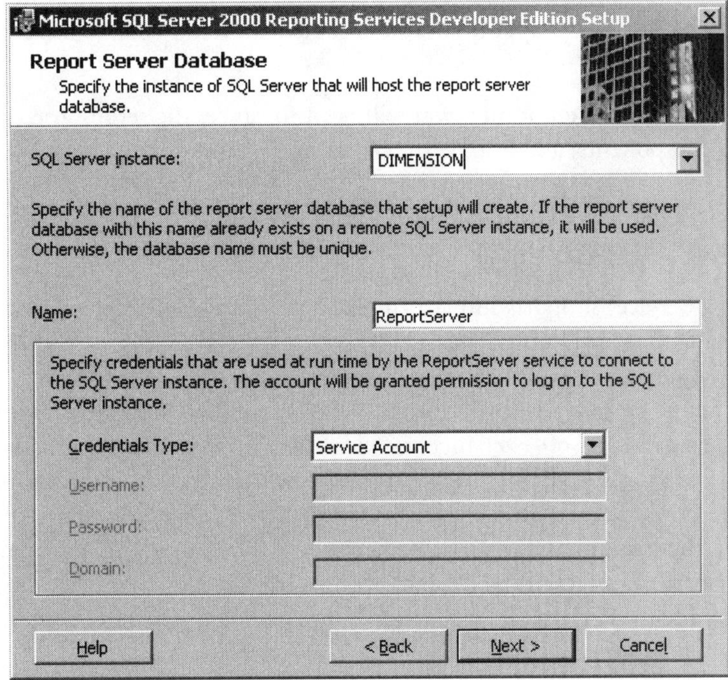

Figure A.4 In the Report Server Database step you specify where the ReportServer and ReportServerTempDB databases will be installed and how RS will connect to them.

The login credentials section deserves more attention and some planning on your part. The reason for this is that the Report Server saves the login credentials in encrypted form. If you later change your mind and decide to use different credentials, you'll need to run a special utility (rsconfig.exe) to properly encrypt the new login credentials.

The default Credentials Type is Service Account. This choice is good if RS and the Report Server Database are installed on the same computer. In this case, RS will use a local service account to log in to the Report Server Database using Windows authentication. Using Service Account as a Credentials Type requires you to install SQL Server hotfix 821334 (see the resource in section A.9).

If RS and the Report Server Database reside on separate computers, you need to specify a SQL Server (standard authentication) or Windows (Windows authentication) account that RS will use to connect to the database. If you specify a SQL Server account, Setup creates the account if it does not already exist. If you specify a Windows account, the user account must already exist. The account specified is granted the public and RSExecRole roles for the Report Server Database (ReportServer) and the RSExecRole role for the master, msdb, and ReportServerTempDB databases.

When you click Next, the Setup program will check to see if the target SQL Server meets these prerequisites:

- SQL Server 2000 Service Pack 3a is installed.
- Hotfix 821334 is applied if you specified Service Account for connecting to that server.

If these conditions are not met, you will need to cancel the setup process, install the required components, and resume the setup.

A.5 Configuring Reporting Services for E-mail Delivery

Reporting Services supports subscribed report delivery where reports can be e-mailed to recipients. On the Report Server Delivery Settings screen (figure A.5) you configure the RS Windows Service for e-mail delivery.

The Setup program asks you for the name of the SMTP server or another e-mail server, such as Microsoft Exchange, to which RS will delegate the e-mail delivery. In addition, you can specify the From Address to which the recipients can send e-mail.

If you don't plan to use e-mail subscribed delivery or if you don't know how to configure these settings, you can leave them blank. You can specify them later by making appropriate changes to RSEmailDPConfiguration section in the Report Server configuration file (RSReportConfig.config). We provide more details about how you can set up e-mail delivery in chapter 14.

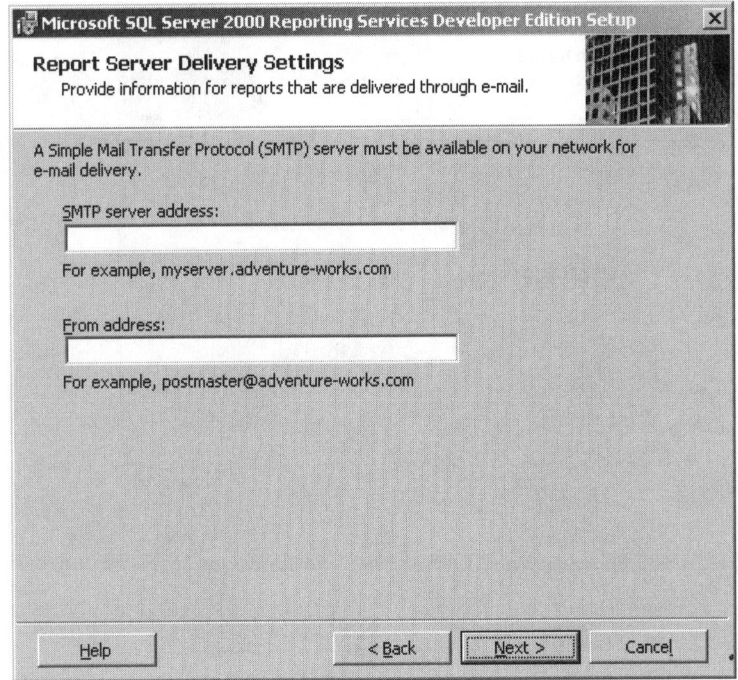

Figure A.5 In the Report Server Delivery Settings step you configure the Report Server for e-mail report delivery.

A.6 SETTING UP THE RS SAMPLES

If you opted to install the RS samples in the Feature Selection step, the Setup program will ask you to specify the SQL Server instance where the sample AdventureWorks2000 database will be installed, as shown in figure A.6.

As we mentioned, you need the AdventureWorks2000 database in order to run the sample reports included with the book's source code.

A.7 CONFIGURING RS LICENSING MODE

We are almost finished. In the Licensing Mode page you need to specify the type of license you purchased for RS (figure A.7).

You can choose either a per-seat license or a per-processor license. For more information about RS licensing, please see the resources in section A.9.

Next, you sit and watch the Setup program install RS. This should result in the creation of two SQL Server 2000 databases (ReportServer and ReportServerTempDB) and two IIS virtual folders named by default Reports and ReportServer.

The Reports virtual folder hosts the Report Manager web application and points by default to C:\Program Files\Microsoft SQL Server\MSSQL\Reporting Services\ReportManager.

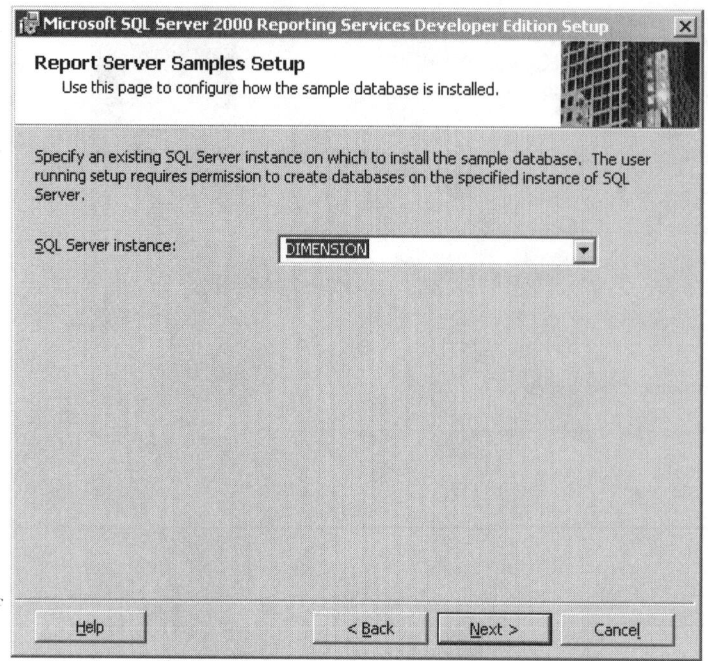

Figure A.6 In the Report Server Samples Setup step you specify the SQL Server that will host the AdventureWorks2000 sample database.

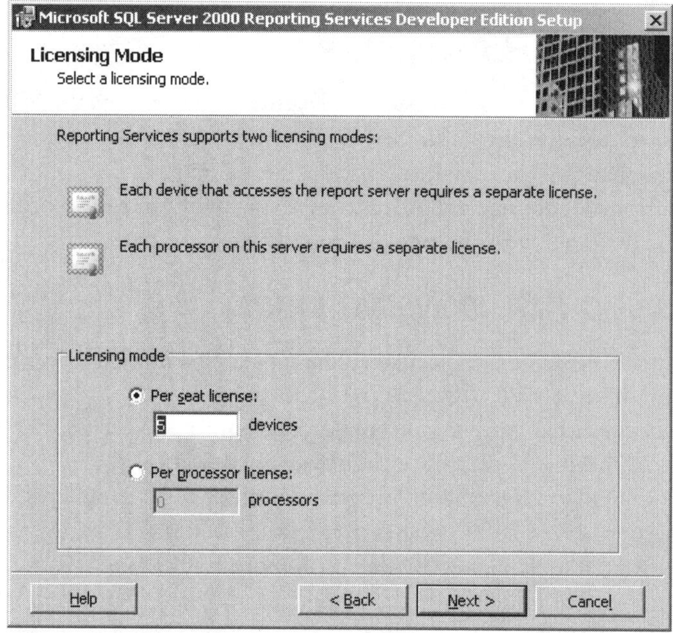

Figure A.7 In the Licensing Mode step you specify the licensing details.

The ReportServer virtual folder represents the ReportServer entry point and points by default to C:\Program Files\Microsoft SQL Server\MSSQL\Reporting Services\ReportServer.

In addition, Setup installs the ReportServer Windows Service and the AdventureWorks2000 SQL Server database for the report samples.

A.8 POST-INSTALLATION STEPS

To verify that RS is installed successfully, please read the steps in the "Verifying an Installation of Reporting Services" topic in RS Books Online (see the resources in section A.9).

A.8.1 Installing RS sample reports

The Setup program doesn't upload the sample reports that come with RS to the report catalog. If you are new to RS and you want to run these reports, follow these steps (you will need local administrator rights to the machine where RS is installed):

Step 1 Open the SampleReports.sln solution in Visual Studio .NET 2003.

Step 2 Right-click the SampleReports project node in the Solution Explorer, and choose Properties from the context menu.

Step 3 In the SampleReports Property Pages dialog, enter the URL address of the Report Server to which the reports will be uploaded in the TargetServerURL setting. Optionally, if you don't want to name the folder SampleReports, specify the name of the folder that will include the sample reports in the TargetFolder setting. Click OK to close the dialog.

Step 4 Back in the Solution Explorer, double-click the AdventureWorks.rds shared data source to open the Shared Data Source dialog.

Step 5 Switch to the Credentials tab and verify the credentials to connect to the AdventureWorks2000 database. You need to specify Windows or SQL Server credentials of an account that has at least Read rights to the tables in the AdventureWorks2000 database. Click OK to close the dialog.

Step 6 Right-click the SampleReports project node in the Solution Explorer and choose Deploy. This will build the reports and upload them to the report catalog.

Step 7 To verify that the sample reports are installed correctly, navigate to the Report Manager web application (http://<servername>/reports), open the SampleReports folder, and run some reports.

To set up the book's source code, follow the directions listed in the "Source Code" section in this book's Preface section.

A.8.2 Backing up the encryption key

We would strongly advise all report server administrators to use the rskeymgmt utility to extract and back up the public encryption key as one of your first post-installation tasks. The Report Server uses this key to encrypt data in the Report Server Database or catalog.

What is the encryption key good for? Chances are that you may need to change the account under which the RS Windows Service (ReportingServicesService.exe) runs, or you may want to set up a new RS installation to use an existing report catalog. If the encryption key is different, the Report Server will not initialize. Therefore, it is absolutely crucial that you store the encryption key in a safe place. Please consult the RS product documentation about how to use the rskeymgmt utility to back up the encryption key.

A.9 RESOURCES

"SQL Server 2000 Reporting Services Deployment Guide"
(http://www.microsoft.com/technet/prodtechnol/sql/2000/deploy/rsdepgd.mspx)

"Installing Reporting Services" section from RS Books Online
(http://msdn.microsoft.com/library/default.asp?url=/library/en-us/RSINSTALL/htm/gs_installingrs_v1_8jom.asp)

Hotfix 821334 for Windows authentication using a local service account
http://support.microsoft.com/default.aspx?scid=kb;en-us;821334&Product=sql

"How to License Reporting Services"
(http://www.microsoft.com/sql/reporting/howtobuy/howtolicensers.asp)

"Verifying the Reporting Services Installation"
(http://msdn.microsoft.com/library/default.asp?url=/library/en-us/rsinstall/htm/gs_installingrs_v1_4q61.asp)

"Installing a Report Server Web Farm"
(http://msdn.microsoft.com/library/default.asp?url=/library/en-us/rsinstall/htm/gs_installingrs_v1_2ckm.asp)

index

Symbols

A

D

E

J

K

L

M

Q

R

S

T

U

V

W

X

Y

Z